Writing Device Drivers: Tutorial and Reference

Writing Device Drivers: Tutorial and Reference

Tim Burke
Mark A. Parenti
Al Wojtas

Digital Press
Boston Oxford Melbourne Singapore Toronto Munich New Delhi Tokyo

Digital Press™ is an imprint of Butterworth–Heinemann, Publisher for Digital Equipment Corporation.

The following are trademarks of Digital Equipment Corporation:
ALL-IN-1, Alpha AXP, AlphaGeneration, AlphaServer, AlphaStation, AXP, Bookreader, CDA, DDIS, DEC, DEC Ada, DEC Fortran, DEC FUSE, DECnet, DECstation, DECsystem, DECterm, DECUS, DECwindows, DTIF, MASSBUS, MicroVAX, OpenVMS, POLYCENTER, Q-bus, TURBOchannel, ULTRIX, ULTRIX Mail Connection, ULTRIX Worksystem Software, UNIBUS, VAX, VAXstation, VMS, XUI, and the DIGITAL logo.

UNIX is a registered trademark in the United States and other countries licensed exclusively through X/Open Company Ltd.

All other trademarks and registered trademarks are the property of their respective holders.

∞ Recognizing the importance of preserving what has been written, Butterworth-Heinemann prints its books on acid-free paper whenever possible.

Library of Congress Cataloging-in-Publication Data

Burke, Tim (Timothy Francis)
    Writing device drivers : tutorial and reference / Tim Burke, Mark
A. Parenti, Al Wojtas.
        p. cm.
    Includes index.
    ISBN 1-55558-141-2 (alk. paper)
        1. UNIX device drivers (Computer programs)   I. Parenti, Mark A.
(Mark Alan)   II. Wojtas, Al (Alphonse Joseph)   III. Title.
QA676.76.D49B87   1995
005.7'11--dc20   95-15954
                                                                CIP

The publisher offers discounts on bulk orders of this book.
For information, please write:

Manager of Special Sales, Digital Press
Butterworth–Heinemann
313 Washington Street
Newton, MA 02158–1626

Order number: EY–S796E–DP

10 9 8 7 6 5 4 3 2 1

Printed in the United States of America

Contributing Authors

Joe Amato

Jeff Anuszcyk

Jim Crapuchettes

Al Delorey

Andrew L. Duane

Gary Dupuis

Don Dutile

Karl Ebner

Barbara J. Glover

Tim Hoskins

Todd Katz

Robin W. Lewis

Debby Haeck

Ashoke Rampuria

Larry Robinson

Brian Stevens

Tim Tierney

Maria DiCenso Vella

Farrell Woods

Joe Yuen

Technical Editors: Henry Blacklock and Emmalyn Bentley

Graphic Artist: Susanna Ries

Contents

About This Book

Part 1 Overview

1 Introduction to Device Drivers

Part 2 Anatomy of a Device Driver

2 Developing a Device Driver

3   Analyzing the Structure of a Device Driver

4 Coding, Configuring, and Testing a Device Driver

Part 3 Hardware Environment

5 Hardware-Independent Model and Device Drivers

6 Hardware Components and Hardware Activities

Part 4 Kernel Environment

7   Device Autoconfiguration

8   Data Structures Used in I/O Operations

9   Using Kernel Interfaces with Device Drivers

Part 5 Device Driver Example

10   Writing a Character Device Driver

Part 6 Device Driver Configuration

11 Device Driver Configuration Models

12 Device Driver Configuration Syntaxes and Mechanisms

13   Device Driver Configuration Examples

Part 7 Device Driver Reference

14   Header Files Related to Device Drivers

15   Kernel Interfaces, ioctls, and Global Variables That Device Drivers Use

16   Structures Related to Device Drivers

17   Device Driver and Bus Configuration Interfaces

Part 8 Appendixes

A   Device Driver Example Source Listings

B   Device Driver Development Worksheets

Glossary

Index

Figures

Tables

About This Book

This book discusses how to write device drivers for computer systems running the Digital UNIX (formerly known as DEC OSF/1) operating system.

Audience

This book is intended for systems engineers who:

- Use standard library interfaces to develop programs in the C language
- Know the Bourne or some other shell based on the UNIX operating system
- Understand basic Digital UNIX concepts such as kernel, shell, process, configuration, and autoconfiguration
- Understand how to use the Digital UNIX programming tools, compilers, and debuggers
- Develop programs in an environment that involves dynamic memory allocation, linked list data structures, and multitasking
- Understand the hardware device for which the driver is being written
- Understand the basics of the CPU hardware architecture, including interrupts, direct memory access (DMA) operations, and I/O

Although the book assumes a strong background in UNIX-based operating systems and C programming, it does not assume any background in device drivers. In addition, the book assumes that the audience has no source code licenses.

A secondary audience is systems engineers who need to implement a new bus or make changes to the implementation of an existing bus. Topics of interest to this audience include descriptions of the bus structure members.

Scope of the Book

The book is directed towards users of the Digital UNIX operating system on computer systems developed by Digital Equipment Corporation. However, the book provides information on designing drivers, on data structures, and kernel interfaces that would be useful to any systems engineer interested in

Chapter 11	Device Driver Configuration Models
	Provides an overview of the two configuration models: the third-party device driver configuration model and the traditional device driver configuration model. Read this chapter to obtain a general overview of the two models. The third-party driver configuration model is particularly well suited for driver developers who want to deliver Digital UNIX device drivers to their customers.
Chapter 12	Device Driver Configuration Syntaxes and Mechanisms
	Describes the syntaxes and mechanisms used to populate the files needed for device driver configuration. Read this chapter if you are not familiar with these syntaxes and mechanisms.
Chapter 13	Device Driver Configuration Examples
	Provides step-by-step instructions for configuring the example device drivers, using the third-party and traditional models. Read this chapter to learn how to configure the example drivers.

Part 7 Device Driver Reference

Part 7 contains four chapters, whose combined goal is to provide reference information on the header files, kernel interfaces, driver interfaces, and data structures used in writing device drivers on Digital UNIX.

Chapter 14	Header Files Related to Device Drivers
	Presents, in reference (man) page style, descriptions of the header files that device drivers most commonly use.
Chapter 15	Kernel Interfaces, ioctls, and Global Variables That Device Drivers Use
	Presents, in reference (man) page style, descriptions of the kernel support interfaces, ioctl commands, and global variables that device drivers use.
Chapter 16	Structures Related to Device Drivers
	Presents, in reference (man) page style, descriptions of the data structures that device drivers initialize and reference.
Chapter 17	Device Driver and Bus Configuration Interfaces
	Presents, in reference (man) page style, descriptions of the device driver and bus configuration interfaces.

writing UNIX-based device drivers.

The book presents a variety of examples including:

* A simple device driver that introduces the driver development process

* A character device driver operating on a TURBOchannel bus that illustrates a minimal implementation of all the TURBOchannel hardware functions

The book does not emphasize any specific types of device drivers. However, mastering the concepts and examples presented in this book would be very useful preparation for writing a variety of device drivers, including drivers for disk and tape controllers as well as more specialized drivers such as array processors.

Organization

The book contains the following chapters and appendixes.

Part 1 Overview

Part 1 contains one chapter, whose goal is to provide you with an overview of device drivers.

Chapter 1   Introduction to Device Drivers
Provides an overview of device drivers. Read this chapter to obtain introductory information on device drivers and to understand the place of a device driver in Digital UNIX.

Part 2 Anatomy of a Device Driver

Part 2 contains three chapters, whose combined goal is to provide enough information to allow you to write a simple Digital UNIX device driver.

Chapter 2   Developing a Device Driver
Describes how to design a device driver. Read this chapter if you are not familiar with the driver development process on Digital UNIX. Even if you have written UNIX device drivers, you may want to read the sections that describe the design issues related to loadable drivers, to CPU architectures, and to porting drivers from ULTRIX to Digital UNIX.

Chapter 3	Analyzing the Structure of a Device Driver
	Analyzes the sections that make up character and block device drivers. Read this chapter if you are not familiar with the sections that make up character and block drivers on Digital UNIX. If you have experience in writing UNIX device drivers, you may want to read selected sections, particularly the section that describes how to set up a `configure` interface for loadable device drivers.
Chapter 4	Coding, Configuring, and Testing a Device Driver
	Using a simple example, describes how to code, configure, and test a device driver. Read this chapter if you have never written a UNIX-based driver before. If you have written a UNIX-based driver, you may want to read only selected sections.

Part 3 Hardware Environment

Part 3 contains two chapters, whose combined goal is to provide you with a view into the device drivers' hardware environment.

Chapter 5	Hardware-Independent Model and Device Drivers
	Provides an overview of the hardware-independent model and how it relates to device drivers. Read this chapter to gain an understanding of how device drivers fit into the hardware-independent model.
Chapter 6	Hardware Components and Hardware Activities
	Describes the hardware components and activities related to device drivers. Read this chapter to obtain an understanding or to refresh your knowledge about the individual hardware components you will work with when writing your drivers.

Part 4 Kernel Environment

Part 4 contains three chapters, whose combined goal is to provide information about the kernel environment.

Chapter 7	Device Autoconfiguration
	Discusses the events that occur during the autoconfiguration of devices, with an emphasis on how autoconfiguration relates to static and loadable device drivers. In addition, the chapter provides detailed information on the data structures related to autoconfiguration. Read this chapter if you are not familiar with autoconfiguration on Digital UNIX. If you have experience in writing UNIX device drivers, you may want to read selected sections, especially the sections that discuss data structure members that are not familiar to you.
Chapter 8	Data Structures Used in I/O Operations
	Describes members of the structures used in input/output (I/O). Read this chapter if you are not familiar with the I/O-related data structures. If you are experienced with other UNIX I/O subsystems, you may want to read selected sections, especially those sections that will refresh your memory about the I/O data structures.
Chapter 9	Using Kernel Interfaces with Device Drivers
	Discusses the kernel interfaces most commonly used by device drivers, including those interfaces used to move data and to allocate and to free memory. Read this chapter if you need examples of when, how, and why you would use these kernel interfaces in device drivers.

Part 5 Device Driver Example

Part 5 contains one chapter, whose goal is to offer a more complex and challenging device driver for you to analyze.

Chapter 10	Writing a Character Device Driver
	Describes how to code a character device driver for a real device that operates on a TURBOchannel bus. Read this chapter if you want source code examples that exemplify a driver implementation for a real device. If you have experience in writing TURBOchannel device drivers, you may want to study only selected sections of the code.

Part 6 Device Driver Configuration

Part 6 contains three chapters, whose combined goal is to provide enough information to allow you to choose the driver configuration procedure most suitable for your development environment.

Chapter 11	Device Driver Configuration Models
	Provides an overview of the two configuration models: the third-party device driver configuration model and the traditional device driver configuration model. Read this chapter to obtain a general overview of the two models. The third-party driver configuration model is particularly well suited for driver developers who want to deliver Digital UNIX device drivers to their customers.
Chapter 12	Device Driver Configuration Syntaxes and Mechanisms
	Describes the syntaxes and mechanisms used to populate the files needed for device driver configuration. Read this chapter if you are not familiar with these syntaxes and mechanisms.
Chapter 13	Device Driver Configuration Examples
	Provides step-by-step instructions for configuring the example device drivers, using the third-party and traditional models. Read this chapter to learn how to configure the example drivers.

Part 7 Device Driver Reference

Part 7 contains four chapters, whose combined goal is to provide reference information on the header files, kernel interfaces, driver interfaces, and data structures used in writing device drivers on Digital UNIX.

Chapter 14	Header Files Related to Device Drivers
	Presents, in reference (man) page style, descriptions of the header files that device drivers most commonly use.
Chapter 15	Kernel Interfaces, ioctls, and Global Variables That Device Drivers Use
	Presents, in reference (man) page style, descriptions of the kernel support interfaces, ioctl commands, and global variables that device drivers use.
Chapter 16	Structures Related to Device Drivers
	Presents, in reference (man) page style, descriptions of the data structures that device drivers initialize and reference.
Chapter 17	Device Driver and Bus Configuration Interfaces
	Presents, in reference (man) page style, descriptions of the device driver and bus configuration interfaces.

Part 8 Appendixes

Part 8 contains two appendixes and a glossary.

Appendix A	Device Driver Example Source Listings Contains the source code listings for the examples presented in this book.
Appendix B	Device Driver Development Worksheets Provides worksheets for use in designing and coding a device driver.
Glossary	Glossary Provides definitions of terms used in the book.

Related Documentation

The printed version of the DEC OSF/1 documentation set is color coded to help specific audiences quickly find the books that meet their needs. (You can order the printed documentation from Digital.) This color coding is reinforced with the use of an icon on the spines of books. The following list describes this convention:

Audience	Icon	Color Code
General Users	G	Teal
System Administrators	S	Red
Network Administrators	N	Yellow
Programmers	P	Blue
Reference Page Users	R	Black

Some books in the documentation set help meet the needs of several audiences. For example, the information in some system books is also used by programmers. Keep this in mind when searching for information on specific topics.

The *Documentation Overview* provides information on all of the books in the DEC OSF/1 documentation set.

Writing device drivers is a complex task; driver writers require knowledge in a variety of areas. One way to acquire this knowledge is to have at least the following categories of documentation available:

• Hardware documentation

- Bus-specific device driver documentation
- Operating system overview documentation
- Programming tools documentation
- System management documentation
- Porting documentation
- Reference pages

The following sections list the documentation associated with each of these categories.

Hardware Documentation

You should have available the hardware manual associated with the device for which you are writing the device driver. You should also have access to the manual that describes the architecture associated with the CPU that the driver operates on, for example, the *Alpha Architecture Reference Manual*.

Bus-Specific Device Driver Documentation

Writing Device Drivers: Tutorial and Reference is the core manual for developing device drivers on the Digital UNIX operating system. It contains information needed for developing drivers on any bus that operates on Digital platforms. It also provides reference (man) page style descriptions of the header files, kernel interfaces, data structures, and other interfaces that device drivers use. The following books provide information about writing device drivers for a specific bus that is beyond the scope of the core tutorial and reference:

- *Writing EISA and ISA Bus Device Drivers*

   This manual provides information for systems engineers who write device drivers for the EISA/ISA bus. The manual describes EISA/ISA bus-specific topics, including EISA/ISA bus architecture and data structures that EISA/ISA bus device drivers use.

- *Writing PCI Bus Device Drivers*

   This manual provides information for systems engineers who write device drivers for the PCI bus. The manual describes PCI bus-specific topics, including PCI bus architecture and data structures that PCI bus device drivers use.

- *Writing Device Drivers for the SCSI/CAM Architecture Interfaces*

   This manual provides information for systems engineers who write device drivers for the SCSI/CAM Architecture interfaces.

   The manual provides an overview of the DEC OSF/1 SCSI/CAM

Architecture and describes User Agent routines, data structures, common and generic routines and macros, error handling and debugging routines. The manual includes information on configuration and installation. Examples show how programmers can define SCSI/CAM device drivers and write to the SCSI/CAM special I/O interface supplied by Digital to process special SCSI I/O commands.

- *Writing TURBOchannel Device Drivers*

  This manual contains information systems engineers need to write device drivers that operate on the TURBOchannel bus. The manual describes TURBOchannel-specific topics, including TURBOchannel kernel interfaces that TURBOchannel device drivers use.

- *Writing VMEbus Device Drivers*

  This manual contains information systems engineers need to write device drivers that operate on the VMEbus. The manual describes VMEbus-specific topics, including VMEbus architecture and kernel interfaces that VMEbus device drivers use. A VMEbus device driver example illustrates the use of these kernel interfaces.

Operating System Overview Documentation

Refer to the *Technical Overview* for a technical introduction to the Digital UNIX operating system (formerly DEC OSF/1). This manual provides a technical overview of the DEC OSF/1 system, focusing on the networking subsystem, the file system, virtual memory, and the development environment. In addition, the manual lists all system limits.

This manual does not supersede the Software Product Description (SPD), which is the definitive description of the DEC OSF/1 system.

Programming Tools Documentation

To create your device drivers, you use a number of programming development tools and should have on hand the manuals that describe how to use these tools. The following manuals provide information related to programming tools used in the Digital UNIX operating system environment:

- *Kernel Debugging*

  This manual provides information about debugging kernels. The manual describes using the dbx, kdbx, and kdebug debuggers to find problems in kernel code. It also describes how to write a kdbx utility extension and how to create and analyze a crash dump file.

  This manual is for system administrators responsible for modifying, rebuilding, and debugging the kernel configuration. It is also for system programmers who need to debug their kernel space programs.

- *Programming Support Tools*

  This manual describes several commands and utilities in the DEC OSF/1 system, including facilities for text manipulation, macro and program generation, source file management, and software kit installation and creation.

  The commands and utilities described in this manual are primarily for programmers, but some of them (such as `grep`, `awk`, `sed`, and the Source Code Control System (SCCS)) are useful for other users. This manual assumes that you are a moderately experienced user of UNIX systems.

- *Programmer's Guide*

  This manual describes the programming environment of the DEC OSF/1 operating system, with an emphasis on the C programming language.

  This manual is for all programmers who use the DEC OSF/1 operating system to create or maintain programs in any supported language.

System Management Documentation

Refer to the *System Administration* manual for information about building a kernel and for general information on system administration. This manual describes how to configure, use, and maintain the DEC OSF/1 operating system. It includes information on general day-to-day activities and tasks, changing your system configuration, and locating and eliminating sources of trouble.

This manual is for the system administrators responsible for managing the operating system. It assumes a knowledge of operating system concepts, commands, and configurations.

Porting Documentation

Refer to the *DEC OSF/1 Migration Guide* for a discussion of the differences between the Digital UNIX and ULTRIX operating systems. This manual compares the DEC OSF/1 operating system to the ULTRIX operating system by describing the differences between the two systems.

This manual has three audiences, as follows:

- General users can read this manual to determine the differences between using an ULTRIX system and using the DEC OSF/1 system.

- System and network administrators can read this manual to determine the differences between ULTRIX and DEC OSF/1 system administration.

- Programmers can read this manual to determine the differences between the ULTRIX programming environment and the DEC OSF/1 programming environment.

This manual assumes you are familiar with the ULTRIX operating system.

Reference Pages

The following reference (man) pages are of interest to device driver writers:

- *Reference Pages Section 2*

  This section defines system calls (entries into the DEC OSF/1 kernel) that programmers use. The introduction to Section 2, intro(2), lists error numbers with brief descriptions of their meanings. The introduction also defines many of the terms used in this section. This section is for programmers.

- *Reference Pages Section 3*

  This section describes the routines available in DEC OSF/1 programming libraries, including the C library, Motif library, and X library. This section is for programmers. In printed format, this section is divided into five volumes.

- *Reference Pages Section 4*

  Section 4 describes the format of system files and how the files are used. The files described include assembler and link editor output, system accounting, and file system formats. This section is for programmers and system administrators.

- *Reference Pages Sections 5 and 7*

  Section 5 contains miscellaneous information, including ASCII character codes, mail-addressing formats, text-formatting macros, and a description of the root file system. This section is for programmers and system administrators.

  Section 7 describes special files, related device driver functions, databases, and network support. This section is for programmers and system administrators.

- *Reference Pages Section 8*

  This section describes commands for system operation and maintenance. It is for system administrators. In printed format, this section is divided into two volumes.

Reader's Comments

Digital welcomes your comments on this or any other DEC OSF/1 manual. A Reader's Comment form is located in the back of each printed DEC OSF/1 manual and on line in the following location:

`/usr/doc/readers_comment.txt`

You can send your comments in the following ways:

* Internet electronic mail: `readers_comment@zk3.dec.com`

* Fax: 603-881-0120 Attn: UEG Publications, ZK03-3/Y32

* Mail:

  Digital Equipment Corporation
  UEG Publications Manager
  ZK03-3/Y32
  110 Spit Brook Road
  Nashua, NH 03062-9987

  The Reader's Comment form located in the back of each printed manual is postage paid if you mail it in the United States.

If you have suggestions for improving particular sections or find any errors, please indicate the manual title, order number, and section numbers. Digital also welcomes general comments.

Conventions

The following conventions are used in this book:

. . . (vertical ellipsis)	A vertical ellipsis indicates that a portion of an example that would normally be present is not shown.
. . . (horizontal ellipsis)	In syntax definitions, a horizontal ellipsis indicates that the preceding item can be repeated one or more times.
filename	In examples, syntax descriptions, and function definitions, this typeface indicates variable values.
buf	In function definitions and syntax definitions used in driver configuration, this typeface is used to indicate names that you must type exactly as shown.
[ ]	In formal parameter declarations in function definitions and in structure declarations, brackets indicate arrays. Brackets are also used to specify ranges for device minor numbers and device special files in `stanza.loadable` file fragments. However, for the syntax definitions used in driver configuration, these brackets indicate items that are optional.

Vertical bars separating items that appear in the syntax definitions used in driver configuration indicate that you choose one item from among those listed.

This book uses the word kernel "interface" instead of kernel "routine" or kernel "macro."

Acknowledgments

A number of people contributed their talents to the writing of this book. At the risk of offending some of the individuals by exclusion, we would like to acknowledge those people who deserve special recognition. We apologize to anyone inadvertently overlooked. We thank Larry Robinson and Jim Crapuchettes for writing the /dev/cb device driver. This example device driver gives readers the opportunity to study a real character device driver that implements many of the character device driver interfaces described in the book.

A number of people were responsible for the design and implementation of the third-party device driver configuration model. Thanks go to Robin Lewis and Debby Haeck for their work on the third-party model for static drivers. Jeff Anuszczyk helped with the implementation of the third-party model for loadable drivers. Thanks to Joe Yuen for critiquing and offering suggestions for improving the chapters related to the device driver configuration models.

We also thank Karl Ebner for creating the examples directory and associated README files that instruct engineers on how to configure the example loadable drivers. Thus, engineers can learn how to configure loadable drivers not only by reading the appropriate chapters in the book but also by using the different configuration utilities.

Al Delorey, Andrew Duane, and Tim Hoskins provided us with information related to understanding the CPU issues that influence device driver design. Specifically, Tim provided us with information and examples related to how a device driver accesses device registers on certain Alpha CPUs. Al Delorey supplied us with the details concerning 64-bit versus 32-bit issues. Andrew Duane provided us with information and examples related to memory barriers.

We also thank Joe Amato, Gary Dupuis, Don Dutile, Todd Katz, Ashoke Rampuria, and Tom Tierney for providing us with information on the data structures and kernel interfaces that device driver writers use.

Through their careful reviews, Barbara Glover, Maria DiCenso Vella, and Dick Buttlar offered us better ways to reword potentially ambiguous sections. Brian Stevens reviewed and provided input on configuring static kernels and on building loadable drivers.

We also thank Farrell Woods for performing extensive testing on the /dev/cb driver. Farrell's testing allowed us to learn more about how the driver operated on the Alpha platforms.

We also thank Paul Hammerstrom, documentation manager of the USG publications group at Digital, for initiating the idea for publishing the book through Digital Press (an imprint of Butterworth Heinemann). Thanks to Margaret Barham, also from USG publications, for copy editing the book. Thanks also to Ann Boland for her help in preparing the final copy of the book.

We extend our thanks to Henry Blacklock and Emmalyn Bentley, our technical editors, and to Susanna Ries, our graphic artist. Henry and Emmalyn are our chief user advocates and their editorial suggestions helped make this a more readable book. Susanna created a great number of illustrations that make it easier to understand abstract concepts. In addition, she never once complained when asked to make change after change to more than 80 illustrations.

We also extend our thanks to Bob Fontaine and Barbara Staines, who codeveloped the document object compiler with one of the authors of this book. This document object compiler allowed us to create the /dev/none and /dev/cb device driver source code examples as document objects and reuse them in the chapters without inline comments, in the appendix source code listings with inline comments, and as device driver source files that could be compiled. This object-oriented technique greatly reduced the chances for errors and guaranteed consistency for the different presentations of the example drivers.

Part 1

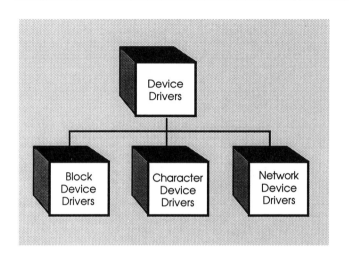

Introduction to Device Drivers   1

This chapter presents an overview of device drivers by discussing:

- The purpose of a device driver
- The types of device drivers
- Static versus loadable device drivers
- When a device driver is called
- The place of a device driver in the Digital UNIX operating system

The chapter concludes with an example of how a device driver in Digital UNIX reads a single character.

1.1 Purpose of a Device Driver

The purpose of a device driver is to handle requests made by the kernel with regard to a particular type of device. There is a well-defined and consistent interface for the kernel to make these requests. By isolating device-specific code in device drivers and by having a consistent interface to the kernel, adding a new device is easier.

1.2 Types of Device Drivers

A device driver is a software module that resides within the Digital UNIX kernel and is the software interface to a hardware device or devices. A hardware device is a peripheral, such as a disk controller, tape controller, or network controller device. In general, there is one device driver for each type of hardware device. Device drivers can be classified as:

- Block device drivers
- Character device drivers (including terminal drivers)
- Network device drivers
- Pseudodevice drivers

The following sections briefly discuss each type.

1.2.1 Block Device Driver

A block device driver is a driver that performs I/O by using file system block-sized buffers from a buffer cache supplied by the kernel. The kernel also provides for the device driver support interfaces that copy data between the buffer cache and the address space of a process.

Block device drivers are particularly well-suited for disk drives, the most common block devices. For block devices, all I/O occurs through the buffer cache.

1.2.2 Character Device Driver

A character device driver does not handle I/O through the buffer cache, so it is not tied to a single approach for handling I/O. You can use a character device driver for a device such as a line printer that handles one character at a time. However, character drivers are not limited to performing I/O one character at a time (despite the name ''character'' driver). For example, tape drivers frequently perform I/O in 10K chunks. You can also use a character device driver when it is necessary to copy data directly to or from a user process.

Because of their flexibility in handling I/O, many drivers are character drivers. Line printers, interactive terminals, and graphics displays are examples of devices that require character device drivers.

A terminal device driver is actually a character device driver that handles I/O character processing for a variety of terminal devices. Like any character device, a terminal device can accept or supply a stream of data based on a request from a user process. It cannot be mounted as a file system and, therefore, does not use data caching.

1.2.3 Network Device Driver

A network device driver attaches a network subsystem to a network interface, prepares the network interface for operation, and governs the transmission and reception of network frames over the network interface. This book does not discuss network device drivers.

1.2.4 Pseudodevice Driver

Not all device drivers control physical hardware. Such device drivers are called ''pseudodevice'' drivers. Like block and character device drivers, pseudodevice drivers make use of the device driver interfaces. Unlike block and character device drivers, pseudodevice drivers do not operate on a bus. One example of a pseudodevice driver is the pseudoterminal or pty terminal driver, which simulates a terminal device. The pty terminal driver is a character device driver typically used for remote logins.

1.3 Static Versus Loadable Device Drivers

Traditional kernels require that device drivers be installed by performing tasks that include rebuilding the kernel, shutting down the system, and rebooting. In these kinds of environments, device drivers can be viewed as static, that is, they are linked directly into the kernel at build time. Historically, this was necessary because many kernel interfaces consisted of static tables with no means of dynamic expansion. Thus, when changes are made to these device drivers, the only way to link them into the kernel is to go through the previously listed steps.

A design goal of OSF/1 was to provide cleanly architected kernel interfaces that would make it easier to add functionality to the kernel. To accomplish the task of allowing functional enhancements at kernel run time rather than at kernel build time, it was necessary for these kernel interfaces not to rely exclusively on statically configured tables. Thus, a set of kernel subsystems was defined.

A subsystem is a kernel module that defines a set of kernel framework interfaces that allow for the dynamic configuration and unconfiguration (adding and removal) of subsystem functionality. Examples of subsystems include (but are not restricted to) device drivers, file systems, and network protocols. The ability to dynamically add subsystem functionality is utilized by loadable drivers to allow the driver to be configured and unconfigured without the need for kernel rebuilds and reboots.

The Digital UNIX operating system embraces and builds on this portability and configurability philosophy by providing the ability for device drivers to be installed dynamically at run time without having to rebuild the kernel, shut down the system, and reboot. You must know the bus type and CPU architecture when deciding to make your device driver loadable. For Digital UNIX, loadable drivers are supported on the Alpha architecture on the EISA, PCI, and TURBOchannel buses. The example drivers in this book implement the loadable driver code.

1.4 When a Device Driver Is Called

Figure 1-1 shows that the kernel calls a device driver during:

- Autoconfiguration

  The kernel calls a device driver at autoconfiguration time to determine what devices are available and to initialize them.

- I/O operations

  The kernel calls a device driver to perform I/O operations on the device. These operations include opening the device to perform reads and writes and closing the device.

- Interrupt handling

  The kernel calls a device driver to handle interrupts from devices capable of generating them.

- Special requests

  The kernel calls a device driver to handle special requests through ioctl calls.

- Reinitialization

  The kernel calls a device driver to reinitialize the driver, the device, or both when the bus (the path from the CPU to the device) is reset.

Figure 1-1: When the Kernel Calls a Device Driver

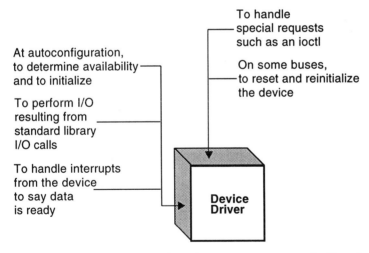

Some of these requests, such as input or output, result directly or indirectly from corresponding system calls in a user program. Other requests, such as the calls at autoconfiguration time, do not result from system calls but from activities that occur at boot time.

1.4.1 Place of a Device Driver in Digital UNIX

Figure 1-2 shows the place of a device driver in the Digital UNIX operating system relative to the device:

- User program or utility

  A user program, or utility, makes calls on the kernel but never directly calls a device driver.

- Kernel

  The kernel runs in supervisor mode and does not communicate with a device except through calls to a device driver.

Figure 1-2: Place of a Device Driver in Digital UNIX

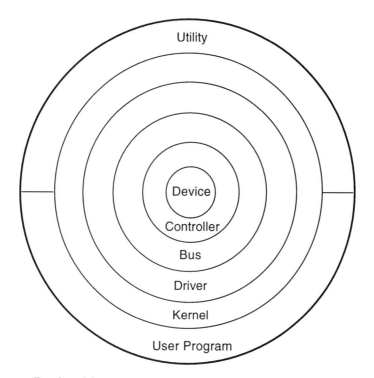

- Device driver

  A device driver communicates with a device by reading and writing through a bus to peripheral device registers.

- Bus

  The bus is the data path between the main processor and the device controller.

- Controller

  A controller is a physical interface for controlling one or more devices. A controller connects to a bus.

- Peripheral device

  A peripheral device is a device that can be connected to a controller, for example, a disk or tape drive. Other devices (for example, the network) may be integral to the controller.

The following sections describe these parts, with an emphasis on how a device driver relates to them.

1.4.2 User Program or Utility

User programs, or utilities, make system calls on the kernel that result in the kernel making requests of a device driver. For example, a user program can make a `read` system call, which calls the driver's `read` interface.

1.4.3 Kernel

The kernel makes requests to a device driver to perform operations on a particular device. Some of these requests result directly from user program requests. For example:

- Block I/O (open, strategy, close)

- Character I/O (open, write, close)

Autoconfiguration requests, such as `probe` and `attach`, do not result directly from a user program, but result from activities performed by the kernel. At boot time, for example, the kernel calls the driver's `probe` interface.

A device driver may call on kernel support interfaces to support such tasks as:

- Sleeping and waking (process rescheduling)

- Scheduling events

- Managing the buffer cache

- Moving or initializing data

- Configuring loadable drivers

1.4.4 Device Driver

A device driver, run as part of the kernel software, manages each of the device controllers on the system. Often, one device driver manages an entire set of identical device controller interfaces. With Digital UNIX, you can configure more device drivers than there are physical devices configured into the hardware system. At boot time, the autoconfiguration software determines which of the physical devices are accessible and functional and can produce a correct run-time configuration for that instance of the running kernel. Similarly, when a driver is dynamically loaded, the kernel performs the configuration sequence for each instance of the physical device.

As stated previously, the kernel makes requests of a driver by calling the driver's standard entry points (such as the `probe`, `attach`, `open`, `read`, `write`, `close` entry points). In the case of I/O requests such as `read` and `write`, it is typical that the device causes an interrupt upon completion of each I/O operation. Thus, a `write` system call from a user program may result in several calls on the `interrupt` entry point in addition to the original call on the `write` entry point. This is the case when the write request is segmented into several partial transfers at the driver level.

Device drivers, in turn, make calls upon kernel support interfaces to perform the tasks mentioned earlier.

The structure declaration giving the layout of the control registers for a device is part of the source for a device driver. Device drivers, unlike the rest of the kernel, can access and modify these registers. The Digital UNIX operating system also provides generic CSR I/O access kernel interfaces that allow device drivers to read from and write to these registers.

1.4.5 Bus

When a device driver reads or writes to the hardware registers of a controller, the data travels across a bus.

A bus is a physical communication path and an access protocol between a processor and its peripherals. A bus standard, with a predefined set of logic signals, timings, and connectors, provides a means by which many types of device interfaces (controllers) can be built and easily combined within a computer system. The term *OPENbus* refers to those buses whose architectures and interfaces are publicly documented, allowing a vendor to easily plug in hardware and software components. The TURBOchannel bus the EISA bus, the PCI bus, and the VMEbus, for example, can be classified as having OPENbus architectures.

Device driver writers must understand the bus that the device is connected to. This book covers topics that all driver writers need to know regardless of the bus.

1.4.6 Device Controller

A device controller is the hardware interface between the computer and a peripheral device. Sometimes a controller handles several devices. In other cases, a controller is integral to the device.

1.4.7 Peripheral Device

A peripheral device is hardware, such as a disk controller, that connects to a computer system. It can be controlled by commands from the computer and can send data to the computer and receive data from it. Examples of peripheral devices include:

- A data acquisition device, like a digitizer
- A line printer
- A disk or tape drive

1.5 Example of Reading a Character

This section provides an example of how Digital UNIX processes a read request of a single character in raw mode from a terminal. (Raw mode returns single characters.) Although the example takes a simplified view of character processing, it does show how control can pass from a user program to the kernel to the device driver. It also shows that interrupt processing occurs asynchronously from other device driver activity.

Figure 1-3 summarizes the flow of control between a user program, the kernel, the device driver, and the hardware. The figure shows the following sequence of events:

- A read request is made to the device driver (C–1 to C–3).
- The character is captured by the hardware (I–4 and I–5).
- The interrupt is generated (I–6).
- The interrupt service interface handles the interrupt (I–7 to I–9).
- The character is returned (C–10 to C–13).

Figure 1-3 provides a snapshot of the processing that occurs in the reading of a single character. The following sections elaborate on this sequence.

Figure 1-3: Simple Character Driver Interrupt Example

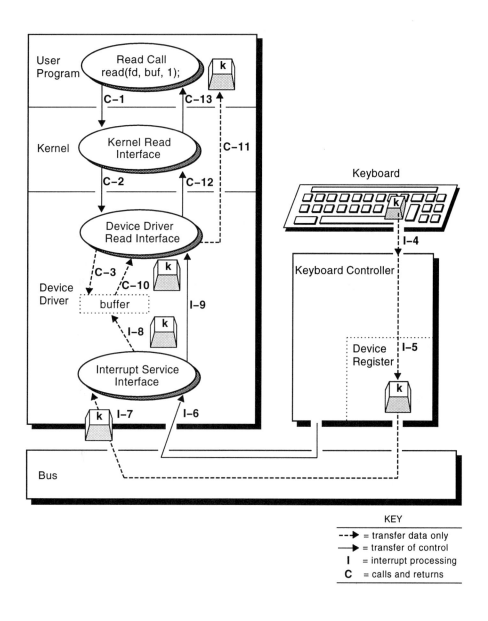

1.5.1 A Read Request Is Made to the Device Driver

A user program issues a read system call (C–1). The figure shows that the read system call passes three arguments: a file descriptor (the fd argument), the character pointer to where the information is stored (the buf argument), and an integer (the value 1) that tells the driver's read interface how many bytes to read. The calling sequence is blocked inside the device driver's read interface because the buffer where the data is stored is empty, indicating that there are currently no characters available to satisfy the read. The kernel's read interface makes a request of the device driver's read interface to perform a read of the character based on the arguments passed by the read system call (C–2). Essentially, the driver read interface is waiting for a character to be typed at the terminal's keyboard. The currently blocked process that caused the kernel to call the driver's read interface is not running in the CPU (C–3).

1.5.2 The Character Is Captured by the Hardware

Later, a user types the letter k on the terminal keyboard (I–4). The letter is stored in the device's data register (I–5).

1.5.3 The Interrupt Is Generated

When the user types a key, the console keyboard controller alters some signals on the bus. This action notifies the CPU that something has changed inside the console keyboard controller. This condition causes the CPU to immediately start running the console keyboard controller's interrupt service interface (I–6). The state of the interrupted process (either some other process or the idle loop) is saved so that the process can be returned to its original state as though it had never been interrupted in the first place.

1.5.4 The Interrupt Service Interface Handles the Interrupt

The console device driver's interrupt service interface first checks the state of the driver and notices that a pending read operation exists for the original process. The console device driver manipulates the controller hardware by way of the bus hardware in order to obtain the value of the character that was typed. This character value was stored somewhere inside the console controller's hardware (I–7). In this case, the value 107 (the ASCII representation for the k character) is stored. The interrupt service interface stores this character value into a buffer that is in a location known to the rest of the console driver interfaces (I–8). It then awakens the original, currently sleeping, process so that it is ready to run again (I–9). The interrupt service interface returns, in effect restoring the interrupted process (not the original process yet) so that it may continue where it left off.

1.5.5 The Character Is Returned

Later, the kernel's process scheduler notices that the original process is ready to run, and so allows it to run. After the original process resumes running (after the location where it was first blocked), it knows which buffer to look at to obtain the typed character (C–10). It removes the character from this buffer and puts it into the user's address space (C–11). The device driver's read interface returns control to the kernel's read interface (C–12). The kernel read interface returns control to the user program that previously initiated the read request (C–13).

1.5.6 Summary of the Example

Although this example presents a somewhat simplified view of character processing, it does illustrate how control passes from a user program to the kernel to the device driver. It also shows clearly that interrupt processing occurs asynchronously from other device driver activity.

Part 2

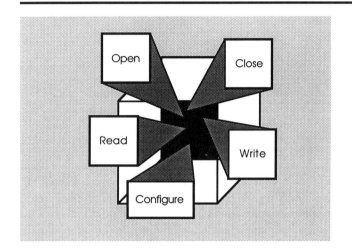

Developing a Device Driver 2

This chapter discusses how you develop a device driver. Included is a simple example called /dev/none, which is written by a fictitious third-party driver company called EasyDriver Incorporated. The /dev/none device driver is a simple device driver that performs the following tasks:

- Determines if the none device exists on the system

- Checks to ensure that the open request is unique and marks the device as open

- Copies data from the specified address space to the device

- Obtains and clears the count of bytes previously written to the device

- Closes the device

- Implements the tasks associated with the loadable version of the driver

The chapter uses worksheets to illustrate the kinds of information you need to gather to make developing the device driver easier. Appendix B provides these same worksheets for use in developing your own device drivers. If you use the worksheets for your driver development, consider organizing them in a device driver project binder. This will make them available to systems engineers who need to maintain the driver.

Specifically, the chapter describes the following tasks associated with developing any device driver:

- Gathering information

- Designing the device driver

- Understanding system data and address types that device drivers use

- Specifying the method for registering device interrupt handlers

- Determining the structure allocation technique

- Understanding CPU issues that influence device driver design

- Understanding bus issues that influence device driver design

- Creating a device driver development environment

The chapter concludes with a section on porting device drivers. This task is only for device driver writers who want to port device drivers from ULTRIX to Digital UNIX systems.

2.1 Gathering Information

The first task in writing a device driver is to gather pertinent information about the host system and the device for which you are writing the driver. You need to:

- Specify information about the host system
- Identify the conventions used in writing the driver
- Specify characteristics of the device
- Describe device usage
- Provide a description of the device registers
- Identify support in writing the driver

The following sections describe how you would fill out the worksheets provided for each of these tasks, using the /dev/none device driver as an example.

2.1.1 Specifying Information About the Host System

Figure 2-1 and Figure 2-2 show the host system information associated with the /dev/none driver. As the worksheets show, you gather the following information about the host system:

- The host CPU or CPUs your driver operates on
- The operating system or systems your driver operates on
- The bus or buses that your driver connects to

2.1.1.1 Specifying the Host CPU or CPUs on Which Your Driver Operates

The /dev/none driver will be developed for use on a DEC 3000 Model 500 AXP Workstation.

The goal should always be to write any device driver to operate on more than one CPU hardware platform, so you should be aware of any differences presented by different CPU architectures. By identifying the hardware platforms you want the driver to operate on, you can address any driver design decisions related to the CPU hardware architecture. This identification can help you determine whether one driver, with appropriate conditional compilation statements, can handle the CPU hardware platforms you want the driver to operate on. You might decide that it would be easier to write two device drivers.

Section 2.6 discusses some device driver design issues that are affected by CPU architectures.

Figure 2-1: Host System Worksheet for /dev/none

HOST SYSTEM WORKSHEET

Specify the Host CPU

Alpha–based CPUs:

DEC 3000 Model 400 AXP Workstation ☐

DEC 3000 Model 500 AXP Workstation ☑

DEC 4000 Model 600 AXP Distributed/ ☐
    Departmental Server

DEC 7000 Model 600 AXP Server ☐

DEC 10000 Model 600 AXP Server ☐

Other Alpha–based CPUs: _____

Other CPUs: _____

Figure 2-2: Host System Worksheet for /dev/none (Cont.)

```
HOST SYSTEM WORKSHEET (Cont.)

Other CPU Architectures:

_____     ☐
_____     ☐
_____     ☐
_____     ☐
_____     ☐


Specify the host operating system:

Digital UNIX          ☑

DEC OSF/1             ☐

ULTRIX               ☐

Other operating systems _____
_____


Specify the bus or buses you plan to
connect to the driver:

TURBOchannel          ☑

VMEbus               ☐

EISA bus             ☑

PCI bus              ☑

SCSI                 ☐

Pseudodevice drivers ☐

Other buses _____
_____
```

2.1.1.2 Specifying the Operating System or Systems on Which Your Driver Operates

The /dev/none driver will be developed for use on the Digital UNIX operating system. This is an important consideration because data structures and kernel interfaces differ among operating systems. For example, device drivers developed for Digital UNIX systems initialize a driver structure, while drivers developed for other versions of UNIX systems would initialize a different structure. This identification can help you determine the amount of work that is involved in porting an existing device driver from some other UNIX operating system to the Digital UNIX operating system.

Section 2.9 provides information to help you understand the tasks involved in porting from ULTRIX to Digital UNIX systems.

The host CPU types you select may dictate which host operating system you can use. For example, VAX-based CPUs do not support the Digital UNIX operating system. When you choose a CPU type, ensure that it supports the chosen operating system.

2.1.1.3 Specifying the Bus or Buses to Which Your Driver Connects

You must identify the bus that the device is connected to. Different buses require different approaches to writing the driver. For example, a VMEbus device driver writer must know how to allocate the VMEbus address space. This task is not applicable for drivers that operate on other buses. On the other hand, you may want to write one device driver that operates on several different bus architectures if these bus architectures exhibit enough common features. To show you how to write such a driver, comments and descriptions for the /dev/none driver point out differences in the coding for the following buses: EISA, PCI, and TURBOchannel.

Section 2.7 discusses some device driver design issues that are affected by bus architectures.

You must know the bus type and CPU architecture when deciding to make your device driver loadable. For Digital UNIX, loadable drivers are supported on the Alpha architecture on the EISA, PCI, and TURBOchannel buses. The example drivers in this book implement the loadable driver code.

Note that the worksheet provides a space for pseudodevice drivers. A pseudodevice driver, such as the pty terminal driver, is structured like any other driver. The difference is that a pseudodevice driver does not operate on a bus. Although this book does not specifically address pseudodevice drivers, the /dev/none driver discussed in Chapter 4 can be considered a pseudodevice driver because it does not connect to a real device.

2.1.2 Identifying the Standards Used in Writing the Driver

Figure 2-3 and Figure 2-4 show the device driver conventions worksheet for the /dev/none driver. As the worksheets show:

- You specify a naming scheme.

- You choose an approach for writing comments and documentation.

2.1.2.1 Specifying a Naming Scheme

The /dev/none driver uses the name none as the prefix for device driver interface names.

Device driver interfaces written for Digital UNIX can use the following naming conventions:

- A prefix that represents the name of some device. In this example, the device is called none; therefore, each driver interface begins with that prefix.

- The name of the interface, for example, open and close. Thus, the example driver has interface names such as noneopen and noneclose.

The /dev/none driver uses the name none as the prefix for data structures internal to the device driver. These structures include a data structure (often referred to as a softc structure) to store driver-specific information.

If you decide to use the CSR I/O access interfaces to read from and write to a device's CSR addresses, you create device register offset names. You can also use the prefix to create names for each of the device register offsets. Because the /dev/none driver uses the CSR I/O access interfaces, it uses the name none as the prefix to the device register offset name.

The /dev/none driver uses the prefix DN for device driver constant names. The prefix matches the first two characters in the driver name, /dev/none. These constants can represent values or macros. For example, the constant DN_SIZE might represent the size of the device register area.

The previously described naming schemes are recommendations, not requirements. The one naming requirement you must follow concerns the name of the configure interface, which for the /dev/none driver is none_configure. This interface is the configuration entry point called when the driver is dynamically loaded. For the configure interface, the underscore character (_) must follow the driver's name. This underscore character in the name is a requirement of the configuration process for loadable drivers and is the OSF/1 convention.

Before choosing a naming scheme, you have to make sure that these names do not conflict with other driver interface and structure names. To help you determine what names are currently used by the system, run the nm command on the kernel image file. This image file is usually called /vmunix. If you follow the third-party device driver configuration model described in Chapter 11, you should be particularly careful about choosing a naming scheme, ensuring that it does not conflict with that of other third-party driver vendors.

Also, if you follow the third-party device driver configuration model, you must choose a naming scheme for specifying device connectivity information in the following files: system configuration file and the stanza.static file fragment for static drivers and the stanza.loadable file fragment for loadable drivers. Chapter 12 discusses a naming scheme and these files. However, a brief discussion here can prepare you for a better understanding of the naming scheme when you encounter it in Chapter 12.

Third-party driver writers may need to specify bus, controller, and device information in the previously mentioned files. If you are supporting Digital devices, you specify valid strings listed in the *System Administration* guide. These strings represent the buses, controllers, and devices supported by Digital.

If you are supporting non-Digital devices, you can select any string other than those already chosen by Digital to represent the device. However, without an exclusive naming scheme, your choices could conflict with those of other third-party driver vendors. To avoid these conflicts, you can select a string that includes the vendor and product names and, possibly, the version and release numbers. This type of naming scheme minimizes the potential for name conflicts. For example, the driver writers at EasyDriver Incorporated might specify `edgd` for an internally developed device.

Figure 2-3: Device Driver Conventions Worksheet for /dev/none

DEVICE DRIVER CONVENTIONS WORKSHEET

Describe the naming scheme you are following for

Device driver interfaces:

The prefix for the /dev/none driver is none

Device driver structures:

The prefix for structures internal to the
/dev/none driver is none

Device driver constants:

The naming scheme for device driver constants
is DN (for Device None)

Device connectivity information:

The naming scheme for this information uses the
first two characters of the company name and
characters that represent the product name.
For devices supported by Digital, the naming scheme
follows that specified by Digital.

2.1.2.2 Choosing an Approach for Writing Comments and Documentation

The /dev/none driver takes two approaches to supplying comments in the driver code examples used in the book. In the first approach, the /dev/none driver contains no inline comments. Instead, the following convention is used:

```
int unit = minor(dev); 1
```

1 A number appears after a line of code in the /dev/none device driver example. Following the example, a corresponding number appears that contains an explanation of the associated line or lines. The device driver examples in Chapter 4 and Chapter 10 use the first approach to make the source code easier to read.

In the second approach, the /dev/none device driver supplies appropriate inline comments. The source code listings in Appendix A use the second approach.

In addition to providing background information and detailed explanations of the /dev/none driver, this book also offers information on device driver concepts, kernel interfaces, data structures, and so forth. Your approach to writing device driver documentation may be different.

Figure 2-4: Device Driver Conventions Worksheet for /dev/none (Cont.)

DEVICE DRIVER STANDARDS WORKSHEET (Cont.)

Describe the approach to writing comments in the device driver:

The /dev/none device driver will take two

approaches for supplying comments :

   1) The first approach has no inline comments
(source code examples in chapters)

   2) The second approach uses inline comments
(source code examples in appendix)

Describe the approach to writing device driver documentation:

The book that describes /dev/none also provides

information on driver concepts, device driver

interfaces, kernel structures, and so forth.

2.1.3 Specifying Characteristics of the Device

Figure 2-5 and Figure 2-6 show the device characteristics for the none device associated with the /dev/none driver.

As the worksheets show, you specify the following characteristics associated with the device:

- Whether the device is capable of block I/O
- Whether the device supports a file system
- Whether the device supports byte stream access
- Actions to take on interrupts
- How to reset the device
- Other device characteristics

2.1.3.1 Specifying Whether the Device Is Capable of Block I/O

If the device is capable of block I/O, then you would write a block device driver. A block device is one that stores data on its media in a standard way. For example, most disk drives store data in disk sectors (typically 512 bytes). Tape drives sometimes store data in a standard-size tape record.

Typically, block devices are random access devices (that is, disks) because the file system does not always perform I/O to sequential disk sectors. Tape devices are typically sequential access devices and, therefore, not suitable for using as a block device.

The none device is not capable of handling blocks of data so the No box on the worksheet is marked.

Figure 2-5: Device Characteristics Worksheet for the none Device

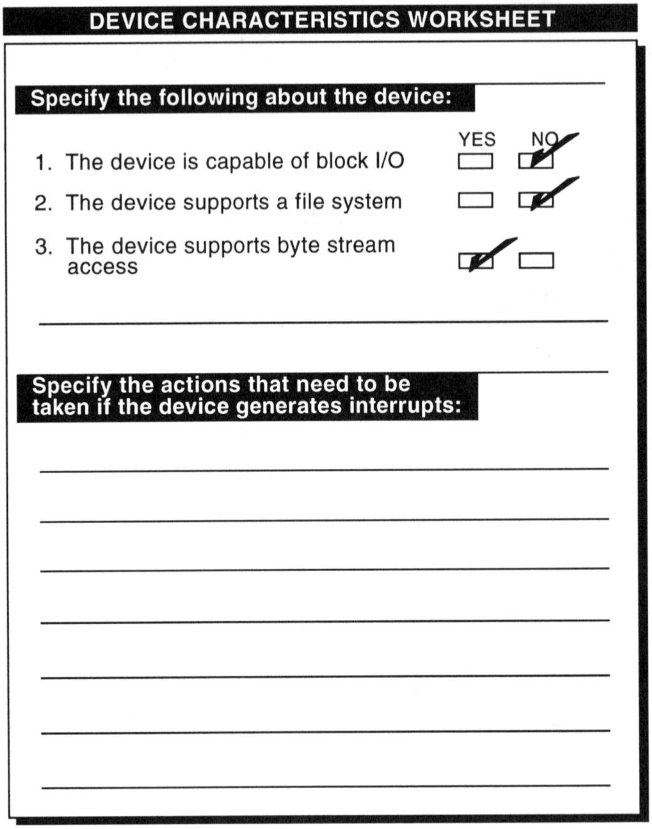

DEVICE CHARACTERISTICS WORKSHEET

Specify the following about the device:

		YES	NO
1.	The device is capable of block I/O	☐	☑
2.	The device supports a file system	☐	☑
3.	The device supports byte stream access	☑	☐

Specify the actions that need to be taken if the device generates interrupts:

_____

_____

_____

_____

_____

_____

_____

2.1.3.2 Specifying Whether the Device Supports a File System

Most block devices can support file systems. If a block device supports a file system, it must be able to map between file system blocks and the underlying structure on the device. In Digital UNIX, this mapping is accomplished through partition tables.

The `none` device is not capable of supporting file systems, so the No box on the worksheet is marked.

2.1.3.3 Specifying Whether the Device Supports Byte Stream Access

Most devices support byte stream access. You can view this access as sequentially accessing data through the device. For example, a sequence of characters typed at a terminal constitutes a byte stream. Most block devices can also be accessed in this manner. When a block device is accessed as a stream of bytes, the access is typically called "raw" access. When accessed this way, the data on the block device is accessed sequentially without any underlying structure being placed on the data (for example, disk sectors).

For the `none` device, the Yes box on the worksheet is marked.

2.1.3.4 Specifying Actions to Take on Interrupts

Use this space to summarize what the driver interrupt interfaces will do when the device generates an interrupt. For example, a terminal-type character driver's interrupt service interface (ISI) can receive a character that was typed on a user's keyboard. Typically, the ISI must determine the source of the interrupt, respond to the interrupt (for example, by reading in the data), and perform the appropriate actions to cause the interrupt to be dismissed.

Some other issues concerning interrupts are:

- Locking out interrupts when performing vulnerable operations
- Not locking out interrupts for an extended period of time
- Queueing the data so that the data-handling operation can be interrupted

Because the `none` device has no underlying physical hardware, it cannot generate interrupts. Therefore, this part of the worksheet is left blank.

Figure 2-6: Device Characteristics Worksheet for the none Device (Cont.)

DEVICE CHARACTERISTICS WORKSHEET (Cont.)

Specify how the device should be reset:

This characteristic is of no concern to the

/dev/none driver

_____

_____

_____

Use the remainder of the worksheet to specify any other device characteristics:

_____

_____

_____

_____

_____

2.1.3.5 Specifying How to Reset the Device

If the bus that the device controller is connected to supports the reset function, the device driver must be able to stop all current work and place the device connected to the controller in a known, quiescent state.

For example purposes, the none device can be connected to the following buses: EISA, PCI, and TURBOchannel. To keep the example driver simple, the reset function will not be implemented as part of the /dev/none device driver. Thus, this characteristic is of no concern to the /dev/none device driver.

2.1.3.6 Specifying Other Device Characteristics

Use this space to identify other characteristics of the device that might influence how you design your device driver.

2.1.4 Describing Device Usage

Figure 2-7 shows the device usage information for the none device associated with the /dev/none driver. As the worksheet shows, you gather the following information about device usage:

- The documentation you have on the device
- The number of instances of this device type that can reside on the system
- The purpose of the device

Figure 2-7: Device Usage Worksheet for the none Device

DEVICE USAGE WORKSHEET

List the documentation you have on the device (the device documentation can help you answer subsequent questions):

_____   _____

_____   _____

_____   _____

_____   _____

_____   _____

Answer the following questions about the usage of the device:

1. How many of this device type can reside on the system?

   The dev/none driver supports four instances of the none device

2. What will the device be used for?

   Not applicable to the none device

2.1.4.1 Listing the Device Documentation

For a real device, you should have on hand the manual for the device that is supplied by the manufacturer. The `none` device is a fictitious device; therefore, this section of the worksheet is left blank.

2.1.4.2 Specifying the Number of Device Types to Reside on the System

The number of devices that can be supported has a direct effect on the design of the driver. If only one will be supported, the driver need not worry about determining which device is being accessed. If a small number (for example, 2 – 5) is supported, the driver can use simple data structures and indexing to keep track of device access. If a greater number is to be supported, the driver must use more sophisticated methods to keep track of which device is being accessed.

The `/dev/none` driver is written to accommodate more than one instance. It will allocate fixed storage for four instances of the `none` device.

2.1.4.3 Describing the Purpose of the Device

For this device usage item, enter a short description of the purpose of the device. For example, the purpose of most disk devices is to provide storage for user data and files. The purpose of most terminal devices is to provide a means for interacting with users of the system.

This item is not applicable to the `none` device because it is a fictitious device.

2.1.5 Providing a Description of the Device Registers

Figure 2-8 and Figure 2-9 show the device register information for the `/dev/none` driver. As the worksheets show, you gather the following information about the device registers:

- A description or sketch of the layout of the device registers

  The manual supplied with the device would most likely have the following:

  - The layout of the registers and their offset
  - How the registers are used

  The worksheet shows a device register offset definition of the device register for the `none` device along with a comment as to its function. In previous versions of the Digital UNIX operating system (formerly known as DEC OSF/1), device drivers directly accessed the device registers through the members of a device register structure. The Digital UNIX operating system no longer supports this method of accessing device registers. Digital recommends that device drivers access the device registers by defining device register offsets and passing them as arguments to the `read_io_port` and `write_io_port` interfaces. The `/dev/none` driver now accesses the device registers for the `none` device by calling these interfaces. See Section 9.8.1 for more information on `read_io_port` and `write_io_port`.

- A mapping of the device register with the memory address

Figure 2-8: Device Register Worksheet for /dev/none

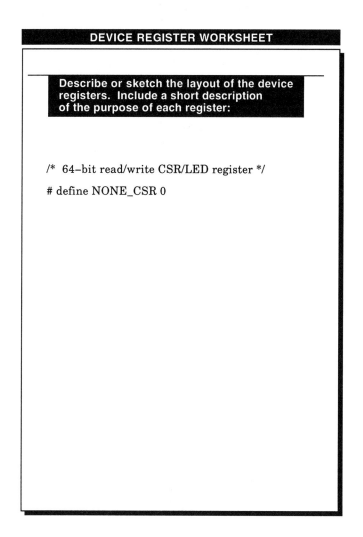

DEVICE REGISTER WORKSHEET

Describe or sketch the layout of the device
registers. Include a short description
of the purpose of each register:

/* 64–bit read/write CSR/LED register */

define NONE_CSR 0

Figure 2-9: Device Register Worksheet for /dev/none (Cont.)

DEVICE REGISTER WORKSHEET (Cont.)

Specify which memory address the registers are associated with:

Device Register	Memory Address
csr	base address + 0x2000

2.1.6 Identifying Support in Writing the Driver

Figure 2-10 shows the support associated with writing the `/dev/none` driver.

Figure 2-10: Device Driver Support Worksheet for /dev/none

```
┌───────────────────────────────────────────────────────────┐
│            DEVICE DRIVER SUPPORT WORKSHEET                 │
├───────────────────────────────────────────────────────────┤
│  Specify one of the following                             │
│  about the device driver:                                 │
│                                            YES   NO        │
│  1. There is no driver for this device.    [✓]  [ ]       │
│     You are going to write it from scratch.               │
│                                                           │
│  2. The driver for this device was previously  [ ]  [✓]   │
│     written for an ULTRIX system and the code             │
│     is available.                                         │
│                                                           │
│  3. The driver for this device was previously  [ ]  [✓]   │
│     written for a UNIX system and the code                │
│     is available.                                         │
│                                                           │
│  4. The driver for this device was previously  [ ]  [✓]   │
│     written for another operating system                  │
│     and the code is available.                            │
│                                                           │
│  5. The existing device driver has documentation. [ ] [✓] │
│                                                           │
│     If the answer is yes, specify the title               │
│     and location of documentation:                        │
│             Title:_____        │
│             Location:_____        │
│  6. If the source code is available,                      │
│     specify the location:                                 │
│             Location: _____        │
├───────────────────────────────────────────────────────────┤
│  7. Identify any experts available whose   Expert's Name, │
│     experience you can draw on for:        Number, Location:│
│     The device:       Colonel Green                       │
│     The design:       Professor Plum                      │
│     The coding:       Colonel Green, Mrs. White           │
│     The installation: Lieutenant Lemon, Colonel Green     │
│     The debugging:    Professor Plum                      │
│     The testing:      Professor Plum                      │
└───────────────────────────────────────────────────────────┘
```

As the worksheet shows, you gather the following information about device driver support:

- Whether you are writing the driver from scratch

  Answering this question can help determine the amount of time you need to spend writing the driver. Most device drivers are written by modifying an existing device driver that contains similar functionality. However, if source code for an existing driver is not available, it may take you more time to develop the driver. The /dev/none driver will be developed from scratch; therefore, the Yes box on the worksheet is marked.

- Whether the driver for the device was written previously for an ULTRIX system

  If the source code is available, you can update the device driver to reflect the Digital UNIX operating system. Section 2.9 provides information to help you understand the tasks involved in porting from an ULTRIX system to Digital UNIX. In this case, no source code is available so the No box on the worksheet is marked.

- Whether the driver for the device was written previously for a UNIX system

  If the source code is available, you can begin updating the device driver by identifying areas that are different from Digital UNIX. Other versions of the UNIX operating system would probably have different data structures and some of the kernel interfaces would probably behave differently and expect different arguments. In this case, no source code is available so the No box on the worksheet is marked.

- Whether the driver for the device was written previously for another operating system

  If the source code is available, you must study the differences between writing a device driver on that operating system and on the Digital UNIX operating system. This would probably be more difficult than the previous two situations. For the /dev/none device driver, the No box is marked.

- Whether the existing driver has documentation

  If the existing driver has documentation, specify the title and where it is located. Look for chapters on data structures and the use of kernel interfaces. These chapters might help in the porting task. For the /dev/none device driver, the No box is marked.

- Location of the existing driver source code

  This information is important. It allows systems engineers added to the project to locate the source code quickly. This item is left blank for the /dev/none device driver.

• Experts available

Writing complex device drivers is always easier when you have access not only to documentation but also to other device driver experts. The worksheet shows the experts who helped in writing the /dev/none device driver. Identifying your experts will make it easier for any future driver writers who work on your driver projects.

2.2 Designing the Device Driver

After you gather information about the host system and the device, your next task is to design the device driver. You need to:

• Specify the type of device driver

• Identify device driver entry points

• Specify the locking method for SMP-safe device drivers

• Specify the method for registering device interrupt handlers

The following sections describe how you would fill out the worksheets provided for each of the above tasks, using the /dev/none device driver as an example.

2.2.1 Specifying the Device Driver Type

Figure 2-11 shows the types of device drivers you can write on a Digital UNIX operating system. As the worksheet shows, you identify your driver as one of the following:

• Character

• Block

• Block and character

• Network

When using the buffer cache to perform I/O on blocks of data, you use block device drivers. Otherwise, you use character device drivers. Most device drivers are character drivers. Some device drivers are both character and block drivers. The network driver is another type of device driver. This book does not discuss network device drivers.

The Character box is marked for the /dev/none device driver because it has no requirements to handle blocks of data.

The worksheet also shows that these types of device drivers can be both loadable and static. When a driver is both loadable and static, the system manager decides at installation time whether to configure the driver as loadable or static. By designing and writing the driver to be both loadable and static, you offer customers maximum flexibility.

The Loadable and Static boxes are marked for the /dev/none device
driver.

Figure 2-11: Device Driver Type Worksheet for /dev/none

DEVICE DRIVER TYPE WORKSHEET

Specify the type of driver:

Character ☑

Block ☐

Character and Block ☐

Network ☐

- -

Loadable ☑

Static ☑

2.2.2 Identifying Device Driver Entry Points

Figure 2-12 shows the device driver entry points for the /dev/none device driver. The worksheet is divided into parts because the possible entry points vary depending on whether the driver is a block, character, or network driver. Because the /dev/none driver is a character driver, the worksheet shows the following entry points:

- noneprobe

  This interface determines if the device exists.

- nonecattach

  This interface would perform initialization for the none controller if the none device was a real device. Instead, nonecattach is a stub for future development.

- none_configure

  This interface is the configuration entry point called when the driver is dynamically loaded. For the configure interface, the underscore character (_) must follow the driver's name. This underscore character in the name is a requirement of the configuration process for loadable drivers and is the OSF/1 convention.

- noneopen

  This interface turns on the open flag.

- noneclose

  This interface turns off the open flag.

- noneioctl

  This interface handles the following special requests:
  - Reinitializes the count to zero
  - Returns the current count

- noneread

  This interface returns an EOF (end-of-file).

- nonewrite

  This interface adds to the count the number of characters written.

- noneintr

  This interface is a stub for future development.

Chapter 3 shows you how to set up the interfaces associated with character and block device drivers. Chapter 4 explains how the previous interfaces are implemented for the /dev/none driver.

You may want to describe the goals of the interfaces for your driver in a more formal device driver development specification. Consider adding this specification along with the worksheets to the device driver project binder.

Figure 2-12: Device Driver Entry Points Worksheet for /dev/none

DEVICE DRIVER ENTRY POINTS WORKSHEET

Block driver entry points:

Entry point:	Name:
probe	_____
slave	_____
cattach	_____
dattach	_____
configure	_____
open	_____
close	_____
strategy	_____
ioctl	_____
interrupt	_____
psize	_____
dump	_____

Character driver entry points:

Entry point:	Name:
probe	noneprobe
slave	_____
cattach	nonecattach (stub)
dattach	_____
configure	none_configure
open	noneopen
close	noneclose
strategy	_____
ioctl	noneioctl
stop	_____
reset	_____
read	noneread
write	nonewrite
mmap	_____
interrupt	noneintr (stub)

2.2.3 Specifying the Locking Method for SMP-Safe Device Drivers

Figure 2-13 shows the methods available in Digital UNIX to make your device drivers operate safely in a symmetric multiprocessing (SMP) environment. The worksheet shows that no method is chosen for the /dev/none device driver, which means it cannot operate safely in an SMP environment.

Writing Device Drivers: Advanced Topics describes the methods available for making your drivers operate safely in an SMP environment.

Figure 2-13: Locking Methods

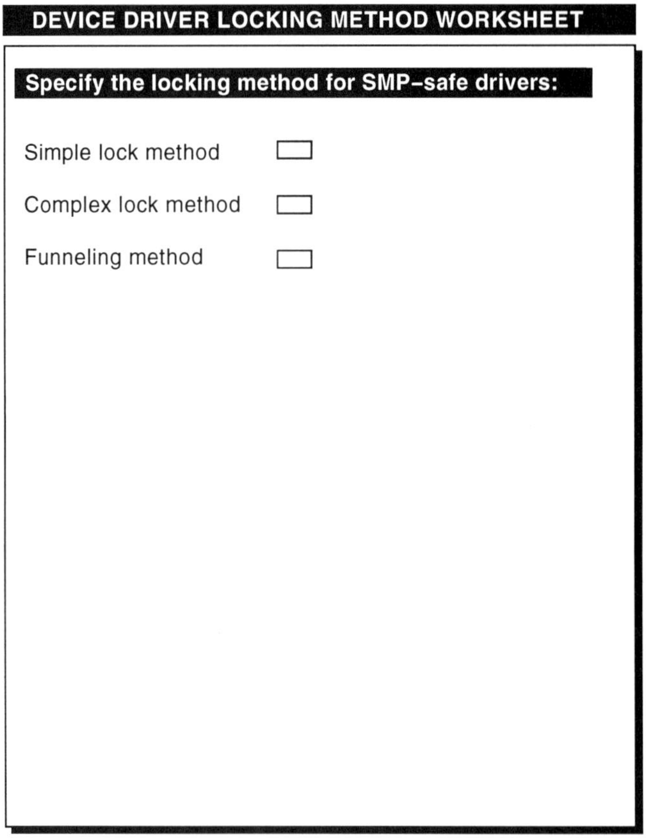

DEVICE DRIVER LOCKING METHOD WORKSHEET

Specify the locking method for SMP–safe drivers:

Simple lock method ☐

Complex lock method ☐

Funneling method ☐

2.3 Understanding System Data and Address Types that Device Drivers Use

When you design a device driver, you need to understand the following system data types and addresses that device drivers use:

- I/O handle data type
- Kernel-unmapped virtual address
- Kernel physical address
- Sparse space address
- Dense space address
- Bus physical address
- Memory address
- I/O address

The following sections discuss each of these system data types and addresses.

2.3.1 I/O Handle Data Type

To provide device driver binary compatibility across different bus architectures, different CPU architectures, and different CPU types within the same CPU architecture, Digital UNIX represents I/O bus address spaces through an I/O handle. An I/O handle is a data entity that is of type io_handle_t. Device drivers use the I/O handle to reference bus address space (either I/O space or memory space). The I/O or memory spaces contain either sparse space or dense space addresses. Section 2.3.4 and Section 2.3.5 describe sparse space and dense space addresses.

The bus configuration code passes the I/O handle to the device driver's xxprobe interface during device autoconfiguration. The number of I/O handles that the bus configuration code passes to the device driver depends on the bus the device operates on. The I/O handle passed to the driver's xxprobe interface describes how to access (address) that device on a particular Alpha CPU.

The properties associated with an I/O handle depend on what slot, bus, or child bus the device resides in.

An I/O handle has properties similar to memory-mapped registers on other UNIX-based systems (for example, TURBOchannel base address regions on ULTRIX MIPS). See the bus-specific device driver books for information on the I/O handle or handles a specific bus passes to a device driver's xxprobe interface.

You can perform standard C mathematical operations on the I/O handle. For example, you can add an offset to or subtract an offset from the I/O handle.

The following list points out restrictions on the use of the I/O handle:

- You cannot add two I/O handles.

- You cannot pass an I/O handle directly to the PHYS_TO_KSEG interface.

You call the iohandle_to_phys interface to convert an I/O handle into a valid system physical address that resides in sparse space, dense space, or bus physical address space.

One purpose of the I/O handle is to hide CPU-specific architecture idiosyncracies that describe how to access a device's control status registers (CSRs) and how to perform I/O copy operations. For example, rather than perform an I/O copy operation according to a specific CPU architecture, you call an I/O copy interface that uses the I/O handle. The use of the I/O handle guarantees device driver portability across those CPUs on which the I/O copy interface is implemented.

2.3.2 Kernel-Unmapped Virtual Address

A kernel-unmapped virtual address is an address that resides in kernel space. This address is sometimes referred to as a kseg address. A kernel-unmapped virtual address makes use of the virtual memory (VM) mapping registers. You can also use a kernel-unmapped virtual address to operate on sparse space, dense space, and I/O spaces available on different Alpha CPUs.

The KSEG_TO_PHYS interface converts a kernel-unmapped virtual address to a physical address. Device drivers can use this physical address in DMA operations.

The PHYS_TO_KSEG interface converts a physical address to a kernel-unmapped virtual address.

2.3.3 Kernel Physical Address

A kernel physical address is an address that resides in kernel space but does not use the virtual memory (VM) mapping registers.

2.3.4 Sparse Space Address

A sparse space address is an address that resides in sparse space. Sparse space contains addresses that reside in bus address space (either I/O space or memory space). All Alpha CPUs support sparse space. As a result, all bus configuration code should supply an I/O handle that references bus address space.

The Digital UNIX operating system provides the following interfaces that allow device drivers to perform copy operations on addresses, zero blocks of memory on addresses, read from addresses, and write to addresses that reside in sparse space. All of these interfaces take one or more I/O handles that reference addresses in sparse space as arguments.

- `io_copyin`

  Copies data from bus address space to system memory

- `io_copyio`

  Copies data from bus address space to bus address space

- `io_copyout`

  Copies data from system memory to bus address space

- `io_zero`

  Copies data from bus address space to system memory

- `READ_BUS_D8`

  Reads a byte (8 bits) from a device register

- **`READ_BUS_D16`**

  Reads a word (16 bits) from a device register

- `READ_BUS_D32`

  Reads a longword (32 bits) from a device register

- `READ_BUS_D64`

  Reads a quadword (64 bits) from a device register

- `read_io_port`

  Reads data from a device register

- `WRITE_BUS_D8`

  Writes a byte (8 bits) to a device register

- `WRITE_BUS_D16`

  Writes a word (16 bits) to a device register

- `WRITE_BUS_D32`

  Writes a longword (32 bits) to a device register

- `WRITE_BUS_D64`

  Writes a quadword (64 bits) to a device register

- `write_io_port`

  Writes data to a device register

Chapter 9 provides examples on how to use the `io_copyin`, `io_copyio`, `io_copyout`, `read_io_port`, and `write_io_port` interfaces.

2.3.5 Dense Space Address

A dense space address is an address that resides in dense space. Dense space is an area of I/O space or memory space that device drivers can access as if it were memory. Not all Alpha CPUs support dense space.

The Digital UNIX operating system provides the following interfaces that allow device drivers to perform copy operations on and zero blocks of memory on addresses that reside in dense space:

- bcopy

  Copies a series of bytes with a specified limit

- blkclr and bzero

  Zeros a block of memory

- copyin

  Copies data from a user address space to a kernel address space

- copyinstr

  Copies a null-terminated string from a user address space to a kernel address space

- copyout

  Copies data from a kernel address space to a user address space

- copyoutstr

  Copies a null-terminated string from a kernel address space to a user address space

2.3.6 Bus Physical Address

A bus physical address is an address that the device driver can pass to another device on the bus. A device driver can use a bus physical address to reference the I/O or memory space of other cards that reside on the same bus as the card that the device driver controls.

2.3.7 Memory Address

A memory address is either a sparse space or dense space address that performs a memory cycle on a specific bus.

2.3.8 I/O Address

An I/O address is either a sparse space or dense space address that performs an I/O cycle on a specific bus.

2.4 Specifying the Method for Registering Device Interrupt Handlers

An interrupt service interface (ISI) is a device driver routine (sometimes called an interrupt handler) that handles hardware interrupts. In previous versions of the Digital UNIX operating system (formerly known as DEC OSF/1), driver writers implementing static-only device drivers specified a device driver's ISI in the system configuration file if they followed the traditional device driver configuration model; they specified the ISI in the config.file file fragment if they followed the third-party device driver configuration model. Loadable device drivers, on the other hand, must call a number of kernel interfaces and use specific data structures to register, deregister, enable, and disable a device driver's ISI.

Digital recommends that all new drivers (static and loadable) call the handler interfaces to dynamically register ISIs.

The dynamic registration of ISIs involves the use of the following data structures:

*   ihandler_t
*   handler_intr_info

Section 7.5 describes the data structures you use to dynamically register ISIs. Section 9.6 shows examples of how to call the handler interfaces to dynamically register ISIs.

See the bus-specific book to determine the interrupt handler registration method(s) supported by the bus your driver operates on. The TURBOchannel bus, for example, supports both methods: through the system configuration file and by calling the handler interfaces.

2.5 Determining the Structure Allocation Technique

Another design consideration is the technique you plan to use for allocating data structures. Generally, there are two techniques you can follow: dynamic allocation and static allocation. Dynamic allocation is the recommended method; however, static allocation is discussed in this book because many existing drivers allocate their data structures statically. Table 2-1 lists the structure allocation techniques discussed in this book along with some guidelines to help you choose the best method for your device drivers. Sections that provide examples of each follow the table.

Table 2-1: Structure Allocation Technique Guidelines

Technique	Guidelines for Using
Static allocation model 1	Use this technique if you do not plan to implement loadable device drivers now or in the future.
Static allocation model 2	Use this technique if you: • Plan to implement loadable drivers now or in the future • Know that the maximum number of devices is five or less • Know that the driver does not use numerous data structures
Dynamic allocation	Use this technique if you: • Plan to implement loadable drivers now or in the future • Know that the maximum number of devices is greater than five • Know that the driver uses numerous data structures

2.5.1 Static Allocation Model 1 Technique

The static allocation model 1 technique lets you statically allocate data structures by using the compile time variable. The following code fragment uses the none_softc structure associated with the /dev/none device driver to illustrate the static allocation model 1 technique:

```
        .
        .
        .
/*****************************************************
 * softc structure used to compare static and       *
 * dynamic allocation techniques                     *
 *****************************************************/
struct none_softc {
        int sc_openf;
        int sc_count;
        int sc_state;
}; 1
        .
        .
        .
```

```
/**************************************************
 * Declarations using the static technique    * 2
 **************************************************/
struct controller *noneinfo[NNONE];
struct none_softc none_softc[NNONE];
    .
    .
    .
```

1 Defines a structure called none_softc, which is used to share data
between the different /dev/none device driver interfaces. The
members of this data structure are not important to the discussion of the
static allocation model 1 technique.

2 These declarations appear in the driver source none.c. The declarations
show that the main characteristic of this structure allocation technique is
the use of the compile time variable to size the structure arrays. Thus, in
the example, the array of pointers to controller structures and the
none_softc structure array use the compile time variable NNONE.
Note that in the none_softc structure array there is one structure for
each instance of the device as specified in the system configuration file.

The config program defines the compile time variable for statically
configured drivers and stores it in the device driver header file. In the
example, the device driver header file created by config would contain
the following entry if there were four devices on the system:

```
#define NNONE 4
```

Section 3.1.1 provides additional details about the device driver header
file and the compile time variable. The major drawback to statically
allocating the data structures is that the number of configured devices is
not available when loadable drivers are built. If you want your drivers to
be both static and loadable, you need to dynamically allocate the data
structures or statically allocate enough data structures to match the
maximum configuration.

2.5.2 Static Allocation Model 2 Technique

The static allocation model 2 technique lets you statically allocate enough
data structures to accommodate the maximum configuration. To make access
to the data structures as easy as possible, you statically declare an array of
pointers to the data structures. The only difference between the static
allocation techniques is that static allocation model 1 technique uses the
compile time variable created by config and static allocation model 2
technique uses a constant that defines the maximum number of devices.

The following code fragment illustrates the static allocation model 2
technique:

```
/***********************************************
 * structure declarations to illustrate the    *
 * static allocation model 2 technique          *
 ***********************************************/
        .
        .
        .
#define MAX_NONE 4 /* Define maximum number of */
                   /* devices */ ①
/***********************************************
 * Use the constant to size the arrays         * ②
 ***********************************************/
struct controller *noneinfo[MAX_NONE];
struct none_softc none_softc[MAX_NONE];
        .
        .
        .
```

① If you knew that your device driver supported at most four instances of
some device (for example, four controllers), you would first declare a
constant to represent this maximum number. Thus, the example defines a
MAX_NONE constant and assigns it the maximum value 4.

You would probably want to declare this constant in a *name_data.c*
file. See Section 3.1.5 for a description of the *name_data.c* file.

② The next two lines use the MAX_NONE constant to size the respective
arrays. In the first line, MAX_NONE sizes the array of pointers to
controller structures, and in the second line it sizes an array of
none_softc structures.

The disadvantage of the static allocation model 2 technique is that, if you
have only one instance of the device on the system, you are wasting three of
the four declared none_softc data structures. If the number of these data
structures does not exceed five and if they contain no more than a reasonable
number of data members, the static allocation model 2 technique is
acceptable.

2.5.3 Dynamic Allocation Technique

The previously described static allocation model 2 technique is suitable for
device drivers that support a small number of devices (five or less). Some
device drivers, however, support more than five devices and declare a
significant number of data structures that might contain a large amount of
data. For example, the Digital Storage Architecture (DSA) subsystem can
support up to 256 disks and at least 16 controllers. Clearly, it would not be
desirable to always allocate all the required data structures because for most

configurations there are not nearly that many devices present. Statically
allocating the maximum number of data structures would waste too much
space. The DSA subsystem and systems like it are good examples of where
dynamic configuration of the required data structures would be beneficial.

In this model of dynamically allocating the data structures, you need to:

- Determine the maximum configuration

- Statically declare an array of pointers to the data structures

- Allocate the data structures

- Access the members of the dynamically allocated data structures

- Free up the dynamically allocated memory

2.5.3.1 Determining the Maximum Configuration

The first task is to determine the maximum number of instances of the device
that can exist on your system. In the example, suppose that there can be a
maximum of 16 none devices. Thus, there is one driver that handles, at
most, 16 instances of the device. In this case, you could define a constant
similar to the following in the name_data.c file:

```
#define MAX_NONE 16
```

2.5.3.2 Statically Declaring an Array of Pointers to the Data Structures

Your next task is to statically declare an array of pointers to the data
structures that the device driver will use. The example declares an array of
pointers to controller and none_softc data structures as follows:

```
struct controller *noneinfo[MAX_NONE];
struct none_softc *none_softc[MAX_NONE];
```

These declarations are pointers to the data structures, not the data structures
themselves. Although this approach is not required, it is chosen for the
example because having the static array of pointers makes access to the data
structures easy.

2.5.3.3 Allocating the Data Structures

The next task is to allocate the data structures in the Autoconfiguration
Support Section of the device driver. This section is where you implement
the driver's probe, attach, and slave interfaces. The following
example shows how to allocate the data structures with the probe interface.

The driver's probe interface is called for each instance of the device that is
actually present on the system. This makes the probe interface one place to

dynamically allocate the data structures, as in the following example:

```
noneprobe(handle, ctlr)
    io_handle_t handle; /* I/O handle */
    struct controller *ctlr; 1
{
    if (ctlr->ctlr_num > MAX_NONE) /* Is unit greater *
                                    * than 16? */ 2
            return(0);
    .
    .
    .
/*************************************************
 * Allocate the softc structure associated      *
 * with this instance                           * 3
 *************************************************/
    if (none_softc[ctlr->ctlr_num] == (struct none_softc *)NULL) {
            struct none_softc *sc;
            MALLOC(sc, struct none_softc *,
                sizeof(struct none_softc),
                M_DEVBUF, M_NOWAIT);
            if (sc) == (struct none_softc *)NULL) {
                    return(0);
            }
    }
    return(1);
}
```

1. The bus configuration code passes the controller structure associated with this device as a parameter to the noneprobe interface. The noneprobe interface uses the ctlr_num member to tell you which instance of the controller you are referring to.

2. Determines if there are more than 16 controllers. If there are, noneprobe returns the value zero (0) to indicate an error. Otherwise, it allocates the data structures.

3. Now you allocate the data structures associated with this instance. The first if statement is a test to make sure that the noneprobe interface has not already been called for this unit.

   You then dynamically allocate the memory to accommodate the none_softc data structures by calling the MALLOC interface and passing to it the number of bytes to allocate.

   The second if statement checks the return value from MALLOC. The return value is NULL if there is no memory available to be dynamically allocated for this instance of the driver. The driver will not be operational without its data structures. In this case, return the value zero (0) to indicate that the driver's probe interface failed.

2.5.3.4   Accessing the Members of the Dynamically Allocated Data Structures

After you dynamically allocate the data structures in the `probe` interface, you need to correctly access them. When using the compile time variable to size the arrays, the declaration appears as follows:

```
struct none_softc none_softc[NNONE];
```

The declaration for dynamically allocating the data structures appears as follows:

```
struct none_softc *none_softc[MAX_NONE];
```

The difference is that one declares the actual data structures while the other declares pointers to an array of the data structures. Thus, to access the data structures, you must reference the data structures as an array of pointers. For example:

```
        .
        .
        .
/************************************************
 * Accessing statically allocated data          *
 * structures                                    *
 ************************************************/
struct controller *ctlr = noneinfo[ctlr->ctlr_num];
struct none_softc *sc = &none_softc[ctlr->ctlr_num];
        .
        .
        .
/************************************************
 * Accessing dynamically allocated data          *
 * structures                                    *
 ************************************************/
struct controller *ctlr = noneinfo[ctlr->ctlr_num]; /* No change from *
                                                     * static allocation */
struct none_softc *sc = none_softc[ctlr->ctlr_num]; /* Different from static *
                                                     * allocation */
```

The reference to the `none_softc` structures uses the address operator in the static case. The address operator is not used in the dynamic case.

2.5.3.5   Freeing Up the Dynamically Allocated Memory

Loadable drivers have a `ctlr_unattach` or a `dev_unattach` interface. When the driver is unloaded, these interfaces are called for each instance of the controller or device present on the system. When these interfaces are called, they should free up the dynamically allocated memory. For the `/dev/none` device driver, the `ctlr_unattach` interface frees up memory as follows:

```
       .
       .
       .
if (ctlr->ctlr_num < MAX_NONE) {
/************************************************
 * Free up the dynamically allocated memory    * 1
 ************************************************/
if (none_softc[ctlr->ctlr_num] != (struct none_softc *)NULL) {
    FREE(none_softc[ctlr->ctlr_num], sizeof(struct none_softc));
/************************************************
 * Set the array element to NULL               * 2
 ************************************************/
    none_softc[ctlr->ctlr_num] = (struct none_softc *)NULL;
    }
       .
       .
       .

}
```

[1] This example of a `ctlr_unattach` interface uses the `ctlr_num`
      member to refer to the specific instance of the controller that the
      `/dev/none` driver operates on. The `if` statement is included as a
      safety check. Note that the `FREE` interface is used to free the memory
      previously allocated in a call to `MALLOC`.

[2] After the dynamically allocated memory has been freed, the following
      line sets the `none_softc` array to NULL. This ensures that there will
      be no dangling references to the memory.

2.6 Understanding CPU Issues That Influence Device Driver Design

Whenever possible, you should design a device driver so that it can
accommodate peripheral devices that operate on more then one CPU
architecture. You need to consider the following issues to make your drivers
portable across CPU architectures:

- Control status register (CSR) access
- I/O copy operation
- Direct memory access (DMA) operation
- Memory mapping
- 64-bit versus 32-bit
- Memory barriers

The discussion centers around Alpha and MIPS CPU platforms, but the
topics may be applicable to other CPU architectures. The following sections

discuss each of these issues.

2.6.1 Control Status Register Issues

Many device drivers based on the UNIX operating system access a device's
control status register (CSR) addresses directly through a device register
structure. This method involves declaring a device register structure that
describes the device's characteristics, which include a device's control status
register. After declaring the device register structure, the driver accesses the
device's CSR addresses through the member that maps to it. In the
following code fragment, the device driver accesses the none device's CSR
address through the status member of the device register structure:

```
        .
        .
        .
/***********************************************
 * Device register structure                  *
 ***********************************************/
typedef volatile struct {
  int status;
  int error;
}some_registers;
     .
     .
     .
/***********************************************
 * noneprobe interface                         *
 ***********************************************/
noneprobe(handle, ctlr)
io_handle_t handle; /* I/O handle */
struct controller *ctlr; /* controller structure */
                         /* for this unit */
/***********************************************
 * Initialize pointer to none_registers        *
 * structure                                   *
 ***********************************************/
register some_registers *reg = (struct some_registers *) handle;
     .
     .
     .
/***********************************************
 * If device error, return 0                   *
 ***********************************************/
if (reg->status & SOME_ERROR)
{
  return(0);
}
/***********************************************
 * Otherwise, initialize the csr               *
 ***********************************************/
reg->status = 0;
```

There are some CPU architectures that do not allow you to access the device
CSR addresses directly. If you want to write your device driver to operate on
both types of CPU architectures, you can write one device driver with the

appropriate conditional compilation statements. You can also avoid the potentially confusing proliferation of conditional compilation statements by using the CSR I/O access kernel interfaces provided by Digital UNIX to read from and write to the device's CSR addresses. Because the CSR I/O access interfaces are designed to be CPU hardware independent, their use not only simplifies the readability of the driver, but also makes the driver more portable across different CPU architectures and different CPU types within the same architecture.

Section 9.8.1 shows you how to use the CSR I/O access kernel interfaces to read from and write to the device's CSR addresses.

Digital recommends that device drivers access the device registers by defining device register offsets and passing them as arguments to the I/O access interfaces.

2.6.2 I/O Copy Operation Issues

I/O copy operations can differ markedly from one device driver to another because of the differences in CPU architectures. Using techniques other than the generic kernel interfaces that Digital provides for performing I/O copy operations, you would probably not be able to write one device driver that operates on more than one CPU architecture or more than one CPU type within the same architecture.

To provide portability when performing I/O copy operations, Digital UNIX provides generic kernel interfaces to the system-level interfaces required by device drivers to perform an I/O copy operation. Because these I/O copy interfaces are designed to be CPU hardware independent, their use makes the driver more portable across different CPU architectures and more than one CPU type within the same architecture.

Section 9.8.2 shows you how to call these I/O copy operation interfaces.

2.6.3 Direct Memory Access Operation Issues

Direct memory access (DMA) operations can differ markedly from one device driver to another because of the DMA hardware support features for buses on Alpha systems and because of the diversity of the buses themselves. Using the current techniques for performing DMA, you would probably not be able to write one device driver that operates on more than one CPU architecture or more than one CPU type within the same architecture.

To provide portability with regard to DMA operations, Digital UNIX provides generic kernel interfaces to the system-level interfaces required by device drivers to perform a DMA operation. These generic interfaces are typically called ''mapping interfaces.'' This is because their historical background is to acquire the hardware and software resources needed to map contiguous I/O bus addresses and accesses into discontiguous system memory addresses and accesses. Because these interfaces are designed to be CPU hardware independent, their use makes the driver more portable across different CPU architectures and more than one CPU type within the same architecture.

Section 9.9 shows you how to use these mapping interfaces to achieve device driver portability across different CPU architectures.

2.6.4 Memory Mapping Issues

Many device drivers based on the UNIX operating system provide a memory map section to handle applications that make use of the mmap system call. An application calls mmap to map a character device's memory into user address space. Some CPU architectures, including the Alpha architecture, do not support an application's use of the mmap system call. If your device driver operates only on CPUs that support the mmap feature, you can continue writing a memory map section. If, however, you want the device driver to operate on CPUs that do not support the mmap feature, you should design the device driver so that it uses something other than a memory map section.

2.6.5 32-Bit Versus 64-Bit Issues

This section describes issues related to declaring data types for 32-bit and 64-bit CPU architectures. By paying careful attention to data types, you can make your device drivers work on both 32-bit and 64-bit systems. Table 2-2 lists the C compiler data types and bit sizes for the MIPS 32-bit and the Alpha 64-bit CPUs.

Table 2-2: C Compiler Data Types and Bit Sizes

C Type	MIPS 32-Bit Data Size	Alpha 64-Bit Data Size
short	16 bits	16 bits
int	32 bits	32 bits
long	32 bits	64 bits
* (pointer)	32 bits	64 bits
long long	64 bits	64 bits

Table 2-2: (continued)

C Type	MIPS 32-Bit Data Size	Alpha 64-Bit Data Size
char	8 bits	8 bits

The following sections describe some common declaration situations:

- Declaring 32-bit variables
- Declaring 32-bit and 64-bit variables
- Declaring arguments to C interfaces (functions)
- Declaring register variables
- Performing bit operations on constants
- Using NULL and zero (0) values
- Modifying type `char`
- Declaring bit fields
- Using `printf` formats
- Using `mb` and `wbflush`
- Using the `volatile` compiler keyword

Note

The `/usr/sys/include/io/common/iotypes.h` file defines constants used for 64-bit conversions. See Chapter 14 for a description of the contents of this file.

2.6.5.1 Declaring 32-Bit Variables

Declare any variable that you want to be 32 bits in size as type `int`, not type `long`. The size of variables declared as type `int` is 32 bits on both the 32-bit MIPS systems and the 64-bit Alpha systems.

Look at any variables declared as type `int` in your existing device drivers to determine if they hold an address. On Alpha systems, `sizeof (int)` is not equal to `sizeof (char *)`.

In your existing device drivers, also look at any variable declared as type `long`. If it must be 32 bits in size, you have to change the variable declaration to type `int`.

2.6.5.2 Declaring 32-Bit and 64-Bit Variables

If a variable should be 32 bits in size on a 32-bit MIPS system and 64 bits in size on a 64-bit Alpha system, declare it as type `long`.

2.6.5.3 Declaring Arguments to C Functions

Be aware of arguments to C interfaces (functions) where the argument is not explicitly declared and typed. You should explicitly declare the formal parameters to C interfaces; otherwise, their sizes may not match up with the calling program. The default size is type `int`, which truncates 64-bit addresses.

2.6.5.4 Declaring Register Variables

When you declare variables with the `register` keyword, the compiler defaults its size to that of type `int`. For example:

```
register somevariable;
```

Remember that these variable declarations also default to type `int`. For example:

```
unsigned somevariable;
```

Thus, if you want the variable to be 32 bits in size on both the 32-bit MIPS and 64-bit Alpha systems, the above declarations are correct. However, if you want the variable to be 32 bits in size on a 32-bit MIPS system and 64 bits in size on a 64-bit Alpha system, declare the variables explicitly, using the type `long`.

2.6.5.5 Performing Bit Operations on Constants

By default, constants are 32-bit quantities. When you perform shift or bit operations on constants, the compiler gives 32-bit results. If you want a 64-bit result, you must follow the constant with an `L`. Otherwise, you get a 32-bit result. For example, the following is a left shift operation that uses the `L`:

```
long foo, bar;
foo = 1L << bar;
```

2.6.5.6 Using NULL and Zero Values

Using the value zero (0) where you should use the value NULL means that you get a 32-bit constant. On Alpha systems, this usage could mean the value zero (0) in the low 32 bits and indeterminate bit values in the high 32 bits. Using NULL from the `types.h` file allows you to obtain the correct value for both the MIPS and Alpha CPUs.

2.6.5.7 Modifying Type char

Modifying a variable declared as type `char` is not atomic on Alpha systems. You will get a load of 32 or 64 bits and then byte operations to extract, mask, and shift the byte, followed by a store of 32 or 64 bits.

2.6.5.8 Declaring Bit Fields

Bit fields declared as type `int` on Alpha systems generate a load/store of longword (32 bits). Bit fields declared as type `long` on Alpha systems generate a load/store of quadword (64 bits).

2.6.5.9 Using printf Formats

The `printf` formats %d and %x will print 32 bits of data. To obtain 64 bits of data, use %ld and %lx.

2.6.5.10 Using mb and wbflush

Device drivers used the `wbflush` interface with ULTRIX systems on MIPS CPUs. Although `wbflush` is aliased to the `mb` (memory barrier) interface for Alpha CPUs, Digital recommends that all new device drivers call the `mb` interface. The remainder of this section discusses when to call the `mb` interface on Alpha CPUs.

In most situations that would require a cache flush on other CPU architectures, you should call the `mb` interface on Digital UNIX Alpha systems. The reason is not that `mb` is equivalent to a cache flush (as it is not). Rather, a common reason for doing a cache flush is to make data that the host CPU wrote available in main memory for access by the DMA device or to access from the host CPU data that was put in main memory by a DMA device. In each case, on an Alpha CPU you should use a memory barrier to synchronize with that event.

A call to `mb` is occasionally needed even where a call to `wbflush` was not needed. In general, a memory barrier causes loads/stores to be serialized (not out-of-order), empties memory pipelines and write buffers, and ensures that the data cache is coherent.

You should use the `mb` interface to synchronize DMA buffers. Use it before the host releases the buffer to the device and before the host accesses a buffer filled by the device.

Alpha CPUs do not guarantee to preserve write ordering, so memory barriers are required between multiple writes to I/O registers where order is important. The same is also true for read ordering.

Use the memory barrier to prevent writes from being collapsed in the write buffer, that is, to prevent bytes, shorts, and ints from being merged into one 64-bit write.

Alpha CPUs require that data caches be transparent. Because there is no way to explicitly flush the data cache on an Alpha platform, you need not call mb before or after. The following code fragment illustrates the use of a memory barrier:

```
       .
       .
       .

     bcopy (data, DMA_buffer, nbytes);
     mb();
     device->csr = GO;
     mb();

       .
       .
       .
```

Another example is presented in the following code fragment:

```
       .
       .
       .
device_intr()
{
     mb();
     bcopy (DMA_buffer, data, nbytes);
     /* If we need to update a device register, do: */
     mb();
     device->csr = DONE;
     mb();
}
```

Another way to look at this issue is to recognize that Alpha CPUs maintain cache coherency for you. However, Alpha CPUs are free to do the cache coherency in any manner and time. The events that cause you to want to read buffers, or the events you want to trigger to release a buffer you have written, are not guaranteed to occur at a time consistent with when the hardware maintains cache coherency. You need the memory barrier to achieve this synchronization.

2.6.5.11 Using the volatile Compiler Keyword

The volatile keyword prevents compiler optimizations from being performed on data structures and variables; such actions could result in unexpected behavior. The following example shows the use of the volatile keyword on a device register structure:

```
typedef volatile struct {
    unsigned adder;
    unsigned pad1;
    unsigned data;
    unsigned pad2;
    unsigned csr;
    unsigned pad3;
```

```
        unsigned test;
        unsigned pad4;
} CB_REGISTERS;
```

The following variables or data structures should be declared as volatile by device drivers:

- Any variable or data structure that can be changed by a controller or processor other than the system CPU

- Variables that correspond to hardware device registers

- Any variable or data structure shared with a controller or coprocessor

The purpose of using the volatile keyword on the example data structure is to prevent compiler optimizations from being performed on it; such actions could result in unexpected behavior.

2.6.6 Memory Barrier Issues

The Alpha architecture, unlike traditional CPU architectures, does not guarantee read/write ordering. That is, the memory subsystem is free to complete read and write operations in any order that is optimal, without regard for the order in which they were issued. Read/write ordering is not the same as cache coherency, which is handled separately and is not an issue.

The Alpha architecture also contains a write buffer (as do many high-performance RISC CPUs, including the MIPS R3000). This write buffer can coalesce multiple writes to identical or adjacent addresses into a single write, effectively losing earlier write requests. Similarly, multiple reads to the same identical or adjacent addresses can be coalesced into a single read.

This coalescing has implications for multiprocessor systems, as well as systems with off-board I/O or DMA engines that can read or modify memory asynchronously or that can require multiple writes to actually issue multiple data items. The mb (memory barrier) interface guarantees ordering of operations. The mb interface is derived from the MB instruction, which is described in the *Alpha Architecture Reference Manual*.

The mb interface is a superset of the wbflush interface that MIPS CPUs use. For compatibility, wbflush is aliased to mb on Digital UNIX Alpha systems.

You call mb in a device driver under the following circumstances:

- To force a barrier between load/store operations

- After the CPU has prepared a data buffer in memory and before the device driver tries to perform a DMA out of the buffer

- Before attempting to read any device CSRs after taking a device interrupt

- Between writes

Each of these is briefly discussed in the following sections.

Note

> Device drivers and the Digital UNIX operating system are the
> primary users of the mb interface. However, some user
> programs, such as a graphics program that directly maps the
> frame buffer and manipulates registers, might need to call mb.
> The Digital UNIX operating system does not provide a C library
> interface for mb. User programs that require use of mb should
> use the following asm construct:
>
> ```
> #include <c_asm.h>
>
> asm ("mb");
> ```

2.6.6.1 Forcing a Barrier Between Load/Store Operations

You can call the mb interface to force a barrier between load/store operations.
This call ensures that all previous load/store operations access memory or I/O
space before any subsequent load/store operations. The following call to mb
ensures that the first register is physically written before the load attempts to
read the second register. The call assumes that device is an I/O handle that
you can use to reference a device register or memory located in bus address
space (either I/O space or memory space). You can perform standard C
mathematical operations on the I/O handle. For example, this code fragment
adds the I/O handle and general register 1 and general register 2 in the calls
to write_io_port and read_io_port.

```
     .
     .
     .
#define csr 0   /* Command/Status register */
#define reg1 8  /* General register 1 */
#define reg2 16 /* General register 2 */

io_handle_t device;
     .
     .
     .
write_io_port(device + reg1, 8, 0, value); 1
mb (); 2
next_value = read_io_port(device + reg2, 8, 0); 3
     .
     .
     .
```

1 Writes the first value to general register 1 by calling the
   write_io_port interface. In previous versions of the Digital UNIX
   operating system (formerly known as DEC OSF/1), this code fragment
   directly accessed the device registers. The code fragment now accesses

the device registers by calling `write_io_port`. See Section 9.8.1.2 for a discussion of `write_io_port`.

[2] Calls the `mb` interface to ensure that the write of the value is completed.

[3] Reads the new value from general register 2 by calling the `read_io_port` interface. In previous versions of the Digital UNIX operating system (formerly known as DEC OSF/1), this code fragment directly accessed the device registers. The code fragment now accesses the device registers by calling the `read_io_port` interface. See Section 9.8.1.1 for a discussion of `read_io_port`.

2.6.6.2 After the CPU Has Prepared a Data Buffer in Memory

You call the `mb` interface after the CPU has prepared a data buffer in memory and before the device driver tries to perform a DMA out of the buffer. You also call `mb` in device drivers that perform a DMA into memory and before using the data in the DMA buffer. The following calls to `mb` ensure that data is available (out of memory pipelines/write buffers) and that the data cache is coherent. The call assumes that `device` is an I/O handle that you can use to reference a device register or memory located in bus address space (either I/O space or memory space). You can perform standard C mathematical operations on the I/O handle. For example, this code fragment adds the I/O handle and the command/status register in the call to `read_io_port`.

```
        .
        .
        .
#define csr 0    /* Command/Status register */
#define reg1 8   /* General register 1 */
#define reg2 16 /* General register 2 */

io_handle_t device;
        .
        .
        .
bcopy (data, dma_buf, nbytes); [1]
mb (); [2]
write_io_port(device + csr, 8, 0, START_DMA); [3]

/* or */ [4]

if (read_io_port(device + csr, 8, 0) | DMA_DONE) {
    mb ();
    bcopy (dma_buf, data, nbytes);
}
        .
        .
        .
```

[1] Writes the data into the DMA buffer.

2 Calls the mb interface to ensure that the write of the data is completed.

3 Issues the start command to the device.

4 This sequence of code presents another way to accomplish the same thing. In previous versions of the Digital UNIX operating system (formerly known as DEC OSF/1), this code fragment directly accessed the device registers. The code fragment now accesses the device registers by calling the read_io_port interface. See Section 9.8.1.1 for a discussion of read_io_port.

If the DMA is finished:

– Calls the mb interface to ensure that the buffer is correct

– Gets the data from the DMA buffer

2.6.6.3   Before Attempting to Read Any Device CSRs

You call the mb interface before attempting to read any device CSRs after taking a device interrupt. The call assumes that device is an I/O handle that you can use to reference a device register or memory located in bus address space (either I/O space or memory space). You can perform standard C mathematical operations on the I/O handle. For example, this code fragment adds the I/O handle and the command/status register in the call to read_io_port.

```
    .
    .
    .
#define csr 0    /* Command/Status register */
#define reg1 8  /* General register 1 */
#define reg2 16 /* General register 2 */

io_handle_t device;
    .
    .
    .
device_intr()
{
      mb(); 1
      stat = read_io_port(device + csr, 8, 0); 2

      /* or */ 3

      mb();
      bcopy (dma_buf, data, nbytes);
}
    .
    .
    .
```

1 Calls the mb interface to ensure that the device CSR write has completed.

2 Reads the status from the device. In previous versions of the Digital UNIX operating system (formerly known as DEC OSF/1), this code fragment directly accessed the device registers. The code fragment now accesses the device registers by calling the `read_io_port` interface. See Section 9.8.1.1 for a discussion of `read_io_port`.

3 This sequence of code presents another way to accomplish the same thing. It calls the `mb` interface to ensure that the buffer is correct. It then gets the data from the DMA buffer by calling the `bcopy` interface.

Note

Digital UNIX on an Alpha system provides a memory barrier in the interrupt stream before calling any device interrupt service interfaces. Thus, a call to `mb` is not strictly necessary in the device interrupt case. For performance reasons in the device interrupt case, you can omit the call to `mb`.

2.6.6.4 Between Writes

You call the `mb` interface between writes if you do not want a write buffer to collapse the writes (merge bytes/shorts/ints/quads or reorder). The call assumes that `device` is an I/O handle that you can use to reference a device register or memory located in bus address space (either I/O space or memory space). You can perform standard C mathematical operations on the I/O handle. For example, this code fragment adds the I/O handle and general register 1 and general register 2 in the calls to `write_io_port`.

```
      .
      .
      .
#define csr 0   /* Command/Status register */
#define reg1 8  /* General register 1 */
#define reg2 16 /* General register 2 */

io_handle_t device;
      .
      .
      .
        *ptr = value; 1
        mb (); 2
        *(ptr+1) = value2; 3

/* or */ 4

        write_io_port(device + reg1, 8, 0, value);
```

```
            mb ();
            write_io_port(device + reg2, 8, 0, value2);
    .
    .
    .
```

1 Writes the first location.

2 Calls the mb interface to force a write out of the write buffer.

3 Writes the second location.

4 This sequence of code illustrates an example more specifically tailored to
   device drivers. Note that this use of mb is exactly equivalent to
   wbflush.

   In previous versions of the Digital UNIX operating system (formerly
   known as DEC OSF/1), this code fragment directly accessed the device
   registers. The code fragment now accesses the device registers by calling
   the write_io_port interface. See Section 9.8.1.2 for a discussion of
   write_io_port. This sequence:

   – Writes the first location by calling write_io_port

   – Calls mb to force a write out of the write buffer

   – Writes the second location by calling write_io_port a second
     time

Note

The *Alpha Architecture Reference Manual* (1992 edition) has a
technical error in the description of the MB instruction. It
specifies that MB is needed only on multiprocessor systems. This
statement is not accurate. The MB instruction must be used in
any system to guarantee correctly ordered access to I/O registers
or memory that can be accessed via off-board DMA. All such
off-board I/O and DMA engines are considered ''processors'' in
the Alpha architecture's definition of multiprocessor.

2.7 Understanding Bus Issues That Influence Device Driver Design

Whenever possible, you should design a device driver so that it can
accommodate peripheral devices that can operate on more than one bus
architecture. You can achieve portability across bus architectures particularly
when the bus architectures themselves exhibit common features and
attributes. For example, you should be able to write one device driver for a
device that operates on the Industry Standard Architecture (ISA) and
Extended Industry Standard Architecture (EISA) buses because their

architectures exhibit common features and attributes. In other cases, it may not be feasible to write one device driver for multiple bus architectures if these architectures exhibit dissimilar features and attributes.

You must consider the following issues to make your drivers portable across bus architectures:

- Bus-specific header file issues

- Bus-specific constant name issues

- Bus-specific option structure issues

- Bus-specific issues related to implementing the `probe` interface

- Bus-specific issues related to implementing the `slave` interface

- Bus-specific issues for implementing the `configure` interface

The discussion centers around EISA, ISA, the Peripheral Component Interconnect (PCI), and TURBOchannel bus architectures, but the topics may be applicable to other bus architectures. The following sections discuss each of these issues.

2.7.1 Bus-Specific Header File Issues

Each bus implemented on Alpha processors and the Digital UNIX operating system has a specific header file. To write portable loadable and static device drivers across multiple bus architectures, you need to consider how to include bus-specific header files in the Include Files Section of your device driver.

The following list describes some of the bus-specific header files:

- `/usr/sys/include/io/dec/eisa/eisa.h`

    Contains definitions for EISA/ISA bus support

- `/usr/sys/include/io/dec/pci/pci.h`

    Contains definitions for PCI bus support

- `/usr/sys/include/io/dec/tc/tc.h`

    Contains definitions for TURBOchannel bus support

You include the header file for the bus that your driver operates on. For example, if your device driver controls a device that connects to a controller that operates on an EISA and PCI bus, you include the files `eisa.h` and `pci.h`.

Section 3.3.1 provides an example of how to write a `probe` interface to support multiple buses.

2.7.2 Bus-Specific Constant Name Issues

To write portable loadable device drivers across multiple bus architectures, you need to consider creating bus-specific constant names to pass to the `ldbl_ctlr_configure` and `ldbl_ctlr_unconfigure` interfaces. Loadable device drivers call these interfaces to configure and unconfigure a specified controller. Typically, you define a bus constant that represents the bus name that you specify in the system configuration file or `stanza.static` file fragment. You usually define these bus-specific constants in the Loadable Driver Configuration Support Declarations and Definitions Section. Section 4.1.4 further discusses bus-specific constant issues as they relate to the `/dev/none` driver. Section 4.1.7.2 shows how the `/dev/none` driver passes the bus-specific constant for the TURBOchannel bus to the `ldbl_stanza_resolver` and `ldbl_ctlr_configure` interfaces. Section 4.1.7.3 shows how the `/dev/none` driver passes the bus-specific constant for the TURBOchannel bus to the `ldbl_ctlr_unconfigure` interface.

2.7.3 Bus-Specific Option Structure Issues

Many buses implemented on Alpha processors and the Digital UNIX operating system have an associated bus-specific option data structure defined in the bus-specific header file. Some members of these bus-specific option structures are identical (for example, the `driver_name` and `intr_b4_probe` members). Other members are specific to the bus.

The following list identifies the option structures for the EISA, PCI, and TURBOchannel buses:

- `eisa_option`

  Contains EISA bus options

- `pci_option`

  Contains PCI bus options

- `tc_option`

  Contains TURBOchannel bus options

Digital declares and initializes an array of bus-specific option structures in a device-specific *name*_data.c file. For example, the following list associates the *name*_data.c files with the previously listed bus-specific option structures:

- The `/usr/sys/data/eisa_option_data.c` file contains the declaration and initialization of the array of `eisa_option` structures.

- The `/usr/sys/data/pci_option_data.c` file contains the declaration and initialization of the array of `pci_option` structures.

- The /usr/sys/data/tc_option_data.c file contains the declaration and initialization of the array of tc_option structures.

See Section 3.1.5 for a discussion of the name_data.c file.

To write portable static device drivers across multiple bus architectures, you need to add device entries to the bus-specific option arrays. You can use a text editor to edit these option arrays. See Section 13.1.3.1 for instructions on how to do this. You can also use the mkdata utility to automatically add the device entry to a copy of the bus-specific option array in the bus-specific name_data.c file. This technique requires you to populate a bus-specific data file with the device information. For example, on the TURBOchannel bus you add the device information to a tc_data file. See the bus-specific book for information on what items to include in the bus-specific data file.

To write portable loadable drivers across multiple bus architectures, you need to declare and initialize a bus-specific option snippet. The bus-specific option snippet is an element of the option table. You declare this snippet in the Loadable Driver Configuration Support Declarations and Definitions Section. You pass the snippet to the ldbl_stanza_resolver interface. Section 4.1.4 further discusses bus-specific option structure issues as they relate to the /dev/none driver. Section 4.1.7.2 shows how the /dev/none driver passes the TURBOchannel bus option snippet to the ldbl_stanza_resolver interface.

2.7.4 Bus-Specific Issues Related to Implementing the probe Interface

The arguments associated with a device driver's probe interface are bus specific. To write portable loadable and static device drivers across multiple bus architectures, you need to know the arguments associated with the probe interface for that bus. See the bus-specific device driver book for a description of the arguments associated with the probe interface for the bus. Section 3.3.1 provides an example of how to write a probe interface to support multiple buses. Section 4.1.6.1 further discusses bus-specific issues related to implementing the probe interface for the /dev/none driver.

2.7.5 Bus-Specific Issues Related to Implementing the slave Interface

The arguments associated with a device driver's slave interface are bus specific. To write portable loadable and static device drivers across multiple bus architectures, you need to know the arguments associated with the slave interface for that bus. See the bus-specific device driver book for a description of the arguments associated with the slave interface for the bus.

2.7.6 Bus-Specific Issues Related to Implementing the configure Interface

To write portable loadable device drivers across multiple bus architectures, you need to know that the `ldbl_stanza_resolver`, `ldbl_ctlr_configure`, and `ldbl_ctlr_unconfigure` interfaces take as an argument the bus name. You define the bus names for the buses you want the driver to operate on as constants that you pass to the previously listed interfaces. Section 4.1.4 further discusses bus-specific issues related to implementing the `configure` interface for the `/dev/none` driver. Section 4.1.7.2 shows how the `/dev/none` driver passes the bus-specific constant for the TURBOchannel bus to the `ldbl_stanza_resolver` and `ldbl_ctlr_configure` interfaces. Section 4.1.7.3 shows how the `/dev/none` driver passes the bus-specific constant for the TURBOchannel bus to the `ldbl_ctlr_unconfigure` interface.

2.8 Creating a Device Driver Development and Kitting Environment

When you are ready to write your driver, you will probably want to design a logical directory structure to hold the different files associated with the driver. Chapter 11 discusses the device driver configuration models and provides examples of driver development environments suitable for the third-party and traditional device driver configuration models.

2.9 Porting ULTRIX Device Drivers to the Digital UNIX Operating System

This section discusses the tasks you need to perform when porting device drivers from the ULTRIX operating system (running on Digital hardware) to the Digital UNIX operating system (also running on Digital hardware). The section does not discuss how to port drivers running on other UNIX operating systems, such as System V, or running on other hardware platforms, such as Sun Microsystems. Specifically, you need to:

- Write test suites
- Check header files
- Review device driver configuration
- Check driver interfaces
- Check kernel interfaces
- Check data structures

These tasks are discussed in the following sections.

2.9.1 Writing Test Suites

Porting a device driver requires that you understand the hardware device and the associated driver you want to port. One way to learn about the hardware device and its associated driver is to run a test suite, if it exists, on the machine and the operating system you are porting from (the source machine and the source operating system). If the test suite does not exist, you need to write a full test suite for that device on the source machine and the source operating system. For example, if you port a device driver written for a Digital CPU running the ULTRIX operating system, write the full test suite on that Digital CPU.

Write the test suite so that only minimal changes are necessary when you move it to the Digital CPU running the Digital UNIX operating system you are porting to (the target machine and the target operating system). The test suite represents a cross section of your users, and they should not have to modify their applications to work with the ported driver. You need to have both the source machine and source operating system and the target machine and target operating system on a network or make them accessible through a common interface, such as the Small Computer System Interface (SCSI).

After writing the test suite on the source machine, move the driver and the test suite to the target machine. Move only the .c and the .h files that were created for the driver. Do not copy any header or binary executable files because these files on the source machine will probably not be compatible on the target machine.

2.9.2 Checking Header Files

Check the header files in the driver you want to port with those in the Digital UNIX device drivers. Section 3.1 provides information on the header files that Digital UNIX uses, including those header files related to loadable device drivers. Chapter 14 provides reference (man) page-style descriptions of the header files that Digital UNIX device drivers use most frequently.

The following example summarizes the differences in the way header files are included in device drivers on ULTRIX and Digital UNIX systems:

```
/* Header Files Included in ULTRIX */ 1
#include "../h/types.h"

/* Header Files Included in Digital UNIX */ 1
#include <sys/types.h>
```

1 This example shows that drivers written for Digital UNIX use left (<) and right (>) angle brackets, instead of the begin (") and end (") quotes used in ULTRIX pathnames. Note also that the location of the file has changed for Digital UNIX.

2.9.3   Reviewing Device Driver Configuration

Device driver configuration on ULTRIX systems follows what this book refers to as the traditional model. The Digital UNIX operating system supports both the traditional model and the third-party device driver configuration model, as described in Chapter 11. Chapter 13 gives examples on configuring drivers by using both the third-party and the traditional models.

2.9.4   Checking Driver Interfaces

You need to compare the driver interfaces that ULTRIX device drivers use with those that Digital UNIX device drivers use. Section 17.2 provides reference (man) page-style descriptions of the driver interfaces that Digital UNIX device drivers use. Use this information to compare the interface's behavior, number and type of arguments, return values, and so forth with its associated ULTRIX driver interface.

2.9.5   Checking Kernel Interfaces

You need to compare the kernel interfaces that ULTRIX device drivers use with those that Digital UNIX device drivers use. Chapter 15 provides reference (man) page-style descriptions of the kernel interfaces that Digital UNIX device drivers use. Use this information to compare the interface's behavior, number and type of arguments, return values, and so forth with its associated ULTRIX kernel interface. Table 2-3 lists some of these differences.

Table 2-3:   Highlights of Differences Between Digital UNIX and ULTRIX Kernel Interfaces

Kernel Interface	Remarks
BADADDR	Device drivers written for ULTRIX systems use the BADADDR interface in the Autoconfiguration Support Section to determine if a device is present on the system. For an example of how noneprobe uses such a variable (called *none_is_dynamic*), see Section 4.1.6.1.
bufflush	ULTRIX BSD device drivers written for platforms based on MIPS use the bufflush interface. This interface is not used for Alpha platforms. Therefore, delete this interface from your device driver.

Table 2-3: (continued)

Kernel Interface	Remarks
KM_ALLOC	A previous version of the Digital UNIX operating system (formerly known as DEC OSF/1) instructed you to replace calls to KM_ALLOC with calls to kalloc. The Digital UNIX operating system supports a new memory allocator. Thus, replace calls to KM_ALLOC with calls to MALLOC.
KM_FREE	A previous version of the Digital UNIX operating system (formerly known as DEC OSF/1) instructed you to replace calls to KM_FREE with calls to kfree. The Digital UNIX operating system supports a new memory allocator. Thus, replace calls to KM_FREE with calls to FREE.
printf interfaces	ULTRIX device drivers can call cprintf, mprintf, printf, and uprintf. Digital UNIX device drivers can call printf and uprintf.
selwakeup	The selwakeup interface is not used in Digital UNIX. Replace calls to selwakeup with calls to select_wakeup. Note that the formal parameters for the two interfaces are different.

Table 2-3: (continued)

Kernel Interface	Remarks
useracc	The useracc interface is obsolete on Digital UNIX. If you called useracc with vslock, replace both interfaces with a call to vm_map_pageable. Typically, the useracc interface was called by the driver's *xx*strategy interface. In most cases, the driver's *xx*strategy interface would be called indirectly from the physio interface (in response to read and write system calls or file-system access).
	In Digital UNIX, the physio interface verifies access permissions to the user buffer and locks down the memory. For this reason, in existing drivers that may have historically called useracc, it is no longer necessary to perform such a check and subsequent locking of memory with vslock. The general rule is that any interface called from the physio interface (that is, the driver's *xx*strategy interface) should not call useracc or its replacement vm_map_pageable because the physio interface performs those functions.
	If you called useracc prior to accessing user data, replace it with calls to copyin and copyout to access user space. Calling useracc simply verifies access permissions to the specified memory at the time the useracc interface is called. It is possible that immediately after the useracc interface has returned back to the driver that the corresponding memory could be invalid. The memory could be invalid if it was swapped out or otherwise remapped by the virtual memory management portion of the kernel. Therefore, a driver should not assume that the memory region whose access permissions are verified through a call to useracc is persistent.
	In Digital UNIX, calls to useracc are either unnecessary (as previously explained) or should be replaced by direct calls to vm_map_pageable. This interface performs functions for both verifying access permissions and for locking down the memory so that it cannot be invalidated until it is unlocked by subsequent calls to vm_map_pageable for this memory region.
vslock	The vslock interface is obsolete on Digital UNIX. Therefore, replace calls to vslock with calls to vm_map_pageable.

Table 2-3: (continued)

Kernel Interface	Remarks
vsunlock	The vsunlock interface is obsolete on Digital UNIX. Therefore, replace calls to vsunlock with calls to vm_map_pageable.

2.9.6 Checking Data Structures

You need to compare the data structures that ULTRIX device drivers use with those that Digital UNIX device drivers use. Chapter 16 provides reference (man) page-style descriptions of the data structures that Digital UNIX device drivers use. Use this information to compare the data structure's members with its associated ULTRIX data structure. Table 2-4 lists some of these differences.

Table 2-4: Highlights of Differences Between Digital UNIX and ULTRIX Data Structures

Data Structure	Remarks
uba_ctlr	Replace references to the uba_ctlr structure and its associated members with references to the controller structure and its associated members.
uba_device	Replace references to the uba_device structure and its associated members with references to the device structure and its associated members. Make sure that the reference is to a slave, for example, a disk or tape drive. If the reference is to a controller, reference the controller structure, not the device structure.
uba_driver	Replace references to the uba_driver structure and its associated members with references to the driver structure and its associated members.

Analyzing the Structure of a Device Driver   **3**

Before implementing the sample device driver discussed in the previous chapter, you need to understand the sections of a Digital UNIX device driver. Analyzing the sections of a device driver gives you the opportunity to learn how to set up the device driver interfaces in preparation for writing your own device drivers. This chapter mentions some structures (for example, the `device` structure) that may be unfamiliar to you. However, to learn how to set up the device driver interfaces, you do not need an intimate understanding of the structures. Chapter 7 discusses these structures in more detail.

The sections that make up a Digital UNIX device driver differ depending on whether the driver is a block, character, or network driver. Figure 3-1 shows the sections that a character device driver can contain and the possible sections for a block device driver. Device drivers are not required to use all of the sections and more complex drivers can have additional sections.

Both types of drivers contain:

- An include files section
- A declarations section
- An autoconfiguration support section
- A configure section (only for loadable drivers)
- An open and close device section
- An ioctl section
- An interrupt section

The block device driver can also contain a strategy section, a `psize` section, and a dump section.

The character device driver contains the following sections not contained in a block device driver:

- A read and write device section
- A reset section
- A stop section
- A select section
- A memory map section (only for CPUs that include map registers)

Figure 3-1: Sections of a Character Device Driver and a Block Device Driver

Character Device Driver	Block Device Driver
/* Include Files Section */ . . . /* Declarations Section */ . . . /* Autoconfiguration Support Section */ . . . /* Configure Section */ . . /* Open and Close Device Section */ . . /* ioctl Section */ . . . /* Interrupt Section */ . . /* Read and Write Device Section */ . . . /* Reset Section */ . . . /* Stop Section */ . . . /* Select Section */ . . . /* Memory Map (mmap) Section */ . . .	/* Include Files Section */ . . . /* Declarations Section */ . . . /* Autoconfiguration Support Section */ . . . /* Configure Section */ . . /* Open and Close Device Section */ . . /* ioctl Section */ . . . /* Interrupt Section */ . . . /* Strategy Section */ . . . /* psize Section */ . . /* Dump Section */ . . .

Each device driver section is described in the following sections. For convenience in referring to the names for the driver interfaces, the chapter uses the prefix *xx*. For example, xxprobe refers to a probe interface for some XX device.

3.1 Include Files Section

Data structures and constant values are defined in header files that you include in the include files section of the driver source code. The number and types of header files you specify in the include files section vary, depending on such things as what structures, constants, and kernel interfaces your device driver references. You need to be familiar with:

- The device driver header file
- The common driver header files
- The loadable driver header files
- The device register header file
- The *name_data.c* file
- Bus-specific header files

The following sections describe these categories of header files. Chapter 14 provides reference (man) page-style descriptions of the header files that Digital UNIX device drivers use most frequently.

3.1.1 Device Driver Header File

The device driver header file contains #define statements for as many devices as are configured into the system. This file is generated by the config program during static configuration of the device driver. This file need not be included if you configure the driver as a loadable driver.

The config program creates the name for this file by using the name of the controller or device that you specify in the system configuration file. For example, if you specified rd as the device in the system configuration file, config creates a header file called rd.h. The following example shows the possible contents for the rd.h device driver header file:

```
#define NRD 1
```

The config program creates a compile time variable, in this example NRD, which defines how many devices exist on the system. This variable is set to the value zero (0) to indicate that no devices exist on the system; or, it is set to a specific number (for example, 4 would indicate that four devices exist on the system). Many existing ULTRIX-based drivers use this compile-time variable in device driver code to refer to the number of this type of device on the system. This usage most frequently occurs in structure array declarations and in condition (for example, if and while) statements.

3.1.2 Common Driver Header Files

The following example lists the header files that device drivers use most frequently:

```
#include <sys/types.h>
#include <sys/errno.h>
#include <io/common/devdriver.h>
#include <sys/uio.h>
#include <machine/cpu.h>
```

The example shows that device drivers should not use explicit pathnames. Using angle brackets (< and >) means you will not have to make changes to your device driver if the file path changes.

The following sections contain brief descriptions of the previously listed common driver header files.

3.1.2.1 The types.h Header File

The header file /usr/sys/include/sys/types.h defines system data types used to declare members in the data structures referenced by device drivers. Table 3-1 lists the system data types defined in this file that device drivers use most frequently.

Table 3-1: System Data Types Defined in types.h That Device Drivers Use Frequently

Data Type	Meaning
daddr_t	Block device address
caddr_t	Main memory virtual address
ino_t	Inode index
dev_t	Device major and minor numbers
off_t	File offset
paddr_t	Main memory physical address
time_t	System time
u_short	unsigned short

The /usr/sys/include/sys/types.h header file includes the file /mach/machine/vm_types.h. This file defines the data type vm_offset_t, which driver writers should use when addresses are treated as arithmetic quantities (that is, as ints and longs). The vm_offset_t data type is defined as unsigned long on Alpha systems and as unsigned `int` on MIPS systems.

3.1.2.2   The errno.h Header File

The header file `/usr/sys/include/sys/errno.h` defines the error
codes returned to a user process by a device driver. Examples of these error
codes include `EINVAL` (invalid argument), `ENODEV` (no such device), and
`EIO` (I/O error).

3.1.2.3   The devdriver.h Header File

The header file `/usr/sys/include/io/common/devdriver.h`
defines structures, constants, data types, and external interfaces that device
drivers and the autoconfiguration software use. Two opaque data types that
you can use to make your device drivers more portable are `io_handle_t`
and `dma_handle_t`.

Section 9.8 and Section 9.9.1 discuss the I/O and DMA handles.

3.1.2.4   The uio.h Header File

The header file `/usr/sys/include/sys/uio.h` contains the definition
of the `uio` structure. The kernel sets up and uses the `uio` structures to read
and write data. Character device drivers include this file because they may
reference the `uio` structure.

3.1.2.5   The cpu.h Header File

The `cpu.h` file defines a variety of structures and constants related to the
CPU. You include the `cpu.h` file in block and character device drivers
when calling any of the `spl` interfaces. The reason for this is that the `spl`
interfaces map to an assembler interface.

3.1.3   Loadable Driver Header Files

You need to include the following files related to loadable device drivers:

```
#include <sys/conf.h>
#include <sys/sysconfig.h>
```

The following sections contain brief descriptions of these files.

3.1.3.1   The conf.h Header File

The header file `/usr/sys/include/sys/conf.h` defines the `bdevsw`
(block device switch) and `cdevsw` (character device switch) tables. You
should include the `conf.h` file in loadable block and character device
drivers because these drivers later add driver entry points to the `bdevsw` and
`cdevsw` arrays declared and initialized by Digital in the

`/usr/sys/io/common/conf.c` file. In the case of loadable device drivers, the driver declares and initalizes a `bdevsw` or `cdevsw` structure and then passes the address of this initialized structure to the `bdevsw_add` or `cdevsw_add` kernel interfaces. These interfaces add the driver entry points to the in-memory `bdevsw` or `cdevsw` arrays.

Section 8.2 describes the device switch tables.

3.1.3.2 The sysconfig.h Header File

The header file `/usr/sys/include/sys/sysconfig.h` defines operation codes and data structures used in loadable device driver configuration. The operation codes define the action to be performed by the driver `configure` interface. Examples of the operation types include configure, unconfigure, and query. This file also defines many of the constants that are shared between the device driver method and the drivers themselves. Within this file also appears the definition of the data structure that is passed to the driver's `configure` interface and the definition of the data structure that device drivers initialize.

Section 3.4 shows how to set up the `configure` interface.

3.1.4 Device Register Header File

The device register header file contains any public declarations that the device driver uses. This file usually contains the device register structure associated with the device. A device register structure is a C structure whose members map to the registers of some device. These registers are often referred to as the device's control status register (or CSR) addresses. The device driver writer creates the device register header file.

The following example shows a device register structure contained in a device register header file for a device driver written for a TURBOchannel test board:

```
typedef volatile struct {
    unsigned adder;
    unsigned pad1;
    unsigned data;
    unsigned pad2;
    unsigned csr;
    unsigned pad3;
    unsigned test;
    unsigned pad4;
} CB_REGISTERS;
```

The example shows the use of the compiler `volatile` keyword. Section 2.6.5.11 provides guidelines for which variables and data strucures device drivers should declare as volatile.

The device register structure is most often used in device drivers that directly access a device's CSR addresses. There are some CPU architectures that do not allow you to access the device CSR addresses directly. If you want to write your device driver to operate on both types of CPU architectures, you can write one device driver with the appropriate conditional compilation statements. You can also avoid the potentially confusing proliferation of conditional compilation statements by using the CSR I/O access kernel interfaces provided by Digital UNIX to read from and write to the device's CSR addresses. Because the CSR I/O access interfaces are designed to be CPU hardware independent, their use not only simplifies the readability of the driver, but also makes the driver more portable across different CPU architectures and different CPU types within the same architecture.

Section 9.8.1 shows you how to use the CSR I/O access kernel interfaces to read from and write to the device's CSR addresses.

This technique of calling kernel interfaces to access a device's CSR addresses also requires defining the registers of a device, usually through constants that map to these device registers. The following example shows the device register definitions contained in a device register header file for a device driver that uses the CSR I/O access kernel interfaces to access a device's CSR addresses:

```
/***************************************************
 * Define offsets to nvram device registers       *
 ***************************************************/
#define ENVRAM_CSR      0xc00  /* CSR */
#define ENVRAM_BAT      0xc04  /* Battery Disconnect */
#define ENVRAM_HIBASE   0xc08  /* Ext. Mem Config */
#define ENVRAM_CONFIG   0xc0c  /* EISA config reg */
#define ENVRAM_ID       0xc80  /* EISA ID reg */
#define ENVRAM_CTRL     0xc84  /* EISA control */
#define ENVRAM_DMA0     0xc88  /* DMA addr reg 0 */
#define ENVRAM_DMA1     0xc8c  /* DMA addr reg 1 */
```

For this version of the Digital UNIX operating system, Digital recommends that you not directly access a device's CSR addresses. Instead, use the indirect method by defining device register offsets (not by defining a device register structure) and by using the CSR I/O access kernel interfaces.

3.1.5 The name_data.c File

The *name_data.c* file provides a convenient place to size the data structures and data structure arrays that device drivers use. In addition, the file can contain definitions that third-party driver writers might want their customers to change. This file is particularly convenient for third-party driver writers who do not want to ship device driver sources. The device driver writer creates the *name_data.c* file.

The *name* argument is usually based on the device name. For example, the none device's `name_data.c` file is called `none_data.c`. The CB device's `name_data.c` file is called `cb_data.c`. The edgd device's `name_data.c` file is called `edgd_data.c`.

The `name_data.c` files supplied by Digital Equipment Corporation are found in the `/usr/sys/data` directory. The following example shows some of the `name_data.c` files contained in the `/usr/sys/data` directory for Digital UNIX:

```
audit_data.c            ga_data.c              np_data.c
autoconf_data.c         gvp_data.c             pci_option_data.c
binlog_data.c           gw_screen_data.c       presto_data.c
cam_data.c              gx_data.c              scc_data.c
cam_special_data.c      if_fta_data.c          scs_data.c
ci_data.c               if_fza_data.c          sysap_data.c
cippd_data.c            if_ln_data.c           tc_option_data.c
eisa_option_data.c      if_mfa_data.c          tga_data.c
```

Third-party device driver writers can place their `name_data.c` file in a products directory with all of the other files they plan to ship to customers.

Figure 11-2 shows a sample directory structure for the fictitious driver development company, EasyDriver Incorporated.

The bus-specific option arrays for the EISA, PCI, and TURBOchannel buses are contained in the `/usr/sys/data/eisa_option_data.c`, `/usr/sys/data/pci_option_data.c`, and `/usr/sys/data/tc_option_data.c` files. See Section 2.7 for a discussion of the issues you need to be aware of to write one driver for multiple bus architectures.

3.1.6   Bus-Specific Header Files

The bus-specific header files contain `#define` statements, data structure definitions, and other information associated with a specific bus. The following are the bus-specific files that Digital supplies:

```
#include <io/dec/eisa/eisa.h> /* EISA/ISA bus */
#include <io/dec/pci/pci.h>    /* PCI bus */
#include <io/dec/tc/tc.h>      /* TURBOchannel bus */
```

You include the header file for the bus that your driver operates on. For example, if your device driver controls a device that connects to a controller that operates on an EISA and PCI bus, you include the files `eisa.h` and `pci.h`.

3.2   Declarations Section

The declarations section of a block or character device driver contains:

- Definitions of symbolic names

- Variable declarations

- Structure declarations

- Declarations of driver interfaces

The following example shows the declarations section for a device driver. The example provides declarations and initializations that would be provided in any device driver:

```
/* Definitions of symbolic names */
define MAX_XFR 4
     .
     .
     .
/* Variable declarations */
extern int hz;
     .
     .
     .
/* Structure declarations */
struct controller *cbinfo[NCB];
     .
     .
     .
/* Declarations of driver interfaces */
int cbstart(), cbprobe(), cbattach(), cbstrategy(), cbminphys();
     .
     .
     .
```

Note that the compile time variable NCB is used to size the array of pointers to controller structures. This usage is an example of statically allocating data structures. Section 2.5 provides information to help you choose an appropriate data structure allocation technique.

3.3   Autoconfiguration Support Section

When Digital UNIX boots, the kernel determines what devices are connected to the computer. After finding a device, the kernel initializes it so that the device can be used at a later time. The probe interface determines if a particular device is present and the attach interface initializes the device.

The system performs a functionally equivalent process when a loadable driver is configured. A loadable driver, like the static driver, has a probe, attach, and possibly a slave interface. From the device driver writer's point of view, these interfaces are the same for static and loadable drivers.

The autoconfiguration support section of a device driver contains the code that implements these interfaces and the section applies to both character and block device drivers. It can contain:

- A `probe` interface
- A `slave` interface
- An `attach` interface

For loadable drivers, the autoconfiguration support section also contains a controller `unattach` or a device `unattach` interface, which is called when the driver is unloaded. You define the entry point for each of these interfaces in the `driver` structure.

Section 7.3.4 describes the `driver` structure. The following sections show you how to set up each of these interfaces.

3.3.1 Setting Up the probe Interface

The way you set up a `probe` interface depends on the bus on which the driver operates. The following code fragment shows you how to set up a `probe` interface for a driver that operates on a TURBOchannel bus:

```
xxprobe(bus_io_handle, ctlr)
io_handle_t bus_io_handle;    /* I/O handle for a specific bus */
struct controller *ctlr;      /* Pointer to controller */
                              /* structure */
{
    /* Variable and structure declarations */
    .
    .
    .
    /* Code to perform necessary checks */
    .
    .
    .
}
```

The code fragment declares the two arguments associated with a `probe` interface that operates on a TURBOchannel bus. To learn what arguments you would specify for other buses, see the bus-specific device driver manual. The code fragment also sets up the sections where you declare local variables and structures and where you write the code to implement the `probe` interface.

Section 4.1.6.1 shows you how to implement a `probe` interface for the `/dev/none` device driver that operates on a TURBOchannel bus. Section 10.8.1 shows you how to implement a `probe` interface for a character device driver that operates on a TURBOchannel bus. Section 17.2 provides a reference (man) page that gives additional information on the arguments and tasks associated with an `xxprobe` interface.

If you want to write one device driver that operates on multiple buses, the driver's `probe` interface must handle any differences related to the bus. The following example shows you how to set up a `probe` interface to handle multiple buses:

```
xxprobe(bus_io_handle, ctlr)
io_handle_t bus_io_handle;   1
struct controller *ctlr;     2
    .
    .
    .
int unit = ctlr->ctlr_num;   3
    .
    .
    .
    switch (ctlr->bus_hd->bus_type) {  4

        case BUS_TC:  5
    .
    .
    .
            break;

        case BUS_EISA:  6
    .
    .
    .
            break;
        default:  7
            printf("xx%d: xxprobe: unknown device0,unit);
            return 0;  8
    .
    .
    .
}
```

1 Specifies an I/O handle that you can use to reference a device register located in the bus address space. The bus configuration code passes this I/O handle to the driver's *xxprobe* interface during device autoconfiguration.

2 Specifies a pointer to the `controller` structure for this controller. This structure contains such information as the controller type, the controller name, and the current status of the controller. The bus configuration code passes the filled in `controller` structure pointer to the driver's *xxprobe* interface.

3 Stores the controller number for this controller in the *unit* variable.

4 Evaluates the `bus_type` member to determine which bus this controller connects to. Note that *xxprobe* references the bus type through the `bus_hd` member of the `controller` structure pointer.

The `bus_hd` member specifies a pointer to the `bus` structure that this controller is connected to. Section 7.2.1.6 discusses the bus_hd and other members of the bus and controller structures as they relate to the creation of the system configuration tree.

[5] If the switch statement evaluates to the bus type BUS_TC, then this controller connects to a TURBOchannel bus. The *xxprobe* interface performs tasks specific to the TURBOchannel bus. The /usr/sys/include/io/common/devdriver.h file defines the bus type definitions.

[6] If the switch statement evaluates to the bus type BUS_EISA, then this controller connects to an EISA bus. The *xxprobe* interface performs tasks specific to the EISA bus.

[7] If the switch statement evaluates to something other than the bus type, then this controller connects to some unknown device. The *xxprobe* interface calls the printf interface to print an appropriate message on the console terminal. Note that the interface prints the controller number for this controller, which was obtained from the ctlr_num member.

[8] Returns the value zero (0) to the bus configuration code to indicate that the driver did not complete the probe operation.

3.3.2 Setting Up the slave Interface

A device driver's slave interface is called only for a controller that has slave devices connected to it. This interface is called once for each slave attached to the controller. The way you set up a slave interface depends on the bus on which the driver operates. The following code fragment shows you how to set up a slave interface for a driver that operates on a TURBOchannel bus:

```
xxslave(device, bus_io_handle)
struct device *device;      /* Pointer to device structure */
io_handle_t bus_io_handle; /* I/O handle for a specific bus */
{
     /* Variable and structure declarations */
     .
     .
     .
     /* Code to check that the device is valid */
     .
     .
     .
}
```

The code fragment declares the two arguments associated with a slave interface that operates on a TURBOchannel bus. To learn what arguments you would specify for other buses, see the bus-specific device driver manual. The code fragment also sets up the sections where you declare local variables and structures and where you write the code to implement the slave interface. Section 17.2 provides a reference (man) page that gives additional information on the arguments and tasks associated with an xxslave interface.

3.3.3 Setting Up the attach Interface

A device driver's attach interface establishes communication with the device. There are two attach interfaces: an xxcattach interface for controller-specific initialization (called once for each controller) and an xxdattach interface for device-specific initialization (called once for each slave device connected to a controller). The following code fragment shows you how to set up an xxdattach interface:

```
xxdattach(device)
struct *device; /* Pointer to device structure */
{
    /* Variable and structure declarations */
    .
    .
    .

    /* Code to perform tasks associated with establishing */
    /* communication with the device */
    .
    .
    .
}
```

The code fragment declares the argument associated with a device attach interface. If the controller attach interface were used, the bus configuration code passes a pointer to a controller structure instead of a pointer to a device structure. The code fragment also sets up the sections where you declare local variables and structures and where you write the code to implement the device attach interface.

Section 4.1.6.2 shows you how to implement an attach interface for the /dev/none device driver. Section 10.8.2 shows you how to implement an attach interface for a character device driver that operates on a TURBOchannel bus. Section 17.2 provides a reference (man) page that gives additional information on the arguments and tasks associated with the xxcattach and xxdattach interfaces.

3.3.4 Setting Up the Controller unattach Interface

A device driver's controller unattach interface removes the specified controller structure from the list of controllers it handles.

The following code fragment shows you how to set up a controller
unattach interface:

```
xxctrl_unattach(bus_struct, ctlr_struct)
struct bus *bus_struct;          /* Pointer to bus structure */
struct controller *ctlr_struct;  /* Pointer to controller */
                                 /* structure */
{
    /* Variable and structure declarations */
    .
    .
    .
    /* Code to perform controller unattach tasks */
    .
    .
    .
}
```

The code fragment declares the two arguments associated with a controller
unattach interface. The code fragment also sets up the sections where you
declare local variables and structures and where you write the code to
implement the controller unattach interface.

Section 4.1.6.3 shows how to implement a controller unattach interface
for the /dev/none device driver. Section 10.8.3 shows how to implement
a controller unattach interface for a character device driver that operates
on a TURBOchannel bus. Section 17.2 provides a reference (man) page that
gives additional information on the arguments and tasks associated with an
xxctrl_unattach interface.

3.3.5   Setting Up the Device unattach Interface

A device driver's device unattach interface removes the specified
device structure from the list of devices it handles. The following code
fragment shows you how to set up a device unattach interface:

```
xxdev_unattach(ctlr_struct, dev_struct)
struct controller *ctlr_struct;  /* Pointer to controller */
                                 /* structure */
struct device *dev_struct;       /* Pointer to device */
                                 /* structure */
{
    /* Variable and structure declarations */
    .
    .
    .
```

```
        /* Code to perform device unattach tasks */
    .
    .
    .
}
```

The code fragment declares the two arguments associated with a device unattach interface that operates on a TURBOchannel bus. The code fragment also sets up the sections where you declare local variables and structures and where you write the code to implement the device unattach interface.

Section 17.2 provides a reference (man) page that gives additional information on the arguments and tasks associated with an *xx*dev_unattach interface.

3.4 Configure Section

The configure section applies to the loadable versions of both character and block device drivers and it contains a configure interface. A device driver's configure interface is called as a result of a user-level request to the sysconfig utility to dynamically load, unload, and query a device driver. The following code fragment shows you how to set up a configure interface:

```
xx_configure(optype, indata, indatalen, outdata, outdatalen)
cfg_op_t optype;        /* Configure operation */
cfg_attr_t *indata;     /* Input data structure */
size_t indatalen;       /* Size of input data structure */
cfg_attr_t *outdata;    /* Parameter not used */
size_t outdatalen;      /* Parameter not used */
{
    /* Variable and structure declarations */
    .
    .
    .

    /* Code to perform configure tasks */
    .
    .
    .
}
```

The code fragment declares the five arguments associated with a configure interface. The code fragment also sets up the sections where you declare local variables and structures and where you write the code to implement the configure interface.

Section 4.1.7.1 shows you how to set up the configure interface for the /dev/none device driver. Section 10.9.1 shows you how to implement a configure interface for a character device driver that operates on a TURBOchannel bus. Section 17.2 provides a reference (man) page that gives additional information on the arguments and tasks associated with an *xx_configure* interface.

3.5   Open and Close Device Section

The open and close device section applies to both character and block device drivers. This section contains:

- An open interface

- A close interface

You specify the entry for the driver's open and close interfaces in the bdevsw for block device drivers and the cdevsw for character device drivers. Section 8.2 describes the device switch tables. The following sections discuss how to set up each of these interfaces.

3.5.1   Setting Up the open Interface

A device driver's open interface is called as the result of an open system call. The following code fragment shows you how to set up an open interface:

```
xxopen(dev, flag, format)
dev_t dev;   /* Major/minor device number */
int flag;    /* Flags from /usr/sys/h/file.h */
int format;  /* Format of special device */
{
    /* Variable and structure declarations */
    .
    .
    .
    /* Code to open the device */
    .
    .
    .
}
```

The code fragment declares the three arguments associated with an open interface that operates on any bus. The code fragment also sets up the sections where you declare local variables and structures and where you write the code to implement the open interface.

Section 4.1.8.1 shows you how to implement an open interface for the /dev/none device driver. Section 10.10.1 shows you how to implement an open interface for a character device driver that operates on a TURBOchannel bus. Section 17.2 provides a reference (man) page that gives additional information on the arguments and tasks associated with an *xx*open interface.

3.5.2 Setting Up the close Interface

The `open` interface is called every time that any user initiates an action that invokes the `open` system call. The `close` interface, however, is called only when the last user initiates an action that closes the device. The reason for this difference is to allow the driver to take some special action when there is no work left to perform. The following code fragment shows you how to set up a `close` interface:

```
xxclose(dev, flag, format)
dev_t dev;   /* Major/minor device number */
int flag;    /* Flags from /usr/sys/h/file.h */
int format;  /* Format of special device */
{
     /* Variable and structure declarations */
  .
  .
  .
     /* Code to correctly close the device */
  .
  .
  .
}
```

The code fragment declares the three arguments associated with a `close` interface that operates on any bus. It also sets up the sections where you declare local variables and structures and where you write the code to implement the `close` interface.

Section 4.1.8.2 shows you how to implement a `close` interface for the `/dev/none` device driver. Section 10.10.2 shows you how to implement a `close` interface for a character device driver that operates on a TURBOchannel bus. Section 17.2 provides a reference (man) page that gives additional information on the arguments and tasks associated with an `xxclose` interface.

3.6 Read and Write Device Section

The read and write device section applies only to character device drivers. This section contains:

- A `read` interface
- A `write` interface

You specify the entry for the driver's `read` and `write` interfaces in the `cdevsw` table. Section 8.2.1 describes the `cdevsw` table. The following sections discuss how to set up each of these interfaces.

3.6.1 Setting Up the read Interface

The read interface is called from the I/O system as the result of a read system call. The following code fragment shows you how to set up a read interface:

```
xxread(dev, uio)
dev_t dev;        /* Major/minor device number */
struct uio *uio; /* Pointer to uio structure */
{
     /* Variable and structure declarations */
     .
     .
     .
     /* Code to read data from the device */
     .
     .
     .
}
```

The code fragment declares the two arguments associated with a read interface that operates on any bus. It also sets up the sections where you declare local variables and structures and where you write the code to implement the read interface.

Section 4.1.9.1 shows you how to implement a read interface for the /dev/none device driver. Section 10.11.1 shows you how to implement a read interface for a character device driver that operates on a TURBOchannel bus. Section 17.2 provides a reference (man) page that gives additional information on the arguments and tasks associated with an xxread interface.

3.6.2 Setting Up the write Interface

The write interface is called from the I/O system as the result of a write system call. The following code fragment shows you how to set up a write interface:

```
xxwrite(dev, uio)
dev_t dev;        /* Major/minor device number */
struct uio *uio; /* Pointer to uio structure */
{
     /* Variable and structure declarations */
     .
     .
     .
     /* Code to write data to the device */
}
```

The code fragment declares the two arguments associated with a write interface that operates on any bus. It also sets up the sections where you declare local variables and structures and where you write the code to implement the `write` interface.

Section 4.1.9.2 shows you how to implement a `write` interface for the /dev/none device driver. Section 10.11.2 shows you how to implement a `write` interface for a character device driver that operates on a TURBOchannel bus. Section 17.2 provides a reference (man) page that gives additional information on the arguments and tasks associated with an *xx*write interface.

3.7 The ioctl Section

The `ioctl` interface typically performs all device-related operations other than read or write operations. A device driver's `ioctl` interface is called as a result of an `ioctl` system call. Only those `ioctl` commands that are device specific or that require action on the part of the device driver result in a call to the driver's `ioctl` interface. You specify the entry for the driver's `ioctl` interface in the `cdevsw` table for character drivers and in the `bdevsw` table for block device drivers. Section 8.2 describes the device switch tables.

The following code fragment shows you how to set up an `ioctl` interface:

```
xxioctl(dev, cmd, data, flag)
dev_t dev;              /* Major/minor device number */
unsigned int cmd;       /* The ioctl command */
caddr_t data;           /* ioctl command-specified data */
int flag;               /* Access mode of the device */
{
    /* Variable and structure declarations */
    .
    .
    .
    /* Code to perform device-related operations */
    .
    .
    .
}
```

The code fragment declares the four arguments associated with an `ioctl` interface that operates on any bus. It also sets up the sections where you declare local variables and structures and where you write the code to implement the `ioctl` interface.

Section 4.1.11 shows you how to implement an `ioctl` interface for the /dev/none device driver. Section 10.14 shows you how to implement an `ioctl` interface for a character device driver that operates on a TURBOchannel bus. Section 17.2 provides a reference (man) page that gives additional information on the arguments and tasks associated with an *xx*ioctl interface.

3.8 Strategy Section

The strategy section applies to block device drivers and contains a `strategy` interface. However, character device drivers can also contain a `strategy` interface that is called by the character driver's `read` and `write` interfaces.

The `strategy` interface performs block I/O for block devices and initiates read and write operations for character devices. You specify the entry point for the `strategy` interface in the `bdevsw` table. Section 8.2.2 describes the `bdevsw` table. For character drivers, you do not specify the entry point for the `strategy` interface because it is called only by the character driver's `read` and `write` interfaces. There is no entry point defined in the `cdevsw` table.

The following code fragment shows you how to set up a `strategy` interface:

```
xxstrategy(bp)
struct buf *bp; /* Pointer to buf structure */
{
     /* Variable and structure declarations */
    .
    .
    .
     /* Code to perform block I/O or read/write operations */
    .
    .
    .
}
```

The code fragment declares the argument associated with a `strategy` interface that operates on any bus. It also sets up the sections where you declare local variables and structures and where you write the code to implement the `strategy` interface.

Section 10.12 shows you how to implement a `strategy` interface for a character device driver that operates on a TURBOchannel bus. Section 17.2 provides a reference (man) page that gives additional information on the arguments and tasks associated with an `xxstrategy` interface.

3.9 Stop Section

The stop section applies only to character device drivers and it contains a `stop` interface. Terminal device drivers use the `stop` interface to suspend transmission on a specified line. You specify the entry for a driver's `stop` interface in the `cdevsw` table. Section 8.2.1 describes the `cdevsw` table.

The following code fragment shows you how to set up a stop interface:

```
xxstop(tp, flag)
struct tty *tp; /* Pointer to tty structure */
int flag;       /* Output flag */
{
     /* Variable and structure declarations */
     .
     .
     .
     /* Code to suspend transmission on the specified line */
     .
     .
     .
}
```

The code fragment declares the two arguments associated with a stop interface that operates on any bus. It also sets up the sections where you declare local variables and structures and where you write the code to implement the stop interface.

Section 17.2 provides a reference (man) page that gives additional information on the arguments and tasks associated with an xxstop interface.

3.10 Reset Section

The reset section applies only to character device drivers and it contains a reset interface. The reset interface is used to force a device reset to place the device in a known state after a bus reset. You specify the entry for a driver's reset interface in the cdevsw table. Section 8.2.1 describes the cdevsw table.

The following code fragment shows you how to set up a reset interface:

```
xxreset(busnum)
int busnum; /* Logical unit number of bus */
{
     /* Variable and structure declarations */
     .
     .
     .
     /* Code to force the device to reset */
     .
     .
     .
}
```

The code fragment declares the argument associated with a reset interface that operates on any bus. It also sets up the sections where you declare local variables and structures and where you write the code to implement the reset interface.

Section 17.2 provides a reference (man) page that gives additional information on the arguments and tasks associated with an xxreset interface.

3.11 Interrupt Section

The interrupt section applies to both character and block device drivers and it contains a device interrupt handler, which this book refers to as the driver's interrupt service interface (ISI). The ISI is called as a result of a hardware interrupt. In previous versions of the Digital UNIX operating system (formerly known as DEC OSF/1), driver writers implementing static-only device drivers specified a device driver's ISI in the system configuration file if they followed the traditional device driver configuration model; they specified the ISI in the config.file file fragment if they followed the third-party device driver configuration model. Loadable device drivers, on the other hand, must call a number of kernel interfaces and use specific data structures to register, deregister, enable, and disable a device driver's ISI. Section 12.2 describes the system configuration file.

Digital recommends that all new drivers (static and loadable) call the handler interfaces to dynamically register ISIs.

The following code fragment shows you how to set up an ISI:

```
xxintr(parameter)
caddr_t parameter; /* Logical controller number */
{
    /* Variable and structure declarations */
    .
    .
    .
    /* Code to handle a hardware interrupt */
    .
    .
    .
}
```

The code fragment declares the argument associated with an ISI that operates on any bus. The code fragment also sets up the sections where you declare local variables and structures and where you write the code to implement the ISI.

Section 10.16 shows you how to implement an ISI for a character device driver that operates on a TURBOchannel bus. Section 17.2 provides a reference (man) page that gives additional information on the arguments and tasks associated with an xxintr interface. It also provides information on the handler interfaces.

3.12 Select Section

The select section applies only to character device drivers and it contains a
`select` interface. A device driver's `select` interface is called to
determine whether data is available for reading and whether space is available
for writing data. You specify the entry point for a driver's `select` interface
in the `cdevsw` table. Section 8.2.1 describes the `cdevsw` table.

Because the `/dev/none` and `/dev/cb` device drivers do not implement a
select section, the following code fragment not only shows you how to set up
a `select` interface, but it also illustrates some typical tasks. For example
purposes, the code refers to some `xx` device.

```
      .
      .
      .
struct {
      .
      .
      .
 sel_queue_t * sel_q;
      .
      .
      .
} xx_softc[NXX];        1
xxselect(dev, events, revents, scanning)
 dev_t dev;             2
 short *events;         3
 short *revents;        4
 int scanning;          5
{
        int nread;      6
        register int unit = minor(dev);         7
        struct xx_softc *sc = &xx_softc[unit];  8
        queue_init(&sc->sel_q.links);           9

/******************************************************
 *         Poll for input reads                       *
 ******************************************************/
        if (*events & POLLNORM) {       10
                if (scanning) {         11
                        nread = xxnread(dev);   12
                        if (nread > 0)
                                *revents |= POLLNORM;   13
                        else
                                select_enqueue(&sc->sel_q);     14
                } else
                        select_dequeue(&sc->sel_q);     15
        }
/******************************************************
 *         Poll for output write                      *
 ******************************************************/
        if (*events & POLLOUT) {        16
                if (scanning) {         17
                        if (xxnwrite(dev))      18
                                *revents |= POLLOUT;    19
                        else
                                select_enqueue(&sc->sel_q);     20
```

```
            } else
                    select_dequeue(&sc->sel_q);  21
        }
        return (0);  22
}
```

1   Declares an array of `softc` structures and calls it `xx_softc`. One of the members of the `xx_softc` structure is a pointer to a `sel_queue` data structure. The `sel_queue` data structure provides device driver writers with a generic queue of select events. You must initialize the `links` member prior to using the `select_enqueue` and `select_dequeue` interfaces.

2   Declares an argument that specifies the major and minor device numbers for a specific `xx` device. The minor device number is used to determine the logical unit number for the `xx` device on which the select call is to be performed.

3   Declares a pointer to an argument that specifies the events to be polled. This argument is an input to the device driver. A user-level process issues a `select` system call. The `select` system call then calls the driver's `xxselect` interface. The kernel can set this argument to the bitwise inclusive OR of one or more of the polling bit masks defined in the file `/usr/sys/include/sys/poll.h`: POLLNORM, POLLOUT, and POLLPRI.

4   Declares a pointer to an argument that specifies the events that are ready. The driver writer sets this value in the driver's `xxselect` interface. The driver writer can set this argument to the bitwise inclusive OR of one or more of the polling bit masks defined in `/usr/sys/include/sys/poll.h`: POLLNVAL, POLLHUP, POLLNORM, and POLLOUT.

5   Declares an argument that specifies the initiation and termination of a select call. The kernel sets this argument to the value 1 to indicate initiation of a select call. A user-level process issues a `select` system call. The `select` system call then calls the driver's `xxselect` interface.

6   Declares a variable to contain the number of characters available for input.

7   Calls the `minor` interface to obtain the minor device number associated with this `xx` device.

8   Declares a pointer to an `xx_softc` structure and calls it `sc`. Initializes `sc` to the address of the `xx_softc` structure associated with this `xx` device. The minor device number, *unit*, is used as an index into the array of `xx_softc` structures to determine which `xx_softc` structure is associated with this `xx` device.

9 Calls the `queue_init` interface. The `queue_init` interface initializes the specified queue. Device drivers call this interface prior to calling `select_enqueue` to initialize a pointer to a `sel_queue` data structure.

10 Determines if the kernel set the read input select bit, which indicates that the caller of the driver's `select` interface wants to know if input data is available on this device. A user-level process issues a `select` system call. The `select` system call then calls the driver's `xxselect` interface.

11 If the kernel sets this argument to the value 1 (true), then a user-level process has initiated a `select` request (which causes the kernel to issue a `select` system call).

12 For the purpose of this example, assume that the `xx` driver has a separate interface called `xxnread`, which returns the count of the number of characters available for input.

13 If the count is greater than zero (0), there are characters available for input. Set the read input select bit in the pointer to the *revents* argument. The `select` system call can be completed without waiting for input to be available.

14 If the count is not greater than zero (0), there are no characters available for input. Call the `select_enqueue` interface to allow the `select` system call to remember that the user-level process that initiated the `select` request wants to be notified when input is available to be read.

This interface takes one argument: a pointer to a `sel_queue` structure. You previously initialized the `links` member of this structure by calling the `queue_init` interface. The `select_enqueue` interface adds the current kernel thread to the list of kernel threads waiting for a select-related event on this `xx` device. When input is available, the `select` request can be completed.

At a different interface in the `xxdriver` (typically, either the interrupt section or an interface called by the interrupt section), when new input has been received on the device the driver calls the `select_wakeup` interface. The driver passes to it the same parameter passed to `select_enqueue` to notify the upper levels of the `select` system call that the user-level process that initiated the `select` request can now be notified that the driver has new input available to be read.

15 Executes when the kernel sets the *scanning* parameter to the value zero (0). This indicates that the upper level `select` system call code is no longer interested in being notified when input is available on this device. The `/dev/xx` driver calls the `select_dequeue` interface to remove any instances of this `xx` device registered as waiting for notification of input.

This interface takes one argument: a pointer to a `sel_queue` structure.

16 Determines if the kernel set the write output select bit, which indicates that the user-level process that initiated the `select` request wants to know if the device is ready to accept data to be output. Typically, this involves verifying that the device's output buffers have sufficient space to accept additional characters to be transmitted.

17 If the kernel sets the *scanning* argument to the value 1 (true), then a user-level process has initiated a `select` request (which causes the kernel to issue a `select` system call).

18 For the purpose of this example, assume that the `/dev/xx` driver has a separate interface called `xxnwrite`, which returns a nonzero value if the device is in a state where it is ready to output data.

19 To indicate that this instance of the `xx` device is ready to accept additional output, sets the *revents* argument to the polling bit `POLLOUT`.

20 The device is not ready to accept additional output. Therefore, the `/dev/xx` driver calls the `select_enqueue` interface to cause the `select` system call to be notified later when the device is ready to accept output. At a different interface in the `/dev/xx` driver (typically, either the interrupt section or an interface called by the interrupt section), after previous output transmission has completed the driver calls the `select_wakeup` interface. The driver passes a pointer to a `sel_queue` structure to notify the upper levels of the `select` system call that the user-level process that initiated the `select` request can now be notified that the driver has new output available to be written.

21 If the kernel sets the *scanning* argument to the value zero (false), then a `select` system call is being terminated. This indicates that the upper level `select` system call code is no longer interested in being notified when the device is ready to accept output characters. The `/dev/xx` driver calls the `select_dequeue` interface to remove any instances of this `xx` device registered as waiting for notification of output ready status.

This interface takes one argument: a pointer to a `sel_queue` structure.

22 The driver's `xxselect` interface returns the value zero (0) to indicate success.

Section 17.2 provides a reference (man) page that gives additional information on the arguments and tasks associated with an `xxselect` interface.

3.13 Dump Section

The dump section applies only to block device drivers and it contains a `dump` interface. A device driver's `dump` interface is called to copy system memory to the dump device. You specify the entry point for a driver's `dump` interface in the `bdevsw` table. Section 8.2.2 describes the `bdevsw` table.

The following code fragment shows you how to set up a `dump` interface:

```
xxdump(dumpdev)
dev_t dumpdev;   /* Device to dump system memory to */
{
     /* Variable and structure declarations */
   .
   .
   .
     /* Code to copy system memory to the dump device */
   .
   .
   .
}
```

The code fragment declares the argument associated with a `dump` interface that operates on any bus. It also sets up the sections where you declare local variables and structures and where you write the code to implement the `dump` interface.

Section 17.2 provides a reference (man) page that gives additional information on the arguments and tasks associated with an *xx*dump interface.

Note

The Digital UNIX operating system does not currently support an *xx*dump interface's ability to copy the contents of system memory to the specified device. Device driver writers should not provide an *xx*dump interface for this version of Digital UNIX.

3.14 The psize Section

The psize section applies only to block device drivers and it contains a `psize` interface. A device driver's `psize` interface is called to return the size of a disk partition. You specify the entry point for a driver's `psize` interface in the `bdevsw` table. Section 8.2.2 describes the `bdevsw` table.

The following code fragment shows you how to set up a `psize` interface:

```
xxpsize(dev)
dev_t dev;  /* Device and partition for which size */
            /* is requested */
{
    /* Variable and structure declarations */
    .
    .
    .

    /* Code to return the size of a disk partition */
    .
    .
    .

}
```

The code fragment declares the argument associated with a `psize` interface that operates on any bus. It also sets up the sections where you declare local variables and structures and where you write the code to implement the `psize` interface.

Section 17.2 provides a reference (man) page that gives additional information on the arguments and tasks associated with an `xxpsize` interface.

3.15 Memory Map Section

Alpha CPUs do not support an application's use of the `mmap` system call. Therefore, if you are writing a device driver that operates on such CPUs, you need to use a mechanism other than the memory map interface. The memory map section applies only to character device drivers, and it contains a memory map interface. The memory map interface is invoked by the kernel as the result of an application calling the `mmap` system call. You specify the entry for the driver's `xxmmap` interface in the `cdevsw` table. Section 8.2.1 describes the `cdevsw` table.

The following code fragment shows you how to set up a memory map interface:

```
xxmmap(dev, offset, prot)
dev_t dev;     /* Major/minor device number */
off_t offset;  /* Offset into device memory */
int prot;      /* Protection flag */
{
    /* Variable and structure declarations */
    .
    .
    .
```

```
    /* Code to map kernel space to user space */
    .
    .
    .
}
```

The code fragment declares the three arguments associated with a memory map interface that operates on any bus. It also sets up the sections where you declare local variables and structures and where you write the code to implement the memory map interface.

Section 17.2 provides a reference (man) page that gives additional information on the arguments and tasks associated with an xxmmap interface.

Coding, Configuring, and Testing a Device Driver 4

The previous chapter showed you how to set up the interfaces associated with a device driver. This chapter shows you how to implement some of those interfaces for the /dev/none device driver. Specifically, the chapter shows you how to:

- Code a device driver

- Configure a device driver

- Test a device driver

4.1 Coding a Device Driver

The /dev/none device driver is a simple device driver that performs the following tasks:

- Determines if the none device exists on the system

- Checks to ensure that the open request is unique and marks the device as open

- Copies data from the specified address space to the device

- Obtains and clears the count of bytes previously written to the device

- Closes the device

- Implements the tasks associated with the loadable version of the driver

The /dev/none device driver is implemented as one driver that operates on a TURBOchannel bus and can be configured either as a loadable or static driver. However, the code explanations point out bus-specific issues you need to consider to make the driver portable across other bus architectures such as EISA and PCI.

The /dev/none device driver references some structures (for example, the driver structure) that may be unfamiliar to you. However, to understand this simple device driver you do not need an intimate understanding of the structures.

For convenience in learning how this driver is implemented, the source code is divided into parts. Table 4-1 lists the parts of the /dev/none device driver and the sections of the chapter where each is described. For those who prefer to read the /dev/none source code with inline comments, see

Section A.1. The /dev/none source code is also available to you in the /usr/examples/devdriver directory. See the README file in this directory, which explains where you can access the device driver kits for the /dev/none device driver.

Note

The /dev/none device driver shows how to write a device driver that controls an example hardware device (that is, the device does not exist). This driver is for example and illustrative purposes only. Therefore, you should never build this driver into a static kernel. You can dynamically load the /dev/none driver, but you cannot execute it because the hardware device it controls does not exist.

Table 4-1: Parts of the /dev/none Device Driver

Part	Section
The nonereg.h Header File	Section 4.1.1
Include Files Section	Section 4.1.2
Autoconfiguration Support Declarations and Definitions Section	Section 4.1.3
Loadable Driver Configuration Support Declarations and Definitions Section	Section 4.1.4
Loadable Driver Local Structure and Variable Definitions Section	Section 4.1.5
Autoconfiguration Support Section	Section 4.1.6
Loadable Device Driver Section	Section 4.1.7
Open and Close Device Section	Section 4.1.8
Read and Write Device Section	Section 4.1.9
Interrupt Section	Section 4.1.10
The ioctl Section	Section 4.1.11

4.1.1   The nonereg.h Header File

The `nonereg.h` file is the device register header file for the `/dev/none` device driver. It contains public declarations and the device register offset for the `none` device. The following declarations are applicable to the loadable or static version of the driver:

```
#define DN_GETCOUNT   _IOR(0,1,int) 1
#define DN_CLRCOUNT   _IO(0,2)       2

#define NONE_CSR 0 3
```

1. Uses the `_IOR` macro to construct an `ioctl` macro called
   DN_GETCOUNT. The `_IOR` macro defines `ioctl` types for situations
   where data is transferred from the kernel into the user's buffer.
   Typically, this data consists of device control or status information
   returned to the application program. Section 15.3 provides reference
   (man) page-style descriptions of the `_IO`, `_IOR`, `_IOW`, and `_IOWR`
   `ioctl` macros.

   Section 4.1.11 shows how the `noneioctl` interface uses
   DN_GETCOUNT.

2. Uses the `_IO` macro to construct an `ioctl` macro called
   DN_CLRCOUNT. The `_IO` macro defines `ioctl` types for situations
   where no data is actually transferred between the application program and
   the kernel. For example, this could occur in a device control operation.
   Section 4.1.11 shows how the `noneioctl` interface uses
   DN_CLRCOUNT.

3. Defines the device register offset for the `none` device. All real devices
   have registers and the offsets defining the layout of these registers are
   usually defined in the device register header file. Although the `none`
   device is not a real device, the example shows how a device register
   offset would be defined.

   The NONE_CSR offset is a 64-bit read/write CSR/LED register.

4.1.2 Include Files Section

The Include Files Section is applicable to the loadable or static version of the /dev/none device driver. It identifies the following header files that the /dev/none device driver needs:

```
#include <sys/param.h>
#include <sys/systm.h>
#include <sys/ioctl.h>
#include <sys/tty.h>
#include <sys/user.h>
#include <sys/proc.h>
#include <sys/map.h>
#include <sys/buf.h>
#include <sys/vm.h>
#include <sys/file.h>
#include <sys/uio.h>
#include <sys/types.h>
#include <sys/errno.h>
#include <sys/conf.h>
#include <sys/kernel.h>
#include <sys/devio.h>
#include <hal/cpuconf.h>
#include <sys/exec.h>
#include <io/common/devdriver.h>
#include <sys/sysconfig.h>

#include <io/dec/tc/tc.h>        1

#include <machine/cpu.h>
#include <io/ESA100/nonereg.h>   2

#define NNONE 4                  3
```

1   Includes the header file tc.h, which is the header file associated with the TURBOchannel bus. If you are writing the driver to operate on multiple bus architectures, you must include the bus-specific header file. For example, to write the /dev/none driver to operate on EISA and PCI buses, you need to include the following header files:

```
#include <io/dec/eisa/eisa.h>

#include <io/dec/pci/pci.h>
```

2   Includes the device register header file, which is discussed in Section 4.1.1. The directory specification adheres to the third-party device driver configuration model discussed in Section 11.1.2. If the traditional device driver configuration model is followed, the directory specification is <io/EasyInc/nonereg.h>. The directory specification you make here depends on where you put the device register file.

The previous lines include the common header files.

Chapter 14 provides reference (man) page-style descriptions of the header files that Digital UNIX device drivers use most frequently.

3 Defines a constant called NNONE that is used to allocate data structures needed by the /dev/none driver. There can be at most four instances of the none controller on the system. This value represents a small number of instances of the driver on the system and the data structures themselves are not large, so it is acceptable to allocate for the maximum configuration. This example uses the static allocation model 2 technique described in Section 2.5.2. Note that you could also define this constant in a name_data.c file.

4.1.3 Autoconfiguration Support Declarations and Definitions Section

The Autoconfiguration Support Declarations and Definitions Section is applicable to the loadable or static version of the /dev/none device driver. It contains the following declarations that the /dev/none device driver needs. The decision as to whether it is loadable or static is made at run time by the system manager and not at compile time by the driver writer. Thus, the driver writer can implement one device driver that is loadable or static.

```
#define DN_RESET 0001 1
#define DN_ERROR 0002 2


#define DN_OPEN  1 3
#define DN_CLOSE 0 4



int noneprobe(), nonecattach(), noneintr();
int noneopen(),  noneclose(),  noneread(), nonewrite();
int noneioctl(), none_ctlr_unattach(); 5



struct controller *noneinfo[NNONE]; 6


struct driver nonedriver = {
        noneprobe,
        0,
        nonecattach,
        0,
        0,
        0,
        0,
        0,
        "none",
        noneinfo,
        0,
        0,
        0,
        0,
        0,
        none_ctlr_unattach,
        0
}; 7


struct none_softc {
      int sc_openf;
```

```
      int sc_count;
      int sc_state;
} none_softc[NNONE];  8
```

1 Declares a constant called DN_RESET to indicate that the specified none
   device is ready for data transfer. Section 4.1.6.1 shows that the
   noneprobe interface uses this constant to set the NONE_CSR device
   register offset associated with a specific none device. If this driver
   operated on actual hardware, setting the DN_RESET bit could force the
   device to reset.

2 Declares a constant called DN_ERROR to indicate when an error occurs.
   Section 4.1.6.1 shows that the noneprobe interface uses this constant in
   a bitwise AND operation with the NONE_CSR device register offset
   associated with a specific none device. An actual hardware device could
   set this bit in the NONE_CSR device register offset to indicate that an
   error condition occurred.

3 Declares a constant called DN_OPEN to represent the device open bit.
   Section 4.1.8.1 shows that the noneopen interface uses this constant to
   set the open bit for a specific none device. This bit represents the
   driver's software state.

4 Declares a constant called DN_CLOSE to represent the device close bit.
   Section 4.1.8.2 shows that the noneclose interface uses this constant to
   clear the open bit for a specific none device. This bit represents the
   driver's software state.

5 Declares the driver interfaces for the /dev/none driver. Note that the
   nonecattach and noneintr interfaces are merely stubs. These
   interfaces have no associated code but are declared here to handle any
   future development.

6 Declares an array of pointers to controller structures and calls it
   noneinfo. The controller structure represents an instance of a
   controller entity, one that connects logically to a bus. A controller can
   control devices that are directly connected or can perform some other
   controlling operation, such as a network interface or terminal controller
   operation. Section 7.3.2 describes the controller structure.

   Note that the NNONE constant is used to represent the maximum number
   of none controllers. This number is used to size the array of pointers to
   controller structures.

7 Declares and initializes the driver structure called nonedriver.
   This structure is used to connect the driver entry points and other
   information to the Digital UNIX code. This structure is used primarily
   during autoconfiguration. Some members of this structure are not used
   by the /dev/none device driver. Section 7.3.4 describes the driver
   structure.

The value zero (0) indicates that the /dev/none driver does not make use of a specific member of the driver structure. The following list describes those members initialized to a nonzero value by the example driver:

- noneprobe, the driver's probe interface

  Section 4.1.6.1 shows how to implement noneprobe.

- nonecattach, the driver's cattach interface

  The none device does not need an attach interface. However, Section 4.1.6.2 provides a nonecattach interface stub for future expansion.

- none, the device name

- noneinfo, which references the array of pointers to the previously declared controller structures

  You index this array with the controller number as specified in the ctlr_num member of the controller structure.

- none_ctlr_unattach, the driver's controller unattach interface

  The none_ctlr_unattach interface removes the controller structure associated with specific none devices from the list of controller structures that it handles. Section 4.1.6.3 shows how to implement none_ctlr_unattach.

8 Declares an array of softc structures and calls it none_softc. Like noneinfo, the none_softc structure's size is the value represented by the NNONE constant. The softc structure is found in many device drivers to allow driver interfaces to share data. The none_softc structure contains the following members:

- sc_openf

  Stores a constant value that indicates that the none device is open. This member is set by the noneopen and noneclose interfaces discussed in Section 4.1.8.1 and Section 4.1.8.2, respectively.

- sc_count

  Stores the count of characters. This member is set by the nonewrite and noneioctl interfaces discussed in Section 4.1.9.2 and Section 4.1.11, respectively.

- sc_state

  Stores a constant value that indicates the state the driver is in. This member is not currently used.

4.1.4 Loadable Driver Configuration Support Declarations and Definitions Section

The Loadable Driver Configuration Support Declarations and Definitions Section is applicable only to the loadable version of the /dev/none device driver. It contains the following declarations that the loadable version of the /dev/none device driver uses:

```
static int cmajnum = 0;  1
static int bmajnum = 0;
static int begunit = 0;
static int numunit = 0;
static int dsflags = 0;
static int noneversion = 0;
static unsigned char mcfgname[CFG_ATTR_NAME_SZ] = "";  2
static unsigned char modtype[CFG_ATTR_NAME_SZ] = "";
static unsigned char devcmajor[CFG_ATTR_NAME_SZ] = "";
static unsigned char devmgrreq[CFG_ATTR_NAME_SZ] = "";
static unsigned char devblkmaj[CFG_ATTR_NAME_SZ] = "";
static unsigned char devblkminor[CFG_ATTR_NAME_SZ] = "";
static unsigned char devblkfiles[CFG_ATTR_NAME_SZ] = "";
static unsigned char devcminor[CFG_ATTR_NAME_SZ] = "";
static unsigned char devcfiles[CFG_ATTR_NAME_SZ] = "";
static unsigned char devuser[CFG_ATTR_NAME_SZ] = "";
static unsigned char devgroup[CFG_ATTR_NAME_SZ] = "";
static unsigned char devmode[CFG_ATTR_NAME_SZ] = "";

cfg_subsys_attr_t none_attributes[] = {  3


{"Module_Config_Name",   CFG_ATTR_STRTYPE, CFG_OP_CONFIGURE,
                         (caddr_t)mcfgname,2,CFG_ATTR_NAME_SZ,0},
{"Module_Type",          CFG_ATTR_STRTYPE, CFG_OP_CONFIGURE,
                         (caddr_t)modtype,2,CFG_ATTR_NAME_SZ,0},
{"Device_Char_Major",    CFG_ATTR_STRTYPE, CFG_OP_CONFIGURE,
                         (caddr_t)devcmajor,0,CFG_ATTR_NAME_SZ,0},
{"Device_Major_Req",     CFG_ATTR_STRTYPE, CFG_OP_CONFIGURE,
                         (caddr_t)devmgrreq,0,CFG_ATTR_NAME_SZ,0},
{"Device_Block_Major",   CFG_ATTR_STRTYPE, CFG_OP_CONFIGURE,
                         (caddr_t)devblkmaj,0,CFG_ATTR_NAME_SZ,0},
{"Device_Block_Minor",   CFG_ATTR_STRTYPE, CFG_OP_CONFIGURE,
                         (caddr_t)devblkminor,0,CFG_ATTR_NAME_SZ,0},
{"Device_Block_Files",   CFG_ATTR_STRTYPE, CFG_OP_CONFIGURE,
                         (caddr_t)devblkfiles,0,CFG_ATTR_NAME_SZ,0},
{"Device_Char_Minor",    CFG_ATTR_STRTYPE, CFG_OP_CONFIGURE,
                         (caddr_t)devcminor,0,CFG_ATTR_NAME_SZ,0},
{"Device_Char_Files",    CFG_ATTR_STRTYPE, CFG_OP_CONFIGURE,
                         (caddr_t)devcfiles,0,CFG_ATTR_NAME_SZ,0},
{"Device_User",          CFG_ATTR_STRTYPE, CFG_OP_CONFIGURE,
                         (caddr_t)devuser,0,CFG_ATTR_NAME_SZ,0},
{"Device_Group",         CFG_ATTR_STRTYPE, CFG_OP_CONFIGURE,
                         (caddr_t)devgroup,0,CFG_ATTR_NAME_SZ,0},
{"Device_Mode",          CFG_ATTR_STRTYPE, CFG_OP_CONFIGURE,
```

```
                                  (caddr_t)devmode,0,CFG_ATTR_NAME_SZ,0},

    {"cmajnum",                   CFG_ATTR_INTTYPE, CFG_OP_QUERY,
                                  (caddr_t)&cmajnum,0,99,0},
    {"bmajnum",                   CFG_ATTR_INTTYPE, CFG_OP_QUERY,
                                  (caddr_t)&bmajnum,0,99,0},
    {"begunit",                   CFG_ATTR_INTTYPE, CFG_OP_QUERY,
                                  (caddr_t)&begunit,0,8,0},
    {"numunit",                   CFG_ATTR_INTTYPE, CFG_OP_QUERY,
                                  (caddr_t)&numunit,0,8,0},
    {"dsflags",                   CFG_ATTR_INTTYPE, CFG_OP_QUERY,
                                  (caddr_t)&dsflags,0,8,0},
    {"version",                   CFG_ATTR_INTTYPE, CFG_OP_QUERY,
                                  (caddr_t)&noneversion,0,9999999,0},
    {"",0,0,0,0,0,0}
    };

    extern int nodev(), nulldev(); 4
    ihandler_id_t *none_id_t[NNONE]; 5



    #define DN_BUSNAME    "tc" 6

    int none_is_dynamic = 0; 7

    struct tc_option none_option_snippet [] =
    /******************************************************/
    {
    /*  module       driver  intr_b4 itr_aft      adpt    */
    /*  name         name    probe   attach  type config  */
    /*  ------       ------  ------- ------- ---- ------   */
    {   "NONE    ",  "none",    0,      1,    'C',    0},
    {   "",          ""       } /* Null terminator in the */
                                /* table */
    }; 8
    int num_none = 0;    9
```

1️⃣ Declares and initializes to the value zero (0) an integer variable used as an attribute in the `none_attributes` structure. The five lines that follow also declare and initialize to the value zero (0) variables used as attributes in the `none_attributes` structure.

The `cfgmgr` daemon modifies these attributes during a configure operation and uses these attributes to provide the special files that loadable drivers need.

2️⃣ Declares and initializes to the null string a character string used as an attribute in the `none_attributes` structure. The lines that follow also declare and initialize to the null string character strings used as attributes in the `none_attributes` structure.

The `cfgmgr` daemon fills in the attributes specified in `none_attributes` because the designated operation types are `CFG_OP_CONFIGURE`. The `cfgmgr` daemon gets the entries for the `/dev/none` driver from the `/etc/sysconfigtab` database by locating the `none:` entry. The driver writers at EasyDriver Incorporated create a `stanza.loadable` file fragment for the `/dev/none` driver. The `sysconfigdb` utility appends this `stanza.loadable` file fragment to the `/etc/sysconfigtab` database.

To determine if `cfgmgr` initialized attributes correctly, the `/dev/none` driver verifies each from the `cfg_attr_t` structure that `cfgmgr` passes into the `none_configure` interface's *indata* argument.

3 Declares an array of `cfg_subsys_attr_t` structures and calls it `none_attributes`. The loadable device driver subsystem requires this data structure. Section 7.4.1 describes the members of the `cfg_subsys_attr_t` structure.

4 Declares external references for the `nodev` and `nulldev` interfaces, which are used to initialize members of the `cdevsw` table under specific circumstances. The `cdevsw_add` kernel interface, called by the driver's `none_configure` interface, initializes the `cdevsw` table. Section 8.2.1 provides a description of the `cdevsw` table and examples of the `nodev` and `nulldev` interfaces.

5 Declares a pointer to an array of IDs used to deregister the interrupt handlers. The NNONE constant represents the maximum number of `none` controllers. This number sizes the array of IDs. Thus, there is one ID per `none` device. Section 4.1.6.1 shows how `noneprobe` uses the *none_id_t* array.

6 Defines a constant that represents a 2-character string that indicates this is a driver that operates on the TURBOchannel bus. This constant is passed as an argument to the `ldbl_stanza_resolver`, `ldbl_ctlr_configure`, and `ldbl_ctlr_unconfigure` interfaces. This bus name is used in calls to the configuration code. Other bus types can use a different name. Section 4.1.7.2 shows how to call `ldbl_stanza_resolver` and `ldbl_ctlr_configure`. Section 4.1.7.3 shows how to call `ldbl_ctlr_unconfigure`.

If you are writing the driver to operate on multiple bus architectures, you must include the bus-specific constant. For example, to write the `/dev/none` driver to operate on EISA and PCI buses, you need to define the following constants:

```
#define DN_BUSNAME "eisa"
```

```
#define DN_BUSNAME "pci"
```

7 Declares a variable called *none_is_dynamic* and initializes it to the value zero (0). This variable is used to control any differences in the

tasks performed by the static and loadable versions of the /dev/none device driver at run time. Thus, the /dev/none driver can be compiled once for the loadable and static versions. The decision as to whether it is loadable or static is made at run time by the system manager and not at compile time by the driver writer.

Section 4.1.6.1 shows how noneprobe uses *none_is_dynamic*. Section 4.1.6.3 shows how none_ctlr_unattach uses *none_is_dynamic*. Section 4.1.7.2 shows how none_configure uses *none_is_dynamic*.

8 Declares a tc_option structure snippet that provides an entry for the loadable version of this driver. For the static version, a similar entry is made in the tc_option structure located in the tc_option_data.c file. The entry in the tc_option structure is used only when the driver is configured statically; the none_option_snippet entry is used only when the driver is configured dynamically.

The tc_option structure and tc_option structure snippet is for the /dev/none driver that operates on the TURBOchannel bus. The tc_option structure is declared and initialized in the tc_option_data.c files. To write device drivers to operate on the EISA and PCI buses you need to declare the option structure snippet associated with these buses. See the bus-specific driver book for a description of the option structure associated with the specific bus.

The option structures for the EISA and PCI buses are:

– eisa_option

– pci_option

These option structures are declared and initialized in the following files:

– eisa_option_data.c

– pci_option_data.c

These option structures contain the bus-specific ROM module name for the driver. This information forms the bus-specific parameter that the driver passes to the ldbl_stanza_resolver interface to look for matches in the eisa_slot, pci_slot, or tc_slot table.

It is not an error if this entry already exists in the table(s). The entry in eisa_option, pci_option, or tc_option is used only when the driver is configured statically. A loadable device driver declares and initializes a snippet structure that is an element of the option table. A loadable device driver initializes the snippet structure with an entry for the loadable version of the driver. The example shows a snippet structure for the option structure associated with the TURBOchannel bus.

The tc_option structure contains the bus-specific ROM module name for the driver. This information forms the bus-specific parameter that is passed to the `ldbl_stanza_resolver` interface to search for matches in the `tc_option` structure. The bus configuration interfaces associated with the TURBOchannel bus use the `tc_option` structure.

The items in the `tc_option` structure snippet are identical to those in the `tc_option` structure. These items have the following meanings:

– **module name**

In this column, you specify the device name in the ROM on the hardware device. The module name can be up to 8 characters in length. You must blank pad the name to 8 bytes for those names that are less than 8 characters in length. Thus, the entry for the `/dev/none` driver consists of the letters "NONE" followed by four spaces.

– **driver name**

In this column, you specify the driver name as it appears in the `Module_Config_Name` field of the `stanza.loadable` file fragment. In this example, the driver name is `none`. Because you specify the same name in the `Module_Config_Name` field and the driver name field of the `tc_option` structure snippet, the bus configuration code initializes the correct `controller` and `device` structures during device autoconfiguration for loadable drivers.

– **intr_b4 probe**

In this column, you specify whether the device needs interrupts enabled during execution of the driver's `probe` interface. A zero (0) value indicates that the device does not need interrupts enabled; a value of 1 indicates that the device needs interrupts enabled. In the example, the value zero (0) is specified to indicate that the `none` device does not need interrupts enabled.

– **itr_aft attach**

In this column, you specify whether the device needs interrupts enabled after the driver's `probe` and `attach` interfaces have completed. A zero (0) value indicates that the device does not need interrupts enabled; a value of 1 indicates that the device needs interrupts enabled. In the example, the value 1 is specified to indicate that the `none` device needs interrupts enabled after its `noneprobe` and `nonecattach` interfaces have completed.

– **type**

In this column, you specify the type of device: `C` (controller) or `A` (adapter). In the example, the value `C` is specified.

– **adpt config**

If the device in the type column is `A` (adapter), you specify the name of the interface to configure the adapter. Otherwise, you specify the value zero (0). In the example, the value zero (0) is specified because the device in the previous column is a controller. Section 4.1.7.2 shows how the `none_configure` interface uses `none_option_snippet`.

9 Declares a variable called *num_none* to store the count on the number of controllers probed during autoconfiguration. This variable is initialized to the value zero (0) to indicate that no instances of the controller have been initialized yet. Section 4.1.6.3 shows how `none_ctlr_unattach` uses this variable. Section 4.1.7.2 shows how `none_configure` uses this variable.

4.1.5 Loadable Driver Local Structure and Variable Definitions Section

The Loadable Driver Local Structure and Variable Definitions Section is applicable only to the loadable version of the /dev/none device driver. It contains the following declaration of the /dev/none driver's cdevsw entry that will be dynamically added to the cdevsw table:

```
int none_config = FALSE;    1
dev_t none_devno = NODEV;   2

struct cdevsw none_cdevsw_entry = {
        noneopen,
        noneclose,
        noneread,
        nonewrite,
        noneioctl,
        nodev,
        nodev,
        0,
        nodev,
        0,
        DEV_FUNNEL_NULL,
        0,
        0,
};  3
```

1 Declares a variable called *none_config* to store state flags indicating whether the /dev/none driver is configured as a loadable driver. The *none_config* variable is initialized to the value FALSE. Section 4.1.7.2 shows that none_configure sets *none_config* to the value TRUE to indicate that the /dev/none driver has successfully configured as a loadable driver. Section 4.1.7.3 shows that none_configure sets *none_config* to the value FALSE to indicate that the /dev/none driver has been successfully unconfigured.

2 Declares a variable called *none_devno* to store the cdevsw table entry slot to use. The *none_devno* variable is initialized to the value NODEV to indicate that no major number for the device has been assigned. Section 4.1.7.2 shows that none_configure sets *none_devno* to the table entry slot.

3 Declares and initializes the cdevsw structure called none_cdevsw_entry. Section 8.2.1 describes the cdevsw table. The following list describes those members initialized to a nonzero value by the /dev/none device driver:

– noneopen, the driver's open interface

   Section 4.1.8.1 shows how to implement noneopen.

- noneclose, the driver's close interface

  Section 4.1.8.2 shows how to implement noneclose.

- noneread, the driver's read interface

  Section 4.1.9.1 shows how to implement noneread.

- nonewrite, the driver's write interface

  Section 4.1.9.2 shows how to implement nonewrite.

- noneioctl, the driver's ioctl interface

  Section 4.1.11 shows how to implement noneioctl.

- DEV_FUNNEL_NULL

  This constant signifies that the operating system schedules a device driver onto a multiprocessor configuration.

4.1.6 Autoconfiguration Support Section

The Autoconfiguration Support Declarations and Definitions Section is applicable to the loadable or static version of the /dev/none device driver. The decision as to whether it is loadable or static is made at run time by the system manager and not at compile time by the driver writer. Thus, the driver writer can implement one device driver that is loadable or static. Table 4-2 lists the interfaces implemented as part of the Autoconfiguration Support Section along with the sections in the book where each is described.

Table 4-2: Interfaces Implemented as Part of the Autoconfiguration Support Section

Part	Section
Implementing the noneprobe Interface	Section 4.1.6.1
Implementing the nonecattach Interface	Section 4.1.6.2
Implementing the none_ctlr_unattach Interface	Section 4.1.6.3

4.1.6.1 Implementing the noneprobe Interface

The noneprobe interface is applicable to the loadable or static version of the /dev/none device driver. The bus configuration code calls noneprobe during boot time for the static version of the driver. For the loadable version of the driver, the loadable subsystem code calls noneprobe indirectly during the driver loading process.

The noneprobe interface's main task is to dynamically register the driver's interrupt handlers by calling the handler interfaces. For the static version, noneprobe calls the BADADDR interface to determine if the device is present. If the device is present, noneprobe returns a nonzero value. If the device is not present, noneprobe returns the value zero (0). Because the loadable version of the driver does not perform this task, a conditional if statement tests the *none_is_dynamic* variable.

The following code implements the noneprobe interface:

```
noneprobe(addr1, ctlr)
io_handle_t addr1;  1
struct controller *ctlr;  2
{
     ihandler_t handler;          3
     struct handler_intr_info info;   4
     int unit = ctlr->ctlr_num;  5
     register io_handle_t reg = addr1;  6


     num_none++;  7
     return(0);   8
     handler.ih_bus = ctlr->bus_hd;  9

     info.configuration_st = (caddr_t)ctlr;  10

     info.config_type = CONTROLLER_CONFIG_TYPE;  11

     info.intr = noneintr;  12

     info.param = (caddr_t)unit;  13
     handler.ih_bus_info = (char *)&info;  14

     none_id_t[unit] = handler_add(&handler);  15
     if (none_id_t[unit] == NULL) {  16
            return(0);
            }
            if (handler_enable(none_id_t[unit]) != 0) {  17
                   handler_del(none_id_t[unit]);
                   return(0);
            }

     num_none++;  18
     return(0);   19

     if (!none_is_dynamic) {  20
```

```
              if (BADADDR( (caddr_t) reg + NONE_CSR, sizeof(long), NULL) !=0)
              {
                      return (0);
              } 21
                  }
      write_io_port(reg + NONE_CSR, 8, 0, DN_RESET); 22
      mb();                          23
      if(read_io_port(reg + NONE_CSR, 8, 0) & DN_ERROR)
      {
          return (0);
      } 24
      write_io_port(reg + NONE_CSR, 8, 0, 0); 25
      mb();          26
      return (1); 27
}
```

1 Declares an `addr1` argument that specifies an I/O handle that you can
use to reference a device register or memory located in bus address space
(either I/O space or memory space). This I/O handle references the
device's I/O address space for the bus where the read operation originates
(in calls to the `read_io_port` interface) and where the write operation
occurs (in calls to the `write_io_port` interface).

In previous versions of the Digital UNIX operating system (formerly
known as DEC OSF/1), this first argument was of type `caddr_t`. The
argument specifies the system virtual address (SVA) that corresponds to
the base slot address. The interpretation of this argument depends on the
bus that your driver operates on. Although there is no real bus connected
to the `/dev/none` driver, the example uses arguments associated with a
TURBOchannel bus. Other buses may require a different argument in
this position. See the bus-specific book for descriptions of these
arguments.

2 Declares a pointer to a `controller` structure. Again, the argument
specified in this position of the `noneprobe` interface depends on the bus
the driver operates on.

3 Declares an `ihandler_t` data structure called `handler` to contain
information associated with the `/dev/none` device driver interrupt
handling. Section 7.5.1 describes the `ihandler_t` structure. The
`noneprobe` interface initializes two members of this data structure.

4 Declares a `handler_intr_info` data structure called `info`. The
`handler_intr_info` structure contains interrupt handler information
for device controllers connected to a bus. In previous versions of the
Digital UNIX operating system (formerly known as DEC OSF/1), the
`/dev/none` driver declares a `tc_intr_info` structure, which is
specific to the TURBOchannel bus. The `handler_intr_info`
structure is a generic structure that contains interrupt handler information
for buses connected to a device controller. Use of the

`handler_intr_info` structure makes the driver more portable across different bus architectures.

The /dev/none device driver uses this interrupt handler structure to dynamically register the device interrupt handlers for the static and loadable version of the driver. Section 7.5.2 describes the `handler_intr_info` structure.

⑤ Declares a *unit* variable and initializes it to the controller number. This controller number identifies the specific none controller that is being probed.

The controller number is contained in the `ctlr_num` member of the `controller` structure associated with this none device. Section 7.3.2.3 describes the `ctlr_num` member.

⑥ Declares a variable called *reg* and initializes it to the I/O handle passed to the driver's `probe` interface by the bus configuration code. In this case, the I/O handle describes the system virtual address (SVA) for the none device.

⑦ Increments the *num_none* variable to indicate that noneprobe performed a probe operation on at least one controller.

⑧ Returns the value zero (0) to the bus configuration code to indicate that noneprobe did not complete the probe operation.

⑨ Registers the interrupt handlers by setting up the interrupt handler structure. This line specifies the bus that this controller is attached to. The `bus_hd` member of the `controller` structure contains a pointer to the `bus` structure that this controller is connected to. After the initialization, the `ih_bus` member of the `ihandler_t` structure contains the pointer to the `bus` structure associated with the /dev/none device driver.

⑩ Sets the `configuration_st` member of the `info` data structure to the pointer to the `controller` structure associated with this none device. This `controller` structure is the one for which an associated interrupt will be written.

This line also performs a type-casting operation that converts `ctlr` (which is of type pointer to a `controller` structure) to be of type `caddr_t`, the type of the `configuration_st` member.

⑪ Sets the `config_type` member of the `info` data structure to the constant `CONTROLLER_CONFIG_TYPE`, which identifies the /dev/none driver type as a controller.

⑫ Sets the `intr` member of the `info` data structure to noneintr, the /dev/none device driver's interrupt service interface.

⑬ Sets the `param` member of the `info` data structure to the controller number for the `controller` structure associated with this none device.

This line also performs a type-casting operation that converts *unit* (which is of type `int`) to be of type `caddr_t`, the type of the `param` member.

|14| Sets the `ih_bus_info` member of the `handler` data structure to the address of the bus-specific information structure, `info`.

This line also performs a type-casting operation that converts `info` (which is of type `ihandler_t`) to be of type `char *`, the type of the `ih_bus_info` member.

|15| Calls the `handler_add` interface and saves its return value for use later by the `handler_del` interface.

The `handler_add` interface takes one argument: a pointer to an `ihandler_t` data structure, which in the example is the initialized `handler` structure.

This interface returns an opaque `ihandler_id_t` key, which is a unique number used to identify the interrupt service interfaces to be acted on by subsequent calls to `handler_del`, `handler_disable`, and `handler_enable`. Note that this key is stored in the *none_id_t* array, which is discussed in Section 4.1.4. Section 4.1.6.3 shows how to call `handler_del` and `handler_disable`.

|16| If the return value from `handler_add` equals NULL, returns a failure status to indicate that there are no interrupt service interfaces for the `/dev/none` driver.

|17| If the `handler_enable` interface returns a nonzero value, returns the value zero (0) to indicate that it could not enable a previously registered interrupt service interface.

The `handler_enable` interface takes one argument: a pointer to the interrupt service interface's entry in the interrupt table. In this example, this ID is contained in the *none_id_t* array.

If the call to `handler_enable` failed, removes the previously registered interrupt handler by calling `handler_del` prior to returning an error status.

|18| Increments the *num_none* variable to indicate that `noneprobe` performed a probe operation on at least one controller.

|19| Returns the value zero (0) to the bus configuration code to indicate that `noneprobe` did not complete the probe operation.

|20| Because the loadable version of the driver cannot use the BADADDR interface, the `noneprobe` interface uses an *if* statement that tests the *none_is_dynamic* variable. The *none_is_dynamic* variable contains a value to control any differences in tasks performed by the

static or loadable version of the /dev/none device driver. This approach means that any differences are made at run time and not at compile time. The *none_is_dynamic* variable is initialized and set by the none_configure interface, discussed in Section 4.1.7.2.

21 The next sequence of code calls the BADADDR interface to determine if the device is present.

The BADADDR interface takes three arguments. However, only two are needed in this call.

— The first argument specifies the address of the device whose existence you want to check.

— The second argument specifies the length of the data to be checked.

In this call to BADADDR, the I/O handle plus the NONE_CSR device register offset maps to the 64-bit control/status register for this none device. The length is the value returned by the sizeof operator, in this case the number of bytes needed to contain a value of type long.

Because the first argument to BADADDR is of type caddr_t, this line also performs a type-casting operation that converts the type of the *reg* variable (which is of type io_handle_t) to type caddr_t.

If a device is present, BADADDR returns the value zero (0).

For some buses (for example, PCI and VMEbus), you must do the following before calling BADADDR:

— Call the iohandle_to_phys interface to convert the I/O handle to a valid system physical address.

— Call the PHYS_TO_KSEG interface to convert the valid system physical address to a kernel-unmapped virtual address.

— Call the BADADDR interface, passing this kernel-unmapped virtual address as the first argument.

22 Calls the write_io_port interface to write the bit represented by the constant DN_RESET to the none device's control/status register. This bit instructs the device to reset itself in preparation for data transfer operations.

The write_io_port interface takes four arguments:

— The first argument specifies an I/O handle that you can use to reference a device register or memory located in bus address space (either I/O space or memory space). This I/O handle references a device register in the bus address space where the write operation occurs. In this call, the /dev/none driver specifies the device's I/O address space by adding the I/O handle (stored in the *reg* variable) to the device register offset (represented by the NONE_CSR bit).

- The second argument specifies the width (in bytes) of the data to be
  written. Valid values are 1, 2, 3, 4, and 8. Not all CPU platforms or
  bus adapters support all of these values. In this call, the /dev/none
  driver passes the value 8.

- The third argument specifies flags to indicate special processing
  requests. Because this argument is not currently used, the
  /dev/none driver passes the value zero (0).

- The fourth argument specifies the data to be written to the specified
  device register in bus address space. In this call, the /dev/none
  driver passes the bit represented by the constant DN_RESET.

[23] Calls the mb interface to perform a memory barrier on Alpha CPUs. On
MIPS CPUs, the wbflush interface is called to ensure that a write to
I/O space has completed. A call to mb is not equivalent to a call to
wbflush. However, it is generally recommended that drivers that
operate on other CPU architectures requiring a cache flush call the mb
interface. See Section 2.6.5.10 for a discussion of the mb and wbflush
interfaces.

[24] If the result of the bitwise AND operation produces a nonzero value (that
is, the error bit is set), then noneprobe returns the value zero (0) to the
configuration code to indicate that the device is broken. To determine if
the error bit is set, the /dev/none driver reads the device register by
calling the read_io_port interface.

The read_io_port interface takes three arguments:

- The first argument specifies an I/O handle that you can use to
  reference a device register or memory located in bus address space
  (either I/O space or memory space). This I/O handle references a
  device register in the bus address space where the read operation
  originates. In this call, the /dev/none driver specifies the device's
  I/O address space by adding the I/O handle (stored in the reg
  variable) to the device register offset (represented by the NONE_CSR
  bit).

- The second argument specifies the width (in bytes) of the data to be
  read. Valid values are 1, 2, 3, 4, and 8. Not all CPU platforms or
  bus adapters support all of these values. In this call, the /dev/none
  driver passes the value 8.

- The third argument specifies flags to indicate special processing
  requests. Currently, no flags are used. Because this argument is not
  currently used, the /dev/none driver passes the value zero (0).

[25] If the result of the bitwise AND operation produces a zero value (that is,
the error bit is not set), then noneprobe initializes the device's
CSR/LED register to the value zero (0) by calling the write_io_port
interface. The /dev/none driver passes the same arguments to

write_io_port as in the previous call except for the fourth argument. In this call, write_io_port passes the value zero (0) to the fourth argument.

26 The mb interface is called a second time to perform a memory barrier.

27 The noneprobe interface returns to the autoconfiguration code a nonzero value, which indicates that the device is present and that the probe operation is successful.

4.1.6.2 Implementing the nonecattach Interface

The `nonecattach` interface has no code associated with it and is included as a stub for future expansion. It would be applicable to the loadable or static version of the `/dev/none` device driver.

```
nonecattach(ctlr)
struct controller *ctlr; 1
{
      /* Attach interface goes here. */
    .
    .
    .
    return;
}
```

1 The `none` device does not need an `attach` interface. However, this line shows that your `cattach` interface would declare a pointer to a `controller` structure. Your device driver could then send any information contained in this structure to the controller. Section 7.3.2 describes the `controller` structure.

4.1.6.3 Implementing the none_ctlr_unattach Interface

The `none_ctlr_unattach` interface is a loadable driver-specific interface called indirectly from the bus code when a system manager specifies that the loadable driver is to be unloaded. In other words, this interface would never be called if the `/dev/none` device driver were configured as a static driver because static drivers cannot be unconfigured. This interface's main tasks are to deregister the interrupt handlers associated with the `/dev/none` device driver and to remove the specified `controller` structure from the list of controllers the `/dev/none` driver handles.

The following code implements the `none_ctlr_unattach` interface:

```
int none_ctlr_unattach(bus, ctlr)
    struct bus *bus;        1
    struct controller *ctlr; 2
{
        register int unit = ctlr->ctlr_num; 3

        if ((unit > num_none) || (unit < 0)) { 4
                return(1);
        }

        if (none_is_dynamic == 0) { 5
                return(1);
        }

        if (handler_disable(none_id_t[unit]) != 0) { 6
                return(1);
        }

        if (handler_del(none_id_t[unit]) != 0) { 7
                return(1);
        }
        return(0); 8
}
```

1. Declares a pointer to a `bus` structure and calls it `bus`. The `bus` structure represents an instance of a bus entity. A bus is a real or imagined entity to which other buses or controllers are logically attached. All systems have at least one bus, the system bus, even though the bus may not actually exist physically. The term *controller* here refers both to devices that control slave devices (for example, disk or tape controllers) and to devices that stand alone (for example, terminal or network controllers). Section 7.3.1 describes the `bus` structure.

2. Declares a pointer to a `controller` structure and calls it `ctlr`. This `controller` structure is the one you want to remove from the list of controllers handled by the `/dev/none` device driver. Section 7.3.2 describes the `controller` structure.

③ Declares a *unit* variable and initializes it to the controller number. This controller number identifies the specific none controller whose associated `controller` structure is to be removed from the list of controllers handled by the `/dev/none` driver. Section 7.3.2.3 describes the `ctlr_num` member.

The controller number is contained in the `ctlr_num` member of the `controller` structure associated with this none device.

④ If the controller number is greater than the number of controllers found by the `noneprobe` interface or the number of controllers is less than zero (0), returns the value 1 to the bus code to indicate an error.

This sequence of code validates the controller number. The *num_none* variable contains the number of instances of the none controller found by the `noneprobe` interface. Section 4.1.6.1 describes the implementation of `noneprobe`.

⑤ If *none_is_dynamic* is equal to the value zero (0), returns the value 1 to the bus code to indicate an error.

This sequence of code validates whether the `/dev/none` driver is a loadable driver. The *none_is_dynamic* variable contains a value to control any differences in tasks performed by the static or loadable version of the `/dev/none` device driver. This approach means that any differences are made at run time and not at compile time. The *none_is_dynamic* variable is initialized and set by the `none_configure` interface, discussed in Section 4.1.7.2.

⑥ If the return value from the call to the `handler_disable` interface is not equal to the value zero (0), returns the value 1 to the bus code to indicate an error. Otherwise, the `handler_disable` interface makes the `/dev/none` device driver's previously registered interrupt service interfaces unavailable to the system. Section 9.6.2 provides additional information on `handler_disable`.

This sequence of code is executed if *none_is_dynamic* is not equal to the value zero (0), indicating that the `/dev/none` device driver is a loadable driver.

The `handler_disable` interface takes one argument: a pointer to the interrupt service's entry in the interrupt table. In this call, the ID is accessed through the *none_id_t* array. Section 4.1.6.1 shows that `handler_add` fills in this array. Note that the *unit* variable is used as an index to identify the interrupt service interface associated with a specific `controller` structure. Section 4.1.6.1 shows that `noneprobe` initializes this variable to the controller number.

⑦ If the return value from the call to the `handler_del` interface is not equal to the value zero (0), returns the value 1 to the bus code to indicate an error. Otherwise, the `handler_del` interface deregisters the

/dev/none device driver's interrupt service interface from the bus-specific interrupt dispatching algorithm. Section 9.6.2 provides additional information on handler_del.

This sequence of code is executed if *none_is_dynamic* is not equal to the value zero (0), indicating that the /dev/none device driver is a loadable driver.

The handler_del interface takes the same argument as the handler_disable interface: a pointer to the interrupt service's entry in the interrupt table.

⑧ Returns the value zero (0) to the bus code upon successful completion of the tasks performed by the none_ctlr_unattach interface.

4.1.7 Loadable Device Driver Section

The Loadable Device Driver Section is applicable only to the loadable version of the /dev/none device driver. It implements the none_configure interface. Table 4-3 lists the tasks associated with implementing the Loadable Device Driver Section along with the sections in the book where each task is described.

Table 4-3: Loadable Device Driver Section

Part	Section
Setting Up the none_configure Interface	Section 4.1.7.1
Configuring (Loading) the /dev/none Device Driver	Section 4.1.7.2
Unconfiguring (Unloading) the /dev/none Device Driver	Section 4.1.7.3
Querying the /dev/none Device Driver	Section 4.1.7.4

4.1.7.1 Setting Up the none_configure Interface

The following code shows how to set up the `none_configure` interface:

```
none_configure(op,indata,indatalen,outdata,outdatalen)
    cfg_op_t op;                1
    cfg_attr_t *indata;         2
    size_t indatalen;           3
    cfg_attr_t *outdata;        4
    size_t outdatalen;          5
{
        dev_t   cdevno;  6
        int     retval;  7
        int     i;       8

#define MAX_DEVICE_CFG_ENTRIES 18  9

#define NONE_DEBUG
#ifdef NONE_DEBUG
        cfg_attr_t cfg_buf[MAX_DEVICE_CFG_ENTRIES];  10
#endif /* NONE_DEBUG */
```

1 Declares an argument called *op* to contain a constant that describes the configuration operation to be performed on the loadable driver. This argument is used in a `switch` statement and evaluates to one of the following valid constants: `CFG_OP_CONFIGURE`, `CFG_OP_UNCONFIGURE`, or `CFG_OP_QUERY`.

2 Declares a pointer to a `cfg_attr_t` data structure called `indata` that consists of inputs to the `none_configure` interface. The `cfgmgr` daemon fills in this data structure. The `cfg_attr_t` data structure is used to represent a variety of information, including the `/dev/none` driver's major number requirements. Section 7.4.2 describes the `cfg_attr_t` structure.

3 Declares an argument called *indatalen* to store the size of this input data structure. This argument represents the number of `cfg_attr_t` structures included in *indata*.

4 This formal parameter is not currently used.

5 This formal parameter is not currently used.

6 Declares a variable called *cdevno* to temporarily store the major device number for the `none` device.

7 Declares a variable called *retval* to store the return value from the `cdevsw_del` interface.

8 Declares a variable called *i* used in the `for` loop when `none_configure` unconfigures the loadable driver.

⑨ Defines a constant that represents the number of configuration lines in the `stanza.loadable` file fragment.

⑩ Declares an array of `cfg_attr_t` data structures and calls it `cfg_buf`. The number of `cfg_attr_t` structures in the array matches the number of configuration lines specified in the `stanza.loadable` file fragment for this loadable device driver subsystem. The `cfgmgr` daemon passes the `cfg_attr_t` array to the input data argument of the driver's `configure` interface. This array contains the strings that are stored in the `sysconfigtab` database for this loadable device driver subsystem.

Thus, for the `/dev/none` device driver, the `cfgmgr` daemon passes the `cfg_attr_t` array to the *indata* argument and the number of `cfg_attr_t` structures in the array to the argument of the `none_configure` interface.

4.1.7.2 Configuring (Loading) the /dev/none Device Driver

The following code shows how to implement the loadable driver's configure or loading operation. This section of code executes when the system manager requests that the /dev/none device driver be dynamically configured.

```
switch (op) {

    case CFG_OP_CONFIGURE: 1

#ifdef NONE_DEBUG 2

            bcopy(indata, cfg_buf[0].name,
                indatalen*(sizeof(cfg_attr_t)));
        printf(" The none_configure routine was called.  op = %x\n",op);
        for( i=0; i < indatalen; i++){
            printf("%s: ",cfg_buf[i].name);
            switch(cfg_buf[i].type){
                case CFG_ATTR_STRTYPE:
                    printf("%s\n",cfg_buf[i].attr.str.val);
                    break;

                default:
                  switch(cfg_buf[i].status){
                    case CFG_ATTR_EEXISTS:
                        printf("**Attribute does not exist\n");
                        break;

                    case CFG_ATTR_EOP:
                        printf("**Attribute does not support operation\n");
                        break;

                    case CFG_ATTR_ESUBSYS:
                        printf("**Subsystem Failure\n");
                        break;

                    case CFG_ATTR_ESMALL:
                        printf("**Attribute size/value too small\n");
                        break;

                    case CFG_ATTR_ELARGE:
                        printf("**Attribute size/value too large\n");
                        break;

                    case CFG_ATTR_ETYPE:
                        printf("**Attribute invalid type\n");
                        break;

                    case CFG_ATTR_EINDEX:
                        printf("**Attribute invalid index\n");
                        break;

                    case CFG_ATTR_EMEM:
                        printf("**Attribute memory allocation error\n");
                        break;

                    default:
                        printf("**Unknown attribute: ");
                        printf("%x\n", cfg_buf[i].status);
```

```
                              break;
                          }
                    break;
                 }
            }
#endif

            if(strcmp(modtype,"Dynamic")==0) {
                    none_is_dynamic = 1;
                } 3

            if (none_is_dynamic) { 4
                    if(strcmp(mcfgname,"")==0) {
                        printf("none_configure, null config name.\n");
                        return(EINVAL);
                        }
            if (ldbl_stanza_resolver(mcfgname, DN_BUSNAME,
                &nonedriver,
                (caddr_t *)none_option_snippet) != 0) {
                return(EINVAL);
                } 5
            if (ldbl_ctlr_configure(DN_BUSNAME,
                        LDBL_WILDNUM, mcfgname,
                        &nonedriver, 0)) {
                        return(EINVAL);
            } 6
            num_none++; 7
            if (num_none == 0) { 8
                 return(EINVAL);
            }
        }

        if(strcmp(devcmajor,"")!=0) { 9
            if((strcmp(devcmajor,"-1")==0) ||
                (strcmp(devcmajor,"?")==0) ||
                (strcmp(devcmajor,"any")==0) ||
                (strcmp(devcmajor,"ANY")==0)){
                cdevno = NODEV;
                }
            else { 10
                cdevno = atoi(devcmajor);
                cdevno = makedev(cdevno,0);
                }
        }
    else
            return EINVAL; 11
        cdevno = cdevsw_add(cdevno,&none_cdevsw_entry);
        if (cdevno == NODEV) {
                        return(ENODEV);
    } 12

    none_devno = cdevno; 13

    cmajnum = major(none_devno); 14

    begunit = 0; 15

    numunit = num_none; 16
```

```
bmajnum = NODEV; [17]

none_config = TRUE; [18]
break;
```

[1] Specifies the CFG_OP_CONFIGURE constant to indicate that this section of code implements the configure loadable driver operation. The file /usr/sys/include/sys/sysconfig.h contains the definition of this constant.

[2] The /dev/none device driver requests that the cfgmgr daemon initialize the none_attributes structure with all of the attributes specified for the none entry in the /etc/sysconfigtab database.

Attributes passed through the none_attributes structure are not known to be valid until the device driver can check their status in the indata argument. A status other than CFG_FRAME_SUCCESS is an error condition. The code that follows #ifdef NONE_DEBUG does the following:

– Debugs cfgmgr loading problems with the none_attributes structure

– Displays the contents and status of the attributes in the /etc/sysconfigtab database for the /dev/none driver on the console terminal

– Reports the cfgmgr daemon's status that indicates a failure to load any of the attribute fields into the none_attributes structure

[3] If the string associated with the modtype variable equals the string Dynamic, then this is the loadable version of the driver. The strcmp interface compares the two null-terminated strings. To indicate this state, the code sets the none_is_dynamic variable to the value 1.

[4] If none_is_dynamic evaluates to true, executes the operation code passed to the op argument. In this case, the operation code is CFG_OP_CONFIGURE.

[5] If the ldbl_stanza_resolver interface returns a value not equal to zero, it did not find matches in the tc_slot table. This condition indicates that ldbl_stanza_resolver failed to find the kernel structure required to configure the option snippet structure, none_option_snippet. The interface returns the constant EINVAL to indicate an invalid argument. Otherwise, ldbl_stanza_resolver allows the device driver to merge the system configuration data structure created by the device method into the hardware topology tree created at static configuration time.

The ldbl_stanza_resolver interface takes four arguments:

- The name of the driver specified by the driver writer in the `stanza.loadable` file fragment in the `Module_Config_Name` field

  In this call, the driver name is obtained from the `name` member of the `none_attributes` structure. Section 4.1.4 shows the initialization of the `none_attributes` structure.

- The name of the parent `bus` structure associated with this controller

  In this call, the constant `DN_BUSNAME` represents the characters "tc", indicating that the parent `bus` structure is a TURBOchannel bus. Section 4.1.4 shows the definition of the bus name. To write a device driver so that it can operate on multiple bus architectures, you must call `ldbl_stanza_resolver` for each bus architecture the driver operates on. In these calls, you pass a constant that defines characters that represent the bus structure associated with the bus architecture.

- A pointer to the `driver` structure for the controlling device driver

  In this call, the address of the `nonedriver` structure is passed.

- A bus-specific parameter

  The bus-specific parameter for a TURBOchannel bus is usually a `tc_option` snippet structure. In this call, the address of the `none_option_snippet` structure is passed. This structure contains the appropriate entry for the loadable version of the `/dev/none` device driver. Section 4.1.4 shows the declaration of this structure.

  To write a device driver so that it can operate on multiple bus architectures, you must call `ldbl_stanza_resolver` for each bus architecture the driver operates on. In these calls, you pass the option snippet structure associated with the bus.

  Note that a type-casting operation converts `none_option_snippet` (which is of type `struct tc_option`) to be of type `caddr_t *`, the type of the bus-specific argument. However, `ldbl_stanza_resolver` does not do anything with this argument but pass it to the bus configuration code that performs the correct type-casting operation to handle `none_option_snippet`. Section 9.7.3 provides additional information on the `ldbl_stanza_resolver` interface.

6️⃣ Calls the `ldbl_ctlr_configure` interface to cause the driver's `noneprobe` interface to be called once for each instance of the controller found on the system. If `ldbl_ctlr_configure` fails, no instances of the controller exist on the bus and it returns the `EINVAL` constant.

The `ldbl_ctlr_configure` interface takes five arguments:

- The bus name

  In this call, the bus name "tc" is represented by the `DN_BUSNAME` constant. Section 4.1.4 shows the definition of the bus name.

- The bus number

  In this call, the bus number is represented by the wildcard constant `LDBL_WILDNUM`. This wildcard allows for the configuration of all instances of the `none` device present on the system. This constant is defined in the file `/usr/sys/include/io/common/devdriver.h`.

- The name of the controlling device driver

  In this call, this name is obtained from the `name` member of the `none_option_snippet` data structure.

- A pointer to the `driver` structure for the controlling device driver, which in this call is `nonedriver`

- Miscellaneous flags from `/usr/sys/include/io/common/devdriver_loadable.h`

  In this call, the value zero (0) is passed to indicate that no flags are specified.

⑦ Increments the *num_none* variable to indicate that `noneprobe` performed a probe operation on at least one controller.

⑧ If the `noneprobe` interface does not find any controllers, sets the variable that keeps count of the number of controllers found to the value zero (0) and returns the constant `EINVAL` to indicate no controllers were found.

⑨ Checks for the existence of the device major number for the `none` device. If the device major number for the `none` device exists, then a call to `makedev` makes the device number.

⑩ Calls the `makedev` interface, which makes a device number of type `dev_t` based on the specified major and minor numbers. Upon successful completion, `makedev` returns the major number for this `none` device in the *cdevno* variable. Note that the driver configuration is performed before obtaining the device major number to prevent user-level programs from gaining access to the `/dev/none` driver's entry points in the `cdevsw`.

The `makedev` interface takes two arguments:

- The first argument is the major number for the device, which in this call is obtained from the `name` member of the `none_attributes` data structure associated with this device. Section 4.1.4 shows the declaration of this structure.

- The second argument is the minor number for the device, which in this call is also obtained from the `name` member of the `none_attributes` structure, indicating that the major and minor numbers are identical. This interface does not make use of the minor number.

Section 15.2 provides a reference (man) page-style description of `makedev`.

11 Returns an error constant if the device major number does not exist.

12 Calls the `cdevsw_add` interface to add the driver entry points for the `/dev/none` driver to the `cdevsw` table.

The `cdevsw_add` interface takes two arguments:

- The first argument specifies the device switch table entry (slot) to use. This entry represents the requested major number. In this call, the slot to use was obtained in a previous call to `makedev`.
- The second argument is the character device switch structure that contains the character device driver's entry points.

In this call, this structure is called `none_cdevsw_entry`. Upon successful completion, `cdevsw_add` returns the device number associated with the device switch table. Section 9.7.2 provides additional information on `cdevsw_add`.

If the device number associated with the device switch table is equal to the constant NODEV, returns the error constant ENODEV. The NODEV constant indicates that the requested major number is currently in use or that the `cdevsw` table is currently full. The NODEV constant is defined in `/usr/sys/include/sys/param.h`, and `/usr/sys/include/sys/errno.h` contains the ENODEV constant.

13 Stores the `cdevsw` table entry slot for this `none` device in the `none_devno` variable. Section 4.1.7.3 shows that `cdevsw_del` uses this slot value when the device is unconfigured.

14 Sets `cmajnum` to the major number for this device by calling the `major` interface. In this call, the number of the device is contained in the `none_devno` variable. The device method's post process can query the major number. The system administrator can also query the major number by using the following:

```
sysconfig -q
```

Section 9.10.2 provides additional information on `major`.

15 Sets `begunit` to the first minor device number in the range. In this case, the first minor number is zero (0).

16 Sets *numunit* to the number of instances of the controller that the noneprobe interface found. In this case, this number is contained in the *numunit* variable, which was incremented by noneprobe upon locating each controller on the system.

17 Sets *bmajnum* to the constant NODEV. The none device is a character device and, therefore, has no block device major number.

18 Sets the state flag to indicate that the /dev/none device driver is now configured as a loadable device driver.

4.1.7.3 Unconfiguring (Unloading) the /dev/none Device Driver

The following code shows how to implement the loadable driver's unconfigure or unloading operation. This section of code executes when the system manager requests that the currently loaded /dev/none device driver be unconfigured.

```
case CFG_OP_UNCONFIGURE: 1

    if (none_config != TRUE) {
            return(EINVAL);
    } 2

    for (i = 0; i < num_none; i++) {
            if (none_softc[i].sc_openf != 0) {
                    return(EBUSY);
            } 3
    }

    retval = cdevsw_del(none_devno);
    if (retval) {
            return(ESRCH);
    } 4

    if (none_is_dynamic) { 5

            if (ldbl_ctlr_unconfigure(DN_BUSNAME,
                    LDBL_WILDNUM, &nonedriver,
                    LDBL_WILDNAME, LDBL_WILDNUM) != 0) { 6

                    return(ESRCH);
            }
    }
    none_config = FALSE; 7
    break;
```

1 Specifies the CFG_OP_UNCONFIGURE constant to indicate that this section of code implements the unconfigure operation of the loadable driver. The file /usr/sys/include/sys/sysconfig.h contains the definition of this constant.

2 If the /dev/none device driver is not currently configured or loaded, it fails the unconfiguration by returning the EINVAL constant. This error code is defined in /usr/sys/include/sys/errno.h.

3 Prevents the system manager from unloading the device driver if it is currently active. To determine if the driver is active, the code checks the sc_openf member of this none device's none_softc structure to determine if the device is opened. If so, the code returns the EBUSY constant. This error code is defined in /usr/sys/include/sys/errno.h.

4. Calls the `cdevsw_del` interface to delete the `/dev/none` driver's entry points from the `cdevsw` table.

The `cdevsw_del` interface takes one argument: the device switch table entry (slot) to use. In this call, the slot is contained in the *none_devno* variable, which was set when the driver was configured. If `cdevsw_del` fails, returns ESRCH to indicate that the driver is not currently present in the `cdevsw` table.

5. If *none_is_dynamic* evaluates to TRUE, calls the `ldbl_ctlr_unconfigure` interface to unconfigure the specified controller. Section 4.1.7.2 shows that the *none_is_dynamic* variable was previously set to TRUE (the value 1) when the driver was configured.

6. If the `ldbl_ctlr_unconfigure` interface returns a nonzero value, returns the error constant ESRCH to indicate that it did not successfully unconfigure the specified controller. Otherwise, it unconfigures the controller. A call to this interface results in a call to the driver's `none_ctlr_unattach` interface for each instance of the controller. Section 4.1.6.3 describes `none_ctlr_unattach`.

The `ldbl_ctlr_unconfigure` interface takes five arguments:

– The bus name

  In this call, the bus name is represented by the constant DN_BUSNAME.

– The bus number

  In this call, the wildcard constant indicates that the interface `ldbl_ctlr_unconfigure` deregisters all instances of the controllers connected to the TURBOchannel bus.

– A pointer to the `driver` structure for the controlling device driver, which in this call is `nonedriver`

– The controller name and controller number

  In this call, the wildcard constants indicate that `ldbl_ctlr_unconfigure` scans all `controller` structures. Section 9.7.4 provides additional information on `ldbl_ctlr_unconfigure`.

7. Sets the *none_config* variable to the value FALSE to indicate that the `/dev/none` device driver is now unconfigured.

4.1.7.4 Querying the /dev/none Device Driver

The following code shows how to implement the loadable driver's query operation. This section of code executes when the system manager requests a query of information associated with the loadable version of the driver. The code is also a program request to the loadable subsystem support interfaces. The driver method uses this code to make the device special files after the none_configure interface executes.

Note that the CFG_OP_QUERY case statement does not perform any explicit operations. The reason for this is the configuration management framework returns the values associated with a query request.

```
            case CFG_OP_QUERY:  1
            break;

            default:
                return(EINVAL);  2
        }

    return(0);  3
}
```

1 Specifies the CFG_OP_QUERY operation to indicate that this section of code implements the query operation of the loadable driver. The file /usr/sys/include/sys/sysconfig.h contains the definition of this constant.

2 Defines an unknown operation type and returns the error constant EINVAL to indicate this condition. This section of code is called if the *op* argument is set to anything other than CFG_OP_CONFIGURE, CFG_OP_UNCONFIGURE, or CFG_OP_QUERY.

3 To indicate that the /dev/none driver's none_configure interface has completed the requested operation of CFG_OP_CONFIGURE, CFG_OP_UNCONFIGURE, or CFG_OP_QUERY successfully, returns the value zero (0).

4.1.8 Open and Close Device Section

The Open and Close Device Section is applicable to the loadable or static version of the /dev/none device driver. The decision as to whether it is loadable or static is made at run time by the system manager and not at compile time by the driver writer. Thus, the driver writer can implement one device driver that is loadable or static. Table 4-4 lists the two interfaces implemented as part of the Open and Close Device Section along with the sections in the book where each is described.

Table 4-4: Interfaces Implemented as Part of the Open and Close Device Section

Part	Section
Implementing the noneopen Interface	Section 4.1.8.1
Implementing the noneclose Interface	Section 4.1.8.2

4.1.8.1 Implementing the noneopen Interface

The noneopen interface is called as the result of an c [...]
noneopen interface performs the following tasks: che [...]
open is unique, marks the device as open, and returns tl [...]
the open system call to indicate success.

The following code implements the noneopen interfac[...]

```
noneopen(dev, flag, format)
dev_t dev;   1
int flag;    2
int format;  3
{
      register int unit = minor(dev);               4
      struct controller *ctlr = noneinfo[unit];     5
      struct none_softc *sc = &none_softc[unit];    6

      if(unit >= NNONE)
            return ENODEV;   7

      if (sc->sc_openf == DN_OPEN)
            return (EBUSY);   8

      if ((ctlr !=0) && (ctlr->alive & ALV_ALIVE))
      {
            sc->sc_openf = DN_OPEN;
            return(0);   9
      }
      else return(ENXIO);   10
}
```

1 Declares an argument that specifies the major and minor device numbers
   for a specific none device. The minor device number is used to
   determine the logical unit number for the none device that is to be
   opened.

2 Declares an argument to contain flag bits from the file
   /usr/sys/include/sys/file.h. These flags indicate whether the
   device is being opened for reading, writing, or both.

3 Declares an argument to contain a constant that identifies whether the
   device is a character or a block device. These constants are defined in
   /usr/sys/include/sys/mode.h.

4 Declares a *unit* variable and initializes it to the device minor number.
   Note the use of the minor interface to obtain the device minor number.

   The minor interface takes one argument: the number of the device for
   which an associated device minor number will be obtained. The minor
   number is encoded in the *dev* argument. Section 9.10.3 provides

tional information on `minor`.

Declares a pointer to a `controller` structure and calls it `ctlr`. Initializes `ctlr` to the `controller` structure associated with this `none` device. The minor device number, *unit*, is used as an index into the array of `controller` structures to determine which `controller` structure is associated with this `none` device.

⑥ Declares a pointer to a `none_softc` structure and calls it `sc`. Initializes `sc` to the address of the `none_softc` structure associated with this `none` device. The minor device number, *unit*, is used as an index into the array of `none_softc` structures to determine which `none_softc` structure is associated with this `none` device.

⑦ The `none` device requires no real work to open; therefore, the code could simply ignore the call and return the value zero (0). To demonstrate some of the checking that a real driver might perform, the example provides code that checks to be sure that the device exists.

If the device minor number, *unit*, is greater than or equal to the number of devices configured by the system, returns the error code ENODEV, which indicates there is no such device on the system. This error code is defined in `/usr/sys/include/sys/errno.h`.

⑧ If the `sc_openf` member of the `sc` pointer is equal to DN_OPEN, returns the error code EBUSY, which indicates that the `none` device has already been opened. This error code is defined in `/usr/sys/include/sys/errno.h`. This example test is used to ensure that this unit of the driver can be opened only once at a time. This type of open is referred to as an exclusive access open.

⑨ If the `ctlr` pointer is not equal to 0 and the `alive` member of `ctlr` has the ALV_ALIVE bit set, then the device exists. If this is the case, the `noneopen` interface sets the `sc_openf` member of the `sc` pointer to the open bit DN_OPEN and returns zero (0) to indicate a successful open.

⑩ If the device does not exist, `noneopen` returns the error code ENXIO, which indicates that the device does not exist. This error code is defined in `/usr/sys/include/sys/errno.h`.

4.1.8.2 Implementing the noneclose Interface

The noneclose interface uses the same arguments as noneopen, gets the device minor number in the same way, and initializes the controller and none_softc structures identically. The purpose of noneclose is to turn off the open flag for the specified none device.

The following code implements the noneclose interface:

```
noneclose(dev, flag, format)
dev_t dev;     [1]
int flag;      [2]
int format;    [3]
{
        register int unit = minor(dev);              [4]
        struct controller *ctlr = noneinfo[unit];  [5]
        struct none_softc *sc = &none_softc[unit];  [6]
            register io_handle_t reg =
            (io_handle_t) ctlr->addr;  [7]
        sc->sc_openf = DN_CLOSE;  [8]
            write_io_port(reg + NONE_CSR, 8, 0, 0);  [9]
        mb();  [10]
        return(0);  [11]
}
```

[1] Like the noneopen interface, the noneclose interface declares an argument that specifies the major and minor numbers for a specific none device. The minor device number is used to determine the logical unit number for the none device to be closed.

[2] Like the noneopen interface, the noneclose interface also declares an argument to contain flag bits from the file /usr/sys/include/sys/file.h. Typically, a driver's close interface does not make use of this argument.

[3] Although the *format* argument is shown here, a driver's close interface does not typically make use of this argument.

[4] Declares a *unit* variable and initializes it to the device minor number. Note the use of the minor interface to obtain the device minor number.

The minor interface takes one argument: the number of the device for which an associated device minor number will be obtained. The minor number is encoded in the *dev* argument. Section 9.10.3 provides additional information on minor.

⑤ Declares a pointer to a `controller` structure and calls it `ctlr`. Initializes `ctlr` to the `controller` structure associated with this `none` device. The minor device number, `unit`, is used as an index into the array of `controller` structures to determine which `controller` structure is associated with this `none` device.

⑥ Declares a pointer to a `none_softc` structure and calls it `sc`. Initializes `sc` to the address of the `none_softc` structure associated with this `none` device. The minor device number, `unit`, is used as an index into the array of `none_softc` structures to determine which `none_softc` structure is associated with this `none` device.

⑦ Section 4.1.6.1 shows that the `/dev/none` device driver stored the I/O handle passed to its `probe` interface in the `reg` variable. The `/dev/none` device driver now initializes `reg` to the system virtual address (SVA) for the `none` device. This address is obtained from the `addr` member of the `controller` structure associated with this `none` device.

Because the data types are different, this line performs a type-casting operation that converts the `addr` member (which is of type `caddr_t`) to be of type `io_handle_t`.

⑧ Turns off the open flag by setting the `sc_openf` member of the `sc` pointer to the close bit `DN_CLOSE`. This action frees up the unit so that subsequent calls to `noneopen` will succeed.

⑨ The `none` device is not a real device and therefore would not initiate interrupts. However, this line shows how to turn off interrupts by writing the value zero (0) to the device's control/status register. To accomplish the write operation, the `/dev/none` device driver calls the `write_io_port` interface.

The `write_io_port` interface takes four arguments:

– The first argument specifies an I/O handle that you can use to reference a device register or memory located in bus address space (either I/O space or memory space). This I/O handle references a device register in the bus address space where the write operation occurs. In this call, the `/dev/none` driver specifies the device's I/O address space by adding the system virtual address (SVA) (stored in the `reg` variable) to the device register offset (represented by the `NONE_CSR` bit).

– The second argument specifies the width (in bytes) of the data to be written. Valid values are 1, 2, 3, 4, and 8. Not all CPU platforms or bus adapters support all of these values. In this call, the `/dev/none` driver passes the value 8.

– The third argument specifies flags to indicate special processing requests. Because this argument is not currently used, the

/dev/none driver passes the value zero (0).

 – The fourth argument specifies the data to be written to the specified
   device register in bus address space. In this call, the /dev/none
   driver passes the value zero (0).

10 Calls the mb interface to perform a memory barrier on Alpha CPUs. On
MIPS CPUs, the wbflush interface is called to ensure that a write to
I/O space has completed. A call to mb is not equivalent to a call to
wbflush. However, it is generally recommended that drivers that
operate on other CPU architectures requiring a cache flush call the mb
interface. See Section 2.6.5.10 for a discussion of the mb and wbflush
interfaces.

11 The noneclose interface returns the value zero (0) to the close
system call to indicate a successful close of the none device.

4.1.9 Read and Write Device Section

The Read and Write Device Section is applicable to the loadable or static
version of the /dev/none device driver. The decision as to whether it is
loadable or static is made at run time by the system manager and not at
compile time by the driver writer. Thus, the driver writer can implement one
device driver that is loadable or static. Table 4-5 lists the two interfaces
implemented as part of the Read and Write Device Section along with the
sections in the book where each is described.

**Table 4-5: Interfaces Implemented as Part of the Read and Write
Device Section**

Part	Section
Implementing the noneread Interface	Section 4.1.9.1
Implementing the nonewrite Interface	Section 4.1.9.2

4.1.9.1 Implementing the noneread Interface

The noneread interface simply returns success to the read system call because the /dev/none driver always returns EOF (end-of-file) on read operations.

The following code implements the noneread interface:

```
noneread(dev, uio, flag)
dev_t dev;        1
struct uio *uio;  2
int flag;
{
     return (0);  3
}
```

1 Declares an argument that specifies the major and minor device numbers for a specific none device. The minor device number is used to determine the logical unit number for the none device on which the read operation is performed.

2 Declares a pointer to a uio structure. This structure contains the information for transferring data to and from the address space of the user's process. You typically pass this pointer unmodified to the uiomove or physio kernel interface.

3 Returns success to the read system call. Because the /dev/none driver always returns EOF on read operations, the noneread interface simply returns zero (0). More complicated drivers would need to copy data from the device into the address space pointed to by the uio structure.

4.1.9.2   Implementing the nonewrite Interface

The `nonewrite` interface copies data from the address space pointed to by the `uio` structure to the device. Upon a successful write, `nonewrite` returns the value zero (0) to the write system call.

The following code implements the `nonewrite` interface:

```
nonewrite(dev, uio, flag)
dev_t dev;          1
struct uio *uio;    2
int flag;
{
        int unit = minor(dev);                    3
        struct controller *ctlr = noneinfo[unit]; 4
        struct none_softc *sc = &none_softc[unit]; 5
        unsigned int count;                       6
        struct iovec *iov;                        7

        while(uio->uio_resid > 0) {         8
            iov = uio->uio_iov;       9
            if(iov->iov_len == 0) { 10
                    uio->uio_iov++;
                    uio->uio_iovcnt--;
                    if(uio->uio_iovcnt < 0) 11
                            panic("none write");
                    continue;
            }

        count = iov->iov_len; 12

        iov->iov_base += count; 13
        iov->iov_len -= count; 14
        uio->uio_offset += count; 15
        uio->uio_resid -= count; 16

        sc->sc_count +=count; 17
        }
        return (0);
}
```

1 Declares an argument that specifies the major and minor device numbers for a specific `none` device. The minor device number is used to determine the logical unit number for the device on which the write operation is performed.

2 Declares a pointer to a `uio` structure. This structure contains the information for transferring data to and from the address space of the user's process. You typically pass this pointer unmodified to the `uiomove` or `physio` kernel interface.

③ Declares a *unit* variable and initializes it to the device minor number. Note the use of the `minor` interface to obtain the device minor number.

The `minor` interface takes one argument: the number of the device for which an associated device minor number will be obtained. The minor number is encoded in the *dev* argument.

④ Declares a pointer to a `controller` structure and calls it `ctlr`. Initializes `ctlr` to the `controller` structure associated with this `none` device. The minor device number, *unit*, is used as an index into the array of `controller` structures to determine which `controller` structure is associated with this `none` device.

⑤ Declares a pointer to a `none_softc` structure and calls it `sc`. Initializes `sc` to the address of the `none_softc` structure associated with this `none` device. The minor device number, *unit*, is used as an index into the array of `none_softc` structures to determine which `none_softc` structure is associated with this `none` device.

⑥ Declares a variable that stores the size of the write request.

⑦ Declares a pointer to an `iovec` structure and calls it `iov`.

⑧ Checks the size of the remaining logical buffer (represented by the `uio_resid` member) to determine if `nonewrite` must copy data from the address space pointed to by the `uio` structure to the device. The loop continues until all the bytes of data are copied to the device.

⑨ Sets the `iov` pointer to the address of the current logical buffer segment (represented by the `uio_iov` member).

⑩ If the remaining size of the current segment (represented by the `iov_len` member) is equal to zero (0), increments the address of the current logical buffer segment (represented by the `uio_iov` member) and decrements the number of remaining logical buffer segments (represented by the `uio_iovcnt` member).

⑪ If the number of remaining logical buffer segments is less than zero (0), there is no data to write; therefore, calls the `panic` interface to cause a system crash and displays the message ''none write'' on the console terminal. This code represents an error condition that should never occur.

⑫ Sets the *count* variable to the number of bytes contained in the current segment (represented by the `iov_len` member). This value is the size of the write request.

⑬ Adds the number of bytes in the write request to the address of the current byte within the logical buffer segment (represented by the `iov_base` member).

⑭ Subtracts the number of bytes in the write request from the current segment (represented by the `iov_len` member).

15 Adds the number of bytes in the write request to the current offset into the full logical buffer (represented by the `uio_offset` member).

16 Subtracts the number of bytes in the write request from the size of the remaining logical buffer (represented by the `uio_resid` member).

17 Adds the number of bytes in the write request to the `sc_count` member of the `sc` pointer. When there are no more bytes, `nonewrite` returns the value zero (0) to indicate a successful write. Otherwise, it returns an appropriate error code that identifies the problem. You obtain the error codes from the file `/usr/sys/include/sys/errno.h`. Because there is no physical device associated with `/dev/none`, `nonewrite` does not actually copy data anywhere.

4.1.10 Interrupt Section

The interrupt entry point for the /dev/none device driver is a stub because there is no physical device to generate an interrupt. However, most devices can generate interrupts. For example, a terminal might generate an interrupt when a character is keyed into it. There is an interrupt entry point for those drivers that are written for devices that generate interrupts.

There are a number of important issues relating to interrupts, which are discussed in Section 2.1.3.4. In addition, Section 2.4 discusses the methods for registering device interrupt handlers. Some devices generate more than one type of interrupt. Thus, drivers controlling these devices can contain more than one interrupt section.

For the /dev/none driver, these issues are not relevant because there are no interrupts, but they will be important for most drivers.

The following shows the interrupt section for the /dev/none device driver:

```
noneintr(ctlr_num)
int ctlr_num; 1

{
       struct controller *ctlr = noneinfo[ctlr_num]; 2
       struct none_softc *sc = &none_softc[ctlr_num];
/* Code to perform the interrupt processing */
       .
       .
       .
}
```

1 Declares an argument to contain the controller number passed by the operating system interrupt code. This logical unit number would have been previously specified in the system configuration file or when the ISI was dynamically registered.

2 This line and the following line show some of the typical data structures you would define for an interrupt interface.

4.1.11 The ioctl Section

The `ioctl` Section is applicable to the loadable or static version of the `/dev/none` device driver. The decision as to whether it is loadable or static is made at run time by the system manager and not at compile time by the driver writer. Thus, the driver writer can implement one device driver that is loadable or static. The `ioctl` Section implements the `noneioctl` interface, which obtains and clears the count of bytes that was previously written by `nonewrite`. When a user program issues the command to obtain the count, the `/dev/none` driver returns the count through the data pointer passed to the `noneioctl` interface. When a user program asks to clear the count, the `/dev/none` driver does so.

The following code implements the `noneioctl` interface:

```
noneioctl(dev, cmd, data, flag)
dev_t dev;               1
unsigned int cmd;        2
caddr_t data;            3
int flag;                4
{
    int unit = minor(dev); 5

    int *res; 6

    struct none_softc *sc = &none_softc[unit]; 7

    res = (int *) data; 8

    if(cmd == DN_GETCOUNT)
        *res = sc->sc_count; 9

    if(cmd == DN_CLRCOUNT)
        sc->sc_count = 0;   10

    return (0); 11
}
```

1. Declares an argument that specifies the major and minor device numbers for a specific `none` device. The minor device number is used to determine the logical unit number for the `none` device on which the `ioctl` operation is to be performed.

2. Declares an argument to contain the `ioctl` command as specified in `/usr/sys/include/sys/ioctl.h` or in another include file that you define.

3. Declares a pointer to the `ioctl` command-specified data that is to be passed to the device driver or filled in by the device driver. This argument is a kernel address. The size of the data cannot exceed the size of a page (currently 8 kilobytes (KB) on Alpha systems). At least 128 bytes are guaranteed. Any size between 128 bytes and the page size may

fail if memory cannot be allocated. The particular `ioctl` command implicitly determines the action to be taken. The `ioctl` system call performs all the necessary copy operations to move data to and from user space.

4 Declares an argument that holds the access mode of the device. The access modes are represented by flag constants defined in `/usr/sys/include/sys/file.h`.

5 Declares a *unit* variable and initializes it to the device minor number. Note the use of the `minor` interface to obtain the device minor number.

The `minor` interface takes one argument: the number of the device for which an associated device minor number will be obtained. The minor number is encoded in the *dev* argument. Section 9.10.3 provides additional information on `minor`.

6 Declares a pointer to a variable that will store the character count. The `nonewrite` interface stores this character count in the `sc_count` member of the `softc` structure associated with this `none` device.

7 Declares a pointer to a `none_softc` structure and calls it `sc`. Initializes `sc` to the address of the `none_softc` structure associated with this `none` device. The minor device number, *unit*, is used as an index into the array of `none_softc` structures to determine which `none_softc` structure is associated with this `none` device.

8 Sets the *res* variable to point to the kernel memory allocated by the `ioctl` system call. The `ioctl` system call copies the data to and from user address space.

Because the data types are different, this line performs a type-casting operation that converts the *data* argument (which is of type `caddr_t`) to be of type pointer to an `int`.

9 If the `ioctl` command is equal to the `DN_GETCOUNT` macro, sets *res* to the number of bytes in the write request. This count was previously set by the `nonewrite` interface in the `sc_count` member of the `sc` pointer.

10 If the `ioctl` command is equal to the `DN_CLRCOUNT` macro, sets the count of characters written to the device to the value zero (0). This line has the effect of clearing the `sc_count` member of the `softc` structure associated with this `none` device.

11 Returns success to the `ioctl` system call.

4.2 Configuring the Device Driver

The Digital UNIX operating system provides two models for configuring device drivers: the third-party device driver configuration model and the traditional device driver configuration model. Chapter 11 describes each of these models. Chapter 12 reviews the files associated with configuring device drivers and describes the syntaxes and mechanisms used to populate these files. Chapter 13 provides instructions for configuring the /dev/none device driver, using the third-party and the traditional models.

You can also see the README file in the /usr/examples/devdriver directory for instructions on how to configure and load the loadable version of the /dev/none device driver.

4.3 Testing a Device Driver

One way to test a device driver is to write a test program. Implementing the test program involves the following tasks:

* Writing the test program
* Deciding on more rigorous testing
* Tracking down problems in testing

Each of these tasks is discussed in the following sections.

4.3.1 Writing the Test Program

The test program for the /dev/none device driver performs the following tasks:

* Opens the none device for both reading and writing.
* Gets the count of bytes written to the device.
* Writes 100 bytes.
* Gets the byte count a second time. The byte count should be 100 more than the first time.
* Resets the count to the value zero (0).
* Gets the count again, to verify that the reset worked.

- Tries to read 100 bytes. The test program should not be able to read any because /dev/none returns EOF on a read.

The test program follows:

```
/******************************************************
 * testdevnone.c - Test program for /dev/none         *
 *                 driver                              *
 ******************************************************/
/******************************************************
 *                                                     *
 * Author: Digital Equipment Corporation               *
 *                                                     *
 ******************************************************/
/******************************************************
 *             INCLUDE FILES                           *
 *                                                     *
 ******************************************************/
/******************************************************
 *                                                     *
 *                                                     *
 * Header files required by testdevnone.c              *
 *                                                     *
 *                                                     *
 ******************************************************/

#include <stdio.h>
#include <sys/ioctl.h>  1
#include <sys/file.h>
#include <sys/limits.h>
#include </usr/opt/ESA100/nonereg.h>  2

char buf[100];  3
main()
{
     int d;  4
     int count;  5
     if((d = open("/dev/none",O_RDWR)) == -1)  6
     {
          perror("/dev/none");
               exit(1);
     }
     ioctl(d,DN_GETCOUNT,&count);  7
     printf("saw %d bytes\n",count);  8

     write(d,&buf[0],100);  9
     printf("wrote 100 bytes\n");  10

     ioctl(d,DN_GETCOUNT,&count);  11
     printf("saw %d bytes\n",count);  12

     ioctl(d,DN_CLRCOUNT,&count);  13
     printf("set count\n");  14

     ioctl(d,DN_GETCOUNT,&count);  15
```

```
            printf("saw %d bytes\n",count);
        count = read(d,&buf[0],100); 16
            printf("was able to read %d bytes\n",count); 17
        exit(0); 18
}
```

1. Includes the `ioctl.h` header file because the test program uses the `ioctl` macros defined in the device register header file `nonereg.h`.

2. Includes the device register header file, which is discussed in Section 4.1.1. The directory specification adheres to the third-party device driver configuration model discussed in Section 11.1.2. If the traditional device driver configuration model is followed, the directory specification is `<io/EasyInc/nonereg.h>`. The directory specification you make here depends on where you put the device register file.

3. Declares an array that contains 100 character elements. This array is used to store the 100 bytes written by the `nonewrite` interface.

4. Declares a variable to contain the return from the `open` system call.

5. Declares a variable to store the character count.

6. Calls the `open` system call, which in this example opens the device for read/write operations.

    The example passes two arguments:

    – The first argument is the pathname that identifies the file to be opened. In the example, `/dev/none` is passed. This path causes the kernel to:

    Look up `/dev/none` in the file system

    Notice that `/dev/none` is a character-special device

    Look up the driver entry for `/dev/none` in the `cdevsw` table

    Locate the pointer to the `noneopen` interface that was put there when the `cdevsw` table was edited for the static version of the driver or inserted by the `cdevsw_add` kernel interface for the loadable version of the driver

    Call the `noneopen` interface, passing to it a data structure that describes the device being opened

    – The second argument is a flag to tell the kernel how to open the file. In the example, the constant O_RDWR is passed. This constant tells the kernel to open `/dev/none` for reading and writing.

    If the `open` system call executes successfully, it opens the device and returns a nonnegative value to the test program. However, if the system call fails, the kernel (in cooperation with the driver's `noneopen` interface) will have set the global variable *errno* to a constant value that describes the error. If an error occurs, the test program prints the error, using the `perror` interface, and quits.

7. After the device is opened, gets the initial character count that was written to it. Although the count should be zero, it may not be if other users have already written data to the device.

Remember that the `noneioctl` interface in the driver is used to read or clear the count of characters written to /dev/none. Here, the `ioctl` system call is used to read the count of characters written to the device. The kernel notices that the file associated with the descriptor *d* is actually a special file, looks up its `ioctl` interface in the `cdevsw` table, and invokes the driver's `noneioctl` interface. The kernel copies the return value from `noneioctl` back to the *count* variable defined in the test program because the bitmask for DN_GETCOUNT instructs it to do so.

8. Calls the `printf` interface to display on the console terminal a message that indicates the number of bytes.

9. Writes 100 bytes of data to /dev/none. The kernel invokes `nonewrite` because the file descriptor *d* is associated with a special file. The `nonewrite` interface counts these characters.

10. Calls the `printf` interface to display on the console terminal a message that indicates that `nonewrite` wrote 100 bytes.

11. Reads the count of characters written to the device now. The count should be 100 higher than it was in the previous section of code. The `noneioctl` interface is used exactly the same as it was to get the initial count.

12. Calls the `printf` interface to display on the console terminal the number of bytes.

13. The next test is to clear the count of characters written to the `none` device. The DN_CLRCOUNT macro is used to accomplish this task. This time, no data will be returned by the device driver, so the kernel will not copy any data back to the test program. All three arguments are passed to the `ioctl` system call for the sake of correctness. When this `ioctl` call returns, the test program expects the current count to be the value zero (0).

14. Calls the `printf` interface to display the message ''set count'' on the console terminal.

15. To determine if the previous code cleared the count to zero (0), the test program reads the characters from the `none` device again. The `printf` interface is used to display the count.

16. One design goal for the /dev/none device driver is that it should always return EOF on read operations. The test program checks this action by trying to read 100 bytes from the device. If the design goal

was met, the `read` system call should return zero (0) bytes.

The test program passes three arguments to the `read` system call:

- The first argument is the file descriptor.
- The second argument points to where the data is stored.
- The final argument tells how many bytes to read, in this example 100 bytes.

As discussed previously, the kernel notices that the file descriptor `d` is associated with a device and finds the `cdevsw` entry for the device's `read` interface, `noneread`. The kernel calls `noneread` to service the read request. The number of bytes successfully read is returned by the `read` system call.

17 The `printf` interface prints the number of bytes that were read.

18 The test program exits and the kernel automatically calls the `noneclose` interface.

The following shows the output from a sample run of the test program, which verifies that the driver is working correctly:

```
saw 0 bytes
wrote 100 bytes
saw 100 bytes
set count
saw 0 bytes
was able to read 0 bytes
```

4.3.2 Deciding on More Rigorous Testing

You can expand the test program for the `/dev/none` device driver to do even more complete testing. For example, the test program could check the character count between each of several writes.

Because `/dev/none` is a simple driver, the test program is relatively straightforward. More complicated drivers require more complicated test programs, but the strategy is the same: for each interface you provide in the driver, test it independently from the other interfaces.

4.3.3 Tracking Problems in Testing

If the driver fails to behave as expected, you need to track down the problem and correct it. Here are several aids and hints:

- Refer to the *Kernel Debugging* for guidelines in debugging the driver.
- Use the `printf` kernel interface to display descriptive messages on the console terminal when the driver calls different interfaces. The messages that appear on the console should give you some insight into the problem.

The `syslog` utility also logs these messages into a message file.

You cannot use the `printf` interface to debug all driver types. For example, `printf` frequently is not useful in debugging terminal drivers because use of the terminal driver may be required to display the contents of `printf` to the terminal.

- Recompile and reinstall the kernel.

- Rerun the test program with the reinstalled kernel.

- Use synchronous traces of flow and variables where practical.

- Do not use synchronous traces in the interrupt handler. This means you should not use the `printf` interface in the interrupt handler.

- Use asynchronous traces where synchronous traces cannot be used.

Figure 4-1 shows the device driver testing worksheet for the `/dev/none` device driver. This worksheet is provided in Appendix B for use in identifying the scope of your driver test programs.

Figure 4-1: Testing Worksheet for /dev/none

DEVICE DRIVER TESTING WORKSHEET

Specify the scope of the driver test program:

		YES	NO
1.	The test program checks all entry points	☑	☐
2.	The test program checks all ioctl requests separately	☑	☐
3.	The test program checks multiple devices	☐	☑
4.	The test program was run with multiple users using the device	☐	☑
5.	The test program includes debug code to check for impossible situations	☐	☑
6.	The test program tests which entry points are available through the system call interface	☐	☑

Part 3

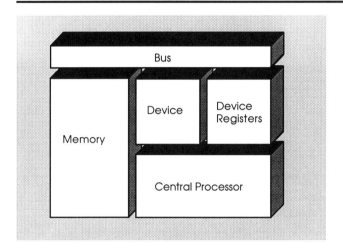

Hardware-Independent Model and Device Drivers 5

One of the goals of an open systems environment is to provide hardware and software platforms that promote the use of standards. By adhering to a set of standard interfaces, these platforms make it easier for third-party application programmers to write applications that can run on a variety of operating systems and hardware. This open systems environment can also make it easier for systems engineers to write device drivers for numerous peripheral devices that operate on this same variety of operating systems and hardware.

The hardware-independent model describes the hardware and software components that make up an open systems environment. This chapter provides an overview of the hardware-independent model and shows how it relates to device drivers. Although you do not need to know all of the details of this model, a high-level discussion can help to clarify how device drivers fit into the independent model.

Figure 5-1 shows that the hardware-independent model consists of a:

- Hardware-independent subsystem
- Hardware-dependent subsystem
- Bus support subsystem
- Device driver subsystem

The sections following Figure 5-1 briefly describe these subsystems as they relate to device drivers.

Figure 5-1: Hardware-Independent Model

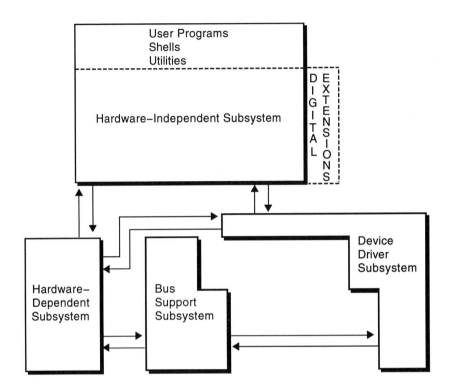

5.1 Hardware-Independent Subsystem

The hardware-independent subsystem contains all of the hardware-independent pieces of an operating system, including the hardware-independent kernel interfaces, user programs, shells, and utilities. Figure 5-1 shows, however, this subsystem also contains extensions and enhancements made by Digital Equipment Corporation. Examples of these extensions are DECnet and support for CD–ROM file systems.

Writing device drivers becomes easier in such an open systems environment because the system design standardizes interfaces and data structures whenever possible. For example, the hardware-independent subsystem contains those kernel interfaces (such as MALLOC and timeout) and data structures (such as buf and uio) that are not affected by the hardware. On the other hand, those interfaces (such as fubyte and suword) and data structures (such as the timer and memory management structures) affected by the hardware are contained in the hardware-dependent subsystem.

Figure 5-1 shows that the hardware-independent subsystem communicates with:

- The hardware-dependent subsystem

  The hardware-independent subsystem communicates with the hardware-dependent subsystem by calling interfaces and referencing data structures and global variables provided by the hardware-dependent subsystem.

- The device driver subsystem

  The hardware-independent subsystem communicates with the device driver subsystem by using specific data structures to make calls into the device driver subsystem. These data structures are the device switch tables `bdevsw` and `cdevsw`.

5.2 Hardware-Dependent Subsystem

The hardware-dependent subsystem contains all of the hardware-dependent pieces of an operating system with the exception of device drivers. This subsystem provides the code that supports a specific CPU platform and, therefore, is implemented by specific vendors. In the case of Digital Equipment Corporation, this code supports the Alpha architecture. However, code could be written to support other CPU architectures. Writing device drivers becomes easier in such an open systems environment because the CPU-specific changes are hidden in the hardware-dependent layer, so minimal or no changes would need to be made to device drivers.

Figure 5-1 shows that the hardware-dependent subsystem communicates with:

- The hardware-independent subsystem

  The hardware-independent subsystem initiates communication with the hardware-dependent subsystem by calling interfaces and referencing data structures and global variables provided by the hardware-dependent subsystem.

- The device driver subsystem

  The device driver subsystem initiates communication with the hardware-dependent subsystem by calling some of the same interfaces and referencing some of the same data structures as the hardware-independent subsystem.

- The bus support subsystem

  The hardware-dependent subsystem initiates communication with the bus support subsystem by calling the bus configuration interfaces. The bus support subsystem also initiates communication with the device driver by calling the driver's autoconfiguration entry points. These entry points are the driver's `probe`, `attach`, and `slave` interfaces.

5.3 Bus Support Subsystem

The bus support subsystem contains all of the bus adapter-specific code. Many buses provide interfaces that are publicly documented and, therefore, allow vendors to more easily plug in hardware and software components. However, the way one vendor implements the bus-specific code can be different from another vendor. For example, the implementation of the VMEbus on Digital Alpha systems is different from Sun Microsystem's implementation of the VMEbus. Isolating the bus-specific code and data structures into a bus support subsystem makes it easier for independent software vendors to implement different bus adapters.

Figure 5-1 shows that the bus support subsystem communicates with:

- The hardware-dependent subsystem

  The bus support subsystem communicates with the hardware-dependent subsystem by calling interfaces and referencing data structures and global variables provided by the hardware-dependent subsystem.

- The device driver subsystem

  The bus support subsystem communicates with the device driver subsystem during device autoconfiguration through the driver's `probe`, `slave`, and `attach` interfaces. In addition, the bus support subsystem provides interfaces that allow drivers to perform bus-specific tasks.

5.4 Device Driver Subsystem

The device driver subsystem contains all of the driver-specific code. This subsystem is supplied by Digital Equipment Corporation and includes device drivers for hardware supported by Digital. Third-party device driver writers would place their drivers in the device driver subsystem.

Figure 5-1 shows that the device driver subsystem communicates with:

- The hardware-dependent subsystem

  The device driver subsystem communicates with the hardware-dependent subsystem by calling interfaces and referencing data structures and global variables provided by the hardware-dependent subsystem.

- The bus support subsystem

  The device driver subsystem communicates with the bus support subsystem during device autoconfiguration. This is accomplished through the driver's `probe`, `slave`, and `attach` interfaces. In addition, device drivers can call bus-specific interfaces to perform a variety of tasks. For

example, a TURBOchannel device driver calls the
`tc_isolate_memerr` interface to log memory-related errors. Other
buses have their own specific interfaces that drivers use to communicate
with this subsystem.

Device drivers can also call generic interfaces such as `enable_option`
to enable a device's interrupt line to the CPU. The advantage to calling
the generic interface as opposed to the bus-specific interface is that the
generic interface makes the driver more portable across different bus
architectures.

- The hardware-independent subsystem

  The device driver subsystem communicates with the hardware-
  independent subsystem through calls to interfaces and data structures
  provided by the hardware-independent subsystem.

Hardware Components and Hardware Activities   6

This chapter discusses the hardware environment from the point of view of the device driver writer. Specifically, the chapter describes the following hardware components:

- The central processing unit (CPU)
- The bus
- The device

The chapter also discusses a variety of hardware activities of interest to a device driver writer.

6.1 Hardware Components

Figure 6-1 shows the following hardware components:

- The central processing unit (CPU)
- Memory
- The bus
- The device

Each of these components is discussed briefly following Figure 6-1.

Figure 6-1: Hardware Components of Interest to a Device Driver Writer

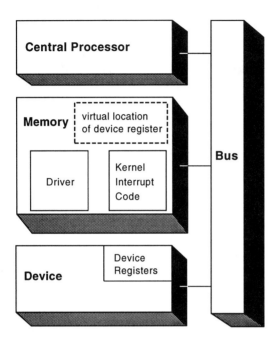

6.1.1 Central Processing Unit

The central processing unit (CPU) is the main computational unit in a computer and the one that executes instructions. The CPU is of interest to device driver writers because its associated architecture influences the design of the driver. Writing device drivers for OPENbus architectures in an open systems environment means that you may need to become familiar with a variety of CPU architectures, such as Alpha and MIPS. Section 2.6 describes the CPU issues that influence the design of device drivers.

6.1.2 Memory

Figure 6-1 shows that both the kernel and device drivers reside in memory, as does the kernel interrupt code that determines what driver will handle each interrupt from a device. The device driver accesses device registers (often referred to as control status register or CSR addresses) as though they were in memory; however, these registers are not really in memory but are located in the device. Figure 6-1 shows this arrangement by identifying a virtual location for the device registers. The hardware manual for the device you are writing the driver for should describe these device register addresses or offsets.

For the TURBOchannel bus, the address is encoded in the form of an I/O handle. The data type `io_handle_t` represents this I/O handle. The I/O handle for the TURBOchannel bus represents an address that is based on the slot. The bus configuration code passes the I/O handle to the device driver through the `probe` interface.

A device driver that operates on the EISA, PCI, or TURBOchannel bus accesses the device registers by referencing this I/O handle in calls to `read_io_port` and `write_io_port`. See the bus-specific book to determine if the bus you are writing the driver for uses an I/O handle or some other mechanism.

6.1.3 Bus

The bus is the path for all communication among the CPU, memory, and devices. Thus, when a device driver reads from or writes to a device's registers, the information transfer is by way of the bus. If you write device drivers for OPEN systems, you will probably need to know about a variety of buses, including the following:

- EISA
- PCI
- SCSI
- TURBOchannel
- VMEbus

There are three situations when the bus is of concern to you:

- When specifying which bus a device is on
- When writing `probe` and `slave` interfaces
- When a device does direct memory access (DMA)

Each of these situations is briefly considered in the following sections.

6.1.3.1 Specifying Which Bus a Device Is On

For the most part, you can think of the bus as a single path, but at kernel configuration time this view is not adequate. The bus, as used in this book, includes:

- The system bus
- Other buses attached to the system bus, for example, a VMEbus

When adding a device driver, you very well may be adding a device to the system. If you are, you will need to know what bus to attach its device controller to.

You specify which bus a device controller is connected to in the following files:

- The system configuration file, for static drivers that follow the traditional device driver configuration model. Section 11.2 describes the traditional device driver configuration model and Section 12.2.1.2 discusses the syntax for specifying which bus is connected to a device controller.

- The config.file file fragment, for static device drivers that follow the third-party device driver configuration model. Section 11.1 describes the third-party device driver configuration model. Section 11.1.2.3 discusses the config.file file fragment. Section 12.2.1.2 discusses the syntax for specifying which bus is connected to a device controller.

- The stanza.loadable file fragment, for loadable drivers that follow the third-party device driver configuration model. Section 11.1.2.5 describes this file fragment and Section 12.6.2.18 explains the syntax for specifying which bus is connected to a device controller.

6.1.3.2   Writing probe and slave Interfaces

When writing probe and slave interfaces, you need to consider the bus on which the driver will operate. The bus affects the formal parameters you specify for these interfaces. Section 3.3.1 and Section 3.3.2 show you how to set up probe and slave interfaces for the TURBOchannel bus. See the bus-specific driver manual to learn how to set up these interfaces for the bus your driver operates on.

6.1.3.3   A Device Does Direct Memory Access

Some devices are capable of directly accessing memory, generally to transfer large blocks of data. Section 6.1.4.5 discusses DMA as it relates to devices.

6.1.4   Device

A device (often referred to as a peripheral device) can be a printer, an acquisition device, terminal, and so forth. Whatever the device is, it has:

- One or more device registers for communicating with other hardware

- The ability (in most devices) to generate interrupts

Major distinctions between devices are the type of device (block, character, or network) and whether the device is capable of directly accessing memory. A direct memory access (DMA) device is one that can directly access (read from and write to) CPU memory, without CPU intervention. Non-DMA devices cannot directly access CPU memory.

The following sections briefly discuss the device registers, block and character devices, terminal devices, network devices, and DMA and non-DMA devices.

6.1.4.1 Device Registers

A device register is commonly referred to as a control status register, or CSR. The device register can be used to:

- Control what a device does

- Report the status of a device

- Transfer data to or from the device

The device register can be in the device or in a separate controller. In most cases, the location of the device register is of no concern to the device driver writer.

The types of device registers can vary widely, depending on the device used. Most devices have multiple registers. A device register can be read-only, such as for device status or the results of an I/O operation; it can be a write-only command/control register; or it can be both readable and writeable.

It is often the case that after writing to a read/write register, the subsequent read from it will return a completely different value. The read value will be defined to be a status or result, while the write value will be command or control information to the device. In many cases, reading a control status register once will clear that register's values. A second read may, in fact, return unexpected or unwanted results. See the documentation for the device to determine if this situation exists.

Digital provides the `read_io_port` and `write_io_port` interfaces to read and write data from a device register located in the bus I/O or memory address space. These interfaces make the device driver more portable across different bus architectures, different CPU architectures, and different CPU types within the same CPU architecture.

6.1.4.2 Block and Character Devices

A block device is one that is designed to operate in terms of the block I/O supported by Digital UNIX. It is accessed through the buffer cache. A block device has an associated block device driver that performs I/O by using file system block-sized buffers from a buffer cache supplied by the kernel. Block device drivers are particularly well-suited for disk drives, the most common block devices.

A character device is any device that can have streams of characters read from or written to it. A character device has a character device driver associated with it that can be used for a device such as a line printer that handles one character at a time. However, character drivers are not limited to performing I/O a single character at a time (despite the name "character" driver). For example, tape drivers frequently perform I/O in 10K chunks. A character device driver can also be used where it is necessary to copy data directly to or from a user process. Because of their flexibility in handling I/O, many drivers are character drivers. Line printers, interactive terminals, and graphics displays are examples of devices that require character device drivers.

6.1.4.3   Terminal Devices

A terminal device is a special type of character device that can have streams of characters read from or written to it. Terminal devices have terminal (character) device drivers associated with them. A terminal device driver is actually a character device driver that handles I/O character processing for a variety of terminal devices. Like any character device, a terminal device can accept or supply a stream of data based on a request from a user process. It cannot be mounted as a file system and, therefore, does not use data caching.

6.1.4.4   Network Devices

A network device is any device associated with network activities and is responsible for both transmitting and receiving frames to and from the network medium. Network devices have network device drivers associated with them. A network device driver attaches a network subsystem to a network interface, prepares the network interface for operation, and governs the transmission and reception of network frames over the network interface.

6.1.4.5   DMA and non-DMA Devices

A direct memory access (DMA) device is one that can directly access (read from and write to) CPU memory, without CPU intervention. Non-DMA devices cannot directly access CPU memory. The object of DMA is faster data transfer. When character drivers perform DMA, they do it to or from the user's address space. When block drivers perform DMA, they do it to or from the buffer cache.

6.2 Hardware Activities

When writing device drivers, you need to consider the following hardware-related activities:

- How a device driver accesses device registers
- How the device uses the registers
- How the device driver interrupts the CPU

The following sections discuss each of these activities as they relate to device drivers.

6.2.1 How a Device Driver Accesses Device Registers

Alpha CPU platforms vary in the mechanisms available to access device registers. Some platforms, such as the DEC 4000 and DEC 7000 series, use the mailbox mechanism. Other platforms, such as the DEC 3000 series, allow ''direct'' access to device registers through special address spaces. The following discussion applies to those platforms that use special address spaces.

Alpha CPUs can access longwords (32 bits) and quadwords (64 bits) atomically. However, many devices have CSRs that are only 16- or 8-bits wide. Program fragments accessing those CSRs will actually be sequences of Alpha instructions that fetch longwords and mask out bytes. For example, for adjacent 16-bit CSRs this longword access is probably not what is intended. The fetch of the longword may result in the reading of multiple CSRs, with unwanted side effects.

6.2.2 How a Device Uses the Registers

Devices use their registers to report status and to return data. DMA devices can move data to or from memory directly. DMA device drivers typically request this type of data transfer by:

- Writing a base address and a count of characters in the device register to specify what data to move
- Setting a bit that requests that the transfer begin

The device requests access to memory and then manages a sequence of data transfers to memory. Upon completion of the transfer, the device:

- Sets a bit indicating that the transfer is done
- Issues an interrupt

You do not need to know the details of how the device and the bus interact to handle these transfers of data. However, you do need to know the exact register fields to use to make the request. This information should be in the hardware manual for the device.

6.2.3 How a Device Driver Interrupts the CPU

The specifics of how interrupts are generated varies from bus to bus and even from CPU architecture to CPU architecture. The following is a general description of how interrupts are processed by the kernel on some systems. The important point to remember is that the end result of an interrupt is the calling of the device driver's interrupt handling interface.

When a device generates an interrupt, it also provides an interrupt index. This interrupt index is passed by the bus to the kernel assembly language interface that does initial handling of interrupts. That interface uses the interrupt index to determine which entry in the interrupt vector table contains the address of the interrupt interface for the device driver that handles this device. Among other things, the assembly language interface uses that address to transfer control to the appropriate driver. The `config` program adds a static device driver's interrupt service interface to the system interrupt vector table if you specify the interrupt handlers in the system configuration file. Calling the `handler` interfaces to dynamically register the interrupt handlers for the static and loadable version of a driver also causes the the interrupt handlers to be added to this table. Section 2.4 describes the methods for registering device interrupt handlers.

6.3 Parts of the System Accessing Hardware

Only two parts of the system access hardware:

*   The bus support subsystem

    There are specific bus support interfaces that access the device registers of the bus adapter.

*   The device driver subsystem

    There are specific device driver interfaces that access the device registers of specific devices attached to a controller.

Part 4

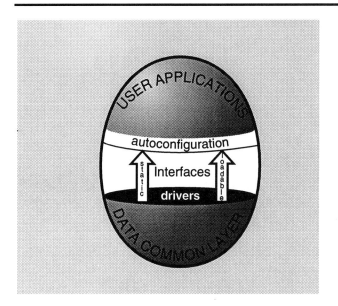

Device Autoconfiguration 7

Autoconfiguration is a process that determines what hardware actually exists during the current instance of the running kernel. This chapter discusses the events that occur during the autoconfiguration of devices, with an emphasis on how autoconfiguration relates to static and loadable drivers. In addition, the chapter provides detailed information on the data structures related to autoconfiguration.

The chapter frequently uses the generic term autoconfiguration software. The autoconfiguration software consists of the programs that accomplish the tasks associated with the events that occur during the autoconfiguration of devices. In most cases, it is not necessary for device driver writers to know the specific programs that execute during autoconfiguration.

The chapter also describes the data structures related to loadable drivers and the data structures associated with the dynamic registration of interrupt handlers.

Specifically, this chapter discusses:

- Files that the autoconfiguration software uses
- The autoconfiguration process
- Data structures that the autoconfiguration software uses
- Data structures that loadable device drivers use
- Data structures that device drivers use to register interrupt handlers

7.1 Files That the Autoconfiguration Software Uses

The autoconfiguration software reads the following files pertinent to device drivers during the autoconfiguration process:

- The `config.file` file fragment and/or the system configuration file (for static device drivers)

  The `config.file` file fragment and the system configuration file (sometimes referred to as the *NAME* file) identify, among other things, device connectivity information. Section 12.2 describes the parts of these files pertinent to device drivers and provides details on the syntaxes that specify each current or planned device on the system.

- The /etc/sysconfigtab database (for loadable device drivers)

  The sysconfigtab database contains the information provided in the stanza.loadable file fragments. This information is appended to the sysconfigtab database when the system manager runs the sysconfigdb utility during the installation of the device driver kit.

  The stanza.loadable file fragment contains an entry for each device driver, providing such information as the driver's name, location of the loadable object, device connectivity information, and device special file information. Parts of the stanza.loadable file fragment are functionally similar to the system configuration file in that the fragment uses a subset of the syntaxes that the system configuration file uses to specify each current or planned device on the system. Section 12.6 describes the valid device syntaxes for the stanza.loadable file fragment.

The following example shows a sample system configuration file and a sample /etc/sysconfigtab database:

```
/* Example system configuration file */
bus           tc0     at      nexus
controller    fb0     at      tc0
controller    ipi0    at      tc0
device disk ip1       at      ipi0 unit 1
device disk ip2       at      ipi0 unit 2
bus           vba0    at      tc0   slot 2 vector vbaerrors
controller    sk0     at      vba0 csr 0x8000 vector skintr 0xc8
bus           vba1    at      tc0   slot 1
controller    cb0     at      vba1 csr 0x80001000 vector cbintr 0x45


/* Example sysconfigtab database */
Module_Config2 = controller  fb0     at       tc0
Module_Config3 = controller  ipi0    at       tc0
Module_Config4 = device disk ip1     at       ipi0    unit 1
Module_Config5 = device disk ip2     at       ipi0    unit 2
```

The two samples are shown together so that you can clearly see the similarities and differences. Note that these samples show only a subset of all the possible syntaxes.

The autoconfiguration software uses the information in this system configuration file and database to create the associated bus, controller, and device structures. These structures are designed so that they are generic enough to handle not only autoconfiguration for static and loadable drivers but also to simplify configuration management. It is important to note that the kernel doubly links these structures top-down and bottom-up to make the traversal of the configuration tree more efficient. Section 7.2 discusses the links the kernel makes between these structures during the autoconfiguration process.

Note

In previous versions of the Digital UNIX operating system (formerly known as DEC OSF/1), the example system configuration file specified the interrupt service interfaces (ISIs) `fbintr` and `ipiintr` for the `fb0` and `ipi0` controllers. The example system configuration file does not specify these ISIs in the Digital UNIX operating system. The drivers associated with these controllers register their ISIs by calling the `handler` interfaces, usually in the Autoconfiguration Support Section.

Some buses (for example, the TURBOchannel bus) support two methods for registering ISIs: through the system configuration file and by calling the `handler` interfaces. Other buses (for example, the PCI bus) support registration of ISIs by calling only the `handler` interfaces.

The example system configuration file continues to specify the ISIs for the `sk0` and the `cb0` controllers to show the differences. See the bus-specific driver book to determine which methods the bus your driver operates on supports.

Digital recommends that all new drivers (and all previously written static drivers that you want to make loadable) register ISIs by calling the `handler` interfaces. Section 7.5 describes the data structures that device drivers use to dynamically register ISIs. Section 9.6 provides examples of how to dynamically register ISIs by calling the `handler` interfaces. In addition, the static versions of the `/dev/none` and `/dev/cb` drivers dynamically register their ISIs by calling the `handler` interfaces instead of specifying them in the system configuration file.

Figure 7-1 shows the structures created by the autoconfiguration software after it reads the sample system configuration file and `sysconfigtab` database. Of course, the autoconfiguration software does not store these structures in memory with the structure names as identified in the figure. These names and the figure are used to make it easier to understand how these structures are created and manipulated.

Figure 7-1: Structures Created from the Example

Structure Arrays Created from Example System Configuration File

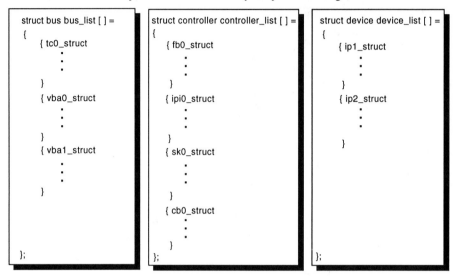

Individual Structures Created from Example sysconfigtab Database

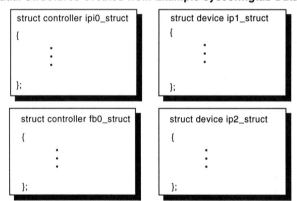

The following sections discuss the similarities and differences between the structures created by the autoconfiguration software for static and loadable drivers.

7.1.1 For bus Structures

For each bus (specified with the `bus` keyword in the system configuration file), the autoconfiguration software creates an array of `bus` structures called `bus_list`, which it stores in `ioconf.c`. As the figure shows, the autoconfiguration software fills this array with the following `bus` structures it finds in the system configuration file: `tc0_struct`, `vba0_struct`, and `vba1_struct`.

Similarly, for each bus (specified with the `bus` keyword in the `stanza.loadable` file fragment), the autoconfiguration software dynamically creates individual `bus` structures, instead of an array, and stores these structures in memory. As the figure shows, `tc0_struct` is not created during the autoconfiguration of loadable drivers. The system bus would have already been created during the autoconfiguration of static drivers.

In this example, `tc0_struct` already exists in the `bus_list` array. The system bus must be in the system configuration file because a loadable system bus is not supported. Here, the `controller` structures are dynamically created and linked through the pointer to the system bus structure that was statically allocated in `bus_list`. Because `tc0_struct` represents the system bus, there is no need to specify it in the `stanza.loadable` file fragment. However, if the system bus was not specified in the system configuration file (for static drivers), no `bus` structures are created. The autoconfiguration software always detects a system bus during autoconfiguration of loadable drivers.

7.1.2 For controller Structures

For each controller (specified with the `controller` keyword in the system configuration file), the autoconfiguration software creates an array of `controller` structures called `controller_list`, which it stores in `ioconf.c`. As the figure shows, the autoconfiguration software fills this array with the following `controller` structures it finds in the system configuration file: `fb0_struct`, `ipi0_struct`, `sk0_struct`, and `cb0_struct`.

Similarly, for each controller (also specified with the `controller` keyword in the `stanza.loadable` file fragment), the autoconfiguration software dynamically creates individual `controller` structures, instead of an array, and stores these structures in memory. As the figure shows, the autoconfiguration software creates the following `controller` structures it finds in the `stanza.loadable` file fragment: `fb0_struct` and `ipi0_struct`.

7.1.3 For device Structures

For each device (specified with the `device` keyword in the system configuration file), the autoconfiguration software creates an array of `device` structures called `device_list`, which it stores in `ioconf.c`. As the figure shows, the autoconfiguration software fills this array with the following `device` structures it finds in the system configuration file: `ip1_struct` and `ip2_struct`.

Similarly, for each device (also specified with the `device` keyword in the `stanza.loadable` file fragment), the autoconfiguration software dynamically creates individual `device` structures, instead of an array, and stores these structures in memory. As the figure shows, the autoconfiguration software creates the following `device` structures it finds in the `stanza.loadable` file fragment: `ip1_struct` and `ip2_struct`.

7.2 Autoconfiguration Process

When the kernel boots, the autoconfiguration software determines what hardware actually exists during the current instance of the running kernel. System managers often create (compile and link) kernels that define the greatest possible amount and variety of hardware available on the system. For example, a large and complex system with many bus adapters might alternately run a certain device on one bus adapter at a certain time and on another bus adapter later for testing purposes.

The following sections describe autoconfiguration from the static and loadable driver points of view.

7.2.1 Autoconfiguration for Static Device Drivers

This section describes autoconfiguration from the point of view of static device drivers. When the kernel boots, the autoconfiguration software configures all the buses on the system by performing the following tasks:

- Locating the `bus` structure for the system bus
- Calling the level 1 bus configuration interfaces
- Configuring all devices
- Calling the level 1 configuration interfaces for any other buses
- Calling the level 2 configuration interfaces for any other buses
- Creating a system configuration tree

Each of these tasks is discussed in the following sections.

7.2.1.1   Locating the bus Structure for the System Bus

The autoconfiguration software searches `bus_list`, the array of `bus` structures created from the system configuration file, to locate the structure for the system bus. The system `bus` structure is identified with a backpointer of –1 indicating that it is connected to the keyword `nexus` in the system configuration file. The `nexus` keyword indicates the top of the system configuration tree.

All systems have a system bus, even if there is no physical bus. For example, workstations that do not have a physical bus have a logical `ibus` to which the onboard devices are connected.

7.2.1.2   Calling the Level 1 Bus Configuration Interfaces

After the autoconfiguration software locates the `bus` structure for the system bus, it calls the level 1 bus configuration interface specified in the `bus` structure. If a bus supports autoconfiguration (that is, the devices support a device type identifier and the bus supports a well-defined search algorithm), the autoconfiguration software searches `controller_list`, the array of `controller` structures created from the system configuration file, to locate a match for each controller on the system bus. If a match is found, the `controller` structure for that controller is linked to the `bus` structure and a back link to the `bus` structure is placed in the `controller` structure. This action continues until all controllers have been configured.

If the bus does not support autoconfiguration, the `controller_list` array is searched for controllers that were attached to the bus in the system configuration file. In both cases, the driver's `probe` interface (as specified in the `driver` structure) for each device is called to verify the existence of the controller. If the `probe` interface returns success, the controller's `attach` interface (if one exists) is called.

7.2.1.3   Configuring All Devices

After a successful probe, the autoconfiguration software searches `device_list`, the array of `device` structures created from the system configuration file, to locate a match for each device connected to a controller. If a match is found, the `device` structure is connected to its respective `controller` structure. For each device found, the autoconfiguration software calls the driver's `slave` and `attach` interfaces.

7.2.1.4   Calling the Level 1 Configuration Interfaces for Any Other Buses

Any other buses located during the configuration of the system bus are handled in the same manner as that described in Section 7.2.1.2. The level 1 configuration interface for each bus is called at this time. All configured buses are also connected by means of a linked list.

7.2.1.5 Calling the Level 2 Configuration Interfaces for Any Other Buses

After all the buses have been configured, the autoconfiguration software calls the system bus level 2 configuration interface specified in the bus structure. This interface then calls the level 2 configuration interface for each directly connected bus. Each of those buses performs any second pass configuration work and calls the level 2 configuration interface of any connected bus.

7.2.1.6 Creating a System Configuration Tree

The end result of this process is to have a completely connected tree that represents the current system configuration. Note that there may be buses, controllers, and devices that are not connected. This indicates the entity was not physically connected on this system.

Figure 7-2 shows the configuration tree the autoconfiguration software would create, based on the entries in the example system configuration file. The figure shows the members of the bus, controller, and device structures used to establish the correct links.

Figure 7-2: Configuration Tree Based on Example System Configuration File

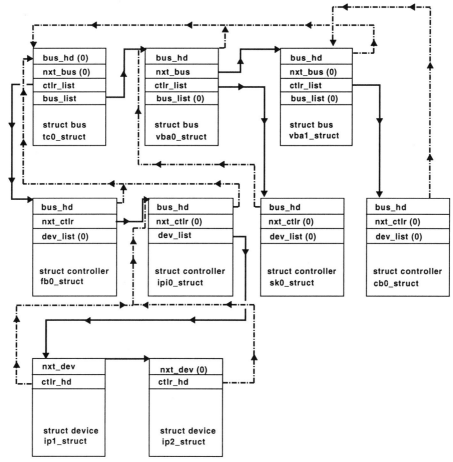

The following text provides information on how to traverse this configuration tree.

Pointing to the bus Structure to Which This Bus Is Connected

The `bus_hd` member specifies a pointer to the bus structure that this bus is connected to. The `vba0` and `vba1` buses are both connected to the system bus. The autoconfiguration software establishes this connection by setting each `bus_hd` member to the address of the system `bus` structure, `tc0_struct`. Figure 7-2 uses a broken arrow to show the setting of the `bus_hd` members.

The system bus is not connected to any other bus and the figure indicates that, as a result, the autoconfiguration software sets this bus_hd member to the value zero (0).

Pointing to the Next Bus at This Level

The nxt_bus member specifies a pointer to the next bus at this level. The vba1 bus follows the vba0 bus, thus making it the next bus at this level. The autoconfiguration software establishes this relationship by setting the nxt_bus member of vba0_struct to the address of vba1_struct. Figure 7-2 uses a solid arrow to show the setting of the nxt_bus member.

No buses follow the system bus and the vba1 bus and the figure indicates that, as a result, the autoconfiguration software sets their nxt_bus members to the value zero (0).

Pointing to a Linked List of Controllers Connected to This Bus

The ctlr_list member specifies a linked list of controllers connected to this bus. The fb0 and ipi0 controllers are connected to the system bus. The autoconfiguration software establishes the linked list by setting the ctlr_list member of tc0_struct to the address of fb0_struct. Figure 7-2 uses a solid arrow to show the setting of the ctlr_list member.

The sk0 controller is connected to the vba0 bus and the cb0 controller is connected to the vba1 bus. As it did with the system bus, the autoconfiguration software establishes the linked lists by setting the ctlr_list member for each bus to the address of its associated controller structure. Figure 7-2 uses a solid arrow to show the setting of the ctlr_list members.

Pointing to the Linked List of Buses Connected to This Bus

The bus_list member specifies a linked list of buses connected to this bus. The vba0 and vba1 buses are connected to the system bus. The autoconfiguration software establishes the linked list by setting the bus_list member of tc0_struct to the address of vba0_struct. Figure 7-2 uses a solid arrow to show the setting of the bus_list member.

The vba0 and vba1 buses do not have a linked list of buses and the figure indicates that, as a result, the autoconfiguration software sets their bus_list members to the value zero (0).

Pointing to the bus Structure to Which This Controller Is Connected

The bus_hd member appears not only in the bus structure, but also in the controller structure. In this case, bus_hd specifies a pointer to the bus structure that this controller is connected to. The fb0 and ipi0 controllers are connected to the system bus. The autoconfiguration software establishes the backpointer to the system bus by setting the bus_hd members of fb0_struct and ipi0_struct to the address of tc0_struct. Figure 7-2 uses a broken arrow to show the setting of the backpointer.

The sk0 and cb0 controllers are connected to the vba0 and vba1 buses. The autoconfiguration software establishes these backpointers by setting the bus_hd members of sk0_struct and cb0_struct to the address of their associated bus structures. Figure 7-2 uses a broken arrow to show the setting of these backpointers.

Pointing to the Next Controller at This Level

The nxt_ctlr member specifies a pointer to the next controller at this level. The ipi0 controller follows the fb0 controller, thus making it the next controller at this level. The autoconfiguration software establishes this relationship by setting the nxt_ctlr member of fb0_struct to the address of ipi0_struct. Figure 7-2 uses a solid arrow to show this. No controllers follow the ipi0 controller and the figure indicates that, as a result, the autoconfiguration software sets the nxt_ctlr member of ipi0_struct to the value zero (0).

The sk0 and cb0 controllers are the only controllers at their respective levels and the figure indicates that, as a result, the autoconfiguration software sets their nxt_ctlr members to the value zero (0).

Pointing to the Linked List of Devices Connected to This Controller

The dev_list member specifies a linked list of devices connected to this controller. The ipi0 controller has two devices connected to it: device ip1 and device ip2. The autoconfiguration software establishes the linked list by setting the dev_list member of ipi0_struct to the address of ip1_struct. Figure 7-2 uses a solid arrow to show the setting of the linked list.

Because the fb0, sk0, and cb0 controllers have no connected devices, Figure 7-2 shows that the autoconfiguration software sets the dev_list member in their respective structures to the value zero (0).

Pointing to the Next Device at This Level

The nxt_dev member specifies a pointer to the next device at this level. The ip2 device follows the ip1 device, thus making it the next device at this level. The autoconfiguration software establishes this relationship by setting the nxt_dev member of ip1_struct to the address of ip2_struct. Figure 7-2 uses a solid arrow to show the setting of the nxt_dev member.

Because there are no devices that follow device ip2, Figure 7-2 shows that the autoconfiguration software sets the nxt_dev member of ip2_struct to the value zero (0).

Pointing to the controller Structure to Which This Device Is Connected

The ctlr_hd member specifies a pointer to the controller structure that this device is connected to. Both the ip1 and ip2 devices are connected to the same controller, ipi0. The autoconfiguration software establishes these backpointers by setting the ctlr_hd member of ip1_struct and ip2_struct to the address of ipi0_struct. Figure 7-2 uses a broken arrow to show the setting of the backpointers.

7.2.2 Autoconfiguration for Loadable Device Drivers

Figure 7-3 shows the configuration tree the autoconfiguration software would create, based on the entries in the sysconfigtab database (which is built from entries specified in stanza.loadable file fragments) presented in Section 7.1. The figure shows the members of the bus, controller, and device structures used to establish the correct links. Note that the system bus, tc0_struct, was previously created during the autoconfiguration of static device drivers.

Figure 7-3: Configuration Tree for Loadable Drivers Based on Example sysconfigtab Database

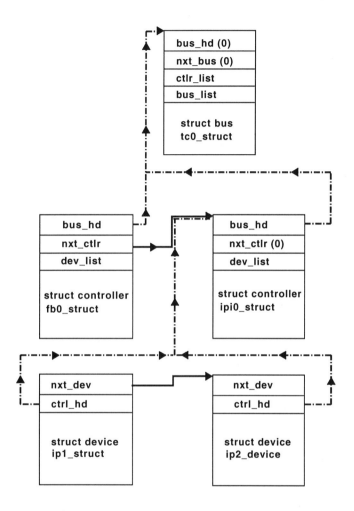

7.3 Data Structures That the Autoconfiguration Software Uses

As discussed in previous sections, the autoconfiguration software creates a configuration tree that represents the current system configuration.

In creating this configuration tree, the autoconfiguration software uses the following data structures:

- `bus`
- `controller`
- `device`
- `driver`
- `port`

The following sections describe each of these data structures.

7.3.1 The bus Structure

The `bus` structure represents an instance of a bus entity. A bus is a real or imagined entity to which other buses or controllers are logically attached. All systems have at least one bus, the system bus, even though the bus may not actually exist physically. The term *controller* here refers both to devices that control slave devices (for example, disk or tape controllers) and to devices that stand alone (for example, terminal or network controllers). You (or the system manager) specify a bus entity as follows:

- For static drivers

  Specify a valid syntax for the bus in the `config.file` file fragment or the system configuration file.

- For loadable drivers

  Specify a valid syntax for the bus in the `stanza.loadable` file fragment.

Chapter 11 discusses the device driver configuration models. Chapter 12 describes the valid syntaxes for a bus specification in these files. Chapter 13 provides examples of how to configure device drivers.

Table 7-1 lists the members of the `bus` structure along with their associated data types.

Table 7-1: Members of the bus Structure

Member Name	Data Type
bus_mbox	u_long *
bus_hd	struct bus *
nxt_bus	struct bus *
ctlr_list	struct controller *

Table 7-1: (continued)

Member Name	Data Type
bus_list	struct bus *
bus_type	int
bus_name	char *
bus_num	int
slot	int
connect_bus	char *
connect_num	int
confl1	int (*confl1)()
confl2	int (*confl2)()
pname	char *
port	struct port *
intr	int (**intr)()
alive	int
framework	struct bus_framework *
driver_name	char *
bus_bridge_dma	void *
private	void * [8]
conn_priv	void * [8]
rsvd	void * [7]

The following sections discuss all of these members except for bus_hd, nxt_bus, ctlr_list, and bus_list, which are presented in Section 7.2.1.6. Chapter 16 provides a reference (man) page-style description of this data structure.

7.3.1.1 The bus_mbox Member

The bus_mbox member specifies a pointer to the mailbox data structure for hardware platforms that access I/O space through hardware mailboxes. The bus adapter code sets this member. As the adapter code probes the buses, the first bus that has a mailbox allocates the initial software mailbox data structure and sets its bus_mbox pointer to that data structure. As the adapter code continues to probe for buses and controllers, the MBOX_GET macro allocates the ctlr_mbox members for devices accessed by mailboxes. Typically, this macro is called in the controller configuration interface after the controller data structure has been found, but before probing the controller. The following code fragment gives an idea of the tasks that occur prior to calling the MBOX_GET macro:

```
config_con(name, node, bus)
{
   register struct controller *ctlr;

   if((ctlr = get_ctlr(name, node, bus->bus_name, bus->bus_num)) ||
         /* other wildcards here */
      (ctlr = get_ctlr(name, -1, "*", -99))) {
   .
   .
   .

      }

/********************************************************
 * Found the controller                                 *
 ********************************************************/

         int savebusnum;
         char *savebusname;
         int saveslot;

         if(ctlr->alive & ALV_ALIVE) {
               printf("config_con: %s%d alive0,
                     ctlr->ctlr_name, ctlr->ctlr_num);
               return(stat);
         }
         savebusnum = ctlr->bus_num;
         savebusname = ctlr->bus_name;
         saveslot = ctlr->slot;
         ctlr->bus_name = bus->bus_name;
         ctlr->bus_num = bus->bus_num;
         ctlr->slot = node;

/********************************************************
 *          Allocate and initialize a software         *
 *          mailbox data structure for the             *
 *          controller if it is attached to a          *
 *          bus that is accessed by mailboxes          *
 ********************************************************/
         MBOX_GET(bus, ctlr);

/********************************************************
 * Now get the controller's driver structure           *
 * and probe                                            *
 ********************************************************/
   .
   .
   .
}
```

7.3.1.2 The bus_type Member

The `bus_type` member specifies the type of bus. The `devdriver.h` file defines constants that represent a variety of bus types.

For the example system configuration file, Figure 7-4 shows that the autoconfiguration software sets the `bus_type` member of `tc0_struct` to `BUS_TC` (a TURBOchannel bus). Also, the autoconfiguration software sets the `bus_type` members of `vba_struct` and `vba1_struct` to `BUS_VME` (a VMEbus).

Similarly for loadable drivers, the autoconfiguration software sets the `bus_type` members for any buses in the `sysconfigtab` database.

Device driver writers seldom need to reference this member. However, bus adapter driver writers might reference this member in their bus adapter code.

Figure 7-4: The bus_type Member Initialized

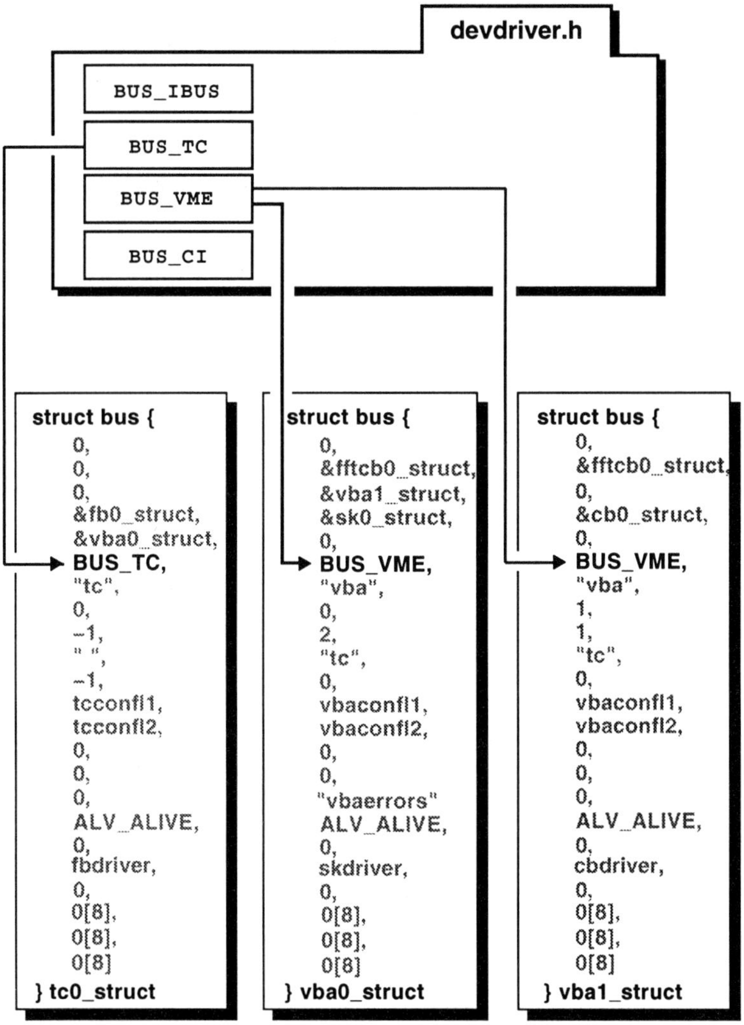

devdriver.h

```
BUS_IBUS
BUS_TC
BUS_VME
BUS_CI
```

```
struct bus {
    0,
    0,
    0,
    &fb0_struct,
    &vba0_struct,
    BUS_TC,
    "tc",
    0,
    -1,
    " ",
    -1,
    tcconfl1,
    tcconfl2,
    0,
    0,
    0,
    ALV_ALIVE,
    0,
    fbdriver,
    0,
    0[8],
    0[8],
    0[8]
} tc0_struct
```

```
struct bus {
    0,
    &fftcb0_struct,
    &vba1_struct,
    &sk0_struct,
    0,
    BUS_VME,
    "vba",
    0,
    2,
    "tc",
    0,
    vbaconfl1,
    vbaconfl2,
    0,
    0,
    "vbaerrors"
    ALV_ALIVE,
    0,
    skdriver,
    0,
    0[8],
    0[8],
    0[8]
} vba0_struct
```

```
struct bus {
    0,
    &fftcb0_struct,
    0,
    &cb0_struct,
    0,
    BUS_VME,
    "vba",
    1,
    1,
    "tc",
    0,
    vbaconfl1,
    vbaconfl2,
    0,
    0,
    0,
    ALV_ALIVE,
    0,
    cbdriver,
    0,
    0[8],
    0[8],
    0[8]
} vba1_struct
```

7.3.1.3 The bus_name and bus_num Members

The bus_name member specifies the bus name. The bus_num member specifies the bus number of this bus.

You (or the system manager) specify the bus name and the bus number by using the keyword bus followed by a character string and number that represent the bus name and bus number. You enter these values in the config.file file fragment or the system configuration file for static drivers and the `stanza.loadable` file fragment for loadable drivers. For example, `tc0` specifies a TURBOchannel bus with a bus number of zero (0).

Figure 7-5 shows the values in the example system configuration file that the autoconfiguration software parses to obtain the bus name and bus number. It also shows that the autoconfiguration software sets the `bus_name` and `bus_num` members to these values for `tc0_struct`, `vba0_struct`, and `vba1_struct`.

The autoconfiguration software performs a similar parsing operation in the `sysconfigtab` database for loadable drivers to obtain the bus name and bus number and to initialize the associated `bus_name` and `bus_num` members.

Device driver writers seldom need to reference the `bus_name` and `bus_num` members in their device drivers. Instead, driver writers often pass a pointer to a `bus` structure to the `handler` interfaces, and the interrupt handlers use the information contained in these members.

Figure 7-5: The bus_name and bus_num Members Initialized

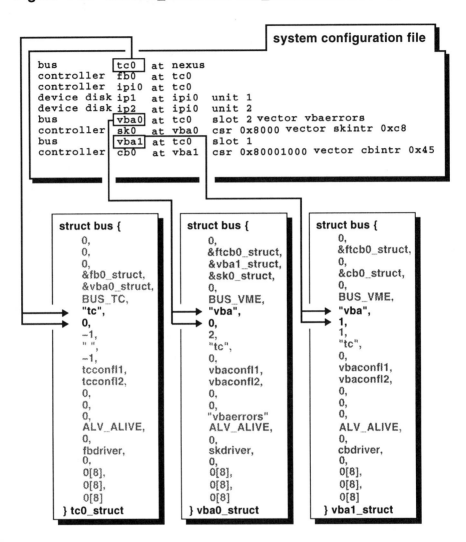

7.3.1.4 The slot, connect_bus, and connect_num Members

The slot member specifies the bus slot or node number. The connect_bus member specifies the name of the bus that this bus is connected to. The connect_num member specifies the number of the bus that this bus is connected to.

You (or the system manager) specify the bus slot or node number by using the slot keyword followed by a valid number. You specify the bus name and bus number that this bus is connected to by using the at keyword followed by:

- A character string that represents the bus name, for example:

  tc

  vba

- A number that represents the bus number, for example:

  vba0

  vba1

- A wildcard character (a question mark (?)) that represents the bus number, for example:

  vba?

You can also specify an asterisk (*) to indicate that the bus or controller connects to any bus. The following example shows an instance of controller type sii0 attached to any bus:

```
controller sii0 *
```

For static drivers, if the bus is the system bus, you use the nexus keyword. For loadable drivers, you never identify the system bus with this keyword because the autoconfiguration software always assumes there is a system bus. Because it is not valid for the system bus to be loadable, the keyword nexus is invalid for loadable drivers. You enter these values in the config.file file fragment or the system configuration file for static drivers and the stanza.loadable file fragment for loadable drivers.

Figure 7-6 shows the values in the example system configuration file that the autoconfiguration software parses to obtain the bus slot, bus connect name, and bus connect number for the system bus. The autoconfiguration software uses the nexus keyword to identify the system bus. Because the slot number is not specified in the system configuration file, the slot member of the system bus structure, tc0_struct, defaults to the value –1. Because the system bus is not connected to any other bus, the autoconfiguration software sets its connect_bus member to the null string and its connect_num member to the value –1.

Figure 7-6 also shows the values in the example system configuration file that the autoconfiguration software parses to obtain the bus slot, bus connect name, and bus connect number for the other specified buses. It uses the slot keyword to set the slot member for vba_struct and vba1_struct to the values 2 and 1. It also sets the connect_bus and connect_num members of vba_struct and vba1_struct to the values tc and zero (0).

The autoconfiguration software performs a similar parsing operation in the `sysconfigtab` database to obtain the bus slot, bus connect name, and bus connect number and to initialize the associated `slot`, `connect_bus`, and `connect_num` members. The only difference is that the autoconfiguration software locates the system bus by name (for example, the string `tc` represents a TURBOchannel bus), without using the `nexus` keyword.

Device driver writers seldom need to reference these members in their device drivers. However, bus adapter driver writers might reference these members in their bus adapter code.

Figure 7-6: The slot, connect_bus, and connect_num Members Initialized

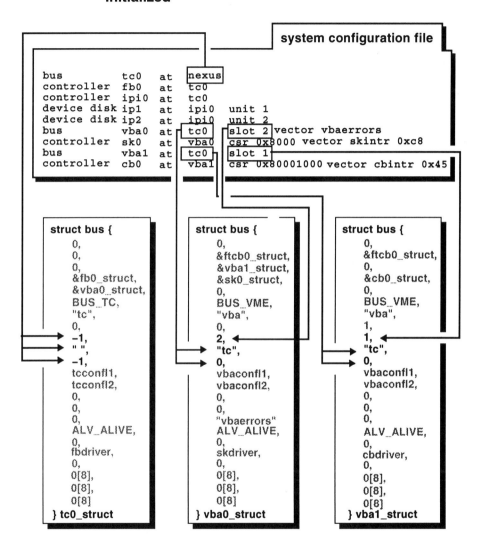

7.3.1.5 The confl1 and confl2 Members

The `confl1` member specifies a pointer to an entry point of the level 1 bus configuration interface. The `confl2` member specifies a pointer to an entry point of the level 2 bus configuration interface. These interfaces are not typically used by device driver writers, but by systems engineers who want to implement a configuration procedure for a specific bus.

Figure 7-7 shows that the autoconfiguration software initializes the `confl1` and `confl2` members of the `tc0_struct`, `vba0_struct`, and `vba1_struct` to their respective level 1 and level 2 bus configuration interfaces.

The autoconfiguration software obtains the names of these interfaces by using the bus name and appending the string `confl1` or `confl2`. Thus, `tcconfl1` and `tcconfl2` are the level 1 and level 2 bus configuration interfaces for the system bus, `tc0_struct`.

The autoconfiguration software performs a similar operation by using entries in the `sysconfigtab` database to initialize the `confl1` and `confl2` members of the associated `bus` structures.

Figure 7-7: The confl1 and confl2 Members Initialized

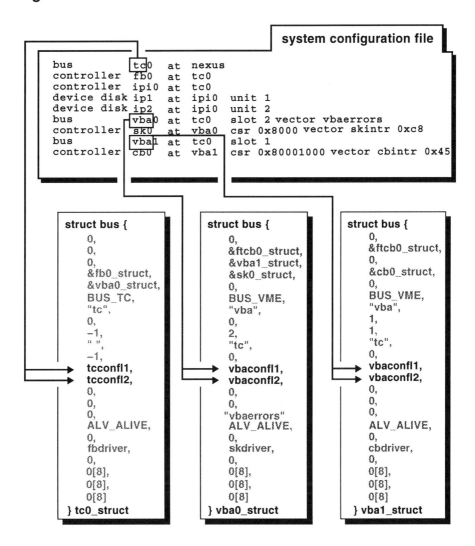

7.3.1.6 The pname and port Members

The `pname` member specifies a pointer to the port name for this bus, if applicable. The `port` member specifies a pointer to the `port` structure for this bus, if applicable.

You (or the system manager) specify the port name by using the `port` keyword followed by a string that represents the name of the port. You enter this keyword and string in the `config.file` file fragment or system configuration file for static drivers. This keyword is not currently supported for loadable drivers; therefore, you cannot specify it in the `stanza.loadable` file fragment.

Figure 7-8 shows that the autoconfiguration software sets these members for all of the structures to the value zero (0) to indicate that no port was specified in the system configuration file. If port names were specified, the autoconfiguration software would initialize the `pname` and `port` members for all of the example `bus` structures to the specified values.

Device driver writers do not reference these members in their device drivers. However, bus adapter writers use the `port` structure to implement the initialization for a class of devices or controllers that have common characteristics.

Figure 7-8: The pname and port Members Initialized

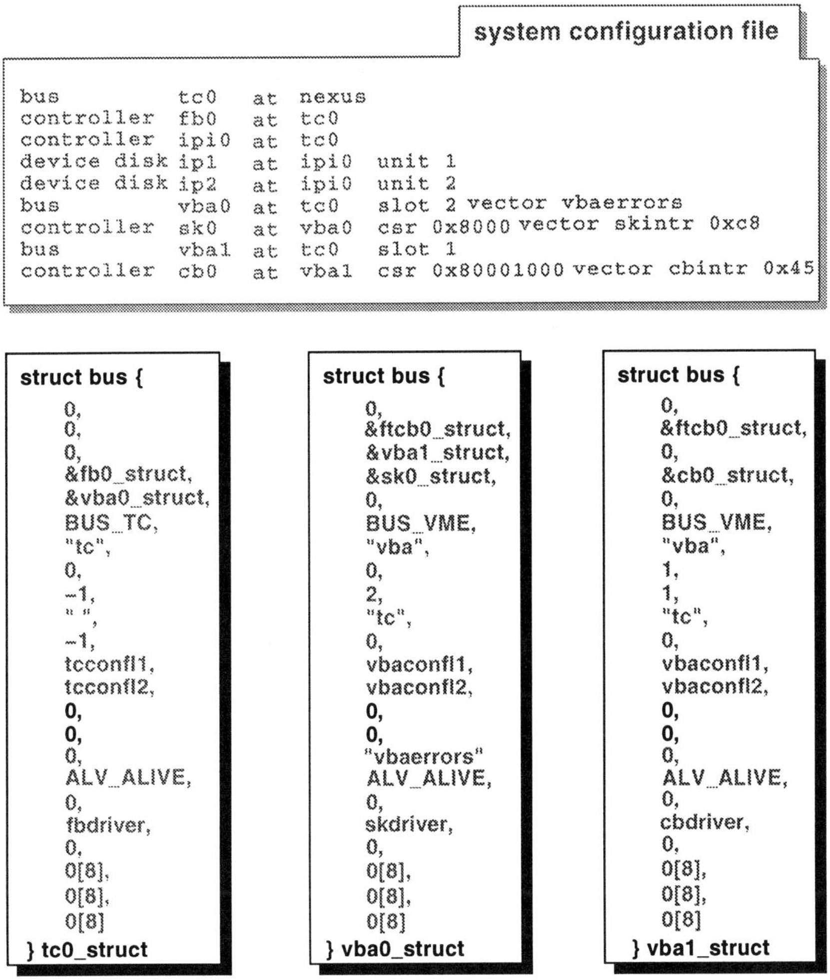

```
                                          ┌──────────────────────────┐
                                          │ system configuration file │
  ┌───────────────────────────────────────┴───────────────────────────────────┐
  │ bus          tc0    at   nexus                                              │
  │ controller   fb0    at   tc0                                                │
  │ controller   ipi0   at   tc0                                               │
  │ device disk  ip1    at   ipi0   unit 1                                     │
  │ device disk  ip2    at   ipi0   unit 2                                     │
  │ bus          vba0   at   tc0    slot 2 vector vbaerrors                    │
  │ controller   sk0    at   vba0   csr 0x8000 vector skintr 0xc8              │
  │ bus          vba1   at   tc0    slot 1                                     │
  │ controller   cb0    at   vba1   csr 0x80001000 vector cbintr 0x45          │
  └───────────────────────────────────────────────────────────────────────────┘
```

struct bus {	struct bus {	struct bus {
0,	0,	0,
0,	&ftcb0_struct,	&ftcb0_struct,
0,	&vba1_struct,	0,
&fb0_struct,	&sk0_struct,	&cb0_struct,
&vba0_struct,	0,	0,
BUS_TC,	BUS_VME,	BUS_VME,
"tc",	"vba",	"vba",
0,	0,	1,
–1,	2,	1,
" ",	"tc",	"tc",
–1,	0,	0,
tcconfl1,	vbaconfl1,	vbaconfl1,
tcconfl2,	vbaconfl2,	vbaconfl2,
0,	**0,**	**0,**
0,	**0,**	**0,**
0,	"vbaerrors"	0,
ALV_ALIVE,	ALV_ALIVE,	ALV_ALIVE,
0,	0,	0,
fbdriver,	skdriver,	cbdriver,
0,	0,	0,
0[8],	0[8],	0[8],
0[8],	0[8],	0[8],
0[8]	0[8]	0[8]
} tc0_struct	} vba0_struct	} vba1_struct

7.3.1.7 The intr Member

The intr member specifies an array that contains an entry point or points
for the bus interrupt interfaces. You specify the bus interrupt interface or
interfaces by using the vector keyword followed by a string that represents
the name of the bus interrupt interface. You enter this keyword and string in
the config.file file fragment or system configuration file for static
drivers.

A device driver knows the name of its bus interrupt interface. A device driver uses the `handler_add` and `handler_enable` interfaces to register its interrupt handlers.

Figure 7-9 shows that the autoconfiguration software initializes this member to the value `vbaerrors` for `vba0_struct`. The figure also shows that the autoconfiguration software initializes this member for all of the other structures in the example to the value zero (0) because there are no bus interrupt interfaces associated with these buses.

Device driver writers seldom need to reference this member in their device drivers. However, bus adapter driver writers might use this member in their bus adapter code to reference the interrupt handlers that handle error interrupts related to the bus.

Figure 7-9: The intr Member Initialized

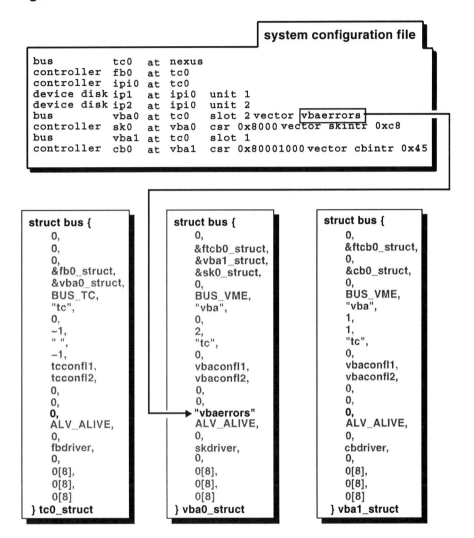

7.3.1.8 The alive Member

The `alive` member specifies a flag word to indicate the current status of the bus. The system sets this member to the bitwise inclusive OR of the valid alive bits defined in `devdriver.h`.

For the example system configuration file, Figure 7-10 shows that the autoconfiguration software initializes the `alive` member for all of the example `bus` structures to the ALV_ALIVE bit. This bit indicates that the device is present and configured on the system.

Similarly for loadable drivers, the autoconfiguration software (specifically, the ldbl_stanza_resolver interface) sets the alive member for any buses in the sysconfigtab database to the bitwise inclusive OR of the valid alive bits defined in devdriver.h. The following list shows the valid alive bits that loadable and static drivers can use:

ALV_FREE	The bus is not yet processed.
ALV_ALIVE	The bus is alive and configured.
ALV_PRES	The bus is present but not yet configured.
ALV_NOCNFG	The bus is not to be configured.
ALV_LOADABLE	The bus is present and resolved as loadable.
ALV_NOSIZER	The sizer program should ignore these bus structures. This bit is set for loadable drivers. It indicates that this bus structure is not part of the static configuration.

Figure 7-10: The alive Member Initialized

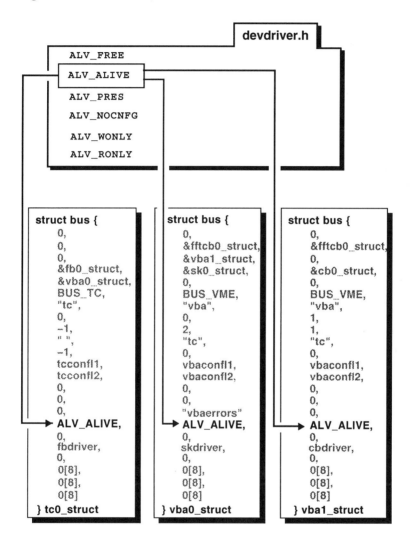

7.3.1.9 The framework and driver_name Members

The `framework` member specifies a pointer to the `bus_framework` structure. This structure contains pointers to bus interfaces for loadable device drivers. These interfaces provide dynamic extensions to bus functionality. They are used in the autoconfiguration of loadable drivers to perform bus-specific tasks, such as the registration of interrupt handlers. The `framework` member is initialized by the bus adapter driver. Device driver writers seldom need to reference this member in their device drivers.

However, bus adapter driver writers might reference this member in their bus adapter code.

The `driver_name` member specifies the name of the controlling device driver. For the example system configuration file, Figure 7-11 shows that the autoconfiguration software initializes the `driver_name` members for the example `bus` structures to the addresses of their respective controlling device drivers: `fbdriver`, `skdriver`, and `cbdriver`. The autoconfiguration software obtains the driver names by using the controller name and appending the string `driver` to it.

Similarly for loadable drivers, the autoconfiguration software sets the `driver_name` members to `xxdriver`, where `xx` is the driver name as specified by the `Module_Config_Name` field in the `stanza.loadable` file fragment. The following example shows one such entry:

```
      .
      .
      .
Module_Config_Name = cb
      .
      .
      .
```

In this case, the autoconfiguration software sets the `driver_name` member to `cbdriver`.

Device driver writers seldom need to reference this member in their device drivers. However, bus adapter driver writers might reference this member in their bus adapter code.

Figure 7-11: The framework and driver_name Members Initialized

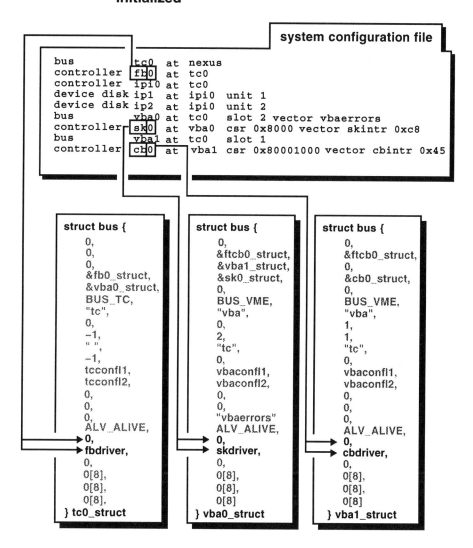

7.3.1.10 The bus_bridge_dma Member

The bus_bridge_dma member specifies that the bus adapter has direct memory access (DMA) mapping support. The bus_bridge_dma member is initialized by the bus adapter driver.

Device driver writers seldom need to reference this member in their device drivers. However, bus adapter driver writers might reference this member in their bus adapter code.

For the example system configuration file, Figure 7-12 shows that the autoconfiguration software initializes the `bus_bridge_dma` member for the example `bus` structures to the value zero (0) to indicate that these buses do not support DMA mapping.

Similarly for loadable drivers, the autoconfiguration software sets the `bus_bridge_dma` members to the value zero (0).

Figure 7-12: The bus_bridge_dma Member Initialized

```
                                                      system configuration file

bus           tc0    at   nexus
controller    fb0    at   tc0
controller    ipi0   at   tc0
device disk ip1      at   ipi0   unit 1
device disk ip2      at   ipi0   unit 2
bus           vba0   at   tc0     slot 2 vector vbaerrors
controller    sk0    at   vba0   csr 0x8000 vector skintr 0xc8
bus           vba1   at   tc0     slot 1
controller    cb0    at   vba1   csr 0x80001000 vector cbintr 0x45
```

```
struct bus {                  struct bus {                  struct bus {
    0,                            0,                            0,
    0,                            &ftcb0_struct,                &ftcb0_struct,
    0,                            &vba1_struct,                 0,
    &fb0_struct,                  &sk0_struct,                  &cb0_struct,
    &vba0_struct,                 0,                            0,
    BUS_TC,                       BUS_VME,                      BUS_VME,
    "tc",                         "vba",                        "vba",
    0,                            0,                            1,
    -1,                           2,                            1,
    " ",                          "tc",                         "tc",
    -1,                           0,                            0,
    tcconfl1,                     vbaconfl1,                    vbaconfl1,
    tcconfl2,                     vbaconfl2,                    vbaconfl2,
    0,                            0,                            0,
    0,                            0,                            0,
    0,                            "vbaerrors"                   0,
    ALV_ALIVE,                    ALV_ALIVE,                    ALV_ALIVE,
    0,                            0,                            0,
    fbdriver,                     skdriver,                     cbdriver,
    0,                            0,                            0,
    0[8],                         0[8],                         0[8],
    0[8],                         0[8],                         0[8],
    0[8]                          0[8]                          0[8]
} tc0_struct                  } vba0_struct                 } vba1_struct
```

7.3.1.11   The private, conn_priv, and rsvd Members

The private member specifies private storage for use by this bus or bus class. The conn_priv member specifies private storage for use by the bus that this bus is connected to. The rsvd member is reserved for future expansion of the data structure.

For the example system configuration file, Figure 7-13 shows that the system initializes these members for all of the structures to the value zero (0). The code controlling the bus can use these members for any storage purposes. The `conn_priv` member is often used by TURBOchannel bus adapter writers as an index to the `tc_option` array.

Figure 7-13: The private, conn_priv, and rsvd Members Initialized

```
                                          system configuration file

bus          tc0    at   nexus
controller   fb0    at   tc0
controller   ipi0   at   tc0
device disk  ip1    at   ipi0   unit 1
device disk  ip2    at   ipi0   unit 2
bus          vba0   at   tc0    slot 2 vector vbaerrors
controller   sk0    at   vba0   csr 0x8000 vector skintr 0xc8
bus          vba1   at   tc0    slot 1
controller   cb0    at   vba1   csr 0x80001000 vector cbintr 0x45
```

struct bus {	struct bus {	struct bus {
0,	0,	0,
0,	&ftcb0_struct,	&ftcb0_struct,
0,	&vba1_struct,	0,
&fb0_struct,	&sk0_struct,	&cb0_struct,
&vba0_struct,	0,	0,
BUS_TC,	BUS_VME,	BUS_VME,
"tc",	"vba",	"vba",
0,	0,	1,
-1,	2,	1,
" ",	"tc",	"tc",
-1,	0,	0,
tcconfl1,	vbaconfl1,	vbaconfl1,
tcconfl2,	vbaconfl2,	vbaconfl2,
0,	0,	0,
0,	0,	0,
0,	"vbaerrors"	0,
ALV_ALIVE,	ALV_ALIVE,	ALV_ALIVE,
0,	0,	0,
fbdriver,	skdriver,	cbdriver,
0,	0,	0,
0[8],	0[8],	0[8],
0[8],	0[8],	0[8],
0[8]	0[8]	0[8]
} tc0_struct	} vba0_struct	} vba1_struct

7.3.2 The controller Structure

The controller structure represents an instance of a controller entity, one that connects logically to a bus. A controller can control devices that are directly connected or can perform some other controlling operation, such as a network interface or terminal controller operation.

You (or the system manager) specify a controller entity as follows:

- For static drivers

  Specify a valid syntax for the controller in the config.file file fragment or the system configuration file.

- For loadable drivers

  Specify a valid syntax for the controller in the stanza.loadable file fragment.

Chapter 11 discusses the device driver configuration models. Chapter 12 describes the valid syntaxes for a controller specification. Chapter 13 provides examples of how to configure device drivers.

Table 7-2 lists the members of the controller structure along with their associated data types.

Table 7-2: Members of the controller Structure

Member Name	Data Type
ctlr_mbox	u_long *
bus_hd	struct bus *
nxt_ctlr	struct controller *
dev_list	struct device *
driver	struct driver *
ctlr_type	int
ctlr_name	char *
ctlr_num	int
bus_name	char *
bus_num	int
rctlr	int
slot	int
alive	int
pname	char *

Table 7-2: (continued)

Member Name	Data Type
port	struct port *
intr	int (**intr)()
addr	caddr_t
addr2	caddr_t
flags	int
bus_priority	int
ivnum	int
priority	int
cmd	int
physaddr	caddr_t
physaddr2	caddr_t
private	void * [8]
conn_priv	void * [8]
rsvd	void * [8]

The following sections discuss all of these members except for bus_hd, nxt_ctlr, and dev_list, which are presented in Section 7.2.1.6. Chapter 16 provides a reference (man) page-style description of this data structure.

7.3.2.1 The ctlr_mbox Member

The ctlr_mbox member specifies a pointer to the mailbox data structure for hardware platforms that access I/O space through hardware mailboxes. The bus adapter code sets this member. As the adapter code probes the buses, the first bus that has a mailbox allocates the initial software mailbox data structure and sets its bus_mbox pointer to that data structure. As the adapter code continues to probe for buses and controllers, the MBOX_GET macro allocates the ctlr_mbox members for devices accessed by mailboxes. Typically, this macro is called in the controller configuration interface after the controller data structure has been found, but before probing the controller.

The following code fragment gives an idea of the tasks that occur prior to calling the MBOX_GET macro:

```
config_con(name, node, bus)
{
    register struct controller *ctlr;

    if((ctlr = get_ctlr(name, node, bus->bus_name, bus->bus_num)) ||
        /* other wildcards here */
       (ctlr = get_ctlr(name, -1, "*", -99))) {
    .
    .
    .
       }

/*******************************************************
* Found the controller                                *
*******************************************************/

        int savebusnum;
        char *savebusname;
        int saveslot;

        if(ctlr->alive & ALV_ALIVE) {
                printf("config_con: %s%d alive0,
                    ctlr->ctlr_name, ctlr->ctlr_num);
                return(stat);
        }
        savebusnum = ctlr->bus_num;
        savebusname = ctlr->bus_name;
        saveslot = ctlr->slot;
        ctlr->bus_name = bus->bus_name;
        ctlr->bus_num = bus->bus_num;
        ctlr->slot = node;

/*******************************************************
*           Allocate and initialize a software       *
*           mailbox data structure for the           *
*           controller if it is attached to a        *
*           bus that is accessed by mailboxes        *
*******************************************************/
        MBOX_GET(bus, ctlr);

/*******************************************************
* Now get the controller's driver structure          *
* and probe                                           *
*******************************************************/
    .
    .
    .
}
```

7.3.2.2 The driver Member

The driver member specifies a pointer to the driver structure for this controller. The device driver writer initializes a driver structure, usually in the Declarations Section of the driver.

For the example system configuration file, Figure 7-14 shows that the autoconfiguration software initializes the `driver` member for the example `controller` structures to their following respective controlling device drivers: `fbdriver`, `ipidriver`, `skdriver`, and `cbdriver`. The autoconfiguration software obtains the driver names by using the keyword for the controller and appending the string `driver` to it.

Similarly for loadable drivers, the driver writer provides the device driver name in the Configure Section of the device driver by calling the `ldbl_stanza_resolver` and `ldbl_ctlr_configure` interfaces. Thus, the autoconfiguration software sets the `driver` members for any controllers specified in the `sysconfigtab` database to the name specified by the driver writer.

Figure 7-14: The driver Member Initialized

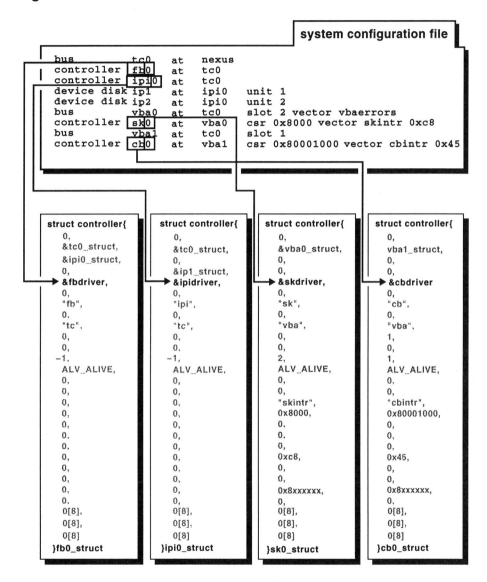

7.3.2.3 The ctlr_type, ctlr_name, and ctlr_num Members

The `ctlr_type` member specifies the controller type. The `ctlr_name` member specifies the controller name. The `ctlr_num` member specifies the controller number.

The ctlr_type member is not currently used by the autoconfiguration software. Thus, Figure 7-15 shows that in the example system configuration file, the autoconfiguration software initializes the ctlr_type members for the example controller structures to the value zero (0).

You (or the system manager) specify the controller name and the controller number by using the controller keyword followed by a character string and number that represent the controller name and controller number. You enter these values in the config.file file fragment or the system configuration file for static drivers and the stanza.loadable file fragment for loadable drivers. For example, fb0 specifies a graphics frame buffer controller with a controller number of zero (0).

Figure 7-15 shows the values in the example system configuration file that the autoconfiguration software parses to obtain the controller name and controller number. It also shows that the autoconfiguration software sets the ctlr_name and ctlr_num members to these values for fb0_struct, ipi0_struct, sk0_struct, and cb0_struct.

The autoconfiguration software performs a similar parsing operation in the sysconfigtab database for loadable drivers to obtain the controller name and controller number and to initialize the associated ctlr_name and ctlr_num members.

Driver writers are unlikely to use the ctlr_name member. Driver writers often use the ctlr_num member as an index to identify which instance of the controller the request is for. The /dev/none and /dev/cb device drivers illustrate the use of the ctlr_num member.

Figure 7-15: The ctlr_type, ctlr_name, and ctlr_num Members Initialized

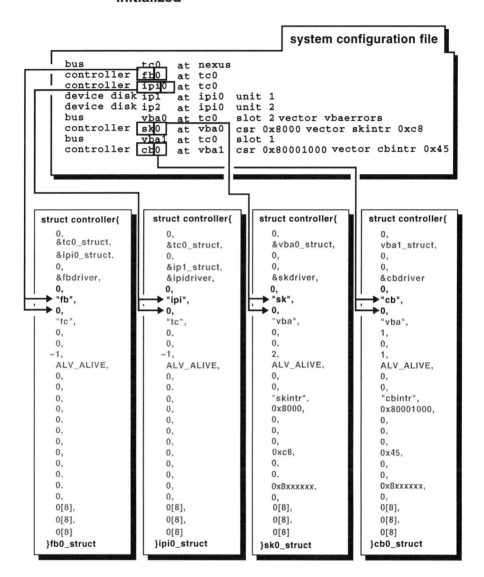

7.3.2.4 The bus_name and bus_num Members

The bus_name member specifies the name of the bus to which this controller is connected. The bus_num member specifies the number of the bus to which the controller is connected.

You (or the system manager) specify the bus name and the bus number by using the `at` keyword followed by a character string and number that represent the bus name and bus number. You enter these values in the `config.file` file fragment or the system configuration file for static drivers and the `stanza.loadable` file fragment for loadable drivers. For example, `tc0` specifies a TURBOchannel bus with a bus number of zero (0).

Figure 7-16 shows the values in the example system configuration file that the autoconfiguration software parses to obtain the bus name and bus number. It also shows that the autoconfiguration software sets the `bus_name` and `bus_num` members to these values for `fb0_struct`, `ipi0_struct`, `sk0_struct`, and `cb0_struct`.

The autoconfiguration software performs a similar parsing operation in the `sysconfigtab` database for loadable drivers to obtain the bus name and bus number and to initialize the associated `bus_name` and `bus_num` members.

Device driver writers seldom need to reference these members in their device drivers. However, bus adapter driver writers might reference these members in their bus adapter code.

Figure 7-16: The bus_name and bus_num Members Initialized

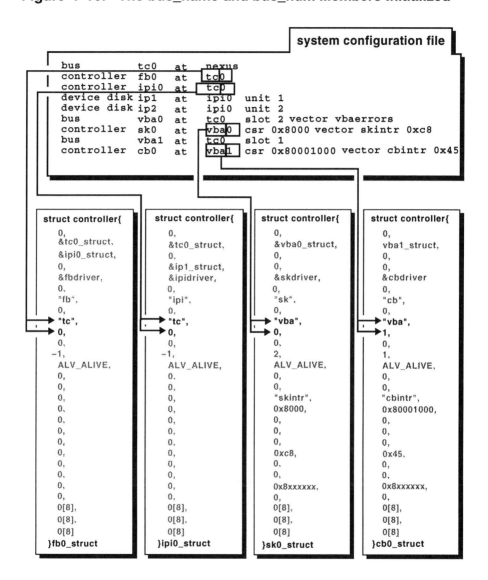

7.3.2.5 The rctlr Member

The `rctlr` member specifies the remote controller number (for example, the SCSI ID).

You (or the system manager) specify the remote controller number by using the `rctlr` keyword followed by a number. You enter this keyword and number in the `config.file` file fragment or system configuration file for static drivers and the `stanza.loadable` file fragment for loadable drivers.

Figure 7-17 shows that the example system configuration file does not contain an entry for the remote controller. Therefore, the autoconfiguration software sets this member to the value zero (0) for each of the controller structures.

Figure 7-17: The rctlr Member Initialized

```
                                    system configuration file

   bus          tc0    at    nexus
   controller   fb0    at    tc0
   controller   ipi0   at    tc0
   device disk  ip1    at    ipi0    unit 1
   device disk  ip2    at    ipi0    unit 2
   bus          vba0   at    tc0     slot 2 vector vbaerrors
   controller   sk0    at    vba0    csr 0x8000 vector skintr 0xc8
   bus          vba1   at    tc0     slot 1
   controller   cb0    at    vba1    csr 0x80001000 vector cbintr 0x45
```

struct controller{	struct controller{	struct controller{	struct controller{
0,	0,	0,	0,
&tc0_struct,	&tc0_struct,	&vba0_struct,	vba1_struct,
&ipi0_struct,	0,	0,	0,
0,	&ip1_struct,	0,	0,
&fbdriver,	&ipidriver,	&skdriver,	&cbdriver
0,	0,	0,	0,
"fb",	"ipi",	"sk",	"cb",
0,	0,	0,	0,
"tc",	"tc",	"vba",	"vba",
0,	0,	0,	1,
0,	**0,**	**0,**	**0,**
-1,	-1,	2,	1,
ALV_ALIVE,	ALV_ALIVE,	ALV_ALIVE,	ALV_ALIVE,
0,	0,	0,	0,
0,	0,	0,	0,
0,	0,	"skintr",	"cbintr",
0,	0,	0x8000,	0x80001000,
0,	0,	0,	0,
0,	0,	0,	0,
0,	0,	0xc8,	0x45,
0,	0,	0,	0,
0,	0,	0,	0,
0,	0,	0x8xxxxxx,	0x8xxxxxx,
0,	0,	0,	0,
0[8],	0[8],	0[8],	0[8],
0[8],	0[8],	0[8],	0[8],
0[8]	0[8]	0[8]	0[8]
}fb0_struct	}ipi0_struct	}sk0_struct	}cb0_struct

7.3.2.6 The slot Member

The slot member specifies the bus slot or node number. Figure 7-18 shows
that the example system configuration file does not contain an entry for the
slot. Because no slots were specified for the controllers connected to these
buses, the kernel sets the slot member to the value −1 for each of the
controller structures.

Figure 7-18: The slot Member Initialized

```
                         system configuration file

bus           tc0    at   nexus
controller    fb0    at   tc0
controller    ipi0   at   tc0
device disk ip1      at   ipi0    unit 1
device disk ip2      at   ipi0    unit 2
bus           vba0   at   tc0     slot 2 vector vbaerrors
controller    sk0    at   vba0    csr 0x8000 vector skintr 0xc8
bus           vba1   at   tc0     slot 1
controller    cb0    at   vba1    csr 0x80001000 vector cbintr 0x45
```

struct controller{	struct controller{	struct controller{	struct controller{
0,	0,	0,	0,
&tc0_struct,	&tc0_struct,	&vba0_struct,	vba1_struct,
&ipi0_struct,	0,	0,	0,
0,	&ip1_struct,	0,	0,
&fbdriver,	&ipidriver,	&skdriver,	&cbdriver
0,	0,	0,	0,
"fb",	"ipi",	"sk",	"cb",
0,	0,	0,	0,
"tc",	"tc",	"vba",	"vba",
0,	0,	0,	1,
0,	0,	0,	0,
−1,	−1,	−1,	−1,
ALV_ALIVE,	ALV_ALIVE,	ALV_ALIVE,	ALV_ALIVE,
0,	0,	0,	0,
0,	0,	0,	0,
0,	0,	"skintr",	"cbintr",
0,	0,	0x8000,	0x80001000,
0,	0,	0,	0,
0,	0,	0,	0,
0,	0,	0,	0,
0,	0,	0xc8,	0x45,
0,	0,	0,	0,
0,	0,	0,	0,
0,	0,	0x8xxxxxx,	0x8xxxxxx,
0,	0,	0,	0,
0[8],	0[8],	0[8],	0[8],
0[8],	0[8],	0[8],	0[8],
0[8]	0[8]	0[8]	0[8]
}fb0_struct	}ipi0_struct	}sk0_struct	}cb0_struct

7.3.2.7   The alive Member

The alive member specifies a flag word to indicate the current status of the
controller. Figure 7-19 shows that the autoconfiguration software sets the
alive member for all of the example controller structures to the
ALV_ALIVE bit. The autoconfiguration software obtains this and the other
alive bits in the file devdriver.h.

Similarly for loadable drivers, the autoconfiguration software (specifically, the `ldbl_stanza_resolver` interface) sets the `alive` member for any controllers in the `sysconfigtab` database to the bitwise inclusive OR of the valid alive bits defined in `devdriver.h`. The following list shows the valid alive bits that loadable and static drivers can use:

ALV_FREE	The controller is not yet processed.
ALV_ALIVE	The controller is alive and configured.
ALV_PRES	The controller is present but not yet configured.
ALV_NOCNFG	The controller is not to be configured.
ALV_LOADABLE	The controller is present and resolved as loadable.
ALV_NOSIZER	The `sizer` program should ignore these `controller` structures. This bit is set for loadable drivers. It indicates that this `controller` structure is not part of the static configuration.
ALV_RONLY	The device is read only. This bit is set for static drivers if the corresponding entry is specified in the `stanza.static` file fragment or system configuration file. This bit is not supported for loadable drivers.
ALV_WONLY	The device is write only. This bit is set for static drivers if the corresponding entry is specified in the `stanza.static` file fragment or system configuration file. This bit is not supported for loadable drivers.

Digital does not make use of the functionality associated with the ALV_RONLY and ALV_WONLY bits. However, the `config` program supports the functionality for third-party driver writers who test for the bits and perform the corresponding logic.

The following examples show situations where third-party driver writers could use the functionality associated with the ALV_RONLY and ALV_WONLY bits:

- You might be implementing a device driver to handle a disk that can be write protected (logically) much the same way as a write-protect button works. Because SCSI disks do not have write-protect buttons, the entry in the system configuration file or `stanza.static` file fragment could look like this:

```
readonly device disk rz7 at asc0 drive 56
```

- You might now have a device that crashes the system every time the system probes it while booting in multiuser mode. You suspect a hardware problem with a disk and you are waiting for field service, but you need the system immediately. However, you do not know if the bad disk is in the critical path. One solution is to mark the disk as not to be configured in the system configuration file, build a kernel, and boot in multiuser mode until field service fixes the problem. Following is the entry in the system configuration file:

```
not device disk rz6 at asc0 drive 55
```

- The following entry in the system configuration file passes a flag to the driver indicating that a terminal device is for display only, will not accept input, and is a write-only device:

```
writeonly device dmb0 at vaxbi? node? flags 0xff
vector dmbsint dmbaint dmblint
```

Figure 7-19: The alive Member Initialized

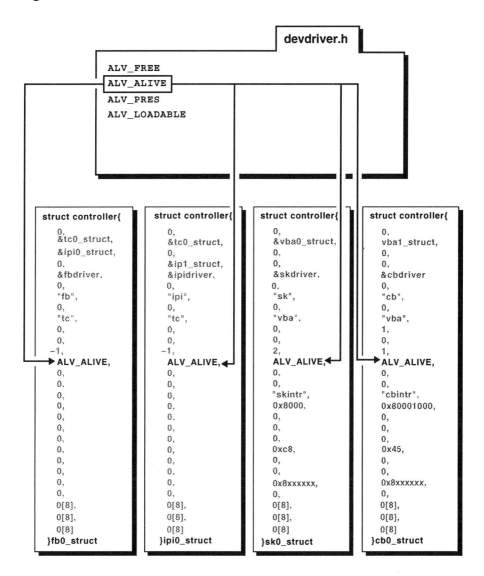

7.3.2.8 The pname and port Members

The pname member specifies a pointer to the port name for this controller, if applicable. The port member specifies a pointer to the port structure for this controller, if applicable.

You (or the system manager) specify the port name by using the `port` keyword followed by a string that represents the name of the port. You enter this keyword and string in the `config.file` file fragment or system configuration file for static drivers. This keyword is not currently supported for loadable drivers; therefore, you cannot specify it in the `stanza.loadable` file fragment.

Figure 7-20 shows that the autoconfiguration software sets these members for all of the structures to the value zero (0) to indicate that no port was specified in the system configuration file. If port names were specified, the autoconfiguration software would initialize the `pname` and `port` members for all of the example `controller` structures to the specified values.

Device driver writers do not reference these members in their device drivers. However, bus adapter writers use the `port` structure to implement the initialization for a class of devices or controllers that have common characteristics.

Figure 7-20: The pname and port Members Initialized

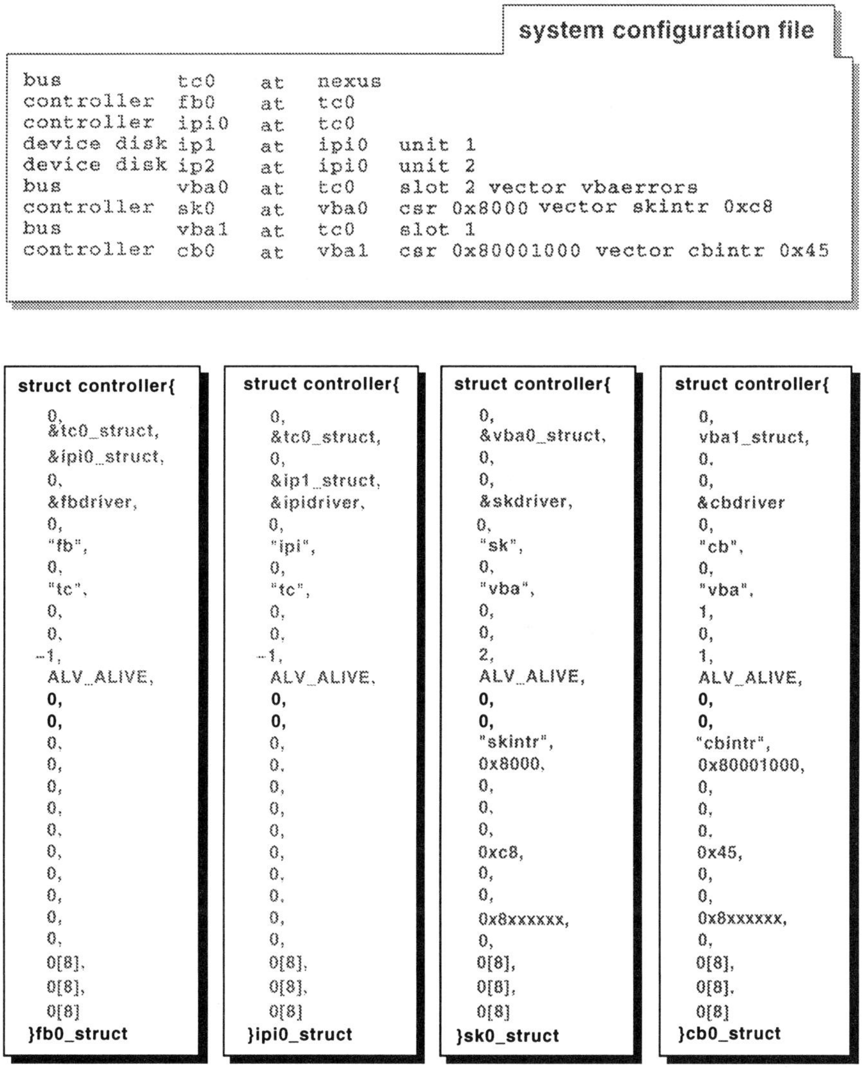

```
                                        ┌──────────────────────────────┐
                                        │  system configuration file   │
┌────────────────────────────────────────┴──────────────────────────────┴──┐
│ bus         tc0    at   nexus                                              │
│ controller  fb0    at   tc0                                               │
│ controller  ipi0   at   tc0                                               │
│ device disk ip1    at   ipi0    unit 1                                     │
│ device disk ip2    at   ipi0    unit 2                                     │
│ bus         vba0   at   tc0     slot 2 vector vbaerrors                    │
│ controller  sk0    at   vba0    csr 0x8000 vector skintr 0xc8              │
│ bus         vba1   at   tc0     slot 1                                     │
│ controller  cb0    at   vba1    csr 0x80001000 vector cbintr 0x45          │
└───────────────────────────────────────────────────────────────────────────┘
```

struct controller{	struct controller{	struct controller{	struct controller{
0,	0,	0,	0,
&tc0_struct,	&tc0_struct,	&vba0_struct,	vba1_struct,
&ipi0_struct,	0,	0,	0,
0,	&ip1_struct,	0,	0,
&fbdriver,	&ipidriver,	&skdriver,	&cbdriver
0,	0,	0,	0,
"fb",	"ipi",	"sk",	"cb",
0,	0,	0,	0,
"tc",	"tc",	"vba",	"vba",
0,	0,	0,	1,
0,	0,	0,	0,
-1,	-1,	2,	1,
ALV_ALIVE,	ALV_ALIVE,	ALV_ALIVE,	ALV_ALIVE,
0,	0,	0,	0,
0,	0,	0,	0,
0,	0,	"skintr",	"cbintr",
0,	0,	0x8000,	0x80001000,
0,	0,	0,	0,
0,	0,	0,	0,
0,	0,	0,	0,
0,	0,	0xc8,	0x45,
0,	0,	0,	0,
0,	0,	0,	0,
0,	0,	0x8xxxxxx,	0x8xxxxxx,
0,	0,	0,	0,
0[8],	0[8],	0[8],	0[8],
0[8],	0[8],	0[8],	0[8],
0[8]	0[8]	0[8]	0[8]
}fb0_struct	}ipi0_struct	}sk0_struct	}cb0_struct

7.3.2.9 The intr Member

The intr member specifies an array that contains one or more entry points
for the controller interrupt service interfaces. Figure 7-21 shows that the
autoconfiguration software initializes the intr members to skintr for
sk0_struct and cbintr for cb0_struct. The autoconfiguration
software obtains these names following the vector keyword in the example

system configuration file.

For loadable drivers and for the static version of the drivers associated with the fb0 and ipi0 controllers, the intr members of these data structures would be set up indirectly through calls to the handler_add interface.

Note

In previous versions of the Digital UNIX operating system (formerly known as DEC OSF/1), the example system configuration file specified the interrupt service interfaces (ISIs) fbintr and ipiintr for the fb0 and ipi0 controllers. The example system configuration file does not specify these ISIs in the Digital UNIX operating system. The drivers associated with these controllers register their ISIs by calling the handler interfaces, usually in the Autoconfiguration Support Section.

Some buses (for example, the TURBOchannel bus) support two methods for registering ISIs: through the system configuration file and by calling the handler interfaces. Other buses (for example, the PCI bus) support registration of ISIs by calling only the handler interfaces.

The example system configuration file continues to specify the ISIs for the sk0 and the cb0 controllers to show the differences. See the bus-specific driver book to determine which methods the bus your driver operates on supports.

Digital recommends that all new drivers (and all previously written static drivers that you want to make loadable) register ISIs by calling the handler interfaces. Section 7.5 describes the data structures that device drivers use to dynamically register ISIs. Section 9.6 provides examples of how to dynamically register ISIs by calling the handler interfaces. In addition, the static versions of the /dev/none and /dev/cb drivers dynamically register their ISIs by calling the handler interfaces instead of specifying them in the system configuration file.

Figure 7-21: The intr Member Initialized

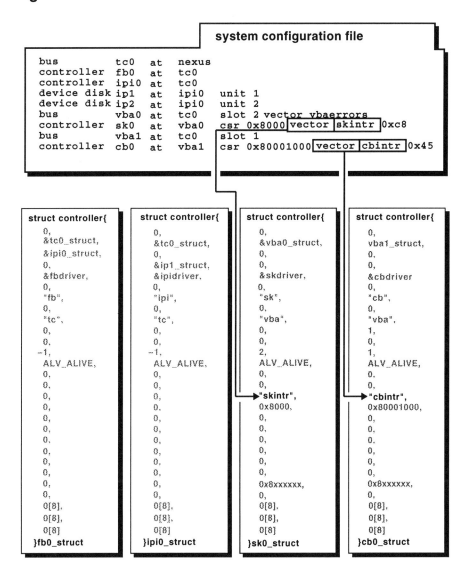

7.3.2.10   The addr and addr2 Members

The addr member specifies the address of the device registers or memory.
Figure 7-22 shows that the autoconfiguration software uses the value
following the csr keyword in the system configuration file to obtain the
address. This address is the first control status register (CSR) for the CPU.
Thus, the autoconfiguration software initializes the addr member to the

value zero (0) for `fb0_struct` and `ipi0_struct` because no CSR addresses were specified. It initializes the `addr` members for `sk0_struct` and `cb0_struct` to the values 0x8000 and 0x80001000.

The `addr2` member specifies an optional second virtual address for this controller. This member is set if there are two CSR spaces. Figure 7-22 shows that because no second CSR address was specified, the autoconfiguration software initializes all of the `addr2` members to the value zero (0). The autoconfiguration software would obtain the second CSR address from the `csr2` keyword.

Note that the addresses that appear in these members may not be the values specified in the system configuration file because the kernel could perform an address-mapping operation to produce different values.

Figure 7-22: The addr and addr2 Members Initialized

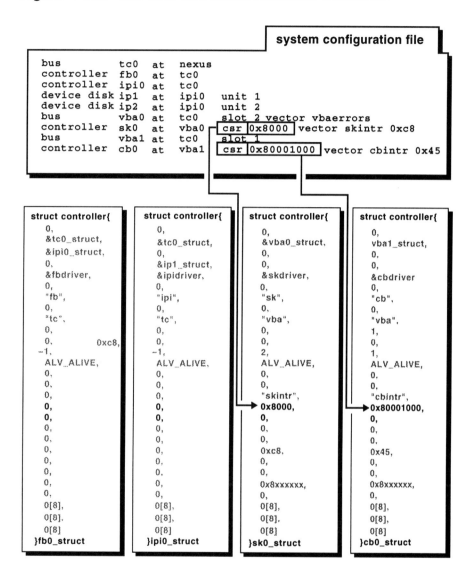

7.3.2.11 The flags Member

The flags member specifies controller-specific flags. The driver writer (or system manager) can specify controller-specific flags by using the flags keyword. Thus, the autoconfiguration software initializes the flags member with the value that follows the flags keyword in the system configuration file.

Figure 7-23 shows that, because no controller-specific flags were specified in the example system configuration file, the autoconfiguration software initializes the `flags` members for all of the `controller` structures to the value zero (0).

Figure 7-23: The flags Member Initialized

```
                                            system configuration file

bus          tc0    at    nexus
controller   fb0    at    tc0
controller   ipi0   at    tc0
device disk ip1     at    ipi0   unit 1
device disk ip2     at    ipi0   unit 2
bus          vba0   at    tc0    slot 2 vector vbaerrors
controller   sk0    at    vba0   csr 0x8000 vector skintr 0xc8
bus          vba1   at    tc0    slot 1
controller   cb0    at    vba1   csr 0x80001000 vector cbintr 0x45
```

struct controller{	struct controller{	struct controller{	struct controller{
0,	0,	0,	0,
&tc0_struct,	&tc0_struct,	&vba0_struct,	vba1_struct,
&ipi0_struct,	0,	0,	0,
0,	&ip1_struct,	0,	0,
&fbdriver,	&ipidriver,	&skdriver,	&cbdriver
0,	0,	0,	0,
"fb",	"ipi",	"sk",	"cb",
0,	0,	0,	0,
"tc",	"tc",	"vba",	"vba",
0,	0,	0,	1,
0,	0,	0,	0,
-1,	-1,	2,	1,
ALV_ALIVE,	ALV_ALIVE,	ALV_ALIVE,	ALV_ALIVE,
0,	0,	0,	0.
0,	0,	0,	0.
0,	0,	"skintr",	"cbintr",
0,	0.	0x8000,	0x80001000,
0,	0,	0,	0,
0,	**0,**	**0,**	**0,**
0,	0,	0,	0.
0,	0,	0xc8,	0x45,
0,	0.	0,	0,
0,	0,	0,	0,
0,	0,	0x8xxxxxx,	0x8xxxxxx,
		0,	0,
0[8],	0[8],	0[8],	0[8].
0[8],	0[8],	0[8],	0[8],
0[8]	0[8]	0[8]	0[8]
}fb0_struct	}ipi0_struct	}sk0_struct	}cb0_struct

7.3.2.12 The bus_priority Member

The `bus_priority` member specifies the configured VMEbus priority level of the device. Only drivers operating on the VMEbus use this member. You (or the system manager) can specify the bus priority by using the `priority` keyword . Thus, the autoconfiguration software initializes the `bus_priority` member with the value that follows the `priority` keyword in the system configuration file.

Figure 7-24 shows that because no bus priorities were specified in the example system configuration file, the autoconfiguration software initializes the `bus_priority` members for all of the `controller` structures to the value zero (0).

Figure 7-24: The bus_priority Member Initialized

```
                                          ┌─────────────────────────────────┐
                                          │   system configuration file     │
                                          │                                 │
 bus         tc0   at   nexus             │                                 │
 controller  fb0   at   tc0                                                  │
 controller  ipi0  at   tc0                                                  │
 device disk ip1   at   ipi0  unit 1                                         │
 device disk ip2   at   ipi0  unit 2                                         │
 bus         vba0  at   tc0   slot 2 vector vbaerrors                        │
 controller  sk0   at   vba0  csr 0x8000 vector skintr 0xc8                  │
 bus         vba1  at   tc0   slot 1                                         │
 controller  cb0   at   vba1  csr 0x80001000 vector cbintr 0x45             │
```

struct controller{	struct controller{	struct controller{	struct controller{
0,	0,	0,	0,
&tc0_struct,	&tc0_struct,	&vba0_struct,	vba1_struct,
&ipi0_struct,	0,	0,	0,
0,	&ip1_struct,	0,	0,
&fbdriver,	&ipidriver,	&skdriver,	&cbdriver
0,	0,	0,	0,
"fb",	"ipi",	"sk",	"cb",
0,	0,	0,	0,
"tc",	"tc",	"vba",	"vba",
0,	0,	0,	1,
0,	0,	0,	0,
-1,	-1,	2,	1,
ALV_ALIVE,	ALV_ALIVE,	ALV_ALIVE,	ALV_ALIVE,
0,	0,	0,	0,
0,	0,	0,	0,
0,	0,	"skintr",	"cbintr",
0,	0,	0x8000,	0x80001000,
0,	0,	0,	0,
0,	0,	0,	0,
0,	0,	0,	0,
0,	0,	0xc8,	0x45,
0,	0,	0,	0,
0,	0,	0,	0,
0,	0,	0x8xxxxxx,	0x8xxxxxx,
0,	0,	0,	0,
0[8],	0[8],	0[8],	0[8],
0[8],	0[8],	0[8],	0[8],
0[8]	0[8]	0[8]	0[8]
}fb0_struct	}ipi0_struct	}sk0_struct	}cb0_struct

7.3.2.13   The ivnum Member

The ivnum member specifies an interrupt vector number. Only drivers operating on the VMEbus use this member. The device driver writer can specify an interrupt vector number after the interrupt interface in the system configuration file. Thus, the autoconfiguration software initializes the ivnum member with the value that follows the interrupt interface in the system configuration file.

Figure 7-25 shows the values in the example system configuration file that the autoconfiguration software parses to obtain the interrupt vector numbers. It also shows that the autoconfiguration software sets the ivnum members to these values for sk0_struct and cb0_struct. Because no interrupt vector numbers were specified in the example system configuration file for fb0_struct and ipi0_struct, the autoconfiguration software initializes their ivnum members to the value zero (0).

Note

VMEbus device drivers (static and loadable) support two methods for registering interrupt service interfaces (ISIs): through the system configuration file and by calling the handler interfaces. If the skdriver and cbdriver drivers called the handler interfaces to register their ISIs, then the ISIs and the associated interrupt vector numbers would not appear in the system configuration file. In this case, the autoconfiguration software sets the ivnum members for the sk0_struct and cb0_struct structures to the value zero (0).

Figure 7-25: The ivnum Member Initialized

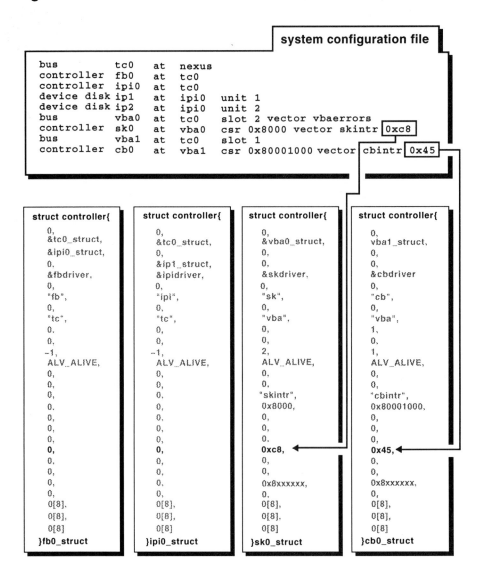

7.3.2.14 The priority Member

The `priority` member specifies the system priority level (spl) to block interrupts from this device. Only drivers operating on the VMEbus use this member. Thus, the autoconfiguration software initializes the `priority` member with an appropriate value based on the value stored in the `bus_priority` member (if specified) and the system implementation.

You use this value as an argument to the `splx` interface to block interrupts for the device. Thus, the autoconfiguration software initializes the `priority` member with an appropriate value based on the value stored in the `bus_priority` member (if specified) and the system implementation. The driver writer uses this value as an argument to the `splx` interface to block interrupts for the device. Figure 7-26 shows that the autoconfiguration software sets the members for all of the `controller` structures to the value zero (0).

Figure 7-26: The priority Member Initialized

```
                                              system configuration file

bus           tc0    at    nexus
controller    fb0    at    tc0
controller    ipi0   at    tc0
device disk   ip1    at    ipi0    unit 1
device disk   ip2    at    ipi0    unit 2
bus           vba0   at    tc0     slot 2 vector vbaerrors
controller    sk0    at    vba0    csr 0x8000 vector skintr 0xc8
bus           vba1   at    tc0     slot 1
controller    cb0    at    vba1    csr 0x80001000 vector cbintr 0x45
```

struct controller{	struct controller{	struct controller{	struct controller{
0,	0,	0,	0,
&tc0_struct,	&tc0_struct,	&vba0_struct,	vba1_struct,
&ipi0_struct,	0,	0,	0,
0,	&ip1_struct,	0,	0,
&fbdriver,	&ipidriver,	&skdriver,	&cbdriver
0,	0,	0,	0,
"fb",	"ipi",	"sk",	"cb",
0,	0,	0,	0,
"tc",	"tc",	"vba".	"vba",
0,	0,	0,	1,
0,	0,	0,	0,
-1,	-1,	2,	1,
ALV_ALIVE,	ALV_ALIVE,	ALV_ALIVE,	ALV_ALIVE,
0,	0,	0,	0,
0,	0,	0,	0,
0,	0,	"skintr",	"cbintr",
0,	0,	0x8000,	0x80001000,
0,	0,	0,	0,
0,	0,	0,	0,
0,	0,	0,	0,
0,	0,	0xc8,	0x45,
0,	**0,**	**0,**	**0,**
0,	0,	0,	0,
0,	0,	0x8xxxxxx,	0x8xxxxxx,
0,	0,	0,	0,
0[8],	0[8],	0[8],	0[8],
0[8],	0[8],	0[8],	0[8],
0[8]	0[8]	0[8]	0[8]
}fb0_struct	}ipi0_struct	}sk0_struct	}cb0_struct

7.3.2.15 The cmd Member

The cmd member specifies a field that is not currently used.

7.3.2.16 The physaddr and physaddr2 Members

The `physaddr` member specifies the physical address that corresponds to the virtual address set in the `addr` member. Because no CSR addresses were specified for `fb0_struct` and `ipi0_struct`, Figure 7-27 shows that the autoconfiguration software initializes their `physaddr` members to the value zero (0). The figure also shows that the autoconfiguration software uses the CSR addresses specified after the `csr` keywords to calculate corresponding physical addresses and to use them to initialize the `physaddr` members for `sk0_struct` and `cb0_struct`.

The `physaddr2` member specifies the physical address that corresponds to the virtual address set in the `addr2` member. The autoconfiguration software would use the CSR addresses specified after the `addr2` keyword to calculate a corresponding second physical address. Because no second CSR addresses were specified in the example system configuration file, Figure 7-27 shows that the autoconfiguration software initializes the `physaddr2` members for all of the `controller` structures to the value zero (0).

Note that the addresses that appear in these members may not be the values specified in the system configuration file because the kernel could perform an address-mapping operation to produce different values.

Figure 7-27: The physaddr and physaddr2 Members Initialized

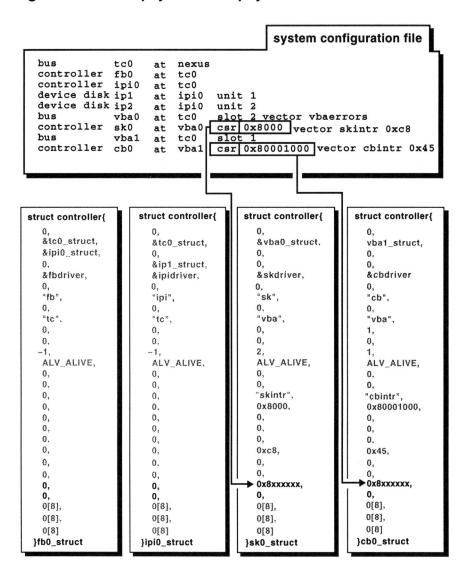

7.3.2.17 The private, conn_priv, and rsvd Members

The private member specifies private storage for use by this controller or controller type. For the example system configuration file, Figure 7-28 shows that the autoconfiguration software initializes these members for all of the structures to the value zero (0). The code controlling the controller can use these members for any storage purpose.

The conn_priv member specifies private storage for use by the bus that this controller is connected to. Figure 7-28 shows that the autoconfiguration software initializes these members for all of the structures to the value zero (0).

The rsvd member is reserved for future expansion of the data structure.

Figure 7-28: The private, conn_priv, and rsvd Members Initialized

```
                                                    system configuration file

bus          tc0    at    nexus
controller   fb0    at    tc0
controller   ipi0   at    tc0
device disk  ip1    at    ipi0    unit 1
device disk  ip2    at    ipi0    unit 2
bus          vba0   at    tc0     slot 2 vector vbaerrors
controller   sk0    at    vba0    csr 0x8000 vector skintr 0xc8
bus          vba1   at    tc0     slot 1
controller   cb0    at    vba1    csr 0x80001000 vector cbintr 0x45
```

```
struct controller{      struct controller{      struct controller{      struct controller{
    0,                      0,                      0,                      0,
    &tc0_struct,            &tc0_struct,            &vba0_struct,           vba1_struct,
    &ipi0_struct,           0,                      0,                      0,
    0,                      &ip1_struct,            0,                      0,
    &fbdriver,              &ipidriver,             &skdriver,              &cbdriver
    0,                      0,                      0,                      0,
    "fb",                   "ipi",                  "sk",                   "cb",
    0,                      0,                      0,                      0,
    "tc",                   "tc",                   "vba",                  "vba",
    0,                      0,                      0,                      1,
    0,                      0,                      0,                      0,
    -1,                     -1,                     2,                      1,
    ALV_ALIVE,              ALV_ALIVE,              ALV_ALIVE,              ALV_ALIVE,
    0,                      0,                      0,                      0,
    0,                      0,                      0,                      0,
    0,                      0,                      "skintr",               "cbintr",
    0,                      0,                      0x8000,                 0x80001000,
    0,                      0,                      0,                      0,
    0,                      0,                      0,                      0,
    0,                      0,                      0xc8,                   0x45,
    0,                      0,                      0,                      0,
    0,                      0,                      0,                      0,
    0,                      0,                      0x8xxxxxx,              0x8xxxxxx,
    0,                      0,                      0,                      0,
    0[8],                   0[8],                   0[8],                   0[8],
    0[8],                   0[8],                   0[8],                   0[8],
    0[8]                    0[8]                    0[8]                    0[8]
}fb0_struct             }ipi0_struct            }sk0_struct             }cb0_struct
```

7.3.3 The device Structure

The device structure represents an instance of a device entity. A device is an entity that connects to and is controlled by a controller. A device does not connect directly to a bus. You (or the system manager) specify a device entity in the system configuration file as follows:

- For static drivers

  Specify a valid syntax for the device in the config.file file fragment or the system configuration file.

- For loadable drivers

  Specify a valid syntax for the device in the stanza.loadable file fragment.

Chapter 11 discusses the device driver configuration models. Chapter 12 describes the valid syntaxes for a device specification. Chapter 13 provides examples of how to configure device drivers.

Table 7-3 lists the members of the device structure along with their associated data types.

Table 7-3: Members of the device Structure

Member Name	Data Type
nxt_dev	struct device *
ctlr_hd	struct controller *
dev_type	char *
dev_name	char *
logunit	int
unit	int
ctlr_name	char *
ctlr_num	int
alive	int
private	void * [8]
conn_priv	void * [8]
rsvd	void * [8]

The following sections discuss all of these members except for nxt_dev and ctlr_hd, which are presented in Section 7.2.1.6. Chapter 16 provides a reference (man) page-style description of this data structure.

7.3.3.1 The dev_type and dev_name Members

The dev_type member specifies the device type (for example, disk or tape). The dev_name member specifies the device name type. You (or the system manager) specify the device type by using any string and the device name by using any string up to a maximum of eight characters. For example, the string disk can indicate that the device is a disk and the string ip can indicate that this is an ip disk. For loadable drivers, the only supported strings are disk and tape.

Figure 7-29 shows the lines in the system configuration file that the autoconfiguration software parses to obtain the device type and device name for the specified devices. It sets the dev_type members of ip1_struct and ip2_struct to the value disk. The autoconfiguration software also sets the dev_name members to the string ip.

Figure 7-29: The dev_type and dev_name Members Initialized

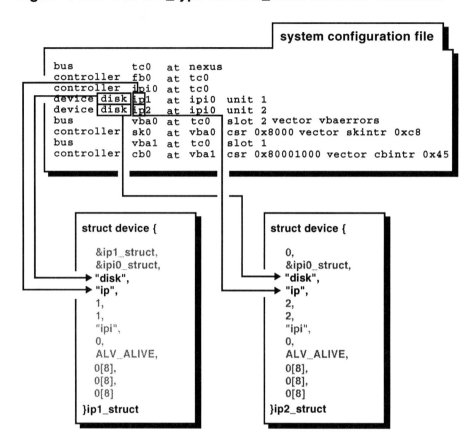

7.3.3.2 The logunit and unit Members

The `logunit` member specifies the device logical unit number. The `unit` member specifies the device physical unit number. You (or the system manager) specify the logical unit number by using a valid number after the device name string and the physical unit number by using a valid number after the `unit` keyword.

Figure 7-30 shows the lines in the system configuration file that the autoconfiguration software parses to obtain the logical unit number and the physical unit number for the specified devices. It sets the `logunit` members of `ip1_struct` and `ip2_struct` to the values 1 and 2.

The figure also shows that the autoconfiguration software sets the `unit` members for these structures to 1 and 2.

Figure 7-30: The logunit and unit Members Initialized

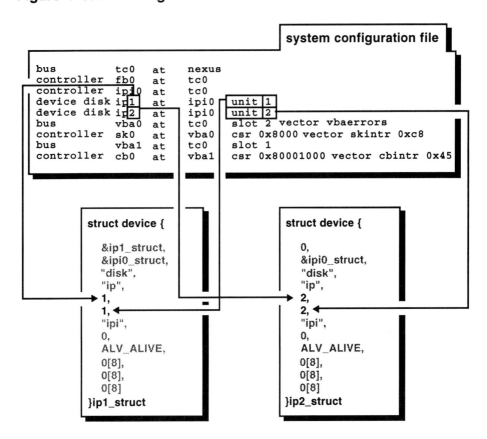

7.3.3.3 The ctlr_name and ctlr_num Members

The `ctlr_name` member specifies the name of the controller that this device is connected to. The `ctlr_num` member specifies the number of the controller that this device is connected to. You (or the system manager) specify the controller name and the controller number by using the `at` keyword followed by a character string and number that represent the controller name and controller number. For example, the character string `ipi` represents a controller supported by Digital. You enter these values in the `config.file` file fragment or the system configuration file for static drivers and the `stanza.loadable` file fragment for loadable drivers.

Figure 7-31 shows the values in the system configuration file that the autoconfiguration software parses to obtain the controller name and the controller number for the specified devices. It sets the `ctlr_name` members of `ip1_struct` and `ip2_struct` to the string `ipi` because both devices are connected to the same controller.

The figure also shows that the autoconfiguration software sets the
ctlr_num members for these structures to the value zero (0).

Figure 7-31: The ctlr_name and ctlr_num Members Initialized

```
                                        ┌──────────────────────────────┐
                                        │  system configuration file   │
┌───────────────────────────────────────┴──────────────────────────────┐
│  bus          tc0    at   nexus                                       │
│  controller   fb0    at   tc0                                         │
│  controller   ipi0   at   tc0                                         │
│  device disk  ip1     at   [ipi0]  unit 1                             │
│  device disk  ip2     at   [ipi0]  unit 2                             │
│  bus          vba0   at   tc0   slot 2 vector vbaerrors               │
│  controller   sk0    at   vba0  csr 0x8000 vector skintr 0xc8         │
│  bus          vba1   at   tc0   slot 1                                │
│  controller   cb0    at   vba1  csr 0x80001000 vector cbintr 0x45     │
└───────────────────────────────────────────────────────────────────────┘


   struct device {                          struct device {

       &ip1_struct,                             0,
       &ipi0_struct,                            &ipi0_struct,
       "disk",                                  "disk",
       "ip",                                    "ip",
       1,                                       2,
       1,                                       2,
       "ipi",   ←                               → "ipi",
       0,       ←                               → 0,
       ALV_ALIVE,                               ALV_ALIVE,
       0[8],                                    0[8],
       0[8],                                    0[8],
       0[8]                                     0[8]
   }ip1_struct                              }ip2_struct
```

7.3.3.4 The alive Member

The alive member specifies a flag word to indicate the current status of the
device. Figure 7-32 shows that the autoconfiguration software sets the
alive member for both of the example device structures to the
ALV_ALIVE bit. The autoconfiguration software obtains this and the other
alive bits in the file /usr/sys/include/io/common/devdriver.h.

Figure 7-32: The alive Member Initialized

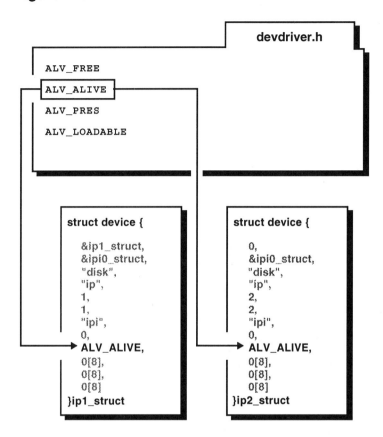

7.3.3.5 The private, conn_priv, and rsvd Members

The `private` member specifies private storage for use by this device or device class. The `conn_priv` member specifies private storage for use by the controller that this device is connected to.

The `rsvd` member is reserved for future expansion of the data structure. For the example system configuration file, Figure 7-33 shows that the autoconfiguration software initializes these members for all of the structures to the value zero (0). The code controlling the device can use these members for any storage purposes.

Figure 7-33: The private, conn_priv, and rsvd Members Initialized

```
                                              system configuration file

bus          tc0    at   nexus
controller   fb0    at   tc0
controller   ipi0   at   tc0
device disk ip1     at   ipi0   unit 1
device disk ip2     at   ipi0   unit 2
bus          vba0   at   tc0    slot 2 vector vbaerrors
controller   sk0    at   vba0   csr 0x8000 vector skintr 0xc8
bus          vba1   at   tc0    slot 1
controller   cb0    at   vba1   csr 0x80001000 vector cbintr 0x45
```

```
struct device {

    &ip1_struct,
    &ipi0_struct,
    "disk",
    "ip",
    1,
    1,
    "ipi",
    0,
    ALV_ALIVE,
    0[8],
    0[8],
    0[8]
}ip1_struct
```

```
struct device {

    0,
    &ipi0_struct,
    "disk",
    "ip",
    2,
    2,
    "ipi",
    0,
    ALV_ALIVE,
    0[8],
    0[8],
    0[8]
}ip2_struct
```

7.3.4 The driver Structure

The driver structure defines driver entry points and other driver-specific information. You declare and initialize an instance of this structure in the device driver. The bus configuration code uses the entry points defined in this structure during system configuration. The bus configuration code fills in the dev_list and ctlr_list arrays. The driver interfaces use these arrays (members of the device and controller structures) to get the structures for specific devices or controllers.

Because driver writers need to be intimately familiar with the members of the `driver` structure, the following shows the C definition:

```
struct driver {
    int      (*probe)();
    int      (*slave)();
    int      (*cattach)();
    int      (*dattach)();
    int      (*go)();
    caddr_t  *addr_list;
    char     *dev_name;
    struct   device **dev_list;
    char     *ctlr_name;
    struct   controller **ctlr_list;
    short    xclu;
    int      addr1_size;
    int      addr1_atype;
    int      addr2_size;
    int      addr2_atype;
    int      (*ctlr_unattach)();
    int      (*dev_unattach)();
};
```

The following sections discuss all of these members. Chapter 16 provides a reference (man) page-style description of this data structure.

7.3.4.1   The probe, slave, cattach, dattach, and go Members

The `probe` member specifies a pointer to the driver's `probe` interface, which is called to verify that the controller exists. The `slave` member specifies a pointer to the driver's `slave` interface, which is called once for each device connected to the controller.

The `cattach` member specifies a pointer to the driver's `cattach` interface, which is called to allow controller-specific initialization. You can set this pointer to NULL. The `dattach` member specifies a pointer to the driver's `dattach` interface, which is called once for each `slave` call that returns success. You use the `dattach` interface for device-specific initialization. You can set this pointer to NULL.

The `go` member specifies a pointer to the driver's `go` interface, which is not currently used. Figure 7-34 shows that the driver writer initializes these members to the values contained in the `cbdriver` structure. This data structure appears in `cb.c`, the source file for the `/dev/cb` device driver.

Figure 7-34: The probe, slave, cattach, dattach, and go Members Initialized

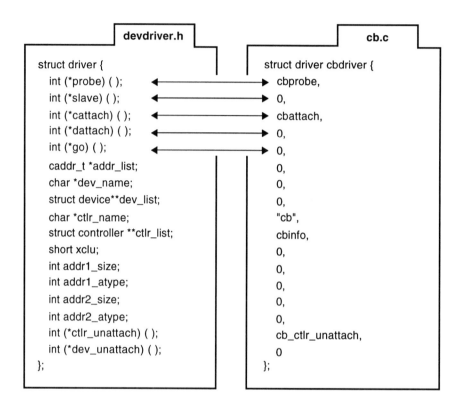

7.3.4.2 The addr_list Member

The addr_list member specifies a list of optional CSR addresses. Figure 7-35 shows that the driver writer initializes this member to the value zero (0) because this entry is not used for TURBOchannel device drivers.

Figure 7-35: The addr_list Member Initialized

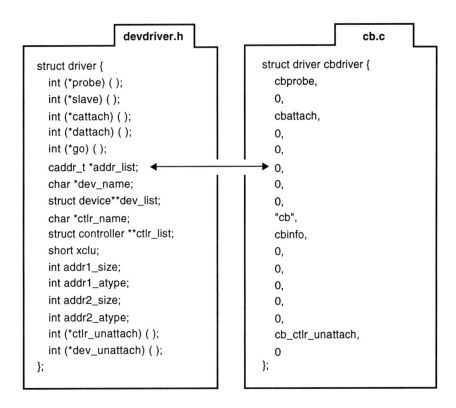

7.3.4.3 The dev_name and dev_list Members

The `dev_name` member specifies the name of the device connected to this controller. The `dev_list` member specifies an array of pointers to device structures currently connected to this controller. This member is indexed through the `logunit` member of the `device` structure associated with this device. Figure 7-36 shows that the driver writer initializes these members to the value zero (0), which indicates that there is no device connected to the controller and that there is no array of pointers to device structures.

Figure 7-36: The dev_name and dev_list Members Initialized

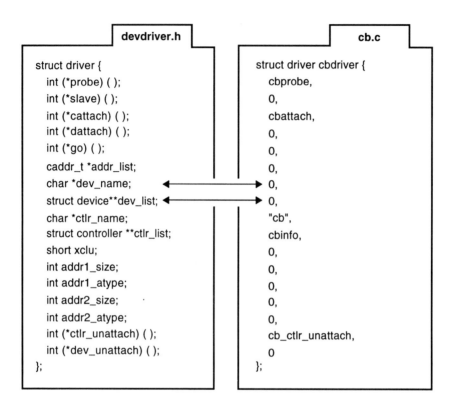

7.3.4.4   The ctlr_name and ctlr_list Members

The ctlr_name member specifies the controller name. The ctlr_list member specifies an array of pointers to controller structures. The system uses this member when multiple controllers are controlled by a single device driver. This member is indexed through the ctlr_num member of the controller structure associated with this device. Figure 7-37 shows that the driver writer initializes these members to the values cb and cbinfo.

Figure 7-37: The ctlr_name and ctlr_list Members Initialized

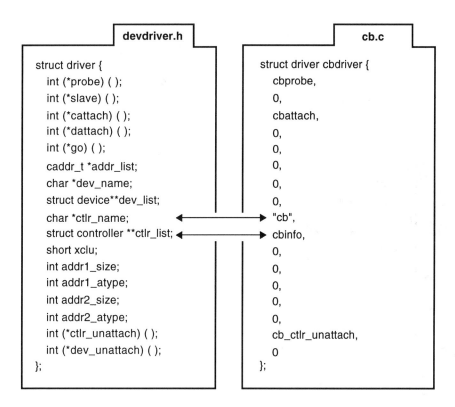

7.3.4.5 The xclu Member

The xclu member specifies a field that is not currently used. Figure 7-38 shows that the driver writer initializes this member to the value zero (0).

Figure 7-38: The xclu Member Initialized

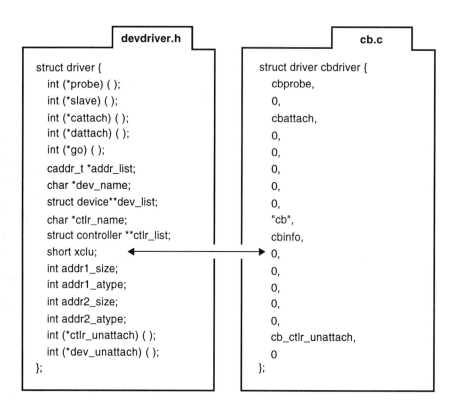

7.3.4.6 The addr1_size, addr1_atype, addr2_size, and addr2_atype Members

The `addr1_size` member specifies the size (in bytes) of the first CSR area. This area is usually the control status register of the device. Only drivers operating on the VMEbus use this member. The `addr1_atype` member specifies the address space, access mode, transfer size, and swap mode of the first CSR area. Note that not all bus adapters use the transfer size. Only drivers operating on the VMEbus use this member.

The `addr2_size` member specifies the size (in bytes) of the second CSR area. This area is usually the data area that the system uses with devices that have two separate CSR areas. Only drivers operating on the VMEbus use this member. The `addr2_atype` member specifies the address space, access mode, transfer size, and swap mode of the second CSR area. Note that not all bus adapters use the transfer size. Only drivers operating on the

VMEbus use this member. Figure 7-39 shows that the driver writer initializes these members to the value zero (0) to indicate that they are not used by the /dev/cb driver.

Figure 7-39: The addr1_size, addr1_atype, addr2_size, and addr2_atype Members Initialized

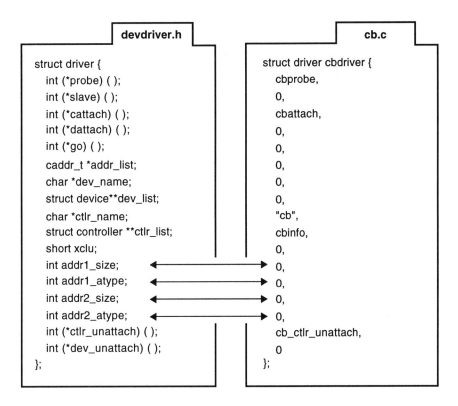

7.3.4.7 The ctlr_unattach and dev_unattach Members

The ctlr_unattach member specifies a pointer to the controller's unattach interface. Loadable drivers use the controller unattach interface. The dev_unattach member specifies a pointer to the device's unattach interface. Loadable drivers use the device unattach interface. Figure 7-40 shows that the driver writer initializes the ctlr_unattach member to the interface cb_ctlr_unattach. The driver writer initializes the dev_unattach member to the value zero (0) to indicate that there is no device unattach interface.

Figure 7-40: The ctlr_unattach and dev_unattach Members Initialized

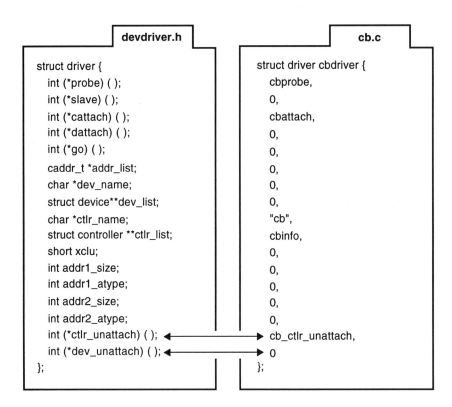

7.3.5 The port Structure

The `port` structure contains information about a port.

Table 7-4 lists the member of the `port` structure along with its associated data type.

Table 7-4: Member of the port Structure

Member Name	Data Type
conf	int (*conf) ()

The `conf` member specifies a pointer to the configuration interface for this port.

7.4 Data Structures That Loadable Device Drivers Use

Loadable device drivers use the `cfg_subsys_attr_t` and `cfg_attr_t` data structures instead of the `device_config_t` structure. In previous versions of the Digital UNIX operating system (formerly known as DEC OSF/1), loadable device drivers used the `device_config_t` data structure to communicate with the device driver method of `cfgmgr` (the configuration manager daemon).

7.4.1 The cfg_subsys_attr_t Structure

The `cfg_subsys_attr_t` data structure contains information that loadable device drivers use to describe a variety of attributes. Device driver writers declare and initialize an array of `cfg_subsys_attr_t` structures in their device drivers. The `cfg_subsys_attr_t` structure is a simplified version of the `cfg_attr_t` structure and is designed to save space in the kernel. Because driver writers need to be intimately familiar with the members of the `cfg_subsys_attr_t` structure, the following shows the C definition:

```
typedef struct {
   char    name[CFG_ATTR_NAME_SZ]; /* attribute name */
   uchar   type;                   /* attribute type */
   uchar   operation;              /* supported operations */
   caddr_t addr;                   /* address of data value */
   ulong   min_val;                /* min size/length/value */
   ulong   max_val;                /* max size/length/value */
   ulong   val_size;               /* binary data size */
} cfg_subsys_attr_t;
```

The `name` member specifies the ASCII name of the attribute. The name must be between 2 and `CFG_ATTR_NAME_SZ` characters in length, including the terminating null character.

The `type` member specifies the data type associated with the `name` attribute. You must set the `type` member to one of the following constants:

Value	Meaning
CFG_ATTR_STRTYPE	Data type is a null-terminated array of characters.
CFG_ATTR_INTTYPE	Data type is a 32-bit signed integer.
CFG_ATTR_UINTTYPE	Data type is a 32-bit unsigned integer.
CFG_ATTR_LONGTYPE	Data type is a 64-bit signed integer.
CFG_ATTR_ULONGTYPE	Data type is a 64-bit unsigned integer.
CFG_ATTR_BINTYPE	Data type is an array of bytes.

The `operation` member specifies the operations that the device driver method of `cfgmgr` can perform on the attribute. You can set this member to one of the following constants:

Value	Meaning
CFG_OP_CONFIGURE	Configures a loadable device driver.
CFG_OP_UNCONFIGURE	Unconfigures a loadable device driver.
CFG_OP_QUERY	Queries the device driver for configuration information.
CFG_OP_RECONFIGURE	The device driver method of `cfgmgr` allows a user to modify the attribute.

The `addr` member specifies the address of the data value associated with the attribute. The `cfgmgr` daemon obtains the data value for this attribute from the `/etc/sysconfigtab` database and stores it at this address. The `cfgmgr` daemon performs this storage operation if the attribute appears in the array with an operation code of `CFG_OP_CONFIGURE`.

In addition, the device driver's `configure` interface initializes (when the driver is dynamically configured) other attributes that appear in the array with an operation code of `CFG_OP_CONFIGURE`.

The `min_val` member specifies the minimum length of the data value.

The `max_val` member specifies the maximum length of the data value.

The `val_size` member specifies the binary data size.

The following code fragment shows how the `/dev/cb` device driver initializes the `cfg_subsys_attr_t` structure:

```
        .
        .
        .
static int cmajnum = 0;
static int bmajnum = 0;
static int begunit = 0;
static int numunit = 0;
static int cbversion = 0;

static unsigned char mcfgname[CFG_ATTR_NAME_SZ] = "";
static unsigned char modtype[CFG_ATTR_NAME_SZ] = "";
static unsigned char devcmajor[CFG_ATTR_NAME_SZ] = "";

cfg_subsys_attr_t cb_attributes[] = {
{"Module_Config_Name", CFG_ATTR_STRTYPE, CFG_OP_CONFIGURE,
                    (caddr_t)mcfgname,2,CFG_ATTR_NAME_SZ,0},
{"Module_Type",        CFG_ATTR_STRTYPE, CFG_OP_CONFIGURE,
                    (caddr_t)modtype,2,CFG_ATTR_NAME_SZ,0},
{"Device_Char_Major",  CFG_ATTR_STRTYPE, CFG_OP_CONFIGURE,
                    (caddr_t)devcmajor,0,CFG_ATTR_NAME_SZ,0},
```

```
{"cmajnum",                      CFG_ATTR_INTTYPE, CFG_OP_QUERY,
                          (caddr_t)&cmajnum,0,99,0},
{"bmajnum",                      CFG_ATTR_INTTYPE, CFG_OP_QUERY,
                          (caddr_t)&bmajnum,0,99,0},
{"begunit",                      CFG_ATTR_INTTYPE, CFG_OP_QUERY,
                          (caddr_t)&begunit,0,8,0},
{"numunit",                      CFG_ATTR_INTTYPE, CFG_OP_QUERY,
                          (caddr_t)&numunit,0,8,0},
{"version",                      CFG_ATTR_INTTYPE, CFG_OP_QUERY,
                          (caddr_t)&cbversion,0,9999999,0},
{"",0,0,0,0,0}
};
    .
    .
    .
```

7.4.2 The cfg_attr_t Structure

The `cfg_attr_t` data structure contains information for managing the
loading and unloading of loadable device drivers. The `cfgmgr` daemon
passes a pointer to this data structure to the device driver's `xxconfigure`
interface. The device driver can parse this structure pointer to check the
validity of the values associated with the driver's associated
`stanza.loadable` file fragment and the `/etc/sysconfigtab`
database. Device driver writers need to be familiar with the following topics
associated with the `cfg_attr_t` structure:

- Members of the `cfg_attr_t` structure

- How to parse the `cfg_attr_t` array

7.4.2.1 Members of the cfg_attr_t Structure

Driver writers need to be intimately familiar with the members of the
`cfg_attr_t` structure. The following shows the C definition:

```
typedef struct cfg_attr {
  char                name[CFG_ATTR_NAME_SZ];
  uchar               type;
  uchar               operation;
  uint                status;
  long                index;
  union {
      struct {
          caddr_t     val;
          ulong       min_size;
          ulong       max_size;
          void        (*disposal)();
          ulong       val_size;
      } bin;

      struct {
          caddr_t     val;
          ulong       min_len;
          ulong       max_len;
```

```
        void      (*disposal)();
    } str;

    struct {
        ulong     val;
        ulong     min_val;
        ulong     max_val;
    } num;
  } attr;
} cfg_attr_t;
```

The name member specifies the ASCII name of the attribute. The name must be between 2 and CFG_ATTR_NAME_SZ characters in length, including the terminating null character.

The type member specifies the data type associated with the name attribute. You must set the type member to one of the following constants:

Value	Meaning
CFG_ATTR_STRTYPE	Data type is a null-terminated array of characters.
CFG_ATTR_INTTYPE	Data type is a 32-bit signed integer.
CFG_ATTR_UINTTYPE	Data type is a 32-bit unsigned integer.
CFG_ATTR_LONGTYPE	Data type is a 64-bit signed integer.
CFG_ATTR_ULONGTYPE	Data type is a 64-bit unsigned integer.
CFG_ATTR_BINTYPE	Data type is an array of bytes.

The operation member specifies the operations that the device driver method of cfgmgr can perform on the attribute. You can set this member to one of the following constants:

Value	Meaning
CFG_OP_CONFIGURE	Configures a loadable device driver.
CFG_OP_UNCONFIGURE	Unconfigures a loadable device driver.
CFG_OP_QUERY	Queries the device driver for configuration information.
CFG_OP_RECONFIGURE	The device driver method of cfgmgr allows a user to modify the attribute.

The `status` member stores the return code (configure, unconfigure, query) from operations performed by the `cfgmgr` daemon. The device driver method of `cfgmgr` can return one of the following operation codes:

Value	Meaning
CFG_ATTR_SUCCESS	Successful operation.
CFG_ATTR_EEXISTS	The attribute you specified in the `name` member does not exist.
CFG_ATTR_EOP	The attribute you specified in the `name` member does support the operation.
CFG_ATTR_ESUBSYS	The device driver method subsystem failed.
CFG_ATTR_ESMALL	The value or size of the attribute you specified in the `name` member is too small.
CFG_ATTR_ELARGE	The value or size of the attribute you specified in the `name` member is too large.
CFG_ATTR_ETYPE	The data type that you specified for the attribute you specified in the `name` member is invalid or is a mismatch.
CFG_ATTR_EINDEX	The index associated with the attribute that you specified in the `name` member is invalid.
CFG_ATTR_EMEM	The device driver method subsystem could not allocate memory for the specified attribute.

The `index` member stores a value that scopes the target for indexed attributes.

The `attr` member specifies a union of the possible attribute types used for storing values, kernel locations, validation criteria, and disposal interfaces.

The `cfgmgr` daemon uses the appropriate union element according to the attribute type. For example, attributes of type `CFG_ATTR_ULONGTYPE` use the union element `num`.

7.4.2.2 How to Parse the cfg_attr_t Array

The following code fragment shows how the `/dev/cb` driver parses the `cfg_attr_t` structure array to determine if any of the attributes failed to load:

```
        .
        .
        .
#define MAX_DEVICE_CFG_ENTRIES 18

/*******************************************************
 * The cfg_attr_t list passed into the                 *
 * cb_configure interface's indata parameter           *
 * contains the strings that are stored in the          *
 * sysconfigtab database for this subsystem (the       *
 * /dev/cb device driver).                             *
 *******************************************************/

#ifdef CB_DEBUG
        cfg_attr_t cfg_buf[MAX_DEVICE_CFG_ENTRIES];
#endif

            case CFG_OP_CONFIGURE:

#ifdef CB_DEBUG
            bcopy(indata, cfg_buf[0].name,
                indatalen*(sizeof(cfg_attr_t)));
            if(op== CFG_OP_CONFIGURE ){
              printf(" The Config routine has been called ... op =
                    %x\n", op);
              for( i=0; i < indatalen; i++){
                printf("%s: ",cfg_buf[i].name);
                switch(cfg_buf[i].type){
                    case CFG_ATTR_STRTYPE:
                        printf("%s\n",cfg_buf[i].attr.str.val);
                        break;
                    default:
                        printf("Unknown attribute: ");
                        printf("%x\n", cfg_buf[i].status);
                        break;
                    }
                }
            }
#endif
        .
        .
        .
```

7.5 Data Structures That Device Drivers Use to Register Interrupt Handlers

An interrupt service interface (ISI) is a device driver routine (sometimes called an interrupt handler) that handles hardware interrupts. In previous versions of the Digital UNIX operating system (formerly known as DEC OSF/1), driver writers implementing static-only device drivers specified a device driver's ISI in the system configuration file if they followed the traditional device driver configuration model; they specified the ISI in the config.file file fragment if they followed the third-party device driver configuration model. Loadable device drivers, on the other hand, must call a number of kernel interfaces and use specific data structures to register, deregister, enable, and disable a device driver's ISI.

Digital recommends that all new drivers (static and loadable) call the `handler` interfaces to dynamically register ISIs.
The dynamic registration of ISIs involves the use of the following data structures:

- `ihandler_t`
- `handler_intr_info`

The following sections describe each of these data structures.

7.5.1 The ihandler_t Structure

The `ihandler_t` structure contains information associated with device driver interrupt handling. In previous versions of the Digital UNIX operating system (formerly known as DEC OSF/1), only loadable drivers used this data structure. Digital recommends that both static and loadable drivers use the `ihandler_t` structure and the `handler` interfaces to dynamically register ISIs. See the bus-specific book for the registration methods supported by the bus on which your driver operates.

This model of interrupt dispatching uses the bus as the means of interrupt dispatching for all drivers. For this reason, all of the information needed to register an interrupt is considered to be bus specific. As a result, no attempt is made to represent all the possible permutations within the `ihandler_t` data structure.

Table 7-5 lists the members of the `ihandler_t` structure along with their associated data types.

Table 7-5: Members of the ihandler_t Structure

Member Name	Data Type
ih_id	ihandler_id_t
ih_bus	struct bus *
ih_bus_info	char *

The `ih_id` member specifies a unique ID.

The `ih_bus` member specifies a pointer to the `bus` structure associated with this device driver. This member is needed because the interrupt dispatching methodology requires that the bus be responsible for dispatching interrupts in a bus-specific manner.

The `ih_bus_info` member specifies bus registration information. Each bus type could have different mechanisms for registering interrupt handlers on that bus. Thus, the `ih_bus_info` member contains the bus-specific information needed to register the interrupt handlers.

For example, on a TURBOchannel bus, the bus-specific information might consist of:

- An interrupt service interface
- A parameter passed to the interrupt service interface
- A slot number

Device driver writers pass the `ihandler_t` structure to the `handler_add` interface to specify how interrupt handlers are to be registered with the bus-specific interrupt dispatcher. This task is usually done within the driver's `probe` interface. The following code fragment shows how the `/dev/cb` driver uses the `ihandler_t` data structure:

```
    .
    .
    .
ihandler_id_t cb_id_t[NCB]; 1
    .
    .
ihandler_t handler; 2
    .
    .
struct handler_intr_info info; 3
    .
    .
handler.ih_bus = ctlr->bus_hd; 4
    .
    .
handler.ih_bus_info = (char *)&info; 5
    .
    .
none_id_t[unit] = handler_add(&handler); 6
```

1. Declares a pointer to an array of IDs used to deregister the interrupt handlers. The NCB constant represents the maximum number of CB controllers. This number sizes the array of IDs. Thus, there is one ID per CB device. Section 10.5 contains the declaration of this array of IDs.

2. Declares an `ihandler_t` data structure called `handler` to contain information associated with the `/dev/cb` device driver interrupt handling.

3. Declares a `handler_intr_info` data structure called `info`. Note that the `ih_bus_info` member is set to the address of this structure.

4. Specifies the bus that this controller is attached to. The `bus_hd` member of the `controller` structure contains a pointer to the `bus` structure that this controller is connected to. After the initialization, the `ih_bus` member of the `ihandler_t` structure contains the pointer to the `bus` structure associated with the `/dev/cb` device driver.

5. Sets the `ih_bus_info` member of the `handler` data structure to the address of the bus-specific information structure, `info`. This setting is necessary because registration of the interrupt handlers will indirectly call bus-specific interrupt registration interfaces.

6. Calls the `handler_add` interface and saves its return value for use later by the `handler_del` interface.

   The `handler_add` interface takes one argument: a pointer to an `ihandler_t` data structure, which in the example is the initialized `handler` structure. Section 10.8.1 provides additional information on the use of the `ihandler_t` structure with the `handler` interfaces.

7.5.2 The handler_intr_info Structure

The `handler_intr_info` structure contains interrupt handler information for device controllers connected to a bus. This generic structure makes device drivers more portable across different buses because it contains all of the necessary information to add an interrupt handler for any bus. Device drivers set the `ih_bus_info` member of the `ihandler_t` structure to the filled-in `handler_intr_info` structure, usually in the driver's `probe` interface.

Both static and loadable device drivers can use the `handler_intr_info` structure and the `handler_add` interfaces to register a device driver's interrupt service interface. The `bus` and `controller` structures contain the bus- and controller-specific information that is not provided in `handler_intr_info`.

Table 7-6 lists the members of the `handler_intr_info` structure along with their associated data types.

Table 7-6: Members of the handler_intr_info Structure

Member Name	Data Type
configuration_st	caddr_t
intr	int (*intr) ()

Table 7-6: (continued)

Member Name	Data Type
param	caddr_t
config_type	unsigned int

The `configuration_st` member specifies a pointer to the `bus` or `controller` structure for which an associated interrupt handler is written.

The `intr` member specifies a pointer to the interrupt handler for the specified bus or controller.

The `param` member specifies a member whose contents are passed to the interrupt service interface.

The `config_type` member specifies the driver type. You can set this member to one of the following constants defined in `handler.h`: CONTROLLER_CONFIG_TYPE (controller) or ADAPTER_CONFIG_TYPE (bus adapter).

Data Structures Used in I/O Operations 8

Data structures are the mechanism used to pass information between the Digital UNIX kernel and device driver interfaces. This chapter describes the data structures used in I/O operations. Specifically, the chapter discusses:

- The `buf` structure

- The device switch tables

- The `uio` structure

- Buffer cache management

- The interrupt code

8.1 The buf Structure

The `buf` structure describes arbitrary I/O, but is usually associated with block I/O and `physio`. A systemwide pool of `buf` structures exists for block I/O; however, many device drivers also include locally defined `buf` structures for use with the `physio` kernel interface. The `buf` structure does not contain data. Instead, it contains information about where the data resides and information about the types of I/O operations. You need to be familiar with the following topics associated with the `buf` structure:

- Using the systemwide pool of `buf` structures

- Declaring locally defined `buf` structures

- Understanding `buf` structure members that device drivers use

8.1.1 Using the Systemwide Pool of buf Structures

The following code fragment shows how the `/dev/cb` driver discussed in Chapter 10 uses the systemwide pool of `buf` structures with the `cbminphys` interface:

```
cbminphys(bp)
register struct buf *bp; 1
{
    .
    .
    .
```

[1] Declares a pointer to a `buf` structure called `bp`. The `cbminphys` interface references the systemwide pool of `buf` structures to perform a variety of tasks, including checking the size of the requested transfer.

8.1.2 Declaring Locally Defined buf Structures

The following code fragment shows how the `/dev/cb` driver discussed in Chapter 10 declares an array of locally defined `buf` structures and references it with the `cbattach` interface:

```
#define NCB TC_OPTION_SLOTS  [1]
   .
   .
   .
struct buf cbbuf[NCB];  [2]
   .
   .
   .
cbattach(ctlr)
struct controller *ctlr;  [3]
{
struct cb_unit *cb;  [4]
   .
   .
   .
cb->cbbuf = &cbbuf[ctlr->ctlr_num];  [5]
```

[1] The NCB constant is used to allocate the `buf` structures associated with the CB devices that currently exist on the system. Section 10.3 shows that this constant is defined in the Include Files Section of the `/dev/cb` device driver.

[2] Declares an array of `buf` structures called `cbbuf`. The NCB constant is used to allocate the `buf` structures for the maximum number of CB devices that currently exist on the system. Thus, there is one `buf` structure per CB device. Section 10.6 shows that this array is declared in the Local Structure and Variable Definitions Section of the `/dev/cb` driver.

[3] Declares a pointer to a `controller` structure associated with a specific CB device. The `ctlr_num` member of this pointer is used as an index to obtain a specific CB device's associated `buf` structure.

[4] Declares a pointer to the `cb_unit` data structure associated with this CB device. Section 10.6 shows the declaration of this data structure. It contains members that store such information as whether the CB device is opened and the CB device's TC slot number. It also declares a pointer to the `cbbuf` structure.

[5] Sets the buffer structure address (the `cbbuf` member of this CB device's `cb_unit` structure) to the address of this CB device's `buf` structure. The `ctlr_num` member is used as an index into the array of `buf`

structures associated with this CB device.

8.1.3 Understanding buf Structure Members That Device Drivers Use

Table 8-1 lists the members of the buf structure along with their associated data types that device drivers might reference.

Table 8-1: Members of the buf Structure

Member Name	Data Type
b_flags	int
b_forw	struct buf *
b_back	struct buf *
av_forw	struct buf *
av_back	struct buf *
b_bcount	int
b_error	short
b_dev	dev_t
b_un.b_addr	caddr_t
b_lblkno	daddr_t
b_blkno	daddr_t
b_resid	int
b_iodone	void (*b_iodone) ()
b_proc	struct proc *

Chapter 16 provides a reference (man) page-style description of this data structure. The following sections discuss all of these members.

8.1.3.1 The b_flags Member

The b_flags member specifies binary status flags. These flags indicate how a request is to be handled and the current status of the request. These status flags are defined in buf.h and get set by various parts of the kernel. The flags supply the device driver with information about the I/O operation.

The device driver can also send information back to the kernel by setting b_flags. Table 8-2 lists the binary status flags applicable to device drivers.

Table 8-2: Binary Status Flags Applicable to Device Drivers

Flag	Meaning
B_READ	This flag is set if the operation is read and cleared if the operation is write.
B_DONE	This flag is cleared when a request is passed to a driver strategy interface. The device driver writer must call iodone to mark a buffer as completed.
B_ERROR	This flag specifies that an error occurred on this data transfer. Device drivers set this flag if an error occurs.
B_BUSY	This flag indicates that the buffer is in use.
B_PHYS	This flag indicates that the associated data is in user address space.
B_WANTED	If this flag is set, it indicates that some process is waiting for this buffer. The device driver should issue a call to the wakeup interface when the buffer is freed by the current process. The driver passes the address of the buffer as an argument to wakeup.

8.1.3.2 The b_forw and b_back Members

The b_forw and b_back members specify a file system buffer hash chain. When the kernel performs an I/O operation on a buffer, the buf structures are not on any list. Device driver writers sometimes use these members to link buf structures to lists.

8.1.3.3 The av_forw and av_back Members

The av_forw and av_back members specify the position on the free list if the b_flags member is not set to B_BUSY. The kernel initializes these members. However, when the driver gets use of the buf structure, these members are available for local use by the device driver.

8.1.3.4 The b_bcount and b_error Members

The b_bcount member specifies the size of the requested transfer (in bytes). This member is initialized by the kernel as the result of an I/O request. The driver writer references this member to determine the size of the I/O request. This member is often used in the driver's strategy interface.

The b_error member specifies that an error occurred on this data transfer. This member is set to an error code if the b_flags member bit was set. The driver writer sets this member with the errors defined in the file errno.h.

8.1.3.5 The b_dev Member

The b_dev member specifies the special device to which the transfer is directed. The data type for this member is dev_t, which maps to major and minor construction macros. The device driver writer should not access the dev_t bits directly. Instead, the driver writer should use the major and minor interfaces to obtain the major and minor numbers for a special device. These numbers are specified by the driver writer in the stanza.static file fragment for static drivers and the stanza.loadable file fragment for loadable drivers. Section 11.1.2.5 and Section 11.1.2.6 describe these file fragments.

8.1.3.6 The b_un.b_addr Member

The b_un.b_addr member specifies the address at which to pull or push the data. This member is set by the kernel and is the main memory address where the I/O occurs. Driver writers use this member when their drivers need to perform DMA operations. It tells the driver where the data comes from and goes to in memory.

8.1.3.7 The b_lblkno and b_blkno Members

The b_lblkno member specifies the logical block number. The b_blkno member specifies the block number on the partition of a disk or on the file system. The b_blkno member is set by the kernel and it indicates the starting block number on the device where the I/O operation is to begin. Device drivers use this member only with block devices. For disk devices, this member is the block number relative to the start of the partition.

8.1.3.8 The b_resid and b_iodone Members

The b_resid member specifies (in bytes) the data not transferred because of some error. The b_iodone member specifies the interface called by iodone. The device driver calls iodone at the completion of an I/O operation. The driver calls the iodone interface, which calls the interface pointed to by the b_iodone member. The driver writer does not need to know anything about the interface pointed to by this argument.

8.1.3.9 The b_proc Member

The b_proc member specifies a pointer to the proc structure that represents the process performing the I/O. A device driver might pass b_proc in a call to the vtop interface in order to obtain the pmap.

8.2 Device Switch Tables

Associated with each device is a unique device number consisting of a major number and a minor number. The major number is used as an index into one of two device switch tables: the cdevsw table for character devices or the bdevsw table for block devices. The device switch tables are located in the file /usr/sys/io/common/conf.c.

The device switch tables have the following characteristics:

- They are arrays of structures that contain device driver entry points. These entry points are actually the addresses of the specific interfaces within the drivers.

- They may contain stubs for device driver entry points for devices that do not exist on a specific machine.

- The location in the table corresponds to the device major number.

The /usr/sys/io/common/conf.c text file is built into the kernel to initialize the bdevsw and cdevsw tables. These tables contain entries for all statically configured drivers. The kernel sizes these tables to include a number of unused entries that will be used at kernel run time to represent loadable drivers. Therefore, loadable device drivers are entered into the memory-resident versions of the bdevsw and cdevsw tables and do not appear in the text file /usr/sys/io/common/conf.c.

The following sections describe the cdevsw and bdevsw tables.

8.2.1 Character Device Switch Table

The character device switch, or cdevsw, table is an array of data structures that contains pointers to device driver entry points for each character device the system supports. In addition, the table can contain stubs for device driver entry points for character mode devices that do not exist or for entry points not used by a device driver.

The following shows the cdevsw structure defined in
/usr/sys/include/sys/conf.h:

```
struct cdevsw
{
   int       (*d_open)();
   int       (*d_close)();
   int       (*d_read)();
   int       (*d_write)();
   int       (*d_ioctl)();
   int       (*d_stop)();
   int       (*d_reset)();
   struct tty *d_ttys;
   int       (*d_select)();
   int       (*d_mmap)();
   int       d_funnel; /* serial code compatibility */
   int       (*d_segmap)(); /* xxx_segmap() entry point */
   int       d_flags; /* if (C_DDIDKI), driver follows
                          SVR4 DDI/DKI interfaces*/
};
```

There are two methods for adding device driver interfaces to the cdevsw
table, depending on whether the system manager chooses to install the device
driver dynamically or statically. Figure 8-1 shows how the device driver
interfaces associated with the loadable version of the /dev/cb driver are
added to the cdevsw table. As the figure shows, the driver writer declares
and initializes a structure called cb_cdevsw_entry that is of type
cdevsw. This data structure is usually declared in a section of the driver
that contains declarations and definitions that the loadable version of the
driver uses. Section 10.7 shows that the /dev/cb driver declares and
initializes cb_cdevsw_entry in the Loadable Driver Local Structure and
Variable Definitions Section.

Figure 8-1: Adding Entries to the cdevsw Table for Loadable Drivers

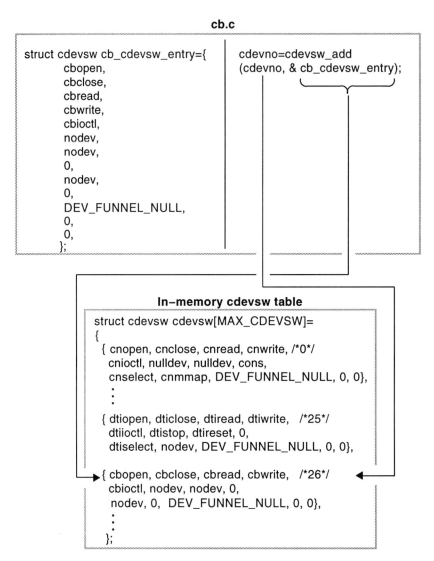

The figure also shows that the driver writer uses cdevsw_add as the mechanism for adding the driver interfaces to the cdevsw table. The first argument to cdevsw_add is the major number associated with the CB device. The second argument is the address of the previously initialized cb_cdevsw_entry structure.

Furthermore, the figure shows that when the loadable version of the driver is configured, cdevsw_add locates the position in the table corresponding to the major number, which in this example is 26, and adds the entries from cb_cdevsw_entry. Note that the cdevsw_add interface adds the driver's entry points into the in-memory resident cdevsw table. It does not change the /usr/sys/io/common/conf.c file, which is used to build the kernel. Thus, the driver's entry points are dynamically added to the cdevsw table for loadable drivers.

The loadable version of the driver usually calls the cdevsw_add interface in a Loadable Device Driver Section. Section 10.9.2 describes in detail the section of the /dev/cb driver that calls cdevsw_add.

For static drivers that follow the traditional device driver configuration model, the device driver writer manually edits the cdevsw table to add the device driver interfaces. For static drivers that follow the third-party device driver configuration model, the device driver interfaces are added by the config program as shown in Figure 8-2.

As the figure shows, config parses the appropriate driver interface entries in the stanza.static file fragment, locates the appropriate major device number (in this case 26), and adds these entries to the table.

The following sections discuss the members of the cdevsw structure.

Figure 8-2: Adding Entries to the cdevsw Table for Static Drivers

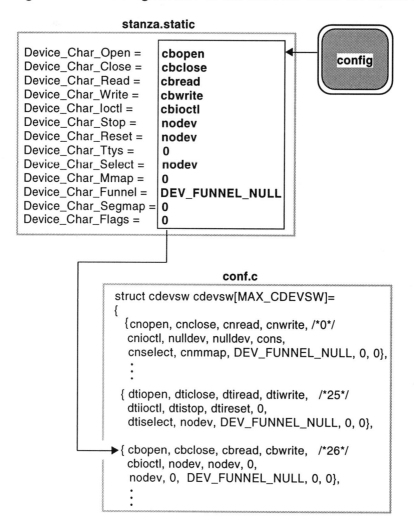

stanza.static

```
Device_Char_Open =        cbopen
Device_Char_Close =       cbclose
Device_Char_Read =        cbread
Device_Char_Write =       cbwrite
Device_Char_Ioctl =       cbioctl
Device_Char_Stop =        nodev
Device_Char_Reset =       nodev
Device_Char_Ttys =        0
Device_Char_Select =      nodev
Device_Char_Mmap =        0
Device_Char_Funnel =      DEV_FUNNEL_NULL
Device_Char_Segmap =      0
Device_Char_Flags =       0
```

config

conf.c

```
struct cdevsw cdevsw[MAX_CDEVSW]=
{
  {cnopen, cnclose, cnread, cnwrite, /*0*/
   cnioctl, nulldev, nulldev, cons,
   cnselect, cnmmap, DEV_FUNNEL_NULL, 0, 0},
   .
   .
   .
  { dtiopen, dticlose, dtiread, dtiwrite,  /*25*/
    dtiioctl, dtistop, dtireset, 0,
    dtiselect, nodev, DEV_FUNNEL_NULL, 0, 0},

  { cbopen, cbclose, cbread, cbwrite,  /*26*/
    cbioctl, nodev, nodev, 0,
    nodev, 0,  DEV_FUNNEL_NULL, 0, 0},
    .
    .
    .
```

8.2.1.1   The d_open and d_close Members

The d_open member specifies a pointer to an entry point for the driver's open interface, which opens a device. As shown in Figure 8-1 and Figure 8-2, the d_open member is initialized to cbopen for both the dynamically configured and statically configured /dev/cb driver.

The cdevsw_add interface is used to dynamically assign device major numbers to loadable character device drivers. The cdevsw_add interface checks the d_open member to determine if the entry is available to be

assigned a dynamic major device number. If your device driver does not
have an `open` interface, you must set this member to `nulldev` to tell
`cdevsw_add` that the entry is not available for dynamic assignment of the
device major number.

The `d_close` member specifies a pointer to an entry point for the driver's
`close` interface, which closes a device. As shown in Figure 8-1 and Figure
8-2, the `d_close` member is initialized to `cbclose` for the dynamically
configured and statically configured `/dev/cb` driver.

8.2.1.2 The d_read and d_write Members

The `d_read` member specifies a pointer to an entry point for the driver's
`read` interface, which reads characters or raw data. As shown in Figure 8-1
and Figure 8-2, the `d_read` member is initialized to `cbread` for both the
dynamically configured and statically configured `/dev/cb` driver.

The `d_write` member specifies a pointer to an entry point for the driver's
`write` interface, which writes characters or raw data. As shown in Figure
8-1 and Figure 8-2, the `d_write` member is initialized to `cbwrite` for
both the dynamically configured and statically configured `/dev/cb` driver.

8.2.1.3 The d_ioctl and d_stop Members

The `d_ioctl` member specifies a pointer to an entry point for the driver's
`ioctl` interface, which performs special functions or I/O control. As shown
in Figure 8-1 and Figure 8-2, the `d_ioctl` member is initialized to
`cbioctl` for both the dynamically configured and statically configured
`/dev/cb` driver.

The `d_stop` member specifies a pointer to an entry point for the driver's
`stop` interface, which suspends other processing on behalf of the current
process. You typically use the `d_stop` member only for terminal drivers.
As shown in Figure 8-1 and Figure 8-2, the `d_stop` member is initialized to
`nodev` for both the dynamically configured and statically configured
`/dev/cb` driver.

The `nodev` entry calls the `nodev` interface, which returns an ENODEV
(error, no such device). You should specify `nodev` when it is not appropriate
to call that interface for a particular driver. For example, a device driver
written for a write-only printer has no need for a `read` interface. Therefore,
the read entry point would contain a `nodev` entry. In this example, it is not
appropriate to call a `stop` interface for the `/dev/cb` driver; therefore, the
`nodev` entry is specified.

You could also specify `nulldev`. The `nulldev` entry calls the `nulldev`
interface, which returns the value zero (0). You should specify `nulldev`
when it is appropriate for the interface to be called, but the driver does not
need to perform any actions to support the interface. If the `stop` interface

has no functionality for the /dev/cb device, the nulldev entry should be specified instead of nodev.

8.2.1.4 The d_reset and d_ttys Members

The d_reset member specifies a pointer to an entry point for the driver's reset interface, which stops all current work and places the device connected to the controller in a known, quiescent state. As shown in Figure 8-1 and Figure 8-2, the d_reset member is initialized to nodev for both the dynamically configured and statically configured /dev/cb driver.

The nodev entry calls the nodev interface, which returns an ENODEV (error, no such device). You should specify nodev when it is not appropriate to call that interface for a particular driver. For example, a device driver written for a write-only printer has no need for a read interface. Therefore, the read entry point would contain a nodev entry. In this example, it is not appropriate to call a reset interface for the /dev/cb driver; therefore, the nodev entry is specified.

The d_ttys member specifies a pointer to driver private data. As shown in Figure 8-1 and Figure 8-2, the d_ttys member is initialized to the value zero (0) for both the dynamically configured and statically configured /dev/cb driver. The value zero (0) indicates that the /dev/cb device does not support the d_ttys member. A possible value for this member is an array of tty data structures. A tty data structure is associated with terminal device drivers, which are not discussed in this book.

8.2.1.5 The d_select and d_mmap Members

The d_select member specifies a pointer to an entry point for the driver's select interface, which determines if a call to a read or write interface will block. As shown in Figure 8-1 and Figure 8-2, the d_select member is initialized to nodev for both the dynamically configured and statically configured /dev/cb driver.

The nodev entry calls the nodev interface, which returns an ENODEV (error, no such device). You should specify nodev when it is not appropriate to call that interface for a particular driver. For example, a device driver written for a write-only printer has no need for a read interface. Therefore, the read entry point would contain a nodev entry. In this example, it is not appropriate to call a select interface for the /dev/cb driver; therefore, the nodev entry is specified.

The d_mmap member specifies a pointer to an entry point for the driver's mmap interface, which maps kernel memory to user address space. As shown in Figure 8-1 and Figure 8-2, the d_mmap member is initialized to the value zero (0) for both the dynamically configured and statically configured /dev/cb driver.

8.2.1.6 The d_funnel Member

The `d_funnel` member schedules a device driver onto a CPU in a multiprocessor configuration. You set this member to one of the following constants:

Value	Meaning
DEV_FUNNEL	Specifies that you want to funnel the device driver because you have not made it SMP safe. This means that the driver is forced to execute on a single (the master) CPU.
	Even if you funnel your device driver, you must follow the SMP locking conventions when accessing kernel data structures external to the driver. Typically, you use kernel interfaces that Digital supplies to indirectly access kernel data structures outside the driver.
DEV_FUNNEL_NULL	Specifies that you do not want to funnel the device driver because you have made it SMP safe. This means that the driver can execute on multiple CPUs. You make a device driver SMP safe by using the simple or complex lock mechanism.

As shown in Figure 8-1 and Figure 8-2, the `d_funnel` member is initialized to the `DEV_FUNNEL_NULL` constant for both the dynamically configured and statically configured /dev/cb device driver.

8.2.1.7 The d_segmap and d_flags Members

The `d_segmap` member specifies the segmap entry point. The `d_flags` member specifies whether this is an SVR4 DDI/DKI-compliant device driver. Set this member to the `C_DDIDKI` constant to indicate that this is an SVR4 DDI/DKI-compliant device driver. As shown in Figure 8-1 and Figure 8-2, the `d_segmap` and `d_flags` members are initialized to the value zero (0) for both the dynamically configured and statically configured /dev/cb device driver.

8.2.2 Block Device Switch Table

The block device switch, or `bdevsw`, table is an array of data structures that contains pointers to device driver entry points for each block mode device supported by the system. In addition, the table can contain stubs for device driver entry points for block mode devices that do not exist or entry points not used by a device driver.

The following shows the bdevsw structure defined in
/usr/sys/include/sys/conf.h:

```
struct bdevsw
{
    int     (*d_open)();
    int     (*d_close)();
    int     (*d_strategy)();
    int     (*d_dump)();
    int     (*d_psize)();
    int     d_flags;
    int     (*d_ioctl)();
    int     d_funnel; /* serial code compatibility */
};
```

The way the bdevsw table gets filled in differs, depending on whether the
system manager configures the loadable or static version of the driver.
Before discussing the members of the bdevsw data structure, it is useful to
describe how entries are added to the bdevsw table for loadable and static
drivers.

The method for adding device driver interfaces to the bdevsw table differs,
depending on whether the system manager chooses to install the device
driver dynamically or statically. Figure 8-3 shows how the device driver
interfaces are added to the bdevsw table when the system manager
dynamically configures the dkip driver. As the figure shows, the driver
writer declares and initializes a structure called dkip_bdevsw_entry that
is of type bdevsw. This data structure is usually declared in a section of the
driver that contains declarations and definitions that the loadable version of
the driver uses.

The figure also shows that the driver writer uses bdevsw_add as the
mechanism for adding the driver interfaces to the bdevsw table. The first
argument to bdevsw_add is the major number associated with the dkip
device. The second argument is the address of the previously initialized
dkip_bdevsw_entry structure. Furthermore, the figure shows that when
the loadable version of the driver is configured, bdevsw_add locates the
major device number in the table, which in this example is zero (0), and adds
the entries from dkip_bdevsw_entry. Note that the bdevsw_add
interface adds the driver's entry points into the in-memory resident bdevsw
table. It does not change the /usr/sys/io/common/conf.c file, which
is used to build the kernel. Thus, the driver's entry points are dynamically
added to the bdevsw table for loadable drivers.

Figure 8-3: Adding Entries to the bdevsw Table for Loadable Drivers

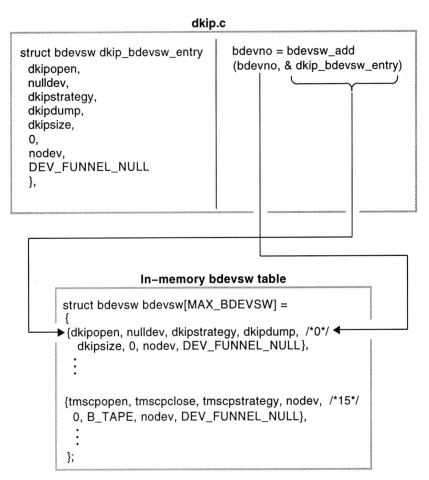

For static drivers that follow the traditional device driver configuration model, the device driver writer manually edits the bdevsw table to add the device driver interfaces. For static drivers that follow the third-party device driver configuration model, the config program adds the device driver interfaces as shown in Figure 8-4.

Figure 8-4: **Adding Entries to the bdevsw Table for Static Drivers**

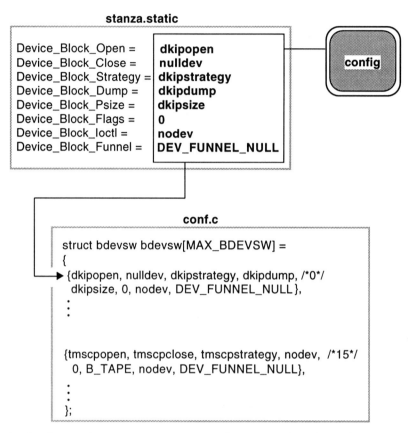

As the figure shows, config parses the appropriate driver interface entries in the stanza.static file fragment, locates the appropriate major device number (in this case 0), and adds these entries to the table.

The following sections discuss the members of the bdevsw structure.

8.2.2.1 The d_open and d_close Members

The d_open member specifies a pointer to an entry point for the driver's open interface, which opens a device. As shown in Figure 8-3 and Figure 8-4, the d_open member is initialized to dkipopen and tmscpopen for both the dynamically configured and statically configured dkip and tmscp drivers.

The bdevsw_add interface is used to dynamically assign device major numbers to loadable block device drivers. The bdevsw_add interface checks the d_open member to determine if the entry is available to be assigned a dynamic major device number. If your device driver does not have an open interface, you must set this member to nulldev to tell bdevsw_add that the entry is not available for dynamic assignment of the device major number.

The d_close member specifies a pointer to an entry point for the driver's close interface, which closes a device. As shown in Figure 8-3 and Figure 8-4, the d_close member is initialized to nulldev for both the dynamically configured and statically configured dkip driver.

The nulldev entry calls the nulldev interface, which returns the value zero (0). You should specify nulldev when it is appropriate for the interface to be called, but the driver does not need to perform any actions to support the interface. The close interface has no functionality for the dkip device; therefore, the nulldev entry is specified.

The figure also shows that d_close is initialized to tmscpclose for both the dynamically configured and statically configured tmscp driver.

8.2.2.2 The d_strategy and d_dump Members

The d_strategy member specifies the device driver's strategy interface for the device. As shown in Figure 8-3 and Figure 8-4, the d_strategy member is initialized to dkipstrategy and tmscpstrategy for both the dynamically configured and statically configured dkip and tmscp drivers.

The d_dump member specifies a pointer to an entry point for the driver's dump interface, which is used for panic dumps of the system image. As shown in Figure 8-3 and Figure 8-4, the d_dump member is initialized to dkipdump for both the dynamically configured and statically configured dkip driver and to nodev for both the dynamically configured and statically configured tmscp driver.

The nodev entry calls the nodev interface, which returns an ENODEV (error, no such device). You should specify nodev when it is not appropriate to call that interface for a particular driver. In this example, it is not appropriate to call a dump interface for the tmscp driver; therefore, the nodev entry is specified.

8.2.2.3 The d_psize and d_flags Members

The d_psize member specifies a pointer to an entry point for the driver's psize interface, which returns the size in physical blocks of a device (disk partition). As shown in Figure 8-3 and Figure 8-4, the d_psize member is initialized to dkipsize for both the dynamically configured and statically configured dkip driver. The figure also shows that d_psize is initialized to the value zero (0) for both the dynamically configured and statically configured tmscp driver. The value zero (0) indicates that the tmscp device does not support disk partitions (because it is a tape device).

The d_flags member specifies device-related and other flags. You set this member to the bitwise inclusive OR of the device-related and other flags. One example of a device-related flag is B_TAPE. This flag is set in the b_flags member of the buf structure. The B_TAPE flag determines whether to use delayed writes, which are not allowed for tape devices. For all other drivers, this member is set to the value zero (0).

Another flag specifies whether this is an SVR4 DDI/DKI-compliant device driver. You set this member to the B_DDIDKI flag to indicate that this is an SVR4 DDI/DKI-compliant device driver. As shown in Figure 8-3 and Figure 8-4, the d_flags member is initialized to the value zero (0) for both the dynamically configured and statically configured dkip driver. The figure also shows that for the tmscp driver the d_flags member is initialized to the B_TAPE constant.

8.2.2.4 The d_ioctl and d_funnel Members

The d_ioctl member specifies a pointer to an entry point for the driver's ioctl interface, which performs special functions or I/O control. As shown in Figure 8-3 and Figure 8-4, the d_ioctl member is initialized to nodev for both the dynamically configured and statically configured dkip and tmscp drivers.

The nodev entry calls the nodev interface, which returns an ENODEV (error, no such device). You should specify nodev when it is not appropriate to call that interface for a particular driver. In this example, it is not appropriate to call an ioctl interface for the dkip and tmscp block drivers; therefore, the nodev entry is specified.

The d_funnel member schedules a device driver onto a CPU in a multiprocessor configuration. You set this member to one of the following constants:

Value	Meaning
DEV_FUNNEL	Specifies that you want to funnel the device driver because you have not made it SMP safe. This means that the driver is forced to execute on a single (the master) CPU.
	Even if you funnel your device driver, you must follow the SMP locking conventions when accessing kernel data structures external to the driver. Typically, you use kernel interfaces that Digital supplies to indirectly access kernel data structures outside the driver.

Value	Meaning
DEV_FUNNEL_NULL	Specifies that you do not want to funnel the device driver because you have made it SMP safe. This means that the driver can execute on multiple CPUs. You make a device driver SMP safe by using the simple or complex lock mechanism.

As shown in Figure 8-3 and Figure 8-4, the d_funnel member is initialized to the DEV_FUNNEL_NULL constant for both the dynamically configured and statically configured dkip and tmscp drivers.

8.3 The uio Structure

The uio structure describes I/O, either single vector or multiple vectors. Typically, device drivers do not manipulate the members of this structure. However, the structure is presented here for the purpose of understanding the uiomove kernel interface, which operates on the members of the uio structure. Table 8-3 lists the members of the uio structure along with their associated data types that you might need to understand.

Table 8-3: Members of the uio Structure

Member Name	Data Type
uio_iov	struct iovec *
uio_iovcnt	int
uio_offset	off_t
uio_segflg	enum uio_seg
uio_resid	int
uio_rw	enum uio_rw

8.3.1 The uio_iov and uio_iovcnt Members

The uio_iov member specifies a pointer to the first iovec structure. The iovec structure has two members: one that specifies the address of the segment and another that specifies the size of the segment. The system allocates contiguous iovec structures for a given transfer.

The uio_iovcnt member specifies the number of iovec structures for this transfer.

8.3.2 The uio_offset and uio_segflg Members

The `uio_offset` member specifies the offset within the file.

The `uio_segflg` member specifies the segment type. This member can be set to one of the following values: `UIO_USERSPACE` (the segment is from the user data space), `UIO_SYSSPACE` (the segment is from the system space), or `UIO_USERISPACE` (the segment is from the user I space).

8.3.3 The uio_resid and uio_rw Members

The `uio_resid` member specifies the number of bytes that still need to be transferred.

The `uio_rw` member specifies whether the transfer is a read or a write. This member is set by `read` and `write` system calls according to the corresponding field in the file descriptor. This member can be set to one of the following values: `UIO_READ` (read transfer) or `UIO_WRITE` (write transfer).

8.4 Buffer Cache Management

When the file system deals with regular files, directories, and block devices, the I/O requests are serviced through the buffer cache system. Because the buffer cache deals with fixed-size buffers, it is often necessary to translate the user's request for I/O into buffer-size pieces called blocks. Only in the case where the size of the user's I/O matches a block and aligns to a block boundary will the underlying request match with the user's size. A large I/O request will be broken down into many block requests, with each block request going to the buffer cache system separately. Both read and write requests smaller than a block force the file system to request a read of the entire block and deal with the small read or write in the buffer.

Regular files and directories go through an extra translation process to map their logical block number into the physical blocks of the disk device. This mapping process itself can generate block requests to the buffer cache system to deal with file extension or to obtain or modify indirect file system blocks.

Buffer reads and buffer writes do not necessarily cause I/O to occur. In the case of buffer reads, the request can be satisfied by data already in the cache. On the other hand, buffer writes can modify or replace data in the cache, but the physical write might be delayed. Using a buffer cache enhances performance because data that changes often in the cache does not require a physical write for each change.

The nature of the buffer cache system's delayed physical I/O requires that each buffer request, or each block read or write, be a self-contained I/O request to the device driver's `strategy` interface. The buffer cache system and the block device driver `strategy` interface cannot assume any particular process context; therefore, the context of the process must be severed from the I/O request. The buffer passed to the buffer interface has all of the context necessary to perform the I/O.

8.4.1 Buffer Header

I/O requests come from a buffer cache interface as follows:

```
(*bdevsw[major](dev).d_strategy)(bp);
```

The `bdevsw` table is referenced and the appropriate driver interface is called through the block device's major number. The driver's `strategy` interface is passed a pointer to a `buf` structure.

8.5 Interrupt Code

When the kernel interrupt interface that does the initial handling of interrupts receives an interrupt, it:

- Saves the state of the CPU (for example, the registers)
- Sets up the argument list for the call to the driver (that is, the unit number)
- Transfers control to the appropriate driver, based on the interrupt vector index provided by the bus

Upon return from the driver's interrupt service interface, the kernel restores the state of the CPU to allow previously running processes to run.

Using Kernel Interfaces with Device Drivers 9

This chapter discusses the kernel interfaces most commonly used by device drivers and provides code fragments to illustrate how to call these interfaces in device drivers. These code fragments and associated descriptions supplement the reference (man) page-style descriptions for these and the other kernel interfaces presented in Chapter 15. Specifically, the chapter discusses the following:

- String interfaces

- Virtual memory interfaces

- Data copying interfaces

- Hardware-related interfaces

- Kernel-related interfaces

- Interfaces related to interrupt handler registration

- Loadable driver interfaces

- Interfaces related to the I/O handle

- Interfaces related to direct memory access

- Miscellaneous interfaces

9.1 String Interfaces

String interfaces allow device drivers to:

- Compare two null-terminated strings

- Compare two strings by using a specified number of characters

- Copy a null-terminated character string

- Copy a null-terminated character string with a specified limit

- Return the number of characters in a null-terminated string

The following sections describe the kernel interfaces that perform these tasks.

9.1.1 Comparing Two Null-Terminated Strings

To compare two null-terminated character strings, call the `strcmp` interface. The following code fragment shows a call to `strcmp`:

```
      .
      .
      .
register struct device *device;
struct controller *ctlr;
      .
      .
      .
if (strcmp(device->ctlr_name, ctlr->ctlr_name)) { 1
      .
      .
      .
}
```

1 Shows that the `strcmp` interface takes two arguments:

– The first argument specifies a pointer to a string (an array of characters terminated by a null character). In this example, this is the controller name pointed to by the `ctlr_name` member of the pointer to the `device` structure.

– The second argument also specifies a pointer to a string (an array of characters terminated by a null character). In the example, this is the controller name pointed to by the `ctlr_name` member of the pointer to the `controller` structure.

The code fragment sets up a condition statement that performs some tasks based on the results of the comparison. Figure 9-1 shows how `strcmp` compares two sample character string values in the code fragment. In item 1, `strcmp` compares the two controller names and returns the value zero (0) because `strcmp` performed a lexicographical comparison between the two strings and they were identical.

In item 2, `strcmp` returns an integer that is less than zero because the lexicographical comparison indicates that the characters in the first controller name, `fb`, come before the letters in the second controller name, `ipi`.

Figure 9-1: Results of the strcmp Interface

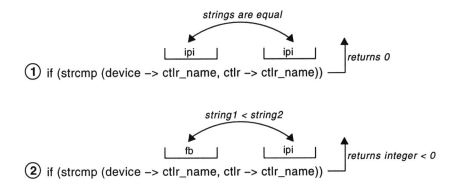

9.1.2 Comparing Two Strings by Using a Specified Number of Characters

To compare two strings by using a specified number of characters, call the `strncmp` interface. The following code fragment shows a call to `strncmp`:

```
      .
      .
      .
register struct device *device;
      .
      .
      .
if( (strncmp(device->dev_name, "rz", 2) == 0)) 1
      .
      .
      .
```

1 Shows that the `strncmp` interface takes three arguments:

- The first argument specifies a pointer to a string (an array of characters terminated by a null character). In the example, this is the device name pointed to by the `dev_name` member of the pointer to the `device` structure.

- The second argument also specifies a pointer to a string (an array of characters terminated by a null character). In the example, this is the character string `rz`.

- The third argument specifies the number of bytes to be compared. In the example, the number of bytes to compare is 2.

The code fragment sets up a condition statement that performs some tasks based on the results of the comparison. Figure 9-2 shows how `strncmp` compares two sample character string values in the code fragment. In item 1, strncmp compares the first two characters of the device name none with the string rz and returns an integer less than the value zero (0). The reason for this is that strncmp makes a lexicographical comparison between the two strings and the string no comes before the string rz. In item 2, strncmp compares the first two characters of the device name rza with the string rz and returns the value zero (0). The reason for this is that strncmp makes a lexicographical comparison between the two strings and the string rz is equal to the string rz.

Figure 9-2: Results of the strncmp Interface

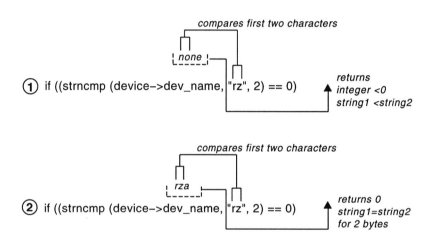

9.1.3 Copying a Null-Terminated Character String

To copy a null-terminated character string, call the strcpy interface. The following code fragment shows a call to strcpy:

```
     .
     .
     .
struct tc_slot   tc_slot[TC_IOSLOTS]; 1
char curr_module_name[TC_ROMNAMLEN + 1]; 2
     .
     .
     .
strcpy(tc_slot[i].modulename, curr_module_name); 3
     .
     .
     .
```

1 Declares an array of tc_slot structures of size TC_IOSLOTS.

2 Declares a variable to store the module name from the ROM of a device on the TURBOchannel bus.

3 Shows that the `strcpy` interface takes two arguments:

- The first argument specifies a pointer to a buffer large enough to hold the string to be copied. In the example, this buffer is the `modulename` member of the `tc_slot` structure associated with the specified bus.

- The second argument specifies a pointer to a string (an array of characters terminated by a null character). This is the string to be copied to the buffer specified by the first argument. In the example, this is the module name from the ROM, which is stored in the *curr_module_name* variable.

Figure 9-3 shows how `strcpy` copies a sample value in the code fragment. The interface copies the string CB (the value contained in *curr_module_name*) to the `modulename` member of the `tc_slot` structure associated with the specified bus. This member is presumed large enough to store the character string. The `strcpy` interface returns the pointer to the location following the end of the destination buffer.

Figure 9-3: Results of the strcpy Interface

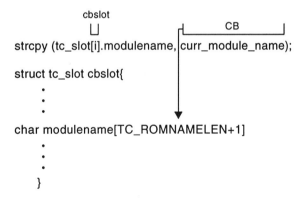

9.1.4 Copying a Null-Terminated Character String with a Specified Limit

To copy a null-terminated character string with a specified limit, call the `strncpy` interface. The following code fragment shows a call to

```
strncpy:
        .
        .
        .
register struct device *device;
char * buffer;
        .
        .
        .
strncpy(buffer, device->dev_name, 2); ⬛1
if (buffer == somevalue)
        .
        .
        .
```

⬛1 Shows that `strncpy` takes three arguments:

  - The first argument specifies a pointer to a buffer of at least the same
    number of bytes as specified in the third argument. In the example,
    this is the pointer to the *buffer* variable.

  - The second argument specifies a pointer to a string (an array of
    characters terminated by a null character). This is the character string
    to be copied and in the example is the value pointed to by the
    `dev_name` member of the pointer to the `device` structure.

  - The third argument specifies the number of characters to copy, which
    in the example is two characters.

The code fragment sets up a condition statement that performs some tasks
based on the characters stored in the pointer to the *buffer* variable.

Figure 9-4 shows how `strncpy` copies a sample value in the code
fragment. The interface copies the first two characters of the string `none`
(the value pointed to by the `dev_name` member of the pointer to the
`device` structure). The `strncpy` interface stops copying after it copies
a null character or the number of characters specified in the third
argument, whichever comes first.

The figure also shows that `strncpy` returns a pointer to the /NULL
character at the end of the first string (or to the location following the last
copied character if there is no NULL). The copied string will not be null
terminated if its length is greater than or equal to the number of
characters specified in the third argument.

Figure 9-4: Results of the strncpy Interface

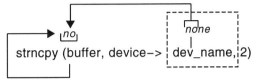

strncpy (buffer, device-> dev_name, 2)

returns pointer to /NULL at end of destination string

9.1.5 Returning the Number of Characters in a Null-Terminated String

To return the number of characters in a null-terminated character string, call the `strlen` interface. The following code fragment shows a call to `strlen`:

```
        .
        .
        .
char *strptr;
        .
        .
        .
if ((strlen(strptr)) > 1) 1
        .
        .
        .
```

1   Shows that the `strlen` interface takes one argument: a pointer to a string (an array of characters terminated by a null character). In the example, this pointer is the variable *strptr*.

The code fragment sets up a condition statement that performs some tasks based on the length of the string. Figure 9-5 shows how `strlen` checks the number of characters in a sample string in the code fragment. As the figure shows, `strlen` returns the number of characters pointed to by the *strptr* variable, which in the code fragment is four. Note that `strlen` does not count the terminating null character.

Figure 9-5: Results of the strlen Interface

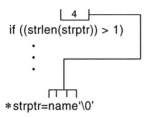

9.2 Virtual Memory Interfaces

In previous versions of the Digital UNIX operating system (formerly known as DEC OSF/1), device drivers could call the following memory allocation-related interfaces:

- `kalloc` and `kfree`

  Device drivers called these interfaces to allocate and free a variable-sized section of kernel virtual memory.

- `kget`

  Device drivers called this interface to perform nonblocking allocation of a variable-sized section of kernel virtual memory.

- `zinit`, `zchange`, `zalloc`, `zfree`, and `zget`

  Device drivers called these interfaces to allocate exact-size sections of kernel virtual memory.

The Digital UNIX operating system still provides backwards compatibility with the `kalloc`, `kfree`, and `kget` interfaces and the `zinit`, `zchange`, `zalloc`, `zfree`, and `zget` interfaces. However, Digital recommends that for new device drivers you use the `MALLOC` and `FREE` interfaces to allocate and to free sections of kernel virtual memory.

The variable-size memory allocator allows you to:

- Allocate a variable-size section of kernel virtual memory
- Deallocate a variable-size section of kernel virtual memory

9.2.1 Allocating a Variable-Size Section of Kernel Virtual Memory

To allocate a variable-size section of kernel virtual memory, call the `MALLOC` interface. The following code fragment shows a call to `MALLOC` in the `probe` interface for a `/dev/xx` device driver. A device driver's `probe` interface is called for each instance of the device that is actually present on the system. This makes the `probe` interface one place to dynamically allocate the data structures.

```
        .
        .
        .
#define MAX_NONE 16
        .
        .
        .
xxprobe (handle, ctlr) 1
   io_handle_t handle;
   struct controller *ctlr;
{
   if (ctlr->ctlr_num > MAX_NONE) 2
           return (0);
        .
        .
        .
if (xx_softc[ctlr->ctlr_num] == (struct xx_softc *) NULL { 3
      register struct xx_softc *sc; 4
      xx_softc[ctlr->ctlr_num] = (struct xx_softc *)MALLOC(sc,
                         struct xx_softc *,
                         sizeof(struct xx_softc), M_DEVBUF,
                         M_NOWAIT); 5
      if (xx_softc[ctlr->ctlr_num] == (struct xx_softc *) NULL { 6
          return (0);
      }
}
return(1); 7
}
        .
        .
        .
```

1 The bus configuration code passes the I/O handle and the `controller` structure associated with this device as parameters to the *xxprobe* interface. The *xxprobe* interface uses the `ctlr_num` member to determine which instance of the controller you are referring to.

2 Determines if there are more than 16 controllers. If there are, *xxprobe* returns the value zero (0) to indicate an error. Otherwise, it allocates the `xx_softc` structure.

3 Is a test to make sure that the bus configuration code has not already called *xxprobe* for this *xx* device.

4 Specifies a pointer to a `softc` structure for which `MALLOC` allocates a variable-size section of kernel virtual memory.

5 The *xxprobe* interface calls `MALLOC` to dynamically allocate the `xx_softc` structure for this *xx* device.

   The `MALLOC` interface takes five arguments:

   – The first argument specifies the memory pointer that points to the allocated memory. In this call, the memory pointer points to the memory allocated for the `xx_softc` structure pointer.

- The second argument specifies the data type for the memory pointer. In this call, the data type is of type `struct xx_softc *`.

- The third argument specifies the size of the memory (in bytes) to allocate. You should pass the size as a constant to speed up the memory allocation.

  This call uses the `sizeof` operator to obtain the size of the `xx_softc` structure.

- The fourth argument specifies the purpose for which the memory is being allocated. The memory types are defined in the file `malloc.h`. Typically, device drivers use the constant `M_DEVBUF` to indicate that device driver memory is being allocated (or freed). This call uses `M_DEVBUF`.

- The fifth argument specifies one of the following flag constants defined in `/usr/sys/include/sys/malloc.h`:

Value	Meaning
M_WAITOK	Allocates memory from the virtual memory subsystem if there is not enough memory in the preallocated pool. This constant signifies that MALLOC can block.
M_NOWAIT	Does not allocate memory from the virtual memory subsystem if there is not enough memory in the preallocated pool. This constant signifies that MALLOC cannot block.

  This call uses the `M_NOWAIT` flag. The *xxprobe* interface defines the return type of MALLOC as `struct xx_softc *`. In this call, MALLOC returns the address of the memory where it allocated the `xx_softc` structure. If the memory allocation request cannot be fulfilled, MALLOC returns a null pointer in the *addr* argument.

6 Checks the return value from MALLOC. The return value is NULL if there is no memory available to be dynamically allocated for the `xx_softc` structure for this *xx* device. Because the device driver is not operational without this data structure, *xxprobe* returns the value zero (0) to indicate that the driver's `probe` interface failed.

7 Otherwise, if MALLOC allocated the memory, *xxprobe* returns to the bus configuration code the value 1 to indicate that the probe succeeded.

9.2.2 Deallocating a Variable-Size Section of Kernel Virtual Memory

To deallocate (free) a variable-size section of kernel virtual memory, call the FREE interface. You use this interface to deallocate the memory space that was previously allocated in a call to MALLOC.

The following code fragment shows a call to FREE in the probe interface for a /dev/xx device driver:

```
    .
    .
    .
#define MAX_NONE 16
    .
    .
    .
xxprobe (handle, ctlr) 1
  io_handle_t handle;
  struct controller *ctlr;
{
  if (ctlr->ctlr_num < MAX_NONE) 2

  if (xx_softc[ctlr->ctlr_num] != (struct xx_softc *) NULL {
      FREE(sc, M_DEVBUF); 3
    .
    .
    .
```

1 The bus configuration code passes the I/O handle and the controller structure associated with this device as parameters to the *xxprobe* interface. The *xxprobe* interface uses the ctlr_num member to determine which instance of the controller you are referring to.

2 Determines if there are less than 16 controllers. If there are, *xxprobe* determines if memory for the xx_softc structure was previously allocated. If so, it deallocates this memory.

3 The FREE interface takes two arguments:

  – The first argument specifies the memory pointer that points to the allocated memory to be freed. You must have previously set this pointer in the call to MALLOC. You also define the data type for this argument in the call to MALLOC. This call passes the sc pointer.

  – The second argument specifies the purpose for which the memory is being allocated. The memory types are defined in the file malloc.h. Typically, device drivers use the constant M_DEVBUF to indicate that device driver memory is being allocated (or freed). This call passes the M_DEVBUF memory type.

9.3 Data Copying Interfaces

The data copying interfaces allow device drivers to:

- Copy a series of bytes with a specified limit
- Zero a block of memory
- Copy data from user address space to kernel address space
- Copy data from kernel address space to user address space
- Move data between user virtual space and system virtual space

The following sections describe the kernel interfaces that perform these tasks.

9.3.1 Copying a Series of Bytes with a Specified Limit

To copy a series of bytes with a specified limit, call the bcopy interface.
The following code fragment shows a call to bcopy:

```
        .
        .
        .
struct tc_slot   tc_slot[TC_IOSLOTS]; 1
        .
        .
        .
char *cp; 2
        .
        .
        .
bcopy(tc_slot[index].modulename, cp, TC_ROMNAMLEN + 1); 3
        .
        .
        .
```

1. Declares an array of tc_slot structures of size TC_IOSLOTS.

2. Declares a pointer to a buffer that stores the bytes of data copied from the first argument.

3. Shows that the bcopy interface takes three arguments:

   – The first argument is a pointer to a byte string (array of characters). In the example, this array is the modulename member of the tc_slot structure associated with this bus.

   – The second argument is a pointer to a buffer that is at least the size specified in the third argument. In the example, this buffer is represented by the pointer to the cp variable.

   – The third argument is the number of bytes to be copied. In the example, the number of bytes is contained in the constant TC_ROMNAMLEN.

Figure 9-6 shows how bcopy copies a series of bytes by using a sample value in the code fragment. As the figure shows, bcopy copies the characters CB to the buffer *cp*. No check is made for null bytes. The copy is nondestructive; that is, the address ranges of the first two arguments can overlap.

Figure 9-6: Results of the bcopy Interface

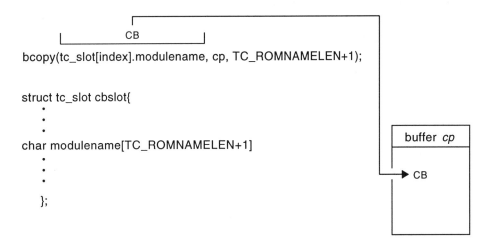

9.3.2 Zeroing a Block of Memory

To zero a block of memory, call the bzero or blkclr interface. The following code fragment shows a call to bzero. (The blkclr interface has the same arguments.)

```
    .
    .
    .
struct bus *new_bus;
    .
    .
    .
bzero(new_bus, sizeof(struct bus)); 1
    .
    .
    .
```

1 Shows that the bzero interface takes two arguments:

–   The first argument is a pointer to a string whose size is at least the size specified in the second argument. In the example, the first argument is a pointer to a bus structure.

- The second argument is the number of bytes to be zeroed. In the example, this size is expressed through the use of the `sizeof` operator, which returns the size of a `bus` structure.

In the example, `bzero` zeros the number of bytes associated with the size of the `bus` structure, starting at the address specified by *new_bus*.

The `blkclr` interface performs the equivalent task.

9.3.3 Copying Data from User Address Space to Kernel Address Space

To copy data from the unprotected user address space to the protected kernel address space, call the `copyin` interface. The following code fragment shows a call to `copyin`:

```
        .
        .
        .
register struct buf *bp;
int err;
caddr_t buff_addr;
caddr_t kern_addr;
        .
        .
        .
if (err = copyin(buff_addr,kern_addr,bp->b_resid)) { 1
        .
        .
        .
```

1 Shows that the `copyin` interface takes three arguments:

- The first argument specifies the address in user space of the data to be copied. In the example, this address is the user buffer's address.
- The second argument specifies the address in kernel space to copy the data to. In the example, this address is the address of the kernel buffer.
- The third argument specifies the number of bytes to copy. In the example, the number of bytes is contained in the `b_resid` member of the pointer to the `buf` structure.

The code fragment sets up a condition statement that performs some tasks based on whether `copyin` executes successfully. Figure 9-7 shows how `copyin` copies data from user address space to kernel address space by using sample data.

As the figure shows, `copyin` copies the data from the unprotected user address space, starting at the address specified by *buff_addr* to the protected kernel address space specified by *kern_addr*. The number of bytes is indicated by the `b_resid` member. The figure also shows that `copyin` returns the value zero (0) upon successful completion. If the address in user address space could not be accessed, `copyin` returns the error EFAULT.

Figure 9-7: Results of the copyin Interface

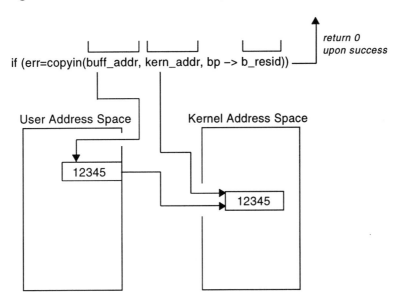

9.3.4 Copying Data from Kernel Address Space to User Address Space

To copy data from the protected kernel address space to the unprotected user address space, call the `copyout` interface. The following code fragment shows a call to `copyout`:

```
    .
    .
    .
register struct buf *bp;
int err;
caddr_t buff_addr;
caddr_t kern_addr;
    .
    .
    .
if (err = copyout(kern_addr,buff_addr,bp->b_resid)) { 1
    .
    .
    .
```

1 Shows that the `copyout` interface takes three arguments:

- The first argument specifies the address in kernel space of the data to be copied. In the example, this address is the kernel buffer's address, which is stored in the *kern_addr* argument.

- The second argument specifies the address in user space to copy the data to. In the example, this address is the user buffer's virtual address, which is stored in the *buff_addr* argument.

- The third argument specifies the number of bytes to copy. In the example, the number of bytes is contained in the b_resid member of the pointer to the buf structure.

Figure 9-8 shows the results of `copyout`, based on the code fragment. As the figure shows, `copyout` copies the data from the protected kernel address space, starting at the address specified by *kern_addr* to the unprotected user address space specified by *buff_addr*. The number of bytes is indicated by the b_resid member. The figure also shows that `copyout` returns the value zero (0) upon successful completion. If the address in kernel address space could not be accessed or if the number of bytes to copy is invalid, `copyout` returns the error EFAULT.

Figure 9-8: Results of the copyout Interface

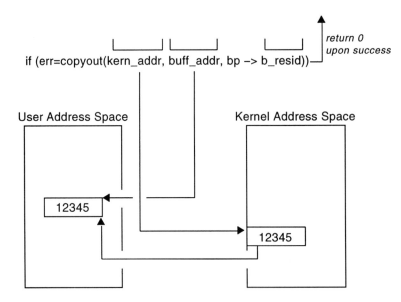

9.3.5 Moving Data Between User Virtual Space and System Virtual Space

To move data between user virtual space and system virtual space, call the uiomove interface. The following code fragment shows a call to uiomove:

```
    .
    .
    .
struct uio *uio;
register struct buf *bp;
int err;
int cnt;
unsigned tmp;
    .
    .
    .
err = uiomove(&tmp,cnt,uio); 1
    .
    .
    .
```

1 Shows that the uiomove interface takes three arguments:

   – The first argument specifies a pointer to the kernel buffer in system virtual space.

   – The second argument specifies the number of bytes of data to be moved. In this example, the number of bytes to be moved is stored in the cnt variable.

   – The third argument specifies a pointer to a uio structure. This structure describes the current position within a logical user buffer in user virtual space.

   Section 10.11.1 shows how you use uiomove with the /dev/cb device driver.

9.4 Hardware-Related Interfaces

The hardware-related interfaces allow device drivers to perform the following tasks related to the hardware:

• Check the read accessibility of addressed data

• Delay the calling interface a specified number of microseconds

• Set the interrupt priority mask

The following sections describe the kernel interfaces that perform these tasks.

9.4.1 Checking the Read Accessibility of Addressed Data

To check the read accessibility of addressed data, call the BADADDR
interface. The following code fragment shows a call to this interface:

```
     .
     .
     .
caddr_t addr1;
     .
     .
     .
typedef volatile struct {
        int csr;
}none_registers;
     .
     .
     .
register struct none_registers *reg = (struct none_registers *) addr1;
if (BADADDR( (caddr_t) &reg->csr, sizeof(int)), NULL !=0) 1
{
     .
     .
     .
}
```

1 Shows that the BADADDR interface takes three arguments:

- The first argument specifies the address of the device registers or
  memory. In the example, this address is that of the csr member of
  the reg pointer. This member maps to the 32-bit control status
  register for this none device.

- The second argument specifies the length (in bytes) of the data to be
  checked. Valid values are 1, 2, and 4 on 32-bit machines and 4 and 8
  on 64-bit machines. In the example, the length is the value returned
  by the sizeof operator — the number of bytes needed to contain a
  value of type int. The reason for this is the csr member is of type
  int.

- The third argument specifies a pointer to a bus_ctlr_common
  structure. You cast this argument as a pointer to either a bus or
  controller structure. Because this example does not use the third
  argument, it passes the value NULL.

The BADADDR interface generates a call to a machine-dependent interface
that does a read access check of the data at the supplied address and
dismisses any machine check exception that may result from the
attempted access. You call this interface to probe for memory or I/O
devices at a specified address during device autoconfiguration.

The BADADDR interface returns the value zero (0) if the data is accessible
and nonzero if the data is not accessible.

This line also sets up a condition statement that performs some tasks
based on BADADDR determining if the data stored in csr is accessible.

Loadable device drivers cannot call the BADADDR interface because it is usable only in the early stages of system booting. Loadable device drivers are loaded during the multiboot stage. If your driver is both loadable and static, you can declare a variable and use it to control any differences in the tasks that the loadable and static drivers perform. Thus, the static driver can still call BADADDR.

9.4.2 Delaying the Calling Interface a Specified Number of Microseconds

To delay the calling interface a specified number of microseconds, call the DELAY interface. The following code fragment shows a call to this interface:

```
    .
    .
    .
DELAY(10000) 1
    .
    .
    .
```

1 Shows that the DELAY interface takes one argument: the number of microseconds for the calling process to spin.

The DELAY interface delays the calling interface a specified number of microseconds. DELAY spins, waiting for the specified number of microseconds to pass before continuing execution. In the example, there is a 10000-microsecond (10-millisecond) delay. The range of delays is system dependent, due to its relation to the granularity of the system clock. The system defines the number of clock ticks per second in the hz variable. Specifying any value smaller than 1/hz to the DELAY interface results in an unpredictable delay. For any delay value, the actual delay may vary by plus or minus one clock tick.

Using the DELAY interface is discouraged because the processor will be consumed for the specified time interval and therefore is unavailable to service other processes. In cases where device drivers need timing mechanisms, you should use the sleep and timeout interfaces instead of the DELAY interface. The most common usage of the DELAY interface is in the system boot path. Using DELAY in the boot path is often acceptable because there are no other processes in contention for the processor.

9.4.3 Setting the Interrupt Priority Mask

To set the interrupt priority level (IPL) mask to a specified level, call one of the spl interfaces. Table 9-1 summarizes the uses for the different spl interfaces.

Table 9-1: Uses for spl Interfaces

spl Interface	Meaning
getspl	Gets the spl value.
splbio	Masks all disk and tape controller interrupts.
splclock	Masks all hardware clock interrupts.
spldevhigh	Masks all device and software interrupts.
splextreme	Blocks against all but halt interrupts.
splhigh	Masks all interrupts except for realtime devices, machine checks, and halt interrupts.
splimp	Masks all Ethernet hardware interrupts.
splnet	Masks all network software interrupts.
splnone	Unmasks (enables) all interrupts.
splsched	Masks all scheduling interrupts (usually hardware clock).
splsoftclock	Masks all software clock interrupts.
spltty	Masks all tty (terminal device) interrupts.
splvm	Masks all virtual memory clock interrupts.
splx	Resets the CPU priority to the level specified by the argument.

The spl interfaces set the CPU priority to various interrupt levels. The current CPU priority level determines which types of interrupts are masked (disabled) and which are unmasked (enabled). Historically, seven levels of interrupts were supported, with eight different spl interfaces to handle the possible cases. For example, calling spl0 would unmask all interrupts and calling spl7 would mask all interrupts. Calling an spl interface between 0 and 7 would mask out all interrupts at that level and at all lower levels.

Specific interrupt levels were assigned for different device types. For example, before handling a given interrupt, a device driver would set the CPU priority level to mask all other interrupts of the same level or lower. This setting meant that the device driver could be interrupted only by interrupt requests from devices of a higher priority.

Digital UNIX currently supports the naming of spl interfaces to indicate the associated device types. Named spl interfaces make it easier to determine which interface you should use to set the priority level for a given device type.

The following code fragment shows the use of `spl` interfaces as part of a disk `strategy` interface:

```
    .
    .
    .
int s;
    .
    .
    .
s = splbio(); 1
    .
    .
    .
[Code to deal with data that can be modified by the disk interrupt code]
splx(s); 2
    .
    .
    .
```

1 Calls the `splbio` interface to mask (disable) all disk interrupts. This interface does not take an argument.

2 Calls the `splx` interface to reset the CPU priority to the level specified by the `s` argument. Note that the one argument associated with `splx` is a CPU priority level, which in the example is the value returned by `splbio`. (The `splx` interface is the only one of the `spl` interfaces that takes an argument.) Upon successful completion, each `spl` interface returns an integer value that represents the CPU priority level that existed before it was changed by a call to the specified `spl` interface.

The binding of any `spl` interface with a specific CPU priority level is highly machine dependent. With the exceptions of the `splhigh` and `splnone` interfaces, knowledge of the explicit bindings is not required to create new device drivers. You always use `splhigh` to mask (disable) all interrupts and `splnone` to unmask (enable) all interrupts.

9.5 Kernel-Related Interfaces

The kernel-related interfaces allow device drivers to:

- Cause a system crash
- Print text to the console and error logger
- Put a calling process to sleep
- Wake up a sleeping process
- Initialize a callout queue element
- Remove the scheduled interface from the callout queues

The following sections describe the kernel interfaces that perform these tasks.

9.5.1 Causing a System Crash

To cause a system crash, call the `panic` interface. The following code fragment shows a call to this interface:

```
        .
        .
        .
panic("vba: no adapter error vector"); 1
        .
        .
        .
```

1 Shows that `panic` takes one argument: the message you want the `panic` interface to display on the console terminal.

The `panic` interface causes a system crash, usually because of fatal errors. It sends to the console terminal and error logger the specified message and, possibly, other system-dependent information (for example, register dumps). It also causes a crash dump to be generated. After displaying the message, `panic` reboots the system if the console environment variables are set appropriately.

9.5.2 Printing Text to the Console and Error Logger

To print text to the console terminal and the error logger, call the `printf` interface. The kernel `printf` interface is a scaled-down version of the C library `printf` interface. The `printf` interface prints diagnostic information directly on the console terminal and writes ASCII text to the error logger. Because `printf` is not interrupt driven, all system activities are suspended when you call it. Only a limited number of characters (currently 128) can be sent to the console display during each call to any section of a driver. The reason is that the characters are buffered until the driver returns to the kernel, at which time they are actually sent to the console display. If more than 128 characters are sent to the console display, the storage pointer may wrap around, discarding all previous characters; or it may discard all characters following the first 128.

If you need to see the results on the console terminal, limit the message size to the maximum of 128 whenever you send a message from within the driver. However, `printf` also stores the messages in an error log file. You can use the `uerf` command to view the text of this error log file. See the reference (man) page for this command.

The messages are easier to read if you use `uerf` with the `-o terse` option. The following code fragment shows a call to this interface:

```
        .
        .
        .
#ifdef CB_DEBUG
printf("CBprobe @ %8x, vbaddr = %8x, ctlr = %8x\n",cbprobe,vbaddr,ctlr);  1
#endif /*CB_DEBUG*/
        .
        .
        .
```

1. Shows a typical use for the `printf` interface in the debugging of device drivers.

The example shows that `printf` takes two arguments:

- The first argument specifies a pointer to a string that contains two types of objects. One object is ordinary characters such as "hello, world", which are copied to the output stream. The other object is a conversion specification such as %d, %o, or %x.

- The second argument specifies the argument list. In this example, the argument list consists of the arguments *cbprobe*, *vbaddr*, and *ctlr*.

The Digital UNIX operating system also supports the `uprintf` interface. The `uprintf` interface prints to the current user's terminal. Interrupt service interfaces should never call `uprintf`. It does not perform any space checking, so you should not use this interface to print verbose messages. The `uprintf` interface does not log messages to the error logger.

9.5.3 Putting a Calling Process to Sleep

To put a calling process to sleep, call the `sleep` interface. The `sleep` and `wakeup` interfaces block and then wake up a process. Generally, device drivers call these interfaces to wait for the transfer to complete an interrupt from the device. That is, the `write` interface of the device driver sleeps on the address of a known location, and the device's interrupt service interface wakes the process when the device interrupts. It is the responsibility of the wakened process to check if the condition for which it was sleeping has been removed. The following code fragment shows a call to this interface:

```
        .
        .
        .
sleep(&ctlr->bus_name, PCATCH);  1
        .
        .
        .
```

[1] Shows that the `sleep` interface takes two arguments:

 - The first argument specifies a unique address associated with the calling kernel thread to be put to sleep. In this example, the `sleep` interface puts the calling process to sleep on the address of the bus that this controller is connected to.

 - The second argument specifies whether the sleep request is interruptible. Setting this argument to the PCATCH flag causes the process to sleep in an interruptible state. Not setting the PCATCH flag causes the process to sleep in an uninterruptible state. The `param.h` file defines the different priorities. The example sets the PCATCH flag to indicate that the sleep request is interruptible.

9.5.4 Waking Up a Sleeping Process

To wake up all processes sleeping on a specified address, call the `wakeup` interface. The following code fragment shows a call to this interface:

```
.
.
.
wakeup(&ctlr->bus_name); [1]
.
.
.
```

[1] Shows that the `wakeup` interface takes one argument: the address on which the wakeup is to be issued. In the example, this address is that of the bus name associated with the bus this controller is connected to. This address was specified in a previous call to the `sleep` interface. All processes sleeping on this address are wakened.

9.5.5 Initializing a Callout Queue Element

To initialize a callout queue element, call the `timeout` interface. The following code fragment shows a call to this interface:

```
.
.
.
#define CBIncSec   1
.
.
.
cb = &cb_unit[unit];
.
.
.
timeout(cbincled, (caddr_t)cb, CBIncSec*hz); [1]
```

.
.
.

[1] Shows that the timeout interface takes three arguments:

– The first argument specifies a pointer to the interface to be called. In the example, timeout will call the cbincled interface on the interrupt stack (not in processor context) as dispatched from the softclock interface.

– The second argument specifies a single argument to be passed to the called interface. In the example, this argument is the pointer to the CB device's cb_unit data structure. This argument is passed to the cbincled interface. Because the data types of the arguments are different, the code fragment performs a type-casting operation that converts the argument type to be of type caddr_t.

– The third argument specifies the amount of time to delay before calling the specified interface. You express time as time (in seconds) * hz. In the example, the constant CBIncSec is used with the *hz* global variable to determine the amount of time before timeout calls cbincled. The global variable *hz* contains the number of clock ticks per second. This variable is a second's worth of clock ticks. The example illustrates a 1-second delay.

9.5.6 Removing the Scheduled Interface from the Callout Queues

To remove the scheduled interfaces from the callout queues, call the untimeout interfaces. The following code fragment shows a call to this interface:

```
.
.
.
untimeout(cbincled, (caddr_t)cb);  [1]
.
.
.
```

[1] Shows that the untimeout interface takes two arguments:

– The first argument specifies a pointer to the interface to be removed from the callout queues. In the example, untimeout removes the cbincled interface from the callout queues. This interface was placed on the callout queue in a previous call to the timeout interface.

– The second argument specifies a single argument to be passed to the called interface. In the example, this argument is the pointer to the CB device's cb_unit data structure. It matches the parameter that was passed in a previous call to timeout. Because the data types of the arguments are different, the code fragment performs a type-casting operation that converts the argument type to be of type `caddr_t`.

The argument is used to uniquely identify which timeout to remove. This is useful if more than one process has called `timeout` with the same interface argument.

9.6 Interfaces Related to Interrupt Handler Registration

An interrupt service interface (ISI) is a device driver routine (sometimes called an interrupt handler) that handles hardware interrupts. In previous versions of the Digital UNIX operating system (formerly known as DEC OSF/1), driver writers implementing static-only device drivers specified a device driver's ISI in the system configuration file if they followed the traditional device driver configuration model; they specified the ISI in the `config.file` file fragment if they followed the third-party device driver configuration model. Loadable device drivers, on the other hand, must call a number of kernel interfaces and use specific data structures to register, deregister, enable, and disable a device driver's ISI.

Digital recommends that all new drivers (static and loadable) call the `handler` interfaces to dynamically register ISIs.

The dynamic registration of ISIs involves the use of the following data structures:

- `ihandler_t`
- `handler_intr_info`

Section 7.5 describes the data structures used to dynamically register ISIs.

The dynamic registration of a device driver's ISI involves the following tasks:

- Registering and enabling a driver's ISI
- Deregistering and disabling a driver's ISI

9.6.1 Registering and Enabling a Driver's Interrupt Service Interface

To register a device driver's ISI, call the `handler_add` interface. To enable a device driver's ISI, call the `handler_enable` interface. The `handler_add` and `handler_enable` interfaces are usually called in the Autoconfiguration Support Section of the device driver. The following code fragment and discussion focus on the data structures and arguments used in the calls to these interfaces. Section 10.8.1 discusses in more detail how these interfaces are implemented for the /dev/cb device driver.

```
·
·
·
ihandler_id_t *cb_id_t[NCB]; 1
·
·
·
ihandler_t handler; 2
struct handler_intr_info info; 3
int unit = ctlr->ctlr_num; 4
·
·
·
info.intr = cbintr; 5
·
·
·
handler.ih_bus_info = (char *)&info; 6
·
·
·
cb_id_t[unit] = handler_add(&handler); 7
·
·
·
if (handler_enable(cb_id_t[unit]) != 0) 8
·
·
·
```

1. Declares a pointer to an array of IDs that are unique numbers for identifying ISIs to be acted on by subsequent calls to handler_enable, handler_disable, and handler_del. This array is filled with the return values from handler_add. These return values are opaque keys of type ihandler_id_t.

2. Declares an ihandler_t data structure called handler to contain information associated with the /dev/cb device driver interrupt handling. Section 7.5.1 describes the ihandler_t structure.

3. Declares a handler_intr_info data structure called info.

4. Declares a *unit* variable and initializes it to the controller number.

5. Sets the intr member of the info data structure to the pointer to the driver's interrupt interface, cbintr.

6. Sets the ih_bus_info member of the handler data structure to the address of the bus-specific information structure, info.

7. Shows that the handler_add interface takes one argument: a pointer to an ihandler_t data structure. In this example, the address of the declared ihandler_t structure is passed.

   The handler_add interface registers a device driver's ISI and its associated `ihandler_t` data structure to the bus-specific interrupt-dispatching algorithm. The `ih_bus` member of the `ihandler_t` structure specifies the parent `bus` structure for the bus controlling the driver being loaded. For controller devices, `handler_add` sets `ih_bus` to the address of the `bus` structure for the bus the controller resides on.

Upon successful completion, the `handler_add` interface returns an opaque `ihandler_id_t` key, which is a unique number that identifies the ISIs to be acted on by subsequent calls to `handler_del`, `handler_disable`, and `handler_enable`. To implement this `ihandler_id_t` key, each call to `handler_add` causes the `handler_key` data structure to be allocated.

In the example, `handler_add` returns this opaque `ihandler_id_t` key to the array of IDs.

8 Shows that the `handler_enable` interface takes one argument: a pointer to the ISI's entry in the interrupt table. In the example, `handler_enable` is passed the IDs that were returned by `handler_add`.

The `handler_enable` interface marks that interrupts are enabled and can be dispatched to the driver's ISIs, as registered in a previous call to `handler_add`. The *id* argument passed to `handler_enable` is used to call a bus-specific `adp_handler_enable` interface to perform the bus-specific tasks needed to enable the ISIs.

Upon successful completion, `handler_enable` returns the value zero (0). Otherwise, it returns the value –1.

9.6.2 Deregistering and Disabling a Driver's Interrupt Service Interface

The deregistration of interrupt handlers consists of two calls. The first is a call to the `handler_disable` interface to disable any further interrupts. The second call is to the `handler_del` interface to remove the interrupt service interfaces. The following code fragments show calls to these interfaces:

```
     .
     .
     .
if (handler_disable(cb_id_t[unit]) != 0) { 1
     .
     .
     .
if (handler_del(cb_id_t[unit]) != 0) { 2
```

.
.
.

1 Shows that the `handler_disable` interface takes one argument: a pointer to the ISI's entry in the interrupt table. In the example, `handler_disable` is passed the IDs that were returned by `handler_add`.

The `handler_disable` interface makes the driver's previously registered interrupt service interfaces unavailable to the system. You must call `handler_disable` prior to calling `handler_del`. The `handler_disable` interface uses the *id* argument to call a bus-specific `adp_handler_disable` interface to perform the bus-specific tasks needed to disable the interrupt service interfaces.

Upon successful completion, `handler_disable` returns the value zero (0). Otherwise, it returns the value –1.

2 Shows that the `handler_del` interface takes the same argument as `handler_disable`. The `handler_del` interface uses the *id* argument to call a bus-specific `adp_handler_del` interface to remove the driver's ISI. Deregistration of an interrupt interface can consist of replacing it with the `stray` interface to indicate that interrupts are no longer expected from this device. The `stray` interface is a generic interface used as the interrupt handler when there is no corresponding ISI.

The `handler_del` interface deregisters a device driver's ISI from the bus-specific interrupt-dispatching algorithm. In addition, the interface unlinks the `handler_key` structure associated with the ISI. Prior to deleting the ISI, the device driver should have disabled it by calling `handler_disable`. If the ISI was not disabled, `handler_del` returns an error.

Upon successful completion, `handler_del` returns the value zero (0). Otherwise, it returns the value –1.

9.7 Loadable Driver Interfaces

The loadable driver interfaces allow loadable drivers to perform a variety of tasks specific to loadable drivers. The most commonly performed loadable driver tasks are to:

- Add or delete entry points in the `bdevsw` table
- Add or delete entry points in the `cdevsw` table
- Merge the configuration data
- Configure and unconfigure the specified controller

9.7.1 Adding or Deleting Entry Points in the bdevsw Table

To dynamically add entry points to the bdevsw (block device switch) table
for loadable drivers, call the bdevsw_add interface. The following code
fragment shows a call to bdevsw_add:

```
    .
    .
    .
struct bdevsw dkip_bdevsw_entry = {
        dkipopen,
        nulldev,
        dkipstrategy,
        dkipdump,
        dkipsize,
        0,
        nodev,
        DEV_FUNNEL_NULL
};
    .
    .
    .
dev_t    dkip_devno;
    .
    .
    .
bdevno = bdevsw_add(bdevno,&dkip_bdevsw_entry); 1
    .
    .
    .
dkip_devno = bdevno; 2
    .
    .
    .
```

1 Shows that bdevsw_add takes two arguments:

– The first argument specifies the device number to use for the bdevsw
  device switch table entry (slot). In this example, the device number is
  stored in the *bdevno* variable. The device number is usually
  obtained in a previous call to the makedev interface.

– The second argument specifies the block device switch structure that
  contains the block device driver's entry points. In this example, the
  dkip_bdevsw_entry structure contains the device driver entry
  points for a dkip driver.

Figure 9-9 shows the results of bdevsw_add, based on the code
fragment. This code would appear in the driver source, dkip.c. As the
figure shows, bdevsw_add identifies as zero the device number for the
dkip device and adds the driver entry points contained in the
dkip_bdevsw_entry structure. The bdevsw_add interface adds the
driver's entry points into the in-memory resident bdevsw table. It does
not change the /usr/sys/io/common/conf.c file, which is used to

build the kernel. Thus, the driver's entry points are dynamically added to the `bdevsw` table for loadable drivers.

Upon successful completion, `bdevsw_add` returns the device number associated with the entry in the `bdevsw` table. In the example, the device number is the value zero (0).

2 Stores the table entry slot for this device in the *dkip_devno* variable for use later by the `bdevsw_del` interface.

Figure 9-9: Results of the bdevsw_add Interface

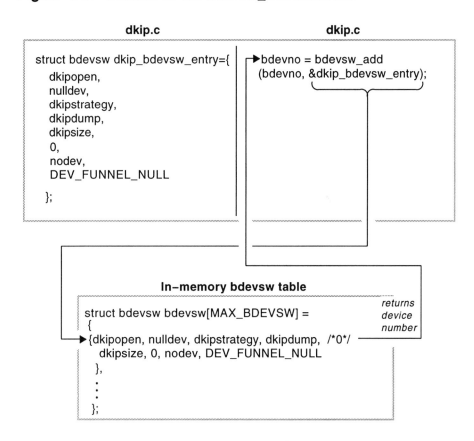

To dynamically delete entry points from the bdevsw (block device switch) table, call the bdevsw_del interface. The following code fragment shows a call to bdevsw_del:

```
         .
         .
         .
int      retval;
         .
         .
         .
retval = bdevsw_del(dkip_devno); 1
         .
         .
         .
```

1 Shows that bdevsw_del takes one argument: the device number specified in a previous call to bdevsw_add. This number was stored in the *dkip_devno* variable.

Figure 9-10 shows the results of bdevsw_del, based on the code fragment. As the figure shows, bdevsw_del identifies as zero the device number for the dkip device and deletes the driver entry points from the bdevsw table. The bdevsw_del interface deletes the driver's entry points from the in-memory resident bdevsw table. It does not change the /usr/sys/io/common/conf.c file, which is used to build the kernel. Thus, the driver's entry points are dynamically deleted from the bdevsw table for loadable drivers.

Upon successful completion, bdevsw_del returns the value zero (0).

Figure 9-10: Results of the bdevsw_del Interface

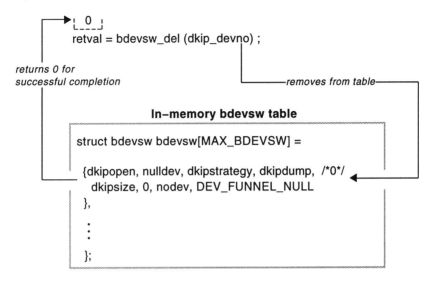

9.7.2 Adding or Deleting Entry Points in the cdevsw Table

To dynamically add entry points to the cdevsw (character device switch)
table for loadable drivers, call the cdevsw_add interface. The following
code fragment shows a call to cdevsw_add:

```
    .
    .
    .
struct cdevsw cb_cdevsw_entry = {
  cbopen,
  cbclose,
  cbread,
  cbwrite,
  cbioctl,
  nodev,
  nodev,
  0,
  nodev,
  0,
  0,
  0,
  0
};
    .
    .
    .
dev_t cb_cdevno;
```

```
        .
        .
        .
cdevno = cdevsw_add(cdevno,&cb_cdevsw_entry);  1
        .
        .
        .
cb_devno = cdevno;  2
```

1 Shows that cdevsw_add takes two arguments:

   – The first argument specifies the device number to use for the cdevsw
      device switch table entry (slot). In this example, the device number is
      stored in the cdevno variable. The device number is usually
      obtained in a previous call to the makedev interface.

   – The second argument specifies the character device switch structure
      that contains the character device driver's entry points. In this
      example, the cb_cdevsw_entry structure contains the device
      driver entry points for the /dev/cb driver.

   Figure 9-11 shows the results of cdevsw_add, based on the code
   fragment. This code would appear in the driver source, cb.c. As the
   figure shows, cdevsw_add identifies as 26 the device number for the
   CB device and adds the driver entry points contained in the
   cb_cdevsw_entry structure. The cdevsw_add interface adds the
   driver's entry points into the in-memory resident cdevsw table. It does
   not change the /usr/sys/io/common/conf.c file, which is used to
   build the kernel. Thus, the driver's entry points are dynamically added to
   the cdevsw table for loadable drivers.

   Upon successful completion, cdevsw_add returns the device number
   associated with the entry in the cdevsw table. In the example, the
   device number is the value 26.

2 Stores the table entry slot for this CB device in the cb_cdevno variable
   for use later by the cdevsw_del interface.

Figure 9-11: Results of the cdevsw_add Interface

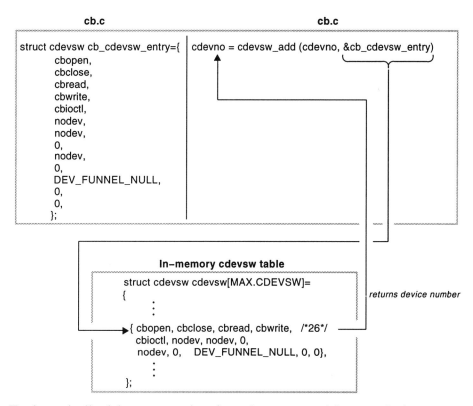

To dynamically delete entry points from the cdevsw (character device switch) table, call the cdevsw_del interface. The following code fragment shows a call to cdevsw_del:

```
   .
   .
   .
int      retval;
   .
   .
   .
retval = cdevsw_del(cb_cdevno);  1
   .
   .
   .
```

1   Shows that cdevsw_del takes one argument: the device number specified in a previous call to cdevsw_add. This number was stored in the *cb_cdevno* variable.

Figure 9-12 shows the results of cdevsw_del, based on the code fragment. As the figure shows, cdevsw_del identifies as 26 the device number for the CB device and deletes the driver entry points from the cdevsw table. The cdevsw_del interface deletes the driver's entry points from the in-memory resident cdevsw table. It does not change the /usr/sys/io/common/conf.c file, which is used to build the kernel. Thus, the driver's entry points are dynamically deleted from the cdevsw table for loadable drivers.

Upon successful completion, cdevsw_add returns the value zero (0).

Figure 9-12: Results of the cdevsw_del Interface

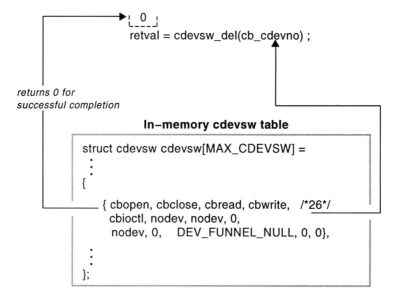

9.7.3 Merging the Configuration Data

To merge the configuration data, call the ldbl_stanza_resolver interface. This interface is generally called in the section of the driver that implements the tasks associated with the configurable (loadable) driver. The following code fragment shows a call to this interface.

Section 10.9.2 discusses in more detail how this interface is implemented for the /dev/cb device driver.

```
        .
        .
        .
#define CB_BUSNAME        "tc"
        .
        .
        .
struct  driver cbdriver = { cbprobe, 0, cbattach, 0, 0, 0, 0, 0,
                            "cb", cbinfo, 0, 0, 0, 0, 0,
                            cb_ctlr_unattach, 0 };
        .
        .
        .
struct tc_option cb_option_snippet [] =
{
    /*  module             driver  intr_b4 itr_aft       adpt    */
    /*  name               name    probe   attach  type  config  */
    /*  ------             ------  ------- ------- ----  ------  */
    {  "CB        ",       "cb",      0,      1,    'C',   0},
    {  "",                 ""         } /* Null terminator in the table */
};
        .
        .
        .
static unsigned char mcfgname[CFG_ATTR_NAME_SZ] = "";
        .
        .
        .
    if(strcmp(mcfgname,"")!=0){
        if (ldbl_stanza_resolver(mcfgname,
                        CB_BUSNAME, &cbdriver,
                        (caddr_t *)cb_option_snippet) != 0) {
                        return(EINVAL);
                        } 1
    }
        .
        .
        .
```

1 Shows that the ldbl_stanza_resolver interface takes four arguments:

– A *driver_name* argument

   The first argument specifies the driver name that was entered as the stanza entry in the stanza.loadable file fragment. The example passes the mcfgname string. The device driver method of cfgmgr fills this string with the name of the controlling device driver, which in the example is the cb driver. The name cb was entered in the stanza.loadable file fragment.

– A *parent_bus* argument

   The second argument specifies the name of the parent bus structure. This name is obtained from the config program. The example specifies that this is a TURBOchannel bus by passing the constant CB_BUSNAME. This constant is defined as the characters tc.

- A *driver_struct* argument

  The third argument specifies a pointer to the `driver` structure for the controlling device driver. The example passes the address of the `cbdriver` structure, which the code fragment shows was previously initialized in the driver.

- A *bus_param* argument

  The fourth argument specifies a bus-specific parameter. The example passes a snippet table, the bus-specific parameter most commonly passed for the TURBOchannel bus. The example shows that the snippet table is initialized in the driver. The snippet table adheres to the same format found in the `tc_option_data.c` table for static drivers.

The `ldbl_stanza_resolver` interface allows device drivers to merge the system configuration data specified in the `stanza.loadable` or `stanza.static` file fragments into the hardware topology tree created at static configuration time. This operation results in a kernel memory resident hardware topology tree that consists of both loadable and static drivers.

The driver later calls the `ldbl_ctlr_configure` interface, which accesses the hardware topology tree. For this reason, device drivers call `ldbl_stanza_resolver` prior to `ldbl_ctlr_configure`. Part of this operation involves calling a bus-specific configuration resolver interface that searches for devices that can be autoconfigured. The *parent_bus* argument is used to locate these bus-specific configuration resolver interfaces.

The `ldbl_stanza_resolver` interface can return the following values:

ESUCCESS
: The interface successfully merged the configuration data.

ENOMEM
: The system is unable to allocate enough memory to complete the resolver operations.

LDBL_ENOBUS
: The specified parent `bus` structure does not exist.

9.7.4 Configuring and Unconfiguring the Specified Controller

To configure the specified controller, call the `ldbl_ctlr_configure` interface. This interface is generally called in the section of the driver that implements the tasks associated with the configurable (loadable) driver. The following code fragment shows a call to this interface. Section 10.9.2

discusses in more detail how this interface is implemented for the /dev/cb device driver.

```
.
.
.
#define CB_BUSNAME          "tc"
.
.
.
struct  driver cbdriver = { cbprobe, 0, cbattach, 0, 0, 0, 0, 0,
                            "cb", cbinfo, 0, 0, 0, 0, 0,
                            cb_ctlr_unattach, 0 };
.
.
.
static unsigned char mcfgname[CFG_ATTR_NAME_SZ] = "";
.
.
.
  if(strcmp(mcfgname,"")!=0){
      if (ldbl_ctlr_configure(CB_BUSNAME,
                              LDBL_WILDNUM, mcfgname,
                              &cbdriver, 0)) {
                              return(EINVAL);
                                  } 1
      }
.
.
.
```

1 Shows that the ldbl_ctlr_configure interface takes five arguments:

- The first argument specifies the bus name. The example specifies that this is a TURBOchannel bus by passing the constant CB_BUSNAME. This constant is defined as the characters tc.

- The second argument specifies the bus number. The example passes the wildcard constant LDBL_WILDNUM, which indicates that all instances of the controller should be configured. This constant is defined in the file devdriver.h.

- The third argument specifies the name of the controlling device driver. The example passes the mcfgname string. The device driver method of cfgmgr fills this string with the name of the controlling device driver, which in the example is the cb driver. The name cb was entered in the stanza.loadable file fragment.

- The fourth argument specifies a pointer to the driver structure for the controlling device driver. The example passes the address of the cbdriver structure, which the code fragment shows was previously initialized in the driver.

- The fifth argument specifies miscellaneous flags contained in the file /usr/sys/include/io/common/devdriver_loadable.h.

The example passes the value zero (0) to indicate that no flags are being passed.

If `ldbl_ctlr_configure` returns an unsuccessful status (a nonzero value), the driver aborts the configuration operation by returning `EINVAL`.

Call the `ldbl_ctlr_unconfigure` interface to unconfigure the specified controller. This interface is generally called in the section of the driver that implements the tasks associated with the unconfiguration of the loadable driver. Section 10.9.3 discusses in more detail how this interface is implemented for the `/dev/cb` device driver.

```
    .
    .
    .
#define CB_BUSNAME          "tc"
    .
    .
    .
struct  driver cbdriver = { cbprobe, 0, cbattach, 0, 0, 0, 0, 0,
                            "cb", cbinfo, 0, 0, 0, 0, 0,
                            cb_ctlr_unattach, 0 };
    .
    .
    .
if (ldbl_ctlr_unconfigure(CB_BUSNAME, LDBL_WILDNUM, &cbdriver,
                  LDBL_WILDNAME, LDBL_WILDNUM) != 0) { 1
    .
    .
    .
```

1 Shows that the `ldbl_ctlr_unconfigure` interface takes five arguments:

- The first argument specifies the bus name. The example specifies that this is a TURBOchannel bus by passing the constant `CB_BUSNAME`. This constant is defined as the characters `tc`.

- The second argument specifies the bus number. The example passes the wildcard constant `LDBL_WILDNUM` to indicate that `ldbl_ctlr_unconfigure` will match any controller.

- The third argument specifies a pointer to the `driver` structure for the controlling device driver. The example passes the address of the `cbdriver` structure, which the code fragment shows was previously initialized in the driver.

- The fourth argument specifies the controller name. You can pass the controller name as it is specified in the `stanza.loadable` file fragment, or you can pass the wildcard constant `LDBL_WILDNAME` to indicate that you want the interface to scan all `controller` structures. The example passes the wildcard constant.

- The fifth argument specifies the controller number.

You can pass the controller number as specified in the
`stanza.loadable` file fragment, or you can pass the wildcard
constant `LDBL_WILDNUM` to indicate that you want the interface to
scan all `controller` structures. The example passes the wildcard
constant.

The call to `ldbl_ctlr_unconfigure` indirectly results in a call to the
driver's `cb_ctlr_unattach` interface, which deregisters the driver's
interrupt handlers.

9.8   Interfaces Related to the I/O Handle

As discussed in Section 2.3.1, you use the I/O handle to provide device
driver binary compatibility across different bus architectures, different CPU
architectures, and different CPU types within the same CPU architecture.
The following categories of kernel interfaces use an I/O handle:

- Control status register (CSR) I/O access interfaces
- I/O copy interfaces

The following sections discuss how the interfaces associated with each
category use the I/O handle.

9.8.1   Control Status Register I/O Access Interfaces

As discussed in Section 2.6.1, one of the issues that influences device driver
design is whether to read from and write to a device's control status register
(CSR) addresses by directly accessing its device registers. To help you write
more portable device drivers, Digital provides a number of kernel interfaces
that allow you to read from and write to a device's CSR addresses without
directly accessing its device registers. Specifically, these interfaces allow you
to:

- Read data from a device register
- Write data to a device register

The following sections describe the kernel interfaces that perform these tasks.

9.8.1.1   Reading Data from a Device Register

To read data from a device register located in bus address space, call the
`read_io_port` interface. The `read_io_port` interface is a generic
interface that maps to a bus- and machine-specific interface that actually
performs the read operation. Using this interface to read data from a device
register makes the device driver more portable across different bus
architectures, different CPU architectures, and different CPU types within the
same CPU architecture.

The following code fragment shows a call to read_io_port:

```
    .
    .
    .
struct xx_softc {
    .
    .
    .
    io_handle_t iohandle; 1
    .
    .
    .
};
    .
    .
    .
xxprobe(iohandle, ctlr)
 io_handle_t iohandle; 2
 struct controller *ctlr;
{
  register struct xx_softc *sc; 3
  u_long hw_id; 4
    .
    .
    .
  sc->iohandle = iohandle; 5
    .
    .
    .
xxwrite(dev, uio, flag)
 dev_t dev;
 register struct uio *uio;
 int flag;
{
 hw_id = read_io_port(sc->iohandle, 4, 0); 6
    .
    .
    .
}
```

1 Defines a softc structure that contains a member that stores the I/O handle. Typically, you define the softc structure in a *name_data.c* file.

2 The bus configuration code passes an I/O handle to the example driver's *xxprobe* interface. An I/O handle is a data entity that is of type io_handle_t. Assume that this example driver operates on a bus that passes the I/O handle to the probe interface's first argument. The arguments you pass to the probe interface differ according to the bus on which the driver operates. See the bus-specific device driver manual, which describes the probe interface as it applies to the specific bus.

3 Declares a pointer to a softc structure and calls it sc. The example device driver uses the iohandle member of the sc pointer to store the

I/O handle for use in future calls to the CSR I/O access kernel interfaces.

4 Declares a variable called *hw_id* to store the data returned by read_io_port.

5 Stores the I/O handle passed in by the bus configuration code in the iohandle member of the sc pointer.

6 Calls read_io_port in the *xxwrite* interface to read a longword (32 bits) from a device register located in the bus I/O address space.

The read_io_port interface takes three arguments:

- The first argument specifies an I/O handle that you can use to reference a device register or memory located in bus address space (either I/O space or memory space). This I/O handle references a device register in the bus address space where the read operation originates.

  You can perform standard C mathematical operations on the I/O handle. For example, you can add an offset to or subtract an offset from the I/O handle. In the example, the I/O handle passed to read_io_port is the one passed to *xxprobe* and stored in the iohandle member of the sc pointer.

- The second argument specifies the width (in bytes) of the data to be read. Valid values are 1, 2, 3, 4, and 8. Not all CPU platforms or bus adapters support all of these values. The example driver passes the value 4 for the width.

- The third argument specifies flags to indicate special processing requests. Currently, no flags are used. Because there are no flags, the example driver passes the value zero (0).

Upon successful completion, read_io_port returns the requested data from the device register located in the bus address space: a byte (8 bits), a word (16 bits), a longword (32 bits), or a quadword (64 bits). This interface returns data justified to the low-order byte lane. For example, a byte (8 bits) is always returned in byte lane 0 and a word (16 bits) is always returned in byte lanes 0 and 1.

In this example, read_io_port returns a longword.

The previous example shows how a device driver reads data from a device register by directly calling read_io_port. Another way to read data from a device register is to use read_io_port to construct driver-specific macros, as in the following example:

```
           .
           .
           .
#define XX_ID      0xc80 1
#define XX_CSR     0xc00
#define XX_BAT     0xc04
#define XX_HIBASE  0xc08
#define XX_CONFIG  0xc0c
#define XX_ID      0xc80
#define XX_CTRL    0xc84
           .
           .
           .
struct xx_softc {
           .
           .
    io_handle_t iohandle;
           .
           .
           .
};
           .
           .
           .
#define XX_READ_D8(a)  read_io_port(sc->iohandle | (io_handle_t)a, 1, 0) 2
#define XX_READ_D16(a) read_io_port(sc->iohandle | (io_handle_t)a, 2, 0)
#define XX_READ_D32(a) read_io_port(sc->iohandle | (io_handle_t)a, 4, 0)
           .
           .
           .
xxprobe(iohandle,ctlr)
  io_handle_t iohandle;
  struct controller *ctlr;
{
   register struct xx_softc *sc;
   unsigned int hw_id;
           .
           .
           .
  sc->iohandle = iohandle; 3
           .
           .
           .
  hw_id = XX_READ_D32(XX_ID); 4
           .
           .
           .
}
```

1 Defines offsets to the device registers. Typically, you define these device register offsets in a device register header file.

2 Constructs driver-specific macros by using the read_io_port interface. The macros construct the first argument by ORing the I/O handle and a device register offset for some XX device. To obtain the correct offset with large offsets like 0xc84, you may need to perform an addition operation instead of an OR operation.

3 Stores the I/O handle passed in by the bus configuration code in the iohandle member of the sc pointer.

4 Calls the XX_READ_D32 macro to read a longword from the device register associated with the XX_ID offset.

9.8.1.2 Writing Data to a Device Register

To write data to a device register located in bus address space, call the write_io_port interface. The write_io_port interface is a generic interface that maps to a bus- and machine-specific interface that actually performs the write operation. Using this interface to write data to a device register makes the device driver more portable across different bus architectures, different CPU architectures, and different CPU types within the same CPU architecture.

The following code fragment shows a call to write_io_port from a device driver's xxprobe interface to write data to some device register located in the bus I/O address space:

```
  .
  .
  .
struct xx_softc {
  .
  .
  .
   io_handle_t iohandle;  1
  .
  .
  .
};
  .
  .
  .
xxprobe(iohandle, ctlr)
 io_handle_t iohandle;  2
 struct controller *ctlr;
{
  register struct xx_softc *sc;  3
  .
  .
  .
 sc->iohandle = iohandle;  4
  .
  .
  .
xxwrite(dev, uio, flag)
 dev_t dev;
 register struct uio *uio;
 int flag;
{
 write_io_port(sc->iohandle, 4, BUS_IO, 0x1);  5
  .
  .
  .
}
```

1 Defines a `softc` structure that contains a member that stores the I/O handle. Typically, you define the `softc` structure in a *name_data.c* file.

2 The bus configuration code passes an I/O handle to the example driver's *xxprobe* interface. An I/O handle is a data entity that is of type `io_handle_t`. Assume that this example driver operates on a bus that passes the I/O handle to the `probe` interface's first argument. The arguments you pass to the `probe` interface differ according to the bus on which the driver operates. See the bus-specific device driver manual, which describes the `probe` interface as it applies to the specific bus.

3 Declares a pointer to a `softc` structure and calls it `sc`. The example device driver uses the `iohandle` member of the `sc` pointer to store the I/O handle for use in future calls to the CSR I/O access kernel interfaces.

4 Stores the I/O handle passed in by the bus configuration code in the `iohandle` member of the `sc` pointer.

5 Calls `write_io_port` in the *xxwrite* interface to write a longword (32 bits) to a device register located in the bus I/O address space.

The `write_io_port` interface takes four arguments:

– The first argument specifies an I/O handle that you can use to reference a device register or memory located in bus address space (either I/O space or memory space).
This I/O handle references a device register in the bus address space where the write operation occurs.

You can perform standard C mathematical operations on the I/O handle. For example, you can add an offset to or subtract an offset from the I/O handle. In the example, the I/O handle passed to `write_io_port` is the one passed to *xxprobe* and stored in the `iohandle` member of the `sc` pointer.

– The second argument specifies the width (in bytes) of the data to be written. Valid values are 1, 2, 3, 4, and 8. Not all CPU platforms or bus adapters support all of these values. The example driver passes the value 4 for the width.

– The third argument specifies flags to indicate special processing requests. Currently, no flags are used. Because no flags are used, the example driver passes the value zero (0).

– The fourth argument specifies the data to be written to the specified device register in bus address space. The example driver passes the value `0x1`.

The `write_io_port` interface has no return value.

The previous example shows how a device driver writes data to a device register by directly calling `write_io_port`. Another way to write data to a device register is to use `write_io_port` to construct driver-specific macros, as in the following example:

```
      .
      .
      .
#define XX_ID     0xc80 1
#define XX_CSR    0xc00
#define XX_BAT    0xc04
#define XX_HIBASE 0xc08
#define XX_CONFIG 0xc0c
#define XX_ID     0xc80
#define XX_CTRL   0xc84
      .
      .
      .
struct xx_softc {
      .
      .
      .
    io_handle_t iohandle;
      .
      .
      .
};
      .
      .
      .
#define XX_WRITE_D8(a,d)  write_io_port(sc->iohandle | (io_handle_t)a, 1, 0, d) 2
#define XX_WRITE_D16(a,d) write_io_port(sc->iohandle | (io_handle_t)a, 2, 0, d)
#define XX_WRITE_D32(a,d) write_io_port(sc->iohandle | (io_handle_t)a, 4, 0, d)
      .
      .
      .
xxprobe(iohandle,ctlr)
 io_handle_t addr;
 struct controller *ctlr;
{
  register struct xx_softc *sc;
      .
      .
      .
 sc->iohandle = iohandle; 3
      .
      .
      .
XX_WRITE_D32(XX_ID, 0); 4
      .
      .
      .
}
```

1 Defines offsets to the device registers. Typically, you define these device register offsets in a device register header file.

2 Constructs driver-specific macros by using the `write_io_port` interface. Note that the macros construct the first argument by ORing the

I/O handle and a device register offset for some XX device. To obtain the correct offset with large offsets like 0xc84, you may need to perform an addition operation instead of an OR operation.

3̄ Stores the I/O handle passed in by the bus configuration code in the iohandle member of the sc pointer.

4̄ Calls the XX_WRITE_D32 macro to write the value zero (0) to the device register associated with the XX_ID offset.

9.8.2 I/O Copy Interfaces

Digital UNIX provides several generic interfaces to copy a block of memory to or from I/O space. These generic interfaces map to bus- and machine-specific interfaces that actually perform the copy operation. Using these interfaces to copy a block of memory to or from I/O space makes the device driver more portable across different CPU architectures and different CPU types within the same architecture. These generic interfaces allow device drivers to:

- Copy a block of memory from I/O address space to system memory
- Copy a block of byte-contiguous system memory to I/O address space
- Copy a memory block of I/O address space to another memory block of I/O address space

Each of these interfaces is discussed in the following sections.

9.8.2.1 Copying a Block of Memory from I/O Address Space to System Memory

To copy data from bus address space to system memory, call the io_copyin interface. The io_copyin interface is a generic interface that maps to a bus- and machine-specific interface that actually performs the copy from bus address space to system memory. Using io_copyin to perform the copy operation makes the device driver more portable across different CPU architectures and different CPU types within the same architecture.

The following code fragment shows a call to io_copyin to copy the memory block:

```
        .
        .
        .
struct xx_softc {
        .
        .
        .
    io_handle_t iohandle; 1̄
```

```
           .
           .
           .
  };
           .
           .
           .
  xxprobe(iohandle, ctlr)
   io_handle_t iohandle;  2
   struct controller *ctlr;
  {
     register struct xx_softc *sc;  3
     int ret_val;  4
           .
           .
           .
   sc->iohandle = iohandle;  5
           .
           .
           .
  xxwrite(dev, uio, flag)
   dev_t dev;
   register struct uio *uio;
   int flag;
  {
   char * buf;
   buf = (char *)kalloc(PAGE_SIZE);
   ret_val = io_copyin(sc->iohandle, buf, PAGE_SIZE);  6
           .
           .
           .
  }
```

1 Defines a `softc` structure that contains a member that stores the I/O
  handle. Typically, you define the `softc` structure in a *name*_data.c
  file.

2 The bus configuration code passes an I/O handle to the example driver's
  *xx*probe interface. An I/O handle is a data entity that is of type
  `io_handle_t`. Assume that this example driver operates on a bus that
  passes the I/O handle to the `probe` interface's first argument. The
  arguments you pass to the `probe` interface differ according to the bus on
  which the driver operates. See the bus-specific device driver manual,
  which describes the `probe` interface as it applies to the specific bus.

3 Declares a pointer to a `softc` structure and calls it `sc`. The example
  device driver uses the `iohandle` member of the `sc` pointer to store the
  I/O handle for use in future calls to the CSR I/O access kernel interfaces.

4 Declares a variable called *ret_val* to store the value returned by
  `io_copyin`.

5 Stores the I/O handle passed in by the bus configuration code in the
  `iohandle` member of the `sc` pointer.

6 Calls `io_copyin` in the *xxwrite* interface to copy a block of memory from I/O address space to system memory.

The `io_copyin` interface takes three arguments:

- The first argument specifies an I/O handle that you can use to reference a device register or memory located in bus address space (either I/O space or memory space). For `io_copyin`, the I/O handle identifies the location in bus address space where the copy originates. You can perform standard C mathematical operations on the I/O handle. For example, you can add an offset to or subtract an offset from the I/O handle.

  In the example, the I/O handle passed to `io_copyin` is the one passed to *xxprobe* and stored in the `iohandle` member of the `sc` pointer.

- The second argument specifies the kernel virtual address where `io_copyin` copies the data to in-system memory.

  The example calls the `kalloc` interface to obtain the kernel virtual address where `io_copyin` copies the data to in-system memory.

- The third argument specifies the number of bytes in the data block to be copied. The interface assumes that the buffer associated with the data block is physically contiguous.

  The example uses the `PAGE_SIZE` constant for the number of bytes in the memory block to be copied.

  Upon successful completion, `io_copyin` returns `IOA_OKAY`. It returns the value −1 on failure.

9.8.2.2   Copying a Block of Byte-Contiguous System Memory to I/O Address Space

To copy data from system memory to bus address space, call the `io_copyout` interface. The `io_copyout` interface is a generic interface that maps to a bus- and machine-specific interface that actually performs the copy to bus address space. Using `io_copyout` to perform the copy operation makes the device driver more portable across different CPU architectures and different CPU types within the same architecture.

The following code fragment shows a call to `io_copyout` to copy the memory block:

```
        .
        .
        .
struct xx_softc {
    .
    .
    .
    io_handle_t iohandle; 1
    .
    .
    .
};
    .
    .
    .
xxprobe(iohandle, ctlr)
  io_handle_t iohandle; 2
  struct controller *ctlr;
{
    register struct xx_softc *sc; 3
    int ret_val; 4
    .
    .
    .
  sc->iohandle = iohandle; 5
    .
    .
    .
xxwrite(dev, uio, flag)
  dev_t dev;
  register struct uio *uio;
  int flag;
{
  char * buf;
  buf = (char *)kalloc(PAGE_SIZE);
  ret_val = io_copyout(buf, sc->iohandle, PAGE_SIZE); 6
    .
    .
    .
}
```

1. Defines a softc structure that contains a member that stores the I/O handle. Typically, you define the softc structure in a *name*_data.c file.

2. The bus configuration code passes an I/O handle to the example driver's *xx*probe interface. An I/O handle is a data entity that is of type io_handle_t. Assume that this example driver operates on a bus that passes the I/O handle to the probe interface's first argument. The arguments you pass to the probe interface differ according to the bus on which the driver operates. See the bus-specific device driver manual, which describes the probe interface as it applies to the specific bus.

3. Declares a pointer to a softc structure and calls it sc. The example device driver uses the iohandle member of the sc pointer to store the

I/O handle for use in future calls to the CSR I/O access kernel interfaces.

4 Declares a variable called `ret_val` to store the value returned by `io_copyout`.

5 Stores the I/O handle passed in by the bus configuration code in the `iohandle` member of the `sc` pointer.

6 Calls `io_copyout` in the *xxwrite* interface to copy a block of byte-contiguous system memory to I/O address space.

The `io_copyout` interface takes three arguments:

– The first argument specifies the kernel virtual address where the copy originates in system memory.

The example calls the `kalloc` interface to obtain the kernel virtual address where the copy originates in system memory.

– The second argument specifies an I/O handle that you can use to reference a device register or memory located in bus address space (either I/O space or memory space). For `io_copyout`, the I/O handle identifies the location in bus address space where the copy occurs. You can perform standard C mathematical operations on the I/O handle. For example, you can add an offset to or subtract an offset from the I/O handle.

In the example, the I/O handle passed to `io_copyout` is the one passed to *xxprobe* and stored in the `iohandle` member of the `sc` pointer.

– The third argument specifies the number of bytes in the data block to be copied. The interface assumes that the buffer associated with the data block is physically contiguous.

The example uses the `PAGE_SIZE` constant for the number of bytes in the memory block to be copied.

Upon successful completion, `io_copyout` returns IOA_OKAY. It returns the value –1 on failure.

9.8.2.3 Copying a Memory Block of I/O Address Space to Another Memory Block of I/O Address Space

To copy data from one location in bus address space to another location in bus address space, call the `io_copyio` interface. The `io_copyio` interface is a generic interface that maps to a bus- and machine-specific interface that actually performs the copy of data from one location in bus address space to another location in bus address space. Using `io_copyio` to perform the copy operation makes the device driver more portable across different CPU architectures and different CPU types within the same architecture.

The following code fragment shows a call to `io_copyio` to copy the memory block:

```
    .
    .
    .
struct xx_softc { 1
    .
    .
    .
   io_handle_t src_addr;
   io_handle_t dest_addr;
    .
    .
    .
};
    .
    .
    .
xxprobe(xxprobe_iohandle, ctlr)
 io_handle_t xxprobe_iohandle; 2
 struct controller *ctlr;
{
   register struct xx_softc *sc; 3
   int ret_val; 4
    .
    .
    .
 sc->src_addr = xxprobe_iohandle; 5
 sc->dest_addr = xxprobe_iohandle + 0x0400; 6
    .
    .
    .
xxwrite(dev, uio, flag)
 dev_t dev;
 register struct uio *uio;
 int flag;
{
 ret_val = io_copyio(sc->src_addr, sc->dest_addr, PAGE_SIZE); 7
    .
    .
    .
}
```

1 Defines a `softc` structure that contains members that store the source and destination addresses associated with the copy operation. Typically, you define the `softc` structure in a *name_data.c* file.

2 The bus configuration code passes an I/O handle to the example driver's *xxprobe* interface. An I/O handle is a data entity that is of type `io_handle_t`. Assume that this example driver operates on a bus that passes the I/O handle to the `probe` interface's first argument. The arguments you pass to the `probe` interface differ according to the bus on which the driver operates. See the bus-specific device driver manual, which describes the `probe` interface as it applies to the specific bus.

3. Declares a pointer to a `softc` structure and calls it `sc`. The example device driver uses the `iohandle` member of the `sc` pointer to store the I/O handle for use in future calls to the CSR I/O access kernel interfaces.

4. Declares a variable called `ret_val` to store the value returned by `io_copyio`.

5. Stores the I/O handle passed in by the bus configuration code in the `xxprobe_iohandle` member of the `sc` pointer.

6. Stores the result of adding the I/O handle passed in by the bus configuration code and a 1K offset in the `dest_addr` member of the `sc` pointer. This is the destination address for the copy operation.

7. Calls `io_copyio` in the `xxwrite` interface to copy a memory block of I/O address space to another memory block of I/O address space.

   The `io_copyio` interface takes three arguments:

   – The first argument specifies an I/O handle that you can use to reference a device register or memory located in bus address space (either I/O space or memory space). For `io_copyio`, this I/O handle identifies the location in bus address space where the copy originates. You can perform standard C mathematical operations on the I/O handle. For example, you can add an offset to or subtract an offset from the I/O handle.

   In the example, the I/O handle passed to `io_copyio` is the one passed to `xxprobe` and stored in the `src_addr` member of the `sc` pointer.

   – The second argument specifies an I/O handle that you can use to reference a device register or memory located in bus address space (either I/O space or memory space). In this case, the I/O handle identifies the location in bus address space where the copy occurs. In the example, the address where the copy operation occurs is stored in the `dest_addr` member of the `sc` pointer.

   – The third argument specifies the number of bytes in the data block to be copied. The interface assumes that the buffer associated with the data block is physically contiguous. The example uses the `PAGE_SIZE` constant for the number of bytes in the memory block to be copied.

   Upon successful completion, `io_copyio` returns IOA_OKAY. It returns the value −1 on failure.

9.9 Interfaces Related to Direct Memory Access

As discussed in Section 2.6.3, one of the issues that influences device driver design is the technique for performing direct memory access (DMA) operations. Whenever possible, you should design device drivers so that they can accommodate DMA devices connected to different buses operating on a variety of Alpha CPUs. The different buses can require different methods for accessing bus I/O addresses and the different Alpha CPUs can have a variety of DMA hardware support features.

To help you overcome the differences in DMA operations across the different buses and Alpha CPUs, Digital UNIX provides a package of mapping interfaces. The mapping interfaces provide a generic abstraction to the kernel- and system-level mapping data structures and to the mapping interfaces that actually perform the DMA transfer operation. This work includes acquiring the hardware and software resources needed to map contiguous I/O bus addresses (accesses) into discontiguous system memory addresses (accesses).

Using the mapping interfaces makes device drivers more portable between major releases of the Digital UNIX operating system (and different hardware support for I/O buses) because it masks out any future changes in the kernel- and system-level DMA mapping data structures. Specifically, these interfaces allow you to:

- Allocate system resources for DMA data transfers
- Load and set allocated system resources for DMA data transfers
- Unload system resources for DMA data transfers
- Release and deallocate resources for DMA data transfers

The DMA mapping package also provides convenience interfaces that allow you to:

- Return a pointer to the current bus address/byte count pair
- Put a new bus address/byte count pair into the list
- Return a kernel segment (kseg) address of a DMA buffer

The following sections describe the kernel interfaces that perform these tasks and also discuss the DMA handle and the `sg_entry` data structure associated with these DMA interfaces.

9.9.1 DMA Handle

To provide device driver binary compatibility across different bus architectures, different CPU architectures, and different CPU types within the same CPU architecture, Digital UNIX represents DMA resources through a DMA handle. A DMA handle is a data entity that is of type dma_handle_t. This handle provides the information to access bus address/byte count pairs. Device driver writers can view the DMA handle as the tag to the allocated system resources needed to perform a DMA operation.

9.9.2 The sg_entry Structure

The sg_entry data structure contains two members: ba and bc. These members represent a bus address/byte count pair for a contiguous block of an I/O buffer mapped onto a controller's bus memory space. The byte count indicates the number of bytes that the address is contiguously valid for on the controller's bus address space. Consider a list entry that has its ba member set to aaaa and its bc member set to nnnn. In this case, the device can perform a contiguous DMA data transfer starting at bus address aaaa and ending at bus address aaaa+nnnn-1.

Table 9-2 lists the members of the sg_entry structure along with their associated data types.

Table 9-2: Members of the sg_entry Structure

Member Name	Data Type
ba	bus_addr_t
bc	u_long

The ba member stores an I/O bus address.

The bc member stores the byte count associated with the I/O bus address. This byte count indicates the contiguous addresses that are valid on this bus.

9.9.3 Allocating System Resources for DMA Data Transfers

To allocate resources for DMA data transfers, call the dma_map_alloc interface. Using the dma_map_alloc interface makes device drivers more portable between DMA hardware-mapping implementations across different hardware platforms because it masks out any future changes in the kernel- and system-level DMA mapping data structures.

The following code fragment taken from a /dev/fd device driver shows the four arguments associated with the call to dma_map_alloc. Two of the arguments passed to dma_map_alloc are defined as members of an `fdcam_class` data structure.

```
    .
    .
    .
#define SECTOR_SIZE 512
    .
    .
    .
struct fdcam_class {
    .
    .
    .
dma_handle_t fc_dma_handle;
    .
    .
    .
struct controller *ctlr;
};
    .
    .
    .
  struct fdcam_class* fcp = &fc_0;
    .
    .
    .
  if (dma_map_alloc(SECTOR_SIZE, fcp->ctlr, &fcp->fc_dma_handle,
                    DMA_SLEEP) == 0) { 1
    .
    .
    .
```

1   Shows that `dma_map_alloc` takes four arguments:

- The first argument specifies the maximum size (in bytes) of the data to be transferred during the DMA transfer operation. The kernel uses this size to determine the resources (mapping registers, I/O channels, and other software resources) to allocate.

  In this example, the *byte_count* is the value defined by the SECTOR_SIZE constant.

- The second argument specifies a pointer to the `controller` structure associated with this controller. The interface uses this pointer to obtain the bus-specific interfaces and data structures that it needs to allocate the necessary mapping resources.

  In this example, *ctlr_p* is the value stored in the `ctlr` member. Assume that the `/dev/fd` driver previously set the `ctlr` member to the `controller` structure pointer associated with this device at probe time.

- The third argument specifies a pointer to a handle to DMA resources associated with the mapping of an in-memory I/O buffer onto a controller's I/O bus. This handle provides the information to access bus address/byte count pairs. A bus address/byte count pair is represented by the `ba` and `bc` members of an `sg_entry` structure pointer. Device driver writers can view the DMA handle as the tag to the allocated system resources needed to perform a DMA operation. The `dma_map_alloc` interface returns to this variable the address of the DMA handle. The device driver uses this address in a call to `dma_map_load`.

In this example, the DMA handle appears as a member in the `fdcam_class` data structure.

– The fourth argument specifies special conditions that the device driver needs the system to perform.

In this example, the bit represented by the `DMA_SLEEP` constant is passed. This bit puts the process to sleep if the system cannot allocate the necessary resources to perform a data transfer of size *byte_count* at the time the driver calls the interface.

The code fragment sets up a condition statement that performs some tasks based on the value returned by `dma_map_alloc`. Upon successful completion, `dma_map_alloc` returns a byte count (in bytes) that indicates the DMA transfer size it can map. It returns the value zero (0) to indicate a failure.

9.9.4 Loading and Setting Allocated System Resources for DMA Data Transfers

To load and set allocated system resources for DMA data transfers, call the `dma_map_load` interface. The `dma_map_load` interface is a generic interface that maps to a bus- and machine-specific interface that actually performs the loading and setting of system resources for DMA data transfers. Using this interface in DMA read and write operations makes the device driver more portable across different bus architectures, different CPU architectures, and different CPU types within the same CPU architecture.

The following code fragment taken from a /dev/fd device driver shows the seven arguments associated with the call to `dma_map_load`. Note that the arguments passed to `dma_map_load` are defined as members of an `fdcam_class` data structure. The /dev/fd driver shows an example of fixed preallocated DMA resources.

```
     .
     .
     .
#define SECTOR_SIZE 512
     .
     .
     .
struct fdcam_class {
     .
     .
     .
int rw_count;
```

```
unsigned char *rw_buf;
struct proc *rw_proc;
dma_handle_t dma_handle;
   .
   .
   .
struct controller *ctlr;
};
   .
   .
   .
  struct fdcam_class* fcp = fsb->fcp;
   .
   .
   .
  flags = (fcp->rw_op == OP_READ) ? DMA_IN : DMA_OUT;
  if (dma_map_load(fcp->rw_count * SECTOR_SIZE, fcp->rw_buf,
                   fcp->rw_proc, fcp->ctlr, &fcp->dma_handle, 0,
                   flags) == 0) { 1
   .
   .
   .
```

1 Shows that dma_map_load takes seven arguments:

 – The first argument specifies the maximum size (in bytes) of the data
   to be transferred during the DMA transfer operation. The kernel uses
   this size to determine the resources (mapping registers, I/O channels,
   and other software resources) to allocate, load, and set.

   In this example, the size is the result of the SECTOR_SIZE and the
   value stored in rw_count. Assume that the /dev/fd driver
   previously set the rw_count member to some value.

 – The second argument specifies the virtual address where the DMA
   transfer occurs. The interface uses this address with the pointer to the
   proc structure to obtain the physical addresses of the system
   memory pages to load into DMA mapping resources. In this
   example, the virtual address is the value stored in the rw_buf
   member. Assume that the /dev/fd driver previously set the
   rw_buf member to some value.

 – The third argument specifies a pointer to the proc structure
   associated with the valid context for the virtual address passed in the
   second argument. The interface uses this pointer to retrieve the pmap
   that is needed to translate this virtual address to a physical address. If
   proc_p is equal to zero (0), the address is a kernel address. In this
   example, proc_p is the value stored in the rw_proc member.
   Assume that the /dev/fd driver previously set the rw_proc
   member to some value.

 – The fourth argument specifies a pointer to the controller structure
   associated with this controller. The dma_map_load interface uses

the pointer to get the bus-specific interfaces and data structures that it needs to load and set the necessary mapping resources.

In this example, `ctlr_p` is the value stored in the `ctlr` member. Assume that the `/dev/fd` driver previously set the `ctlr` member to the `controller` structure pointer associated with this device at probe time.

– The fifth argument specifies a pointer to a handle to DMA resources associated with the mapping of an in-memory I/O buffer onto a controller's I/O bus. This handle provides the information to access bus address/byte count pairs. A bus address/byte count pair is represented by the `ba` and `bc` members of an `sg_entry` structure pointer. Device driver writers can view the DMA handle as the tag to the allocated system resources needed to perform a DMA operation. Typically, the device driver passes an argument of type `dma_handle_t *`.

In this example, the `/dev/fd` device driver simply passes the address of the DMA handle that is a member of the `fdcam_class` structure.

– The sixth argument specifies the maximum-size byte-count value that should be stored in the `bc` members of the `sg_entry` structures.

In this example, the `/dev/fd` driver passes the value zero (0).

– The seventh argument specifies special conditions that the device driver needs the system to perform.

In this example, `flags` is DMA_IN if `rw_op` evaluates to TRUE (that is, this is a DMA read operation). The DMA_IN bit indicates that the system should perform a DMA write into core memory. Otherwise, `flags` is DMA_OUT if `rw_op` evaluates to FALSE (that is, this is a DMA write operation). The DMA_OUT bit indicates that the system should perform a DMA read from the main core memory.

The code fragment sets up a condition statement that performs some tasks based on the value returned by dma_map_load. Upon successful completion, dma_map_load returns a byte count (in bytes) that indicates the DMA transfer size it can support. It returns the value zero (0) to indicate a failure.

9.9.5 Unloading System Resources for DMA Data Transfers

To unload the resources that were loaded and set up in a previous call to dma_map_load, call the dma_map_unload interface. The dma_map_unload interface is a generic interface that maps to a bus- and machine-specific interface that actually performs the unloading of system resources associated with DMA data transfers. Using this interface in DMA read and write operations makes the device driver more portable across different bus architectures, different CPU architectures, and different CPU types within the same CPU architecture.

The following code fragment taken from a /dev/fd device driver shows the two arguments associated with the call to dma_map_unload. One of the arguments passed to dma_map_unload is defined as a member of an fdcam_class data structure.

```
       .
       .
       .
struct fdcam_class {
       .
       .
       .
char rw_use_dma;
       .
       .
       .
dma_handle_t dma_handle;
       .
       .
       .
};
       .
       .
       .
   struct fdcam_class* fcp = fsb->fcp;
       .
       .
       .
   if (fcp->rw_use_dma) {
       dma_map_unload(0, fcp->dma_handle);
   } 1
       .
       .
       .
```

1 Shows that dma_map_unload takes two arguments:

– To cause a deallocation of DMA mapping resources, you set the first argument to the special condition bit DMA_DEALLOC. This bit setting is analogous to setting the *dma_handle_p* argument to the value zero (0) for dma_map_load to allocate the DMA mapping resources.

   In this example, the /dev/fd driver passes the value zero (0) to indicate that it did not want to deallocate the DMA mapping resources.

– The second argument specifies a handle to DMA resources associated with the mapping of an in-memory I/O buffer onto a controller's I/O bus. This handle provides the information to access bus address/byte count pairs. A bus address/byte count pair is represented by the ba and `bc` members of an `sg_entry` structure pointer. Device driver writers can view the DMA handle as the tag to the allocated system resources needed to perform a DMA operation.

In this example, the `/dev/fd` device driver simply passes the DMA handle that is a member of the `fdcam_class` structure.

The code fragment sets up a condition statement that calls `dma_map_unload` if the `rw_use_dma` evaluates to a nonzero (true) value. Upon successful completion, `dma_map_unload` returns the value 1. Otherwise, it returns the value zero (0).

A call to `dma_map_unload` does not release or deallocate the resources that were allocated in a previous call to `dma_map_alloc` unless the driver sets the *flags* argument to the `DMA_DEALLOC` bit.

9.9.6 Releasing and Deallocating Resources for DMA Data Transfers

To release and deallocate the resources that were allocated in a previous call to `dma_map_alloc`, call the `dma_map_dealloc` interface. Using the `dma_map_dealloc` interface makes device drivers more portable between DMA hardware-mapping implementations across different hardware platforms because it masks out any future changes in the kernel- and system-level DMA mapping data structures.

The following code fragment taken from a `/dev/fd` device driver shows the argument associated with the call to `dma_map_dealloc`. This argument is defined as a member of an `fdcam_class` data structure.

```
      .
      .
      .
struct fdcam_class {
      .
      .
      .
char rw_use_dma;
      .
      .
      .
dma_handle_t dma_handle;
      .
      .
      .
};
      .
      .
      .
struct fdcam_class* fcp;
      .
      .
      .
    if (fcp->rw_use_dma) {
```

```
        dma_map_dealloc(fcp->dma_handle_p);
}  1
        .
        .
        .
```

1 Shows that `dma_map_dealloc` takes one argument: a handle to DMA
    resources associated with the mapping of an in-memory I/O buffer onto a
    controller's I/O bus. This handle provides the information to access bus
    address/byte count pairs. A bus address/byte count pair is represented by
    the `ba` and `bc` members of an `sg_entry` structure pointer. Device
    driver writers can view the DMA handle as the tag to the allocated
    system resources needed to perform a DMA operation.

    In this example, the `/dev/fd` device driver simply passes the DMA
    handle that is a member of the `fdcam_class` structure.

The code fragment sets up a condition statement that calls
`dma_map_dealloc` if the `rw_use_dma` evaluates to a nonzero (true)
value. Upon successful completion, `dma_map_dealloc` returns the value
1. Otherwise, it returns the value zero (0).

9.9.7 Returning a Pointer to the Current Bus Address/Byte Count Pair

The DMA handle provides device drivers with a tag to the allocated system
resources needed to perform a DMA operation. In particular, the handle
provides the information for drivers to access bus address/byte count pairs.
The system maintains arrays of `sg_entry` data structures. Some device
drivers may need to traverse the arrays of `sg_entry` data structures to
obtain specific bus address/byte count pairs. The DMA mapping package
provides two convenience interfaces that allow you to traverse the
discontinuous sets of `sg_entry` arrays:

*   The `dma_get_curr_sgentry` interface returns a pointer to an
    `sg_entry` data structure. A device driver can use this pointer to retrieve
    the current bus address/byte count pair for the mapping of a block of an
    in-memory I/O buffer onto the controller's I/O bus.

*   The `dma_get_next_sgentry` interface returns a pointer to an
    `sg_entry` data structure. A device driver can use this pointer to retrieve
    the next valid bus address/byte count pair for the mapping of a block of
    an in-memory I/O buffer onto the controller's I/O bus.

The following example shows the similarities and differences between the calls to `dma_get_curr_sgentry` and `dma_get_next_sgentry`:

```
     .
     .
     .
dma_handle_t dma_handle;  1
sg_entry_t sgentry_curr;  2
vm_offset_t address_curr;  3
long count_curr;  4
     .
     .
     .
sgentry_curr = dma_get_curr_sgentry(dma_handle)  5
     .
     .
     .
address_curr = (vm_offset_t)sgentry_curr->ba;  6
count_curr = sgentry_curr->bc - 1;  7

dma_handle_t dma_handle;  1
sg_entry_t sgentry_next;  2
vm_offset_t address_next;  3
long count_next;  4
     .
     .
     .
sgentry_next = dma_get_next_sgentry(dma_handle)  5
     .
     .
     .
address_next = (vm_offset_t)sgentry_next->ba;  6
count_next = sgentry_next->bc - 1;  7
```

1. Declare a DMA handle called `dma_handle`. The example passes this DMA handle to the `dma_get_curr_sgentry` and `dma_get_next_sgentry` interfaces.

2. Declare pointers to `sg_entry` structures called `sgentry_curr` and `sgentry_next`. The example uses these pointers to store the `sg_entry` structure pointers in the array returned by `dma_get_curr_sgentry` and `dma_get_next_sgentry`.

3. Declare variables called *address_curr* and *address_next* to store the bus addresses associated with the `sg_entry` structure pointers returned by `dma_get_curr_sgentry` and `dma_get_next_sgentry`.

4. Declare variables called *count_curr* and *count_next* to store the byte counts associated with the `sg_entry` structure pointers returned by `dma_get_curr_sgentry` and `dma_get_next_sgentry`.

5. Call the `dma_get_curr_sgentry` and `dma_get_next_sgentry` interfaces passing to them the DMA handle. This argument specifies a handle to DMA resources associated with the mapping of an in-memory I/O buffer onto a controller's I/O bus. This handle provides the

information to access bus address/byte count pairs. A bus address/byte count pair is represented by the `ba` and `bc` members of an `sg_entry` structure pointer. Device driver writers can view the DMA handle as the tag to the allocated system resources needed to perform a DMA operation.

6 Set the *address_curr* and *address_next* variables to the bus addresses associated with the `sg_entry` structure pointers returned by `dma_get_curr_sgentry` and `dma_get_next_sgentry`. In the call to `dma_get_curr_sgentry`, this bus address is associated with the last `sg_entry` structure pointer that the system read in the array. In the call to `dma_get_next_sgentry`, this bus address is associated with the next valid `sg_entry` structure pointer in the array.

7 Set the *count_curr* and *count_next* variables to the byte counts associated with the `sg_entry` structure pointers returned by `dma_get_curr_sgentry` and `dma_get_next_sgentry`. In the call to `dma_get_curr_sgentry`, this byte count is associated with the last `sg_entry` structure pointer that the system read in the array. In the call to `dma_get_next_sgentry`, this byte count is associated with the next valid `sg_entry` structure pointer in the array.

9.9.8 Putting a New Bus Address/Byte Count Pair into the List

The DMA handle provides device drivers with a tag to the allocated system resources needed to perform a DMA operation. In particular, the handle provides the information for drivers to access bus address/byte count pairs. The system maintains arrays of `sg_entry` data structures. Some device drivers may need to traverse the arrays of `sg_entry` data structures to put new bus address/byte count pair values into the `ba` and `bc` members of specific `sg_entry` structures. The DMA mapping package provides two convenience interfaces that allow you to traverse the discontinuous sets of `sg_entry` arrays:

*   The `dma_put_curr_sgentry` interface puts new bus address/byte count values into the `ba` and `bc` members for the existing bus address/byte count pair pointed to by the DMA handle passed in by you. This interface enables device drivers to patch an existing bus address/byte count pair due to an unexpected interruption in a DMA transfer.

*   The `dma_put_prev_sgentry` interface updates an internal pointer index to the linked list of `sg_entry` structures, and then puts new bus address/byte count values into the existing bus address/byte count pair pointed to by the DMA handle passed in by you. This interface enables device drivers to patch existing bus address/byte count pairs due to an unexpected interruption in a DMA transfer.

The following code fragment shows the similarities and differences between the calls to dma_put_curr_sgentry and dma_put_prev_sgentry:

```
         .
         .
         .
dma_handle_t dma_handle; 1
sg_entry_t sgentry_curr; 2
int ret_curr; 3
         .
         .
         .
Call dma_map_load 4
         .
         .
         .
Call kalloc 5
         .
         .
         .
Call dma_map_load a second time 6
         .
         .
         .
Set the ba & bc members 7
         .
         .
         .
ret_curr = dma_put_curr_sgentry(dma_handle, sgentry_curr) 8
         .
         .
         .
Call dma_map_dealloc 9

dma_handle_t dma_handle; 1
sg_entry_t sgentry_prev; 2
int ret_prev; 3
         .
         .
         .
Call dma_map_load 4
         .
         .
         .
Call kalloc 5
         .
         .
         .
Call dma_map_load a second time 6
         .
         .
         .
Set the ba & bc members 7
         .
         .
         .
ret_prev = dma_put_prev_sgentry(dma_handle, sgentry_prev) 8
         .
```

.
.
.
`Call dma_map_dealloc` **9**

1 Declare a DMA handle called `dma_handle`. The example passes this
DMA handle to the `dma_put_curr_sgentry` and
`dma_put_prev_sgentry` interfaces.

2 Declare pointers to `sg_entry` structures called `sgentry_curr` and
`sgentry_prev`. The example uses these pointers to store the new bus
address/byte count pairs passed to `dma_put_curr_sgentry` and
`dma_put_prev_sgentry`.

3 Declare variables to store the values returned by
`dma_put_curr_sgentry` and `dma_put_prev_sgentry`.

4 Call the `dma_map_load` interface to load and set the allocated system
resources for DMA data transfers.

5 Call the `kalloc` interface to allocate a temporary storage buffer.

6 Call `dma_map_load` a second time to load and set the allocated system
resources for the temporary storage buffer. The example makes this
second call to `dma_map_load` to obtain a valid map of the temporary
storage buffer into the system.

7 Set the `ba` and `bc` members of the respective `sg_entry` structures to
the values returned to the `ba` and `bc` members associated with this
mapped buffer.

8 Call the `dma_put_curr_sgentry` and `dma_put_prev_sgentry`
interfaces, passing to them the DMA handle and the `sg_entry`
structures containing the new bus address/byte count pair values.

9 Call the `dma_map_dealloc` interface to release and deallocate the
resources for DMA data transfers associated with the temporary mapped
buffer. The example makes this call after the system transfers the patched
bus address/byte count pair. This call is required to keep the hardware
mapping resources valid during the DMA data transfer.

9.9.9 Returning a Kernel Segment Address of a DMA Buffer

To return a kernel segment (kseg) address of a DMA buffer, call the
`dma_kmap_buffer` interface. The `dma_kmap_buffer` interface takes
an *offset* variable and returns a kseg address. The device driver can use
this kseg address to copy and save the data at the offset in the buffer. The

following code fragment shows a call to dma_kmap_buffer:

```
    .
    .
    .
dma_handle_t dma_handle;
u_long offset;
vm_offset_t kseg_addr;
    .
    .
    .
kseg_addr = dma_kmap_buffer(dma_handle, offset) [1]
```

[1] The dma_kmap_buffer interface takes two arguments:

– The first argument specifies a handle to DMA resources associated
   with the mapping of an in-memory I/O buffer onto a controller's I/O
   bus. This handle provides the information to access bus address/byte
   count pairs. A bus address/byte count pair is represented by the ba
   and bc members of an sg_entry structure pointer. Device driver
   writers can view the DMA handle as the tag to the allocated system
   resources needed to perform a DMA operation. The example passes
   the DMA handle to dma_kmap_buffer.

– The second argument specifies a byte count offset from the virtual
   address passed as the *virt_addr* argument of the dma_map_load
   interface. This virtual address specifies the beginning of a process's
   (or kernel) buffer that a DMA transfer operation is done to or from.
   A device driver determines the smallest DMA transfer size by calling
   the dma_min_boundary interface. The *offset* specifies the
   number of bytes a DMA engine moved. This number is less than the
   number of bytes the dma_map_load interface loaded.

Upon successful completion, dma_kmap_buffer returns a kseg address of
the byte offset pointed to by the addition of the following two values:

virt_addr + offset

where:

• *virt_addr* is the virtual address passed to the *virt_addr* argument
   of dma_map_load

• *offset* is the offset passed to the *offset* argument of
   dma_kmap_buffer

The dma_kmap_buffer interface returns the value zero (0) to indicate
failure to retrieve the kseg address.

9.10 Miscellaneous Interfaces

The miscellaneous interfaces allow device drivers to:

- Indicate that I/O is complete
- Get the device major number
- Get the device minor number
- Implement raw I/O

The following sections describe the kernel interfaces that perform these tasks.

9.10.1 Indicating That I/O Is Complete

To indicate that I/O is complete, call the `iodone` interface. The following code fragment shows a call to this interface. The code fragment verifies read or write access to the user's buffer before beginning the DMA operation.

```
        .
        .
        .
{

                bp->b_error = EACCES;
                bp->b_flags |= B_ERROR;
                iodone(bp);  1
                return;
        }

        .
        .
        .
```

1   Shows that `iodone` takes one argument: a pointer to a `buf` structure. The `iodone` interface indicates that I/O is complete and reschedules the process that initiated the I/O.

9.10.2 Getting the Device Major Number

To get the device major number, call the `major` interface. The following code fragment shows a call to this interface. This code fragment would appear in the section of the driver source that handles the tasks associated with the loadable driver.

```
        .
        .
        .
dev_t cb_devno = NODEV;  1
        .
        .
        .
cb_devno = cdevno;  2
        .
        .
        .
static int cmajnum = 0;  3
```

```
        .
        .
        .
              cmajnum = major(cb_devno);  4
        .
        .
        .
```

1 Initializes the variable cb_devno, which stores the number of the device whose associated major number you want to obtain. The constant NODEV indicates that no device number has yet been assigned.

2 Sets the cb_devno variable to the device number for this device. The device number is obtained in a call to the cdevsw_add interface.

3 Declares and initializes a variable to store the return from the major interface.

4 Shows that the major interface takes one argument: the number of the device whose associated major device number the major interface will obtain. In the example, the device number is stored in the cb_devno variable. Upon successful completion, major returns the major number portion of the dev_t passed as the argument. In this example, the major device number is stored in the cmajnum variable.

9.10.3 Getting the Device Minor Number

To get the device minor number, call the minor interface. The following code fragment shows a call to this interface:

```
     .
     .
     .
int unit = minor(dev);  1
     .
     .
     .
```

1 Shows that the minor interface takes one argument: the number of the device whose associated minor device number the minor interface will obtain. Upon successful completion, minor returns the minor number portion of the dev_t passed as the argument.

9.10.4 Implementing Raw I/O

To implement raw I/O, call the physio interface. This interface maps the raw I/O request directly into the user buffer, without using bcopy. The memory pages in the user address space are locked while the transfer is processed.

The following code fragment shows a call to this interface:

```
   .
   .
   .
return(physio(cbstrategy,cb->cbbuf,dev,B_READ,cbminphys,uio)); 1
   .
   .
   .
```

1 Shows that physio takes six arguments:

– The first argument specifies the device driver's strategy interface for the device. In this call, cbstrategy is the strategy interface for the /dev/cb device driver.

– The second argument specifies a pointer to a buf structure. This structure contains information such as the binary status flags, the major/minor device numbers, and the address of the associated buffer. This buffer is always a special buffer header owned exclusively by the device for handling I/O requests. In this call, the address of the buf structure associated with this CB device is passed.

– The third argument specifies the device number. In this call, the CB device's number is passed.

– The fourth argument specifies the read/write flag. In this call, the binary status flag B_READ is passed. This flag is set if the operation is read and cleared if the operation is write.

– The fifth argument specifies a pointer to a minphys interface. In this call, the cbminphys interface is passed.

– The sixth argument specifies a pointer to a uio structure. This structure describes the current position within a logical user buffer in user virtual space.

Part 5

```
cbclose(dev,flag,format)
dev_t dev;
int flag;
int format;
{
int unit = minor(dev);
cb_unit[unit].opened = 0;
return (0);
}
```

Writing a Character Device Driver **10**

The `/dev/none` device driver described in Chapter 4 had no real device or bus associated with it. All real device drivers are written for some device that operates on a specific bus. This chapter provides you with an opportunity to study a real device driver called `/dev/cb`. The `/dev/cb` device driver provides a simple interface to the TURBOchannel test board. The `/dev/cb` device driver operates on a TURBOchannel bus and implements many of the character device driver interfaces described in Chapter 3. It also implements other device driver sections that the TURBOchannel test board needs.

The chapter begins with an overview of the tasks that the `/dev/cb` device driver performs. Following this overview are descriptions of each piece of the `/dev/cb` device driver. Table 10-1 lists the parts of the `/dev/cb` device driver and the sections of the chapter where each is described.

Table 10-1: Parts of the /dev/cb Device Driver

Tasks	Section
The cbreg.h Header File	Section 10.2
Include Files Section	Section 10.3
Autoconfiguration Support Declarations and Definitions Section	Section 10.4
Loadable Driver Configuration Support Declarations and Definitions Section	Section 10.5
Local Structure and Variable Definitions Section	Section 10.6
Loadable Driver Local Structure and Variable Definitions Section	Section 10.7
Autoconfiguration Support Section	Section 10.8
Loadable Device Driver Section	Section 10.9
Open and Close Device Section	Section 10.10

Table 10-1: (continued)

Tasks	Section
Read and Write Device Section	Section 10.11
Strategy Section	Section 10.12
Start Section	Section 10.13
The ioctl Section	Section 10.14
Increment LED Section	Section 10.15
Interrupt Section	Section 10.16

The source code uses the following convention:

```
extern int hz;  1
```

1   Numbers appear after each line or lines of code in the /dev/cb device driver example. Following the example, a corresponding number appears that contains an explanation for the associated line or lines. The source code does not contain any inline comments. Section A.2 contains the /dev/cb driver source code in its entirety with the inline comments.

10.1 Overview of the /dev/cb Device Driver

The /dev/cb device driver is a character driver that implements a test board on the TURBOchannel bus. The TURBOchannel test board is a minimal implementation of all the TURBOchannel hardware functions: programmed I/O, direct memory access (DMA) read, DMA write, and I/O read/write conflict testing. The software view of the board consists of:

- An EPROM address space
- A 32-bit ADDRESS register with bits scrambled for direct use as a TURBOchannel DMA address
- A 32-bit DATA register used for programmed I/O and as the holding register for DMA
- A 16-bit register used to control four light-emitting diodes (LEDs) on the TURBOchannel option card, a 1-bit TEST register, and a 16-bit control status register (CSR)

All registers must be accessed as 32-bit longwords, even when they are not implemented as 32 bits. The CSR contains bits to enable option DMA read testing, conflict signal testing, I/O interrupt testing, and option DMA write testing. The CSR also contains a bit that indicates that one or more of the tests are enabled, 4-byte mask flag bits, and a DMA done bit.

The /dev/cb device driver:

- Reads from the data register on the test board to words in system memory
- Writes to the data register on the test board from words in system memory
- Tests the interrupt logic on the test board
- Reads one 32-bit word from the test board address (ROM/register) space into system memory
- Updates, reads, and returns the 32-bit CSR value
- Starts and stops clock-driven incrementing of the four spare LEDs on the board

10.2 The cbreg.h Header File

The `cbreg.h` file is the device register header file for the `/dev/cb` device driver. It contains public declarations and the device register offset definitions for the TURBOchannel test board (the CB device). The following declarations are applicable to both the loadable and static versions of the driver:

```
#define CB_REL_LOC 0x00040000  1
#define CB_ADR(n) ((io_handle_t)(n + CB_REL_LOC))  2
#define CB_SCRAMBLE(x) (((unsigned)x<<3)&~(0x1f))|(((unsigned)x>>29)&0x1f)  3

#define CB_INTERUPT 0x0e00  4
#define CB_CONFLICT 0x0d00  5
#define CB_DMA_RD   0x0b00  6
#define CB_DMA_WR   0x0700  7
#define CB_DMA_DONE 0x0010  8

#define CBPIO _IO('v',0)  9
#define CBDMA _IO('v',1)  10
#define CBINT _IO('v',2)  11

#define CBROM _IOWR('v',3,int)  12
#define CBCSR _IOR('v',4,int)   13

#define CBINC _IO('v',5)  14
#define CBSTP _IO('v',6)  15

#define CB_ADDER   0x0  16
#define CB_DATA    0x4  17
#define CB_CSR     0x8  18
#define CB_TEST    0xC  19
```

1. Defines a constant called `CB_REL_LOC`.

2. Defines a macro called `CB_ADR` that the `cbattach` interface calls to convert the register offset to the kernel virtual address. The data type specified in the type-casting operation is of type `io_handle_t`. Section 10.8.2 shows how `cbattach` calls this macro.

3. Defines a macro called `CB_SCRAMBLE` that the `cbstrategy` interface calls to discard the low-order 2 bits of the physical address while scrambling the rest of the address. Section 10.12.2.4 shows how `cbstrategy` calls this macro.

4. Defines a constant called `CB_INTERUPT` that is used to set bits 9, 10, and 11 of the CSR. Section 10.14.4 shows how the `cbioctl` interface uses this constant when it performs interrupt testing.

5. Defines a constant called `CB_CONFLICT` that is used to set bits 9, 8, 10, and 11 of the CSR. This constant is not currently used.

6. Defines a constant called `CB_DMA_RD` that is used to set bits 10, 8, 9, and 11 of the CSR. Section 10.12.2.4 shows how the `cbstrategy` interface uses this constant to set up the DMA enable bits.

7. Defines a constant called `CB_DMA_WR` that is used to set bits 11, 8, 9, and 10 of the CSR. Section 10.12.2.4 shows how the `cbstrategy` interface uses this constant when converting the buffer virtual address.

8. Defines a constant called `CB_DMA_DONE` for use by the `cbstart` interface's timeout loop. Section 10.13 shows how `cbstart` uses this constant in the timeout loop.

9. Uses the `_IO` macro to construct an `ioctl` macro called `CBPIO`. The `_IO` macro defines `ioctl` types for situations where no data is actually transferred between the application program and the kernel. For example, this could occur in a device control operation. Section 15.3 provides information on the `_IO`, `_IOR`, `_IOW`, and `_IOWR` `ioctl` macros.

   The `cbread`, `cbwrite`, and `cbioctl` interfaces use `CBPIO` to set the `iomode` member of the `cb_unit` structure for this `CB` device to the programmed I/O (PIO) read or write code. Section 10.11.1 shows how the `cbread` interface uses this `ioctl`. Section 10.11.2 shows how the `cbwrite` interface uses this `ioctl`. Section 10.14.3 shows how the `cbioctl` interface uses this `ioctl`.

10. Uses the `_IO` macro to construct an `ioctl` macro called `CBDMA`. The `cbread`, `cbwrite`, and `cbioctl` interfaces use `CBDMA` to set the `iomode` member of the `cb_unit` structure for this `CB` device to the DMA I/O read or write code. Section 10.11.1 shows how the `cbread` interface uses this `ioctl`. Section 10.11.2 shows how the `cbwrite` interface uses this `ioctl`. Section 10.14.3 shows how the `cbioctl` interface uses this `ioctl`.

11. Uses the `_IO` macro to construct an `ioctl` macro called `CBINT`. Section 10.14.4 shows how the `cbioctl` interface uses `CBINT` to perform interrupt tests.

12. Uses the `_IOWR` macro to construct an `ioctl` macro called `CBROM`. The `_IOWR` macro defines `ioctl` types for situations where data is transferred from the user's buffer into the kernel. The driver then performs the appropriate `ioctl` operation and returns data of the same size back up to the user-level application. Typically, this data consists of device control or status information passed to the driver from the application program. Section 10.14.5 shows how the `cbioctl` interface uses `CBROM` to perform a variety of tasks.

13. Uses the `_IOR` macro to construct an `ioctl` macro called `CBCSR`. The `_IOR` macro defines `ioctl` types for situations where data is transferred from the kernel into the user's buffer. Typically, this data consists of device control or status information returned to the application program. Section 10.14.5 shows how the `cbioctl` interface uses `_IOR` to perform a variety of tasks.

14 Uses the _IO macro to construct an ioctl macro called CBINC. Section 10.14.2 shows how the cbioctl interface uses CBINC when it starts to increment the lights.

15 Uses the _IO macro to construct an ioctl macro called CBSTP. Section 10.14.5 shows how cbioctl uses CBSTP when it stops incrementing the lights.

16 Defines the device register offset definitions for the CB device. The device registers are aligned on longword (32-bit) boundaries, even when they are implemented with less than 32 bits. The CB_ADDER device register offset represents the 32-bit read/write DMA address register. The CB_ADDER and the following device register offset definitions show the new technique for defining the registers of a device. Previous versions of the /dev/cb device driver defined a device register structure called CB_REGISTERS. The /dev/cb driver used the members of this data structure to directly access the device registers of the CB device.

By defining device register offset definitions, the /dev/cb driver can use the read_io_port and write_io_port interfaces to access the device registers of the CB device. This makes the /dev/cb driver more portable across different bus architectures, different CPU architectures, and different CPU types within the same CPU architecture.

Section 10.12.2.4 shows the use of CB_ADDER in a call to write_io_port.

17 Represents the 32-bit read/write data register. Section 10.11.1 shows the use of CB_DATA in a call to read_io_port. Section 10.11.2 shows the use of CB_DATA in a call to write_io_port.

18 Represents the 16-bit read/write CSR/LED register. Section 10.13, Section 10.15, Section 10.14.4, and Section 10.14.5 show the use of CB_CSR in calls to read_io_port and write_io_port.

19 Represents the go bit set by the cbwrite interface and cleared by the cbread interface. Section 10.13 and Section 10.14.4 show the use of CB_TEST in calls to read_io_port and write_io_port. Section 10.16 shows the use of CB_TEST in a call to read_io_port.

10.3 Include Files Section

The Include Files Section is applicable to the loadable or static version of the /dev/cb device driver. It identifies the following header files that the /dev/cb device driver needs:

```
#include <sys/param.h>
#include <kern/lock.h>
#include <sys/ioctl.h>
#include <sys/user.h>
#include <sys/proc.h>
#include <hal/cpuconf.h>
#include <io/common/handler.h>
#include <sys/vm.h>
#include <sys/buf.h>
#include <sys/errno.h>
#include <sys/conf.h>
#include <sys/file.h>
#include <sys/uio.h>
#include <sys/types.h>

#include <io/common/devdriver.h>
#include <sys/sysconfig.h>
#include <io/dec/tc/tc.h>

#include <io/ESB100/cbreg.h>      1

#define NCB TC_OPTION_SLOTS       2
```

1 Includes the device register header file, which contains the definitions of the device register offsets for the CB device. Section 10.2 shows the definitions of the device register offsets. The directory specification adheres to the third-party device driver configuration model discussed in Section 11.1.2. If the traditional device driver configuration model was followed, the directory specification would be <io/EasyInc/cbreg.h>.

The directory specification you make here depends on where you put the device register file. Chapter 14 provides reference (man) page-style descriptions of the header files that Digital UNIX device drivers use most frequently.

2 Defines a constant called NCB that is used to allocate data structures that the /dev/cb driver needs. The define uses the constant TC_OPTION_SLOTS, which is defined in /usr/sys/include/io/dec/tc/tc.h. There can be at most three instances of the CB controller on the system. This is a small number of instances of the driver on the system and the data structures themselves are not large, so it is acceptable to allocate for the maximum configuration. This example uses the static allocation model 2 technique described in Section 2.5.2. You could also define this constant in a *name_data.c* file.

10.4 Autoconfiguration Support Declarations and Definitions Section

The Autoconfiguration Support Declarations and Definitions Section is applicable to the loadable or static version of the /dev/cb device driver. It contains the following declarations that the /dev/cb device driver needs:

```
extern  int hz; 1

int cbprobe(), cbattach(), cbintr(), cbopen(), cbclose();
int cbread(), cbwrite(), cbioctl(), cbstart(), cbminphys();
int cbincled(), cb_ctlr_unattach(), cbstrategy(); 2

struct controller *cbinfo[NCB];  3

struct  driver cbdriver = {
        cbprobe,
        0,
        cbattach,
        0,
        0,
        0,
        0,
        0,
        "cb",
        cbinfo,
        0,
        0,
        0,
        0,
        0,
        cb_ctlr_unattach,
        0
}; 4
```

1 Declares the global variable hz to store the number of clock ticks per second. The hz global variable is typically used with the timeout kernel interface to schedule interfaces to be run at the time stored in the variable. Section 10.14.2 shows how cbioctl uses this global variable. Section 10.15 shows how cbincled uses this variable.

2 Declares the driver interfaces for the /dev/cb device driver.

3 Declares an array of pointers to controller structures and calls it cbinfo. The controller structure represents an instance of a controller entity, one that connects logically to a bus. A controller can control devices that are directly connected or can perform some other controlling operation, such as a network interface or terminal controller operation. Section 7.3.2 describes the controller structure.

The NCB constant represents the maximum number of CB controllers. This number sizes the array of pointers to controller structures. If you are writing a new device driver (as opposed to porting an existing driver, which is the case for the /dev/cb driver), dynamically allocate the data structures as needed by calling the zalloc interface. See Section 2.5.3 for a discussion of this technique. The structures for the /dev/cb driver are not dynamically allocated.

4 Declares and initializes the driver structure and calls it cbdriver. The value zero (0) indicates that the /dev/cb driver does not make use of a specific member of the driver structure.

The following list describes those members that the /dev/cb device driver initializes to a nonzero value. Section 7.3.4 describes the driver structure.

− cbprobe, the driver's probe interface

 Section 10.8.1 shows how to implement cbprobe.

− cbattach, the driver's cattach interface

 Section 10.8.2 shows how to implement cbattach.

− cb, the device name

− cbinfo, which references the array of pointers to the previously declared controller structures

 You index this array with the controller number as specified in the ctlr_num member of the controller structure.

− cb_ctlr_unattach, the driver's controller unattach interface

 The cb_ctlr_unattach interface removes the controller structure associated with the TURBOchannel test board from the list of controller structures that it handles. Section 10.8.3 shows how to implement cb_ctlr_unattach. Loadable drivers use the controller unattach interface.

10.5 Loadable Driver Configuration Support Declarations and Definitions Section

The Loadable Driver Configuration Support Declarations and Definitions Section contains the following declarations that the /dev/cb device driver uses when it is configured as a loadable driver:

```
static int cmajnum = 0; 1
static int bmajnum = 0;
static int begunit = 0;
static int numunit = 0;
static int cbversion = 0;

static unsigned char mcfgname[CFG_ATTR_NAME_SZ] = ""; 2
static unsigned char modtype[CFG_ATTR_NAME_SZ] = "";
static unsigned char devcmajor[CFG_ATTR_NAME_SZ] = "";

cfg_subsys_attr_t cb_attributes[] = { 3
{"Module_Config_Name", CFG_ATTR_STRTYPE, CFG_OP_CONFIGURE,
                    (caddr_t)mcfgname,2,CFG_ATTR_NAME_SZ,0},
{"Module_Type",           CFG_ATTR_STRTYPE, CFG_OP_CONFIGURE,
                    (caddr_t)modtype,2,CFG_ATTR_NAME_SZ,0},
{"Device_Char_Major",     CFG_ATTR_STRTYPE, CFG_OP_CONFIGURE,
                    (caddr_t)devcmajor,0,CFG_ATTR_NAME_SZ,0},
{"cmajnum",               CFG_ATTR_INTTYPE, CFG_OP_QUERY,
                    (caddr_t)&cmajnum,0,99,0},
{"bmajnum",               CFG_ATTR_INTTYPE, CFG_OP_QUERY,
                    (caddr_t)&bmajnum,0,99,0},
{"begunit",               CFG_ATTR_INTTYPE, CFG_OP_QUERY,
                    (caddr_t)&begunit,0,8,0},
{"numunit",               CFG_ATTR_INTTYPE, CFG_OP_QUERY,
                    (caddr_t)&numunit,0,8,0},
{"version",               CFG_ATTR_INTTYPE, CFG_OP_QUERY,
                    (caddr_t)&cbversion,0,9999999,0},
{"",0,0,0,0,0,0}
};

extern int nodev(), nulldev(); 4
ihandler_id_t *cb_id_t[NCB];    5
#define CB_BUSNAME    "tc" 6

int cb_is_dynamic = 0; 7

struct tc_option cb_option_snippet [] =
{
    /* module          driver  intr_b4 itr_aft       adpt    */
    /* name            name    probe   attach  type   config  */
    /* ------          ------  ------- ------- ----   ------  */
    {   "CB      ",    "cb",     0,      1,    'C',     0},
    {   "",            ""              } /* Null terminator in the table */
}; 8
int num_cb = 0;    9
```

1 Declares and initializes to the value zero (0) an integer variable used as an attribute in the cb_attributes structure. The four lines that follow also declare and initialize to the value zero (0) variables used as

attributes in the `cb_attributes` structure.

The `cfgmgr` daemon modifies these attributes during a configure operation and uses these attributes to provide the special files that loadable drivers need.

2 Declares and initializes to the null string a character string used as an attribute in the `cb_attributes` structure. The two lines that follow also declare and initialize to the null string character strings used as attributes in the `cb_attributes` structure.

The `cfgmgr` daemon fills in the attributes specified in `cb_attributes` because the designated operation types are `CFG_OP_CONFIGURE`. The `cfgmgr` daemon gets the entries for the `/dev/cb` driver from the `/etc/sysconfigtab` database by locating the `cb:` entry. The driver writers at EasyDriver Incorporated create a `stanza.loadable` file fragment for the `/dev/cb` driver. The `sysconfigdb` utility appends this `stanza.loadable` file fragment to the `/etc/sysconfigtab` database.

To determine if `cfgmgr` initialized attributes correctly, the `/dev/cb` driver verifies each from the `cfg_attr_t` structure that `cfgmgr` passes into the `cb_configure` interface's *indata* argument.

3 Declares and initializes an array of `cfg_subsys_attr_t` data structures and calls it `cb_attributes`. The `cfg_subsys_attr_t` structure contains attribute information for loadable drivers.

4 Declares external references for the `nodev` and `nulldev` interfaces, which are used to initialize members of the `cdevsw` table under specific circumstances. The `cdevsw_add` kernel interface, called by the driver's `cb_configure` interface, initializes the `cdevsw` table. Section 8.2.1 provides a description of the `cdevsw` table and examples of the `nodev` and `nulldev` interfaces.

5 Declares a pointer to an array of IDs used to deregister the interrupt handlers. The NCB constant represents the maximum number of CB controllers. This number sizes the array of IDs. Thus, there is one ID per CB device. Section 10.8.1 shows how `cbprobe` uses *cb_id_t*.

If you are writing a new device driver (as opposed to porting an existing driver, which is the case for the `/dev/cb` driver), dynamically allocate the data structures as needed by calling the `zalloc` interface.

6 Defines a constant that represents a 2-character string that indicates this is a driver that operates on the TURBOchannel bus. This constant is passed as an argument to the `ldbl_stanza_resolver`, `ldbl_ctlr_configure`, and `ldbl_ctlr_unconfigure` interfaces. This bus name is used in calls to the configuration code. Other bus types can use a different name. Section 10.9.2 shows how to call `ldbl_stanza_resolver` and `ldbl_ctlr_configure`.

Section 10.9.3 shows how to call ldbl_ctlr_unconfigure.

⑦ Declares a variable called *cb_is_dynamic* and initializes it to the value zero (0). This variable is used to control any differences in the tasks performed by the /dev/cb device driver when it is configured as a loadable or static driver. Thus, the /dev/cb driver can be compiled once. The decision as to whether it is loadable or static is made at kernel configuration time by the system manager and not at compile time by the driver writer.

Section 10.8.1 shows how cbprobe uses *cb_is_dynamic*. Section 10.8.3 shows how cb_ctlr_unattach uses *cb_is_dynamic*. Section 10.9.2 shows how cb_configure uses *cb_is_dynamic*.

⑧ These lines are specific to drivers written for the TURBOchannel bus. Other bus types may use a different mechanism.

Declares a tc_option structure snippet that provides an entry for the loadable version of this driver. For the static version, a similar entry is made in the tc_option structure located in the tc_option_data.c file. The entry in tc_option_data.c is used only when the driver is configured statically; the cb_option_snippet entry is used only when the driver is configured dynamically.

The tc_option structure contains the bus-specific ROM module name for the driver. This information forms the bus-specific parameter that is passed to the ldbl_stanza_resolver interface to search for matches in the tc_option structure. The bus configuration interfaces associated with the TURBOchannel bus use the tc_option structure.

The items in the tc_option structure snippet have the following meanings:

– module name

   In this column, you specify the device name in the ROM on the hardware device. The module name must be no more than 7 characters in length, but you must blank pad the name to 8 bytes. The module name can be up to 8 characters in length. You must blank pad the name to 8 bytes for those names that are less than 8 characters in length. Thus, the entry for the /dev/cb driver consists of the letters ''CB'' followed by six spaces.

– driver name

   In this column, you specify the driver name as it appears in the Module_Config_Name field of the stanza.loadable file fragment. In this example, the driver name is cb. Because you specify the same name in the Module_Config_Name field and the driver name field of the tc_option structure snippet, the bus configuration code initializes the correct controller and device structures during device autoconfiguration for loadable drivers. Section 12.6.2.16 describes the `Module_Config_Name` field.

- intr_b4 probe

  In this column, you specify whether the device needs interrupts enabled during execution of the driver's `probe` interface. A zero (0) value indicates that the device does not need interrupts enabled; a value of 1 indicates that the device needs interrupts enabled. In the example, the value zero (0) is specified to indicate that the CB device does not need interrupts enabled.

- itr_aft attach

  In this column, you specify whether the device needs interrupts enabled after the driver's `probe` and `attach` interfaces have completed. A zero (0) value indicates that the device does not need interrupts enabled; a value of 1 indicates that the device needs interrupts enabled. In the example, the value 1 is specified to indicate that the CB device needs interrupts enabled after its `cbprobe` and `cbattach` interfaces have completed.

- type

  In this column, you specify the type of device: C (controller) or A (adapter). In the example, the value C is specified.

- adpt config

  If the device in the type column is A (adapter), you specify the name of the interface to configure the adapter. Otherwise, you specify the value zero (0). In the example, the value zero (0) is specified because the device in the previous column is a controller. Section 10.9.2 shows how the `cb_configure` interface uses `cb_option_snippet`.

9 Declares a variable called *num_cb* to store the count on the number of controllers probed during autoconfiguration. This variable is initialized to the value zero (0) to indicate that no instances of the controller have been initialized yet. Section 10.8.1 shows how `cbprobe` uses this variable. Section 10.8.3 shows how `cb_ctlr_unattach` uses this variable. Section 10.9.2 shows how `cb_configure` uses this variable.

10.6 Local Structure and Variable Definitions Section

The Local Structure and Variable Definitions Section is applicable to the loadable or static version of the /dev/cb device driver. It contains such declarations as the following cb_unit data structure:

```
struct buf cbbuf[NCB];   1

unsigned tmpbuffer;  2

struct cb_unit {
    int   attached;
    int   opened;
    int   iomode;
    int   intrflag;
    int   ledflag;
    int   adapter;
    caddr_t cbad;
    io_handle_t cbr;
    struct buf    *cbbuf;
} cb_unit[NCB];   3

#define MAX_XFR 4  4
```

1 Declares an array of buf structures and calls it cbbuf. Section 8.1 describes the buf structure.

The NCB constant represents the maximum number of CB devices. This number sizes the array of buf structures. Thus, there is one buf structure per CB device. Section 10.8.2 shows how cbattach references the buf structure. Section 10.11.1 and Section 10.11.2 show the buf structure passed as an argument to the physio kernel interface.

2 Declares a one-word buffer called *tmpbuffer*. Section 10.12.2.2 shows how the cbstrategy interface uses this variable to store the internal buffer virtual address.

3 Declares an array of cb_unit data structures. Again, the NCB constant represents the maximum number of CB devices. This number sizes the array of cb_unit structures. Thus, there is one cb_unit structure per CB device.

The cbattach interface initializes some of the members of the cb_unit data structure, and all of the other /dev/cb driver interfaces reference cb_unit.

The following list describes the members contained in this structure:

— attached

Stores a value to indicate that the specified CB device is attached. Section 10.8.2 shows that the cbattach interface sets this member to a value that indicates the device is attached.

– opened

Stores a value to indicate that the specified CB device is opened. Section 10.10.1 shows that the cbopen interface sets this member to a value that indicates the device is open; and Section 10.10.2 shows that the cbclose interface clears the value to indicate the device is closed.

– iomode

Stores the read/write mode to one of the bits represented by these constants defined in cbreg.h: CBPIO (programmed I/O) and CBDMA (DMA I/O read code). Section 10.14.3 shows that the cbioctl interface sets this member to these constants.

– intrflag

Stores a flag value used to test for an interrupt. Section 10.16 shows that cbintr sets the interrupt flag; and Section 10.14.4 shows that cbioctl clears the interrupt flag.

– ledflag

Stores a flag value for the LED increment function. Section 10.9.3 shows that cb_configure turns off the LED increment function; and Section 10.14.2 shows that cbioctl sets the LED increment flag. Section 10.14.5 shows that cbioctl sets the flag so that it turns off the LED increment function.

– adapter

Stores the TC slot number. Section 10.8.2 shows that cbattach sets this member to the slot number for this CB controller.

– cbad

Stores the ROM base address. Section 10.8.2 shows that cbattach sets this member to the address of the data to be checked for read accessibility.

– cbr

Stores the I/O handle for the device registers associated with this CB device. An I/O handle is a data entity that is of type io_handle_t. You pass this I/O handle to the read_io_port and write_io_port interfaces. Section 10.8.2 shows that cbattach sets this member to point to this CB device's registers. Section 10.2 shows the declaration of the device register offsets used with the I/O handle.

– cbbuf

    Stores a pointer to a `buf` structure. Section 10.8.2 shows that
`cbattach` sets this member to point to this CB device's buffer
header.

4 Defines a constant called `MAX_XFR` that specifies the maximum chunk of
data (in bytes) that can be transferred in read and write operations.
Section 10.11.1 shows how `cbread` uses `MAX_XFR`. Section 10.11.2
shows how `cbwrite` uses this constant. Section 10.12.1 shows that the
`cbminphys` interface uses this constant to set the `b_bcount` member
of the `buf` structure associated with this CB device.

10.7 Loadable Driver Local Structure and Variable Definitions Section

The Loadable Driver Local Structure and Variable Definitions Section is applicable only to the loadable version of the /dev/cb device driver. It contains declarations of the driver interfaces that were previously declared in Section 10.4. It also contains the following declaration of the /dev/cb driver's cdevsw entry that will be dynamically added to the cdevsw table:

```
int cb_config = FALSE;   1
dev_t cb_devno = NODEV;  2

struct cdevsw cb_cdevsw_entry = {
        cbopen,
        cbclose,
        cbread,
        cbwrite,
        cbioctl,
        nodev,
        nodev,
        0,
        nodev,
        nodev,
        DEV_FUNNEL_NULL,
        0,
        0
};  3

#define CB_DEBUG   4
#undef CB_DEBUGx
```

1. Declares a variable called *cb_config* to store state flags that indicate whether the /dev/cb driver is configured as a loadable driver. The *cb_config* variable is initialized to the value FALSE to indicate the driver defaults to being statically configured. Section 10.9.2 shows that cb_configure sets *cb_config* to the value TRUE to indicate that the /dev/cb driver has been successfully configured as a loadable driver. Section 10.9.3 shows that cb_configure sets *cb_config* to the value FALSE to indicate that the /dev/cb driver has been successfully unconfigured.

2. Declares a variable called *cb_devno* to store the cdevsw table entry slot to use. The *cb_devno* variable is initialized to the value NODEV to indicate that no major number for the device has been assigned. Section 10.9.2 shows that cb_configure sets *cb_devno* to the table entry slot.

3. Declares and initializes the cdevsw structure called cb_cdevsw_entry. Section 10.9.2 shows that cdevsw_add uses cb_cdevsw_entry to add the /dev/cb driver interfaces to the in-memory cdevsw table.

The following list describes those members that the /dev/cb device driver initializes to a nonzero value:

- cbopen, the driver's open interface

  Section 10.10.1 shows how to implement cbopen.

- cbclose, the driver's close interface

  Section 10.10.2 shows how to implement cbclose.

- cbread, the driver's read interface

  Section 10.11.1 shows how to implement cbread.

- cbwrite, the driver's write interface

  Section 10.11.2 shows how to implement cbwrite.

- cbioctl, the driver's ioctl interface

  Section 10.14.1 shows how to implement cbioctl.

Section 8.2.1 describes the cdevsw table.

④ Uses two of the C preprocessor statements to define and undefine debug constants. The /dev/cb device driver contains numerous conditional compilation debug statements. This section shows only one of these statements. However, the source code listing in Section A.2 contains all the debug code.

10.8 Autoconfiguration Support Section

The Autoconfiguration Support Section is applicable to the loadable or static version of the /dev/cb device driver. Table 10-2 lists the three interfaces implemented as part of the Autoconfiguration Support Section, along with the sections in the book where each is described.

Table 10-2: Interfaces Implemented as Part of the Autoconfiguration Support Section

Interface	Section
Implementing the cbprobe Interface	Section 10.8.1
Implementing the cbattach Interface	Section 10.8.2
Implementing the cb_ctlr_unattach Interface	Section 10.8.3

10.8.1 Implementing the cbprobe Interface

The cbprobe interface is applicable to both the loadable and static versions of the /dev/cb device driver. However, there are some tasks associated only with loadable drivers. These tasks are identified by a conditional if statement that tests the *cb_is_dynamic* variable. The cbprobe interface's main task is to determine whether any CB devices exist on the system. For the loadable version of the driver, cbprobe also calls the appropriate interfaces to register the interrupt handlers for the loadable driver.

The following code implements the cbprobe interface:

```
cbprobe(addr, ctlr)
io_handle_t addr;            1
struct controller *ctlr;     2
{

        ihandler_t handler;            3
        struct handler_intr_info info;  4
        int unit = ctlr->ctlr_num;     5

/*********************************************************
 *              DEBUG STATEMENT                         *
 *********************************************************/
#ifdef CB_DEBUG 6
printf("CBprobe @ %8x, addr = %8x, ctlr = %8x\n",cbprobe,addr,ctlr);
#endif /* CB_DEBUG */

                handler.ih_bus = ctlr->bus_hd; 7
                info.configuration_st = (caddr_t)ctlr; 8
                info.config_type = CONTROLLER_CONFIG_TYPE; 9

                info.intr = cbintr; 10

                info.param = (caddr_t)unit; 11
                handler.ih_bus_info = (char *)&info; 12

                cb_id_t[unit] = handler_add(&handler); 13
                if (cb_id_t[unit] == NULL) { 14

                        return(0);
                }
                if (handler_enable(cb_id_t[unit]) != 0) { 15
                        handler_del(cb_id_t[unit]); 16

                        return(0);
                }
        num_cb++; 17

        return(1); 18
}
```

1 Declares an *addr* argument that specifies an I/O handle that you can use to reference a device register or memory located in bus address space (either I/O space or memory space). This I/O handle references the

device's I/O address space for the bus where the read operation originates (in calls to the `read_io_port` interface) and where the write operation occurs (in calls to the `write_io_port` interface).

In previous versions of the Digital UNIX operating system (formerly known as DEC OSF/1), this first argument was of type `caddr_t`. The argument specifies the system virtual address (SVA) that corresponds to the base slot address. The interpretation of this argument depends on the bus that your driver operates on. This line is applicable to the loadable or static version of the `/dev/cb` device driver.

2. Declares a pointer to the `controller` structure associated with this CB device. The `controller` structure represents an instance of a controller entity, one that connects logically to a bus. A controller can control devices that are directly connected or can perform some other controlling operation, such as a network interface or terminal controller operation. This line is applicable to the loadable or static version of the `/dev/cb` device driver. Section 7.3.2 describes the `controller` structure.

3. Declares an `ihandler_t` data structure called `handler` to contain information associated with the `/dev/cb` device driver interrupt handling. Section 7.5.1 describes the `ihandler_t` structure. The `cbprobe` interface initializes two members of this data structure. This line is applicable only to the loadable version of the `/dev/cb` device driver.

4. Declares a `handler_intr_info` data structure called `info`. The `handler_intr_info` structure contains interrupt handler information for device controllers connected to a bus. In previous versions of the Digital UNIX operating system (formerly known as DEC OSF/1), the `/dev/cb` driver declares a `tc_intr_info` structure, which is specific to the TURBOchannel bus. The `handler_intr_info` structure is a generic structure that contains interrupt handler information for buses connected to a device controller. Use of the `handler_intr_info` structure makes the driver more portable across different bus architectures.

The `/dev/cb` device driver uses this interrupt handler structure to dynamically register the device interrupt handlers for the static and loadable version of the driver. Section 7.5.2 describes the `handler_intr_info` structure.

5. Declares a *unit* variable and initializes it to the controller number. This controller number identifies the specific CB controller that is being probed. The controller number is contained in the `ctlr_num` member of the `controller` structure associated with this CB device. Section 7.3.2.3 describes the `ctlr_num` member. This member is used as an index into a variety of tables to retrieve information about this instance of

the CB device.

6 Calls the printf interface to print information that is useful for debugging purposes. This line is executed only during debugging of the /dev/cb driver.

Only a limited number of characters (currently 128) can be sent to the console display during each call to any section of a driver. The reason is that the characters are buffered until the driver returns to the kernel, at which time they are actually sent to the console display. If more than 128 characters are sent to the console display, the storage pointer may wrap around, discarding all previous characters; or it may discard all characters following the first 128.

If you need to see the results on the console terminal, limit the message size to the maximum of 128 whenever you send a message from within the driver. However, printf also stores the messages in an error log file. You can use the uerf command to view the text of this error log file. See the reference (man) page for this command.
The messages are easier to read if you use uerf with the -o terse option.

This line is applicable to the loadable or static version of the /dev/cb device driver.

7 This and the following items describe the setup of the loadable and static driver's interrupt handler. In previous versions of the Digital UNIX operating system (formerly known as DEC OSF/1), dynamic registration of interrupt handlers was accomplished only for loadable drivers. For the Digital UNIX operating system, Digital recommends that you dynamically register interrupt handlers for loadable and static drivers by using the handler interfaces. See the bus-specific book to determine the interrupt handler registration method(s) supported by the bus your driver operates on.

Specifies the bus that this controller is attached to. The bus_hd member of the controller structure contains a pointer to the bus structure that this controller is connected to. After the initialization, the ih_bus member of the ihandler_t structure contains the pointer to the bus structure associated with the /dev/cb device driver.

8 Sets the configuration_st member of the info data structure to the pointer to the controller structure associated with this CB device. This controller structure is the one for which an associated interrupt will be written.

This line also performs a type-casting operation that converts ctlr (which is of type pointer to a controller structure) to be of type caddr_t, the type of the configuration_st member.

9 Sets the `config_type` member of the `info` data structure to the constant `CONTROLLER_CONFIG_TYPE`, which identifies the `/dev/cb` driver type as a controller.

10 Sets the `intr` member of the `info` data structure to `cbintr`, the `/dev/cb` device driver's interrupt service interface (ISI).

11 Sets the `param` member of the `info` data structure to the controller number for the `controller` structure associated with this CB device. Once the driver is operational and interrupts are generated, the `cbintr` interface is called with the controller number, which specifies which instance of the controller the interrupt is associated with.

This line also performs a type-casting operation that converts *unit* (which is of type `int`) to be of type `caddr_t`, the type of the `param` member.

12 Sets the `ih_bus_info` member of the `handler` data structure to the address of the bus-specific information structure, `info`. This setting is necessary because registration of the interrupt handlers will indirectly call bus-specific interrupt registration interfaces.

This line also performs a type-casting operation that converts `info` (which is of type `ihandler_t`) to be of type `char *`, the type of the `ih_bus_info` member.

13 Calls the `handler_add` interface and saves its return value for use later by the `handler_del` interface.

The `handler_add` interface takes one argument: a pointer to an `ihandler_t` data structure, which in the example is the initialized `handler` structure.

This interface returns an opaque `ihandler_id_t` key, which is a unique number used to identify the interrupt service interfaces to be acted on by subsequent calls to `handler_del`, `handler_disable`, and `handler_enable`. This key is stored in the *cb_id_t* array (indexed by the unit number), which was declared in Section 10.5. Section 10.8.3 shows how to call `handler_del` and `handler_disable`.

14 If the return value from `handler_add` equals NULL, returns a failure status to indicate that registration of the interrupt handler failed.

15 If the `handler_enable` interface returns a nonzero value, returns the value zero (0) to indicate that it could not enable a previously registered interrupt service interface.

The `handler_enable` interface takes one argument: a pointer to the interrupt service interface's entry in the interrupt table. In this example, the ID associated with the interrupt entry is contained in the *cb_id_t* array.

16 If the call to `handler_enable` failed, removes the previously registered interrupt handler by calling `handler_del` prior to returning an error status.

17 Increments the number of instances of this controller found on the system.

18 Returns the value 1 to indicate success status because the TURBOchannel initialization code already verified that the device was present.

10.8.2 Implementing the cbattach Interface

The cbattach interface is applicable to both the loadable and static versions of the /dev/cb device driver. Its main task is to perform controller-specific initialization.

The following code implements the cbattach interface:

```
cbattach(ctlr)
struct controller *ctlr; 1
{
    struct cb_unit *cb; 2

    cb = &cb_unit[ctlr->ctlr_num]; 3
    cb->attached = 1; 4
    cb->adapter = ctlr->slot; 5
    cb->cbad = ctlr->addr; 6
    cb->cbr = (io_handle_t)CB_ADR(ctlr->addr); 7
    cb->cbbuf = &cbbuf[ctlr->ctlr_num]; 8
    cb->iomode = CBPIO; 9
}
```

1. Declares a pointer to the controller structure associated with this CB device. The controller structure represents an instance of a controller entity, one that connects logically to a bus. A controller can control devices that are directly connected or can perform some other controlling operation, such as a network interface or terminal controller operation. Section 7.3.2 describes the controller structure.

2. Declares a pointer to the cb_unit data structure associated with this CB device and calls it cb. Section 10.6 shows the declaration of cb_unit.

3. Sets the pointer to the cb_unit structure to the address of the unit data structure associated with this CB device. The ctlr_num member of the controller structure pointed to by ctlr holds the controller number for the controller associated with this CB device. Thus, this member is used as an index into the array of cb_unit structures to set the instance that represents this CB device.

4. Indicates that this CB device is attached to its associated controller by setting the attached member of the device's associated cb_unit structure to the value 1.

5. Sets this CB device's TURBOchannel slot number by setting the adapter member of this CB device's cb_unit structure to the slot number contained in the slot member of the device's controller structure. Section 7.3.2.6 describes the slot member.

6. Sets the base address of the device ROM. This location is the address of the data to be checked for read accessibility. The cbattach interface accomplishes this task by setting the cbad member of this CB device's

cb_unit structure to the address contained in the addr member of its controller structure.

7 Sets the pointer to the CB device's registers. The cbattach interface accomplishes this task by setting the cbr member of this device's cb_unit structure to the register address calculated by the CB_ADR macro. The cbr member is an I/O handle. An I/O handle is a data entity that is of type io_handle_t.

Note that CB_ADR takes as an argument the address of the data to be checked for read accessibility, which in this case is stored in the addr member of the controller structure. Section 10.2 shows the definition of the CB_ADR macro.

When CB_ADR completes execution, the cb->cbr pointer is set to the base address plus 20000 hexadecimal because the CB device registers are located at that offset from the base address.

8 Sets the buffer structure address (the cbbuf member of this CB device's cb_unit structure) to the address of this CB device's buf structure. Again, the ctlr_num member is used as an index into the array of buf structures associated with this CB device.

9 Sets the read/write mode to the ioctl represented by CBPIO. This ioctl indicates that the driver starts in programmed I/O (PIO) read or write mode.

10.8.3 Implementing the cb_ctlr_unattach Interface

The cb_ctlr_unattach interface is a loadable driver-specific interface called indirectly from the bus code when a system manager specifies that the loadable driver is to be unloaded using the sysconfig utility. In other words, this interface would never be called if the /dev/cb device driver were configured as a static driver because static drivers cannot be unconfigured. The cb_ctlr_unattach interface's main tasks are to deregister the interrupt handlers associated with the /dev/cb device driver and to remove the specified controller structure from the list of controllers the /dev/cb driver handles.

The following code implements the cb_ctlr_unattach interface:

```
int cb_ctlr_unattach(bus, ctlr)
    struct bus *bus;        1
    struct controller *ctlr; 2
{
        register int unit = ctlr->ctlr_num; 3
        if ((unit > num_cb) || (unit < 0)) { 4
            return(1);
        }
        if (cb_is_dynamic == 0) { 5
            return(1);
        }
        if (handler_disable(cb_id_t[unit]) != 0) { 6
            return(1);
        }
        if (handler_del(cb_id_t[unit]) != 0) { 7
            return(1);
        }
        return(0); 8
}
```

1 Declares a pointer to a bus structure and calls it bus. The bus structure represents an instance of a bus entity. A bus is a real or imagined entity to which other buses or controllers are logically attached. All systems have at least one bus, the system bus, even though the bus may not actually exist physically. The term *controller* here refers both to devices that control slave devices (for example, disk or tape controllers) and to devices that stand alone (for example, terminal or network controllers). Section 7.3.1 describes the bus structure.

2 Declares a pointer to a controller structure and calls it ctlr. This controller structure is the one you want to remove from the list of controllers handled by the /dev/cb device driver. Section 7.3.2 describes the controller structure.

3. Declares a *unit* variable and initializes it to the controller number. This controller number identifies the specific CB controller whose associated `controller` structure is to be removed from the list of controllers handled by the `/dev/cb` driver. Section 7.3.2.3 describes the `ctlr_num` member.

The controller number is contained in the `ctlr_num` member of the `controller` structure associated with this CB device.

4. If the controller number is greater than the number of controllers found by the `cbprobe` interface or the controller number is less than zero, returns the value 1 to the bus code to indicate an error. This sequence of code validates the controller number. The *num_cb* variable contains the number of instances of the CB controller found by the `cbprobe` interface. Section 10.8.1 describes the implementation of `cbprobe`.

5. If *cb_is_dynamic* is equal to the value zero (0), returns the value 1 to the bus code to indicate an error. This sequence of code validates whether the `/dev/cb` driver was dynamically loaded. The *cb_is_dynamic* variable contains a value to control any differences in tasks performed by the static and loadable versions of the `/dev/cb` device driver. This approach means that any differences are made at run time and not at compile time. The *cb_is_dynamic* variable was previously initialized and set by the `cb_configure` interface, discussed in Section 10.9.2.

6. If the return value from the call to the `handler_disable` interface is not equal to the value zero (0), returns the value 1 to the bus code to indicate an error. Otherwise, the `handler_disable` interface makes the `/dev/cb` device driver's previously registered interrupt service interfaces unavailable to the system. Section 9.6.2 provides additional information on `handler_disable`.

7. If the return value from the call to the `handler_del` interface is not equal to the value zero (0), returns the value 1 to the bus code to indicate an error. Otherwise, the `handler_del` interface deregisters the `/dev/cb` device driver's interrupt service interface from the bus-specific interrupt dispatching algorithm. Section 9.6.2 provides additional information on `handler_del`.

The `handler_del` interface takes the same argument as the `handler_disable` interface: a pointer to the interrupt service's entry in the interrupt table.

8. Returns the value zero (0) to the bus code upon successful completion of the tasks performed by the `cb_ctlr_unattach` interface.

10.9 Loadable Device Driver Section

The Loadable Device Driver Section is applicable only to the loadable version of the /dev/cb device driver. It implements the cb_configure interface. Table 10-3 lists the tasks associated with implementing the Loadable Device Driver Section, along with the sections in the book where each task is described.

Table 10-3: Tasks Associated with Implementing the Loadable Device Driver Section

Tasks	Section
Setting Up the cb_configure Interface	Section 10.9.1
Configuring (Loading) the /dev/cb Device Driver	Section 10.9.2
Unconfiguring (Unloading) the /dev/cb Device Driver	Section 10.9.3
Querying the /dev/cb Device Driver	Section 10.9.4

10.9.1 Setting Up the cb_configure Interface

The following code shows how to set up the cb_configure interface:

```
cb_configure(op,indata,indatalen,outdata,outdatalen)
    cfg_op_t op;       1
    cfg_attr_t *indata;  2
    size_t indatalen;    3
    cfg_attr_t *outdata;  4
    size_t outdatalen;    5
{
        dev_t   cdevno;  6
        int     retval;  7
        int     i;        8
        struct cb_unit *cb;  9
        int cbincled();       10


#define MAX_DEVICE_CFG_ENTRIES 18  11


#ifdef CB_DEBUG
        cfg_attr_t cfg_buf[MAX_DEVICE_CFG_ENTRIES];  12
#endif
```

1   Declares an argument called *op* to contain a constant that describes the configuration operation to be performed on the loadable driver. This argument is used in a switch statement and evaluates to one of the following valid constants: CFG_OP_CONFIGURE, CFG_OP_UNCONFIGURE, or CFG_OP_QUERY.

2   Declares a pointer to a cfg_attr_t data structure called indata that consists of inputs to the cb_configure interface. The cfgmgr daemon fills in this data structure. The cfg_attr_t data structure is used to represent a variety of information, including the /dev/cb driver's major number requirements. Section 7.4.2 describes the cfg_attr_t structure.

3   Declares an argument called *indatalen* to store the size of this input data structure. This argument represents the number of cfg_attr_t structures included in *indata*.

4   This formal parameter is not currently used.

5   This formal parameter is not currently used.

6   Declares a variable called *cdevno* to temporarily store the major device number for the CB device.

7   Declares a variable called *retval* to store the return value from the cdevsw_del interface.

8   Declares a variable called *i* to be used in the for loop when cb_configure unconfigures the loadable driver.

9 Declares a pointer to the `cb_unit` data structure associated with this CB device and calls it `cb`. Section 10.6 shows the declaration of `cb_unit`.

10 Declares a forward reference to the `cbincled` interface. Section 10.15 shows the implementation of `cbincled`.

11 Defines a constant that represents the number of configuration lines in the `stanza.loadable` file fragment for the `/dev/cb` device driver.

12 Declares an array of `cfg_attr_t` data structures and calls it `cfg_buf`. The number of `cfg_attr_t` structures in the array matches the number of configuration lines specified in the `stanza.loadable` file fragment for this loadable device driver subsystem. The `cfgmgr` daemon passes the `cfg_attr_t` array to the input data argument of the driver's `configure` interface. This array contains the strings that are stored in the `sysconfigtab` database for this loadable device driver subsystem.

Thus, for the `/dev/cb` device driver, the `cfgmgr` daemon passes the `cfg_attr_t` array of attributes to the *indata* argument and the number of `cfg_attr_t` structures in the array to the *indatalen* argument of the `cb_configure` interface.

10.9.2 Configuring (Loading) the /dev/cb Device Driver

The following code shows how to implement the configurable (loadable) version of the /dev/cb device driver:

```
switch (op) {

        case CFG_OP_CONFIGURE: 1
#ifdef CB_DEBUG 2
            bcopy(indata, cfg_buf[0].name,
                    indatalen*(sizeof(cfg_attr_t)));
            printf(" The cb_configure routine was called.  op = %x\n",op);
            for( i=0; i < indatalen; i++){
                printf("%s: ",cfg_buf[i].name);
                switch(cfg_buf[i].type){
                    case CFG_ATTR_STRTYPE:
                        printf("%s\n",cfg_buf[i].attr.str.val);
                        break;
                    default:
                      switch(cfg_buf[i].status){
                        case CFG_ATTR_EEXISTS:
                            printf("**Attribute does not exist\n");
                            break;
                        case CFG_ATTR_EOP:
                            printf("**Attribute does not support operation\n");
                            break;
                        case CFG_ATTR_ESUBSYS:
                            printf("**Subsystem Failure\n");
                            break;
                        case CFG_ATTR_ESMALL:
                            printf("**Attribute size/value too small\n");
                            break;
                        case CFG_ATTR_ELARGE:
                            printf("**Attribute size/value too large\n");
                            break;
                        case CFG_ATTR_ETYPE:
                            printf("**Attribute invalid type\n");
                            break;
                        case CFG_ATTR_EINDEX:
                            printf("**Attribute invalid index\n");
                            break;
                        case CFG_ATTR_EMEM:
                            printf("**Attribute memory allocation error\n");
                            break;
                        default:
                            printf("**Unknown attribute: ");
                            printf("%x\n", cfg_buf[i].status);
                            break;
                            }
                    break;
                    }
                }
#endif

        if(strcmp(modtype,"Dynamic")==0) {
            cb_is_dynamic = 1;
            } 3
        if (cb_is_dynamic) { 4
```

```
        if(strcmp(mcfgname,"")==0) {
            printf("cb_configure, null config name.\n");
            return(EINVAL);
            }

        if (ldbl_stanza_resolver(mcfgname,
            CB_BUSNAME, &cbdriver,
            (caddr_t *)cb_option_snippet) != 0) {
            return(EINVAL);
            } 5

        if (ldbl_ctlr_configure(CB_BUSNAME,
            LDBL_WILDNUM, mcfgname,
            &cbdriver, 0)) {
            return(EINVAL);
            } 6

            if (num_cb == 0) {
                return(EINVAL);
            }
    } 7


    if(strcmp(devcmajor,"")!=0) { 8
            if((strcmp(devcmajor,"-1")==0) ||
               (strcmp(devcmajor,"?")==0) ||
               (strcmp(devcmajor,"any")==0) ||
               (strcmp(devcmajor,"ANY")==0)){
                cdevno = NODEV;
                }
            else { 9
                cdevno = atoi(devcmajor);
                cdevno = makedev(cdevno,0);
                }
        }
    else
            return EINVAL; 10
cdevno = cdevsw_add(cdevno,&cb_cdevsw_entry); 11
if (cdevno == NODEV) {

        return(ENODEV);
} 12

cb_devno = cdevno; 13

cmajnum = major(cb_devno); 14

begunit = 0; 15

numunit = num_cb; 16

bmajnum = NODEV; 17

cb_config = TRUE; 18
break;
```

1   Specifies the CFG_OP_CONFIGURE constant to indicate that this section
    of code implements the configure loadable driver operation. The file
    /usr/sys/include/sys/sysconfig.h contains the definition of
    this constant.

2 The /dev/cb device driver requests that the cfgmgr daemon initialize the cb_attributes structure with all of the attributes specified for the cb entry in the /etc/sysconfigtab database.

Attributes passed through the cb_attributes structure are not known to be valid until the device driver can check their status in the *indata* argument. A status other than CFG_FRAME_SUCCESS is an error condition. The code:

– Debugs cfgmgr loading problems with the cb_attributes structure

– Displays the contents and status of the attributes in the /etc/sysconfigtab database for the /dev/cb driver on the console terminal

– Reports the cfgmgr daemon's status that indicates a failure to load any of the attribute fields into the cb_attributes structure

3 If the string associated with the *modtype* variable equals the string Dynamic, then this is the loadable version of the driver. The strcmp interface compares the two null-terminated strings. To indicate this state, the code sets the *cb_is_dynamic* variable to 1. The file /usr/sys/include/sys/sysconfig.h contains the definition of this constant.

4 If *cb_is_dynamic* evaluates to true, execute the operation code passed to the *op* argument. In this case, the operation code is CFG_OP_CONFIGURE.

5 If the ldbl_stanza_resolver interface returns a value not equal to zero (0), it did not find matches in the tc_slot table. This condition indicates that ldbl_stanza_resolver failed to find the kernel structure required to configure the option snippet structure, cb_option_snippet. The interface returns the constant EINVAL to indicate an invalid argument. Otherwise, ldbl_stanza_resolver allows the device driver to merge the system configuration data structure created by the device method into the hardware topology tree created at static configuration time.

The ldbl_stanza_resolver interface takes four arguments:

– The name of the driver specified by the driver writer in the stanza.loadable file fragment

   In this call, the driver name is obtained from the name member of the cb_attributes structure. Section 10.5 shows the initialization of the cb_attributes structure.

– The name of the parent bus structure associated with this controller

   In this call, the constant CB_BUSNAME represents the characters ''tc'' indicating that the parent bus structure is a TURBOchannel bus.

Section 10.5 shows the definition of the bus name.

– A pointer to the `driver` structure for the controlling device driver

In this call, the address of the `cbdriver` structure is passed.

– A bus-specific parameter

The bus-specific parameter for a TURBOchannel bus is usually a `tc_option` snippet table. The snippet table is identical in format to the `tc_option` table defined in the `tc_option_data.c` file. In this call, the address of the `cb_option_snippet` table is passed. This table contains the appropriate entry for the loadable version of the `/dev/cb` device driver. Section 10.5 shows the declaration of this table.

Note that a type-casting operation converts `cb_option_snippet` (which is of type `struct tc_option`) to be of type `caddr_t *`, the type of the bus-specific argument. However, `ldbl_stanza_resolver` does not do anything with this argument but pass it to the bus configuration code, which performs the correct type-casting operation to handle `cb_option_snippet`. Section 9.7.3 provides additional information on the `ldbl_stanza_resolver` interface.

6 Calls the `ldbl_ctlr_configure` interface to cause the driver's `cbprobe` interface to be called once for each instance of the controller found on the system. If the call to `ldbl_ctlr_configure` fails, no instances of the controller exist on the bus and it returns the `EINVAL` constant.

The `ldbl_ctlr_configure` interface takes five arguments:

– The bus name

In this call, the bus name is represented by the `CB_BUSNAME` constant, which maps to the character string `tc`. Section 10.5 shows the definition of the bus name.

– The bus number

In this call, the bus number is represented by the wildcard constant `LDBL_WILDNUM`. This wildcard allows for the configuration of all instances of the `CB` device present on the system. This constant is defined in the file `/usr/sys/include/io/common/devdriver.h`.

– The name of the controlling device driver

In this call, this name is obtained from the `name` member of the `cb_option_snippet` data structure.

– A pointer to the `driver` structure for the controlling device driver

In this call, the controlling device driver is `cbdriver`.

- Miscellaneous flags from
  `/usr/sys/include/io/common/devdriver_loadable.h`

  In this call, the value zero (0) is passed to indicate that no flags are specified.

7. If the `cbprobe` interface does not find any controllers, returns the `EINVAL` constant to indicate no controllers were found.

8. Checks for the existence of the device major number for the CB device. If the device major number for the CB device exists, then a call to `makedev` makes the device number.

9. Calls the `makedev` interface, which makes a device number of type `dev_t` based on the specified major and minor numbers. Upon successful completion, `makedev` returns the major number for this CB device in the *cdevno* variable. The driver configuration is performed before obtaining the device major number to prevent user-level programs from gaining access to the `/dev/cb` driver's entry points in the `cdevsw` table.

   The `makedev` interface takes two arguments:

   - The first argument is the major number for the device, which in this call is obtained from the `name` member of the `cb_attributes` data structure associated with this device. Section 10.5 shows the declaration of this structure.

   - The second argument is the minor number for the device, which in this call is also obtained from the `name` member of the `cb_attributes` structure, indicating that the major and minor numbers are identical. This interface does not make use of the minor number.

   Section 15.2 provides a reference (man) page-style description of `makedev`.

10. Returns an error constant if the device major number does not exist.

11. Calls the `cdevsw_add` interface to add the driver entry points for the `/dev/cb` driver to the `cdevsw` table.

    The `cdevsw_add` interface takes two arguments:

    - The first argument specifies the device switch table entry (slot) to use. This entry represents the requested major number. In this call, the slot to use was obtained in a previous call to `makedev`.

    - The second argument is the character device switch structure that contains the character device driver's entry points.

    In this call, this structure is called `cb_cdevsw_entry`. Upon successful completion, `cdevsw_add` returns the device number associated with the device switch table. Section 9.7.2 provides additional information on `cdevsw_add`.

12 If the device number associated with the device switch table is equal to the constant `NODEV`, returns the error constant `ENODEV`. The `NODEV` constant indicates that the requested major number is currently in use or that the `cdevsw` table is currently full. The `NODEV` constant is defined in `/usr/sys/include/sys/param.h`, and `/usr/sys/include/sys/errno.h` contains the `ENODEV` constant.

13 Stores the `cdevsw` table entry slot for this CB device in the *cb_devno* variable. Section 10.9.3 shows that `cdevsw_del` uses this slot value when the device is unconfigured.

14 Sets *cmajnum* to the major number for this device by calling the `major` interface. In this call, the number of the device is contained in the *cdevno* variable. The device method's post process can query the major number. The system administrator can also query the major number by using the following:

```
sysconfig -q
```

15 Sets *begunit* to the first minor device number in the range. In this case, the first minor number is zero (0).

16 Sets *numunit* to the number of instances of the controller that the cbprobe interface found. In this case, this number is contained in the *numunit* variable, which was incremented by cbprobe upon locating each controller on the system.

17 Sets *bmajnum* to the constant `NODEV`. The CB device is a character device and, therefore, has no block device major number.

18 Sets the state flag to indicate that the `/dev/cb` device driver is now configured as a loadable device driver.

10.9.3 Unconfiguring (Unloading) the /dev/cb Device Driver

The following code shows how to implement the unconfiguration of the loadable version of the /dev/cb device driver:

```
case CFG_OP_UNCONFIGURE: 1

    if (cb_config != TRUE) {
            return(EINVAL);
    } 2

    for (i = 0; i < num_cb; i++) {
            if (cb_unit[i].opened != 0) {
                    return(EBUSY);
            } 3
    }

    for (i = 0; i < num_cb; i++) { 4
            cb = &cb_unit[i];
            cb->ledflag = 0;
            untimeout(cbincled, (caddr_t)cb);
    }

            retval = cdevsw_del(cb_devno);
            if (retval) {
            return(ESRCH);
            } 5

    if (cb_is_dynamic) { 6

            if (ldbl_ctlr_unconfigure(CB_BUSNAME,
                    LDBL_WILDNUM, &cbdriver,
                    LDBL_WILDNAME, LDBL_WILDNUM) != 0) { 7

                    return(ESRCH);
            }
    }
    cb_config = FALSE; 8
    break;
```

1. Specifies the CFG_OP_UNCONFIGURE constant to indicate that this section of code implements the unconfigure operation of the loadable driver. The file /usr/sys/include/sys/sysconfig.h contains the definition of this constant.

2. If the /dev/cb device driver is not currently configured or loaded, it fails the unconfiguration by returning the EINVAL constant. This error code is defined in /usr/sys/include/sys/errno.h.

3. Prevents the system manager from unloading the device driver if it is currently active. Checks the opened member of this CB device's cb_unit structure to determine if the device is open and thus active. If the device is open, returns the EBUSY constant. This error code is defined in /usr/sys/include/sys/errno.h.

4. As long as the variable i is less than the number of controllers found by cbprobe, executes the following:

- Specifies the cb_unit structure associated with this CB device
- Turns off the LED increment function

    This is accomplished by setting the member of the cb_unit structure that stores the LED increment function flag. The reason for turning off this function is to ensure that the driver is quiescent. If this function is not turned off, the cbincled interface could be called after its timeout interval expires. If an attempt to execute a driver interface that had already been unloaded is made, a system panic could result.

- Calls the untimeout kernel interface to remove the scheduled interface from the callout queues

    When this call to untimeout is made, the driver does not know if there are any pending calls on the callout queues. If there are any pending calls, they are removed from the callout queues. If there are no pending calls, untimeout simply returns.

    The untimeout interface takes two arguments:

    - The first argument is a pointer to the interface to be removed from the callout queues, which in this call is cbincled.

    - The second argument is a single argument passed to the called interface, which is cbincled.

        In this call, this single argument is the pointer to the cb_unit structure associated with this CB device.

        A type-casting operation converts cb (which is of type cb_unit) to be of type caddr_t, the type of the single argument. Section 9.5.6 provides additional information on untimeout.

5 Calls the cdevsw_del interface to delete the /dev/cb driver's entry points from the cdevsw table. This task is done prior to calling ldbl_ctlr_unconfigure to prevent access to the device in the middle of unconfiguring the driver. If cdevsw_del returns a nonzero value, it returns the error constant ESRCH to indicate there was no such slot in the cdevsw table. Otherwise, it deletes the driver's entry points. Section 9.7.1 provides additional information on the cdevsw_del interface.

The cdevsw_del interface takes one argument: the device switch table entry (slot) to use. In this call, the slot is contained in the cb_devno variable, which was set when the driver was configured.

6 If cb_is_dynamic evaluates to TRUE, calls the ldbl_ctlr_unconfigure interface to unconfigure the specified controller. Section 10.9.2 shows that the cb_is_dynamic variable was previously set to TRUE (the value 1) when the driver was configured.

7 If the `ldbl_ctlr_unconfigure` interface returns a nonzero value, returns the error constant `ESRCH` to indicate that it did not successfully unconfigure the specified controller. Otherwise, it unconfigures the controller. A call to this interface results in a call to the driver's `cb_ctlr_unattach` interface for each instance of the controller. Section 10.8.3 describes `cb_ctlr_unattach`.

The `ldbl_ctlr_unconfigure` interface takes five arguments:

–   The bus name

    In this call, the bus name is represented by the constant `CB_BUSNAME`.

–   The bus number

    In this call, the wildcard constant indicates that the interface `ldbl_ctlr_unconfigure` deregisters all instances of the controllers connected to the TURBOchannel bus.

–   A pointer to the `driver` structure for the controlling device driver

    In this case, the controlling device driver is `cbdriver`.

–   The controller name and controller number

    In this call, the wildcard constants indicate that `ldbl_ctlr_unconfigure` scans all `controller` structures.

Section 9.7.4 provides additional information on `ldbl_ctlr_unconfigure`.

8 Sets the `cb_config` variable to the value FALSE to indicate that the `/dev/cb` device driver is now unconfigured.

10.9.4 Querying the /dev/cb Device Driver

The following code shows how to implement the query section of a loadable device driver. This section of code executes when the system manager queries information associated with the loadable version of the driver. This section of code is also a program request to the loadable subsystem support interfaces. This is how the driver method makes the device special files after the cb_configure interface executes.

```
        case CFG_OP_QUERY: 1
          break;

        default:
          return(EINVAL); 2
          break;
    }

    return(0); 3
  }
```

1 Specifies the CFG_OP_QUERY operation to indicate that this section of code implements the query operation of the loadable driver. The file /usr/sys/include/sys/sysconfig.h contains the definition of this constant.

2 Defines an unknown operation type and returns the error constant EINVAL to indicate this condition. This section of code is called if the *op* argument is set to anything other than CFG_OP_CONFIGURE, CFG_OP_UNCONFIGURE, or CFG_OP_QUERY. To indicate that the /dev/cb driver's cb_configure interface has completed the requested operation of CFG_OP_CONFIGURE, CFG_OP_UNCONFIGURE, or CFG_OP_QUERY successfully, returns the value zero (0).

3 To indicate that the /dev/cb driver's cb_configure interface completed successfully, returns the value zero (0).

10.10 Open and Close Device Section

The Open and Close Device Section is applicable to the loadable or static
version of the /dev/cb device driver. Table 10-4 lists the two interfaces
implemented as part of the Open and Close Device Section along with the
sections in the book where each is described.

**Table 10-4: Interfaces Implemented as Part of the Open and
Close Device Section**

Interfaces	Section
Implementing the cbopen Interface	Section 10.10.1
Implementing the cbclose Interface	Section 10.10.2

10.10.1 Implementing the cbopen Interface

The following code implements the cbopen interface:

```
cbopen(dev, flag, format)
dev_t dev;     1
int flag;      2
int format;    3
{
        int unit = minor(dev); 4
        if ((unit > NCB) || !cb_unit[unit].attached)
                return(ENXIO); 5
        cb_unit[unit].opened = 1; 6
        return(0);                7
}
```

1. Declares an argument that specifies the major and minor device numbers for a specific CB device. The minor device number is used to determine the logical unit number for the CB device that is to be opened.

2. Declares an argument to contain flag bits from the file /usr/sys/include/sys/file.h. These flags indicate whether the device is being opened for reading, writing, or both.

3. Declares an argument that specifies the format of the special device to be opened. The *format* argument is used by a driver that has both block and character interfaces and that uses the same open interface in both the bdevsw and cdevsw tables. The driver uses this argument to distinguish the type of device being opened. The cbopen interface does not use this argument.

4. Declares a *unit* variable and initializes it to the device minor number. Note the use of the minor interface to obtain the device minor number.

   The minor interface takes one argument: the number of the device for which an associated device minor number will be obtained. The minor number is encoded in the *dev* argument.

5. If the device minor number is greater than the number of CB devices configured in this system OR if this CB device is not attached, returns the error code ENXIO, which indicates no such device or address. This error code is defined in /usr/sys/include/sys/errno.h.

   The NCB constant is used in the comparison of the *unit* variable. This constant defines the maximum number of CB devices configured on this system.

   The line also checks the attached member of this CB device's cb_unit structure. Section 10.8.2 shows that the cbattach interface set this member to the value 1.

6. If the previous line evaluates to FALSE, sets the opened member of this CB device's cb_unit structure to the value 1 to indicate that this CB

device is open and ready for operation. Section 10.6 shows the declaration of the cb_unit data structure.

7 Returns success to the open system call, indicating a successful open of this CB device.

10.10.2 Implementing the cbclose Interface

The following code implements the `cbclose` interface:

```
cbclose(dev, flag, format)
dev_t dev;     1
int flag;      2
int format;    3
{
        int unit = minor(dev);       4
        cb_unit[unit].opened = 0;    5
        return(0);                   6
}
```

1 Declares an argument that specifies the major and minor device numbers for a specific CB device. The minor device number is used to determine the logical unit number for the CB device that is to be closed.

2 Declares an argument to contain flag bits from the file `/usr/sys/include/sys/file.h`. The `cbclose` interface does not use this argument.

3 Declares an argument that specifies the format of the special device to be closed. The *format* argument is used by a driver that has both block and character interfaces and that uses the same `close` interface in both the `bdevsw` and `cdevsw` tables. The driver uses this argument to distinguish the type of device being closed.

   The `cbclose` interface does not use this argument.

4 Declares a *unit* variable and initializes it to the device minor number. Note the use of the `minor` interface to obtain the device minor number.

   The `minor` interface takes one argument: the number of the device for which an associated device minor number will be obtained. The minor number is encoded in the *dev* argument.

5 Sets the `opened` member of this CB device's `cb_unit` structure to the value zero (0), indicating that this CB device is now closed. Section 10.6 shows the declaration of the `cb_unit` data structure.

6 Returns success to the `close` system call, indicating a successful close of this CB device.

10.11 Read and Write Device Section

The Read and Write Device Section is applicable to the loadable or static version of the /dev/cb device driver. Table 10-5 lists the interfaces implemented as part of the Read and Write Device Section along with the sections in the book where each is described.

Table 10-5: Interfaces Implemented as Part of the Read and Write Device Section

Interfaces	Section
Implementing the cbread Interface	Section 10.11.1
Implementing the cbwrite Interface	Section 10.11.2

10.11.1 Implementing the cbread Interface

The following code implements the cbread interface:

```
cbread(dev, uio, flag)
dev_t dev;         1
struct uio *uio;   2
int flag;
{
        unsigned tmp;   3
        int cnt, err;   4
        int unit = minor(dev);   5
        struct cb_unit *cb;      6

        err = 0;                    7
        cb = &cb_unit[unit];        8
        if(cb->iomode == CBPIO) {   9

                while((cnt = uio->uio_resid) && (err == 0)) {  10
                        if(cnt > MAX_XFR)cnt = MAX_XFR;  11
                        tmp = read_io_port(cb->cbr | CB_DATA,
                                           4,
                                           0);12

                        err = uiomove(&tmp,cnt,uio);  13
                        }
                return(err);  14
                }
        else if(cb->iomode == CBDMA)  15

            return(physio(cbstrategy,cb->cbbuf,dev,
                        B_READ,cbminphys,uio));
}
```

1. Declares an argument that specifies the major and minor device numbers for a specific CB device. The minor device number is used to determine the logical unit number for the CB device on which the read operation is performed.

2. Declares a pointer to a uio structure. This structure contains the information for transferring data to and from the address space of the user's process. You typically pass this pointer unmodified to the uiomove or physio kernel interface. This driver passes the pointer to both interfaces.

3. Declares a variable called *tmp* to store the 32-bit read/write data register. This variable is passed as an argument to the uiomove kernel interface.

4. Declares a variable called *cnt* to store the number of bytes of data that still need to be transferred. This variable is passed as an argument to the uiomove interface.

   Declares a variable called *err* to store the return value from uiomove.

5. Declares a *unit* variable and initializes it to the device minor number. Note the use of the minor interface to obtain the device minor number.

The `minor` interface takes one argument: the number of the device for which an associated device minor number will be obtained. The minor number is encoded in the `dev` argument.

The `unit` variable is used to select the CB board to be accessed for the read operation.

6 Declares a pointer to the `cb_unit` data structure associated with this CB device and calls it `cb`. Section 10.6 shows the declaration of `cb_unit`.

7 Initializes the `err` variable to the value zero (0) to indicate no error has occurred yet.

8 Sets the pointer to the `cb_unit` structure to the address of the unit data structure associated with this CB device. The `unit` variable contains this CB device's minor number. Thus, this argument is used as an index into the array of `cb_unit` structures associated with this CB device.

9 If the I/O mode bit is `CBPIO`, then this is a programmed I/O read operation. This bit is set in the `iomode` member of the pointer to the `cb_unit` data structure associated with this CB device.

For a programmed I/O read operation, the contents of the data register on the TURBOchannel test board are read into a 32-bit local variable. Then the `uiomove` interface moves the contents of that variable into the buffer in the user's virtual address space.

10 Sets up a `while` loop that allows the `uiomove` interface to transfer bytes from the TURBOchannel test board data register to the user's buffer until all of the requested bytes are moved or until an error occurs.

The `uio_resid` member of the pointer to the `uio` structure specifies the number of bytes that still need to be transferred.

The `while` loop must accomplish this task because the TURBOchannel test board data register can supply only a maximum of MAX_XFR bytes at a time. The MAX_XFR constant was previously defined as 4 bytes. This loop may not be required by other devices.

11 If the number of bytes that still need to be transferred is greater than 4, then forces `cnt` to contain 4 bytes of data. This code causes a read of more than 4 bytes to be divided into a number of 4-byte maximum transfers with a final transfer of 4 bytes or less.

12 Reads the 32-bit read/write data register by calling the `read_io_port` interface. This register value is defined by the CB_DATA device register offset associated with this CB device. The `read_io_port` interface is a generic interface that maps to a bus- and machine-specific interface that actually performs the read operation. Using this interface to read data from a device register makes the device driver more portable across different bus architectures, different CPU architectures, and different CPU types within the same CPU architecture.

The read_io_port interface takes three arguments:

- The first argument specifies an I/O handle that you can use to reference a device register or memory located in bus address space (either I/O space or memory space). This I/O handle references a device register in the bus address space where the read operation originates. You can perform standard C mathematical operations on the I/O handle. In this call, the /dev/cb driver ORs the I/O handle with the 32-bit read/write data register represented by CB_DATA.

- The second argument specifies the width (in bytes) of the data to be read. Valid values are 1, 2, 3, 4, and 8. Not all CPU platforms or bus adapters support all of these values. In this call, the /dev/cb driver passes the value 4.

- The third argument specifies flags to indicate special processing requests. In this call, the /dev/cb driver passes the value zero (0).

Upon successful completion, read_io_port returns the data read from the 32-bit read/write data register to the tmp variable.

[13] Calls the uiomove interface to move the bytes read from the TURBOchannel data register in system virtual space to the user's buffer in user space. The maximum number of bytes moved is 4 and uio_resid is updated as each move is completed.

The uiomove interface takes three arguments:

- A pointer to the kernel buffer in system virtual space

  In this call, this pointer is the 32-bit read/write data contained in the tmp variable.

- The number of bytes to be moved

  In this call, the number of bytes to move is contained in the cnt variable, which is always 4 bytes.

- A pointer to a uio structure

  This structure describes the current position within a logical user buffer in user virtual space.

Section 9.3.5 provides additional information on uiomove.

[14] Returns a zero (0) value whenever the user virtual space described by the uio structure is accessible and the data is successfully moved. Otherwise, it returns an EFAULT error value.

[15] If the I/O mode bit is CBDMA, then this is a DMA I/O read operation. This bit is set in the iomode member of the pointer to the cb_unit data structure associated with this CB device.

For a DMA I/O read operation, the physio kernel interface and the /dev/cb driver's cbstrategy and cbminphys interfaces are called to transfer the contents of the data register on the TURBOchannel test board into the buffer in the user's virtual address space. Because only a single word of 4 bytes can be transferred at a time, both modes of reading include code to limit the read to chunks with a maximum of 4 bytes each. Reading more than 4 bytes will propagate the contents of the data register throughout the words of the user's buffer.

The physio interface takes six arguments:

- A pointer to the driver's strategy interface

  In this call, the driver's strategy interface is cbstrategy. Section 10.12.2 shows how to set up the cbstrategy interface.

- A pointer to a buf structure

  In this call, the buf structure is the one associated with this CB device. This structure contains information such as the binary status flags, the major/minor device numbers, and the address of the associated buffer. This buffer is always a special buffer header owned exclusively by the device for handling I/O requests. Section 8.1 describes the buf structure.

- The device number, which in this call is contained in the *dev* argument

- The read/write flag

  In this call the read/write flag is the constant B_READ.

- A pointer to the minphys interface

  In this call, the driver's minphys interface is cbminphys. Section 10.12.1 shows how to set up the cbminphys interface.

- A pointer to a uio structure

10.11.2 Implementing the cbwrite Interface

The following code implements the cbwrite interface:

```
cbwrite(dev, uio, flag)
dev_t dev;          1
struct uio *uio;    2
int flag;
{
        unsigned tmp;  3
        int cnt, err;  4
        int unit = minor(dev);  5
        struct cb_unit *cb;    6

        err = 0;                        7
        cb = &cb_unit[unit];            8
        if(cb->iomode == CBPIO) {   9

                while((cnt = uio->uio_resid) && (err == 0)) {  10
                        if(cnt > MAX_XFR)cnt = MAX_XFR;   11

                        err = uiomove(&tmp,cnt,uio);   12
                        write_io_port(cb->cbr | CB_DATA,
                                        4,
                                        0,
                                        tmp);   13
                }
                return(err);   14
        }
        else if(cb->iomode == CBDMA)   15

                return(physio(cbstrategy,cb->cbbuf,dev,
                                B_WRITE,cbminphys,uio));
}
```

1 Declares an argument that specifies the major and minor device numbers for a specific CB device. The minor device number is used to determine the logical unit number for the CB device on which the write operation is performed.

2 Declares a pointer to a uio structure. This structure contains the information for transferring data to and from the address space of the user's process. You typically pass this pointer unmodified to the uiomove or physio kernel interface. This driver passes the pointer to both interfaces.

3 Declares a variable called tmp to store the 32-bit read/write data register. This variable is passed as an argument to the uiomove kernel interface.

4 Declares a variable called cnt to store the number of bytes of data that still need to be transferred. This variable is passed as an argument to the uiomove interface.

Declares a variable called err to store the return value from uiomove.

5 Declares a *unit* variable and initializes it to the device minor number. Note the use of the `minor` interface to obtain the device minor number.

The `minor` interface takes one argument: the number of the device for which an associated device minor number will be obtained. The minor number is encoded in the *dev* argument.

The *unit* variable is used to select the TURBOchannel test board to be accessed for the write operation.

6 Declares a pointer to the `cb_unit` data structure associated with this CB device and calls it `cb`. Section 10.6 shows the declaration of `cb_unit`.

7 Initializes the *err* variable to the value zero (0) to indicate no error has occurred yet.

8 Sets the pointer to the `cb_unit` structure to the address of the unit data structure associated with this CB device. The *unit* variable contains this CB device's minor number. Thus, this argument is used as an index into the array of `cb_unit` structures associated with this CB device.

9 If the I/O mode bit is `CBPIO`, then this is a programmed I/O write operation. This bit is set in the `iomode` member of the pointer to the `cb_unit` data structure associated with this CB device.

For a programmed I/O write operation, the `uiomove` interface moves the contents of one word from the buffer in the user's virtual address space to a 32-bit local variable. Then the contents of that variable are moved to the data register on the CB test board.

10 Sets up a `while` loop that allows the `uiomove` interface to transfer bytes from the user's buffer to the TURBOchannel test board data register until all of the requested bytes are moved or until an error occurs.

The `uio_resid` member of the pointer to the `uio` structure specifies the number of bytes that still need to be transferred.

The `while` loop must do this task because the TURBOchannel test board data register can accept only a maximum of MAX_XFR bytes at a time. The MAX_XFR constant was previously defined as 4 bytes. This loop may not be required by other devices.

11 If the number of bytes that still need to be transferred is greater than 4, then forces *cnt* to contain 4 bytes of data. This code causes a write of more than 4 bytes to be divided into a number of 4-byte maximum transfers with a final transfer of 4 bytes or less.

12 Calls the `uiomove` interface to move the bytes from the user's buffer to the local variable, *tmp*. The maximum number of bytes moved is 4 and `uio_resid` is updated as each move is completed.

The `uiomove` interface takes the same three arguments as described for `cbread`.

13 Writes the data to the 32-bit read/write data register by calling the write_io_port interface. This register value is defined by the CB_DATA device register offset associated with this CB device. The write_io_port interface is a generic interface that maps to a bus- and machine-specific interface that actually performs the write operation. Using this interface to write data to a device register makes the device driver more portable across different bus architectures, different CPU architectures, and different CPU types within the same CPU architecture.

The write_io_port interface takes four arguments:

– The first argument specifies an I/O handle that you can use to reference a device register or memory located in bus address space (either I/O space or memory space). This I/O handle references a device register in the bus address space where the write operation occurs. You can perform standard C mathematical operations on the I/O handle. In this call, the /dev/cb driver ORs the I/O handle with the 32-bit read/write data register represented by CB_DATA.

– The second argument specifies the width (in bytes) of the data to be written. Valid values are 1, 2, 3, 4, and 8. Not all CPU platforms or bus adapters support all of these values. In this call, the /dev/cb driver passes the value 4.

– The third argument specifies flags to indicate special processing requests. In this call, the /dev/cb driver passes the value zero (0).

– The fourth argument specifies the data to be written to the specified device register in bus address space. In this call, the /dev/cb driver passes the value stored in the *tmp* variable. Section 10.11.1 shows that the read_io_port interface stored this value in the *tmp* variable.

14 Returns a zero (0) value whenever the user virtual space described by the uio structure is accessible and the data is successfully moved. Otherwise, it returns an EFAULT error value.

15 If the I/O mode bit is CBDMA, then this is a DMA I/O write operation. This bit is set in the iomode member of the pointer to the cb_unit data structure associated with this CB device.

For a DMA I/O write operation, the physio kernel interface and the /dev/cb driver's cbstrategy and cbminphys interfaces are called to transfer the contents of the buffer in the user's virtual address space to the data register on the TURBOchannel test board. Because only a single word of 4 bytes can be transferred at a time, both modes of reading include code to limit the write to chunks with a maximum of 4 bytes. Writing more than 4 bytes has limited usefulness because all the words in the user's buffer will be written into the single data register on the test board.

This call to the `physio` interface takes the same arguments as those passed to `cbread` except the read/write flag is `B_WRITE` instead of `B_READ`.

10.12 Strategy Section

Table 10-6 lists the tasks associated with implementing the Strategy Section along with the sections in the book where each task is described.

Table 10-6: Tasks Associated with Implementing the Strategy Section

Tasks	Section
Setting Up the cbminphys Interface	Section 10.12.1
Setting Up the cbstrategy Interface	Section 10.12.2
Initializing the buf Structure for Transfer	Section 10.12.2.1
Testing the Low-Order Two Bits and Using the Internal Buffer	Section 10.12.2.2
Converting the Buffer Virtual Address	Section 10.12.2.3
Converting the 32-Bit Physical Address	Section 10.12.2.4
Starting I/O and Checking for Timeouts	Section 10.12.2.5

10.12.1 Setting Up the cbminphys Interface

The following code sets up the cbminphys interface, whose major task is to bound the data transfer size to 4 bytes:

```
cbminphys(bp)
register struct buf *bp;  1
{
        if (bp->b_bcount > MAX_XFR)  2
                bp->b_bcount = MAX_XFR;
        return;
}
```

1. Declares a pointer to a buf structure and calls it bp. Section 8.1 describes the buf structure.

2. If the size of the requested transfer is greater than 4 bytes, sets the b_bcount member of bp to 4 bytes and returns.

   The b_bcount member stores the size of the requested transfer (in bytes).

   In the call to physio, the driver writer passes cbminphys as the interface to call to check for size limitations. Section 10.11.1 and Section 10.11.2 discuss the call to physio.

10.12.2 Setting Up the cbstrategy Interface

The `cbstrategy` interface performs the following tasks:

- Initializes the `buf` structure for data transfer
- Tests the low-order 2 bits and uses the internal buffer
- Converts the buffer virtual address
- Converts the 32-bit physical address
- Starts I/O and checks for timeouts

Section 10.11.1 and Section 10.11.2 show that `cbread` and `cbwrite` call the `cbstrategy` interface. The following code implements the `cbstrategy` interface:

```
cbstrategy(bp)
register struct buf *bp; 1
{
        register int unit = minor(bp->b_dev); 2
        register struct controller *ctlr; 3
        struct cb_unit *cb;        4
        caddr_t buff_addr;         5
        caddr_t virt_addr;         6
        unsigned phys_addr;        7
        int cmd;                   8
        int err;                   9
        int status;                10
        unsigned lowbits;          11
        unsigned tmp;              12
        int s;                     13

        ctlr = cbinfo[unit];       14
```

1. Declares a pointer to a `buf` structure and calls it `bp`. Section 8.1 describes the `buf` structure.

2. Gets the minor device number and stores it in the *unit* variable.

   The `minor` kernel interface is used to obtain the minor device number associated with this CB device.

   The `minor` interface takes one argument: the number of the device for which the minor device needs to be obtained. In this call, the device number is stored in the `b_dev` member of the `buf` structure associated with this CB device.

3. Declares a pointer to a `controller` structure and calls it `ctlr`. Section 7.3.2 describes the `controller` structure.

4. Declares a pointer to the `cb_unit` data structure associated with this CB device and calls it `cb`. Section 10.6 shows the declaration of `cb_unit`.

5. Declares a variable called *buff_addr* that stores the user buffer's virtual address. Section 10.12.2.2 shows that *buff_addr* is passed to

the `copyin` kernel interface. Section 10.12.2.5 shows that *buff_addr* is passed to the `copyout` kernel interface.

|6| Declares a variable called *virt_addr* that stores the user buffer's virtual address. Section 10.12.2.2 shows that *virt_addr* is passed to the `copyin` kernel interface. Section 10.12.2.3 shows that *virt_addr* is passed to the `vtop` kernel interface. Section 10.12.2.5 shows that *virt_addr* is passed to the `copyout` kernel interface.

|7| Declares a variable called *phys_addr* that stores the user buffer's physical address. Section 10.12.2.3 shows that this variable stores the value returned by the `vtop` kernel interface.

|8| Declares a variable called *cmd* that stores the current command for the TURBOchannel test board. Section 10.12.2.4 shows that the commands are represented by the constants `CB_DMA_RD` and `CB_DMA_WR`.

|9| Declares a variable called *err* that stores the error status returned by `cbstart`.

|10| Declares a variable called *status* to store the value associated with the 16-bit read/write CSR/LED register. This value is obtained by calling the `read_io_port` interface. Appendix A shows that `cbstrategy` uses this variable in a `CB_DEBUG` statement.

|11| Declares a variable called *lowbits* to store the low 2 virtual address bits. Section 10.12.2.2 and Section 10.12.2.5 show how this variable is used.

|12| Declares a temporary holding variable called *tmp*. Section 10.12.2.4 shows that the `CB_SCRAMBLE` macro uses this variable.

|13| Declares a temporary holding variable called *s*. Section 10.12.2.4 shows that the `splbio` kernel interface uses this variable to store its return value.

|14| Sets the pointer to the `controller` structure to its associated CB device. Note that *unit*, which now contains this CB device's minor device number, is used as an index into the array of `controller` structures to obtain the `controller` structure associated with this device.

10.12.2.1 Initializing the buf Structure for Transfer

The following code initializes the buf structure for transfer:

```
bp->b_resid = bp->b_bcount;   1
bp->av_forw = 0;              2

cb = &cb_unit[unit];          3

virt_addr = bp->b_un.b_addr;  4
buff_addr = virt_addr;        5
```

1 Initializes the bytes not transferred. This is done in case the transfer fails at a later time. The b_resid member of the pointer to the buf structure stores the data (in bytes) not transferred because of some error. The b_bcount member stores the size of the requested transfer (in bytes).

2 Clears the buffer queue forward link. The av_forw member stores the position on the free list if the b_flags member is not set to B_BUSY.

3 Sets the pointer to the cb_unit structure to the address of the unit data structure associated with this CB device. The *unit* variable contains this CB device's minor number. Thus, this argument is used as an index into the array of cb_unit structures associated with this CB device. Section 10.12.2 shows how the minor interface initializes *unit* to the device's minor number.

4 Sets the *virt_addr* variable to the buffer's virtual address. The operating system software sets this address in the b_addr member of the union member b_un in the pointer to the buf structure.

5 Copies the buffer's virtual address into the *buff_addr* variable for use by the driver.

10.12.2.2   Testing the Low-Order Two Bits and Using the Internal Buffer

Direct memory access (DMA) on the TURBOchannel test board can be done
only with full words and must be aligned on word boundaries. Because the
user's buffer can be aligned on any byte boundary, the /dev/cb driver code
must check for and handle the cases where the buffer is not word aligned. In
this context, word aligned means that the address is evenly divisible by 4,
where a word is a 4-byte entity. Any address that is word aligned has its
lowest order 2 bits set to zeros. (If the TURBOchannel interface hardware
included special hardware to handle nonword-aligned transfers, this checking
would not have to be performed.) If the user's buffer is not word aligned, the
driver can:

- Exit with an error

- Take some action to ensure the words are aligned on the transfer

Because virtual-to-physical mapping is done on a page basis, the low-order 2
bits of the virtual address of the user's buffer are also the low 2 bits of the
physical address of the user's buffer. You can determine the buffer alignment
by examining the low 2 bits of the virtual buffer address. If these 2 bits are
nonzero, the buffer is not word aligned and the driver must take the correct
action.

The following code tests the low-order 2 bits:

```
if ((lowbits = (unsigned)virt_addr & 3) != 0) { 1
        virt_addr = (caddr_t)(&tmpbuffer);   2

        if ( !(bp->b_flags&B_READ) ) { 3
                tmpbuffer = 0 ;

                if (err = copyin(buff_addr,virt_addr,
                              bp->b_resid)) { 4
                        bp->b_error = err;          5
                        bp->b_flags |= B_ERROR;     6
                        iodone(bp);                 7
                        return;                     8
                }
        }
}
```

1   This bitwise AND operation uses the low-order 2 bits of the buffer virtual
    address as the word-aligned indicator for this transfer. If the result of the
    bitwise AND operation is nonzero, the user's buffer is not word aligned
    and the next line gets executed.

    Section 10.12.2.1 shows that the *virt_addr* variable gets set to the
    buffer's virtual address. Because *virt_addr* is of type caddr_t and
    lowbits is of type unsigned, the code performs the appropriate
    type-casting operation.

2. Because the user's buffer is not word aligned, uses the internal buffer, `tmpbuffer`. This line replaces the current user buffer virtual address with the internal buffer virtual address. The `physio` kernel interface updates the current user buffer virtual address as each word is transferred. Because DMA to the TURBOchannel test board can be done only a word at a time, the internal buffer needs to be only a single word.

3. If the transfer type is a write, clears the one-word temporary buffer `tmpbuffer`.

4. Calls the `copyin` kernel interface to copy data from the user address space to the kernel address space.

   The `copyin` kernel interface takes three arguments:

   – The address in user space of the data to be copied

   In this call, the address of the data is stored in the `buff_addr` variable. Section 10.12.2.1 discusses how to set this address.

   – The address in kernel space to copy the data to

   In this call, the address in kernel space is stored in the `virt_addr` variable. Section 10.12.2.2 discusses how to set this address.

   – The number of bytes to copy

   In this call, the number of bytes to copy is stored in the `b_resid` member of the pointer to the `buf` structure. Section 10.12.2.1 shows the initialization of this member.

5. Upon success, `copyin` returns the value zero (0). Otherwise, it returns `EFAULT` to indicate that the address specified in `buff_addr` could not be accessed. This line sets the `b_error` member of the pointer to the `buf` structure to the value returned in `err`. Section 10.11.2 shows that `err` was initialized to the value zero (0) to indicate that no error has yet occurred.

6. Sets `b_flags` to the bitwise inclusive OR of the read and error bits.

7. Calls the `iodone` kernel interface to indicate that the I/O operation is complete.

   This interface takes one argument: a pointer to a `buf` structure. Section 9.10.1 provides additional information on the `iodone` kernel interface.

8. Returns with an error to `physio`, which was called by `cbwrite`. Section 10.11.2 shows the call to `physio`.

10.12.2.3 Converting the Buffer Virtual Address

The following code for the cbstrategy interface converts the buffer virtual address to a physical address for DMA by calling the vtop interface. In previous versions of the Digital UNIX operating system (formerly known as DEC OSF/1), the /dev/cb driver made calls to the IS_KSEG_VA, KSEG_TO_PHYS, IS_SEG0_VA, pmap_kernel, and pmap_extract interfaces to accomplish this task. On the Digital UNIX operating system the /dev/cb driver now makes one call to vtop.

```
phys_addr = vtop(bp->b_proc, virt_addr);  1
```

1 Converts the buffer virtual address to a physical address for DMA.

This interface takes two arguments:

– The first argument specifies a pointer to a proc structure. The vtop interface uses the proc structure pointer to obtain the pmap. In this call, the /dev/cb driver passes the b_proc member of the buf structure pointer associated with this CB device. The b_proc member specifies a pointer to the proc structure that represents the process performing the I/O.

– The second argument specifies the virtual address that vtop converts to a physical address. In this call, the /dev/cb driver passes the value stored in *virt_addr*.

Upon successful completion, vtop returns the physical address associated with the specified virtual address.

10.12.2.4 Converting the 32-Bit Physical Address

The following code uses the CB_SCRAMBLE macro to convert the 32-bit physical address to a form suitable for use in the DMA operation:

```
tmp = CB_SCRAMBLE(phys_addr);  1
write_io_port(cb->cbr | CB_ADDER,
              4,
              0,
              tmp);  2

if(bp->b_flags&B_READ)         3
        cmd = CB_DMA_WR;
else
        cmd = CB_DMA_RD;
s = splbio();                  4
```

1. Converts the 32-bit physical address (actually the low 32 bits of the 34-bit physical address) from the linear form to the condensed form that the DMA operation uses to pack 34 address bits onto 32 board lines. TURBOchannel DMA operations can be done only with full words and must be aligned on word boundaries. The CB_SCRAMBLE macro discards the low-order 2 bits of the physical address while scrambling the rest of the address. Therefore, anything that is going to be done to resolve this address must be done before calling CB_SCRAMBLE.

2. Writes the data to the 32-bit read/write DMA address register by calling the write_io_port interface. This register value is defined by the CB_ADDER device register offset associated with this CB device. The write_io_port interface is a generic interface that maps to a bus- and machine-specific interface that actually performs the write operation. Using this interface to write data to a device register makes the device driver more portable across different bus architectures, different CPU architectures, and different CPU types within the same CPU architecture.

   The write_io_port interface takes four arguments:

   – The first argument specifies an I/O handle that you can use to reference a device register or memory located in bus address space (either I/O space or memory space). This I/O handle references a device register in the bus address space where the write operation occurs. You can perform standard C mathematical operations on the I/O handle. In this call, the /dev/cb driver ORs the I/O handle with the 32-bit read/write DMA address register represented by CB_ADDER.

   – The second argument specifies the width (in bytes) of the data to be written. Valid values are 1, 2, 3, 4, and 8. Not all CPU platforms or bus adapters support all of these values. In this call, the /dev/cb driver passes the value 4.

- The third argument specifies flags to indicate special processing requests. In this call, the /dev/cb driver passes the value zero (0).

- The fourth argument specifies the data to be written to the specified device register in bus address space. In this call, the /dev/cb driver passes the value returned by CB_SCRAMBLE in the *tmp* variable.

3 If the read bit is set, initializes the *cmd* argument to the DMA write bit, which is defined in the cbreg.h file. This bit indicates a write to memory.

Otherwise, if the read bit is not set, initializes the *cmd* argument to the DMA read bit, which also is defined in the cbreg.h file. This bit indicates a read from memory.

4 Calls the splbio interface to mask (disable) all controller interrupts. The value returned by splbio is an integer value that represents the CPU priority level that existed prior to the call. The return value stored in *s* becomes the argument passed to splx, which is discussed in Section 10.12.2.5.

10.12.2.5 Starting I/O and Checking for Timeouts

The following code starts the I/O and checks for timeouts:

```
err = cbstart(cmd,cb);        1
splx(s);                      2

if(err <= 0) { 3
        bp->b_error = EIO;
        bp->b_flags |= B_ERROR;
        iodone(bp);
        return;                   4
        }
else { 5
        if ( (lowbits)!=0 && bp->b_flags&B_READ) { 6
                if (err = copyout(virt_addr,buff_addr,
                                bp->b_resid)) { 7
                        bp->b_error = err;
                        bp->b_flags |= B_ERROR;
                }
        }
        bp->b_resid = 0;      8
    }
iodone(bp);                   9

return;

}
```

1 Starts the I/O by calling the driver's cbstart interface, passing to it the current command for the test board and the address of the cb_unit data structure associated with this CB device. Section 10.13 describes the cbstart driver interface.

The *cmd* argument is set either to CB_DMA_WR (the write to memory bit) or to CB_DMA_RD (the read from memory bit).

2 Restores the CPU priority by calling the splx kernel interface, passing to it the value returned in a previous call to splbio. This value is an integer that represents the CPU priority level that existed before the call to splbio.

3 If the return value from cbstart is the value zero (0), the DMA operation did not complete within the timeout period. In this case, cbstart does the following:

– Sets the b_error member in the buf structure pointer to indicate that an I/O error occurred. This error flag, EIO, is defined in /usr/sys/include/sys/errno.h.

– Sets the b_flags member in the buf structure pointer to indicate that an error occurred on this data transfer.

–   Calls the iodone kernel interface to indicate that the I/O transfer is complete.

The iodone interface takes one argument: a pointer to a buf structure. The iodone interface reschedules the process that initiated the I/O.

4   Returns the error status.

5   Else, executes the following lines because the DMA completed successfully.

6   If a read was attempted to an unaligned user buffer, calls copyout to copy the bytes that were read into the user buffer.

7   If the copyout kernel interface was unable to copy data from kernel address space to user address space, copyout does the following:

–   Sets the b_error member in the buf structure pointer to the value returned by copyout. This value indicates that the kernel address specified in the first argument could not be accessed or that the number of bytes to copy specified in the third argument is invalid.

–   Sets the b_flags member in the buf structure pointer to indicate an error occurred on this data transfer.

8   Sets the b_resid member in the buf structure pointer to the value zero (0) to indicate that the read or write operation has completed.

9   Calls iodone to indicate that the I/O transfer has completed and to initiate the return status.

10.13 Start Section

The `cbstart` interface's main task is to load the CSR register of the TURBOchannel test board. Because the `cbincled` interface increments the LEDs in the high 4 bits of the 16-bit CSR register, `cbstart` always loads the 4 bits into whatever value it will be storing into the CSR before doing the actual storage operation. The `cbstart` interface is called with system interrupts disabled; thus, `cbincled` is not called while `cbstart` is incrementing.

The following code shows the implementation of the `cbstart` interface:

```
int cbstart(cmd,cb)
int cmd;                 1
struct cb_unit *cb;      2
{
        int timecnt;  3
        int status;   4

        cmd = (read_io_port(cb->cbr | CB_CSR,
                            4,
                            0)&0xf000)|(cmd&0xfff);  5

        status = read_io_port(cb->cbr | CB_TEST,
                            4,
                            0);  6


        write_io_port(cb->cbr | CB_CSR,
                            4,
                            0,
                            cmd);  7
        mb();            8

        write_io_port(cb->cbr | CB_TEST,
                            4,
                            0,
                            0);  9

        mb();                         10
        timecnt = 10;                 11
        status = read_io_port(cb->cbr | CB_CSR,
                            4,
                            0);  12

        while((!(status & CB_DMA_DONE)) && timecnt > 0) {  13
                write_io_port(cb->cbr | CB_CSR,
                            4,
                            0,
                            cmd);

                mb();
                status = read_io_port(cb->cbr | CB_CSR,
                            4,
                            0);
                timecnt --;
                }
```

```
            return(timecnt); 14
}
```

1 Declares a variable to contain the current command for the test board. Section 10.12.2.4 shows that *cmd* was set to CB_DMA_WR or CB_DMA_RD.

2 Declares a pointer to the cb_unit data structure associated with this CB device and calls it cb. Section 10.6 shows the declaration of cb_unit.

3 Declares a variable to contain the timeout loop count.

4 Declares a variable to contain the CSR contents for status checking.

5 Sets the *cmd* variable to the logical or high 4 LED bits and the command to be performed by calling the read_io_port interface. The read_io_port interface is a generic interface that maps to a bus- and machine-specific interface that actually performs the read operation. Using this interface to read data from a device register makes the device driver more portable across different bus architectures, different CPU architectures, and different CPU types within the same CPU architecture.

Reads the CSR/LED register by calling the read_io_port interface. On the CB device, reading the test register clears the go bit. The test register is defined by the CB_TEST device register offset associated with this CB device.

The read_io_port interface takes three arguments:

– The first argument specifies an I/O handle that you can use to reference a device register or memory located in bus address space (either I/O space or memory space). This I/O handle references a device register in the bus address space where the read operation originates. You can perform standard C mathematical operations on the I/O handle. In this call, the /dev/cb driver ORs the I/O handle with the go bit represented by CB_TEST.

– The second argument specifies the width (in bytes) of the data to be read. Valid values are 1, 2, 3, 4, and 8. Not all CPU platforms or bus adapters support all of these values. In this call, the /dev/cb driver passes the value 4.

– The third argument specifies flags to indicate special processing requests. In this call, the /dev/cb driver passes the value zero (0).

Upon successful completion, read_io_port returns the data read from the go bit register to the *status* variable.

6 Reads the test register by calling the read_io_port interface. On the CB device, reading the test register clears the go bit. This call to read_io_port is the same as the previous call except that here the /dev/cb driver ORs the I/O handle with the go bit represented by the

`CB_TEST` device register offset.

|7| Writes the data to the specified location by calling the `write_io_port` interface. This location is the result of the ORing of the I/O handle with the 16-bit read/write CSR/LED register value. This register value is defined by the `CB_CSR` device register offset associated with this `CB` device. The `write_io_port` interface is a generic interface that maps to a bus- and machine-specific interface that actually performs the write operation. Using this interface to write data to a device register makes the device driver more portable across different bus architectures, different CPU architectures, and different CPU types within the same CPU architecture.

The `write_io_port` interface takes four arguments:

- The first argument specifies an I/O handle that you can use to reference a device register or memory located in bus address space (either I/O space or memory space). This I/O handle references a device register in the bus address space where the write operation occurs. You can perform standard C mathematical operations on the I/O handle. In this call, the `/dev/cb` driver ORs the I/O handle with the 16-bit read/write CSR/LED register represented by `CB_CSR`.

- The second argument specifies the width (in bytes) of the data to be written. Valid values are 1, 2, 3, 4, and 8. Not all CPU platforms or bus adapters support all of these values. In this call, the `/dev/cb` driver passes the value 4.

- The third argument specifies flags to indicate special processing requests. In this call, the `/dev/cb` driver passes the value zero (0).

- The fourth argument specifies the data to be written to the specified device register in bus address space. In this call, the `/dev/cb` driver passes the value stored in the *cmd* variable.

|8| Calls the `mb` kernel interface to ensure that a write to I/O space has completed.

|9| Writes the value zero (0) to the specified location by calling the `write_io_port` interface. This call is the same as the previous call except for the values passed to the first and fourth arguments. For the first argument, the location is the result of ORing the I/O handle with the go bit device register offset. This register value is defined by the `CB_TEST` device register offset associated with this `CB` device. For the fourth argument, the data to be written is the value zero (0). Writing zero (0) to this device register has the effect of setting the go bit.

|10| Calls `mb` again to ensure that a write to I/O space has completed.

|11| Initializes the timeout loop counter variable, *timecnt*, to the value 10.

12 Reads the status for this `CB` device from the specified location by calling the `read_io_port` interface. This call passes the same values as a previous call. For the first argument, the location of the read operation is the result of ORing the I/O handle with the 16-bit read/write CSR/LED register represented by `CB_CSR`.

13 Spins until the DMA has completed or the timeout loop counter expires. Then:

- Writes a value to the specified location by calling the `write_io_port` interface. This call is the same as previous calls. For the first argument, the location is the result of ORing the I/O handle with the 16-bit read/write CSR/LED device register offset. This register value is defined by the `CB_CSR` device register offset associated with this `CB` device. For the fourth argument, the data to be written is stored in the *cmd* variable.

- Calls `mb` a third time to ensure that a write to I/O space has completed.

- Reads the status for this `CB` device from the specified location by calling the `read_io_port` interface. This call passes the same values as a previous call. For the first argument, the location of the read operation is the result of ORing the I/O handle with the 16-bit read/write CSR/LED register represented by `CB_CSR`.

- Decrements the counter.

14 Returns the timeout count. If the command is successful, `cbstart` returns a nonzero value. If the loop exits because of a timeout, `cbstart` returns a zero (0) value.

10.14 The ioctl Section

Table 10-7 lists the tasks associated with implementing the ioctl Section, along with the sections in the book where each task is described.

Table 10-7: Tasks Associated with Implementing the ioctl Section

Part	Section
Setting Up the cbioctl Interface	Section 10.14.1
Incrementing the Lights	Section 10.14.2
Setting the I/O Mode	Section 10.14.3
Performing an Interrupt Test	Section 10.14.4
Returning a ROM Word, Updating the CSR, and Stopping Increment of the Lights	Section 10.14.5

10.14.1 Setting Up the cbioctl Interface

The Read and Write Device Section is applicable to the loadable or static version of the /dev/cb device driver. The following code sets up the cbioctl interface:

```
#define CBIncSec  1    1

cbioctl(dev, cmd, data, flag)
dev_t dev;               2
unsigned int cmd;        3
int *data;               4
int flag;                5
{
        int tmp;                      6
        int *addr;                    7
        int timecnt;                  8
        int unit = minor(dev);        9
        struct cb_unit *cb;           10
        int cbincled();               11

        cb = &cb_unit[unit];          12
```

1 Defines a constant called CBIncSec that indicates the number of seconds between increments of the TURBOchannel test board lights. Section 10.14.2 shows that this constant is passed to the timeout kernel interface.

2 Declares an argument that specifies the major and minor device numbers for a specific CB device. The minor device number is used to determine the logical unit number for the CB device on which the ioctl operation is to be performed.

3 Declares an argument that specifies the ioctl command in the file /usr/sys/include/sys/ioctl.h or in another include file that the device driver writer defines. There are two types of ioctl commands. One type is supported by all drivers of a given class. Another type is specific to a given device. The values of the *cmd* argument are defined by using the _IO, _IOR, _IOW, and _IOWR macros. Section 10.2 shows that the following ioctl commands are defined in the cbreg.h file: CBPIO, CBDMA, CBINT, CBROM, CBCSR, CBINC, and CBSTP.

4 Declares a pointer to ioctl command-specific data that is to be passed to the device driver or filled in by the device driver. This argument is a kernel address. The size of the data cannot exceed the size of a page (currently 8 kilobytes (KB) on Alpha systems). At least 128 bytes are guaranteed. Any size between 128 bytes and the page size may fail if memory cannot be allocated. The particular ioctl command implicitly determines the action to be taken. The ioctl system call performs all the necessary copy operations to move data to and from user space. Section 10.14.5 shows how cbioctl initializes the *data* argument.

5 Declares an argument that specifies the access mode of the device. The /dev/cb driver does not use this argument.

6 Declares a temporary holding variable called *tmp*.

7 Declares a pointer to a variable called *addr* that is used for word access to the TURBOchannel test board. Section 10.14.5 shows that this variable is used with the *data* argument.

8 Declares a variable called *timecnt*. Section 10.14.4 shows that this variable is used in the timeout loop count.

9 Declares a *unit* variable and initializes it to the device minor number. Note the use of the minor interface to obtain the device minor number.

The minor interface takes one argument: the number of the device for which an associated device minor number will be obtained. The minor number is encoded in the *dev* argument.

The *unit* variable is used to select the TURBOchannel test board to be accessed for the ioctl operation.

10 Declares a pointer to the cb_unit data structure associated with this CB device and calls it cb. Section 10.6 shows the declaration of cb_unit.

11 Declares a forward reference to the cbincled interface. Section 10.15 shows the implementation of cbincled.

12 Sets the pointer to the cb_unit structure to the address of the unit data structure associated with this CB device.

10.14.2 Incrementing the Lights

The following code starts incrementing the lights on the TURBOchannel test board:

```
switch(cmd&0xFF) {          1
        case CBINC&0xFF:                  2
                if(cb->ledflag == 0) {   3
                        cb->ledflag++;   4
                        timeout(cbincled, (caddr_t)cb, CBIncSec*hz);  5
                }
                break;
```

1 Uses the *cmd* argument to perform the appropriate ioctl operation.

2 When *cmd* evaluates to CBINC&0xFF, the ioctl operation starts incrementing the lights on the TURBOchannel test board.

3 If the increment function has not started, executes the next two lines. This line of code determines the start of the increment function by checking the ledflag member of the CB structure associated with this CB device.

4 Sets the flag for the LED increment function.

5 Starts the timer by calling the timeout kernel interface.

The timeout kernel interface takes three arguments:

– The first argument is a pointer to the interface to call, which in this case is cbincled.

– The second argument is a single argument to be passed to the interface specified by the first argument when it is called. In this example, the single argument is the pointer to the cb_unit data structure associated with this CB device. Because the second argument to timeout is of type caddr_t, the code performs the appropriate type-casting operation.

– The third argument is the amount of time to delay before calling the cbincled interface. The constant CBIncSec represents some amount of time in seconds.

The timeout interface initializes a callout queue element. Section 9.5.5 provides additional information on timeout.

10.14.3 Setting the I/O Mode

The following code sets the I/O mode for the `ioctl` operations to either programmed I/O or DMA I/O:

```
case CBPIO&0xFF: 1
        cb->iomode = CBPIO;
        break;
case CBDMA&0xFF: 2
        cb->iomode = CBDMA;
        break;
```

1 When *cmd* evaluates to `CBPIO&0xFF`, the `ioctl` operation sets the I/O mode to programmed I/O for this CB device.

2 When *cmd* evaluates to `CBDMA&0xFF`, the `ioctl` operation sets the I/O mode to DMA I/O for this CB device.

10.14.4 Performing an Interrupt Test

The following code tests the interrupt operation:

```
case CBINT&0xFF: 1
        timecnt = 10; 2
        cb->intrflag = 0; 3
        tmp = read_io_port(cb->cbr | CB_TEST,
                            4,
                            0); 4
        tmp = CB_INTERUPT|(read_io_port(cb->cbr | CB_CSR,
                            4,
                            0)&0xf000); 5
        write_io_port(cb->cbr | CB_CSR,
                            4,
                            0,
                            tmp); 6
        mb();                     7
        write_io_port(cb->cbr | CB_TEST,
                            4,
                            0,
                            1); 8
        mb();                     9
        while ((cb->intrflag == 0) && (timecnt > 0)) { 10
                write_io_port(cb->cbr | CB_CSR,
                            4,
                            0,
                            tmp);
                mb();
                timecnt --;
        }
        tmp = read_io_port(cb->cbr | CB_TEST,
                            4,
                            0); 11

        return(timecnt == 0);    12
```

1 When *cmd* evaluates to CBINT&0xFF, the ioctl operation performs an interrupt test.

2 Initializes the timeout loop count variable, *timecnt*, to the value 10.

3 Clears the interrupt flag by setting the intrflag member of the cb_unit structure associated with this CB device to the value zero (0). Section 10.14.1 shows the declaration of the pointer to the cb_unit data structure called cb.

4 Clears the go bit by calling the read_io_port interface. The read_io_port interface is a generic interface that maps to a bus- and machine-specific interface that actually performs the read operation. Using this interface to read data from a device register makes the device driver more portable across different bus architectures, different CPU architectures, and different CPU types within the same CPU architecture.

The read_io_port interface takes three arguments:

- The first argument specifies an I/O handle that you can use to reference a device register or memory located in bus address space (either I/O space or memory space). This I/O handle references a device register in the bus address space where the read operation originates. You can perform standard C mathematical operations on the I/O handle. In this call, the /dev/cb driver ORs the I/O handle with the go bit device register represented by CB_TEST.

- The second argument specifies the width (in bytes) of the data to be read. Valid values are 1, 2, 3, 4, and 8. Not all CPU platforms or bus adapters support all of these values. In this call, the /dev/cb driver passes the value 4.

- The third argument specifies flags to indicate special processing requests. In this call, the /dev/cb driver passes the value zero (0).

Upon successful completion, read_io_port returns the data read from the go bit device register to the *tmp* variable.

5 Performs a bitwise inclusive OR operation that assigns the 16-bit read/write CSR/LED register to the temporary holding variable. This operation uses two values. The first value is represented by the constant CB_INTERUPT. Section 10.2 shows that this constant is currently defined as 0x0e00. The second value is the result of the bitwise AND operation of the value returned by read_io_port and the value 0xf000. These 4 bits contain the current LED state.

The result of these operations produces the value, which is assigned to the *tmp* variable.

6 Calls the write_io_port interface to load enables and LEDs.

The write_io_port interface takes four arguments:

- The first argument specifies an I/O handle that you can use to reference a device register or memory located in bus address space (either I/O space or memory space). This I/O handle references a device register in the bus address space where the write operation occurs. You can perform standard C mathematical operations on the I/O handle. In this call, the /dev/cb driver ORs the I/O handle with the 16-bit read/write CSR/LED register represented by CB_CSR.

- The second argument specifies the width (in bytes) of the data to be written. Valid values are 1, 2, 3, 4, and 8. Not all CPU platforms or bus adapters support all of these values. In this call, the /dev/cb driver passes the value 4.

- The third argument specifies flags to indicate special processing requests. In this call, the /dev/cb driver passes the value zero (0).

- The fourth argument specifies the data to be written to the specified device register in bus address space. In this call, the /dev/cb driver passes the value stored in the *tmp* variable. This value is the bit calculated by the CB_INTERUPT macro and the current LED state.

7️⃣ Calls the mb kernel interface to ensure that a write to I/O space has completed.

8️⃣ Writes the value 1 to the specified location by calling the write_io_port interface. This call is the same as previous calls. For the first argument, the location is the result of ORing the I/O handle with the go bit device register offset. This register value is defined by the CB_TEST device register offset associated with this CB device. For the fourth argument, the data to be written is the value 1.

9️⃣ Calls mb again to ensure that a write to I/O space has completed.

🔟 The interrupt flag, cb->intrflag, is set to a nonzero value by cbintr if an interrupt is received. Section 10.16 discusses cbintr.

While the interrupt flag is equal to the value zero (0) and the timeout loop count variable is greater than zero (0), cbioctl executes the following statements:

– Updates the status of the 16-bit read/write CSR/LED register by calling the write_io_port interface.

– Calls mb again to ensure that a write to I/O space has completed.

– Decrements the timeout loop count variable.

This section of code executes until the interrupt flag is set and the timeout loop counter expires.

1️⃣1️⃣ Ensures that the go bit is cleared by calling the read_io_port interface.

1️⃣2️⃣ Returns to the ioctl system call. If the interrupt is started before the timeout loop count expires, cbioctl returns a zero (0) value to indicate success. If the timeout count expires, cbioctl returns a nonzero (1) value to indicate failure.

10.14.5 Returning a ROM Word, Updating the CSR, and Stopping Increment of the Lights

The following code returns a ROM word, updates the CSR, and then stops incrementing the lights on the TURBOchannel test board:

```
case CBROM&0xFF:              1
        tmp = *data;          2
        if(tmp < 0 || tmp >= 32768*4+4*4) 3
                return(-tmp);
        tmp <<= 1;
        addr = (int *)&(cb->cbad[tmp]); 4
        *data = *addr;        5
        break;
case CBCSR&0xFF: 6
        write_io_port(cb->cbr | CB_CSR,
                      4,
                      0,
                      read_io_port(cb->cbr | CB_CSR,
                                   4,
                                   0)); 7
        mb();                 8
        *data = read_io_port(cb->cbr | CB_CSR,
                             4,
                             0); 9
        break;
case CBSTP&0xFF: 10
        cb->ledflag = 0;
        break;
default: 11
        return(EINVAL);
    }
return(0); 12
}
```

1. When *cmd* evaluates to CBROM&0xFF, the ioctl operation returns a ROM word for this CB device by executing the statements from 2 to 5.

2. Gets the specified byte offset from the argument that is a kernel address.

3. If the byte offset is not in the valid range of 32k words + 4 registers, returns the byte offset to the ioctl system call to indicate that it is out of range.

4. Gets the ROM base address from the cbad member of the CB structure associated with this CB device.

   The cbad member provides the base address of the ROM. Because cbad is type cast as an int *, the *tmp* variable is used as an index to determine how many bytes to go into the ROM, and the resulting address is used to fetch the contents.

5⃞ Returns the word from the TURBOchannel test board.

6⃞ When *cmd* evaluates to CBCSR&0xFF, the ioctl operation updates and returns the CSR for this CB device by executing the statements from 7 to 9.

7⃞ Reads from and writes to this CB device's 16-bit read/write CSR/LED register by calling the read_io_port and write_io_port interfaces.

8⃞ Calls the mb kernel interface to ensure that a write to I/O space has completed.

9⃞ Returns the CSR from the TURBOchannel test board by calling the read_io_port interface.

10⃞ When *cmd* evaluates to CBSTP&0xFF, the ioctl operation stops incrementing the lights on the next timeout by clearing the LED increment function flag.

11⃞ Returns an error to indicate that the default is the error case.

12⃞ Upon successful completion, cbioctl returns the value zero (0) to the ioctl system call.

10.15 Increment LED Section

The `cbincled` interface is applicable to the loadable or static versions of the `/dev/cb` device driver. It is called by the `softclock` kernel interface `CBIncSec` seconds after the last timeout call. If the increment flag is still set, `cbincled` increments the pattern in the high four LEDs of the LED/CSR register and restarts the timeout to recall later.

The following code shows the implementation of the `cbincled` interface:

```
cbincled(cb)
struct cb_unit *cb;  1

{
                int tmp;

                tmp = read_io_port(cb->cbr | CB_CSR,
                                   4,
                                   0);
                                   tmp -= 0x1000;
                write_io_port(cb->cbr | CB_CSR,
                              4,
                              0,
                              tmp);  2
    if(cb->ledflag != 0) {    3
            timeout(cbincled, (caddr_t)cb, CBIncSec*hz);
            }
    return;
}
```

1 Declares a pointer to the `cb_unit` data structure associated with this CB device and calls it `cb`. Section 10.6 shows the declaration of `cb_unit`.

 This argument is specified in the callout to the `timeout` interface.

2 Calls the `read_io_port` and `write_io_port` interfaces to increment the lights. Because the LEDs are on when a bit is zero (0), a subtraction is done to accomplish the increment.

3 If the increment function flag is still set, restarts the timer by calling the `timeout` kernel interface and returns to `softclock`.

 The increment function flag is stored in the `ledflag` member of the `cb_unit` data structure associated with this CB device.

 The `timeout` kernel interface takes three arguments:

 – The first argument is a pointer to the interface to call, which in this case is `cbincled`.

 – The second argument is a single argument to be passed to the interface specified by the first argument when it is called. In this example, the single argument is the pointer to the `cb_unit` data structure associated with this CB device. Because the second argument to `timeout` is of type `caddr_t`, the code performs the appropriate type-casting operation.

– The third argument is the amount of time to delay before calling the cbincled interface. The constant CBIncSec represents some amount of time in seconds.

The timeout interface initializes a callout queue element. Section 9.5.5 provides additional information on timeout.

10.16 Interrupt Section

The `cbintr` interface is applicable to the loadable or static versions of the `/dev/cb` device driver. The interface's tasks are to clear the go bit and set a flag to indicate that an interrupt occurred.

The following code shows the implementation of the `cbintr` interface:

```
cbintr(ctlr)
int ctlr; 1
{
        int tmp; 2
        struct cb_unit *cb;      3
        cb = &cb_unit[ctlr];     4
        tmp = read_io_port(cb->cbr | CB_TEST,
                          4,
                          0); 5
        cb->intrflag++;          6

        return; 7
}
```

1. Declares a variable to contain the controller number, which is passed in by the operating system interrupt code.

2. Declares a temporary variable to hold the go bit.

3. Declares a pointer to the `cb_unit` data structure associated with this CB device and calls it `cb`. Section 10.6 shows the declaration of `cb_unit`.

4. Sets the pointer to the `cb_unit` structure to the address of the unit data structure associated with this CB device. The `ctlr` argument is used as an index into the array of `cb_unit` structures associated with this CB device.

5. Calls the `read_io_port` interface to read the test register to clear the go bit. The `read_io_port` interface is a generic interface that maps to a bus- and machine-specific interface that actually performs the read operation. Using this interface to read data from a device register makes the device driver more portable across different bus architectures, different CPU architectures, and different CPU types within the same CPU architecture.

   The `read_io_port` interface takes three arguments:

   – The first argument specifies an I/O handle that you can use to reference a device register or memory located in bus address space (either I/O space or memory space). This I/O handle references a device register in the bus address space where the read operation originates. You can perform standard C mathematical operations on the I/O handle. In this call, the `/dev/cb` driver ORs the I/O handle with the go bit device register represented by `CB_TEST`.

- The second argument specifies the width (in bytes) of the data to be read. Valid values are 1, 2, 3, 4, and 8. Not all CPU platforms or bus adapters support all of these values. In this call, the /dev/cb driver passes the value 4.

- The third argument specifies flags to indicate special processing requests. In this call, the /dev/cb driver passes the value zero (0).

Upon successful completion, read_io_port returns the data read from the go bit device register to the *tmp* variable.

⑥ Sets the interrupt flag to indicate that an interrupt occurred.

The flag value is contained in the intrflag member of the cb_unit data structure associated with this CB device.

⑦ Returns to the operating system interrupt code.

Part 6

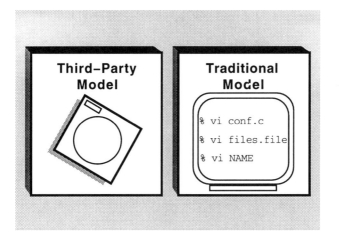

Device Driver Configuration Models 11

Device driver configuration is the process of incorporating device drivers into the kernel and making them available to system management and other utilities. Do not confuse device driver configuration with device autoconfiguration. The former is for incorporating device drivers into the kernel; the latter is what occurs when the kernel boots. Chapter 7 describes device autoconfiguration.

The Digital UNIX operating system provides two models for configuring device drivers:

- The third-party device driver configuration model

  This model is recommended for third-party device driver writers who want to ship loadable and static drivers to customers running the Digital UNIX operating system. Customers then use a variety of system management utilities that automatically configure the static and loadable drivers.

- The traditional device driver configuration model

  This model is suitable for driver writers (or system managers) who simply want to configure static and loadable drivers, without going through the kit-building process. For example, device driver writers developing a driver in a classroom setting may want to use this model. This model is also suitable for driver writers following the third-party model during the initial stages of driver development. Driver writers or system managers manually perform many of the tasks that otherwise are automated in the third-party device driver configuration model.

The following sections describe each of these models. This chapter uses a fictitious device driver development company called EasyDriver Incorporated to illustrate the approach third-party driver developers can take to configure their drivers.

Note

See also the README file in the /usr/examples/devdriver directory for instructions on how to configure and load the loadable versions of the /dev/none and /dev/cb device drivers.

The device driver examples are stored in an optional software subset that the system manager must select when installing the Digital UNIX operating system. If the `/usr/examples/devdriver` directory does not appear on your system, check with your system manager. The system manager can install this optional subset by using the `setld` utility.

11.1 Third-Party Device Driver Configuration Model

The third-party device driver configuration model provides tools that customers use to automate the installation of third-party device drivers. These customers can use the automated mechanism to:

- Install the device driver any time after the installation of the operating system
- Install the device driver without manual edits to system files
- Install static or loadable device drivers
- Integrate into the driver configuration site-specific tasks that are not currently handled by the `config` program

This model requires that third-party driver writers provide a device driver kit to their customers. Figure 11-1 shows the tasks and groups of people involved in the third-party device driver kit delivery process.

The figure shows that the third-party device driver kit delivery process involves at least three different audiences: the device driver writer, the kit developer, and the system manager (who, from the device driver writer's point of view, is the customer). In addition to showing the groups of people, Figure 11-1 also shows the tasks each group does to deliver the device driver:

- The device driver writer creates a driver development environment and writes and tests the driver.
- The device driver writer creates a driver kit development environment.
- The device driver writer provides the contents of the device driver kit.
- The kit developer prepares the device driver kit.
- The customer loads the device driver kit and runs `setld`.

Figure 11-1: Third-Party Device Driver Kit Delivery Process

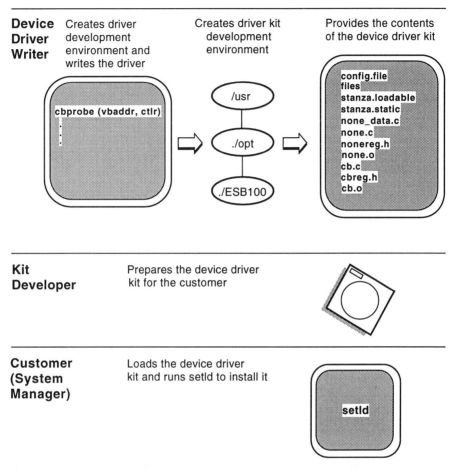

The following sections describe these tasks in more detail. Because these tasks encompass more than one group of people, the following discussions explicitly identify the group typically associated with the specific tasks.

11.1.1 Creating a Driver Development Environment and Writing the Driver

The first task of the driver writer is to write the device driver, using the design and development techniques described in the previous chapters of this book. During the initial stages of driver development, driver writers are probably not interested in going through the kit-building process. Therefore, during the initial driver development stages driver writers can follow the traditional device driver configuration model described in Section 11.2. This model presents a development environment that makes it possible for driver writers to design, write, test, rewrite, and configure the driver without going through the kit-building process.

The driver writers at EasyDriver Incorporated use the traditional model to perform their initial driver development. Their development directory structure is discussed in Section 11.2.

11.1.2   Creating a Driver Kit Development Environment

When all device driver testing (following the traditional model) is complete, the driver writer works with the kit developer to create a driver kit development environment. The driver writers for EasyDriver Incorporated work with their kit developers to create the kit development environment shown in Figure 11-2.

A directory structure, such as the one shown in Figure 11-2, helps the kit developer to prepare the kit and the driver writer to test the driver under conditions similar to those experienced by customers. Figure 11-2 contrasts the directories and files related to the system with the directories and files related to the driver kit development environment.

Figure 11-2: Driver Kit Development Environment for EasyDriver Incorporated

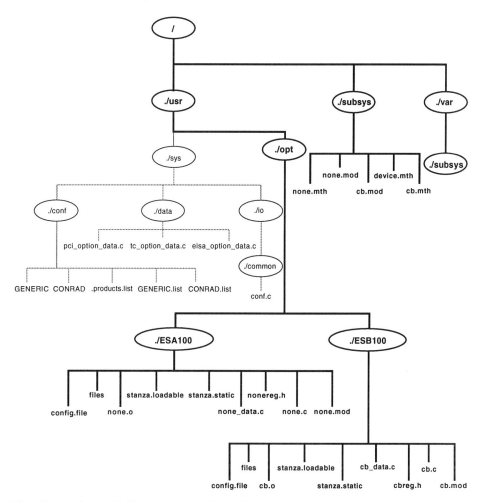

The directories and files related to EasyDriver Incorporated's system are as follows:

- The /usr/sys/conf directory

  This directory contains files that define the kernel configuration for the generic (all-encompassing) and target machine kernels. In the /usr/sys/conf directory for EasyDriver Incorporated, the generic kernel is called GENERIC and the target machine kernel is called CONRAD. This directory also contains the .products.list file and, optionally, a GENERIC.list or CONRAD.list file.

- A /usr/sys/data directory

  This directory contains the *name*_data.c files supplied by Digital. Examples of such files are eisa_option_data.c, pci_option_data.c, and tc_option_data.c.

- A /usr/sys/io/common directory

  This directory contains the conf.c template file, which contains the bdevsw and cdevsw tables.

The directories and files related to EasyDriver Incorporated's driver kit development environment (identified in darker type in the figure) are as follows:

- A /usr/opt directory

  This directory contains subdirectories that represent each of the driver products that EasyDriver Incorporated developed. Figure 11-2 shows two such directories: ESA100 and ESB100.

  Driver writers can follow the naming conventions described in the *Programming Support Tools* book. The driver writers at EasyDriver Incorporated adhere to these conventions by specifying directory names based on 3-character product and version codes. Thus, the driver writers at EasyDriver Incorporated use the product codes ESA and ESB to represent the directories that contain the files associated with the /dev/none and /dev/cb drivers. The version code 100 indicates that this is Version 1.0 of the driver products.

- A /usr/opt/ESA100 directory

  This directory contains the configuration-related file fragments, driver load modules (for loadable drivers), driver object files (for static drivers), and, optionally, driver source code for the /dev/none device driver that EasyDriver Incorporated ships to its customers.

- A /usr/opt/ESB100 directory

  This directory contains the configuration-related file fragments, driver load modules (for loadable drivers), driver object files (for static drivers), and, optionally, driver source code for the /dev/cb device driver that EasyDriver Incorporated ships to its customers.

- A /subsys directory

  This directory contains the loadable modules linked to the files with .mth extensions.

- A /var/subsys directory

  This is a loadable subsystem directory that contains files with .mod and .mth extensions. You can use this directory or the /subsys directory to contain the files with .mod and .mth extensions.

The following sections describe these files.

11.1.2.1 The /usr/sys/conf/NAME File

The /usr/sys/conf/NAME file (referred to as the system configuration file) is an ASCII text file that defines the components of the system. The system configuration file name, NAME, is usually the name of the system. By convention, the system configuration file name is capitalized. There can be more than one system configuration file defined in /usr/sys/conf, each with a capitalized name. As Figure 11-2 shows, EasyDriver Incorporated has two system configuration files: GENERIC and CONRAD. Customers, too, can have more than one system configuration file to represent different configurations.

The GENERIC system configuration file supplied by Digital contains all the possible software and hardware options available to Digital UNIX systems and includes all supported Digital devices. The GENERIC system configuration file is used to build a kernel that represents all possible combinations of statically configured drivers that Digital supports. This kernel is booted during the operating system installation and is often referred to as the generic kernel. While running the generic kernel, the installation software determines which subset of all possible device drivers should be used to build a target kernel to match the hardware attached to the system being installed.

The installation software builds a tailored system configuration file to match the hardware present by calling the sizer program. This tailored system configuration file is later used by doconfig to create a tailored kernel.

Device driver writers following the third-party model do not supply complete system configuration files to their customers. Rather, they supply entries in the config.file file fragment, which is located in the vendor-specific directory and is a logical extension to the system configuration file found in /usr/sys/conf. For the /dev/cb driver product, the vendor-specific directory is /usr/optESB100. Section 12.2 describes the syntaxes driver writers use to specify the necessary information in the config.file file fragment.

11.1.2.2 The .products.list and NAME.list Files

The /usr/sys/conf/.products.list file (for static drivers) stores information about static device driver products. The NAME.list file is a copy of the .products.list file that is created when the system manager installs the device driver kit supplied by a third-party vendor. Device driver writers and kit developers do not supply either of these files; however, an understanding of these files can help during third-party kit development and testing.

Figure 11-3 shows the relationship between these two files during kit installation:

1. The system manager loads the device driver kit and runs the `setld` utility.

2. The `setld` utility reads the device driver kit and calls the subset control program (SCP) provided by the kit developer. The SCP contains path specifications for all of the files related to the driver product. For example, Figure 11-3 shows the path and one file associated with the `/dev/cb` driver product.

3. The SCP calls the `/sbin/kreg` utility, which registers the product on the customer's system. This action makes the device driver product available to system management-related programs such as `doconfig` and `config`.

Figure 11-3: Comparison of .products.list File and NAME.list

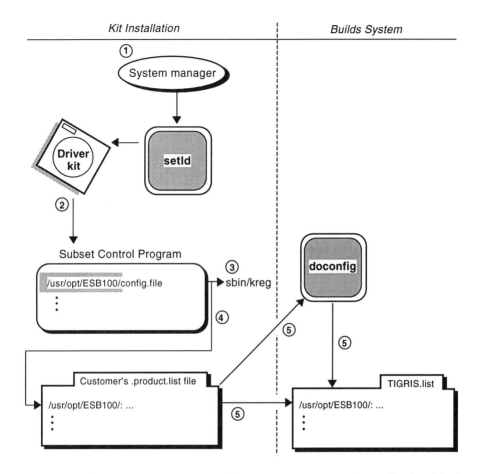

4. As the figure shows, the SCP calls /sbin/kreg and supplies it with the driver path to where the files related to the /dev/cb driver product are located. The /sbin/kreg utility registers the path along with other supporting information in the customer's .products.list file. The three dots in the figure indicate that the supporting information is contained in other fields in the entry. The key piece of information for the driver writer and the kit developer is the location of the files associated with the driver product.

5. The doconfig program, run by the system manager, reads the .products.list file and copies it to a file of the form *NAME*.list. (This occurs only if the system manager does not specify the -c option. If the system manager specifies the -c option, the doconfig program

builds a kernel based on the contents of the file specified by the system manager. In this case, doconfig does not perform the copy operation.) The *NAME* variable usually specifies the name of the system configuration file. For example, TIGRIS.list would be the name for the file that contains information about static device drivers for the customer system described by the system configuration file called TIGRIS.

The fields contained in the /usr/sys/conf/.products.list file are described in Section 12.4.

Customers can edit the *NAME*.list file to exclude a driver entry, thus removing the entry's associated functionality from the rebuilt kernel. Otherwise, customers always get the driver products as they are specified in the /usr/sys/conf/.products.list file. Customers should never edit the /usr/sys/conf/.products.list file directly. Instead, customers make required changes by using the kreg utility or by editing the *NAME*.list file.

11.1.2.3   The config.file File Fragment

You can view the config.file file fragment (for static drivers) as a ''mini'' system configuration file, as shown in Figure 11-4. The figure shows the relationship between a config.file file fragment from EasyDriver Incorporated and a customer system configuration file called TIGRIS. The config.file file fragment from EasyDriver Incorporated contains device definition keywords and callout keyword definitions for the static driver products. The customer's system configuration file contains not only these categories of keywords, but also additional ones. Although config.file can also contain these other keywords, the driver writers at EasyDriver Incorporated specify only keywords related to their device driver product and needed by their customers.

Furthermore, Figure 11-4 shows that the config program run by the customer reads the information contained in both files and makes the options specified in them available to the system. The figure shows that config does not append the information in config.file to the system configuration file, but rather creates a virtual system configuration file of the entries contained in both files. The config program does not alter the supplied third-party config.file file fragment or the customer's system configuration file.

Figure 11-4: Comparison of config.file File Fragment and System Configuration File

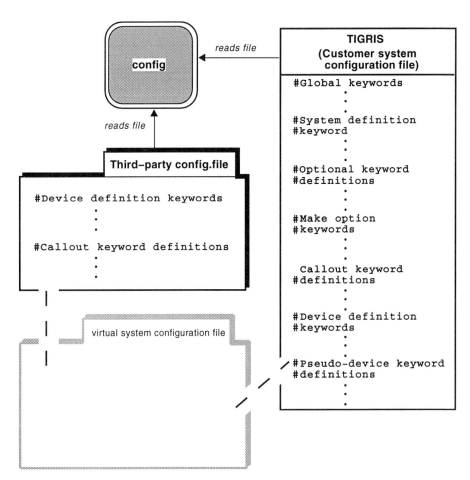

However, driver writers must be particularly careful about choosing appropriate naming conventions for such items as the device connectivity information to avoid name conflicts with other third-party driver vendors. One suggestion is to use extensions to names that minimize the chances for conflict. These extensions could include any combination of the company initials, product name, version number, and release number. For example, the driver writers at EasyDriver Incorporated might specify edcb for an internally developed device. The prefix ed represents the company name and cb is the name of the device.

Section 12.2 discusses the syntaxes that driver writers use to populate the `config.file` file fragment with device- and callout-related information.

11.1.2.4 The files File

You can view the `files` file fragment (for static drivers) as a "mini" `files` file, as shown in Figure 11-5. The figure shows the relationship between a `files` file fragment from EasyDriver Incorporated and a customer's `files` file. The `files` file fragment (for static drivers) from EasyDriver Incorporated contains the following information about the static driver products:

- The location of the source code associated with the product drivers

- Tags indicating when the product drivers are to be loaded into the kernel

- Whether the source code or the binary form of the product drivers is supplied to the customer

The customer's `files` file contains similar entries for other device drivers. To have the `config` program automatically generate the appropriate rules to build the drivers, the driver writer must specify the appropriate information in the `files` file fragment.

Figure 11-5 shows that the `config` program run by the customer reads both `files` files and makes the information specified in them available to the system. The figure also shows that `config` does not append the information in the supplied `files` file fragment to the customer's `files` file, but rather creates a virtual `files` file of the entries contained in both files. It does not alter the supplied third-party `files` file fragment or the customer's `files` file.

This automated mechanism relieves the customer from having to make tedious and potentially error-prone changes to the `files` file. Driver writers must be particularly careful about choosing unique path and file names in this file.

Section 12.5 describes the syntaxes used to specify the previously described information.

Figure 11-5: Comparison of files File Fragment and Customer's files File

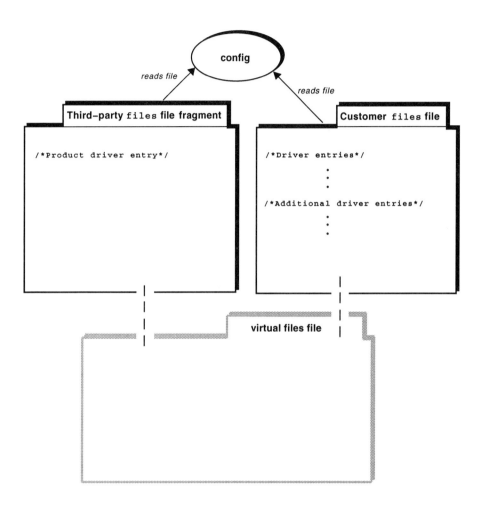

11.1.2.5 The stanza.loadable File Fragment

You can view the stanza.loadable file fragment (for loadable drivers)
as a ''mini'' sysconfigtab database, as shown in Figure 11-6. The
figure shows the relationship between a stanza.loadable file fragment
from EasyDriver Incorporated and a customer /etc/sysconfigtab
database. The stanza.loadable file fragment from EasyDriver
Incorporated contains such items as device connectivity information, the
driver's major number requirements, the names and minor numbers of the
device special files, and the permissions and directory name where the device

special files reside. The customer's /etc/sysconfigtab database contains not only these categories of information, but also additional ones that can represent other loadable drivers. The driver writers at EasyDriver Incorporated specify only options related to their device driver product and needed by their customers.

Furthermore, Figure 11-6 shows that the sysconfigdb utility appends the information contained in the stanza.loadable file fragment to the customer's /etc/sysconfigtab database.

Figure 11-6: Comparison of stanza.loadable File Fragment and sysconfigtab Database

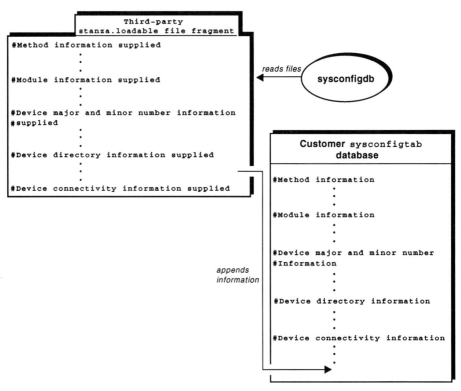

This automated mechanism relieves the customer from having to make tedious and potentially error-prone changes to the /etc/sysconfigtab database. However, driver writers must be particularly careful about choosing appropriate naming conventions for such items as the device connectivity information to avoid name conflicts with other third-party driver vendors. One suggestion is to use extensions to names that minimize the chances for conflict. These extensions could include any combination of the company initials, product name, version number, and release number. For example, the driver writers at EasyDriver Incorporated might specify `edcb` for an internally developed device. The prefix `ed` represents the company name and `cb` is the name of the device.

Section 12.6 discusses the syntaxes that driver writers use to populate the `stanza.loadable` file fragment.

11.1.2.6 The stanza.static File Fragment

The `stanza.static` file fragment (for static drivers) contains such items as the driver's major number requirements, the names and minor numbers of the device special files, the permissions and directory name where the device special files reside, and the driver interface names to be added to the `bdevsw` and `cdevsw` tables.

The `kmknod` utility uses the information in this file fragment to dynamically create device special files for static device drivers.

Section 12.6 discusses the syntaxes that driver writers use to populate the `stanza.static` file fragment.

11.1.2.7 The name_data.c File

The `name_data.c` file (for static drivers) provides a convenient place to size the data structures and data structure arrays that static device drivers use. In addition, this file can contain definitions that customers can change. The `name` argument is usually based on the device name. For example, the none device's `name_data.c` file is called `none_data.c`. The CB device's `name_data.c` file is called `cb_data.c`. The edgd device's `name_data.c` file is called `edgd_data.c`. See Section 3.1.5 for more information on this file and how it relates to loadable drivers.

11.1.2.8 Files Related to the Device Driver Product

The driver writer supplies files related to the device driver product. For the static device driver product, these can include the driver header files, which have `.h` extensions; source files, which have `.c` extensions; and the driver object files, which have `.o` extensions.

The device driver object files are the actual executables associated with the static device driver. To supply the device driver objects and the device driver source code, driver writers specify the valid syntaxes in a `files` file fragment. Section 12.5 discusses these syntaxes.

For the loadable device driver product the driver writer supplies the driver load modules, which have `.mod` extensions.

11.1.2.9 The conf.c File

The `/usr/sys/io/common/conf.c` file contains the `bdevsw` and `cdevsw` tables. The method for adding device driver interfaces to these tables differs according to whether the driver is static or loadable:

- For static drivers

  The driver writer provides the driver interfaces in the `stanza.static` file fragment. The `config` program reads the `stanza.static` file fragment to obtain these interface names and then automatically adds them to these tables for the driver product. Section 12.8 describes how to provide this information for static drivers.

- For loadable drivers

  Loadable drivers use the `devsw` interfaces to add the interfaces to the `bdevsw` and `cdevsw` tables. Section 9.7 describes how to use these interfaces.

- For drivers implemented as static and loadable

  If the driver is implemented as both a loadable and a static driver, the driver writer implements the `devsw` interfaces and specifies the driver interface names in the `stanza.static` file fragment. During the installation of the product drivers, an appropriate prompt would request that the customer specify whether the driver is to be installed as a loadable or static driver. The device driver kit can provide a software subset for the static device driver product and a software subset for the loadable driver product. The customer can then choose to install either the static or the loadable driver product.

11.1.3 Providing the Contents of the Device Driver Kit

The driver writer provides specific items that the kit developer uses as the contents of the device driver kit. These items consist of the files and file fragments discussed in the previous sections. These files and file fragments contain information necessary for system managers (customers) to configure the loadable or static drivers into their systems. Table 11-1 summarizes the files and file fragments the kit developer needs to supply on the device driver kit. The table has the following columns:

- File

  Contains the name of the file or file fragment.

- Static drivers (source)

  A ''Yes'' appears in this column if the file or file fragment should be supplied with static drivers supplied as source. Otherwise, a ''No'' appears.

- Static drivers (binary)

  A "Yes" appears in this column if the file or file fragment should be supplied with static drivers supplied as binary. Otherwise, a "No" appears.

- Loadable drivers (binary)

  A "Yes" appears in this column if the file or file fragment should be supplied with loadable drivers supplied as binary. Otherwise, a "No" appears.

Note

The third-party device driver configuration model does not currently support shipping loadable drivers as source and building them at the customer site. Therefore, the table omits a column for loadable drivers (source).

Table 11-1: Contents of Device Driver Kit

File	Static Drivers (Source)	Static Drivers (Binary)	Loadable Drivers (Binary)
`config.file` file fragment	Yes	Yes	No
`files` file fragment	Yes	Yes	No
`stanza.loadable` file fragment	No	No	Yes
`stanza.static` file fragment	Yes	Yes	No
*name*_data.c	Yes	Yes	No
driver headers	Yes	No*	No
driver sources	Yes	No	No
driver objects	No	Yes	No
driver load modules	No	No	Yes
Subset Control Program (SCP)	Yes	Yes	Yes

* But Yes if needed by data.c

11.1.4 Preparing the Device Driver Kit

The kit developer prepares the distribution medium, which in Figure 11-1 is a CD–ROM. See the *Programming Support Tools* book for a discussion of the media supported by Digital's setld architecture.

In this book, the distribution medium is referred to as the device driver kit. It consists of a hierarchical group of the files and directories provided by the device driver writer. It is the responsibility of the driver writer to work with the kit developer to determine how the files and directories are grouped within the hierarchy. The driver writers for EasyDriver Incorporated worked with their kit developers to create the directory structure shown in Figure 11-2.

The kit developer performs the appropriate tasks for preparing the device driver kit to be used with the setld utility. One of these tasks is to write a subset control program (SCP) that installs and manages software subsets. In addition, this SCP calls /sbin/kreg (for static drivers), which is the utility that registers a subset as a kernel build module and fills the /usr/sys/conf/.products.list file. For loadable drivers, the SCP calls the sysconfigdb utility, which maintains and manages the /etc/sysconfigtab database.

The kit developer should refer to the *Programming Support Tools* book, which contains information about preparing software distribution kits that are compatible with the setld utility. The setld utility installs and manages Digital UNIX software kits and layered product kits.

Section 12.9 provides an example SCP written by EasyDriver Incorporated.

11.1.5 Loading the Distribution Medium and Running setld

To install the device driver kit at the customer site, the system manager (customer) loads the device driver kit and runs setld. This utility transfers the contents of the kit to the customer's file system at a known location, as determined by the device driver kit. The setld utility then calls the SCP supplied by the third-party vendor.

If the driver can be both statically configured and dynamically loaded, the SCP must prompt the system manager to choose. If the system manager chooses static, the SCP calls the kreg utility. The kreg utility creates a /usr/sys/conf/.products.list file or updates an existing one. If the system manager chooses loadable, the SCP calls the sysconfigdb utility. The sysconfigdb utility maintains and manages the /etc/sysconfigtab database.

Both the kreg and sysconfigdb utilities examine the files that were transferred from the device driver kit to determine if the system has the subset loaded or if it has previously been registered.

Table 11-2 summarizes the system management tools that customers use to automatically configure device drivers. Third-party driver writers may want to understand the events that occur when the system manager configures the driver as a static or loadable driver. The sections following the table are designed to promote an understanding of these events.

Table 11-2: Summary of System Management Tools

Tool	Description
doconfig	Creates a new or modifies an existing system configuration file, copies .products.list to *NAME*.list, creates the device special files for static drivers, and builds a new Digital UNIX kernel. (The doconfig program calls config, which actually performs many of the tasks mentioned.)
cfgmgr	Works with kloadsrv, the kernel load server, to manage loadable device drivers.
kmknod	Uses the information from the stanza.static file fragment to dynamically create device special files for static device drivers at boot time.
kreg	Maintains the /sys/conf/.product.list system file, which registers static device driver products.
sysconfig	Modifies the loadable subsystem configuration. The sysconfig utility provides a user interface to the cfgmgr daemon.
sysconfigdb	Maintains the sysconfigtab database. The driver stanza entries in the stanza.loadable file fragment are appended to this database.

11.1.5.1 Installing Static Device Drivers

Figure 11-7 shows the events that occur when the system manager installs a static device driver. The events start after the system manager loads the device driver kit and runs setld.

1. The system manager runs the doconfig program (which calls config) to generate a system configuration file (shown as *NAME* in the figure) and to generate a kernel that contains the statically linked drivers.

2. The config program reads the /usr/sys/conf/.products.list file and copies it to the *NAME*.list file. It uses the entries in *NAME*.list to locate and use the supplied entries contained in the config.file and files file fragments and any source and/or object files.

3. The config program reads the stanza.static file fragment to determine the driver's major and minor number requirements; it reads the system configuration file, *NAME*, to determine the device options and other system parameters. It also saves the device special file characteristics.

4. After determining the major number requirements, config automatically edits the /usr/sys/io/common/conf.c file to place the driver's entry points in the bdevsw and/or cdevsw tables. The assigned major number is saved in a kernel-resident table for later use.

5. The config program completes the kernel makefile to include the new static device driver.

   After doconfig builds the kernel and the system manager boots the system, the third-party static device driver is configured into the kernel. There is an entry in the inittab file that is referenced at boot time to cause the kmknod utility to run. This utility creates the device special files for this driver so that the customer's utilities can access this third-party device driver.

6. The kmknod utility references the kernel-resident table of assigned major numbers to determine what major number has been assigned to this driver. It also gets the device characteristics from this table. All of the other information needed to do the mknods for the device special file is specified in the stanza.static file fragment.

   At this point, the driver is fully configured, the device special files have been created, and the kernel is running.

Figure 11-7: Sequence of Events for Installation of Static Drivers

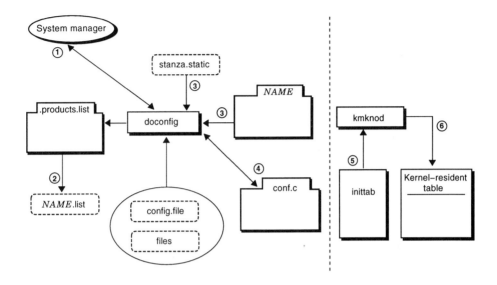

11.1.5.2 Installing Loadable Device Drivers

Figure 11-8 shows the events that occur when the system manager installs a loadable device driver. The events start after the system manager loads the device driver kit. The SCP requests that the system manager specify the driver be installed as loadable. The following events occur:

1. The SCP calls the `sysconfigdb` utility.

   The SCP calls `sysconfigdb`, which adds the entries contained in the `stanza.loadable` file fragment to the `/etc/sysconfigtab` database.

   The `sysconfigdb` utility can be called to add the driver to the list of drivers that are automatically configured each time the system boots. At this point, the loadable driver has been installed on the system.

2. The SCP calls the `sysconfig` utility.

   Although the loadable driver has been installed on the system, it is not currently loaded into the kernel and is therefore not usable by user-level programs. To load the installed loadable driver, the system manager (or the SCP) runs the `sysconfig` utility.

3. The `sysconfig` utility calls the `cfgmgr` daemon.

   The `sysconfig` utility passes the name of the driver to load to the `cfgmgr` daemon through a socket connection. The `cfgmgr` daemon searches the global stanza database, /etc/sysconfigtab, to fetch the stanza entry for the driver. One of the fields of the stanza entry identifies the loadable module as a device driver. This information causes the cfgmgr daemon to use the device driver-specific portion (referred to as the driver method) to perform the specific loading tasks (such as creating the necessary device special files).

4. The cfgmgr daemon calls kloadsrv.

   Another field in the stanza entry lists the pathname of the loadable object (the driver itself). The cfgmgr daemon calls the kernel loader utility kloadsrv to load the driver's object into the kernel's address space.

5. The kloadsrv utility calls the driver's configure interface.

   After loading the driver's object, kloadsrv calls the device driver's configure interface. The driver's configure interface causes the driver to be linked into the autoconfiguration-related data structures: bus, controller, and device. The driver's interrupt interface is registered. The configure interface also calls a bdevsw_add or cdevsw_add interface to provide a major number for this driver. The assignment of a major number includes adding the driver's entry points into the in-memory bdevsw and/or cdevsw tables.

6. The driver's configure interface returns a data structure.

   The driver's configure interface returns a data structure that contains, among other things, the major number or numbers assigned to the driver. This return information is passed back to the cfgmgr daemon.

Figure 11-8: Sequence of Events for Installation of Loadable Drivers

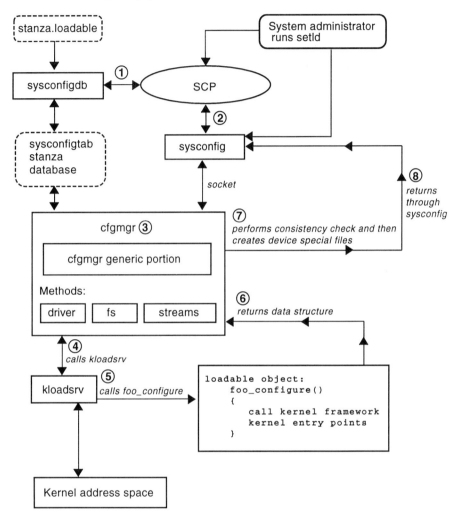

7. The cfgmgr daemon performs a consistency check and then creates device special files.

Once the driver has been loaded into the kernel's address space and prior to creating the device special files for this driver, a consistency check is performed to delete any device special files of the same name or the same driver type and major number.

The cfgmgr daemon then creates the device special files associated with the device by taking the major number returned from the driver's `configure` interface and the information contained in the driver's stanza entry to do the appropriate `mknod` calls.

8. The `cfgmgr` daemon returns through `sysconfig`.

   The `cfgmgr` daemon returns through `sysconfig` and the driver loading is complete. User-level utilities can now access the driver.

11.2 Traditional Device Driver Configuration Model

The traditional device driver configuration model provides a manual mechanism for driver writers or system managers to configure device drivers into the kernel. One advantage of the traditional model is that no device driver kit is needed. Thus, the driver writer can configure the driver almost immediately. The traditional model is particularly suited to a classroom situation, where the goal of the class is to learn how to write device drivers. It is also suited to driver writers following the third-party model during the initial stages of driver development.

The end result of the traditional and third-party models is the same. The disadvantage of the traditional model is that it does not use the automated driver installation interfaces. Thus, the traditional model is potentially error prone.

This model requires that driver writers perform the tasks shown in Figure 11-9. The figure shows that the traditional driver configuration model involves only the device driver writer. The third-party driver configuration model is different in that it involves at least three groups of people. Figure 11-9 also shows the following tasks performed by the driver writer:

- Creating a driver development environment and writing the driver
- Configuring the device driver

The sections following Figure 11-9 describe these tasks in detail.

Figure 11-9: Tasks for Traditional Model

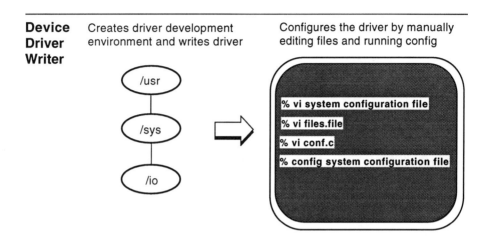

Device Creates driver development   Configures the driver by manually
Driver   environment and writes driver   editing files and running config
Writer

11.2.1   Creating a Driver Development Environment and Writing the Driver

The device driver writer creates a driver development environment and writes the device driver by using the information and techniques described in the previous chapters of this book. Figure 11-10 shows the development environment for EasyDriver Incorporated, using the traditional driver configuration model.

Figure 11-10: Driver Development Environment for EasyDriver Incorporated Using the Traditional Model

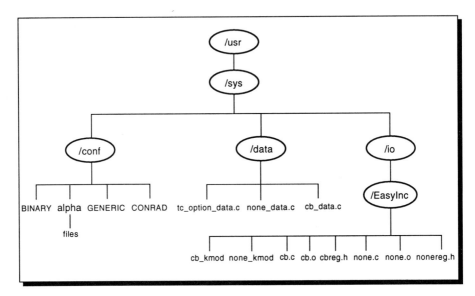

The figure shows the following directory structure:

- The `/usr/sys/conf` directory

  This directory contains files that define the kernel configuration for the generic (all-encompassing) and target machine kernels. In the `/usr/sys/conf` directory for EasyDriver Incorporated, the generic kernel is called `GENERIC` and the target machine kernel is called `CONRAD`. The `/usr/sys/conf/BINARY` system configuration file is shown here because the traditional model requires that entries be added to accommodate loadable device drivers.

- A `/usr/sys/conf/alpha` directory

  This directory contains the `files` file.

- A `/usr/sys/data` directory

  This directory contains the `name_data.c` files supplied by Digital. Examples of such files are `eisa_option_data.c`, `pci_option_data.c`, and `tc_option_data.c`. The figure also shows that EasyDriver Incorporated uses this directory to contain the `name_data.c` files associated with their device drivers.

- A /usr/sys/io/EasyInc directory

  This directory contains the source code, object, header, and load module files for the drivers developed by EasyDriver Incorporated.

The following sections describe each of these files from the traditional model point of view. Previous sections related to the third-party driver configuration model discuss some of these files from the third-party model point of view.

11.2.1.1 The /usr/sys/conf/NAME File

The /usr/sys/conf/NAME file (referred to as the system configuration file) is an ASCII text file that defines the components of the system. The system configuration file name, NAME, is usually the name of the system. By convention, the system configuration file name is capitalized. A device driver writer can have more than one system configuration file defined in /usr/sys/conf, each with a capitalized name. As Figure 11-10 shows, EasyDriver Incorporated has two system configuration files: GENERIC and CONRAD. In addition, there is a system configuration file called /usr/sys/conf/BINARY.

The GENERIC system configuration file supplied by Digital contains all the possible software and hardware options available to Digital UNIX systems and includes all supported Digital devices. The GENERIC system configuration file is used to build a kernel that represents all possible combinations of statically configured drivers that Digital supports. This kernel is booted during the operating system installation and is often referred to as the generic kernel. While running the generic kernel, the installation software determines which subset of all possible device drivers should be used to build a target kernel to match the hardware attached to the system being installed.

The installation software builds a tailored system configuration file to match the hardware present by calling the sizer program. This tailored system configuration file is later used by doconfig to create a tailored kernel.

The BINARY system configuration file supplied by Digital contains a subset of all the possible software and hardware options available to Digital UNIX systems.

In the traditional model, device driver writers manually edit the system configuration file to specify device connectivity information associated with the static device driver. For loadable drivers, device driver writers manually edit the BINARY system configuration file to cause an independent load module (for example, the cb.mod module) to be created. This step contrasts with static device drivers where the driver itself is incorporated into the tailored kernel. Thus, driver writers modify the BINARY system configuration file for loadable drivers and the system configuration file for static drivers. Section 12.2 describes the syntaxes driver writers use to specify the necessary information in the system configuration file.

11.2.1.2 The files File

The device driver writer manually edits the `files` file, which contains the following information:

- Driver source code location
- Conditions under which the driver is to be statically configured
- Whether the device driver sources are supplied

Section 12.5 describes the syntaxes used to specify this information. Note that in the traditional device driver configuration model, the device driver writer specifies information in the `files` file for both loadable and static device drivers. This information is necessary to construct the driver object file for static drivers and the kernel load module for loadable drivers.

The `files` file can reside in one of several directories, based on the architecture. For example:

```
conf/alpha/files
conf/mips/files
```

There may also be one `files` file for each kernel built. In this case, the `files` file takes the name of the system configuration file. For example:

```
conf/files.TIGRIS
conf/files.EUPHRATES
```

The driver writers at EasyDriver Incorporated chose to locate their files in the `/usr/sys/conf/alpha` directory.

11.2.1.3 The name_data.c File

The `name_data.c` file provides a convenient place to size the data structures and data structure arrays that static device drivers use. The `name` argument is usually based on the device name. For example, the `none` device's `name_data.c` file is called `none_data.c`. The CB device's `name_data.c` file is called `cb_data.c`. The `edgd` device's `name_data.c` file is called `edgd_data.c`. See Section 3.1.5 for more information on this file and how it relates to static drivers.

11.2.1.4 Driver Header, Source, Object, and Load Module Files

The driver writer creates a directory to contain the files related to the device driver. For the static device driver product, these can include the driver header files, which have `.h` extensions; source files, which have `.c` extensions; and the driver object files, which have `.o` extensions. The device driver object files are the actual driver executables. Figure 11-10 shows that driver writers for EasyDriver Incorporated place these files in the `/usr/sys/io/EasyInc` directory.

For the loadable device driver product, there are driver load modules, which have `.mod` extensions.

Device Driver Configuration Syntaxes and Mechanisms   **12**

The previous chapter described the third-party and traditional device driver configuration models, which included brief descriptions of the file fragments the driver writer needs to supply on the device driver kit for the third-party model and the files the driver writer manually edits for the traditional model. This chapter reviews these files and describes the syntaxes and mechanisms used to populate them.

Specifically, the chapter discusses how to:

- Review device driver configuration-related files

- Specify information in the `config.file` file fragment and system configuration file

- Specify information in the `BINARY` system configuration file

- Understand the format of the *NAME*.`list` file

- Specify information in the `files` file fragment and `files` file

- Specify information in the `stanza` files

- Specify information in the *name_data.c* file

- Specify information in the `conf.c` file

- Supply the subset control program (SCP)

12.1 Reviewing Device Driver Configuration-Related Files

Table 12-1 reviews the files and file fragments related to device driver configuration and provides a summary of how the driver writer populates these files with the necessary information. Subsequent sections in the chapter describe the actual syntaxes and mechanisms used to populate these files and file fragments. The table also indicates whether the file is applicable to the third-party or traditional model.

Table 12-1: Contents of Device Driver Configuration-Related Files

File	Information/Mechanisms	Third-Party Model	Traditional Model
system configuration file	For static drivers, you specify a valid syntax for the device connectivity information contained in this file. This file is not applicable to loadable drivers.	No	Yes
config.file file fragment	For static drivers, you specify a valid syntax for the device connectivity and callout information contained in this file. This file is not applicable to loadable drivers.	Yes	No
BINARY system configuration file	For loadable drivers, you specify a valid syntax to ensure that loadable drivers build successfully. This file is not applicable to static drivers.	No	Yes
NAME.list file	For static drivers, this file contains such information as where the files for the driver product are located. This file is not supplied on the device driver kit. This file is not applicable to loadable drivers.	Yes	No
files file	For static drivers, you specify a valid syntax for when the driver is to be loaded into the kernel, the location of the driver source code, and whether the driver sources are supplied. For loadable drivers using the traditional model, you specify a valid syntax for when the driver source is to be compiled into a dynamic load module and the location of the driver source code. This file is not applicable to loadable drivers shipped in binary form.	No	Yes
files file fragment	For static drivers shipped in source form, you specify a valid syntax for when the driver is to be loaded into the kernel, the location of the driver source code, and whether the driver sources are supplied. This file is not applicable to loadable drivers shipped in binary form.	Yes	No

Table 12-1:   (continued)

File	Information/Mechanisms	Third-Party Model	Traditional Model
`stanza.loadable` file fragment	For loadable drivers, you specify a valid syntax for device connectivity information, the driver's major number requirements, the names and minor numbers of the device special files, and the permissions and directory name where the device special files are created. This file fragment is not applicable to static drivers.	Yes	Yes
`stanza.static` file fragment	For static drivers, you specify a valid syntax for the driver's major number requirements, the names and minor numbers of the device special files, the permissions and directory name where the device special files reside, and the driver interfaces to be added to the `bdevsw` and `cdevsw` tables. This file is not applicable to loadable drivers.	Yes	No
`name_data.c` file	For static drivers, you specify data structure sizes in this file. Loadable drivers should dynamically allocate memory to accommodate data structure sizes.	Yes	Yes
driver sources and driver objects	The driver writer supplies the `.c` (optional), `.h` (optional), `.o` (for static drivers), and `.mod` (for loadable drivers) driver files.	Yes	Yes
`conf.c`	For static drivers using the traditional model, you edit the `conf.c` file with the device driver entry points in the appropriate `devsw` table. For static drivers using the third-party model, you use a valid syntax in the `stanza.static` file fragment to automatically add device driver entry points to the `bdevsw` and `cdevsw` tables. This file is not used for loadable drivers. Instead, for loadable drivers, use the `bdevsw_add` and `cdevsw_add` interfaces to dynamically add device driver entry points to the in-memory `bdevsw` and `cdevsw` tables.	No	Yes

Table 12-1:   (continued)

File	Information/Mechanisms	Third-Party Model	Traditional Model
Subset Control Program (SCP)	The kit developer writes an SCP that installs and manages the files and file fragments supplied to customers.	Yes	No

12.2   Specifying Information in the config.file File Fragment and the System Configuration File

The config.file file fragment uses the same syntax as the system configuration file to specify device connectivity information and command callout options. For the third-party model, driver writers specify in config.file only the information needed for their driver product. For the traditional model, driver writers manually edit the system configuration file to include the necessary information. The following sections discuss the syntaxes for the device options and the callout options available to device driver writers. For descriptions of the other options and definitions that could be specified in these files, see the *System Administration* guide.

12.2.1   Specifying Device Definitions

The device definition keywords, part of the config.file file fragment and the system configuration file, contain descriptions of each current or planned device on the system. That is, these definitions describe such things as bus, controller, disk, and tape mnemonics and logical unit numbers for devices connected to the system. When the system is initially configured, the doconfig and sizer utilities identify all of the devices supplied by Digital that are attached to the system and place their associated entries in the specified system configuration file.

For the third-party driver configuration model, device driver writers must make their device definitions available to their customer's system through the config.file file fragment. For the traditional model, driver writers must manually edit the system configuration file to make the appropriate device definitions. In either case, the keywords and values for making these entries are identical.

Device driver writers must know the syntax for making:

- A bus specification
- A controller specification

- A device specification

The syntaxes for each category are discussed in the following sections. Section 12.2.1.4 provides examples of the device options syntaxes for the CB and none devices.

12.2.1.1 Bus Specification

The following is the syntax for specifying a bus in the config.file file fragment and the system configuration file:

bus *bus_name#* **at** *bus_connection#*

bus
> The keyword that precedes a bus name and its associated unit number.

bus_name#
> Specifies the name and number of the bus. The bus name can be any string. For buses supported by Digital, the bus name is one of the valid strings listed in the *System Administration* guide. For example, the string tc represents a TURBOchannel bus.
>
> Third-party driver writers who write drivers that operate on non-Digital buses can select a string that might include the vendor and product names. The string could also include version and release numbers. This type of naming scheme reduces the chance of name conflicts with other vendors. For example, the driver writers at EasyDriver Incorporated might specify edgb for an internally developed bus.
>
> The number for a bus is any positive integer, for example, 0 or 1.

at
> The keyword that precedes the bus connection.

bus_connection#
> Specifies the name and number of the bus that this bus is connected to. The keyword nexus indicates that the specified bus is the system bus.
>
> A wildcard syntax for the bus specification is also allowed, as shown in the following examples:
>
> bus tc?
>
> bus tc? at nexus
>
> The first example specifies any TURBOchannel bus. The second example specifies the top-level or system bus.

12.2.1.2 Controller Specification

The following is the syntax for specifying a controller in the `config.file` file fragment and the system configuration file:

controller *ctlr_name#* **at** *bus_name#* [**csr** *addr*] [**flags** *flag_value*] [**slot** *slot#*] **vector** *vec...*

`controller`
> The keyword that precedes a controller name and its associated logical unit number. A controller identifies either a physical or logical connection with zero or more slaves (that is, disk and tape drives) attached to it.

`ctlr_name#`
> Specifies the controller's name and associated logical unit number. The controller name can be any string. For controllers supplied by Digital, the controller name is one of the valid strings listed in the *System Administration* guide. For example, the string `hsc` represents an HSC controller.
>
> Third-party driver writers who write drivers for non-Digital controllers can select a string that might include the vendor and product names. The string could also include version and release numbers. This type of naming scheme reduces the chance of name conflicts with other vendors. For example, the driver writers at EasyDriver Incorporated might specify `edgc` for an internally developed controller.
>
> The logical unit number for a controller is any positive integer, for example, 0 or 1.

`at`
> The keyword that precedes the bus to which the controller is connected.

`bus_name#`
> Specifies the name and number of the bus the controller is connected to. The bus name can be any string. For buses supported by Digital, the bus name is one of the valid strings listed in the *System Administration* guide. For example, the string `tc` represents a TURBOchannel bus.
>
> Third-party driver writers who write drivers that operate on non-Digital buses can select a string that might include the vendor and product names. The string could also include version and release numbers. This type of naming scheme reduces the chance of name conflicts with other vendors. For example, the driver writers at EasyDriver Incorporated might specify `edgc` for an internally developed controller.
>
> A wildcard syntax for the bus specification is also allowed, as shown in the following examples:
>
> ```
> controller sii0 at tc?
> ```

```
controller sii0 at *
```
The first example specifies an instance of a controller of type `sii` attached to any TURBOchannel bus. The second example specifies an instance of a controller of type `sii` attached to any bus type (that is, not restricted to a TURBOchannel bus).

`csr`
Specifies an optional keyword that precedes a control status register value for some device.

addr
Specifies the address of the control status register for the device. This address is required if the `csr` keyword was specified.

`flags`
An optional keyword that precedes some value that directs the system to perform some request.

flag_value
Specifies the value for the flag. Possible values are decimal numbers and hexadecimal numbers.

The format of the hexadecimal number is $0xnn$, where nn is a hexadecimal number consisting of digits from 0 to 9 inclusive and of the letters a to f inclusive.

`slot`
The keyword that precedes the bus slot or node number.

slot#
Specifies the bus slot or node number.

`vector`
The keyword that precedes the name or names of the interrupt handlers for the device. This keyword is for static drivers. Loadable drivers register their interrupt handlers through the `handler_add` and `handler_enable` interfaces. Section 9.6.1 shows how to register the interrupt service interface for the `/dev/cb` driver by calling `handler_add` and `handler_enable`.

vec...
Specifies the name or names of the interrupt handlers for the device.

12.2.1.3 Device Specification

The following is the syntax for specifying a device (for example, disk or tape) in the `config.file` file fragment and the system configuration file:

device *device_spec device_name#* **at** *ctlr_name#* **drive** *phys#*

device
The keyword that precedes the string that identifies the device.

device_spec
Specifies a keyword that precedes a device name and its logical unit number. This keyword can be any string. Digital uses the keywords `disk` and `tape` to represent disk and tape devices.

device_name#
Specifies the device's name and associated logical unit number. The device name can be any string. For devices supported by Digital, the device name is one of the valid strings listed in the *System Administration* guide. For example, the strings `ra` and `tz` represent SCSI disk and tape drives supported by Digital.

Third-party driver writers who write drivers that operate on non-Digital devices can select a string that might include the vendor and product names. The string could also include version and release numbers. This type of naming scheme reduces the chance of name conflicts with other vendors. For example, the driver writers at EasyDriver Incorporated might specify `edgd` for an internally developed disk device.

The logical unit number for a disk drive is any positive integer, for example, 0 or 1.

at
The keyword that precedes the controller to which the device is attached.

ctlr_name#
Specifies the name and logical unit number of the controller to which the device is attached. The controller name can be any string. For controllers supplied by Digital, the controller name is one of the valid strings listed in the *System Administration* guide. For example, the string `hsc` represents an HSC controller.

Third-party driver writers who write drivers for non-Digital controllers can select a string that might include the vendor and product names. The string could also include version and release numbers. This type of naming scheme reduces the chance of name conflicts with other vendors. For example, the driver writers at EasyDriver Incorporated might specify `edgc` for an internally developed controller.

The logical unit number for a controller is any positive integer, for example, 0 or 1.

drive
The keyword that precedes the physical unit number of the device.

phys#
Specifies the physical unit number of the device, if required.

12.2.1.4 Device Options Syntaxes Example

The driver writers from EasyDriver Incorporated supply the following `config.file` file fragment to their customers. This file fragment shows entries for the `none` and `CB` device controllers, which operate on the customer's TURBOchannel bus:

```
# Entries in config.file for none and CB devices

controller none0 at tc?  1
controller cb0   at tc? vector cbintr   2
```

1 Indicates that the `CB` controller is connected to the customer's TURBOchannel bus. Note the use of the wildcard character to indicate that the `none` controller can be connected to any TURBOchannel bus.

For this version of the Digital UNIX operating system, Digital recommends that all new device drivers (loadable and static) register their device interrupt handlers by calling the `handler_add` and `handler_enable` interfaces and referencing the handler-specific data structures.

For backward compatibility, some buses (for example, the TURBOchannel bus) allow device drivers to register device interrupt handlers by specifying an appropriate syntax in the system configuration file or `stanza.static` file fragment. Digital no longer recommends this method for new drivers. See the bus-specific device driver book for more details on how to register interrupt handlers for the bus your driver operates on.

The interrupt handler for the `/dev/none` device driver controlling the `none` controller is called `noneintr`. Because the TURBOchannel bus supports both methods for registering interrupt handlers, the previous example shows the interrupt handler, `noneintr`, specified in the `config.file` file fragment. Section 4.1.6.1 shows how to register `noneintr` by calling `handler_add` and `handler_enable`.

2 Indicates that the `/dev/cb` controller is connected to the customer's TURBOchannel bus. Because the TURBOchannel bus supports both methods for registering interrupt handlers, the previous example shows the interrupt handler, `cbintr`, specified in the `config.file` file fragment. Section 10.8.1 shows how to register `cbintr` by calling `handler_add` and `handler_enable`.

Following the traditional device driver configuration model, the driver writers at EasyDriver Incorporated edit their system configuration file with the following entries:

```
.
.
.
controller none0 at tc0 slot? vector noneintr
.
.
.
controller cb0 at tc0 slot? vector cbintr
.
.
.
```

Note that the `slot` keyword is used because these controllers are connected to the TURBOchannel bus.

12.2.2 Specifying Callouts

The `callout` keyword provides driver writers with a mechanism for handling customer-specific tasks related to driver configuration that are not currently handled by the `config` program. The `config.file` file fragment and the system configuration file can contain one or more callout keyword definitions that invoke a subprocess. While the subprocess executes, `config` suspends its execution. It resumes execution when the subprocess has completed.

The driver writer can invoke any subprocess with a `callout` keyword. The following list describes issues to consider when using the callout mechanism:

- The command must be in the search path or you must specify the full pathname.

- System resources such as memory, disks, or tapes must be available.

- The subprocess must handle all error conditions because the `config` program behaves as if the subprocess always succeeds.

- If more than one callout is used with the same keyword value, the order of execution is determined by the order in the system configuration file from top to bottom.

The `callout` keyword specifies the point in the configuration sequence at which to invoke the subprocess. The subprocess that is called out has the CONFIG_NAME environment variable set to specify the system configuration file that called it.

Table 12-2 describes the `callout` keywords and the times at which they are invoked by `config`.

Table 12-2: The callout Keywords

callout Keyword	Invocation Time
at_start	After config has parsed the system configuration file syntax, but before processing any other input such as stanza.static file fragments
at_exit	Immediately before config exits, regardless of its exit status
at_success	Before the at_exit process, if specified, and only if config exits with a success exit status
before_h	Before config creates any *.h files
after_h	After config creates any *.h files
before_c	Before config creates any *.c files
after_c	After config creates any *.c files
before_makefile	Before config creates the makefile
after_makefile	After config creates the makefile
before_conf	Before config creates the /usr/sys/*NAME*/conf.c file
after_conf	After config creates the /usr/sys/*NAME*/conf.c file

The following example shows one possible entry in a config.file file fragment and system configuration file:

```
        .
        .
        .
bus tc0 at nexus?
callout after_c "../bin/mkdata"  1
        .
        .
        .
```

1 In this example, the callout keyword invokes a subprocess (C program) called mkdata. The purpose of mkdata is to automatically add third-party devices registered through the kreg utility to the tc_option table.

12.3 Specifying Information in the BINARY System Configuration File

To build a loadable driver load module, using the traditional device driver configuration model, the BINARY system configuration file must be edited.

The following syntax specifies a loadable driver entry in the `BINARY` system configuration file:

pseudo-device *driver_name* **dynamic** *driver_name*

`pseudo-device`
> Specifies a keyword that causes the appropriate `makefile` to be generated for the specified device driver.

driver_name
> Specifies the name of the loadable driver. This name is the *entry_name* that was specified in the `stanza.loadable` file fragment.

`dynamic`
> The keyword that specifies that the device driver is built as a dynamic load module (loadable driver).

The following example shows an entry for the `/dev/cb` device driver:

```
pseudo-device    cb    dynamic    cb
```

12.4 Understanding the Format of the NAME.list File

In the third-party device driver configuration model, the `kreg` utility sets up the `.products.list` and *NAME*.`list` files on the customer's system. Although third-party driver writers and kit developers do not supply these files, it is useful to understand the files' format. Note that these files are not used by driver writers following the traditional device driver configuration model. Figure 12-1 shows the format of such a file for EasyDriver Incorporated.

Figure 12-1: A NAME.list File for EasyDriver Incorporated

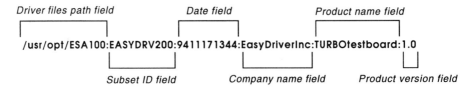

The figure shows that the *NAME*.`list` file has fields separated by colons (:), as follows:

* Driver files path field

    The driver files path field contains the path that points to the location of the files associated with the driver product, which in the figure is

`/usr/opt/ESA100`. The value in the driver files path field must be unique.

- Subset ID field

  The subset ID field contains the subset ID associated with the `setld` utility, which in the figure is `EASYDRV200`.

- Date field

  The date field contains the date when the product is ready for distribution. The date has the form *yymmddhhmm*, where *yy* represents the year, *mm* represents the month, *hh* represents the hour (24-hour time), and *mm* represents the minutes. For EasyDriver Incorporated, the date field translates to:

  ```
  November 17, 1994 1:44 PM
  ```

- Company name field

  The company name field contains the company's name, which in the figure is abbreviated to EasyDriverInc.

- Product name field

  The product name field contains the name of the product, which in the figure is `TURBOtestboard`.

- Product version field

  The product version field contains the version number of the product, which in the figure is 1.0.

  Note that the configuration software (namely, the `config` program) uses the information only in the path field. Although editing the *NAME*.`list` file is not supported, driver writers can add an entry to this file. Doing so would be useful if for some reason the driver writer did not want to use the `setld` utility for kit processing.

12.5 Specifying Information in the files File Fragment and files File

The `files` file fragment contains the same kind of information that appears in the `files` file. For the third-party model, driver writers specify in the `files` file fragment only the information needed for their driver product. For the traditional model, driver writers manually edit the `files` file to include the necessary information.

The following syntax specifies an entry in the `files` file fragment and the `files` file for static device drivers:

path_name **optional** *key_string* | **standard device-driver Binary** | **Notbinary**

The following syntax specifies an entry in the `files` file for loadable device drivers:

path_name **optional** *key_string* | **standard device-driver if_dynamic** *key_string* **Binary**

`path_name`
Specifies the file specification indicating where the device driver sources reside.

`optional`
The keyword that indicates that this software module will be included in those kernels whose system configuration files specify the `key_string` that follows the keyword `optional`.

`standard`
The keyword that indicates that this software module will be included in every kernel.

`device-driver`
The keyword that directs the `config` program to create the `makefile` entry that builds the kernel object so that the C compiler builds the object code unoptimized. You need to use this keyword only if you want to build your driver code unoptimized (that is, without compiler optimizations). You do not need to specify this keyword in the `files` file if your device drivers follow the guidelines presented in Section 2.6.5.11 for using the `volatile` keyword.

`if_dynamic`
The keyword that marks the specified device driver source files such that the resulting object files can be built as either static or loadable.

`Binary`
The keyword that causes symbolic links to be made to existing object modules. This implies that the file is installed as an already compiled module. In this case the source files are not installed because they are not system specific.

`Notbinary`
The keyword that causes the `config` program to create a `makefile` that compiles the object from source. Static device drivers written by third-party vendors can use either `Binary` or `Notbinary`, depending on whether they want to supply the driver sources or to compile their `name_data.c` files, if shipped.

Third-party vendors must use the `Binary` keyword, as shown in the syntax, for loadable drivers.

The following examples show how the driver writers at EasyDriver
Incorporated specify entries in the `files` file fragment (third-party model)
and the `files` file (traditional model) for the static versions of the
`/dev/none` and `/dev/cb` drivers.

```
# This example illustrates the third-party model
# by showing a files file fragment for static
# drivers developed by EasyDriver Incorporated.

ESA100/none.c standard none if_dynamic none Binary 1

ESB100/cb.c optional cb Binary 2


# This example illustrates the traditional model
# by showing a files file for static drivers
# developed by  EasyDriver Incorporated.

io/EasyInc/none.c standard none Notbinary 1
io/EasyInc/cb.c optional cb device-driver Binary 2
```

1.   In the third-party model example, shows that the `/dev/none` device
driver object is located in the directory `ESA100`. The `kreg` utility puts
the path `/usr/opt/ESA100` in the customer's `.products.list`
file.

   The corresponding line in the traditional model example shows that the
`/dev/none` device driver object is located in the directory
`/usr/sys/io/EasyInc`. In both cases, the name of the driver source
is `none.c`.

   In the third-party model example, the `standard` keyword indicates that
the `/dev/none` driver will be included in every customer kernel. In the
traditional model example, the `standard` keyword indicates that the
`/dev/none` driver will be included in every kernel at EasyDriver
Incorporated.

   The `Notbinary` keyword indicates that the `none.c` file will be
supplied to customers.

2.   In both the third-party and traditional models, shows the syntax for the
`/dev/cb` driver. The syntax is identical to that specified for the
`/dev/none` driver except that in both models it uses the `optional`
and `Binary` keywords.

   The `optional` keyword indicates that the `/dev/cb` driver will be
included in those kernels whose system configuration files specify `cb` as
a device entry.

   The `Binary` keyword indicates that the `cb.c` file will not be compiled
and need not exist but that the kernel links in a supplied `cb.o` object file.

The following example shows how the driver writers at EasyDriver Incorporated specify entries in the `files` file (traditional model) for the loadable versions of the `/dev/none` and `/dev/cb` drivers.

```
# This example illustrates the traditional model
# by showing a files file for loadable drivers
# developed by EasyDriver Incorporated.

io/EasyInc/none.c optional none if_dynamic none Binary 1

io/EasyInc/cb.c optional cb if_dynamic cb Binary 2
```

1. Shows that the `/dev/none` device driver object is located in the directory `io/EasyInc`.

   The `optional` keyword indicates that the `/dev/none` device driver will be included in those kernels whose system configuration files specify `none` as a device entry.

   The `if_dynamic` keyword marks the `/dev/none` device driver source files such that the resulting object files can be built as either static or loadable.

   The `Binary` keyword causes symbolic links to be made to existing load modules.

2. Specifies the keywords for the `/dev/cb` driver. They are the same as the ones used for the `/dev/none` driver.

12.6 Specifying Information in the Stanza Files

Device driver writers must understand the following topics associated with the stanza files:

- Stanza file format
- Stanza file syntax

Section 12.6.3 provides examples of the syntaxes for the `stanza.static` and `stanza.loadable` file fragments.

12.6.1 Stanza File Format

Figure 12-2 shows the format associated with the fields in the stanza files separated by colons (:). It also shows that the syntax for a stanza entry contains:

- *entry_name*

  Specifies the name of the device driver. The figure shows one sample driver entry called `tdc`.

  Typically, each driver contains a separate stanza entry. If more than one stanza entry is supplied in a single `stanza.loadable` or `stanza.static` file fragment, separate them with one or more blank lines.

Third-party driver writers who write drivers for non-Digital controllers can select a name that might include the vendor and product names. The string could also include version and release numbers. This type of naming scheme reduces the chance of name conflicts with other third-party drivers. For example, the driver writers at EasyDriver Incorporated might specify `edgd` for a device driver developed for an internally developed device.

- Comments

  A number sign (#) at the beginning of a line indicates a comment. You can include comments at the beginning or the end of a driver stanza entry. The figure shows an example of a comment at the beginning of the entry for the `tdc` driver. Comments are not allowed within the body of the stanza entry.

- Trailing blanks

  Tabs are allowed at the beginning or end of lines and, as the figure shows, trailing blanks are allowed at the end of lines.

- *Attribute_name* and *Attribute_value*

  Specifies a valid stanza field. The figure shows that a valid stanza entry consists of a keyword that identifies the field, an equal sign (=) separator, and one or more values. The values can be strings (as in the figure) or valid keywords described in this book.

  Driver writers interested in learning about the other valid stanza keywords should see `sysconfigtab` in *Reference Pages Section 4*.

- New lines

  The figure also shows that a new line terminates an attribute name and value pair.

The following list describes restrictions associated with a `stanza.loadable` and `stanza.static` file fragment:

- An individual stanza entry can be a maximum of 40960 bytes in length. The system ignores all bytes in excess of this limit.

- An individual line (attribute) within a stanza entry cannot exceed 500 bytes.

- An individual stanza entry cannot consist of over 2048 lines (attributes).

- At least one blank line is required between stanza entries.

Figure 12-2: Format of the Stanza Files

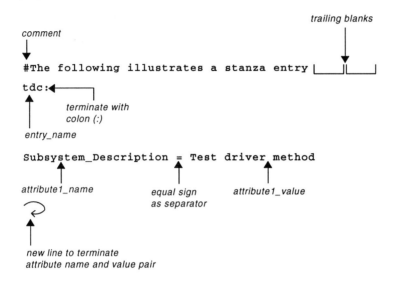

12.6.2 Stanza File Syntax

Table 12-3 lists the stanza file fields driver writers must be familiar with. The table has the following columns:

- Field

  This column lists the stanza field.

- `stanza.loadable`

  A Yes appears in this column if the field is applicable to the `stanza.loadable` file fragment. Otherwise, a No appears.

- `stanza.static`

  A Yes appears in this column if the field is applicable to the `stanza.static` file fragment. Otherwise, a No appears.

Table 12-3: The Stanza File Fields

Field	stanza.loadable	stanza.static
Subsystem_Description	Yes	Yes
Module_Type	Yes	No

Table 12-3: (continued)

Field	stanza.loadable	stanza.static
Module_Path	Yes	No
Device_Dir	Yes	Yes
Device_Subdir	Yes	Yes
Device_Block_Subdir	Yes	Yes
Device_Char_Subdir	Yes	Yes
Device_Major_Req	Yes	Yes
Device_Block_Major	Yes	Yes
Device_Block_Minor	Yes	Yes
Device_Block_Files	Yes	Yes
Device_Char_Major	Yes	Yes
Device_Char_Minor	Yes	Yes
Device_Char_Files	Yes	Yes
Device_User	Yes	Yes
Device_Group	Yes	Yes
Device_Mode	Yes	Yes
Module_Config_Name	Yes	Yes
Module_Config	Yes	Yes
Device_Block_Open	No	Yes
Device_Block_Close	No	Yes
Device_Block_Strategy	No	Yes
Device_Block_Dump	No	Yes
Device_Block_Psize	No	Yes
Device_Block_Flags	No	Yes
Device_Block_Ioctl	No	Yes
Device_Block_Funnel	No	Yes
Device_Char_Open	No	Yes
Device_Char_Close	No	Yes
Device_Char_Read	No	Yes
Device_Char_Write	No	Yes
Device_Char_Ioctl	No	Yes
Device_Char_Stop	No	Yes
Device_Char_Reset	No	Yes
Device_Char_Ttys	No	Yes

Table 12-3:   (continued)

Field	stanza.loadable	stanza.static
Device_Char_Select	No	Yes
Device_Char_Mmap	No	Yes
Device_Char_Funnel	No	Yes
Device_Char_Segmap	No	Yes
Device_Char_Flags	No	Yes

Each of the fields from Subsystem_Description to Module_Config is discussed in the following sections. The remainder of the fields are related to the conf.c file; therefore, they are discussed in Section 12.8.2. Note that you can include fields that are not used because the system ignores them.

12.6.2.1   Subsystem_Description Field

The following is the syntax for specifying the Subsystem_Description field in the stanza.loadable or stanza.static file fragment:

Subsystem_Description = *description*

The Subsystem_Description field is optional, and it specifies a short literal string used as a description. If specified in the stanza.static file, the description is used as the comment in the entry to the bdevsw or cdevsw table.

12.6.2.2   Module_Type Field

The following syntax specifies the Module_Type field in a stanza.loadable file fragment:

Module_Type = Dynamic ǀ Static

The Module_Type field is required, and it specifies a subsystem type of Dynamic or Static. The Dynamic type indicates that the driver subsystem is a loadable module. Loadable device drivers should specify this value type.

The Static type indicates that the driver subsystem is statically configured into the kernel. This type enables statically configured subsystems to be included in the global stanza database, /etc/sysconfigtab, and to be controlled by the cfgmgr daemon.

12.6.2.3 Module_Path Field

The following syntax specifies the `Module_Path` field in a `stanza.loadable` file fragment:

Module_Path = *path_name*

The `Module_Path` field specifies the full pathname where the loadable driver subsystem resides. This field is required if `Dynamic` is specified in the `Module_Type` field.

12.6.2.4 Device_Dir Field

The following syntax specifies the `Device_Dir` field in the `stanza.loadable` and `stanza.static` file fragments:

Device_Dir = *directory*

The `Device_Dir` field is optional, and it specifies a valid directory specification for the location of the device special files. This directory is typically `/dev` for both block and character devices. If you do not specify a directory for this field, it defaults to `/dev` for both block and character devices.

12.6.2.5 Device_Subdir Field

The following syntax specifies the `Device_Subdir` field in the `stanza.loadable` and `stanza.static` file fragments:

Device_Subdir = *subdirectory*

The `Device_Subdir` field is optional, and it is appended to the directory specified or defaulted to in the `Device_Dir` field. The `Device_Subdir` field specifies a single directory location for the placement of the device special files associated with both character and block drivers. If you do not specify a directory for this field, the device special files are placed in the directory specified or defaulted to in the `Device_Dir` field.

If the device special files for both block and character drivers should not reside in a single directory, use the `Device_Block_Subdir` and `Device_Char_Subdir` fields.

12.6.2.6 Device_Block_Subdir Field

The following syntax specifies the `Device_Block_Subdir` field in the `stanza.loadable` and `stanza.static` file fragments:

Device_Block_Subdir = *subdirectory*

The `Device_Block_Subdir` field is optional, and it specifies a subdirectory for the directory specified in `Device_Dir`. The `Device_Block_Subdir` field overrides any directory specification made in the `Device_Subdir` field for device special files associated with block device drivers. This directory is used to place the device special files for block drivers to keep them separate from the device special files for character drivers. If you do not specify a directory for this field, the device special files are placed in the directory specified or defaulted to in the `Device_Dir` field and the `Device_Subdir` field, if specified.

If the device special files for block device drivers reside in the same directory as the device special files for character drivers, use the `Device_Subdir` field.

12.6.2.7 Device_Char_Subdir Field

The following syntax specifies the `Device_Char_Subdir` field in the `stanza.loadable` and `stanza.static` file fragments:

Device_Char_Subdir = *subdirectory*

The `Device_Char_Subdir` field is optional, and it specifies a subdirectory for the directory specified in `Device_Dir`. The `Device_Char_Subdir` field overrides any directory specification made in the `Device_Subdir` field for device special files associated with character device drivers. This directory is used to place the device special files for character drivers to keep them separate from the device special files for block drivers. If you do not specify a directory for this field, the device special files are placed in the directory specified or defaulted to in the `Device_Dir` field and the `Device_Subdir` field, if specified.

If the device special files for character device drivers reside in the same directory as the device special files for block drivers, use the `Device_Subdir` field.

12.6.2.8 Device_Major_Req Field

The following syntax specifies the `Device_Major_Req` field in the `stanza.loadable` and `stanza.static` file fragments:

Device_Major_Req = None | Same

The `Device_Major_Req` field is optional, and it specifies the requirements that relate to major number assignment. Specify `None` or omit this field if there are no major number requirements.

Specify `Same` if the driver needs the same major number in both the `bdevsw` and `cdevsw` tables. If `Same` is specified, the values of the `Device_Block_Major` and `Device_Char_Major` fields must be identical. Otherwise, the attempt to load the driver fails.

12.6.2.9 Device_Block_Major Field

The following syntax specifies the `Device_Block_Major` field in the `stanza.loadable` and `stanza.static` file fragments:

Device_Block_Major = Any | *major#*

The `Device_Block_Major` field is required only if the driver is a block device driver, and it specifies the block major number for the device driver. Specify the value `Any`, which indicates that the system dynamically assigns the next available block device major number; or, specify a number (for example, 24) and the system assigns this major number to the driver if it is not currently in use. If the specified number is in use, the attempt to dynamically load the driver fails.

12.6.2.10 Device_Block_Minor Field

The following syntax specifies the `Device_Block_Minor` field in the `stanza.loadable` and `stanza.static` file fragments:

Device_Block_Minor = *minor#*

The `Device_Block_Minor` field is optional, and it specifies the minor numbers used to create the device special files for the driver. Each minor number must be paired with a file name specified in the `Device_Block_Files` field.

The following example shows four ways to specify the block device minor numbers:

```
# One device minor number 1
Device_Block_Minor = 1
# More than one device minor number 2
Device_Block_Minor = 0,1,2,3
# A range of device minor numbers 3
Device_Block_Minor = [0-10]
# More than one range of device minor numbers 4
Device_Block_Minor = [0-10],[21-30]
```

1 To specify a single device minor number, simply specify the number. The device minor number must be a positive integer that cannot exceed 99999. A maximum of 512 device special files can be created for a device major number, unless a driver is both a block and character device. In this case, the maximum is 1024 device special files (512 for the block and 512 for the character drivers).

2 To specify more than one device minor number, specify the numbers separated by commas. Each device minor number must be greater than the one previously specified.

3 To specify a range of device minor numbers, enclose the range within brackets ([]) and separate the beginning and ending values with a dash (–).

The following rules apply to numbers specified in a range:

- The ending number must be greater than the beginning number, as in the example. Thus, [10-0] is an invalid range specification.

- The numbers specified in the range must be greater than the value zero (0). Thus, [-1-10] is also an invalid range specification because the first number is less than the value zero (0).

- The largest allowable number in the range is 99999.

- A maximum of 512 device special files can be created for any device major number. Thus, [0-511] and [1000-1500] are valid range specifications while [0-600] is invalid.

4 To specify more than one range of device minor numbers, enclose the first range within brackets ([]) and separate the range with a dash (–). Follow the first range with a comma (,). Specify the second range in the same manner as the first and omit the comma (unless there are additional ranges).

12.6.2.11   Device_Block_Files Field

The following syntax specifies the Device_Block_Files field in the stanza.loadable and stanza.static file fragments:

Device_Block_Files = *devspecialfilename*

The Device_Block_Files field is optional, and it specifies the device special files to be created. Each device special file name must be paired with a minor number specified in the Device_Block_Minor field. If a driver is both a block and character driver, specify device special files in both the Device_Block_Files and Device_Char_Files fields.

The following example shows four ways to specify the block device special file names:

```
# One device special file name 1
Device_Block_Files = rz1

# More than one device special file name 2
Device_Block_Files = rz1,rz2,rz3

# A range of device special file names 3
Device_Block_Files = rz1[a-h]
```

```
# More than one range of device special file names 4
Device_Block_Files = rz1[a-h],rz2[a-h]
```

1 To specify a single file name, simply specify the name.

2 To specify more than one file name, specify the names separated by commas.

3 To specify a range of file names, enclose the range within brackets ([]) and separate the beginning and ending names with a dash (–).

The following rules apply to letters specified in a range:

- Both letters must be either lowercase or uppercase. Thus, [a-h] or [A-H] are valid range specifications while [A-h] and [a-H] are invalid.

- Only one letter is allowed in the range specification, as in the example. Thus, [aa-hh] is not a valid range specification.

- The ending letter must be greater than the beginning letter. Thus, [z-a] is not a valid range specification.

4 To specify more than one range of file names, enclose the first range within brackets ([]) and separate the range with a dash (–). Follow the first range with a comma (,). Specify the second range in the same manner as the first and omit the comma (unless there are additional ranges).

As stated previously, the Device_Block_Files field must be paired with corresponding minor numbers specified in the Device_Block_Minor field. The ranges for each must represent an equal number of file-to-minor number associations. The following example shows a correct match:

```
Device_Block_Files = rz0[a-h]
Device_Block_Minor = [0-7]
```

The following shows an invalid match:

```
Device_Block_Files = rz0[a-c]
Device_Block_Minor = [0-7]
```

The following shows a match that uses more than one range. Note that the gap in the minor numbers is valid:

```
Device_Block_Files = rz0[a-h],rz1[a-h],rz2[a-h],rt5[a-h]
Device_Block_Minor = [0-7],[8-15],[16-23],[40-47]
```

The number of files must equal the number of minor numbers, just as in a single range specification.

In addition, the maximum number of devices is 512. Thus, the following range specifications are invalid:

```
Device_Block_Files = rz0[0-300],rz1[301-600]
Device_Block_Minor = [0-300],[301-600]
```

If you violate any of the previously discussed rules, none of the device special files will be created.

12.6.2.12 Device_Char_Major Field

The following syntax specifies the Device_Char_Major field in the stanza.loadable and stanza.static file fragments:

Device_Char_Major = Any | *major#*

The Device_Char_Major field is required only if the driver is a character driver and it specifies the character major number for the device driver. Specify the value Any, which indicates that the system dynamically assigns the next available character device major number; or, specify a number (for example, 24) and the system assigns this major number to the driver if it is not currently in use. If the specified number is in use, the attempt to dynamically load the driver fails.

12.6.2.13 Device_Char_Minor Field

The following syntax specifies the Device_Char_Minor field in the stanza.loadable and stanza.static file fragments:

Device_Char_Minor = *minor#*

The Device_Char_Minor field is optional, and it specifies the minor numbers used to create the device special files for the driver. Each minor number must be paired with a file name specified in the Device_Char_Files field.

The following example shows four ways to specify the character device minor numbers:

```
# One device minor number 1
Device_Char_Minor = 1

# More than one device minor number 2
Device_Char_Minor = 0,1,2,3

# A range of device minor numbers 3
Device_Char_Minor = [0-10]

# More than one range of device minor numbers 4
Device_Char_Minor = [0-10],[21-30]
```

1. To specify a single device minor number, simply specify the number. The device minor number must be a positive integer that cannot exceed 99999. A maximum of 512 device special files can be created for a device major number, unless a driver is both a block and character device. In this case, the maximum is 1024 device special files (512 for the block and 512 for the character drivers).

2. To specify more than one device minor number, specify the numbers separated by commas. Each device minor number must be greater than the one previously specified.

3. To specify a range of device minor numbers, enclose the range within brackets ([]) and separate the beginning and ending values with a dash (−).

The following rules apply to numbers specified in a range:

- The ending number must be greater than the beginning number, as in the example. Thus, [10-0] is an invalid range specification.

- The numbers specified in the range must be greater than the value zero (0). Thus, [-1-10] is also an invalid range specification because the first number is less than the value zero (0).

- The largest allowable number in the range is 99999.

- A maximum of 512 device special files can be created for any device major number. Thus, [0-511] and [1000-1500] are valid range specifications while [0-600] is invalid.

4. To specify more than one range of device minor numbers, enclose the first range within brackets ([]) and separate the range with a dash (−). Follow the first range with a comma (,). Specify the second range in the same manner as the first and omit the comma (unless there are additional ranges).

12.6.2.14 Device_Char_Files Field

The following syntax specifies the Device_Char_Files field in the stanza.loadable and stanza.static file fragments:

Device_Char_Files = *devspecialfilename*

The Device_Char_Files field is optional, and it specifies the device special files to be created. Each device special file name must be paired with a minor number specified in the Device_Char_Minor field. If a driver is both a block and character driver, specify device special files in both the Device_Block_Files and Device_Char_Files fields.

The following example shows four ways to specify the character device special file names:

```
# One device special file name 1
Device_Char_Files = rrz1

# More than one device special file name 2
Device_Char_Files = rrz1,rrz2,rrz3

# A range of device special file names 3
Device_Char_Files = rrz1[1-10]

# More than one range of device special file names 4
Device_Char_Files = rrz1[a-h],rrz2[i-t]
```

1. To specify a single file name, simply specify the name.

2. To specify more than one file name, specify the names separated by commas.

3. To specify a range of file names, enclose the range within brackets ([])
   and separate the beginning and ending names with a dash (–).

   The following rules apply to letters specified in a range:

   – Both letters must be either lowercase or uppercase. Thus, [a-h] or
     [A-H] are valid range specifications while [A-h] and [a-H] are
     invalid.

   – Only one letter is allowed in the range specification, as in the
     example. Thus, [aa-hh] is not a valid range specification.

   – The ending letter must be greater than the beginning letter. Thus,
     [z-a] is not a valid range specification.

4. To specify more than one range of file names, enclose the first range
   within brackets ([]) and separate the range with a dash (–). Follow the
   first range with a comma (,). Specify the second range in the same
   manner as the first and omit the comma (unless there are additional
   ranges).

As stated previously, the Device_Char_Files field must be paired with
corresponding minor numbers specified in the Device_Char_Minor field.
The ranges for each must represent an equal number of file-to-minor number
associations. The following example shows a correct match:

```
Device_Char_Files = rrz0[a-h]
Device_Char_Minor = [0-7]
```

The following shows an invalid match:

```
Device_Char_Files = rrz0[a-c]
Device_Char_Minor = [0-7]
```

The following shows a match that uses more than one range. Note that the gap in the minor numbers is valid:

```
Device_Char_Files = rrz0[a-h],rrz1[a-h],rrz2[a-h],rrt5[a-h]
Device_Char_Minor = [0-7],[8-15],[16-23],[40-47]
```

The number of files must equal the number of minor numbers, just as in a single range specification.

In addition, the maximum number of devices is 512. Thus, the following range specifications are invalid:

```
Device_Char_Files = rrz0[0-300],rrz1[301-600]
Device_Char_Minor = [0-300],[301-600]
```

If you violate any of the previously discussed rules, none of the device special files will be created.

12.6.2.15 Device_User, Device_Group, and Device_Mode Fields

The following is the syntax for specifying the `Device_User`, `Device_Group`, and `Device_Mode` fields for block and character device special files in `stanza.loadable` and `stanza.static` file fragments:

Device_User = *name*
Device_Group = *group*
Device_Mode = *mode*

If these optional fields are omitted, the system uses the values specified in the default stanza entry of the `/etc/sysconfigtab` database to create the device special files for loadable drivers. The system does not use the values specified in `/etc/sysconfigtab` for static drivers.

The `Device_User` field is optional, and it specifies the user ID (UID) that owns the device special files for block and character devices. You can specify a decimal number or a string of alphabetic characters. The default is the value zero (0).

The `Device_Group` field is optional, and it specifies the group ID (GID) to which the device special files associated with the block and character devices belong. You can specify a decimal number or a string of alphabetic characters. The default is the value zero (0).

The `Device_Mode` field is optional, and it specifies the protection mode for the device special files. You must specify an octal number. The default is the octal number 0664.

12.6.2.16 Module_Config_Name Field

The following is the syntax for specifying the `Module_Config_Name` field in `stanza.loadable` and `stanza.static` file fragments:

Module_Config_Name = *name*

The `Module_Config_Name` field specifies the driver name. This field can be set to the same name that was specified for the *entry_name* field in the `stanza.loadable` and `stanza.static` file fragments. The following list describes the interpretation of this field for loadable and static drivers:

- For loadable drivers

  This field is used to identify the driver's configuration *NAME* and is required only if the `Module_Config` field is specified.

- For static drivers

  This field is required because it indicates that this stanza entry is to be added through the use of the automated configuration tools. If no driver name is specified in this field, the entire stanza entry is skipped. Ignoring the entire stanza entry is not considered an error, and no error message will be generated.

12.6.2.17 Module_Config Field for Bus Specification

The following syntax specifies the `Module_Config` field for buses in the `stanza.loadable` file fragment. This field is not used for static drivers because device connectivity information for static drivers is specified in the `config.file` file fragment or the system configuration file. Section 12.2 describes the syntax for specifying the device connectivity information in the `config.file` file fragment and the system configuration file.

Module_Config*n* = *device_connectivity_info*

The `Module_Config` field is optional, and it specifies the device connectivity information. The *n* argument is a number in the range of 0 to 499, for example, `Module_Config2`. The argument *device_connectivity_info* has the following format for bus specification. Note that this format is a subset of those used in the `config.file` file fragment and the system configuration file.

bus *bus_name#* **at** *bus_connection#*

bus
    The keyword that precedes a bus name and its associated unit number.

bus_name#
    Specifies the name and number of the bus. The bus name can be any string. For buses supported by Digital, the bus name is one of the valid

strings listed in the *System Administration* guide. For example, the string `tc` represents a TURBOchannel bus.

Third-party driver writers who write drivers that operate on non-Digital buses can select a string that might include the vendor and product names. The string could also include version and release numbers. This type of naming scheme reduces the chance of name conflicts with other vendors.

The number for a bus is any positive integer, for example, 0 or 1.

`at`
> The keyword that precedes the bus connection.

bus_connection#
> Specifies the name and number of the bus that this bus is connected to. The bus name can be any string. For buses supported by Digital, the bus name is one of the valid strings listed in the *System Administration* guide. For example, the string `tc` represents a TURBOchannel bus.
>
> Third-party driver writers who write drivers that operate on non-Digital buses can select a string that might include the vendor and product names. The string could also include version and release numbers. This type of naming scheme reduces the chance of name conflicts with other vendors.
>
> The number for a bus is any positive integer, for example, 0 or 1.
>
> A wildcard syntax for the bus specification is also allowed, as shown in the following examples:
>
> `bus tc?`
>
> `bus tc0 at bus tc1`
>
> The first example specifies any TURBOchannel bus. The second example specifies that TURBOchannel bus number 1 is connected to TURBOchannel bus number 0.

12.6.2.18 Module_Config Field for Controller Specification

The following syntax specifies the `Module_Config` field for controllers in the `stanza.loadable` file fragment. This field is not used for static drivers because device connectivity information for static drivers is specified in the `config.file` file fragment or the system configuration file. Section 12.2 describes the syntax for specifying the device connectivity information in the `config.file` file fragment and the system configuration file.

Module_Config*n* = *device_connectivity_info*

The `Module_Config` field is optional, and it specifies the device connectivity information. The *n* argument is a number in the range of 0 to

499, for example, `Module_Config2`. The argument
`device_connectivity_info` has the following format for controller
specification. Note that this format is a subset of those used in the
`config.file` file fragment and the system configuration file.

controller *ctlr_name#* **at** *bus_name* [**slot** *slot#*]

`controller`
> The keyword that precedes a controller name and its associated logical
> unit number. A controller identifies either a physical or logical
> connection with zero or more slaves (that is, disk and tape drives)
> attached to it.

`ctlr_name#`
> Specifies the controller's name and associated logical unit number. The
> controller name can be any string. For controllers supplied by Digital,
> the controller name is one of the valid strings listed in the *System
> Administration* guide. For example, the string `hsc` represents an HSC
> controller.
>
> Third-party driver writers who write drivers for non-Digital controllers
> can select a string that might include the vendor and product names.
> The string could also include version and release numbers. This type of
> naming scheme reduces the chance of name conflicts with other vendors.
> For example, the driver writers at EasyDriver Incorporated might specify
> `edgc` for an internally developed controller.
>
> The logical unit number for a controller is any positive integer, for
> example, 0 or 1.

`at`
> The keyword that precedes the bus to which the controller is connected.

`bus_name#`
> Specifies the name and number of the bus the controller is connected to.
> The bus name can be any string that matches the previously specified
> string for the bus entry as described in Section 12.6.2.17. For buses
> supported by Digital, the bus name is one of the valid strings listed in
> the *System Administration* guide. For example, the string `tc` represents
> a TURBOchannel bus.
>
> Third-party driver writers who write drivers that operate on non-Digital
> buses can select a string that might include the vendor and product
> names. The string could also include version and release numbers. This
> type of naming scheme reduces the chance of name conflicts with other
> vendors.
>
> A wildcard syntax for the bus specification is also allowed, as shown in
> the following examples:
>
> ```
> controller sii0 at tc?
> ```

```
controller sii0 at *
```

The first example specifies an instance of a controller of type sii attached to any TURBOchannel bus. The second example specifies an instance of a controller of type sii attached to any bus type (that is, not restricted to a TURBOchannel bus).

slot
> The keyword that precedes the bus slot or node number.

slot#
> Specifies the bus slot or node number.

12.6.2.19   Module_Config Field for Device Specification

The following syntax specifies the Module_Config field for devices. This field is not used for static drivers because device connectivity information for static drivers is specified in the config.file file fragment or the system configuration file. Section 12.2 describes the syntax for specifying the device connectivity information in the config.file file fragment and the system configuration file.

Module_Config*n = device_connectivity_info*

The Module_Config field is optional, and it specifies the device connectivity information. The *n* argument is a number in the range of 0 to 499, for example, Module_Config2. The argument *device_connectivity_info* has the following format for device specification. Note that this format is a subset of those used in the config.file file fragment and the system configuration file.

device *device_spec device_name#* **at** *ctlr_name#* **drive** *phys#*

device
> The keyword that precedes the string that identifies the device.

device_spec
> Specifies a keyword that precedes a device name and its logical unit number. This keyword can be any string. Digital uses the keywords disk and tape to represent disk and tape devices.

device_name#

Specifies the device's name and associated logical unit number. The device name can be any string. For devices supported by Digital, the device name is one of the valid strings listed in the *System Administration* guide. For example, the strings `ra` and `tz` represent SCSI disk and tape drives supported by Digital.

Third-party driver writers who write drivers that operate on non-Digital devices can select a string that might include the vendor and product names. The string could also include version and release numbers. This type of naming scheme reduces the chance of name conflicts with other vendors. For example, the driver writers at EasyDriver Incorporated might specify `edgd` for an internally developed disk device.

The logical unit number for a disk drive is any positive integer, for example, 0 or 1.

`at`

The keyword that precedes the controller to which the device is attached.

ctlr_name#

Specifies the name and logical unit number of the controller to which the device is attached. The controller name can be any string that matches the previously specified string for the controller entry as described in Section 12.6.2.18. For controllers supplied by Digital, the controller name is one of the valid strings listed in the *System Administration* guide. For example, the string `hsc` represents an HSC controller.

Third-party driver writers who write drivers for non-Digital controllers can select a string that might include the vendor and product names. The string could also include version and release numbers. This type of naming scheme reduces the chance of name conflicts with other vendors. For example, the driver writers at EasyDriver Incorporated might specify `edgc` for an internally developed controller.

The logical unit number for a controller is any positive integer, for example, 0 or 1.

`drive`

The keyword that precedes the physical unit number of the device.

phys#

Specifies the physical unit number of the device, if required.

12.6.3   Stanza File Fragment Examples

The following example shows a `stanza.loadable` file fragment for the
`/dev/none` device driver. The driver writers at EasyDriver Incorporated
create this file in the directory `/usr/opt/ESA100`, as discussed in Section
11.1.2.

```
none:
        Subsystem_Description = none device driver
        Module_Type = Dynamic
        Module_Path = /usr/opt/ESA100/none.mod
        Module_Config_Name = none
        Module_Config1 = controller none0 at tc?
        Module_Config2 = controller none0 at eisa?
        Module_Config3 = controller none0 at pci?
        Device_Dir = /dev
        Device_Char_Major = Any
        Device_Char_Minor = 0
        Device_Char_Files = none
        Device_User = root
        Device_Group = 0
        Device_Mode = 666
```

The following example shows a `stanza.loadable` file fragment for the
`/dev/cb` device driver. The driver writers at EasyDriver Incorporated
create this file in the directory `/usr/opt/ESB100`, as discussed in Section
11.1.2.

```
cb:
        Subsystem_Description = cb device driver
        Module_Type = Dynamic
        Module_Config_Name = cb
        Module_Config1 = controller cb0 at tc?
        Module_Path = /usr/opt/ESB100/cb.mod
        Device_Dir = /dev
        Device_Char_Major = Any
        Device_Char_Minor = 0
        Device_Char_Files = cb
        Device_User = root
        Device_Group = 0
        Device_Mode = 666
```

The following example shows a `stanza.static` file fragment for the
`/dev/none` device driver. The driver writers at EasyDriver Incorporated
create this file in the directory `/usr/opt/ESA100`, as discussed in Section
11.1.2. For descriptions of the fields that contain the driver interfaces, see

Section 12.8.2.

```
none:
        Subsystem_Description = none device driver
        Module_Config_Name = none
        Device_Char_Major = Any
        Device_Char_Minor = 0
        Device_Char_Files = none
        Device_Char_Open = noneopen
        Device_Char_Close = noneclose
        Device_Char_Read = noneread
        Device_Char_Write = nonewrite
        Device_Char_Ioctl = noneioctl
        Device_Char_Stop = nulldev
        Device_Char_Reset = nulldev
        Device_Char_Ttys = 0
        Device_Char_Select = nodev
        Device_Char_Mmap = nodev
        Device_Char_Funnel = DEV_FUNNEL_NULL
        Device_Char_Segmap = NULL
        Device_Char_Flags = NULL
```

The following example shows a stanza.static file fragment for the
/dev/cb device driver. The driver writers at EasyDriver Incorporated
create this file in the directory /usr/opt/ESB100, as discussed in Section
11.1.2. For descriptions of the fields that contain the driver interfaces, see
Section 12.8.2.

```
cb:
        Subsystem_Description = cb device driver
        Module_Config_Name = cb
        Device_Char_Major = Any
        Device_Char_Minor = 0
        Device_Char_Files = cb
        Device_Char_Open = cbopen
        Device_Char_Close = cbclose
        Device_Char_Read = cbread
        Device_Char_Write = cbwrite
        Device_Char_Ioctl = cbioctl
        Device_Char_Stop = nulldev
        Device_Char_Reset = nulldev
        Device_Char_Ttys = 0
        Device_Char_Select = nodev
        Device_Char_Mmap = nodev
        Device_Char_Funnel = DEV_FUNNEL_NULL
        Device_Char_Segmap = NULL
        Device_Char_Flags = NULL
```

12.7 Specifying Information in the name_data.c File

A *name_data.c* file is compiled when the kernel is made and it is usually used to size data structures for static-only drivers. The *name_data.c* file is typically not used for loadable drivers. Driver writers are encouraged to dynamically allocate data structures, as described in Section 2.5.

The *name* argument is usually based on the device name. For example, the none device's *name_data.c* file is called `none_data.c`. The CB device's *name_data.c* file is called `cb_data.c`. The edgd device's *name_data.c* file is called `edgd_data.c`.

12.8 Specifying Information in the conf.c File

The `conf.c` file contains two device switch tables called `bdevsw` and `cdevsw`. Section 8.2.1 and Section 8.2.2 describe in detail each of the members contained in these tables. This section is concerned with the mechanisms that device driver writers use to populate the device switch tables with the device driver entry points associated with their device drivers. The mechanisms are as follows:

- For static drivers

  For the third-party model, specify the device driver entry points in the `stanza.static` file fragment. For the traditional model, edit the `bdevsw` and/or `cdevsw` tables in the `conf.c` file with the driver entry points.

- For loadable drivers

  For block device drivers, add the entry points to the `bdevsw` table by calling the `bdevsw_add` interface in the configure section of the device driver.

  For character device drivers, add the entry points to the `cdevsw` table by calling the `cdevsw_add` interface in the configure section of the device driver.

The following sections show you how to populate the `cdevsw` table by using the `cdevsw_add` interface for loadable drivers and the `stanza.static` file fragment for static drivers.

12.8.1 Using cdevsw_add to Add Entries to the cdevsw Table

The following code fragment shows how a loadable driver uses the `cdevsw_add` interface to add a character device driver's entry points into the `cdevsw` table. This code fragment would appear in the configure section of the device driver.

```
/* Device switch structure for dynamic configuration */
        .
        .
        .
#include <sys/conf.h>
        .
        .
        .
struct cdevsw cb_cdevsw_entry = { 1
    cbopen,             /* d_open */
    cbclose,            /* d_close */
    cbread,             /* d_read */
    cbwrite,            /* d_write */
    cbioctl,            /* d_ioctl */
    nodev,              /* d_stop */
    nodev,              /* d_reset */
    0,                  /* d_ttys */
    nodev,              /* d_select */
    nodev,              /* d_mmap */
    DEV_FUNNEL_NULL     /* d_funnel */
};
        .
        .
        .
cdevno = cdevsw_add(cdevno,&cb_cdevsw_entry); 2
        .
        .
        .
```

1   Declares a cdevsw structure called cb_cdevsw_entry and initializes
    it to the device driver entry points associated with the /dev/cb device
    driver.

    The cdevsw and bdevsw structures are defined in
    /usr/sys/include/sys/conf.h.

2   Calls the cdevsw_add interface to register the device driver entry
    points indicated in the comments in the cb_cdevsw_entry structure.

    The code fragment shows that there are two arguments:

    –   The first argument is the device switch table entry (slot) to use. This
        slot would be obtained in a previous call to the makedev interface.
        Section 10.9.2 provides more details on how this is accomplished in
        the /dev/cb driver. This argument represents the device driver's
        major number requirements. For most drivers, this argument is set in
        the stanza entry in such a way that the next available major number
        gets assigned.

    –   The second argument is the address of the previously initialized
        cb_cdevsw_entry data structure. This structure is dynamically
        added to the cdevsw table by the cdevsw_add interface. The
        cdevsw_add interface adds the driver's entry points to the in-

memory resident `cdevsw` table.

Upon return from the call to `cdevsw_add`, the *cdevno* variable is set to the assigned device major number. If this value is `NODEV`, the call to `cdevsw_add` failed. This prevents the driver from being configured as a loadable driver.

Using the `bdevsw_add` interface is the same as using `cdevsw_add`, except that the entries get filled in the in-memory resident `bdevsw` table instead of the in-memory resident `cdevsw` table. The device driver writer would initialize a structure of type `bdevsw` with the block driver's entry points.

12.8.2 Using the stanza.static File Fragment to Add Entries to the Device Switch Tables

Use the following syntax for adding static device driver interfaces to the `bdevsw` table:

Device_Block_Open = *d_open*
Device_Block_Close = *d_close*
Device_Block_Strategy = *d_strategy*
Device_Block_Dump = *d_dump*
Device_Block_Psize = *d_psize*
Device_Block_Flags = *d_flags*
Device_Block_Ioctl = *d_ioctl*
Device_Block_Funnel = *d_funnel*

`Device_Block_Open`	Specifies the block driver's `open` interface.
`Device_Block_Close`	Specifies the block driver's `close` interface.
`Device_Block_Strategy`	Specifies the block driver's `strategy` interface.
`Device_Block_Dump`	Specifies the block driver's `dump` interface.
`Device_Block_Psize`	Specifies the block driver's `psize` interface.
`Device_Block_Flags`	Specifies whether this is an SVR4 DDI/DKI-compliant device driver. Set this field to the `B_DDIDKI` constant to indicate that this is an SVR4 DDI/DKI-compliant device driver.
`Device_Block_Ioctl`	Specifies the block driver's `ioctl` interface.

`Device_Block_Funnel`	Schedules a device driver onto a CPU in a multiprocessor configuration. Set this field to one of the following constants: `DEV_FUNNEL` or `DEV_FUNNEL_NULL`. The `DEV_FUNNEL` constant specifies that you want to funnel the device driver because you have not made it SMP safe. This means that the driver is forced to execute on a single CPU.

Note that the `DEV_FUNNEL` constant was not supported in previous versions of the Digital UNIX operating system (formerly DEC OSF/1). Therefore, if you need to supply a `stanza.static` file to customers running a previous version and the current version of Digital UNIX, specify the value 1 instead of `DEV_FUNNEL`.

The `DEV_FUNNEL_NULL` constant specifies that you do not want to funnel the device driver because you have made it SMP safe. This means that the driver can execute on multiple CPUs. You make a device driver SMP safe by using the simple or complex lock mechanism. If you do not specify one of these constants in your `stanza.static` file, the default is `DEV_FUNNEL_NULL`.

Use the following syntax to add static device driver interfaces to the `cdevsw` table. Any field not present is filled in with the `nulldev` interface. No particular field is required, but at least one must be present.

Device_Char_Open = *d_open*
Device_Char_Close = *d_close*
Device_Char_Read = *d_read*
Device_Char_Write = *d_write*
Device_Char_Ioctl = *d_ioctl*
Device_Char_Stop = *d_stop*
Device_Char_Reset = *d_reset*
Device_Char_Ttys = *d_ttys*
Device_Char_Select = *d_select*
Device_Char_Mmap = *d_mmap*
Device_Char_Funnel = *d_funnel*
Device_Char_Segmap = *d_segmap*
Device_Char_Flags = *d_flags*

`Device_Char_Open`	Specifies the character driver's `open` interface.
`Device_Char_Close`	Specifies the character driver's `close` interface.
`Device_Char_Read`	Specifies the character driver's `read` interface.
`Device_Char_Write`	Specifies the character driver's `write` interface.
`Device_Char_Ioctl`	Specifies the character driver's `ioctl` interface.
`Device_Char_Stop`	Specifies the character driver's `stop` interface.
`Device_Char_Reset`	Specifies the character driver's `reset` interface.
`Device_Char_Ttys`	Specifies the character driver's private data. Only terminal drivers use this field.
`Device_Char_Select`	Specifies the character driver's `select` interface.
`Device_Char_Mmap`	Specifies the character driver's memory map interface.

Device_Char_Funnel	Schedules a device driver onto a CPU in a multiprocessor configuration. Set this field to one of the following constants: DEV_FUNNEL or DEV_FUNNEL_NULL. The DEV_FUNNEL constant specifies that you want to funnel the device driver because you have not made it SMP safe. This means that the driver is forced to execute on a single CPU.

Note that the DEV_FUNNEL constant was not supported in previous versions of the Digital UNIX operating system (formerly DEC OSF/1). Therefore, if you need to supply a stanza.static file to customers running a previous version and the current version of Digital UNIX, specify the value 1 instead of DEV_FUNNEL.

The DEV_FUNNEL_NULL constant specifies that you do not want to funnel the device driver because you have made it SMP safe. This means that the driver can execute on multiple CPUs. You make a device driver SMP safe by using the simple or complex lock mechanism. If you do not specify one of these constants in your stanza.static file, the default is DEV_FUNNEL_NULL.

Device_Char_Segmap	Specifies the segmap entry point.
Device_Char_Flags	Specifies whether this is an SVR4 DDI/DKI-compliant device driver. Set this field to the C_DDIDKI constant to indicate that this is an SVR4 DDI/DKI-compliant device driver.

12.9 Supplying the Subset Control Program

Digital provides the tools for creating kits for device driver products as part of the standard operating system distribution. These tools are described in the *Programming Support Tools* book. The kit developer at EasyDriver Incorporated reads the *Programming Support Tools* book to learn how to create a kit for the device driver products developed by EasyDriver Incorporated. The following list summarizes what you must know about the kit-building process:

- Understand the syntax of the `setld` utility.

- Understand the files that the `setld` utility uses.

- Become familiar with the steps the `setld` utility performs when a system manager loads, configures, verifies, and removes the software subset or subsets on the device driver kit by invoking the appropriate option.

- Learn how to effectively use the file system.

- Create a kit for the `setld` utility. This step involves creating a subset control program (SCP) that performs special tasks beyond the basic installation managed by `setld` and building the kit.

The SCP is the program used with the `setld` utility to register third-party device driver subsets. After reading the information on creating and managing software product kits in the *Programming Support Tools* book, the kit developer at EasyDriver Incorporated decides on the strategy to follow for writing the SCPs associated with the driver products. The strategy you choose depends on how you want to market your device driver products. The following list presents some strategies for writing the SCP associated with the driver products developed by EasyDriver Incorporated:

- Write one SCP for a kit that contains the software subset associated with the static `/dev/none` device driver.

- Write one SCP for a kit that contains the software subset associated with the loadable `/dev/none` device driver.

- Write one SCP for a kit that contains the software subset associated with the static `/dev/cb` device driver.

- Write one SCP for a kit that contains the software subset associated with the loadable `/dev/cb` device driver.

- Write one SCP for a kit that contains the software subsets associated with both the static and loadable versions of the `/dev/none` device driver.

- Write one SCP for a kit that contains the software subsets associated with both the static and loadable versions of the `/dev/cb` device driver.

The kit developer at EasyDriver Incorporated chooses to write the SCP as described in bullet items 5 and 6 in the previous list. The following sections provide these SCPs.

12.9.1 Subset Control Program for the /dev/none Device Driver Product

The following example shows the SCP for the /dev/none device driver product:

```
#!/sbin/sh 1
#
#
#   NONE.scp - Install the files associated with the loadable and static
#              /dev/none device driver product 2
#

echo "*********** /dev/none Device Driver Product Installation Menu ***********"
echo "***********                                            ***********"
echo "1. Install the static /dev/none device driver subset."
echo "2. Delete the static /dev/none device driver subset."
echo "3. Install the loadable /dev/none device driver subset."
echo "4. Delete the loadable /dev/none device driver subset."

echo" Type the number corresponding to your choice [] " 3

read answer
case ${answer} in
    1)
    case "$ACT" in 4
    POST_L) 5

      # Register the files associated with the static /dev/none
      # device driver product.
      kreg -l EasyDriverInc EASYDRVNONESTATIC200 /usr/opt/none200 6

      # Reminder
      echo "The /dev/none device driver is installed on your system."
      echo "Before your utilities can make use of the driver, you"
      echo "must build a new kernel by running doconfig." 7
      ;;
    2)
    POST_D) 8
    kreg -d EASYDRVNONESTATIC200 9

      echo "The /dev/none device driver is no longer on the system." 10
      echo "Remember to build a new kernel to remove the /dev/none driver"
      echo "functionality."

      ;;

    3)
    POST_L) 11
    # Add the files associated with the loadable /dev/none device
    # driver product to the customer's sysconfigtab database
    sysconfigdb -a -f /usr/opt/none200/stanza.loadable none 12

    # Cause the /dev/none device driver to be automatically loaded each time
    # the system reboots
    sysconfigdb -on none 13

# Copy the none.mod file to the /subsys directory. Create
# the none.mth driver method by linking to device.mth
# /subsys/none.mth -> /subsys/device.mth
```

```
cp /usr/opt/ESB200/none.mod /subsys/none.mod 14
ln -s device.mth none.mth 15

    # Load the /dev/none device driver and create the device special files
    sysconfig -c none 16

    echo "The /dev/none device driver was added to your global stanza"
    echo "database (sysconfigtab) and will automatically be loaded"
    echo "each time the system reboots." 17

    4)
    POST_D) 18
    # Make sure the /dev/none device driver is not currently loaded
    sysconfig -u none 19

    # Remove the /dev/none device driver from the automatic startup list
    sysconfigdb -off none 20

    # Delete the /dev/none device driver's stanza entry from the global
    # stanza database
    sysconfigdb -d none 21
    ;;
esac
exit 0
```

1 The kit developer for EasyDriver Incorporated follows Digital's
   recommendation to write the SCP as a script for /sbin/sh. Note that
   the kit developer supplies a menu of choices for installing or deleting the
   subsets associated with the /dev/none device driver product. You
   would probably also want to supply an installation booklet that walks the
   customer through the installation and the deletion of the subsets.

2 The name of this SCP is NONE.scp and it copies the files associated
   with the static and loadable versions of the /dev/none device driver to
   a specific directory on the customer's system. It can also delete the
   subsets after they have been installed.

3 To install the software subsets associated with the /dev/none driver
   product, the system manager enters the value 1.

4 The ACT environment variable is set by setld when it invokes the SCP.
   In this SCP, the ACT environment variable can take the value POST_L or
   POST_D.

5 Specifies an ACT environment variable setting that indicates the tasks to
   be performed after loading the software subset. For the static
   /dev/none device driver, the kreg utility performs these tasks.

6 The kreg utility registers a device driver product by creating the
   /usr/sys/conf/.products.list file on the customer's system.
   This file contains registration information associated with the static
   device driver product.

In this call to `kreg`, the following flag and arguments are passed:

- The `-l` flag

  This flag indicates that the subset was loaded and it directs `kreg` to register this device driver product as a new kernel extension.

- The company name

  The company name is `EasyDriverInc`. The `kreg` utility places this name in the company name field of the customer's `/usr/sys/conf/.products.list` file.

- The software subset name

  The software subset name for this device driver product is `EASYDRVNONESTATIC200`. The subset name consists of the product code `EASYDRV`, the subset mnemonic `NONESTATIC`, and the 3-digit version code `200`. The `kreg` utility extracts information from the specified subset data and loads it into the customer's `/usr/sys/conf/.products.list` file.

- The directory name

  The directory on the customer's system where `kreg` copies the files associated with this driver product is `/usr/opt/none200`. The `kreg` utility places this directory in the driver files path field of the customer's `/usr/sys/conf/.products.list` file.

7 This message is displayed on the console terminal after the files contained on the kit have been copied to the appropriate directory.

8 To delete the software subsets associated with the `/dev/none` driver product that were previously installed, the system manager enters the value 2 at the prompt `Type the number corresponding to your choice [ ]`. The `ACT` environment variable is set to `POST_D` by `setld` when it invokes the SCP. The `POST_D` variable indicates the tasks to be performed when deleting the software subset. The `kreg` utility performs these tasks.

9 In this call to `kreg`, the following flag and argument are passed:

- The `-d` flag

  This flag deletes the entry for the specified layered product from the customer's `/usr/sys/conf/.products.list` file when the customer removes the subset from the system.

- The software subset name

  The software subset name, `EASYDRVNONESTATIC200`, indicates that the static `/dev/none` device driver product is to be removed from the customer's `/usr/sys/conf/.products.list` file.

10 This message is displayed on the console terminal after the entry for the device driver product has been removed from the customer's /usr/sys/conf/.products.list file.

11 To add the software subsets associated with the loadable /dev/none driver product, the system manager enters the value 3 at the prompt Type the number corresponding to your choice []. The ACT environment variable is set to POST_L by setld when it invokes the SCP. The POST_L variable indicates the tasks to be performed after loading the software subset.

For the loadable /dev/none device driver, the sysconfigdb utility performs these tasks.

12 The sysconfigdb utility maintains and manages the /etc/sysconfigtab database. For each driver product, this database contains such items as device connectivity information, the driver's major number requirements, the names and minor numbers of the device special files, and the permissions and directory name where the device special files reside.

In this call to sysconfigdb, the following flags and arguments are passed:

- The -a flag

   Specifies that sysconfigdb add the device driver entry to the customer's /etc/sysconfigtab database.

- The -f flag

   Specifies the flag that precedes the name of the stanza.loadable file fragment whose device driver entry is to be added to the /etc/sysconfigtab database. This flag is used with the -a flag.

- The stanza.loadable file fragment

   The kit developer at EasyDriver Incorporated specifies the path /usr/opt/none200/stanza.loadable to indicate the location of the stanza.loadable file fragment for the /dev/none device driver.

- The device driver name

   The kit developer at EasyDriver Incorporated specifies none as the name of the driver whose associated information is added to the /etc/sysconfigtab database. Note that this name is obtained from the *entry_name* field of the stanza.loadable file fragment, as described in Section 12.6.1.

13 The kit developer at EasyDriver Incorporated calls sysconfigdb a second time with the -on flag, which causes the loadable /dev/none device driver to be automatically loaded each time the customer reboots

the system. The name of the driver as specified in the
`stanza.loadable` file fragment follows the flag.

14. The kit developer at EasyDriver Incorporated uses the appropriate
commands to copy the loadable object file that has a file extension of
`.mod` to the `/subsys` directory.

15. The kit developer at EasyDriver Incorporated uses the appropriate
commands to create the device driver method file. This is accomplished
by linking the device driver method file associated with the driver product
to the `device.mth` file. In this SCP, the kit developer specifies a
device driver method file of `none.mth`.

16. The kit developer at EasyDriver Incorporated calls the `sysconfig`
utility with the `-c` flag, which configures the loadable `/dev/none`
device driver into the running system and creates the device special files.
The name of the driver as specified in the `stanza.loadable` file
follows the flag.

17. This message is displayed on the console terminal after `sysconfigdb`
and `sysconfig` have performed their tasks.

18. To delete the software subsets associated with the loadable `/dev/none`
driver product that were previously installed, the system manager enters
the value 4 at the prompt `Type the number corresponding to`
`your choice []`. The `ACT` environment variable is set to `POST_D`
by `setld` when it invokes the SCP. The `POST_D` variable indicates the
tasks to be performed when deleting the software subset.

The `sysconfig` and `sysconfigdb` utilities perform these tasks.

19. The kit developer at EasyDriver Incorporated calls the `sysconfig`
utility with the `-u` flag, which unconfigures the loadable `/dev/none`
device driver from the running system. The name of the driver as
specified in the `stanza.loadable` file fragment follows the flag.

20. The kit developer at EasyDriver Incorporated calls the `sysconfigdb`
utility with the `-off` flag, which causes the loadable `/dev/none`
device driver to not be automatically configured during an early phase of
system startup. It removes the `/dev/none` driver from the
`automatic` entry in the customer's `/etc/sysconfigtab` database.
The name of the driver as specified in the `stanza.loadable` file
fragment follows the flag.

21. The kit developer at EasyDriver Incorporated calls the `sysconfigdb`
utility with the `-d` flag, which deletes the loadable `/dev/none` device
driver from the customer's `/etc/sysconfigtab` database. The name
of the driver as specified in the `stanza.loadable` file fragment
follows the flag.

12.9.2 Subset Control Program for the /dev/cb Device Driver Product

The following example shows the SCP for the /dev/cb device driver product:

```
#!/sbin/sh 1
#
#
#    CB.scp - Install the files associated with the loadable and static
#             /dev/cb device driver product 2
#

echo "*********** /dev/cb Device Driver Product Installation Menu ***********"
echo "***********                                         ***********"
echo "1. Install the static /dev/cb device driver subset."
echo "2. Delete the static /dev/cb device driver subset."
echo "3. Install the loadable /dev/cb device driver subset."
echo "4. Delete the loadable /dev/cb device driver subset."

echo" Type the number corresponding to your choice [] " 3

read answer
case ${answer} in
   1)
   case "$ACT" in 4
   POST_L) 5

    # Register the files associated with the static /dev/cb
    # device driver product.
    kreg -l EasyDriverInc EASYDRVCBSTATIC100 /usr/opt/cb100 6

    # Reminder
    echo "The /dev/cb device driver is installed on your system."
    echo "Before your utilities can make use of the driver, you"
    echo "must build a new kernel by running doconfig." 7
    ;;
   2)
   POST_D) 8
   kreg -d EASYDRVCBSTATIC100 9

    echo "The /dev/cb device driver is no longer on the system." 10
    echo "Remember to build a new kernel to remove the /dev/cb driver"
    echo "functionality."

    ;;

   3)
   POST_L) 11
   # Add the files associated with the loadable /dev/cb device
   # driver product to the customer's sysconfigtab database
   sysconfigdb -a -f /usr/opt/cb100/stanza.loadable cb 12

    # Cause the /dev/cb device driver to be automatically loaded each time
    # the system reboots
    sysconfigdb -on cb 13

# Copy the cb.mod file to the /subsys directory. Create
# the cb.mth driver method by linking to device.mth
```

```
# /subsys/cb.mth -> /subsys/device.mth
cp /usr/opt/cb100/cb.mod /subsys/cb.mod 14
ln -s /subsys/device.mth /subsys/cb.mth 15

    # Load the /dev/cb device driver and create the device special files
    sysconfig -c cb 16

    echo "The /dev/cb device driver was added to your global stanza"
    echo "database (sysconfigtab) and will automatically be loaded"
    echo "each time the system reboots." 17

    4)
    POST_D) 18
    # Make sure the /dev/cb device driver is not currently loaded
    sysconfig -u cb 19

    # Remove the /dev/cb device driver from the automatic startup list
    sysconfigdb -off cb 20

    # Delete the /dev/cb device driver's stanza entry from the global
    # stanza database
    sysconfigdb -d cb 21
    ;;
esac
exit 0
```

1   The kit developer for EasyDriver Incorporated follows Digital's recommendation to write the SCP as a script for /sbin/sh. Note that the kit developer supplies a menu of choices for installing or deleting the subsets associated with the /dev/cb device driver product. You would probably also want to supply an installation booklet that walks the customer through the installation and the deletion of the subsets.

2   The name of this SCP is CB.scp and it copies the files associated with the static and loadable versions of the /dev/cb device driver to a specific directory on the customer's system. It can also delete the subsets after they have been installed.

3   To install the software subsets associated with the /dev/cb driver product, the system manager enters the value 1.

4   The ACT environment variable is set by setld when it invokes the SCP. In this SCP, the ACT environment variable can take the value POST_L or POST_D.

5   Specifies an ACT environment variable setting that indicates the tasks to be performed after loading the software subset. For the static /dev/cb device driver, the kreg utility performs these tasks.

6   The kreg utility registers a device driver product by creating the /usr/sys/conf/.products.list file on the customer's system. This file contains registration information associated with the static device driver product.

In this call to kreg, the following flag and arguments are passed:

- The -l flag

  This flag indicates that the subset was loaded and it directs kreg to register this device driver product as a new kernel extension.

- The company name

  The company name is EasyDriverInc. The kreg utility places this name in the company name field of the customer's /usr/sys/conf/.products.list file.

- The software subset name

  The software subset name for this device driver product is EASYDRVCBSTATIC100. The subset name consists of the product code EASYDRV, the subset mnemonic CBSTATIC, and the 3-digit version code 100. The kreg utility extracts information from the specified subset data and loads it into the customer's /usr/sys/conf/.products.list file.

- The directory name

  The directory on the customer's system where kreg copies the files associated with this driver product is /usr/opt/cb100. The kreg utility places this directory in the driver files path field of the customer's /usr/sys/conf/.products.list file.

7 This message is displayed on the console terminal after the files contained on the kit have been copied to the appropriate directory.

8 To delete the software subsets associated with the /dev/cb driver product that were previously installed, the system manager enters the value 2 at the prompt Type the number corresponding to your choice []. The ACT environment variable is set to POST_D by setld when it invokes the SCP. The POST_D variable indicates the tasks to be performed when deleting the software subset. The kreg utility performs these tasks.

9 In this call to kreg, the following flag and argument are passed:

- The -d flag

  This flag deletes the entry for the specified layered product from the customer's /usr/sys/conf/.products.list file when the customer removes the subset from the system.

- The software subset name

  The software subset name, EASYDRVCBSTATIC100, indicates that the static /dev/cb device driver product is to be removed from the customer's /usr/sys/conf/.products.list file.

10 This message is displayed on the console terminal after the entry for the device driver product has been removed from the customer's

`/usr/sys/conf/.products.list` file.

11 To add the software subsets associated with the loadable `/dev/cb` driver
product, the system manager enters the value 3 at the prompt `Type the`
`number corresponding to your choice []`. The ACT
environment variable is set to POST_L by `setld` when it invokes the
SCP. The POST_L variable indicates the tasks to be performed after
loading the software subset.

For the loadable `/dev/cb` device driver, the `sysconfigdb` utility
performs these tasks.

12 The `sysconfigdb` utility maintains and manages the
`/etc/sysconfigtab` database. For each driver product, this database
contains such items as device connectivity information, the driver's major
number requirements, the names and minor numbers of the device special
files, and the permissions and directory name where the device special
files reside.

In this call to `sysconfigdb`, the following flags and arguments are
passed:

- The `-a` flag

  Specifies that `sysconfigdb` add the device driver entry to the
  customer's `/etc/sysconfigtab` database.

- The `-f` flag

  Specifies the flag that precedes the name of the `stanza.loadable`
  file fragment whose device driver entry is to be added to the
  `/etc/sysconfigtab` database. This flag is used with the `-a` flag.

- The `stanza.loadable` file fragment

  The kit developer at EasyDriver Incorporated specifies the path
  `/usr/opt/cb100/stanza.loadable` to indicate the location
  of the `stanza.loadable` file fragment for the `/dev/cb` device
  driver.

- The device driver name

  The kit developer at EasyDriver Incorporated specifies cb as the
  name of the driver whose associated information is added to the
  `/etc/sysconfigtab` database. Note that this name is obtained
  from the *entry_name* field of the `stanza.loadable` file
  fragment, as described in Section 12.6.1.

13 The kit developer at EasyDriver Incorporated calls `sysconfigdb` a
second time with the `-on` flag, which causes the loadable `/dev/cb`
device driver to be automatically loaded each time the customer reboots
the system. The name of the driver as specified in the
`stanza.loadable` file fragment follows the flag.

[14] The kit developer at EasyDriver Incorporated uses the appropriate commands to copy the loadable object file that has a file extension of `.mod` to the `/subsys` directory.

[15] The kit developer at EasyDriver Incorporated uses the appropriate commands to create the device driver method file. This is accomplished by linking the device driver method file associated with the driver product to the `device.mth` file. In this SCP, the kit developer specifies a device driver method file of `cb.mth`.

[16] The kit developer at EasyDriver Incorporated calls the `sysconfig` utility with the `-c` flag, which configures the loadable `/dev/cb` device driver into the running system and creates the device special files. The name of the driver as specified in the `stanza.loadable` file follows the flag.

[17] This message is displayed on the console terminal after `sysconfigdb` and `sysconfig` have performed their tasks.

[18] To delete the software subsets associated with the loadable `/dev/cb` driver product that were previously installed, the system manager enters the value 4 at the prompt `Type the number corresponding to your choice []`. The `ACT` environment variable is set to `POST_D` by `setld` when it invokes the SCP. The `POST_D` variable indicates the tasks to be performed when deleting the software subset.

The `sysconfig` and `sysconfigdb` utilities perform these tasks.

[19] The kit developer at EasyDriver Incorporated calls the `sysconfig` utility with the `-u` flag, which unconfigures the loadable `/dev/cb` device driver from the running system. The name of the driver as specified in the `stanza.loadable` file fragment follows the flag.

[20] The kit developer at EasyDriver Incorporated calls the `sysconfigdb` utility with the `-off` flag, which causes the loadable `/dev/cb` device driver to not be automatically configured during an early phase of system startup. It removes the `/dev/cb` driver from the `automatic` entry in the customer's `/etc/sysconfigtab` database. The name of the driver as specified in the `stanza.loadable` file fragment follows the flag.

[21] The kit developer at EasyDriver Incorporated calls the `sysconfigdb` utility with the `-d` flag, which deletes the loadable `/dev/cb` device driver from the customer's `/etc/sysconfigtab` database. The name of the driver as specified in the `stanza.loadable` file fragment follows the flag.

Device Driver Configuration Examples 13

This chapter ties together the device driver configuration models presented in Chapter 11 and the device driver syntaxes and mechanisms presented in Chapter 12 by walking you through device driver configuration as it is accomplished by EasyDriver Incorporated. You can choose to follow this model or devise an alternate one that matches your device driver development environment. Figure 13-1 shows the steps the driver writer, kit developer, and system manager perform at EasyDriver Incorporated to configure the /dev/none and /dev/cb device drivers.

If you have access to the current version of the Digital UNIX operating system, see the README file in the /usr/examples/devicedriver directory for instructions on how to load and configure the loadable versions of the /dev/cb and /dev/none device drivers.

Figure 13-1: Device Driver Configuration as Done by EasyDriver Incorporated

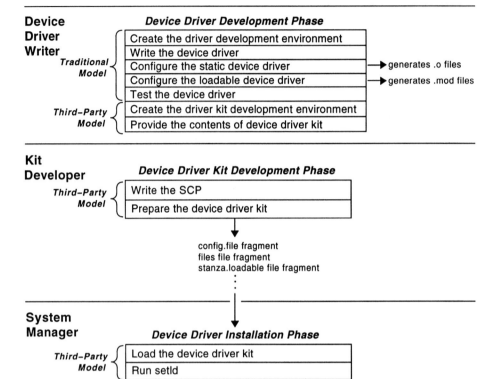

As the figure shows, EasyDriver Incorporated organizes its driver development into a:

- Device driver development phase
- Kit development phase
- Driver installation phase

Note that the figure identifies the audiences expected to complete each of the tasks. The figure also identifies which tasks are associated with the traditional and third-party device driver configuration models. The tasks associated with each phase are discussed in the following sections.

13.1 Device Driver Development Phase

The device driver writers at EasyDriver Incorporated perform the following tasks during the device driver development phase:

- Create the device driver development environment
- Write the device driver
- Configure the static device driver
- Configure the loadable device driver
- Test the device driver
- Create the device driver kit development environment
- Provide the contents of the device driver kit

13.1.1 Creating the Device Driver Development Environment

The driver writers at EasyDriver Incorporated create a device driver development environment following the traditional device driver configuration model discussed in Section 11.2. Section 11.2 discusses one possible directory structure for locating the files associated with the device driver.

Follow the guidelines presented in Section 11.2 to create a driver development environment suitable to your needs.

13.1.2 Writing the Device Driver

The driver writers at EasyDriver Incorporated use the techniques described in this book to write their device drivers. They use the guidelines presented in Section 2.1.2.1 for naming the device driver source file. For the /dev/none device driver, the source file is called none.c. For the /dev/cb device driver, the source file is called cb.c.

Follow the guidelines presented in Section 2.1.2.1 for naming your device driver source files.

13.1.3 Configuring the Static Device Driver

The driver writers at EasyDriver Incorporated configure the static versions of the /dev/none and /dev/cb device drivers by following the steps provided for the traditional device driver configuration model:

1. Make an entry in the tc_option_data.c table (TURBOchannel specific).
2. Compile and link the static device driver.

3. Back up the new kernel.

The steps described in the following sections apply to device drivers written for the TURBOchannel bus. These steps might differ for drivers written for other buses. See the bus-specific device driver manual on how to configure drivers for the specific bus, using the traditional model.

13.1.3.1   Step 1: Make an Entry in the tc_option Structure Array

The driver writers at EasyDriver Incorporated make an entry in the tc_option structure array, located in the file /usr/sys/data/tc_option_data.c.

The tc_option structure array provides a mapping between the device name in the read-only memory (ROM) on the hardware device module and the driver in the Digital UNIX kernel. This step is specific to drivers written for the TURBOchannel bus. Other buses may require some other task to be performed.

The following shows the tc_option structure array in the Digital-provided tc_option_data.c file:

```
struct tc_option tc_option [] =
{
/* module      driver     intr_b4    itr_aft          adpt    */
/* name        name       probe      attach    type   config  */
/* ------      ------     -------     -------   ----   ------  */

{ "PMTNV-AA", "nvtc",    0,          1,         'C',   0}, /* TCNVRAM */
{ "PMAP-AA ", "nvtc",    0,          1,         'C',   0}, /* TCNVRAM temp */
{ "PMAD-AA ", "ln",      0,          1,         'C',   0}, /* Lance */
{ "PMAF-AA ", "fza",     1,          1,         'C',   0}, /* FDDI */
{ "PMAF-FA ", "fta",     0,          1,         'C',   0}, /* FDDI */
{ "PMAZ-AA ", "asc",     0,          1,         'C',   0}, /* SCSI */
{ "PMAZ-DS ", "asc",     1,          1,         'A',   tscsiconf}, /* TCDS */
{ "PMAZB-AA", "asc",     1,          1,         'A',   tscsiconf}, /* TCDS */
{ "PMAZB-AB", "asc",     1,          1,         'A',   tscsiconf}, /* TCDS */
{ "PMAG-BA ", "fb",      0,          0,         'C',   0}, /* CFB */
{ "PMAG-AA ", "fb",      0,          0,         'C',   0}, /* MFB */
{ "PMAGB-BA", "fb",      0,          1,         'C',   0}, /* SFB */
{ "PMAG-RO ", "fb",      0,          0,         'C',   0}, /* RO*/
{ "PMAG-JA ", "fb",      0,          0,         'C',   0}, /* RO*/
{ "PMAG-CA ", "px",      0,          1,         'C',   0}, /* 2DA */
{ "PMAG-DA ", "px",      0,          1,         'C',   0}, /* LM-3DA */
{ "PMAG-FA ", "px",      0,          1,         'C',   0}, /* HE-3DA */
{ "PMAG-FB ", "px",      0,          1,         'C',   0}, /* HE+3DA */
{ "PMAGB-FA", "px",      0,          1,         'C',   0}, /* HE+3DA */
{ "PMAGB-FB", "px",      0,          1,         'C',   0}, /* HE+3DA */
{ "PMAGZ-PV", "pv",      0,          1,         'C',   0}, /* PV+3DA */
#ifdef mips
{ "PMABV-AA", "vba",     1,          1,         'A',   xviaconf}, /* VME */
{ "CITCA-AA", "ci",      0,          1,         'A',   tcciconf},/* CI */
#endif /* mips */


/*
```

```
* Do not delete any table entries above this line or your system
* will not configure properly.
*
* Add any new controllers or devices here.
* Remember, the module name must be blank padded to 8 bytes.
*/

    /*
%%%Used by mktcdata as placemarker for automatic installation
    */

/*
* Do not delete this null entry, which terminates the table or your
* system will not configure properly.
*/
{    "",                "" }                /* Null terminator in the table */
};
```

The items in the tc_option table have the following meanings:

module name
> In this column, you specify the device name in the ROM on the
> hardware device. You must blank-pad the names to 8 bytes.

driver name
> In this column, you specify the driver name as it appears in the system
> configuration file.

intr_b4 probe
> In this column, you specify whether the device needs interrupts enabled
> during execution of the driver's probe interface. A zero (0) value
> indicates that the device does not need interrupts enabled; a value of 1
> indicates that the device needs interrupts enabled.

itr_aft attach
> In this column, you specify whether the device needs interrupts enabled
> after the driver's probe and attach interfaces have completed. A
> zero (0) value indicates that the device does not need interrupts enabled;
> a value of 1 indicates that the device needs interrupts enabled.

type
> In this column, you specify the type of device: C (controller) or A
> (adapter).

adpt config
> If the device in the type column is A (adapter), you specify the name of
> the interface to configure the adapter. Otherwise, you specify the value
> zero (0).

The entries for the /dev/none and /dev/cb drivers are as follows:

```
{  "NONE    ", "none", 0, 1, 'C', 0}, /* None */
{  "CB      ", "cb", 0, 1, 'C', 0}, /* cb */
```

Make similar entries in this table if your device driver operates on the TURBOchannel bus.

13.1.3.2 Step 2: Compile and Link the Static Device Driver

To compile and link the static device driver, the driver writers at EasyDriver Incorporated perform the following tasks:

- Back up files
- Make an entry in the system configuration file
- Add the driver source to the files file
- Declare the device driver entry points in /usr/sys/io/common/conf.c
- Modify the bdevsw or cdevsw table
- Run the config program
- Create a device special file
- Create a new kernel

Each of these tasks is discussed in the following sections.

Step 2a: Back Up Files

The driver writers at EasyDriver Incorporated use the traditional device driver configuration model to configure their device drivers during the initial stages of development. Because they will later test the third-party device driver configuration model, the driver writers do not want to make permanent edits to their system configuration file, files file, and conf.c file. If your driver development environment resembles that of EasyDriver Incorporated, you will probably want to back up these files. The following shows one way to accomplish this task:

```
%cd /usr/sys/conf/CONRAD
%cp CONRAD CONRAD.save
%cd /usr/sys/conf/alpha
%cp files files.save
%cd /usr/sys/io/common
%cp conf.c conf.c.save
```

In this example, CONRAD is the name of the system configuration file. You replace this name with the name of your system configuration file.

Step 2b: Make an Entry in the System Configuration File

Make an entry in /usr/sys/conf/*NAME*, the system configuration file, to add the device to the system. The *NAME* variable represents the name of the system you want to configure, for example, CONRAD. Because the /dev/none and /dev/cb drivers are developed for use on the TURBOchannel bus, the device entry must follow the syntaxes associated with the TURBOchannel, as follows:

```
controller none0 at tc0 slot?
controller cb0 at tc0 slot? vector cbintr
```

You specify a valid syntax for the device entry associated with the bus your driver operates on.

Step 2c: Add the Driver Source to the files File

Make an entry in /usr/sys/conf/alpha/files as either Binary (no driver sources are supplied) or Notbinary (driver sources are supplied). The following example shows the entries for the /dev/none and /dev/cb device drivers without source code:

```
io/EasyInc/none.c optional none device-driver Binary
io/EasyInc/cb.c optional cb device-driver Binary
```

Replace EasyInc with your directory name, none.c and cb.c with your device driver source file name, and none and cb with your device name.

The following example shows the entries for the /dev/none and /dev/cb device drivers with source code:

```
io/EasyInc/none.c  optional  none device-driver Notbinary
io/EasyInc/cb.c  optional  cb device-driver Notbinary
```

Replace EasyInc with your directory name, none.c and cb.c with your device driver source file name, and none and cb with your device name.

Step 2d: Declare the Device Driver Entry Points in conf.c

Declare the device driver entry points for your device by editing the /usr/sys/io/common/conf.c file. The following example shows the device driver interface declarations for the /dev/none and /dev/cb device drivers:

```
#include <none.h>
#if NNONE > 0
int     noneopen(),noneclose(),noneread(),nonewrite(),noneioctl();
int     nonereset();
#else
#define noneopen        nodev
#define noneclose       nodev
#define noneread        nodev
```

```
#define nonewrite          nodev
#define noneioctl          nodev
#define nonereset          nodev
#ENDIF

   .
   .
   .

#include <cb.h>
#if NCB > 0
int     cbopen(),cbclose(),cbread(),cbwrite(),cbioctl();
#else
#define cbopen             nodev
#define cbclose            nodev
#define cbread             nodev
#define cbwrite            nodev
#define cbioctl            nodev
#ENDIF
```

First, you include the device driver header file that was created by `config`. The `config` program creates this header file by using the name of the controller or device that you specified in the system configuration file. In this example, the header files are `none.h` and `cb.h`. These names indicate that the characters ''none'' and ''cb'' were previously specified for these devices in the system configuration file. Replace `none.h` and `cb.h` with the name of the device driver header file created by `config` for your device driver.

Next, you declare the device driver interfaces that were defined in the `bdevsw` or `cdevsw` table if the device constant (or constants) are greater than zero (0), which indicates that the device was actually in the system configuration file. The device constant is also created by `config` in the following way:

- It locates the name of the controller or device that you specified in the system configuration file.

- It converts the lowercase name to uppercase.

- It appends the uppercase name to the letter ''N.''

In this example, the device constants are NNONE and NCB and the `none` and `cb` interfaces defined in the `cdevsw` table are declared to be of type `int`. Otherwise, if the device is not actually in the system configuration file, you declare the entry points as `nodev`.

Replace the device constants NNONE and NCB with the device constants that `config` creates for your device driver. In addition, replace the driver interface declarations for the `/dev/none` and `/dev/cb` device drivers with declarations for your device driver interfaces.

Step 2e: Modify the bdevsw or cdevsw Table

To modify the `bdevsw` or `cdevsw` table, edit the
`/usr/sys/io/common/conf.c` file and search for `struct bdevsw` or
`struct cdevsw`. Add your entries to the end of the table. The easiest
way to add entries to the tables is to copy the previous entry, change the
driver entry point names, and increment the comment by 1. The number in
your comment is your device major number. Keep this number for use in a
subsequent step. The following example shows the entries for the
`/dev/none` and `/dev/cb` device drivers along with the entry that precedes
them:

```
struct cdevsw    cdevsw[MAX_CDEVSW] =
{
    .
    .
    .
/* STREAMS clone device */
{clone_open,    nodev,    nodev,              nodev, /*32*/
 nodev,         nodev,    nodev,              0,
 nodev,         nodev,    DEV_FUNNEL_NULL, NULL, NULL },
    .
    .
    .
/* none device */
{noneopen,     noneclose,    noneread,    nonewrite, /*33*/
 noneioctl,    nodev,        nodev,    0,
 nodev,        nodev,        DEV_FUNNEL_NULL, NULL, NULL },
/* cb device */
{cbopen,       cbclose,      cbread,       cbwrite, /*34*/
 cbioctl,    nodev,      nodev      0,
 nodev,    nodev,      DEV_FUNNEL_NULL, NULL, NULL},
    .
    .
    .
```

The driver writers at EasyDriver Incorporated record the device major
numbers 33 and 34. Replace the device major numbers 33 and 34 with the
device major number associated with your driver entry.

Step 2f: Run config on the System Configuration File

Run `config` on the system configuration file from the `/usr/sys/conf`
directory.

In the following example, the driver writers at EasyDriver Incorporated run config on the system called CONRAD:

```
%cd /sys/conf
%./config CONRAD
```

Replace CONRAD with the system configuration file associated with your system.

Step 2g: Create a Device Special File

Create a device special file for your device, using the mknod command. The following example shows the entries for the devices associated with the /dev/none and /dev/cb device drivers:

```
% mknod /dev/none c 33 0 1
% mknod /dev/cb c 34 1 2
```

1 The first entry describes the none device. The letter c represents character device, as opposed to b for block device. The number 33 is the major device number the driver writers at EasyDriver Incorporated recorded when they added the device to the cdevsw table. The value zero (0) is the minor number associated with this device.

2 The second entry describes the CB device. The number 34 is the major device number the driver writers at EasyDriver Incorporated recorded when they added the device to the cdevsw table. The value 1 is the minor number associated with this device.

Replace none and CB with the name associated with your device. In addition, replace the numbers 33 and 34 with the device major number you recorded in Step 2e.

Note

Before you use the mknod command to create a device special file, determine if there are any existing device special files of the same type with the same major number as your device. If yes, the device special files are probably associated with a device driver that is no longer configured into the kernel. In this case, ensure that the corresponding driver is no longer in use.

For example, suppose you create a device special file called /dev/foo at character major number 38 and minor number zero (0). Before you create this device special file with mknod, perform a check as follows:

```
# cd /dev
# ls -l | grep ^c | grep 38
crw-rw-rw-   1 root      system     38,     0 Apr 13 10:40 fax
```

This check tells you that there is already a device special file called fax that conflicts with your device special file. Verify that the driver associated with /dev/fax is not being used on your system. If not, delete the /dev/fax device special file and issue the mknod command as follows:

```
# mknod foo c 30 0
```

You need to delete these stale /dev entries corresponding to previously configured drivers to prevent unintended access to your driver. For example, your driver /dev/foo might be a terminal type device driver while /dev/fax might be a disk type driver. If any program were to open and start using /dev/fax, the commands would go to /dev/foo through the cdevsw table and cause unexpected behavior in your driver (for example, system panics).

One of the advantages of using the automated driver configuration process is that you do not need to worry about stale /dev entries because the automated tools perform these checks automatically.

Step 2h: Create a New Kernel

Create a new kernel by going to the /usr/sys/NAME directory, which was created by config in Step 2f. The NAME in the directory path represents the name of the system configuration file.

The driver writers at EasyDriver Incorporated specify the following:

```
%cd /usr/sys/CONRAD
%make depend
%make
```

Replace CONRAD with the system configuration file name associated with your system. Errors can occur when you configure a device driver into a kernel from a binary (using the Binary keyword) object build. These error messages might occur from the system configuration file, files file, or the conf.c file. Device driver syntax and code errors can occur when you configure a device driver into a kernel from a source (using the Notbinary keyword) build.

13.1.3.3 Step 3: Back Up the New Kernel

If a new kernel was built successfully, you may still want to back up the existing kernel and then place the new kernel in /vmunix, as in the following example:

```
% mv /vmunix /vmunix.sav
% cp vmunix /vmunix
```

Use the following steps from Section 13.1.3.2 for specific modifications:

- Start with step 2g after modifying any driver source code.
- Start with step 2e to add a new device.
- Perform steps 2a, 2d, 2g, and 3 to change vectors.
- Perform steps 2c, 2d, 2e, 2g, and 3 to add entry points.

13.1.4 Configuring the Loadable Device Driver

The driver writers at EasyDriver Incorporated now configure the loadable versions of the /dev/none and /dev/cb device drivers by following the steps provided for the traditional device driver configuration model:

1. Create a stanza.loadable file fragment.
2. Compile and link the device driver.
3. Run the sysconfigdb utility.
4. Run the sysconfig utility.

The steps described in the following sections apply to device drivers written for the TURBOchannel bus. These steps might differ for drivers written for other buses. See the bus-specific device driver manual on how to configure drivers for the specific bus, using the traditional model.

13.1.4.1 Step 1: Create a stanza.loadable File Fragment

Create a stanza.loadable file fragment for each of your driver products. Section 12.6 discusses the format and syntaxes associated with the stanza.loadable file fragment. The driver writers at EasyDriver Incorporated create the following stanza.loadable file fragment for the /dev/none device driver:

```
none:
        Subsystem_Description = none device driver
        Module_Type = Dynamic
        Module_Path = /usr/opt/ESA100/none.mod
        Module_Config_Name = none
        Module_Config1 = controller none0 at tc?
        Module_Config2 = controller none0 at eisa?
        Module_Config3 = controller none0 at pci?
```

```
Device_Dir = /dev
Device_Char_Major = Any
Device_Char_Minor = 0
Device_Char_Files = none
Device_User = root
Device_Group = 0
Device_Mode = 666
```

They also create the following `stanza.loadable` file fragment for the
`/dev/cb` device driver:

```
cb:
        Subsystem_Description = cb device driver
        Module_Type = Dynamic
        Module_Config_Name = cb
        Module_Config1 = controller cb0 at tc?
        Module_Path = /usr/opt/ESB100/cb.mod
        Device_Dir = /dev
        Device_Char_Major = Any
        Device_Char_Minor = 0
        Device_Char_Files = cb
        Device_User = root
        Device_Group = 0
        Device_Mode = 666
```

Replace the entries for the `/dev/none` and `/dev/cb` device drivers with
appropriate entries for your device driver.

13.1.4.2   Step 2: Compile and Link the Device Driver

To compile and link the loadable device driver, perform the following tasks:

- Add the driver source to the `files` file.
- Make an entry in the `BINARY` system configuration file.
- Run the `config` program.
- Build the driver loadable modules.

Each of these tasks is discussed in the following sections.

Step 2a: Add the Driver Source to the files File

Make an entry in `/usr/sys/conf/alpha/files` as `Binary` (no driver
sources are supplied). The following example shows the entries for the

/dev/none and /dev/cb device drivers without source code:

```
io/EasyInc/none.c optional none if_dynamic none Binary
io/EasyInc/cb.c optional cb if_dynamic cb Binary
```

Note that the specification for a loadable driver in the files file is identical to that for a static driver except for the use of the if_dynamic keyword followed by the *key_string* keyword. This keyword marks the specified device driver source files so that the resulting object files can be built as either static or loadable.

Replace EasyInc with your directory name, none.c and cb.c with your device driver source file name, and none and cb with your device name.

Step 2b: Make an Entry in the BINARY System Configuration File

For the static versions of the /dev/none and /dev/cb device drivers, the driver writers at EasyDriver Incorporated made appropriate entries in the system configuration file that added their associated devices to the system. The config program uses these entries to create a system configuration tree and interrupt handler description for the static kernel.

You do not describe loadable device drivers in the system configuration file in the same way as for static drivers. The reason for this is loadable drivers are dynamically added to the system configuration tree and their interrupt handlers are dynamically registered. In addition, entries for loadable drivers are specified in the BINARY system configuration file. The following syntax shows the entries in the BINARY system configuration file for the /dev/none and /dev/cb device drivers:

```
pseudo-device none dynamic none
pseudo-device cb dynamic cb
```

The use of the pseudo-device keyword ensures that the appropriate makefile is generated. The dynamic keyword specifies that the device driver is built as a dynamic loadable module (loadable driver).

Replace none and cb with your device name.

Step 2c: Run config on the System Configuration File

Run config on the BINARY system configuration file from the /usr/sys/conf directory to create the BINARY Makefile. This Makefile specifies the operations needed to build the loadable module for the driver. These operations include the syntax needed to compile and link the driver.

```
%cd /sys/conf
%./config -s BINARY
```

Step 2d: Build the Driver Loadable Modules

After the `makefile` has been rebuilt in `/usr/sys/BINARY`, you build the driver loadable module by calling `make` followed by the device driver name, as specified in the `stanza.loadable` file fragment. To build the driver loadable modules for the `/dev/none` and `/dev/cb` device drivers, the driver writers at EasyDriver Incorporated specify the following commands:

```
%cd /usr/sys/BINARY
%make none
%make cb
```

Upon successfully completing the previously described steps, the driver writers at EasyDriver Incorporated notice two device driver loadable subsystems in `/usr/sys/BINARY`: `none.mod` and `cb.mod`.

Replace `none` and `cb` with the name of your device driver. Note the resulting loadable modules, which are of the form *xx*.`mod` , where *xx* represents the name of your device driver and `.mod` is the extension that identifies the loadable module.

13.1.4.3   Step 3: Run the sysconfigdb Utility

You use the `sysconfigdb` utility to manage and maintain `/etc/sysconfigtab`, the global stanza database. This database contains the information specified in the `stanza.loadable` file fragment for the loadable driver. To add the information contained in the `stanza.loadable` file fragments for the `/dev/none` and `/dev/cb` device drivers, the driver writers at EasyDriver Incorporated specify the following commands:

```
%sysconfigdb -a -f /usr/opt/ESA100/stanza.loadable none
%sysconfigdb -a -f /usr/opt/ESB100/stanza.loadable cb
```

The `-a` and `-f` flags cause `sysconfigdb` to add the information contained in the `stanza.loadable` file fragments for the `/dev/none` and `/dev/cb` device drivers to EasyDriver Incorporated's `/etc/sysconfigtab` database. See the *Reference Pages Section 8* for additional information on the `sysconfigdb` utility and its associated flags.

Replace the paths specified in the example with the path that identifies the location of your `stanza.loadable` file fragment. In addition, replace `none` and `cb` with your device driver name.

13.1.4.4 Step 4: Run the sysconfig Utility

To dynamically configure the device driver and create the corresponding device special files, use the `sysconfig` utility. To dynamically configure the `/dev/none` and `/dev/cb` device drivers and create their corresponding device special files, the driver writers at EasyDriver Incorporated specify the following commands:

```
%sysconfig -c none
%sysconfig -c cb
```

The `-c` flag causes `sysconfig` to configure the `/dev/none` and `/dev/cb` device drivers into the running system and create the device special files. See the *Reference Pages Section 8* for additional information on the `sysconfig` utility and its associated flags.

Using the previous example as a guide, you type the exact syntax and replace `none` and `cb` with your device driver name.

To verify that their device drivers are currently configured, the driver writers at EasyDriver Incorporated specify the following command:

```
%sysconfig -q none
%sysconfig -q cb
```

The `-q` flag causes `sysconfig` to display information about the `/dev/none` and `/dev/cb` device drivers. Using the previous example as a guide, you type the exact syntax and replace `none` and `cb` with the name(s) of your device driver(s).

To iteratively develop the loadable driver, you can unload the driver, make changes to the device driver source, compile, and then load the driver again. You can unload the driver by using the `sysconfig` utility as follows:

```
%sysconfig -u none
```

To rebuild the loadable driver, follow Step 2d: Build the Driver Loadable Modules. To reload the loadable driver, follow Step 4: Run the sysconfig Utility.

Note

A number of failure conditions can occur when you use `sysconfig -c` to dynamically configure the device driver. One failure condition occurs as a result of unresolved references that exist in the device driver loadable module. The `kloadsrv` utility (which the `sysconfig` utility calls) returns a simple error condition that describes the link problem. However, `kloadsrv` does not generate a detailed list of unresolved symbols or other error conditions. To understand and correct failure conditions related to using `sysconfig -c`, do the following:

- Run the `sysconfig` utility with `kloadsrv` debugging enabled. This debugging enabled feature allows `kloadsrv` to report unresolved references and other lodable subsystem failures. To perform this debugging enabled task, specify the `-v` option. The following example shows how the driver writers at EasyDriver Incorporated specify this option for the `/dev/none` driver:

  ```
  sysconfig -v -c none
  ```

- Use the `nm(1)` utility on the loadable module to search for undefined symbols. The following example shows one way to use the `nm` utility:

  ```
  nm none.mod | grep U
  ```

  Verify that these symbols are defined on the static kernel by also using `nm` on `/vmunix` and by searching for the symbols that were undefined in the loadable module.

- Follow the steps for configuring a static device driver to correct any link-time errors in the device driver. Section 13.1.3 discusses how to configure a static device driver.

13.1.5 Testing the Device Driver

The driver writers at EasyDriver Incorporated test the device driver to ensure that it works with the associated utilities on the Digital UNIX operating system. They repeat the previously described tasks until the device driver works. This ends the device driver development phase.

You should perform similar testing.

13.1.6 Creating the Device Driver Kit Development Environment

The driver writers at EasyDriver Incorporated are now ready to create the device driver kit development environment that was discussed in Section 11.1.2. Create your driver kit development environment by following the recommendations provided in that section.

13.1.7 Providing the Contents of the Device Driver Kit

The driver writers at EasyDriver Incorporated plan to supply their customers with the static and loadable binary versions of the `/dev/none` and `/dev/cb` device drivers. Thus, they provide to their kit developers the following file fragments and files that become the contents of the device driver kit:

- `config.file` file fragment
- `files` file fragment
- `stanza.loadable` file fragment
- `stanza.static` file fragment
- Device driver objects
- Device driver loadable modules

Because the driver writers at EasyDriver Incorporated are shipping the binary versions of the device drivers, they do not provide the header or source files for the `/dev/none` and `/dev/cb` device drivers. Note, also, that they are not supplying any `name_data.c` files because they did not dynamically allocate any data structures. See Table 11-1 in Section 11.1.3 for a summary of the files and file fragments supplied to the kit developer, based on whether the driver is shipped in source or binary versions.

The following sections show the contents of these files as they apply to the driver products for EasyDriver Incorporated.

13.1.7.1 Providing the Contents of the config.file File Fragment

For the static binary versions of the `/dev/none` and `/dev/cb` device drivers, the driver writers at EasyDriver Incorporated provide the following `config.file` file fragment to their kit developers:

```
# Entries in config.file for none and CB devices

controller none0 at tc?
controller cb0   at tc? vector cbintr
```

Using this example as a guide, create a `config.file` file fragment and specify the appropriate syntax that describes your device.

13.1.7.2 Providing the Contents of the files File Fragment

For the static binary versions of the `/dev/none` and `/dev/cb` device drivers, the driver writers at EasyDriver Incorporated provide the following `files` file fragment to their kit developers:

```
# This example illustrates the third-party model
# by showing a files file fragment for static
# drivers developed by EasyDriver Incorporated.

ESA100/none.c standard none if_dynamic none Binary

ESB100/cb.c standard cb device-driver if_dynamic cb Binary
```

Using this example as a guide, create a `files` file fragment by using the keyword syntax shown in the example and replacing `none.c` and `cb.c` with your device driver source file name and `none` and `cb` with your device name.

13.1.7.3   Providing the Contents of the stanza.loadable File Fragment

For the loadable binary versions of the `/dev/none` and `/dev/cb` device drivers, the driver writers at EasyDriver Incorporated provide the following `stanza.loadable` file fragment to their kit developers:

```
none:
        Subsystem_Description = none device driver
        Module_Type = Dynamic
        Module_Path = /usr/opt/ESA100/none.mod
        Module_Config_Name = none
        Module_Config1 = controller none0 at tc?
        Module_Config2 = controller none0 at eisa?
        Module_Config3 = controller none0 at pci?
        Device_Dir = /dev
        Device_Char_Major = Any
        Device_Char_Minor = 0
        Device_Char_Files = none
        Device_User = root
        Device_Group = 0
        Device_Mode = 666


cb:
        Subsystem_Description = cb device driver
        Module_Type = Dynamic
        Module_Config_Name = cb
        Module_Config1 = controller cb0 at tc?
        Module_Path = /usr/opt/ESB100/cb.mod
        Device_Dir = /dev
        Device_Char_Major = Any
        Device_Char_Minor = 0
        Device_Char_Files = cb
        Device_User = root
        Device_Group = 0
        Device_Mode = 666
```

Using this example as a guide, create a `stanza.loadable` file fragment by using the keyword syntax shown in the example and replacing the values with those specific to your device and device driver.

13.1.7.4   Providing the Contents of the stanza.static File Fragment

For the static binary versions of the `/dev/none` and `/dev/cb` device drivers, the driver writers at EasyDriver Incorporated provide the following `stanza.static` file fragment to their kit developers:

```
none:
        Subsystem_Description = none device driver
        Module_Config_Name = none
        Device_Char_Major = Any
        Device_Char_Minor = 0
        Device_Char_Files = none
        Device_Char_Open = noneopen
        Device_Char_Close = noneclose
        Device_Char_Read = noneread
        Device_Char_Write = nonewrite
        Device_Char_Ioctl = noneioctl
        Device_Char_Stop = nulldev
        Device_Char_Reset = nulldev
        Device_Char_Ttys = 0
        Device_Char_Select = nodev
        Device_Char_Mmap = nodev
        Device_Char_Funnel = DEV_FUNNEL_NULL
        Device_Char_Segmap = NULL
        Device_Char_Flags = NULL



cb:
        Subsystem_Description = cb device driver
        Module_Config_Name = cb
        Device_Char_Major = Any
        Device_Char_Minor = 0
        Device_Char_Files = cb
        Device_Char_Open = cbopen
        Device_Char_Close = cbclose
        Device_Char_Read = cbread
        Device_Char_Write = cbwrite
        Device_Char_Ioctl = cbioctl
        Device_Char_Stop = nulldev
        Device_Char_Reset = nulldev
        Device_Char_Ttys = 0
        Device_Char_Select = nodev
        Device_Char_Mmap = nodev
        Device_Char_Funnel = DEV_FUNNEL_NULL
        Device_Char_Segmap = NULL
        Device_Char_Flags = NULL
```

Using this example as a guide, create a `stanza.static` file fragment by using the keyword syntax shown in the example and replacing the values with those specific to your device and device driver.

13.1.7.5 Providing the Device Driver Object Files

For the static binary versions of the /dev/none and /dev/cb device
drivers, the driver writers at EasyDriver Incorporated provide the following
device driver object files. These object files were created as a result of
following the steps beginning in Section 13.1.3.1.

- none.o

- cb.o

Using this example as a guide, the object files you supply should have the
name of your device driver(s) with .o extensions.

13.1.7.6 Providing the Device Driver Loadable Modules

For the loadable binary versions of the /dev/none and /dev/cb device
drivers, the driver writers at EasyDriver Incorporated provide the following
device driver loadable modules. These loadable modules were created as a
result of following the steps beginning in Section 13.1.4.1.

- none.mod

- cb.mod

Using this example as a guide, the device driver loadable modules you
supply should have the name of your device driver(s) with .mod extensions.

13.2 Device Driver Kit Development Phase

The kit developer at EasyDriver Incorporated performs the following tasks
during the device driver kit development phase:

- Writes the SCP

- Prepares the device driver kit

13.2.1 Writing the SCP

As part of the kit development phase, the kit developer at EasyDriver
Incorporated writes a subset control program (SCP) such as the one described
in Section 12.9. Your kit developers can use that example as a guide for
writing their own SCPs. In addition, they can refer to the *Programming
Support Tools* book for details on writing an SCP.

13.2.2 Preparing the Device Driver Kit

As part of the kit development phase, the kit developer at EasyDriver
Incorporated prepares the device driver kit, following the guidelines
presented in Section 11.1.4. This section refers to the *Programming Support
Tools* book, which provides complete details about preparing software

distribution kits that are compatible with the `setld` utility.

Your kit developers can also follow the guidelines presented in that section to prepare their device driver kits.

13.3 Device Driver Installation Phase

The system manager at EasyDriver Incorporated performs the following tasks to install the `/dev/none` and `/dev/cb` device drivers:

- Restores the backed-up files
- Loads the device driver kit
- Runs the `setld` utility

13.3.1 Restoring the Backed-Up Files

The driver writers at EasyDriver Incorporated previously used the traditional device driver configuration model to configure their device drivers during the initial stages of development. They backed up their system configuration file, `files` file, and `conf.c` file, to avoid making permanent edits. Before loading the device driver kit, the system manager at EasyDriver Incorporated restores the previously backed-up files. If you previously backed up these files, you will probably want to restore them at this time. The following shows one way to accomplish this task:

```
%cd /usr/sys/conf/CONRAD
%mv CONRAD.save CONRAD
%cd /usr/sys/conf/alpha
%mv files.save files
%cd /usr/sys/io/common
%mv conf.c.save conf.c
```

Using this example as a guide, follow the instructions exactly except that you should replace CONRAD with the name of your system configuration file.

13.3.2 Loading the Device Driver Kit

The system manager at EasyDriver Incorporated loads the device driver kit, following instructions provided by the device driver writers and kit developer. The system manager ensures that the instructions are clear and concise and that the installation of the device drivers is successful.

You can perform similar testing by having your system manager install the device driver kit. You can also provide instructions on how to install the kit.

13.3.3   Running the setld Utility

The system manager at EasyDriver Incorporated is instructed to type the following command:

```
setld -l /dev/rmt0h
```

The `setld` utility invokes the subset control program (SCP) that copies the driver-related files from the kit to the customer's system. The driver writers at EasyDriver Incorporated created the SCP that was discussed in Section 12.9. That SCP displays a prompt that asks whether to install the static or loadable version of the `/dev/cb` device driver. If the static version is selected, the SCP calls the `kreg` utility, which does the following:

- Registers the device driver product by creating the `/usr/sys/conf/.products.list` file on the system. This file contains registration information associated with the static device driver product.

- Loads the data that controls how to include the device driver product in the kernel build process.

After these tasks are completed, the SCP instructs you to run `doconfig` to build a new kernel and thus make the `/dev/cb` driver available to the system utilities. The driver writers at EasyDriver Incorporated run `doconfig`, which automatically does all of the tasks described in the traditional model.

If the loadable version is selected, the SCP calls the `sysconfigdb` utility, which does the following:

- Adds the files associated with the loadable `/dev/cb` device driver product to the `/etc/sysconfigtab` database

- Causes the `/dev/cb` device driver to be automatically loaded each time the system reboots

The SCP also calls the `sysconfig` utility, which does the following:

- Loads the `/dev/cb` device driver and creates the device special files

- Displays a prompt indicating that the `/dev/cb` device driver was added to the `/etc/sysconfigtab` database and that the loadable driver will automatically be loaded each time the system reboots

Part 7

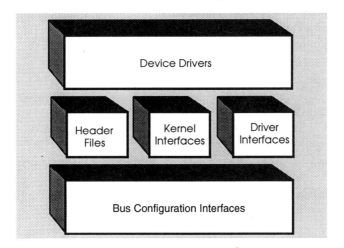

Header Files Related to Device Drivers 14

This chapter describes:

- Conventions for header files that device drivers use
- Header files that device drivers use

14.1 Conventions for Header Files

The descriptions of the header files associated with device drivers are presented in alphabetical order and in reference (man) page style. The descriptions can include the following sections.

Name

This section lists the name of the header file along with a summary description of its contents.

Location

This section presents the pathname for the header file. The pathname makes it easier for you to locate specific header files.

Description

This section briefly describes the contents of the header file.

When to Include

This section explains when to include a header file for block and character drivers.

Of Special Interest

This section lists specific structures, macros, constant values, and so forth that are of interest to device driver writers.

Related Information

This section lists related kernel interfaces, structures, system calls, and so forth.

14.2 Header Files

Table 14-1 lists the header files related to device drivers, along with short descriptions of their contents. For convenience, the files are listed in alphabetical order. Note that device drivers should include header files that use the relative pathname instead of the explicit pathname. For example, although buf.h resides in /usr/sys/include/sys/buf.h, device drivers should include it as:

```
<sys/buf.h>
```

Not all of the header files reside in <sys>. The following include files reside in other directories:

```
<kern/lock.h>
<hal/cpuconf.h>
<io/common/handler.h>
```

Table 14-1: Summary Descriptions of Header Files

Header File	Contents
<sys/buf.h>	Defines the buf structure.
<sys/conf.h>	Defines the bdevsw (block device switch) and cdevsw (character device switch) tables.
<machine/cpu.h>	Defines structures and constants related to the CPU.
<io/common/devdriver.h>	Defines the structures, constants, and external interfaces that device drivers and the autoconfiguration software use.
<io/common/devdriver_loadable.h>	Defines constants and declares external functions associated with loadable drivers.
<io/common/devio.h>	Defines common structures and definitions for device drivers and ioctl requests.
<sys/disklabel.h>	Defines structures and macros that operate on Digital UNIX disk labels.
<sys/errno.h>	Defines the error codes that a device driver returns to a user process.
<sys/fcntl.h>	Defines I/O mode flags that user programs supply to open and fcntl system calls.
<sys/ioctl.h>	Defines commands for ioctl interfaces in different device drivers.
<io/common/iotypes.h>	Defines constants that 64-bit conversions use.
<sys/kernel.h>	Defines global variables that the kernel uses.

Table 14-1: (continued)

Header File	Contents
<kern/lock.h>	Defines simple and complex lock structures.
<sys/malloc.h>	Defines kernel memory allocator-related information.
<sys/map.h>	Defines structures associated with resource allocation maps.
<sys/mman.h>	Defines constants associated with the mmap kernel interface.
<sys/mode.h>	Defines constants that driver interfaces use.
<sys/mtio.h>	Defines commands and structures for magnetic tape operations.
<sys/param.h>	Defines constants and interfaces that the kernel uses.
<sys/poll.h>	Defines polling bit masks.
<sys/proc.h>	Defines the proc structure, which defines a user process.
<kern/sched_prim.h>	Defines scheduling interfaces.
<sys/security.h>	Defines structures, constants, and data types that UNIX security software uses.
<sys/select.h>	Defines select-related data structures and interfaces.
<sys/sysconfig.h>	Defines operation codes and data structures used in loadable device driver configuration.
<sys/systm.h>	Defines generic kernel global variables.
<kern/task.h>	Defines structures that tasks use.
<kern/thread.h>	Defines structures that kernel threads use.
<sys/time.h>	Contains structures and symbolic names that time-related interfaces use.
<sys/types.h>	Defines system data types and major and minor device interfaces.
<sys/uio.h>	Contains the definition of the uio structure.
<sys/user.h>	Defines the user structure.
<sys/vm.h>	Contains a sequence of include statements that includes all of the virtual memory-related files.
<sys/vmmac.h>	Contains definitions for byte conversions.
<kern/zalloc.h>	Defines zone kernel memory allocator-related information.

Name

buf.h – Defines the buf structure

Location

/usr/sys/include/sys/buf.h

Description

The buf.h file defines the buf structure used to pass I/O requests to the strategy interface of a block device driver. Character device drivers can also use the buf structure, typically in the xxstrategy interface.

When to Include

You include the buf.h file in block device drivers because they use file system block-sized buffers from a buffer cache supplied by the kernel to perform I/O.

Of Special Interest

Items of interest to device driver writers are:

- The buf structure
- The BUF_LOCK macro
- The BUF_UNLOCK macro
- Flag definitions for the b_flags member of the buf structure

Related Information

Section 15.2, Kernel Support Interfaces: BUF_LOCK, BUF_UNLOCK

Chapter 16, Structures Related to Device Drivers: buf

Name

conf.h – Defines the bdevsw (block device switch) and cdevsw (character device switch) tables

Location

/usr/sys/include/sys/conf.h

Description

The conf.h file defines the bdevsw (block device switch) and cdevsw (character device switch) tables. This file is included in the source file /usr/sys/io/common/conf.c.

When to Include

You should include the conf.h file in loadable block and character device drivers because these drivers later add driver entry points to the bdevsw and cdevsw arrays declared and initialized by Digital in the /usr/sys/io/common/conf.c file.

Of Special Interest

Items of interest to device driver writers are:

- The bdevsw table
- The cdevsw table
- The define for DEV_FUNNEL_NULL
- The define for DEV_FUNNEL

You use the defines to initialize the d_funnel member of the bdevsw or cdevsw structure.

Related Information

Chapter 16, Structures Related to Device Drivers: bdevsw, cdevsw

Name

cpu.h – Defines structures and constants related to the CPU

Location

/usr/sys/include/machine/cpu.h

Description

The cpu.h file defines a variety of structures and constants related to the
CPU.

When to Include

You include the cpu.h file in block and character device drivers when
calling any of the spl interfaces. The reason for this is that the spl
interfaces map to an assembler interface.

Of Special Interest

The items contained in cpu.h are opaque to device driver writers. In other
words, device driver writers need not know the details of how the spl
interfaces map to the assembler-specific interface.

Related Information

Section 15.2, Kernel Support Interfaces: spl

Name

`devdriver.h` – Defines the structures, constants, and external interfaces that device drivers and the autoconfiguration software use

Location

`/usr/sys/include/io/common/devdriver.h`

Description

The `devdriver.h` file defines the structures, constants, and external interfaces that device drivers and the autoconfiguration software use.

When to Include

You must include the `devdriver.h` file in block and character device drivers because you initialize the `driver` structure and reference the `controller`, `device`, and `bus` structures.

Of Special Interest

Items of interest to device driver writers are:

- The `bus`, `controller`, `device`, and `driver` structures
- The `port` structure
- Bus type constants
- Bit constants for the `alive` member of the `bus`, `controller`, and `device` structures
- The typedefs `io_handle_t` and `dma_handle_t`

Related Information

Chapter 16, Structures Related to Device Drivers: `bus`, `controller`, `device`, `driver`

Name

devdriver_loadable.h – Defines constants and declares external functions associated with loadable drivers

Location

/usr/sys/include/io/common/devdriver_loadable.h

Description

The devdriver_loadable.h file defines constants and declares external functions associated with loadable drivers. The file also defines constants and declares external functions associated with bus support.

When to Include

The devdriver_loadable.h file defines constants that the loadable driver support interfaces use. You do not need to include this file in your device driver.

Of Special Interest

Items of interest to device driver writers are the external definitions for the ldbl_ctlr_configure, ldbl_ctlr_unconfigure, and ldbl_stanza_resolver kernel interfaces.

Items of interest to systems engineers who implement a new bus or make changes to an existing bus are the external declarations ldbl_find_bus, ldbl_search_bus_local, and ldbl_find_ctlr.

Related Information

Section 17.3, Bus Configuration Interfaces: ctlr_configure

Name

devio.h – Defines common structures and definitions for device drivers and ioctl requests

Location

/usr/sys/include/io/common/devio.h

Description

The devio.h file defines common structures and definitions for device drivers and ioctl requests, such as DEVIOCGET. This file also contains descriptions of device types, attributes, and names.

When to Include

You include the devio.h file in your device driver if you plan to use the DEVIOCGET ioctl request.

Of Special Interest

Items of interest to device driver writers are:

- The devget structure
- Status constant definitions for the category and bus members of the devget structure
- Constant definitions for the interface and the device character array members of the devget structure
- Constant definitions for the stat and category_stat members of the devget structure

Related Information

Section 15.3, ioctl Commands: DEVIOCGET

Name

`disklabel.h` – Defines structures and macros that operate on Digital UNIX disk labels

Location

`/usr/sys/include/sys/disklabel.h`

Description

The `disklabel.h` file defines structures and macros that operate on Digital UNIX disk labels. Each disk has a label that includes information about the hardware disk geometry, file system partitions, and drive-specific information.

When to Include

You include the `disklabel.h` file if your block device driver needs to operate on disk labels.

Of Special Interest

Items of interest to device driver writers are:

- The `disklabel` structure

- Constant values for the `d_type` member of the `disklabel` structure

  The values for this member can be set to describe the drive type. Some examples are `DTYPE_MSCP` (the drive type is an MSCP) and `DTYPE_SCSI` (the drive type is a SCSI).

Related Information

Reference Pages Sections 5 and 7: `disktab`

Name

errno.h – Defines the error codes that a device driver returns to a user process

Location

/usr/sys/include/sys/errno.h

Description

The errno.h file defines the error codes returned to a user process by a device driver. Device driver interfaces use the codes EIO, ENXIO, EACCES, EBUSY, ENODEV, and EINVAL.

When to Include

You include the errno.h file in both block and character device drivers to use the systemwide error codes.

Name

fcntl.h – Defines I/O mode flags that user programs supply to open and fcntl system calls

Location

/usr/sys/include/sys/fcntl.h

Description

The fcntl.h file defines I/O mode flags supplied by user programs to the open and fcntl system calls.

When to Include

You include the fcntl.h file in both block and character device drivers because these I/O mode flags get passed to the driver's open, close, and ioctl interfaces.

Related Information

Reference Pages Section 2: fcntl, open

Name

ioctl.h – Defines commands for ioctl interfaces in different device drivers

Location

/usr/sys/include/sys/ioctl.h

Description

The ioctl.h file defines commands for ioctl interfaces in different device drivers. The ioctl commands are driver entry points that perform tasks other than the general I/O operations such as read and write. Thus, you can consider ioctl operations as a way to perform any task other than read/write tasks.

When to Include

You include the ioctl.h file in both block and character device drivers only when there is an ioctl entry point; that is, the driver has an ioctl interface that uses I/O control commands.

Name

iotypes.h – Defines constants that 64-bit conversions use

Location

/usr/sys/include/io/common/iotypes.h

Description

The iotypes.h file defines constants that 64-bit conversions use.

When to Include

You include the iotypes.h file if you use the constants defined for 64-bit conversions in your device driver.

Of Special Interest

The following table lists some of the 64-bit conversion constants:

Constant	Meaning
I8	char
U8	unsigned char
I16	short
U16	unsigned short
I32	int
U32	unsigned int
I64	long long
U64	unsigned long long
I_WORD	long
U_WORD	unsigned long

Name

`kernel.h` – Defines global variables that the kernel uses

Location

`/usr/sys/include/sys/kernel.h`

Description

The `kernel.h` file defines global variables that the kernel uses.

When to Include

You include the `kernel.h` file in both block and character device drivers to make use of the kernel global variables.

Of Special Interest

The kernel global variables that are of particular interest to device driver writers are:

- The `hz` variable
- The `lbolt` variable
- The `time` structure

  This structure is defined as an external structure. This structure is defined in the file `time.h`.

Related Information

Section 15.4, Global Variables: `hz`, `lbolt`

Name

`lock.h` – Defines simple and complex lock structures

Location

`/usr/sys/include/kern/lock.h`

Description

The `lock.h` file defines the simple spin lock and complex lock structures that device drivers use for synchronization on single processor and multiprocessor systems.

When to Include

You include the `lock.h` file in device drivers if you use simple or complex locks to synchronize access to device driver structures and device registers.

Of Special Interest

Items of interest to the device driver writer are:

- The `slock` structure

  This is the simple spin lock structure.

- The typedefs `simple_lock_data_t` and `simple_lock_t`

  The `simple_lock_data_t` typedef is an alternate name for the `slock` structure and the `simple_lock_t` typedef is an alternate name for a pointer to the `slock` structure.

- The `lock` structure

  This is the complex lock structure.

- The typedefs `lock_data_t` and `lock_t`

  The `lock_data_t` typedef is an alternate name for the `lock` structure and the `lock_t` typedef is an alternate name for a pointer to the `lock` structure.

Related Information

Chapter 16, Structures Related to Device Drivers: `lock`, `slock`

Name

malloc.h – Defines kernel memory allocator-related information

Location

/usr/sys/include/sys/malloc.h

Description

The malloc.h file defines the constants, data structures, and interfaces associated with the kernel memory allocator interfaces MALLOC and FREE.

When to Include

You include the malloc.h file in block and character device drivers when calling the interfaces associated with the kernel memory allocator.

Of Special Interest

Items of interest to device driver writers are the defines for the different memory types that device drivers can pass to the *type* argument of the MALLOC interface. For example, you can pass the M_DEVBUF constant to indicate that device driver memory is being allocated (or freed).

Related Information

Section 15.2, Kernel Support Interfaces: FREE, MALLOC

Name

map.h – Defines structures associated with resource allocation maps

Location

/usr/sys/include/sys/map.h

Description

The map.h file defines structures associated with resource allocation maps.

When to Include

You include the map.h file in both block and character device drivers when you need to make reference to the members of the map and mapent structures.

Name

mman.h – Defines constants associated with the mmap kernel interface

Location

/usr/sys/include/sys/mman.h

Description

The mman.h file defines constants associated with the mmap kernel interface. It also defines protection bits that the mmap system call uses.

When to Include

You include the mman.h file in any character device driver that needs to call the mmap kernel interface.

Of Special Interest

Items of interest to device driver writers are the following protection bits:

- PROT_READ
- PROT_WRITE

Related Information

Section 17.2, Block and Character Device Driver Interfaces: xxmmap

Reference Pages Section 2: mmap, munmap

Name

mode.h – Defines constants that driver interfaces use

Location

/usr/sys/include/sys/mode.h

Description

The mode.h file defines constants that driver interfaces use.

When to Include

You include the mode.h file when you use any of the constants defined in this file in your device driver.

Of Special Interest

Items of interest to device driver writers are:

- The S_IFBLK constant

- The S_IFCHR constant

Driver writers can use these constants to check the *format* argument for the *xxclose* and *xxopen* interfaces to determine whether the request is for a block or character special file.

Name

mtio.h – Defines commands and structures for magnetic tape operations

Location

/usr/sys/include/sys/mtio.h

Description

The mtio.h file defines commands and structures for magnetic tape operations.

When to Include

You include the mtio.h file in tape device drivers. Commands defined in this file are used to communicate with the device driver's ioctl interface.

Of Special Interest

Items of interest to device driver writers are:

- The mtop structure
- The mtget structure

Related Information

Reference Pages Section 4: mtio

Name

param.h – Defines constants and interfaces that the kernel uses

Location

/usr/sys/include/sys/param.h

Description

The param.h file defines constants and interfaces that the kernel uses.

When to Include

You include the param.h file in block and character device drivers when calling the sleep interface. The reason for this is that the sleep interface maps to another kernel interface.

Of Special Interest

One item of interest to device driver writers is the PCATCH constant.

Related Information

Section 15.2, Kernel Support Interfaces: sleep

Name

poll.h – Defines polling bit masks

Location

/usr/sys/include/sys/poll.h

Description

The poll.h file defines bit polling bit masks that a device driver's
xxselect interface uses.

When to Include

You include the poll.h file in character device drivers if you want to use
the polling bit masks to determine the state of the specified device.

Of Special Interest

Items of interest to device driver writers are the following polling bit masks:

- POLLNORM
- POLLOUT
- POLLPRI
- POLLNVAL
- POLLHUP

Related Information

Section 15.2, Kernel Support Interfaces: select_dequeue,
select_dequeue_all, select_enqueue, select_wakeup

Section 17.2, Block and Character Device Driver Interfaces: xxselect

Reference Pages Section 2: select

Name

`proc.h` – Defines the `proc` structure, which defines a user process

Location

`/usr/sys/include/sys/proc.h`

Description

The `proc.h` file defines the `proc` structure, which defines a user process.

When to Include

You include the `proc.h` file in block and character device drivers if you want to access different members of the user's process structure.

Name

`sched_prim.h` – Defines scheduling interfaces

Location

`/usr/sys/include/kern/sched_prim.h`

Description

The `sched_prim.h` file defines scheduling interfaces (macros) and kernel threads-related constants.

When to Include

You include the `sched_prim.h` file when your driver references any kernel threads-related constants or scheduling interfaces.

Of Special Interest

Items of interest to driver writers are the following interfaces:

- `assert_wait_mesg`
- `thread_block`
- `thread_wakeup`
- `thread_wakeup_one`

Related Information

Section 15.2, Kernel Support Interfaces: `assert_wait_mesg`, `thread_block`, `thread_wakeup`, `thread_wakeup_one`

Name

security.h – Defines structures, constants, and data types that UNIX security software uses

Location

/usr/sys/include/sys/security.h

Description

The security.h file defines structures, constants, and data types that UNIX security software uses.

When to Include

You include the security.h file in block and character device drivers if you call the privileged kernel interface.

Of Special Interest

Items of interest to device driver writers are the privilege constants. Examples of these constants include:

- SEC_FILESYS
- SEC_OWNER
- SEC_CHPRIV

Related Information

Section 15.2, Kernel Support Interfaces: privileged

Name

select.h – Defines select-related data structures and interfaces

Location

/usr/sys/include/sys/select.h

Description

The select.h file defines the data structure and interfaces that device drivers use in the Select Section.

When to Include

You include the select.h file when your device driver uses the sel_queue data structure and calls the select_enqueue and select_dequeue interfaces.

Of Special Interest

Items of interest to device driver writers are:

- The sel_queue data structure
- The typedef sel_queue_t, which is an alternate name for struct sel_queue

Related Information

Section 15.2, Kernel Support Interfaces: select_dequeue, select_enqueue, sel_queue

Name

sysconfig.h – Defines operation codes and data structures used in loadable device driver configuration

Location

/usr/sys/include/sys/sysconfig.h

Description

The sysconfig.h file defines operation codes and data structures used in loadable device driver configuration. The operation codes define the action to be performed by the device driver's configure interface. Examples of the operation types include configure, unconfigure, and query. This file also defines many of the constants that are shared between the device driver method and the drivers themselves. The definition of the cfg_attr_t data structure that the device driver method of cfgmgr passes to the driver's configure interface appears in this file. The definition of the cfg_subsys_attr_t data structure that a loadable driver's configure interface initializes also appears in this file.

When to Include

You include the sysconfig.h file in loadable block and character device drivers.

Of Special Interest

Items of interest to device driver writers are the following constants:

- CFG_OP_CONFIGURE (configure the loadable driver)
- CFG_OP_UNCONFIGURE (unconfigure the loadable driver)
- CFG_OP_QUERY (query the loadable driver)

Related Information

Chapter 16, Structures Related to Device Drivers: cfg_attr_t, cfg_subsys_attr_t

Section 17.2, Block and Character Device Driver Interfaces: xxconfigure

Name

systm.h – Defines generic kernel global variables

Location

/usr/sys/include/sys/systm.h

Description

The systm.h file defines generic kernel global variables that some kernel interfaces use.

When to Include

You include the systm.h file in character and block device drivers only if you need to reference one of the generic kernel global variables. Most device drivers will not need this file.

Of Special Interest

Items of interest to device driver writers are:

- The *physmem* global variable

  This global variable specifies the physical memory on this CPU.

- The *version* global variable

  This global variable is a character array that specifies the system version.

- Casts for the insque and remque kernel interfaces

  These casts are made to satisfy the lint program.

Related Information

Section 15.2, Kernel Support Interfaces: insque

Name

task.h – Defines structures that tasks use

Location

/usr/sys/include/kern/task.h

Description

The task.h file defines structures that tasks use.

When to Include

You include the task.h file when your driver references any of the data structures related to tasks.

Of Special Interest

One item of interest to the device driver writer is the typedef task_t, which is an alternate name for struct task *.

Related Information

Chapter 16, Structures Related to Device Drivers: task

Name

thread.h – Defines structures that kernel threads use

Location

/usr/sys/include/kern/thread.h

Description

The thread.h file defines structures that kernel threads use.

When to Include

You include the thread.h file when your driver references any of the data structures related to kernel threads.

Of Special Interest

One item of interest to the device driver writer is the typedef thread_t, which is an alternate name for struct thread *.

Related Information

Chapter 16, Structures Related to Device Drivers: thread

Name

time.h – Contains structures and symbolic names that time-related interfaces use

Location

/usr/sys/include/sys/time.h

Description

The time.h file contains structures and symbolic names that time-related interfaces use.

When to Include

You include the time.h file in block and character device drivers if the driver needs to look at:

- The system time
- A process's timeval structures

Of Special Interest

Items of interest to device driver writers are:

- The tm structure
- The timeval structure

Name

types.h – Defines system data types and major and minor device interfaces

Location

/usr/sys/include/sys/types.h

Description

The types.h file defines system data types and major and minor device interfaces.

When to Include

You include the types.h file in most block and character device drivers in order to use the defined data types.

Name

uio.h – Contains the definition of the uio structure

Location

/usr/sys/include/sys/uio.h

Description

The uio.h file contains the definition of the uio structure.

When to Include

You include the uio.h file in character device drivers that access the uio structure.

Of Special Interest

Items of interest to device driver writers are:

- The uio structure
- The uio structure member uio_rw

  This member is an enumerated data type that can be set to the flag UIO_READ or UIO_WRITE.

- The uio structure member uio_segflg

  This member is an enumerated data type that can be set to the flag UIO_USERSPACE, UIO_SYSSPACE, or UIO_USERISPACE.

Related Information

Chapter 16, Structures Related to Device Drivers: uio

Name

user.h – Defines the user structure

Location

/usr/sys/include/sys/user.h

Description

The user.h file defines the user structure.

When to Include

You include the user.h file in block and character device drivers only if the driver needs to access different members of the user's user context structure.

Of Special Interest

Items of interest to device driver writers are:

- The user structure
- The utask structure

Name

vm.h – Contains a sequence of include statements that includes all of the virtual memory-related files

Location

/usr/sys/include/sys/vm.h

Description

The vm.h file contains a sequence of include statements that includes all of the virtual memory-related files.

When to Include

Including the vm.h file is a quick way of including all of the virtual memory-related files.

Name

vmmac.h – Contains definitions for byte conversions

Location

/usr/sys/include/sys/vmmac.h

Description

The vmmac.h file contains definitions for converting from bytes to pages and from pages to bytes.

When to Include

You include the vmmac.h file in device drivers if the driver needs to perform virtual memory calculations directly.

Name

zalloc.h – Defines zone kernel memory allocator-related information

Location

/usr/sys/kernel/kern/zalloc.h

Description

The zalloc.hFMpathfontend file defines information that the zone
kernel memory allocator interfaces use.

When to Include

You include the zalloc.h file in device drivers when using the zone kernel
memory allocator. The zone kernel memory allocator includes the following
kernel interfaces:

- zinit
- zchange
- zalloc
- zfree
- zget

Of Special Interest

Items of interest to the device driver writer are:

- The zone structure

  This is the structure that defines the characteristics associated with a
  fixed-sized element. These characteristics include the sizes of the element
  and the zone.

- The typedef zone_t

  The zone_t typedef is an alternate name for struct zone *.

Related Information

Section 15.2, Kernel Support Interfaces: zalloc, zchange, zfree,
zget, zinit

Chapter 16, Structures Related to Device Drivers: zone

Kernel Interfaces, ioctls, and Global Variables That Device Drivers Use 15

This chapter describes:

- Conventions
- The kernel I/O support interfaces that device drivers use
- The ioctl commands that device drivers use
- Global variables that device drivers use

15.1 Conventions

The following sections describe:

- Conventions for kernel interfaces that device drivers use
- Conventions for ioctl commands that device drivers use
- Conventions for global variables that device drivers use

15.1.1 Conventions for Kernel Interfaces

The descriptions of the kernel interfaces are presented in alphabetical order and in reference (man) page style. The descriptions can include the following sections.

Name

This section lists the name of the kernel interface, along with a summary description of its purpose. In general, there is one interface described for each reference page. However, in some cases it makes sense to describe more than one interface on the same page if the interfaces are related. When this occurs, this section lists the names of all the interfaces it describes.

Synopsis

This section shows the kernel interface function definition. The style used is that of the function definition, not the function call. This book assumes that you understand how to interpret the function definition and how to write an appropriate call for a specific interface.

The following example shows these conventions:

```
int copyin(user_src, kernel_dest, bcount)
caddr_t user_src;
caddr_t kernel_dest;
u_int bcount;
```

The kernel interface function definition gives you the following information:

- Return type

  The data type of the return value, if the kernel interface returns data. If the kernel interface does not return a value, the void data type is used.

- Kernel interface name

  The kernel interface name, for example, copyin. Some kernel interfaces are in uppercase.

- Argument names

  The name of each kernel interface argument name. In the example, the argument names are user_src, kernel_dest, and bcount.

- Argument types

  The types for each of the arguments. In the example, these types are caddr_t and u_int.

This book uses the word kernel "interface" instead of kernel "routine" or kernel "macro."

Arguments

This section provides descriptions for the arguments associated with a given kernel interface. In most cases, argument descriptions begin with the word specifies to indicate that you pass the argument (with some specified value) to the kernel interface. If the type of the argument appears as a void *, the argument description states that you must define the type.

Description

This section contains explanations of the tasks performed by the kernel interface.

Notes

This section discusses information that falls into the following categories:

- Hardware-specific information

  Some kernel interfaces behave differently depending on the architecture of the hardware.

- Operating system-specific information

  Some kernel interfaces behave differently depending on the implementation of the operating system.

- Information pertinent to device drivers

  Some kernel interfaces require specific information important to the device driver writer.

Cautions

This section provides information of particular importance when you use the kernel interface. In many cases, the text in this section alerts you to anything that might cause a panic.

Example

This section provides the section where you can find an example of the kernel interface.

Errors

This section provides the possible error constants a given kernel interface can return, along with a short description of the error.

Side Effects

This section describes special processing performed by the kernel interface. For example, the Side Effects section for the `uiomove` kernel interface describes the members of the `uio` structure that it can update.

Return Values

This section describes the return values that a given kernel interface can return. In most cases, if the kernel interface returns an error value, this value is described in the Return Values section.

Related Information

This section lists related kernel interfaces, structures, system calls, and so forth.

15.1.2 Conventions for ioctl Commands

The description of `ioctl` commands and interfaces (macros) are presented in reference (man) page style. The description can include the following sections.

Name

This section lists the name of the `ioctl` command or interface, along with a summary description of its purpose.

Synopsis

For `ioctl` commands, this section lists the associated header files. For `ioctl` interfaces, this section shows the interface definition. For example:

```
#include <sys/ioctl.h>

_IO(g, n)
```

The interface definition shows the header file where the `ioctl` interface is defined. The definition also shows the arguments passed to the interface.

Arguments

This section provides descriptions for the arguments associated with a given `ioctl` interface. In most cases, argument descriptions begin with the word *specifies* to indicate that you pass the argument (with some specified value) to the `ioctl` interface.

Description

This section describes `ioctl` commands or interfaces. The description could include information on associated structures and members.

Example

This section provides an example showing how to construct a driver-specific interface that uses the specified `ioctl` interface.

Related Information

This section lists related kernel interfaces, structures, system calls, and so forth.

15.1.3 Conventions for Global Variables

The descriptions of the global variables are presented in alphabetical order and in reference (man) page style. The descriptions can include the following sections.

Name

This section lists the name of the global variable, along with a short description of its purpose.

Synopsis

This section provides the declaration of the global variable.

Location

This section presents the pathname for the header file that defines the global variable.

Description

This section describes the purpose of the global variable.

Notes

This section discusses information about the global variable pertinent to the device driver writer.

15.2 Kernel Support Interfaces

Table 15-1 summarizes the kernel interfaces discussed in this chapter.

Note

Device drivers use the following header files most frequently:

```
#include <sys/types.h>
#include <sys/errno.h>
#include <io/common/devdriver.h>
#include <sys/uio.h>
#include <machine/cpu.h>
```

Table 15-1: Summary Descriptions of Kernel Support Interfaces

Kernel Interface	Summary Description
assert_wait_mesg	Asserts that the current kernel thread is about to block (sleep).
BADADDR	Probes the address during device autoconfiguration.
bcmp	Compares two byte strings.
bcopy	Copies a series of bytes with a specified limit.
bdevsw_add	Adds entry points to the block device switch table.
bdevsw_del	Deletes entry points from the block device switch table.
blkclr	Zeros a block of memory.
btop	Converts bytes to number of pages.
BUF_LOCK	Locks the specified I/O buffer.
BUF_UNLOCK	Unlocks the specified I/O buffer.
busphys_to_iohandle	Converts a valid bus physical address to an I/O handle base.
bzero	Zeros a block of memory.
clear_wait	Clears the wait condition.
cdevsw_add	Adds entry points to the character device switch table.
cdevsw_del	Deletes entry points from the character device switch table.
copyin	Copies data from a user address space to a kernel address space.
copyinstr	Copies a null-terminated string from a user address space to a kernel address space.
copyout	Copies data from a kernel address space to a user address space.
copyoutstr	Copies a null-terminated string from a kernel address space to a user address space.
copystr	Copies a null-terminated character string with a specified limit.
copy_to_phys	Copies data from a virtual address to a physical address.
current_task	Returns a pointer to the currently running kernel thread.
decl_simple_lock_data	Declares a simple lock structure.
DELAY	Delays the calling interface a specified number of microseconds.
disable_option	Disables a device's interrupt line to the processor.
dma_get_curr_sgentry	Returns a pointer to the current sg_entry.
dma_get_next_sgentry	Returns a pointer to the next sg_entry.
dma_get_private	Gets a data element from the DMA private storage space.
dma_kmap_buffer	Returns a kernel segment (kseg) address of a DMA buffer.
dma_map_alloc	Allocates resources for DMA data transfers.

Table 15-1: (continued)

Kernel Interface	Summary Description
dma_map_dealloc	Releases and deallocates the DMA resources previously allocated for DMA data transfers.
dma_map_load	Loads and sets allocated DMA resources and sets up a DMA data path for DMA data transfers.
dma_map_unload	Unloads the system DMA resources.
dma_min_boundary	Returns system-level information.
dma_put_curr_sgentry	Puts a new bus address/byte count pair in the linked list of sg_entry structures.
dma_put_prev_sgentry	Updates an internal pointer index to the linked list of sg_entry structures.
dma_put_private	Stores a data element in the DMA private storage space.
do_config	Initializes the device to its assigned configuration.
drvr_register_shutdown	Registers or deregisters a shutdown interface.
dualdevsw_add	Adds entry points to the block device switch and character device switch tables.
dualdevsw_del	Deletes entry points from the block device switch and character device switch tables.
enable_option	Enables a device's interrupt line to the processor.
ffs	Finds the first set bit in a mask.
FREE	Deallocates (frees) the allocated kernel virtual memory.
fubyte	Returns a byte from user address space.
fuibyte	Returns a byte from user instruction address space.
fuiword	Returns a word from user address space.
fuword	Returns a word from user address space.
get_config	Returns assigned configuration data for a device.
get_info	Returns system-specific information.
gsignal	Sends a signal to a process group.
handler_add	Registers a device driver's interrupt service interface.
handler_del	Deregisters a device driver's interrupt service interface.
handler_disable	Disables a previously registered interrupt service interface.
handler_enable	Enables a previously registered interrupt service interface.
htonl	Converts longword values from host-to-network byte order.
htons	Converts word values from host-to-network byte order.
insque	Adds an element to the queue.
io_copyin	Copies data from bus address space to system memory.

Table 15-1: (continued)

Kernel Interface	Summary Description
io_copyio	Copies data from bus address space to bus address space.
io_copyout	Copies data from system memory to bus address space.
io_zero	Zeros a block of memory in bus address space.
iodone	Indicates that I/O is complete.
iohandle_to_phys	Converts an I/O handle to a valid system physical address.
IS_KSEG_VA	Determines if the specified address is located in the kernel-unmapped address space.
IS_SEG0_VA	Determines if the specified address is located in the user-mapped address space.
IS_SEG1_VA	Determines if the specified address is located in the kernel-mapped address space.
kernel_isrthread	Starts a fixed priority kernel thread dedicated to interrupt service.
kernel_thread_w_arg	Starts a kernel thread with a calling argument passed in.
KSEG_TO_PHYS	Converts a kernel-unmapped virtual address to a physical address.
ldbl_ctlr_configure	Configures the specified controller.
ldbl_ctlr_unconfigure	Unconfigures the specified controller.
ldbl_stanza_resolver	Merges the configuration data.
lock_done	Releases a complex lock.
lock_init	Initializes a complex lock.
lock_read	Asserts a complex lock with read-only access.
lock_terminate	Terminates, using a complex lock.
lock_try_read	Tries to assert a complex lock with read-only access.
lock_try_write	Tries to assert a complex lock with write access.
lock_write	Asserts a complex lock with write access.
major	Returns the device major number.
makedev	Returns a dev_t.
MALLOC	Allocates a variable-size section of kernel virtual memory.
mb	Performs a memory barrier.
minor	Returns the device minor number.
minphys	Bounds the data transfer size.
mpsleep	Blocks (puts to sleep) the current kernel thread.
ntohl	Converts longword values from network-to-host byte order.
ntohs	Converts word values from network-to-host byte order.
ovbcopy	Copies a byte string with a specified limit.

Table 15-1: (continued)

Kernel Interface	Summary Description
panic	Causes a system crash.
physio	Implements raw I/O.
PHYS_TO_KSEG	Converts a physical address to a kernel-unmapped virtual address.
pmap_extract	Extracts a physical page address.
pmap_kernel	Returns the physical map handle for the kernel.
pmap_set_modify	Sets the modify bits of the specified physical page.
printf	Prints text to the console and the error logger.
privileged	Checks for proper privileges.
psignal	Sends a signal to a process.
queue_init	Initializes the specified queue.
read_io_port	Reads data from a device register.
remque	Removes an element from the queue.
READ_BUS_D8	Reads a byte (8 bits) from a device register.
READ_BUS_D16	Reads a word (16 bits) from a device register.
READ_BUS_D32	Reads a longword (32 bits) from a device register.
READ_BUS_D64	Reads a quadword (64 bits) from a device register.
rmalloc	Allocates size units from the given resource map.
rmfree	Frees space previously allocated into the specified resource map.
rmget	Allocates size units from the given resource map.
rminit	Initializes a resource map.
round_page	Rounds the specified address.
select_dequeue	Removes the last kernel thread waiting for an event.
select_dequeue_all	Removes all kernel threads waiting for an event.
select_enqueue	Adds the current kernel thread.
select_wakeup	Wakes up a kernel thread.
simple_lock	Asserts a simple lock.
simple_lock_init	Initializes a simple lock structure.
simple_lock_terminate	Terminates, using a simple lock.
simple_lock_try	Tries to assert a simple lock.
simple_unlock	Releases a simple lock.
sleep	Puts a calling process to sleep.
spl	Sets the processor priority to mask different levels of interrupts.
strcmp	Compares two null-terminated character strings.

Table 15-1: **(continued)**

Kernel Interface	Summary Description
strcpy	Copies a null-terminated character string.
strlen	Returns the number of characters in a null-terminated string.
strncmp	Compares two strings, using a specified number of characters.
strncpy	Copies a null-terminated character string with a specified limit.
subyte	Writes a byte into user address space.
suibyte	Writes a byte into user instruction address space.
suiword	Writes a word into user instruction address space.
suser	Checks whether the current user is the superuser.
suword	Writes a word into user address space.
svatophys	Converts a system virtual address to a physical address.
swap_lw_bytes	Performs a longword byte swap.
swap_word_bytes	Performs a short word byte swap.
swap_words	Performs a word byte swap.
thread_block	Blocks (puts to sleep) the current kernel thread.
thread_halt_self	Handles asynchronous traps for self-terminating kernel threads.
thread_set_timeout	Sets a timer for the current kernel thread.
thread_terminate	Stops execution of the specified kernel thread.
thread_wakeup	Wakes up all kernel threads waiting for the specified event.
thread_wakeup_one	Wakes up the first kernel thread waiting on a channel.
timeout	Initializes a callout queue element.
trunc_page	Truncates the specified address.
uiomove	Moves data between user and system virtual space.
unix_master	Forces execution onto the master CPU.
unix_release	Releases binding of the kernel thread.
untimeout	Removes the scheduled interface from the callout queues.
uprintf	Is a nonsleeping kernel printf function.
vm_map_pageable	Sets pageability of the specified address range.
vtop	Converts any virtual address to a physical address.
wakeup	Wakes up all processes sleeping on a specified address.
WRITE_BUS_D8	Writes a byte (8 bits) to a device register.
WRITE_BUS_D16	Writes a word (16 bits) to a device register.
WRITE_BUS_D32	Writes a longword (32 bits) to a device register.
WRITE_BUS_D64	Writes a quadword (64 bits) to a device register.

Table 15-1: **(continued)**

Kernel Interface	Summary Description
write_io_port	Writes data to a device register.
zalloc	Returns an element from the specified zone.
zchange	Changes a zone's flags.
zfree	Frees (deallocates) an element.
zget	Returns an element from the specified zone.
zinit	Initializes a new zone.

Note

The kernel interface descriptions in this section do not discuss how a kernel interface acquires and releases the appropriate symmetric multiprocessing (SMP) lock. The reasons for this approach are that some kernel interfaces such as read_io_port and write_io_port do not need to acquire an SMP lock; some kernel interfaces need to acquire an SMP lock but the device driver writer does not need to know the intricacies of how the kernel interface acquires the SMP lock.

Unless otherwise noted, the kernel interfaces that need to acquire an SMP lock acquire the lock at the start of execution and release the lock when they complete execution.

Name

assert_wait_mesg – Asserts that the current kernel thread is about to block (sleep)

Synopsis

```
void assert_wait_mesg(event, interruptible, message)
vm_offset_t event;
boolean_t interruptible;
char *message;
```

Arguments

event
> Specifies the event associated with the current kernel thread.

interruptible
> Specifies a Boolean value that indicates how the kernel thread is awakened. You can pass one of the following values:

Value	Meaning
TRUE	The current kernel thread is interruptible. This value means that a signal can awaken the current kernel thread.
FALSE	The current kernel thread is not interruptible. This value means that only the specified event can awaken the current kernel thread.

message
> Specifies a mnemonic for the type of wait. The /bin/ps command uses this mnemonic to print out more meaningful messages about a process.

Description

The assert_wait_mesg interface asserts that the current kernel thread is about to block (sleep) until the specified *event* occurs. This interface sets a thread wait bit in the pointer to the thread structure associated with the current kernel thread. This bit signifies that this kernel thread is on the appropriate wait hash queue, waiting for a wakeup call.

To actually block (put to sleep) the current kernel thread, call `thread_block`.

To issue a wakeup call on the specified *event*, call the `thread_wakeup_prim` or `clear_wait` interface.

Cautions

You must not call `assert_wait_mesg` from a device driver's interrupt service interface. The reason for this is that at interrupt context there is no process to be put to sleep.

Example

See *Writing Device Drivers: Advanced Topics* for a code example of the `assert_wait_mesg` interface.

Return Values

None

Related Information

Section 15.2, Kernel Support Interfaces: `clear_wait`, `thread_block`

Chapter 16, Structures Related to Device Drivers: `thread`

Reference Pages Section 1: `ps`

Name

BADADDR – Probes the address during device autoconfiguration

Synopsis

```
int BADADDR(addr, length, ptr)
caddr_t addr;
int length;
struct bus_ctlr_common *ptr;
```

Arguments

addr
　Specifies the address of the device registers or memory.

length
　Specifies the length (in bytes) of the data to be checked. Valid values
　are 1, 2, and 4 on 32-bit machines and 4 and 8 on 64-bit machines.

ptr
　Specifies a pointer to a bus_ctlr_common structure. You cast this
　argument as a pointer to either a bus or controller structure.

Description

The BADADDR interface generates a call to a machine-dependent interface
that does a read access check of the data at the supplied address and
dismisses any machine check exception that may result from the attempted
access. You call this interface to probe for memory or I/O devices at a
specified address during device autoconfiguration.

Notes

Device drivers written for ULTRIX systems use the BADADDR interface in
the Autoconfiguration Support Section to determine if a device is present on
the system. You can use BADADDR in device drivers that are configured
statically on Digital UNIX. However, you cannot use BADADDR in device
drivers that are configured as loadable on Digital UNIX.

Loadable device drivers cannot call the BADADDR interface because it is
usable only in the early stages of system booting. Loadable device drivers
are loaded during the multiboot stage. If your driver is both loadable and
static, you can declare a variable and use it to control any differences in the

tasks that the loadable and static drivers perform. Thus, the static driver can still call BADADDR. The following code fragment shows the use of such a variable used in the probe interface for the /dev/none driver:

```
   .
   .
   .
 if (none_is_dynamic) {

 /* Code to handle loadable driver tasks */
   .
   .
   .
 }
 else {

 /* Code to handler static driver tasks, */
 /* including call to BADADDR          */
 }
   .
   .
   .
```

Some buses (for example, EISA and ISA) do not generate a machine check when BADADDR performs a read access to a nonexistent location. These buses always return success when BADADDR performs a read access to their address space.

For some buses (for example, PCI and VMEbus), you must do the following before calling BADADDR:

- Call the iohandle_to_phys interface to convert the I/O handle to a valid system physical address.

- Call the PHYS_TO_KSEG interface to convert the valid system physical address to a kernel-unmapped virtual address.

- Call the BADADDR interface, passing this kernel-unmapped virtual address as the first argument.

Return Values

The BADADDR interface returns the value zero (0) if the data is accessible and nonzero if the data is not accessible.

Name

bcmp – Compares two byte strings

Synopsis

```
int bcmp(b1, b2, n)
char *b1;
char *b2;
int n;
```

Arguments

b1

Specifies a pointer to a byte string (array of characters).

b2

Specifies a pointer to a byte string (array of characters).

n

Specifies the number of bytes to be compared.

Description

The bcmp interface compares byte string $b1$ to byte string $b2$. The interface compares exactly n bytes. No check is made for null bytes.

Return Values

If the first n bytes of $b1$ and $b2$ are equal, the bcmp interface returns the value zero (0). Otherwise, it returns a nonzero integer.

Related Information

Section 15.2, Kernel Support Interfaces: strcmp

Name

bcopy – Copies a series of bytes with a specified limit

Synopsis

```
void bcopy(b1, b2, n)
char *b1;
char *b2;
int n;
```

Arguments

b1

Specifies a pointer to a byte string (array of characters). This pointer can reside in kernel address space or user address space.

b2

Specifies a pointer to a buffer of at least n bytes. This pointer can reside in kernel address space or user address space.

n

Specifies the number of bytes to be copied.

Description

The bcopy interface copies n bytes from string b1 to buffer b2. No check is made for null bytes. The copy is nondestructive, that is, the address ranges of b1 and b2 can overlap.

Example

See Section 9.3.1 for a code example of the bcopy interface.

Return Values

None

Related Information

Section 15.2, Kernel Support Interfaces: blkclr, copystr, ovbcopy, strcpy, strncpy

Name

bdevsw_add, cdevsw_add, bdevsw_del, cdevsw_del – Add and delete entry points to block and character device switch tables

Synopsis

```
#include <sys/conf.h>
#include <sys/types.h>

dev_t bdevsw_add(devno, blkent)
dev_t devno;
struct bdevsw *blkent;


dev_t cdevsw_add(devno, chrent)
dev_t devno;
struct cdevsw *chrent;


int bdevsw_del(devno)
dev_t devno;


int cdevsw_del(devno)
dev_t devno;
```

Arguments

devno

Specifies the device switch table entry (slot) to use. If you pass NODEV to bdevsw_add or cdevsw_add, the first available slot is used.

blkent

Specifies a pointer to the block device switch structure that contains the block device driver's entry points for the system service's I/O requests.

chrent

Specifies a pointer to the character device switch structure that contains the character device driver's entry points for the system service's I/O requests.

Description

The `devsw` interfaces allow loadable device drivers to add and delete entry points in device switch tables. Separate sets of interfaces are provided for block and character device drivers. The `bdevsw_add` and `cdevsw_add` interfaces take a device number, which determines the device switch slot for the driver entry points. A device driver can supply NODEV instead of a device number. In this case, the add interfaces find the first available device switch slot and return the device number actually used. If a device switch slot is already in use or if there are no slots available, an error is returned. The delete interfaces reference device numbers returned by previous calls to the add interfaces.

Notes

A loadable driver's interrupt service interfaces must be registered with the kernel's interrupt dispatcher. The `handler` interfaces are used for registering the interrupt service interfaces. The system I/O services interfaces are those specified in the device switch tables. For each I/O system call, a driver must provide an entry point in the device switch table. The `devsw` interfaces are provided for configuration of the I/O services interfaces.

A device driver specifies its I/O services interfaces in the `bdevsw` table for block drivers and in the `cdevsw` table for character drivers. You must specify an interface name for each member of these tables. If the driver does not implement a specific interface, there are typically two interfaces you can specify:

- The `nodev` interface

  You specify `nodev` when it is an error for the interface to be called. To indicate the error, `nodev` returns ENODEV.

- The `nulldev` interface

  You specify `nulldev` when it is not an error for the interface to be called, but the driver has no need to implement the interface. The `nulldev` interface returns the value zero (0) and performs no tasks. This value indicates a success status.

Cautions

To prevent the `devsw` interfaces from dynamically reallocating the driver's major number, make sure that the `d_open` member of the `bdevsw` or `cdevsw` structure is set to a driver interface, the `nodev` interface, or the `nulldev` interface. This setting is necessary because the `devsw` interfaces consider any `d_open` member set to NULL as unused and available for dynamically reallocating the major number to another device driver.

Example

See Section 9.7 for code examples of the `bdevsw_add`, `cdevsw_add`, `bdevsw_del`, and `cdevsw_del` interfaces.

Return Values

Upon successful completion, `bdevsw_add` and `cdevsw_add` return the device number associated with the device switch table. Otherwise, they return `NODEV`.

Upon successful completion, `bdevsw_del` and `cdevsw_del` return the value zero (0). Otherwise, they return a nonzero value.

Related Information

Section 15.2, Kernel Support Interfaces: `dualdevsw_add`, `dualdevsw_del`, `handler_add`

Name

blkclr, bzero – Zeros a block of memory

Synopsis

```
void blkclr(b1, n)
char *b1;
unsigned int n;


void bzero(b1, n)
char *b1;
int n;
```

Arguments

b1

Specifies a pointer to a string of at least *n* bytes.

n

Specifies the number of bytes to be zeroed.

Description

The blkclr and bzero interfaces zero *n* bytes of memory beginning at the address specified by *b1*.

Example

See Section 9.3.2 for code examples of the blkclr and bzero interfaces.

Return Values

None

Related Information

Section 15.2, Kernel Support Interfaces: bcopy, copystr, ovbcopy, strcpy, strncpy

Name

btop – Converts bytes to number of pages

Synopsis

```
int btop(virt_addr)
vm_offset_t virt_addr;
```

Arguments

virt_addr
Specifies the virtual address.

Description

The btop interface converts the specified byte address to the number of
pages.

Return Values

The btop interface returns the number of kernel pages associated with the
specified byte address.

Name

BUF_LOCK – Locks the specified I/O buffer

Synopsis

```
void BUF_LOCK(bp)
struct buf *bp;
```

Arguments

bp

Specifies a pointer to a buf structure.

Description

The BUF_LOCK interface locks the specified I/O buffer. The interface masks all disk and tape controller interrupts (by calling the splbio interface). It sets the mutual exclusion buffer lock member, b_lock, of the specified buf structure pointer.

The BUF_LOCK interface then sets the b_flags member of the specified buf structure pointer to B_BUSY to indicate that this buffer is being used. Finally, BUF_LOCK resets the CPU priority level (by calling the splx interface).

Notes

You should make efforts in your device drivers to hold the I/O buffer lock for as short a period of time as possible to allow maximum concurrency. You should also release the I/O buffer lock by calling the BUF_UNLOCK interface before returning from the driver's entry point.

Return Values

None

Related Information

Section 15.2, Kernel Support Interfaces: BUF_UNLOCK

Name

BUF_UNLOCK – Unlocks the specified I/O buffer

Synopsis

```
void BUF_UNLOCK(bp)
struct buf *bp;
```

Arguments

bp
> Specifies a pointer to a buf structure.

Description

The BUF_UNLOCK interface unlocks the specified I/O buffer that was locked in a previous call to BUF_LOCK. The interface masks all disk and tape controller interrupts (by calling the splbio interface). It resets the mutual exclusion buffer lock member, b_lock, of the specified buf structure pointer.

The BUF_UNLOCK interface then resets the b_flags member of the specified buf structure pointer to indicate that this buffer is not being used. Finally, BUF_UNLOCK resets the CPU priority level (by calling the splx interface).

Notes

You must have locked the specified I/O buffer by calling BUF_LOCK prior to calling the BUF_UNLOCK interface.

Return Values

None

Related Information

Section 15.2, Kernel Support Interfaces: BUF_LOCK

Name

busphys_to_iohandle – Converts a valid bus physical address to an I/O handle base

Synopsis

```
io_handle_t busphys_to_iohandle(addr, flags, ctlr_p)
u_long addr;
int flags;
struct controller *ctlr_p;
```

Arguments

addr

Specifies the bus physical address that you want busphys_to_iohandle to translate into an I/O handle base.

flags

Specifies flags to indicate the address space in which the bus physical address that you pass to the addr argument resides. You can pass one of the following address space type flags:

Value	Meaning
BUS_MEMORY	The address is from the bus memory. In this case, busphys_to_iohandle converts the bus physical address to a sparse memory base I/O handle.
BUS_IO	The address is from the bus I/O memory. In this case, busphys_to_iohandle converts the bus physical address to a sparse I/O base handle.
DENSE_MEMORY	The address is from dense space. In this case, busphys_to_iohandle converts the bus physical address to a dense memory base.

ctlr_p

Specifies a pointer to the controller structure associated with the controller that connects to this device. The busphys_to_iohandle interface uses the controller structure pointer to obtain any hardware resource-related information.

Description

The `busphys_to_iohandle` interface converts a valid bus physical address to an I/O handle base that a device driver uses to perform I/O copy operations. The form of this address is CPU specific.

Notes

The `busphys_to_iohandle` interface is a generic interface that maps to a bus-specific interface that actually converts the bus physical address to an I/O handle base. Using this interface to convert the bus physical address makes the device driver more portable across different bus architectures.

Return Values

Upon successful completion, `busphys_to_iohandle` returns the I/O handle associated with the bus physical address. If `busphys_to_iohandle` cannot convert the bus physical address into a base I/O handle, it returns a value of −1.

Related Information

Section 15.2, Kernel Support Interfaces: `io_copyin`, `io_copyio`, `io_copyout`, `iohandle_to_phys`

Name

clear_wait – Clears the wait condition

Synopsis

```
void clear_wait(thread, result, interrupt_only)
thread_t thread;
int result;
boolean_t interrupt_only;
```

Arguments

thread
> Specifies a pointer to the thread structure associated with the kernel thread to awaken.

result
> Specifies the outcome of the wait. You can pass one of the following values:

Value	Meaning
THREAD_AWAKENED	This is a normal wakeup.
THREAD_TIMED_OUT	The timeout period expired.
THREAD_INTERRUPTED	The clear_wait interface interrupted the wakeup.

interrupt_only
> Specifies a Boolean value that indicates how the clear_wait interface clears the wait condition. You can pass one of the following values:

Value	Meaning
TRUE	Clears the wait condition only if the kernel thread is waiting in an interruptible state.
FALSE	Clears the wait condition under any circumstances.

Description

The `clear_wait` interface clears the wait condition for the specified kernel thread and starts executing the kernel thread, if appropriate. If the kernel thread is interruptible and is still waiting for the event, `clear_wait` sets the kernel thread state to `TH_RUN` and places it on the run queue.

Return Values

None

Related Information

Section 15.2, Kernel Support Interfaces: `assert_wait_mesg`, `mpsleep`, `thread_block`, `thread_wakeup`, `thread_wakeup_one`

Name

copyin – Copies data from a user address space to a kernel address space

Synopsis

```
int copyin(user_src, kernel_dest, bcount)
caddr_t user_src;
caddr_t kernel_dest;
u_int bcount;
```

Arguments

user_src
    Specifies the address in user space of the data to be copied.

kernel_dest
    Specifies the address in kernel space to copy the data to.

bcount
    Specifies the number of bytes to copy.

Description

The copyin interface copies a specified amount of data from the unprotected user address space to the protected kernel address space.

Example

See Section 9.3.3 for a code example of the copyin interface.

Return Values

Upon successful completion, copyin returns a value of zero (0). Otherwise, it can return the following error:

EFAULT
    The address in user space that you specified in the *user_src* argument cannot be accessed.

Related Information

Section 15.2, Kernel Support Interfaces: `copyinstr, copyout`

Name

copyinstr – Copies a null-terminated string from a user address space to a kernel address space

Synopsis

```
int copyinstr(user_src, kernel_dest, maxlength,
lencopied)
char *user_src;
char *kernel_dest;
int maxlength;
int *lencopied;
```

Arguments

user_src
:   Specifies the address in user space of the null-terminated string to be copied.

kernel_dest
:   Specifies the address in kernel space to copy the null-terminated string to.

maxlength
:   Specifies the maximum number of bytes to copy.

lencopied
:   Specifies the actual length of the string copied.

Description

The copyinstr copies a specified null-terminated string from the unprotected user address space to a specified address in the protected kernel address space.

Cautions

If the string being copied is not null-terminated, copyinstr copies maxlength bytes into the kernel address space.

Return Values

Upon successful completion, copyinstr returns the value zero (0) and the actual length of the string copied to the *lencopied* argument. Otherwise, it returns one of the following errors:

EFAULT
> The address in user space that you specified in the *user_src* argument cannot be accessed.

ENAMETOOLONG
> The length of the string exceeds the *maxlength* value.

Related Information

Section 15.2, Kernel Support Interfaces: copyoutstr

Name

copyout – Copies data from a kernel address space to a user address space

Synopsis

```
int copyout(kernel_src, user_dest, bcount)
caddr_t kernel_src;
caddr_t user_dest;
u_int bcount;
```

Arguments

kernel_src
Specifies the address in kernel space of the data to be copied.

user_dest
Specifies the address in user space to copy the data to.

bcount
Specifies the number of bytes to copy.

Description

The copyout interface copies a specified amount of data from the protected kernel address space to the unprotected user address space.

Example

See Section 9.3.4 for a code example of the copyout interface.

Return Values

Upon successful completion, copyout returns the value zero (0). Otherwise, it returns the following error:

EFAULT
The address in kernel space that you specified in the kernel_src argument cannot be accessed; or, the length you specified in bcount is invalid.

Related Information

Section 15.2, Kernel Support Interfaces: `copyin, copyoutstr`

Name

copyoutstr – Copies a null-terminated string from a kernel address space to a user address space

Synopsis

```
int copyoutstr(kernel_src, user_dest, maxlength,
lencopied)
char *kernel_src;
char *user_dest;
int maxlength;
int *lencopied;
```

Arguments

kernel_src
   Specifies the address in kernel space of the null-terminated string to be copied.

user_dest
   Specifies the address in user space to copy the null-terminated string to.

maxlength
   Specifies the maximum number of bytes to copy.

lencopied
   Specifies the actual length of the string copied.

Description

The copyoutstr interface copies a specified null-terminated string from the protected kernel address space to the unprotected user address space.

Cautions

If the string being copied is not null-terminated, copyoutstr copies maxlength bytes into the user address space.

Return Values

Upon successful completion, copyoutstr returns the value zero (0) and the actual length of the string copied in *lencopied*. Otherwise, it can return the following errors:

EFAULT
> The address in kernel space that you specified in the *kernel_src* argument cannot be accessed.

ENAMETOOLONG
> The length of the string exceeds the *maxlength* value.

Related Information

Section 15.2, Kernel Support Interfaces: copyinstr

Name

copystr – Copies a null-terminated character string with a specified limit

Synopsis

```
int copystr(s1, s2, maxlength, ncopiedaddr)
char *s1;
char *s2;
u_int maxlength;
u_int *ncopiedaddr;
```

Arguments

s1
> Specifies a pointer to a string (an array of characters terminated by a null character).

s2
> Specifies a pointer to a buffer of at least maxlength characters.

maxlength
> Specifies the maximum number of characters to copy.

ncopiedaddr
> Specifies the address of an integer to receive the number of copied characters.

Description

The copystr interface copies string s1 to the buffer pointed to by s2. The interface stops after copying a null character or after copying maxlength characters, whichever comes first. The s2 buffer is not padded with null characters to maxlength.

The copystr interface returns the number of characters copied in the location pointed to by ncopiedaddr.

Note that the character size is 1 byte.

Return Values

Upon successful completion, `copystr` returns the value zero (0). Otherwise, it can return the following error:

ENAMETOOLONG
> The string length, $s1$, exceeds the maximum number of characters, $maxlength$.

Related Information

Section 15.2, Kernel Support Interfaces: `bcopy, blkclr, ovbcopy, strcpy, strncpy`

Name

`copy_to_phys` – Copies data from a virtual address to a physical address

Synopsis

```
void copy_to_phys(virt_src, phys_dest, bcount)
vm_offset_t virt_src;
vm_offset_t phys_dest;
unsigned int bcount;
```

Arguments

virt_src
Specifies the virtual address of the data to be copied.

phys_dest
Specifies the physical address to copy the data to.

bcount
Specifies the number of bytes to copy.

Description

The `copy_to_phys` interface copies a specified amount of virtually addressed memory to physically addressed memory. The addresses reside only in system memory space and not in the memory space on I/O buses.

Cautions

If there is any overlap between *virt_src* and *phys_dest*, the `copy_to_phys` interface panics.

Return Values

None

Related Information

Section 15.2, Kernel Support Interfaces: `copyin`, `copyout`, `io_copyin`, `io_copyio`, `io_copyout`

Name

current_task – Returns a pointer to the currently running kernel thread

Synopsis

```
struct task * current_task();
```

Arguments

None

Description

The current_task interface returns a pointer to the task structure associated with the currently running kernel thread. A device driver typically calls this interface in preparation for doing a DMA operation to a user's buffer. The device driver uses the pointer returned by current_task in the call to the vm_map_pageable interface.

Cautions

You must not call the current_task interface from a driver's interrupt service interface.

Return Values

The current_task interface returns a pointer to the task structure for the currently running kernel thread.

Related Information

Section 15.2, Kernel Support Interfaces: round_page, trunc_page, vm_map_pageable

Chapter 16, Structures Related to Device Drivers: thread

Name

decl_simple_lock_data – Declares a simple lock structure

Synopsis

```
#include <kern/lock.h>
void decl_simple_lock_data(class, name)
char class;
char name;
```

Arguments

class
> Specifies the class of the declaration. For example, you pass the keyword extern if you want to declare the simple lock structure as an external structure.

name
> Specifies the name you want the decl_simple_lock_data interface to assign to the declaration of the simple lock structure.

Description

The decl_simple_lock_data interface declares a simple lock structure, slock, of the specified *name*. You declare a simple lock structure for the purpose of protecting device driver data structures and device register access. You use decl_simple_lock_data to declare a simple lock structure and then pass it to the following simple lock-specific interfaces: simple_lock_init, simple_lock, simple_lock_try, simple_unlock, and simple_lock_terminate.

Example

See *Writing Device Drivers: Advanced Topics* for a code example of the decl_simple_lock_data interface.

Return Values

None

Related Information

Chapter 14, Header Files Related to Device Drivers: `lock.h`

Section 15.2, Kernel Support Interfaces: `simple_lock`, `simple_lock_try`, `simple_lock_init`, `simple_unlock`

Chapter 16, Structures Related to Device Drivers: `slock`

Name

DELAY – Delays the calling interface a specified number of microseconds

Synopsis

```
void DELAY(n)
int n;
```

Arguments

n

Specifies the number of microseconds for the calling process to spin.

Description

The DELAY interface delays the calling interface a specified number of microseconds. DELAY spins, waiting for the specified number of microseconds to pass before continuing execution. For example, the following code results in a 10000-microsecond (10-millisecond) delay:

```
.
.
.
DELAY(10000);
.
.
.
```

The range of delays is system dependent, due to its relation to the granularity of the system clock. The system defines the number of clock ticks per second in the hz variable. Specifying any value smaller than 1/hz to the DELAY interface results in an unpredictable delay. For any delay value, the actual delay may vary by plus or minus one clock tick.

Using the DELAY interface is discouraged because the processor will be consumed for the specified time interval and therefore is unavailable to service other processes. In cases where device drivers need timing mechanisms, you should use the sleep and timeout interfaces instead of the DELAY interface. The most common usage of the DELAY interface is in the system boot path. Using DELAY in the boot path is often acceptable because there are no other processes in contention for the processor.

Return Values

None

Related Information

Section 15.2, Kernel Support Interfaces: `sleep`, `timeout`

Section 15.4, Global Variables: *hz*

Name

disable_option – Disables a device's interrupt line to the processor

Synopsis

```
void disable_option(ctlr_p)
struct controller *ctlr_p;
```

Arguments

ctlr_p
Specifies a pointer to the controller structure associated with the controller to be configured. The disable_option interface obtains the device whose interrupt line is to be disabled through its controller's associated controller structure pointer.

Description

The disable_option interface disables a device's interrupt line to the processor. Use this interface only if the device must have its interrupts alternately enabled or disabled during device autoconfiguration. Otherwise, interrupts may be generated before the device is ready to receive them.

Notes

The disable_option interface is a generic interface that maps to a bus- and machine-specific interface that actually disables a device's interrupt line to the processor. Using this interface to disable interrupts makes the driver more portable across different bus architectures, different CPU architectures, and different CPU types within the same CPU architecture.

Return Values

None

Related Information

Section 15.2, Kernel Support Interfaces: enable_option

Chapter 16, Structures Related to Device Drivers: controller

Name

dma_get_curr_sgentry – Returns a pointer to the current sg_entry

Synopsis

```
#include <io/common/devdriver.h>
sg_entry_t dma_get_curr_sgentry(dma_handle)
dma_handle_t dma_handle;
```

Arguments

dma_handle
Specifies a handle to DMA resources associated with the mapping of an in-memory I/O buffer onto a controller's I/O bus. This handle provides the information to access bus address/byte count pairs. A bus address/byte count pair is represented by the ba and bc members of an sg_entry structure pointer. Device driver writers can view the DMA handle as the tag to the allocated system resources needed to perform a DMA operation.

Description

The dma_get_curr_sgentry interface returns a pointer to an sg_entry data structure. A device driver can use this pointer to retrieve the current bus address/byte count pair for the mapping of a block of an in-memory I/O buffer onto the controller's I/O bus. A bus address/byte count pair is represented by the ba and bc members of an sg_entry structure pointer.

Specifically, dma_get_curr_sgentry returns a pointer to a bus address/byte count pair from the in-kernel DMA mapping data structures. Unlike dma_get_next_sgentry, a call to dma_get_curr_sgentry does not result in incrementing an internal index variable. Thus, subsequent calls to dma_get_curr_sgentry result in a return of the same sg_entry pointer and the same bus address/byte count pair.

Notes

Use of the dma_get_curr_sgentry interface makes device drivers more portable between DMA hardware-mapping implementations across different hardware platforms because it masks out any future changes in the kernel- and system-level DMA mapping data structures.

Example

See Section 9.9.7 for a code example of the `dma_get_curr_sgentry` interface.

Return Values

Upon successful completion, `dma_get_curr_sgentry` returns a pointer to the `sg_entry` structure associated with a mapped region of an I/O buffer on the controller's I/O bus. This `sg_entry` pointer is associated with the current bus address/byte count pair for this DMA handle. Otherwise, `dma_get_curr_sgentry` returns the value zero (0) to indicate it reached the end of bus address/byte count pairs for this DMA handle.

Related Information

Section 15.2, Kernel Support Interfaces: `dma_get_next_sgentry`

Chapter 16, Structures Related to Device Drivers: `sg_entry`

Name

dma_get_next_sgentry – Returns a pointer to the next sg_entry

Synopsis

```
#include <io/common/devdriver.h>
sg_entry_t dma_get_next_sgentry(dma_handle)
dma_handle_t dma_handle;
```

Arguments

dma_handle

Specifies a handle to DMA resources associated with the mapping of an in-memory I/O buffer onto a controller's I/O bus. This handle provides the information to access bus address/byte count pairs. A bus address/byte count pair is represented by the ba and bc members of an sg_entry structure pointer. Device driver writers can view the DMA handle as the tag to the allocated system resources needed to perform a DMA operation.

Description

The dma_get_next_sgentry interface returns a pointer to an sg_entry data structure. A device driver can use this pointer to retrieve the next valid bus address/byte count pair for the mapping of a block of an in-memory I/O buffer onto the controller's I/O bus. A bus address/byte count pair is represented by the ba and bc members of an sg_entry structure pointer.

Specifically, dma_get_next_sgentry returns a pointer to a bus address/byte count pair from the in-kernel DMA mapping data structures. After each call to dma_get_next_sgentry, the interface increments an internal index variable. This contrasts with the dma_get_curr_sgentry interface, which does not perform an increment operation. This increment operation ensures that the next call to dma_get_next_sgentry gets the next sg_entry pointer and thus the next bus address/byte count pair for this DMA handle.

Notes

Use of the `dma_get_next_sgentry` interface makes device drivers more portable between DMA hardware-mapping implementations across different hardware platforms because it masks out any future changes in the kernel- and system-level DMA mapping data structures.

Example

See Section 9.9.7 for a code example of the `dma_get_next_sgentry` interface.

Return Values

Upon successful completion, `dma_get_next_sgentry` returns a pointer to the `sg_entry` structure associated with a mapped region of an I/O buffer on the controller's I/O bus. This `sg_entry` pointer is associated with the next bus address/byte count pair for this DMA handle. Otherwise, `dma_get_next_sgentry` returns the value zero (0) to indicate it reached the end of bus address/byte count pairs for this DMA handle.

Related Information

Section 15.2, Kernel Support Interfaces: `dma_get_curr_sgentry`

Chapter 16, Structures Related to Device Drivers: `sg_entry`

Name

dma_get_private – Gets a data element from the DMA private storage space

Synopsis

```
#include <io/common/devdriver.h>
int dma_get_private(dma_handle, index, data)
dma_handle_t dma_handle;
int index;
u_long *data;
```

Arguments

dma_handle
> Specifies a handle to DMA resources associated with the mapping of an in-memory I/O buffer onto a controller's I/O bus. This handle provides the information to access bus address/byte count pairs. A bus address/byte count pair is represented by the ba and bc members of an sg_entry structure pointer. Device driver writers can view the DMA handle as the tag to the allocated system resources needed to perform a DMA operation.

index
> Specifies an index to the DMA private storage area for an internal kernel data structure associated with this DMA handle. Currently, you can pass only the value zero (0) as the index.

data
> Specifies the address of the location to retrieve the 64-bit data element from the DMA private storage area. You put this 64-bit data element in the DMA private storage area in a previous call to dma_put_private.

Description

The dma_get_private interface retrieves a 64-bit data element from the DMA private storage area of the internal kernel data structure associated with the specified DMA handle. Device drivers can put a 64-bit data element in the DMA private storage area of this internal kernel data structure by calling dma_put_private. Currently, the internal kernel data structure provides only one member to store a 64-bit data element.

DMA engines that make multiple calls to dma_map_alloc and dma_map_load can use the dma_get_private and dma_put_private pair of interfaces. Each call to dma_map_alloc and dma_map_load returns the address of the allocated DMA handle. The device driver calls dma_put_private to store each returned address as the 64-bit data element in each internal kernel data structure's DMA private storage area. By storing each address as the 64-bit data element in each internal kernel data structure's DMA private storage area, the device driver creates a linked list of DMA handles that it can pass to some lower software layer. This lower software layer then calls dma_get_private to retrieve the resources contained in the linked list of DMA handles.

Notes

Use of the dma_get_private interface makes device drivers more portable between DMA hardware-mapping implementations across different hardware platforms because it masks out any future changes in the kernel- and system-level DMA mapping data structures.

Return Values

Upon successful completion, dma_get_private returns the value zero (0). If the *index* to the private storage area is greater than zero (0), dma_get_private returns the value 1, indicating a failure status.

Related Information

Section 15.2, Kernel Support Interfaces: dma_put_private

Chapter 16, Structures Related to Device Drivers: sg_entry

Name

dma_kmap_buffer – Returns a kernel segment (kseg) address of a DMA buffer

Synopsis

```
#include <io/common/devdriver.h>
vm_offset_t dma_kmap_buffer(dma_handle, offset)
dma_handle_t dma_handle;
u_long offset;
```

Arguments

dma_handle
> Specifies a handle to DMA resources associated with the mapping of an in-memory I/O buffer onto a controller's I/O bus. This handle provides the information to access bus address/byte count pairs. A bus address/byte count pair is represented by the ba and bc members of an sg_entry structure pointer. Device driver writers can view the DMA handle as the tag to the allocated system resources needed to perform a DMA operation.

offset
> Specifies a byte count offset from the virtual address passed as the *virt_addr* argument of the dma_map_load interface. This virtual address specifies the beginning of a process's (or kernel) buffer that a DMA transfer operation is done to or from. A device driver determines the smallest DMA transfer size by calling the dma_min_boundary interface. The *offset* specifies the number of bytes a DMA engine moved. This number is less than the number of bytes the dma_map_load interface loaded.

Description

The dma_kmap_buffer interface takes an *offset* variable and returns a kseg address. The device driver can use this kseg address to copy and save the data at the offset in the buffer.

A device driver calls dma_kmap_buffer when the following occurs:

- A DMA device on a CPU or bus interrupts a transfer before the full transfer has completed

- The value returned by dma_min_boundary is greater than 1
- The transfer is interrupted within the region of the value returned by dma_min_boundary.

For example, a SCSI device performs a disconnect in the second byte of a longword on a TURBOchannel-based SCSI subsystem. The device driver uses the kseg address to read the valid data transferred so far, saves it in a dma_min_boundary sized buffer, and merges it back into the DMA buffer once the rest of the transfer has completed.

Example

See Section 9.9.9 for a code example of the dma_kmap_buffer interface.

Return Values

Upon successful completion, dma_kmap_buffer returns a kseg address of the byte offset pointed to by the addition of the following two values:

virt_addr + offset

where:

- *virt_addr* is the virtual address passed to the *virt_addr* argument of dma_map_load
- *offset* is the offset passed to the *offset* argument of dma_kmap_buffer

The dma_kmap_buffer interface returns the value zero (0) to indicate failure to retrieve the kseg address.

Related Information

Section 15.2, Kernel Support Interfaces: dma_map_load, dma_min_boundary

Chapter 16, Structures Related to Device Drivers: sg_entry

Name

dma_map_alloc – Allocates resources for DMA data transfers

Synopsis

```
#include <io/common/devdriver.h>
u_long dma_map_alloc(byte_count, ctlr_p, dma_handle_p, flags)
u_long byte_count;
struct controller *ctlr_p;
dma_handle_t *dma_handle_p;
int flags;
```

Arguments

byte_count
: Specifies the maximum size (in bytes) of the data to be transferred during the DMA transfer operation. The kernel uses this size to determine the resources (mapping registers, I/O channels, and other software resources) to allocate.

ctlr_p
: Specifies a pointer to the controller structure associated with this controller. The interface uses this pointer to obtain the bus-specific interfaces and data structures that it needs to allocate the necessary mapping resources.

dma_handle_p
: Specifies a pointer to a handle to DMA resources associated with the mapping of an in-memory I/O buffer onto a controller's I/O bus. This handle provides the information to access bus address/byte count pairs. A bus address/byte count pair is represented by the ba and bc members of an sg_entry structure pointer. Device driver writers can view the DMA handle as the tag to the allocated system resources needed to perform a DMA operation.

  Typically, the device driver passes an argument of type dma_handle_t *. The dma_map_alloc interface returns to this variable the address of the DMA handle. The device driver uses this address in a call to dma_map_load.

flags
: Specifies special conditions that the device driver needs the system to perform.

You can pass the bitwise inclusive OR of the following special condition bits defined in `/usr/sys/include/io/common/devdriver.h`:

Value	Meaning
DMA_GUARD_UPPER	Allocates additional resources so that contiguous data overruns are captured by the system map error functions. This bit is probably most useful during device driver development and debugging.
DMA_GUARD_LOWER	Allocates additional resources so that contiguous data underruns are captured by the system map error functions. This bit is probably most useful during device driver development and debugging.
DMA_SLEEP	Puts the process to sleep if the system cannot allocate the necessary resources to perform a data transfer of size *byte_count* at the time the driver calls the interface.
DMA_IN	Sets up a DMA write into main core memory.
DMA_OUT	Sets up a DMA read from main core memory.
DMA_ALL	Returns a nonzero value, only if the system can satisfy a DMA transfer of size *byte_count*.

Description

The dma_map_alloc interface allocates the resources (mapping registers, I/O channels, and other hardware and software resources) for DMA data transfers. You specify the size of the DMA data transfer in the *byte_count* argument.

The dma_map_alloc interface returns to the *dma_handle_p* argument a handle to DMA resources associated with the mapping of an in-memory I/O buffer onto a controller's I/O bus. Device driver writers can view the DMA handle as the tag to the allocated system resources needed to perform a DMA operation.

The dma_map_alloc interface allocates only the necessary resources for a device driver to perform a maximum transfer of size *byte_count*. However, the maximum transfer size is the size of the returned byte count if the returned byte count is not equal to *byte_count*. All drivers must be prepared for a returned byte count that is less than *byte_count*. The reason for this is that system resources can have physical limits that may never satisfy an allocation request of size *byte_count*. To actually initialize and set up the resources, the driver must make a call to dma_map_load.

The dma_map_alloc interface does not put the process to sleep and returns the value zero (0) if:

- The driver writer sets the *flags* argument to DMA_SLEEP

  AND

- The specified *byte_count* exceeds all available system resources; that is, the system cannot provide the resources for a data transfer of size *byte_count*

Notes

Use of the dma_map_alloc interface makes device drivers more portable between DMA hardware-mapping implementations across different hardware platforms because it masks out any future changes in the kernel- and system-level DMA mapping data structures.

Example

See Section 9.9.3 for a code example of the dma_map_alloc interface.

Return Values

Upon successful completion, dma_map_alloc returns a byte count (in bytes) that indicates the DMA transfer size it can map. It returns the value zero (0) to indicate a failure.

If the device driver sets *flags* to DMA_ALL, then dma_map_alloc returns a nonzero value only if the system can satisfy a transfer size of *byte_count*. This means that if the system cannot support a transfer of size *byte_count* (even if all DMA resources were made available), dma_map_alloc refuses to allocate any portion of the resources associated with the specified *byte_count* and returns a byte count of zero (0). This behavior — no allocation of resources unless dma_map_alloc can allocate the resources needed to do an uninterruptible transfer of the requested size — avoids extra calls to dma_map_dealloc.

If the returned byte count equals *byte_count*, then dma_map_alloc has allocated all of the resources necessary to allow the DMA transfer, without additional system resource allocation. If the returned byte count does not equal *byte_count*, the device driver can perform one of the following tasks:

- Partition the DMA data transfer

  A device driver can partition the DMA data transfer into a *byte_count* that is less than or equal to the returned byte count and then perform a sequence of DMA data transfer operations until the transfer has completed.

- Release and deallocate resources

  If the device driver needs more resources associated with the specified *byte_count* than dma_map_alloc can allocate, the driver calls dma_map_dealloc to release and deallocate these resources. The driver then recalls dma_map_alloc (possibly with the DMA_SLEEP flag set) until the necessary resources are available.

- Set the DMA_SLEEP bit

  A system can have the necessary resources to perform a DMA transfer of size *byte_count*. However, the resources might not be available at the time of the driver's call to dma_map_alloc. In this case, you set the DMA_SLEEP bit in the *flags* argument. This causes dma_map_alloc to block (sleep) until all the resources necessary to perform a DMA transfer of size *byte_count* are available to be allocated.

Related Information

Section 15.2, Kernel Support Interfaces: dma_map_dealloc, dma_map_load

Chapter 16, Structures Related to Device Drivers: controller, sg_entry

Name

dma_map_dealloc – Releases and deallocates the DMA resources
previously allocated for DMA data transfers

Synopsis

```
#include <io/common/devdriver.h>
int dma_map_dealloc(dma_handle)
dma_handle_t dma_handle;
```

Arguments

dma_handle

    Specifies a handle to DMA resources associated with the mapping of an
in-memory I/O buffer onto a controller's I/O bus. This handle provides
the information to access bus address/byte count pairs. A bus
address/byte count pair is represented by the ba and bc members of an
sg_entry structure pointer. Device driver writers can view the DMA
handle as the tag to the allocated system resources needed to perform a
DMA operation.

Description

The dma_map_dealloc interface releases and deallocates the resources for
DMA data transfers that were previously allocated in a call to
dma_map_alloc or dma_map_load.

Notes

Use of the dma_map_dealloc interface makes device drivers more
portable between DMA hardware-mapping implementations across different
hardware platforms because it masks out any future changes in the kernel-
and system-level DMA mapping data structures.

Example

See Section 9.9.6 for a code example of the dma_map_dealloc interface.

Return Values

Upon successful completion, dma_map_dealloc returns the value 1. Otherwise, it returns the value zero (0).

Related Information

Section 15.2, Kernel Support Interfaces: dma_map_alloc, dma_map_load, dma_map_unload

Chapter 16, Structures Related to Device Drivers: sg_entry

Name

dma_map_load – Loads and sets allocated DMA resources and sets up a
DMA data path for DMA data transfers

Synopsis

```
#include <io/common/devdriver.h>
u_long dma_map_load(byte_count, virt_addr, proc_p, ctlr_p, dma_handle_p,
max_byte_count, flags)
u_long byte_count;
vm_offset_t virt_addr;
struct proc *proc_p;
struct controller *ctlr_p;
dma_handle_t *dma_handle_p;
u_long max_byte_count;
int flags;
```

Arguments

byte_count

Specifies the maximum size (in bytes) of the data to be transferred
during the DMA transfer operation. The kernel uses this size to
determine the resources (mapping registers, I/O channels, and other
software resources) to allocate, load, and set.

virt_addr

Specifies the virtual address where the DMA transfer occurs. The
interface uses this address with the pointer to the proc structure to
obtain the physical addresses of the system memory pages to load into
DMA mapping resources.

proc_p

Specifies a pointer to the proc structure associated with the valid
context for the virtual address specified in virt_addr. The interface
uses this pointer to retrieve the pmap that is needed to translate this
virtual address to a physical address. If proc_p is equal to zero (0),
the address is a kernel address.

ctlr_p

Specifies a pointer to the controller structure associated with this
controller. The dma_map_load interface uses the pointer to get the
bus-specific interfaces and data structures that it needs to load and set
the necessary mapping resources.

dma_handle_p

Specifies a pointer to a handle to DMA resources associated with the
mapping of an in-memory I/O buffer onto a controller's I/O bus. This

handle provides the information to access bus address/byte count pairs. A bus address/byte count pair is represented by the `ba` and `bc` members of an `sg_entry` structure pointer. Device driver writers can view the DMA handle as the tag to the allocated system resources needed to perform a DMA operation.

Typically, the device driver passes an argument of type `dma_handle_t *`. If the device driver called `dma_map_alloc` prior to calling `dma_map_load`, then `dma_map_alloc` returns to this argument the address of the allocated DMA handle. The `dma_map_load` interface can then use this handle to load the appropriate DMA mapping resources. If the device driver did not call `dma_map_alloc` prior to calling `dma_map_load`, then you must set the *dma_handle_p* argument to the value zero (0). Upon completing execution, `dma_map_load` returns a valid DMA handle to *dma_handle_p*.

max_byte_count
> Specifies the maximum-size byte-count value that should be stored in the `bc` members of the `sg_entry` structures.

flags
> Specifies special conditions that the device driver needs the system to perform. You can pass the bitwise inclusive OR of the following special condition bits defined in `/usr/sys/include/io/common/devdriver.h`:

Value	Meaning
DMA_GUARD_UPPER	Allocates additional resources so that contiguous data overruns are captured by the system map error functions. This bit is probably most useful during device driver development and debugging.
DMA_GUARD_LOWER	Allocates additional resources so that contiguous data underruns are captured by the system map error functions. This bit is probably most useful during device driver development and debugging.
DMA_SLEEP	Puts the process to sleep if the system cannot allocate the necessary resources to perform a data transfer of size *byte_count* at the time the driver calls the interface.
DMA_IN	Sets up a DMA write into main core memory.
DMA_OUT	Sets up a DMA read from main core memory.
DMA_ALL	Returns a nonzero value, only if the system can satisfy a DMA transfer of size *byte_count*.

Description

The dma_map_load interface loads and sets the system resources necessary to perform a DMA transfer of size *byte_count* to the virtual address specified in the *virt_addr* argument. This virtual address must be valid in the context of the process's proc structure, specified in the *proc_p* argument.

If the device driver calls dma_map_alloc prior to calling dma_map_load, then dma_map_alloc returns to *dma_handle_p* the address of the allocated DMA handle. The dma_map_load interface uses this handle to load and set the appropriate DMA mapping resources. If the device driver did not call dma_map_alloc prior to calling dma_map_load, then you must set *dma_handle_p* to the value zero (0). In this case, dma_map_load allocates the appropriate DMA mapping resources (just as if the allocation were done in a previous call to the dma_map_alloc interface) and loads and sets the resources as necessary.

Notes

Use of the dma_map_load interface makes device drivers more portable between DMA hardware-mapping implementations across different hardware platforms because it masks out any future changes in the kernel- and system-level DMA mapping data structures.

Example

See Section 9.9.4 for a code example of the dma_map_load interface.

Return Values

Upon successful completion, dma_map_load returns a byte count (in bytes) that indicates the DMA transfer size it can support. It returns the value zero (0) to indicate a failure.

If the device driver sets *flags* to DMA_ALL, then dma_map_load returns a nonzero value only if the system can satisfy a transfer size of *byte_count*. This means that if the system cannot support a transfer of size *byte_count* (even if all DMA resources were made available), dma_map_load refuses to allocate any portion of the resources associated with the specified *byte_count* and returns a byte count of zero (0). This behavior — no allocation of resources unless dma_map_load can allocate the resources needed to do an uninterruptible transfer of the requested size — avoids extra calls to dma_map_dealloc.

If the returned byte count equals *byte_count*, then dma_map_load has allocated, loaded, and set all of the resources necessary to allow the DMA transfer, without additional system resource allocation.

If the returned byte count does not equal *byte_count*, the device driver can perform one of the following tasks:

- Release and deallocate resources

  If the device driver needs more resources associated with the specified *byte_count* than dma_map_load can allocate, the driver calls dma_map_unload, dma_map_dealloc, or both to unload, release, and deallocate these resources. The driver then recalls dma_map_alloc (possibly with the DMA_SLEEP flag set) until the necessary resources are available.

- Use the resources already allocated

  The device driver can use the resources already allocated, loaded, and set to perform the DMA data transfers. This data was indicated as mapped by dma_map_alloc in the *dma_handle_p* argument.

- Set the DMA_SLEEP bit

  A system can have the necessary resources to perform a DMA transfer of size *byte_count*. However, the resources might not be available at the time of the driver's call to dma_map_load. In this case, you set the DMA_SLEEP bit in the *flags* argument. This causes dma_map_load to block (sleep) until all the resources necessary to perform a DMA transfer of size *byte_count* are available to be allocated, loaded, and set.

Related Information

Section 15.2, Kernel Support Interfaces: dma_map_alloc, dma_map_dealloc, dma_map_unload

Chapter 16, Structures Related to Device Drivers: sg_entry

Name

dma_map_unload – Unloads the system DMA resources

Synopsis

```
#include <io/common/devdriver.h>
int dma_map_unload(flags, dma_handle)
int flags;
dma_handle_t dma_handle;
```

Arguments

flags
> To cause a deallocation of DMA mapping resources, you set the first argument to the special condition bit DMA_DEALLOC.
>
> This bit setting is analogous to setting the dma_handle_p argument to the value zero (0) for dma_map_load to allocate the DMA mapping resources.

dma_handle
> Specifies a handle to DMA resources associated with the mapping of an in-memory I/O buffer onto a controller's I/O bus. This handle provides the information to access bus address/byte count pairs. A bus address/byte count pair is represented by the ba and bc members of an sg_entry structure pointer. Device driver writers can view the DMA handle as the tag to the allocated system resources needed to perform a DMA operation.

Description

The dma_map_unload interface unloads (invalidates) the resources that were loaded and set up in a previous call to dma_map_load. A call to dma_map_unload does not release or deallocate the resources that were allocated in a previous call to dma_map_alloc unless the driver sets the flags argument to the DMA_DEALLOC bit.

Notes

Use of the dma_map_unload interface makes device drivers more portable between DMA hardware-mapping implementations across different hardware platforms because it masks out any future changes in the kernel- and system-level DMA mapping data structures.

Example

See Section 9.9.5 for a code example of the dma_map_unload interface.

Return Values

Upon successful completion, dma_map_unload returns the value 1.
Otherwise, it returns the value zero (0).

Related Information

Section 15.2, Kernel Support Interfaces: dma_map_alloc,
dma_map_dealloc, dma_map_load

Chapter 16, Structures Related to Device Drivers: sg_entry

Name

`dma_min_boundary` – Returns system-level information

Synopsis

```
#include <io/common/devdriver.h>
int dma_min_boundary(ctlr_p)
struct controller *ctlr_p;
```

Arguments

ctlr_p
Specifies a pointer to the `controller` structure associated with this controller. The `dma_min_boundary` interface uses this pointer to obtain the system and bus-specific information needed to return the mask or integer value.

Description

The `dma_min_boundary` interface returns an integer value that provides the information necessary for a device driver to determine the smallest DMA transfer that can be done atomically on a CPU or bus. The value returned by `dma_min_boundary` depends on the type of CPU or bus. For example, on a DEC 3000 Model 500 AXP Workstation connected to a TURBOchannel bus, this interface returns a value of 4. This indicates that a TURBOchannel DMA operation is atomic at the longword level (not the byte or word level). On a DEC 2000 Model 300 connected to an EISA bus, for example, this interface returns a value of 1 to indicate byte atomicity. Subbyte atomicity is not supported.

On a DEC 3000 Model 500 AXP Workstation connected to a TURBOchannel bus, this return value of 4 informs a device driver about how to handle a DMA transfer that involves a buffer that begins and/or ends within a nonlongword aligned, nonintegral longword-sized (DMA) transfer. The device driver handles this DMA transfer by redirecting the beginning and/or end of the DMA transfer, respectively, to other buffers that must be merged to the main (aligned longword block) buffer through calls to `bcopy`.

Return Values

The dma_min_boundary interface returns the value zero (0) to indicate that the system initialization code did not set up this field. Otherwise, dma_min_boundary returns the byte-size atomicity value that the system supports for DMA operations for all controllers on the respective bus.

Related Information

Chapter 16, Structures Related to Device Drivers: controller

Name

`dma_put_curr_sgentry` – Puts a new bus address/byte count pair in the
linked list of `sg_entry` structures

Synopsis

```
#include <io/common/devdriver.h>
int dma_put_curr_sgentry(dma_handle, sg_entryp)
dma_handle_t dma_handle;
sg_entry_t sg_entryp;
```

Arguments

dma_handle
>   Specifies a handle to DMA resources associated with the mapping of an
>   in-memory I/O buffer onto a controller's I/O bus. This handle provides
>   the information to access bus address/byte count pairs. A bus
>   address/byte count pair is represented by the `ba` and `bc` members of an
>   `sg_entry` structure pointer. Device driver writers can view the DMA
>   handle as the tag to the allocated system resources needed to perform a
>   DMA operation.

sg_entryp
>   Specifies a pointer to the `sg_entry` structure that contains the bus
>   address/byte count values to replace the corresponding bus address/byte
>   count of the `sg_entry` structure associated with this DMA handle.
>   You set the bus address/byte count in the `ba` and `bc` members of the
>   `sg_entry` structure and then pass its address to
>   `dma_put_curr_sgentry`.

Description

The `dma_put_curr_sgentry` interface puts new bus address/byte count
values into the `ba` and `bc` members for the existing bus address/byte count
pair pointed to by the DMA handle passed in by you. This interface enables
device drivers to patch an existing bus address/byte count pair due to an
unexpected interruption in a DMA transfer. A bus address/byte count pair is
represented by the `ba` and `bc` members of an `sg_entry` structure pointer.

This interface is useful for DMA engines that do not have total control of a
DMA transfer. For example, a SCSI device doing an unexpected disconnect
in the middle of a block transfer can interrupt a SCSI controller. Such a
disconnect can require the driver to do one or more patches to the list of bus

address/byte count pairs in order to restart the DMA transfer (without starting from the beginning of the list). Device drivers call the `dma_put_curr_sgentry` and `dma_put_prev_sgentry` interfaces to accomplish these patch operations. Typically, only buses that do not have byte atomicity transfers (for example, the TURBOchannel bus on Alpha CPUs) require these patch operations.

Example

See Section 9.9.8 for a code example of the `dma_put_curr_sgentry` interface.

Return Values

Upon successful completion, `dma_put_curr_sgentry` returns the value 1. Otherwise, `dma_put_curr_sgentry` returns the value zero (0) to indicate a failure. This failure indicates that the index into the DMA handle points past the end of the last bus address/byte count pair. The DMA handle can point past the end of the valid portion of the list when the previous call to `dma_get_next_sgentry` returned the pointer to the DMA handle associated with the last byte address/byte count pair.

Related Information

Section 15.2, Kernel Support Interfaces: `dma_get_curr_sgentry`, `dma_get_next_sgentry`, `dma_put_prev_sgentry`

Chapter 16, Structures Related to Device Drivers: `sg_entry`

Name

dma_put_prev_sgentry – Updates an internal pointer index to the linked list of sg_entry structures

Synopsis

```
#include <io/common/devdriver.h>
int dma_put_prev_sgentry(dma_handle, sg_entryp)
dma_handle_t dma_handle;
sg_entry_t sg_entryp;
```

Arguments

dma_handle

Specifies a handle to DMA resources associated with the mapping of an in-memory I/O buffer onto a controller's I/O bus. This handle provides the information to access bus address/byte count pairs. A bus address/byte count pair is represented by the ba and bc members of an sg_entry structure pointer. Device driver writers can view the DMA handle as the tag to the allocated system resources needed to perform a DMA operation.

sg_entryp

Specifies a pointer to the sg_entry structure that contains the bus address/byte count values to replace the corresponding bus address/byte count of the sg_entry structure associated with this DMA handle. The device driver writer sets the bus address/byte count in the ba and bc members of the sg_entry structure and then passes its address to dma_put_prev_sgentry.

Description

The dma_put_prev_sgentry interface updates an internal pointer index to the linked list of sg_entry structures, and then puts new bus address/byte count values into the existing bus address/byte count pair pointed to by the DMA handle passed in by you. This interface enables device drivers to patch existing bus address/byte count pairs due to an unexpected interruption in a DMA transfer. A bus address/byte count pair is represented by the ba and bc members of an sg_entry structure pointer.

This interface is useful for DMA engines that do not have total control of a DMA transfer. For example, a SCSI device doing an unexpected disconnect in the middle of a block transfer can interrupt a SCSI controller. Such a disconnect can require the driver to do one or more patches to the list of bus address/byte count pairs in order to restart the DMA transfer (without starting from the beginning of the list). Device drivers call the dma_put_curr_sgentry and dma_put_prev_sgentry interfaces to accomplish these patch operations. Typically, only buses that do not have byte atomicity transfers (for example, the TURBOchannel bus on Alpha CPUs) require these patch operations.

The dma_put_prev_sgentry differs from dma_put_curr_sgentry in that it updates an internal pointer index before inserting the new bus address/byte count values into the existing bus address/byte count pair. The pointer-index retains this updated value after dma_put_prev_sgentry returns.

Example

See Section 9.9.8 for a code example of the dma_put_prev_sgentry interface.

Return Values

Upon successful completion, dma_put_prev_sgentry returns the value 1. Otherwise, dma_put_prev_sgentry returns the value zero (0) to indicate failure. This failure indicates that the index into the DMA handle points to the first element in the byte address/byte count list. In this case, there is no previous byte address/byte count entry to patch.

Related Information

Section 15.2, Kernel Support Interfaces: dma_put_curr_sgentry

Chapter 16, Structures Related to Device Drivers: sg_entry

Name

dma_put_private – Stores a data element in the DMA private storage space

Synopsis

```
#include <io/common/devdriver.h>
int dma_put_private(dma_handle, index, data)
dma_handle_t dma_handle;
int index;
u_long data;
```

Arguments

dma_handle
Specifies a handle to DMA resources associated with the mapping of an in-memory I/O buffer onto a controller's I/O bus. This handle provides the information to access bus address/byte count pairs. A bus address/byte count pair is represented by the ba and bc members of an sg_entry structure pointer. Device driver writers can view the DMA handle as the tag to the allocated system resources needed to perform a DMA operation.

index
Specifies an index to the DMA private storage area for an internal kernel data structure associated with this DMA handle. Currently, you can pass only the value zero (0) as the index.

data
Specifies the address of the location to return the 64-bit data element from the DMA private storage area. The 64-bit data element is put in the DMA private storage area by a previous call to dma_get_private.

Description

The dma_put_private interface stores a 64-bit data element in the DMA private storage area of the internal kernel data structure associated with the specified DMA handle. Device drivers call dma_get_private to retrieve a 64-bit data element from the DMA private storage of this internal kernel data structure. Currently, the internal kernel data structure provides only one member to store a 64-bit data element.

DMA engines that make multiple calls to dma_map_alloc and dma_map_load can use the dma_get_private and dma_put_private pair of interfaces. Each call to dma_map_alloc and dma_map_load returns the address of the allocated DMA handle. The device driver calls dma_put_private to store each returned address as the 64-bit data element in each internal kernel data structure's DMA private storage area. By storing each address as the 64-bit data element in each internal kernel data structure's DMA private storage area, the device driver creates a linked list of DMA handles that it can pass to some lower software layer. This lower software layer then calls dma_get_private to retrieve the resources contained in the linked list of DMA handles.

Notes

Use of the dma_put_private interface makes device drivers more portable between DMA hardware-mapping implementations across different hardware platforms because it masks out any future changes in the kernel- and system-level DMA mapping data structures.

Return Values

Upon successful completion, dma_put_private returns the value 1. If the *index* to the private storage area is greater than zero (0), dma_put_private returns the value zero (0), indicating a failure status.

Related Information

Section 15.2, Kernel Support Interfaces: dma_get_private

Chapter 16, Structures Related to Device Drivers: sg_entry

Name

do_config – Initializes the device to its assigned configuration

Synopsis

```
void do_config(ctlr_p)
struct controller *ctlr_p;
```

Arguments

ctlr_p

Specifies a pointer to the controller structure associated with the controller to be configured. The do_config interface obtains the device to initialize through its controller's associated controller structure pointer.

Description

The do_config interface initializes the specified controller based on its power-up resource assignments. If the device uses either an interrupt or a DMA channel, then do_config also performs any setup requirements. For example, for controllers that connect to the EISA bus, do_config initializes the controller according to the parameters specified in the EISA configuration file.

Notes

The do_config interface is a generic interface that maps to a bus-specific interface that actually initializes the specified device. Using this interface to initialize a device makes the driver more portable across different bus architectures. Not all buses support the do_config interface.

Return Values

None

Related Information

Section 15.2, Kernel Support Interfaces: get_config, get_info

Chapter 16, Structures Related to Device Drivers: controller

Name

drvr_register_shutdown – Registers or deregisters a shutdown
interface

Synopsis

void drvr_register_shutdown(*callback*, *parameter*,
flags)
void (**callback*) ();
caddr_t *parameter*;
int *flags*;

Arguments

callback

Specifies the name of the device driver interface to be registered or
deregistered by drvr_register_shutdown. When registered, this
is the interface that the kernel calls when the system shuts down or
halts.

parameter

Specifies a parameter that the kernel passes to the device driver's
shutdown interface. For example, the kernel could pass a pointer to a
unit-specific data structure.

flags

Specifies whether to register or deregister the device driver's shutdown
interface. You can pass one of the following constants:

Value	Meaning
DRVR_REGISTER	Registers a device driver shutdown interface.
DRVR_UNREGISTER	Deregisters a device driver shutdown interface.

Description

The drvr_register_shutdown interface registers or deregisters a
shutdown interface for the calling device driver. Device drivers call
drvr_register_shutdown to register a device driver shutdown

interface that the kernel calls at system shutdown time (or when the user halts the system).

The `drvr_register_shutdown` interface allows device drivers to register interfaces that turn off the hardware device before the system shuts down. For example, a device driver that operates on a SCSI bus connected to two host CPUs (Available Server Environment) must ensure that the SCSI adapter on the shutdown host CPU is not doing work on the bus.

Cautions

The `drvr_register_shutdown` interface causes a system crash and displays an appropriate message on the console terminal if the device driver writer sets an invalid bit in the *flags* argument.

Return Values

None

Name

dualdevsw_add – Adds entry points to the block device switch and character device switch tables

Synopsis

```
dev_t dualdevsw_add(devno, chrent, blkent)
dev_t devno;
struct cdevsw *chrent;
struct bdevsw *blkent;
```

Arguments

devno
> Specifies the device switch table entry (slot) to use. If you pass NODEV to dualdevsw_add, the first available slot is used.

chrent
> Specifies a pointer to the character device switch structure that contains the character device driver's entry points for the system service's I/O requests.

blkent
> Specifies a pointer to the block device switch structure that contains the block device driver's entry points for the system service's I/O requests.

Description

The dualdevsw_add interface adds a device driver's entry points to both the block device and character device switch tables. One example of such a driver is a disk driver that has a character driver entry point for access to the ''raw'' device and a block driver entry point for access to the block device.

The only drivers that should call this interface are those drivers that strictly require that the assigned major number be the same in both the block device and the character device switch tables. The dualdevsw_add interface adds the entry points into the switch tables only if the same major number can be allocated for both the block and character device. If a device driver does not require that the major number be the same in both tables, it should use separate calls to the bdevsw_add and cdevsw_add interfaces.

Return Values

Upon successful completion, the `dualdevsw_add` interface returns the assigned major number. If the interface fails to allocate the major numbers, it returns the constant NODEV.

Related Information

Section 15.2, Kernel Support Interfaces: `bdevsw_add`, `dualdevsw_del`

Name

dualdevsw_del – Deletes entry points from the block device switch and
character device switch tables

Synopsis

```
int dualdevsw_del(devno)
dev_t devno;
```

Arguments

devno
Specifies the device switch table entry you want to remove.

Description

The dualdevsw_del interface deletes a device driver's entry points from
both the block device and character device switch tables.

Device drivers should call dualdevsw_del only if their entry points were
added to the device switch tables through a call to dualdevsw_add. The
dualdevsw_del interface assumes that the major number for the driver is
the same in both the block device and character device switch tables. If this
is not the case, calling dualdevsw_del could erroneously remove the
entry points for another device driver.

Return Values

If *devno* is a valid registered device number, dualdevsw_del removes
the device from both device switch tables and returns the value zero (0). If
the interface fails, it returns a nonzero value.

Related Information

Section 15.2, Kernel Support Interfaces: bdevsw_add, dualdevsw_add

Name

enable_option – Enables a device's interrupt line to the processor

Synopsis

```
void enable_option(ctlr_p)
struct controller *ctlr_p;
```

Arguments

ctlr_p

Specifies a pointer to the controller structure associated with the controller to be configured. The enable_option interface obtains the device whose interrupt line is to be enabled through its controller's associated controller structure pointer.

Description

The enable_option interface enables a device's interrupt line to the processor. Use this interface only if the device must have its interrupts alternately enabled or disabled during device autoconfiguration. Otherwise, interrupts may be generated before the device is ready to receive them.

Notes

The enable_option interface is a generic interface that maps to a bus- and machine-specific interface that actually enables a device's interrupt line to the processor. Using this interface to enable interrupts makes the driver more portable across different bus architectures, different CPU architectures, and different CPU types within the same CPU architecture.

Return Values

None

Related Information

Section 15.2, Kernel Support Interfaces: disable_option

Chapter 16, Structures Related to Device Drivers: controller

Name

ffs – Finds the first set bit in a mask

Synopsis

```
int ffs(mask)
long mask;
```

Arguments

mask
Specifies a bit mask with zero (0) or more bits set.

Description

The ffs interface returns the bit position of the first bit you set in the *mask* argument. The scan proceeds from the least significant bit to the most significant bit of the mask.

Notes

The ffs interface duplicates the behavior of the ffs instruction on the Digital VAX series computers. It is not present in architectures that implement its function in hardware or through compiler inline substitution.

The ffs interface is useful for translating bits in a bit mask into bit positions. For example, the signal handling code uses it to analyze the signal mask.

Return Values

Upon successful completion, ffs returns the bit position of the first bit set in the mask. If no bits were set in the mask, ffs returns the value zero (0).

Name

FREE – Deallocates (frees) the allocated kernel virtual memory

Synopsis

```
#include <sys/malloc.h>
void FREE(addr, type)
void *addr;
int type;
```

Arguments

addr
> Specifies the memory pointer that points to the allocated memory to be freed. You must have previously set this pointer in the call to MALLOC. You also define the data type for this argument in the call to MALLOC.

type
> Specifies the purpose for which the memory is being allocated. The memory types are defined in the file malloc.h. Typically, device drivers use the constant M_DEVBUF to indicate that device driver memory is being allocated (or freed).

Description

The FREE interface deallocates (frees) the allocated kernel virtual memory, which you allocated in a previous call to MALLOC. The FREE interface is actually a wrapper that calls free. A device driver should not directly call the free interface.

Notes

In previous versions of the Digital UNIX operating system (formerly known as DEC OSF/1), device drivers could call the following memory allocation-related interfaces:

- kalloc and kfree

  Device drivers called these interfaces to allocate and free a variable-sized section of kernel virtual memory.

- kget

  Device drivers called this interface to perform nonblocking allocation of a variable-sized section of kernel virtual memory.

- `zinit`, `zchange`, `zalloc`, `zfree`, and `zget`

  Device drivers called these interfaces to allocate exact-size sections of kernel virtual memory.

The Digital UNIX operating system still provides backwards compatibility with the `kalloc`, `kfree`, and `kget` interfaces and the `zinit`, `zchange`, `zalloc`, `zfree`, and `zget` interfaces. However, Digital recommends that for new device drivers you use the `MALLOC` and `FREE` interfaces to allocate and to free sections of kernel virtual memory.

A memory corruption can occur if a device driver continues to use the memory after freeing it. The Digital UNIX operating system provides a built-in mechanism to debug such erroneous use of memory. You can enable this debugging feature at boot time by providing the following boot parameter: `kmem_debug=1`. When you enable this debugging feature, the `free` interface stores the following in the last word of freed memory:

- The program counter (pc) of the module that last freed the memory
- The checksum of the memory content

The `malloc` interface checks the checksum of the memory content before reallocating this corrupted memory. If the checksum of the memory content does not match the corrupted memory, `malloc` stores the debug information and then causes the kernel to panic. The `malloc` interface stores the address and size of the corrupted memory and the pc of the interface that last freed it in a `kmem_corrupt_data` structure.

You should consider the following when using this debugging feature:

- This debugging feature does not detect cases where the corruption occurs after `malloc` reallocates the freed memory to some other module.
- There is a small chance that the pc of the interface that freed the memory (stored in the last word of freed memory) may itself get corrupted.

Example

See Section 9.2.2 for a code example of the `FREE` interface.

Return Values

None

Related Information

Section 15.2, Kernel Support Interfaces: MALLOC, zalloc, zchange, zfree, zget, zinit

Name

`fubyte` – Returns a byte from user address space

Synopsis

```
int fubyte(user_src)
char *user_src;
```

Arguments

`user_src`
Specifies the address in user space from which to read the byte.

Description

The `fubyte` interface returns 1 byte from the unprotected user address space to the calling program.

Notes

If the size of the return value is larger than 1 byte, the byte actually used for the return value is implementation defined.

Return Values

Upon successful completion, `fubyte` returns a value greater than zero (0). Otherwise, it returns –1, indicating that the user address specified in `user_src` cannot be accessed.

Related Information

Section 15.2, Kernel Support Interfaces: `copyinstr`, `fuword`, `subyte`, `suword`

Name

fuibyte – Returns a byte from user instruction address space

Notes

The fuibyte interface is for machines that have separate address spaces for code and data. Because the Alpha architecture does not have separate address spaces for code and data, fuibyte is mapped to fubyte. The fuibyte interface is provided for compatibility reasons. See the interface description for fubyte for a complete description of fuibyte.

Name

`fuiword` – Returns a word from user instruction address space

Notes

The `fuiword` interface is for machines that have separate address spaces for code and data. Because the Alpha architecture does not have separate address spaces for code and data, `fuiword` is mapped to `fuword`. The `fuiword` interface is provided for compatibility reasons. See the interface description for `fuword` for a complete description of `fuiword`.

Name

fuword – Returns a word from user address space

Synopsis

```
int fuword(user_src)
char *user_src;
```

Arguments

user_src
> Specifies the address in user space from which to read the word.

Description

The fuword interface returns one word from the unprotected user address space to the calling program.

Return Values

Upon successful completion, fuword returns a value greater than zero (0). Otherwise, it returns −1, indicating that the user address specified in user_src cannot be accessed.

Related Information

Section 15.2, Kernel Support Interfaces: copyinstr, fubyte, subyte, suword

Name

get_config – Returns assigned configuration data for a device

Synopsis

```
int get_config(ctlr_p, config_item, func_type,
data_p, handle)
struct controller *ctlr_p;
uint_t config_item;
char *func_type;
void *data_p;
int handle;
```

Arguments

ctlr_p

Specifies a pointer to the controller structure associated with the controller to be configured. The get_config interface obtains the device whose assigned configuration data you want through its controller's associated controller structure pointer.

config_item

Specifies the configuration data item you want to obtain for the specified device. You can pass one of the following constants:

Value	Meaning
RES_MEM	Obtains bus memory characteristics.
RES_IRQ	Obtains interrupt channel characteristics assigned to the device.
RES_DMA	Obtains the DMA channel assigned to the device.
RES_PORT	Obtains the I/O port assignments for the device.

func_type

Specifies a bus-specific argument. Some bus or bus adapters do not use this argument. For the EISA bus, this argument specifies the function type string that appears in the device's eisa_option structure.

data_p

Specifies a pointer to a structure appropriate for storing the requested data. The void * data type means that you cast the *data_p* argument's data type to the structure that stores the requested data.

handle
Specifies a handle returned by get_config if there is more configuration data of the type requested in the *config_item* argument. You must pass the value zero (0) on the first call to get_config. On subsequent calls to get_config for this configuration data type, you pass the value returned in the previous call to get_config.

Description

The get_config interface returns configuration data information assigned to the specified device.

Notes

The get_config interface is a generic interface that maps to a bus-specific interface that actually returns the assigned configuration data for the specified device. Using this interface to obtain configuration information makes the driver more portable across different bus architectures.

Return Values

If the bus option has only one resource of the requested *config_item*, get_config stores its value in the *data_p* argument and returns the value zero (0).

If the bus option has multiple resources of the requested *config_item*, get_config stores the value at the top of the list in the *data_p* argument and returns a handle that points to the next element in the list. To obtain the next element in the list, call get_config again and pass the returned handle to the *handle* argument. After reading all of the elements in the list, get_config returns the value zero (0).

If the bus option does not have a resource of the requested *func_type*, get_config returns the value –1.

Related Information

Section 15.2, Kernel Support Interfaces: do_config, get_info

Chapter 16, Structures Related to Device Drivers: controller

Name

get_info – Returns system-specific information

Synopsis

```
#include <devdriver.h>
u_int get_info(item_list)
struct item_list *item_list;
```

Arguments

item_list
Specifies a linked list of information requests.

Description

The get_info interface returns system-specific data assigned to the hardware platform that the driver operates on. For example, a device driver might request system-specific information for the following Alpha hardware platforms: DEC 3000 Model 300 AXP Workstation, DEC 3000 Model 500 AXP Workstation, and DEC 4000 Model 610 AXP System.

The get_info interface checks the function code that you pass in the function member of the item_list data structure. If the hardware platform that the driver operates on supports the system item associated with this function code, get_info returns the system-specific data for the system item in the output_data member of the item_list structure. For example, get_info returns the TURBOchannel clock speed in the output_data member of the item_list structure if you specify the constant GET_TC_SPEED in the function member of the item_list structure.

The get_info interface then performs the identical checks for the rest of the item_list structures in the linked list.

Notes

The get_info interface is a generic interface that maps to a hardware platform-specific interface that actually returns the assigned CPU-specific data for the specified CPU. Using this interface to obtain CPU-specific information makes the driver more portable across different CPU architectures and different CPU types within the same architecture.

Return Values

The return value from the get_info interface depends on the following issues:

- The hardware platform supports get_info

  In this case, get_info returns the value TRUE.

- The hardware platform does not support get_info

  In this case, get_info returns the value NOT_SUPPORTED.

If get_info returns the value TRUE, it returns one of the following values in the rtn_status member of the item_list data structure:

Value	Meaning
INFO_RETURNED	Indicates that the hardware platform that the driver currently operates on supports the requested system item.
NOT_SUPPORTED	Indicates that the hardware platform that the driver operates on does not support the requested system item.

Related Information

Section 15.2, Kernel Support Interfaces: do_config, get_config

Chapter 16, Structures Related to Device Drivers: item_list

Name

gsignal – Sends a signal to a process group

Synopsis

```
void gsignal(pgroup, signal)
pid_t pgroup;
int signal;
```

Arguments

pgroup
Specifies the process group to which you want to send a specified signal.

signal
Specifies the signal that you want to send to the specified process group.
You can specify any of the signals defined in
/usr/sys/include/sys/signal.h.

Description

The gsignal interface sends a signal to a process group, invoking
psignal for each process that is a member of the specified process group.

Return Values

None

Related Information

Section 15.2, Kernel Support Interfaces: psignal

Name

`handler_add` – Registers a device driver's interrupt service interface

Synopsis

```
ihandler_id_t * handler_add(handler)
ihandler_t *handler;
```

Arguments

handler
Specifies a pointer to an `ihandler_t` data structure.

Description

The `handler_add` interface registers a device driver's ISI and its associated `ihandler_t` data structure to the bus-specific interrupt-dispatching algorithm. The `ih_bus` member of the `ihandler_t` structure specifies the parent `bus` structure for the bus controlling the driver being loaded. For controller devices, `handler_add` sets `ih_bus` to the address of the `bus` structure for the bus the controller resides on.

Notes

Loadable and static device drivers call the `handler_add` interface to register a device driver's interrupt service interface.

Example

See Section 9.6.1 for a code example of the `handler_add` interface.

Return Values

Upon successful completion, the `handler_add` interface returns an opaque `ihandler_id_t` key, which is a unique number that identifies the ISIs to be acted on by subsequent calls to `handler_del`, `handler_disable`, and `handler_enable`. To implement this `ihandler_id_t` key, each call to `handler_add` causes the `handler_key` data structure to be allocated.

The `handler_add` interface returns the value NULL if it cannot allocate the appropriate resources or if it detected an error.

Related Information

Section 15.2, Kernel Support Interfaces: `handler_del`, `handler_disable`, `handler_enable`

Chapter 16, Structures Related to Device Drivers: `ihandler_t`

Name

handler_del – Deregisters a device driver's interrupt service interface

Synopsis

```
int handler_del(id)
ihandler_id_t *id;
```

Arguments

id

Specifies a pointer to the ISI's entry in the interrupt table.

Description

The handler_del interface deregisters a device driver's ISI from the bus-specific interrupt-dispatching algorithm. In addition, the interface unlinks the handler_key structure associated with the ISI. Prior to deleting the ISI, the device driver should have disabled it by calling handler_disable. If the ISI was not disabled, handler_del returns an error.

The handler_del interface uses the *id* argument to call a bus-specific adp_handler_del interface to remove the driver's ISI. Deregistration of an interrupt interface can consist of replacing it with the stray interface to indicate that interrupts are no longer expected from this device. The stray interface is a generic interface used as the interrupt handler when there is no corresponding ISI.

Notes

Loadable device drivers call the handler_del interface to deregister a device driver's interrupt service interface. It is not necessary for static device drivers to call the handler_del interface.

Example

See Section 9.6.2 for a code example of the handler_del interface.

Return Values

Upon successful completion, `handler_del` returns the value zero (0). Otherwise, it returns the value −1.

Related Information

Section 15.2, Kernel Support Interfaces: `handler_add`, `handler_disable`, `handler_enable`

Chapter 16, Structures Related to Device Drivers: `ihandler_t`

Section 17.3, Bus Configuration Interfaces: `adp_handler_del`

Name

handler_disable – Disables a previously registered interrupt service interface

Synopsis

```
int handler_disable(id)
ihandler_id_t *id;
```

Arguments

id
> Specifies a pointer to the ISI's entry in the interrupt table.

Description

The handler_disable interface makes the driver's previously registered interrupt service interfaces unavailable to the system. You must call handler_disable prior to calling handler_del. The handler_disable interface uses the *id* argument to call a bus-specific adp_handler_disable interface to perform the bus-specific tasks needed to disable the interrupt service interfaces.

Notes

Loadable device drivers call the handler_disable interface to disable a previously registered interrupt service interface. It is not necessary for static device drivers to call handler_disable.

Example

See Section 9.6.2 for a code example of the handler_disable interface.

Return Values

Upon successful completion, handler_disable returns the value zero (0). Otherwise, it returns the value –1.

Related Information

Section 15.2, Kernel Support Interfaces: `handler_add, handler_del, handler_enable`

Chapter 16, Structures Related to Device Drivers: `ihandler_t`

Name

handler_enable – Enables a previously registered interrupt service interface

Synopsis

```
int handler_enable(id)
ihandler_id_t *id;
```

Arguments

id
Specifies a pointer to the ISI's entry in the interrupt table.

Description

The handler_enable interface marks that interrupts are enabled and can be dispatched to the driver's ISIs, as registered in a previous call to handler_add. The id argument passed to handler_enable is used to call a bus-specific adp_handler_enable interface to perform the bus-specific tasks needed to enable the ISIs.

Notes

Loadable and static device drivers call the handler_enable interface to enable a previously registered interrupt service interface.

Example

See Section 9.6.1 for a code example of the handler_enable interface.

Return Values

Upon successful completion, handler_enable returns the value zero (0). Otherwise, it returns the value –1.

Related Information

Section 15.2, Kernel Support Interfaces: handler_add, handler_del, handler_disable

Chapter 16, Structures Related to Device Drivers: `ihandler_t`

Section 17.3, Bus Configuration Interfaces: `adp_handler_enable`

Name

htonl, htons – Convert word and longword values from host-to-network byte order

Synopsis

```
#include <sys/param.h>
```

unsigned int htonl(*longword*)
unsigned int *longword*;

unsigned short htons(*word*)
unsigned short *word*;

Arguments

longword
Specifies a 32-bit value to be conditionally byte swapped.

word
Specifies a 16-bit value to be conditionally byte swapped.

Description

The htonl interface converts the specified longword value from host-to-network byte order. The htons interface converts the specified word value from host-to-network byte order.

The TCP/IP protocols specify the canonical network byte order, which is big endian (meaning that the most significant byte is leftmost in memory).

Return Values

Upon successful completion, the htonl interface returns the converted longword value in network byte order. Similarly, upon successful completion, the htons interface converts the specified word value in network byte order.

Related Information

Section 15.2, Kernel Support Interfaces: `ntohl`

Name

insque, remque – Adds or removes an element from the queue

Synopsis

```
struct generic_qheader {
                        struct generic_qheader *q_forw;
                        struct generic_qheader *q_back;
                        };


    int insque(elem, pred)
    struct generic_qheader *elem;
    struct generic_qheader *pred;


    int remque(elem)
    struct generic_qheader *elem;
```

Arguments

elem
Specifies the address of the queue header that contains the element to be manipulated.

pred
Specifies the address of the queue header that contains the element to precede the one specified by *elem* in the queue.

Description

The insque interface adds the element that the *elem* argument specifies to the queue. The interface inserts *elem* in the next position after *pred* in the queue.

The remque interface removes the element that the *elem* argument specifies from the queue it is currently in.

Queues are built from doubly linked lists. Each element is linked into the queue through a queue header. All queue headers are of the generic form struct generic_qheader. A given element may have multiple queue headers. This allows each element to be simultaneously linked onto multiple queues.

Any driver interface that manipulates these queues must call an appropriate spl interface to ensure that the spl level is high enough to block out any interrupts for other device drivers that may access these queues.

Return Values

None

Related Information

Section 15.2, Kernel Support Interfaces: spl

Name

io_copyin – Copies data from bus address space to system memory

Synopsis

int io_copyin(*srcaddr, destaddr, byte_count*)
io_handle_t *srcaddr*;
vm_offset_t *destaddr*;
u_long *byte_count*;

Arguments

srcaddr
> Specifies an I/O handle that you can use to reference a device register or memory located in bus address space (either I/O space or memory space). For io_copyin, the I/O handle identifies the location in bus address space where the copy originates. You can perform standard C mathematical operations on the I/O handle. For example, you can add an offset to or subtract an offset from the I/O handle.

destaddr
> Specifies the kernel virtual address where io_copyin copies the data to in-system memory.

byte_count
> Specifies the number of bytes in the data block to be copied. The interface assumes that the buffer associated with the data block is physically contiguous.

Description

The io_copyin interface copies data from bus address space to system memory. The interface optimizes the copy operation for 32-bit transfers. The I/O handle you pass to *srcaddr* identifies where the copy originates in bus address space, and the address you pass to *destaddr* identifies where the copy occurs in system memory. The io_copyin interface assumes no alignment of data associated with *srcaddr* and *destaddr*.

Notes

The `io_copyin` interface is a generic interface that maps to a bus- and machine-specific interface that actually performs the copy from bus address space to system memory. Using `io_copyin` to perform the copy operation makes the device driver more portable across different CPU architectures and different CPU types within the same architecture.

Cautions

The I/O handle that you pass to the *srcaddr* argument of the `io_copyin` interface must be an I/O handle that references addresses residing in sparse space. All Alpha CPUs support sparse space. As a result, all bus configuration code should supply an I/O handle that references bus address space.

If you pass an I/O handle to the *srcaddr* argument that references addresses residing in some other space (for example, dense space) the results of the copy operation are unpredictable.

The Digital UNIX operating system provides the following interfaces that allow device drivers to perform copy operations on and zero blocks of memory on addresses that reside in dense space:

*   `bcopy`

    Copies a series of bytes with a specified limit

*   `blkclr` and `bzero`

    Zeros a block of memory

*   `copyin`

    Copies data from a user address space to a kernel address space

*   `copyinstr`

    Copies a null-terminated string from a user address space to a kernel address space

*   `copyout`

    Copies data from a kernel address space to a user address space

*   `copyoutstr`

    Copies a null-terminated string from a kernel address space to a user address space

Example

See Section 9.8.2.1 for a code example of the io_copyin interface.

Return Values

Upon successful completion, io_copyin returns IOA_OKAY. It returns the value −1 on failure.

Related Information

Section 15.2, Kernel Support Interfaces: io_copyio, io_copyout

Name

io_copyio – Copies data from bus address space to bus address space

Synopsis

```
int io_copyio(srcaddr, destaddr, byte_count)
io_handle_t srcaddr;
io_handle_t destaddr;
u_long byte_count;
```

Arguments

srcaddr
> Specifies an I/O handle that you can use to reference a device register or memory located in bus address space (either I/O space or memory space). For io_copyio, this I/O handle identifies the location in bus address space where the copy originates. You can perform standard C mathematical operations on the I/O handle. For example, you can add an offset to or subtract an offset from the I/O handle.

destaddr
> Specifies an I/O handle that you can use to reference a device register or memory located in bus address space (either I/O space or memory space). In this case, the I/O handle identifies the location in bus address space where the copy occurs.

byte_count
> Specifies the number of bytes in the data block to be copied. The interface assumes that the buffer associated with the data block is physically contiguous.

Description

The io_copyio interface copies data from one location in bus address space to another location in bus address space. The I/O handles you pass to srcaddr and destaddr identify the locations in bus address space where the copy originates and where the copy occurs. The io_copyio interface assumes no alignment of data associated with srcaddr and destaddr.

Notes

The `io_copyio` interface is a generic interface that maps to a bus- and machine-specific interface that actually performs the copy of data from one location in bus address space to another location in bus address space. Using `io_copyio` to perform the copy operation makes the device driver more portable across different CPU architectures and different CPU types within the same architecture.

Cautions

The I/O handles that you pass to the *srcaddr* and *destaddr* arguments of the `io_copyio` interface must be I/O handles that reference addresses residing in sparse space. All Alpha CPUs support sparse space. As a result, all bus configuration code should supply an I/O handle that references bus address space.

If you pass I/O handles to the *srcaddr* and *destaddr* arguments that reference addresses residing in some other space (for example, dense space) the results of the copy operation are unpredictable.

The Digital UNIX operating system provides the following interfaces that allow device drivers to perform copy operations on and zero blocks of memory on addresses that reside in dense space:

- `bcopy`

  Copies a series of bytes with a specified limit

- `blkclr` and `bzero`

  Zeros a block of memory

- `copyin`

  Copies data from a user address space to a kernel address space

- `copyinstr`

  Copies a null-terminated string from a user address space to a kernel address space

- `copyout`

  Copies data from a kernel address space to a user address space

- `copyoutstr`

  Copies a null-terminated string from a kernel address space to a user address space

Example

See Section 9.8.2.3 for a code example of the `io_copyio` interface.

Return Values

Upon successful completion, `io_copyio` returns `IOA_OKAY`. It returns the value −1 on failure.

Related Information

Section 15.2, Kernel Support Interfaces: `io_copyin`, `io_copyout`

Name

io_copyout – Copies data from system memory to bus address space

Synopsis

```
int io_copyout(srcaddr, destaddr, byte_count)
vm_offset_t srcaddr;
io_handle_t destaddr;
u_long byte_count;
```

Arguments

srcaddr
Specifies the kernel virtual address where the copy originates in system memory.

destaddr
Specifies an I/O handle that you can use to reference a device register or memory located in bus address space (either I/O space or memory space). For io_copyout, the I/O handle identifies the location in bus address space where the copy occurs. You can perform standard C mathematical operations on the I/O handle. For example, you can add an offset to or subtract an offset from the I/O handle.

byte_count
Specifies the number of bytes in the data block to be copied. The interface assumes that the buffer associated with the data block is physically contiguous.

Description

The io_copyout interface copies data from system memory to bus address space. The interface optimizes the copy operation for 32-bit transfers. The address you pass to *srcaddr* identifies the kernel virtual address where the copy originates in system memory, and the I/O handle you pass to *destaddr* identifies the address where the copy occurs in bus address space. The io_copyout interface assumes no alignment of data associated with *srcaddr* and *destaddr*.

Notes

The `io_copyout` interface is a generic interface that maps to a bus- and machine-specific interface that actually performs the copy to bus address space. Using `io_copyout` to perform the copy operation makes the device driver more portable across different CPU architectures and different CPU types within the same architecture.

Cautions

The I/O handle that you pass to the *destaddr* argument of the `io_copyout` interface must be an I/O handle that references addresses residing in sparse space. All Alpha CPUs support sparse space. As a result, all bus configuration code should supply an I/O handle that references bus address space.

If you pass an I/O handle to the *destaddr* argument that references addresses residing in some other space (for example, dense space) the results of the copy operation are unpredictable.

The Digital UNIX operating system provides the following interfaces that allow device drivers to perform copy operations on and zero blocks of memory on addresses that reside in dense space:

- `bcopy`

  Copies a series of bytes with a specified limit

- `blkclr` and `bzero`

  Zeros a block of memory

- `copyin`

  Copies data from a user address space to a kernel address space

- `copyinstr`

  Copies a null-terminated string from a user address space to a kernel address space

- `copyout`

  Copies data from a kernel address space to a user address space

- `copyoutstr`

  Copies a null-terminated string from a kernel address space to a user address space

Example

See Section 9.8.2.2 for a code example of the io_copyout interface.

Return Values

Upon successful completion, io_copyout returns IOA_OKAY. It returns the value −1 on failure.

Related Information

Section 15.2, Kernel Support Interfaces: io_copyin, io_copyio

Name

io_zero – Zeros a block of memory in bus address space

Synopsis

```
int io_zero(destaddr, byte_count)
io_handle_t destaddr;
u_long byte_count;
```

Arguments

destaddr
> Specifies an I/O handle that you can use to reference a device register or memory located in bus address space (either I/O space or memory space). For io_zero, this I/O handle identifies the location in bus address space where the zero operation occurs. You can perform standard C mathematical operations on the I/O handle. For example, you can add an offset to or subtract an offset from the I/O handle.

byte_count
> Specifies the number of bytes in the data block to be zeroed. The interface assumes that the buffer associated with the data block is physically contiguous.

Description

The io_zero interface zeros byte_count bytes of memory beginning at the bus address specified by destaddr. The I/O handle you pass to destaddr identifies where the zero operation occurs in bus address space. The interface optimizes the copy operation for 32-bit transfers.

Notes

The io_zero interface is a generic interface that maps to a machine-specific interface that actually writes zeros to some location in bus address space. Using io_zero to perform the zero operation makes the device driver more portable across different CPU architectures and different CPU types within the same architecture.

Cautions

The I/O handle that you pass to the *destaddr* argument of the `io_zero` interface must be an I/O handle that references addresses residing in sparse space. All Alpha CPUs support sparse space. As a result, all bus configuration code should supply an I/O handle that references bus address space.

If you pass an I/O handle to the *destaddr* argument that references addresses residing in some other space (for example, dense space) the results of the copy operation are unpredictable.

The Digital UNIX operating system provides the following interfaces that allow device drivers to perform copy operations on and zero blocks of memory on addresses that reside in dense space:

- `bcopy`

  Copies a series of bytes with a specified limit

- `blkclr` and `bzero`

  Zeros a block of memory

- `copyin`

  Copies data from a user address space to a kernel address space

- `copyinstr`

  Copies a null-terminated string from a user address space to a kernel address space

- `copyout`

  Copies data from a kernel address space to a user address space

- `copyoutstr`

  Copies a null-terminated string from a kernel address space to a user address space

Return Values

Upon successful completion, `io_zero` returns `IOA_OKAY`. It returns the value −1 on failure.

Related Information

Section 15.2, Kernel Support Interfaces: `io_copyin`, `io_copyio`, `io_copyout`

Name

iodone – Indicates that I/O is complete

Synopsis

```
void iodone(bp)
struct buf *bp;
```

Arguments

bp

Specifies a pointer to a buf structure.

Description

The iodone interface indicates that I/O is complete and reschedules the process that initiated the I/O.

Return Values

None

Name

iohandle_to_phys – Converts an I/O handle to a valid system physical address

Synopsis

```
u_long iohandle_to_phys(io_handle, flags)
io_handle_t io_handle;
long flags;
```

Arguments

io_handle

Specifies the I/O handle that you want converted to a valid system physical address. To convert the I/O handle to a valid system physical address, you must pass the bitwise inclusive OR of one of the valid conversion flag bits and one of the data type flag bits described in the *flags* argument. See the bus-specific device driver book for the type of I/O handle associated with that bus.

flags

Specifies a flag that indicates the conversion type and data size. This flag is the bitwise inclusive OR of a valid conversion type value and a valid data size value. To indicate the conversion type, pass one of the following conversion type values defined in /usr/sys/include/io/common/devdriver.h:

Conversion Type Value	Meaning
HANDLE_DENSE_SPACE	Converts the I/O handle to a dense space physical address.
HANDLE_SPARSE_SPACE	Converts the I/O handle to a sparse space physical address.
HANDLE_BUSPHYS_ADDR	Converts the I/O handle to a bus physical address.

In addition to one of the conversion type values, you OR in one of the following data size values defined in /usr/sys/include/io/common/devdriver.h. This bit is required for compatibility across Alpha CPU architectures. Some Alpha CPUs encode size information in the physical address used in I/O or memory bus accesses.

Data Size Value	Meaning
HANDLE_BYTE	Converts the I/O handle to a system physical address that points to a byte address. This byte address resides in bus address space (either I/O space or memory space).
HANDLE_WORD	Converts the I/O handle to a system physical address that points to a word address. This word address resides in bus address space (either I/O space or memory space).
HANDLE_LONGWORD	Converts the I/O handle to a system physical address that points to a longword address. This longword address resides in bus address space (either I/O space or memory space).
HANDLE_QUADWORD	Converts the I/O handle to a system physical address that points to a quadword address. This quadword address resides in bus address space (either I/O space or memory space).
HANDLE_TRIBYTE	Converts the I/O handle to a system physical address that points to a tribyte address. This tribyte address resides in bus address space (either I/O space or memory space).

Description

The `iohandle_to_phys` interface converts an I/O handle to a valid system physical address that a device driver uses to perform I/O copy operations. You use this physical address in the I/O copy operations associated with calls to `bcopy`, `copyin`, `copyout`, or a copy interface that you supply. Do not use the physical address returned by `iohandle_to_phys` in calls to `io_copyin`, `io_copyio`, and `io_copyout`. These interfaces take an I/O handle instead of a physical address and are to bus address space what `bcopy` is to system memory.

Notes

The `iohandle_to_phys` interface is a generic interface that maps to a bus- and machine-specific interface that actually converts the I/O handle to a system physical address. Using this interface to convert the I/O handle makes the device driver more portable across different bus architectures, different CPU architectures, and different CPU types within the same CPU architecture.

Return Values

Upon successful completion, `iohandle_to_phys` returns the physical address indicated by the conversion type value that you passed to the *flags* argument. If a failure occurs, `iohandle_to_phys` returns the value zero (0). A return value of zero (0) can occur as a result of the following conditions:

- The CPU that the driver operates on does not support the physical address space indicated by the conversion type value.

- The data type indicated by the data type value does not exist in the physical address space on this CPU or bus.

Related Information

Section 15.2, Kernel Support Interfaces: `io_copyin`, `io_copyio`, `io_copyout`

Name

IS_KSEG_VA, IS_SEG0_VA, IS_SEG1_VA – Determine if the specified address is located in the kernel-unmapped address space, the user-mapped address space, and the kernel-mapped address space.

Synopsis

```
void IS_KSEG_VA(addr)
unsigned long addr;


void IS_SEG0_VA(addr)
unsigned long addr;


void IS_SEG1_VA(addr)
unsigned long addr;
```

Arguments

addr
> Specifies the virtual address.

Description

The IS_KSEG_VA interface determines if the specified address is located in the kernel-unmapped address space. The IS_SEG0_VA interface determines if the specified address is located in the user-mapped address space. The IS_SEG1_VA interface determines if the specified address is located in the kernel-mapped address space.

Example

The following code fragment shows a call to IS_KSEG_VA:

```
    .
    .
    .
caddr_t virt_addr;  1
unsigned phys_addr; 2
    .
    .
    .
    if(IS_KSEG_VA(virt_addr)) { 3
```

```
              phys_addr = KSEG_TO_PHYS(virt_addr); 4
          •
          •
          •
```

1 Declares a variable to store the user buffer's virtual address.

2 Declares a variable to store the physical address returned by
   KSEG_TO_PHYS.

3 Before calling KSEG_TO_PHYS, calls IS_KSEG_VA to determine if the
   virtual address is from the kernel-unmapped address space.

4 If the virtual address is from the kernel-unmapped address space, then
   calls KSEG_TO_PHYS to convert the address to a corresponding physical
   address.

Return Values

None

Related Information

Section 15.2, Kernel Support Interfaces: KSEG_TO_PHYS,
PHYS_TO_KSEG

Name

kernel_isrthread – Starts a fixed priority kernel thread dedicated to interrupt service

Synopsis

```
thread_t kernel_isrthread(task, start, pri)
task_t task;
void (*start) ();
int pri;
```

Arguments

task

Specifies a pointer to a task structure. This pointer identifies the task in which the kernel_isrthread interface starts the newly created kernel thread dedicated to interrupt service handling.

start

Specifies a pointer to an interface that is the entry point for the newly created kernel thread.

pri

Specifies the scheduling priority level for the newly created kernel thread.

The priority usage table describes the possible scheduling priorities. The first column shows a range of priorities. The second column shows an associated scheduling priority constant defined in <src/kernel/kern/sched.h> (if applicable). The third column describes the usage of the priority ranges. To specify a scheduling priority of 38, you pass the constant BASEPRI_SYSTEM as shown in the example. To specify a scheduling priority of 33, you can pass the following: BASEPRI_HIGHEST + 1.

Priority	Constant	Usage
0	N/A	Realtime kernel threads
.		
.		
.		
31		

Priority	Constant	Usage
32	BASEPRI_HIGHEST	Operating system kernel threads
.	.	
.	.	
.	.	
38	BASEPRI_SYSTEM	
44	BASEPRI_USER	User kernel threads
.	.	
.	.	
.	.	
64	BASEPRI_LOWEST	

Description

The `kernel_isrthread` interface creates and starts a kernel thread at the specified entry point. This kernel thread handles only interrupt service requests in the specified task and at the specified priority level. A device driver should always attach a kernel thread to the "first task."

Example

See *Writing Device Drivers: Advanced Topics* for a code example of the `kernel_isrthread` interface.

Return Values

Upon successful completion, `kernel_isrthread` returns a pointer to the `thread` structure associated with the kernel thread started at the specified entry point. Device drivers can use this pointer as a handle to a specific kernel thread in calls to other kernel threads-related interfaces.

Related Information

Section 15.2, Kernel Support Interfaces: `kernel_thread_w_arg`

Chapter 16, Structures Related to Device Drivers: `task`, `thread`

Name

kernel_thread_w_arg – Starts a kernel thread with a calling argument passed in

Synopsis

thread_t kernel_thread_w_arg(*task, start, argument*)
task_t *task;*
void *(*start) ();*
void **argument;*

Arguments

task
> Specifies a pointer to a task structure. This pointer identifies the task in which the kernel_thread_w_arg interface starts the newly created kernel thread.

start
> Specifies a pointer to an interface that is the entry point for the newly created kernel thread.

argument
> Specifies the argument that kernel_thread_w_arg passes to the entry point specified in *start*.

Description

The kernel_thread_w_arg interface creates and starts a kernel thread in the specified task at the specified entry point with a specified argument. The kernel_thread_w_arg interface passes the specified argument to the newly created kernel thread. The kernel_thread_w_arg interface creates and starts a kernel thread with timeshare scheduling. A kernel thread created with timeshare scheduling means that its priority degrades if it consumes an inordinate amount of CPU resources. A device driver should call kernel_thread_w_arg only for long-running tasks. A device driver should always attach a kernel thread to the "first task."

Notes

This interface is actually a convenience wrapper for the `thread_create` interface (which creates the kernel thread) and the `thread_start` interface (which starts the newly created kernel thread).

The `kernel_thread_w_arg` interface behaves identically to `kernel_isrthread` except that with `kernel_thread_w_arg` you can pass an argument to the entry point for the newly created kernel thread.

Example

See *Writing Device Drivers: Advanced Topics* for a code example of the `kernel_thread_w_arg` interface.

Return Values

Upon successful completion, `kernel_thread_w_arg` returns a pointer to the `thread` structure associated with the kernel thread started at the specified entry point. Device drivers can use this pointer as a handle to a specific kernel thread in calls to other kernel threads-related interfaces.

Related Information

Section 15.2, Kernel Support Interfaces: `kernel_isrthread`

Chapter 16, Structures Related to Device Drivers: `task`, `thread`

Name

KSEG_TO_PHYS – Converts a kernel-unmapped virtual address to a physical address

Synopsis

vm_offset_t KSEG_TO_PHYS(*addr*)
vm_offset_t *addr*;

Arguments

addr
Specifies the buffer virtual address to convert to a physical address.

Description

The KSEG_TO_PHYS interface converts a kernel-unmapped virtual address to a physical address. Device drivers can use this physical address in DMA operations. Prior to calling KSEG_TO_PHYS, device driver writers often call one of the following interfaces to determine whether the address passed is a virtual address in the addressed kernel segment:

- IS_KSEG_VA

  Determines if the specified address is located in the kernel-unmapped address space

- IS_SEG0_VA

  Determines if the specified address is located in the user-mapped address space

- IS_SEG1_VA

  Determines if the specified address is located in the kernel-mapped address space

Example

The following code fragment shows a call to KSEG_TO_PHYS:

```
    .
    .
    .
caddr_t virt_addr;   1
unsigned phys_addr;  2
    .
    .
    .
    if(IS_KSEG_VA(virt_addr)) {  3
        phys_addr = KSEG_TO_PHYS(virt_addr);  4
    .
    .
    .
```

1   Declares a variable to store the user buffer's virtual address.

2   Declares a variable to store the physical address returned by
    KSEG_TO_PHYS.

3   Before calling KSEG_TO_PHYS, calls IS_KSEG_VA to determine if the
    virtual address is from the kernel-unmapped address space.

4   If the virtual address is from the kernel-unmapped address space, then
    calls KSEG_TO_PHYS to convert the address to a corresponding physical
    address.

Return Values

Upon successful completion, KSEG_TO_PHYS returns the physical address.

Related Information

Section 15.2, Kernel Support Interfaces: IS_KSEG_VA, PHYS_TO_KSEG

Name

ldbl_ctlr_configure – Configures the specified controller

Synopsis

int ldbl_ctlr_configure(*bus_name*, *bus_num*,
driver_name, *driver_struct*, *flags*)
char **bus_name;*
int *bus_num;*
char **driver_name;*
struct driver **driver_struct;*
int *flags;*

Arguments

bus_name
    Specifies the bus name.

bus_num
    Specifies the bus number.

driver_name
    Specifies the name of the controlling device driver.

driver_struct
    Specifies a pointer to the driver structure for the controlling device
    driver. The device driver writer initializes this driver structure,
    usually in the Declarations Section of the device driver.

flags
    Specifies miscellaneous flags contained in the file
    /usr/sys/include/io/common/devdriver_loadable.h.

Description

The ldbl_ctlr_configure interface scans the hardware topology tree
for bus structures whose bus_name and bus_num members contain
values that match those specified by the *bus_name* and *bus_num*
arguments. For each bus whose values match, ldbl_ctlr_configure
searches for controller structures with the following characteristics:

- Their alive members are set to the bitwise inclusive OR of the
  following valid alive bits:

ALV_PRES
  Controller present but not configured as loadable

ALV_LOADABLE
  Controller present and resolved as loadable

These bits indicate that the specified device driver controls the controller structures. The ldbl_stanza_resolver interface, which the device driver previously called, sets these bits.

For each controller structure found, ldbl_ctlr_configure calls the bus-specific ctlr_configure interface to complete the configuration process.

Notes

Loadable device drivers call the ldbl_ctlr_configure interface to configure the specified controller.

Example

See Section 9.7.4 for a code example of the ldbl_ctlr_configure interface.

Return Values

The ldbl_ctlr_configure interface can return the following values:

ESUCCESS
  The interface successfully configured the specified controller or controllers.

Status value
  This return value is a status value from the bus-specific ctlr_configure interface.

Related Information

Section 15.2, Kernel Support Interfaces: ldbl_ctlr_unconfigure, ldbl_stanza_resolver

Chapter 16, Structures Related to Device Drivers: driver

Section 17.3, Bus Configuration Interfaces: ctlr_configure

Name

ldbl_ctlr_unconfigure – Unconfigures the specified controller

Synopsis

```
int ldbl_ctlr_unconfigure(bus_name, bus_num,
driver_struct, ctlr_name, ctlr_num)
char *bus_name;
int bus_num;
struct driver *driver_struct;
char *ctlr_name;
int ctlr_num;
```

Arguments

bus_name
> Specifies the bus name.

bus_num
> Specifies the bus number. To indicate that you want the interface to match any controller, pass the wildcard constant LDBL_WILDNUM.

driver_struct
> Specifies a pointer to the driver structure for the controlling device driver. The device driver writer initializes this driver structure, usually in the Declarations Section of the device driver.

ctlr_name
> Specifies the controller name. The controller name can be any string. You can pass the controller name as it is specified in the stanza.loadable file fragment, or you can pass the wildcard constant LDBL_WILDNAME to indicate that you want the interface to scan all controller structures.

ctlr_num
> Specifies the controller number. You can pass the controller number as specified in the stanza.loadable file fragment, or you can pass the wildcard constant LDBL_WILDNUM to indicate that you want the interface to scan all controller structures.

Description

The `ldbl_ctlr_unconfigure` interface scans the hardware topology tree for `bus` structures with one or both of the following characteristics:

- Their `bus_name` members match the value specified in the *bus_name* argument

- Their `bus_num` members match the value specified in the *bus_num* argument

For each bus found, `ldbl_ctlr_unconfigure` searches for `controller` structures to determine if:

- Their `driver` members are set to the address of the device driver structure specified in the *driver_struct* argument

- Their `ctlr_name` members match the controller name specified in the *ctlr_name* argument

- Their `ctlr_num` members match the controller number specified in the *ctlr_num* argument

- Their `alive` members are set to the bitwise inclusive OR of the following valid alive bits:

  `ALV_ALIVE`
  > The controller is present and active on the system.

  `ALV_LOADABLE`
  > The controller is configured for use by loadable device drivers.

For each `controller` structure found, `ldbl_ctlr_unconfigure` calls the driver-specific `dev_unattach` interface to process the controller's device list (the `dev_list` members of the `controller` structures). The `dev_unattach` interface deallocates these `device` structures to prevent subsequent autoconfiguration processing (driver loading) from detecting devices that are no longer in the configuration.

After `dev_unattach` deallocates the `device` structures and performs any other cleanup tasks, it calls a driver-specific `ctlr_unattach` interface. The `ctlr_unattach` interface performs such tasks as removing any in-memory data structures and interrupt service interfaces the driver may have established. After `ctlr_unattach` returns successfully, `ldbl_ctlr_unconfigure` sets the `alive` members of the `controller` structures to alive bit `ALV_PRES` (the controller is present on the system, but it is no longer configured for loadable device drivers).

Notes

Loadable device drivers call the `ldbl_ctlr_unconfigure` interface to unconfigure the specified controller.

Example

See Section 9.7.4 for a code example of the `ldbl_ctlr_unconfigure` interface.

Return Values

The `ldbl_ctlr_unconfigure` interface can return the following values:

ESUCCESS
> The interface successfully unconfigured the specified controllers.

Status value
> This return value is a status value from the device driver's `ctlr_unattach` or `dev_unattach` interface.

Status value
> This return value is a status value from the bus-specific `ctlr_unconfigure` interface.

Related Information

Section 15.2, Kernel Support Interfaces: `ldbl_ctlr_configure`, `ldbl_stanza_resolver`

Chapter 16, Structures Related to Device Drivers: `driver`

Section 17.2, Block and Character Device Driver Interfaces: *xx*`ctrl_unattach`, *xx*`dev_unattach`

Name

ldbl_stanza_resolver – Merges the configuration data

Synopsis

```
int ldbl_stanza_resolver(driver_name, parent_bus,
driver_struct, bus_param)
char *driver_name;
char *parent_bus;
struct driver *driver_struct;
caddr_t *bus_param;
```

Arguments

driver_name
> Specifies the driver name that was entered as the stanza entry in the stanza.loadable file fragment.

parent_bus
> Specifies the name of the parent bus structure. This name is obtained from the config program.

driver_struct
> Specifies a pointer to the driver structure for the controlling device driver. The device driver writer initializes this driver structure, usually in the Declarations Section of the device driver.

bus_param
> Specifies a bus-specific parameter. For example, you would probably pass a snippet table as the value to this argument for the TURBOchannel bus.

Description

The ldbl_stanza_resolver interface allows device drivers to merge the system configuration data specified in the stanza.loadable or stanza.static file fragments into the hardware topology tree created at static configuration time. This operation results in a kernel memory resident hardware topology tree that consists of both loadable and static drivers.

The driver later calls the ldbl_ctlr_configure interface, which accesses the hardware topology tree. For this reason, device drivers call ldbl_stanza_resolver prior to ldbl_ctlr_configure. Part of this operation involves calling a bus-specific configuration resolver interface that searches for devices that can be autoconfigured. The *parent_bus* argument is used to locate these bus-specific configuration resolver interfaces.

The `ldbl_stanza_resolver` interface sets the `alive` members of all bus and `controller` structures it creates or uses to the bitwise inclusive OR of the following valid alive bits:

ALV_PRES
> The bus or controller is present but not configured as loadable.

ALV_LOADABLE
> The bus or controller is present and resolved as loadable.

ALV_NOSIZER
> The `sizer` program should ignore these bus and `controller` structures.

Notes

Loadable device drivers call the `ldbl_stanza_resolver` interface to merge the configuration data.

Example

See Section 9.7.3 for a code example of the `ldbl_stanza_resolver` interface.

Return Values

The `ldbl_stanza_resolver` interface can return the following values:

ESUCCESS
> The interface successfully merged the configuration data.

ENOMEM
> The system is unable to allocate enough memory to complete the resolver operations.

LDBL_ENOBUS
> The specified parent bus structure does not exist.

Related Information

Section 15.2, Kernel Support Interfaces: `ldbl_ctlr_configure`, `ldbl_ctlr_unconfigure`

Chapter 16, Structures Related to Device Drivers: `driver`

Name

lock_done – Releases a complex lock

Synopsis

```
#include <kern/lock.h>
void lock_done(lock_structptr)
lock_t lock_structptr;
```

Arguments

lock_structptr
Specifies a pointer to the complex lock structure, lock. The lock
structure is an opaque data structure; that is, its associated members are
referenced and manipulated by the Digital UNIX operating system and
not by the user of the complex lock mechanism.

Description

The lock_done interface releases a lock that was previously asserted by
one of the following complex locking interfaces: lock_read,
lock_try_read, lock_try_write, and lock_write.

Notes

You must hold the lock on the resource before calling lock_done.

Example

See *Writing Device Drivers: Advanced Topics* for a code example of the
lock_done interface.

Return Values

None

Related Information

Chapter 14, Header Files Related to Device Drivers: lock.h

Section 15.2, Kernel Support Interfaces: lock_init, lock_read, `lock_terminate`, `lock_try_read`, `lock_try_write`, `lock_write`

Chapter 16, Structures Related to Device Drivers: `lock`

Name

lock_init – Initializes a complex lock

Synopsis

```
#include <kern/lock.h>
void lock_init(lock_structptr, can_sleep)
lock_t lock_structptr;
boolean_t can_sleep;
```

Arguments

lock_structptr

Specifies a pointer to the complex lock structure, lock. The lock structure is an opaque data structure; that is, its associated members are referenced and manipulated by the Digital UNIX operating system and not by the user of the complex lock mechanism.

can_sleep

Specifies a Boolean value that indicates whether to allow kernel threads to block (sleep) if the complex lock is asserted. You can pass to this argument only the value TRUE (allow kernel threads to block if the lock is asserted).

Description

The lock_init interface initializes a complex lock. You identify this lock by declaring a pointer to a complex lock structure and passing it as the first argument. The complex lock structure pointer must be initialized before you can assert read and write operations on the complex lock.

Example

See *Writing Device Drivers: Advanced Topics* for a code example of the lock_init interface.

Return Values

None

Related Information

Chapter 14, Header Files Related to Device Drivers: `lock.h`

Section 15.2, Kernel Support Interfaces: `lock_done`, `lock_read`, `lock_terminate`, `lock_try_read`, `lock_try_write`, `lock_write`

Chapter 16, Structures Related to Device Drivers: `lock`

Name

lock_read – Asserts a complex lock with read-only access

Synopsis

```
#include <kern/lock.h>
void lock_read(lock_structptr)
lock_t lock_structptr;
```

Arguments

lock_structptr
Specifies a pointer to the complex lock structure, lock. This is the lock structure associated with the resource on which you want to assert a complex lock with read-only access.

The lock structure is an opaque data structure; that is, its associated members are referenced and manipulated by the Digital UNIX operating system and not by the user of the complex lock mechanism.

Description

The lock_read interface asserts a lock with read-only access for the resource associated with the specified lock structure pointer. The lock_read interface allows multiple kernel threads to access the resource read-only at the same time. When a read lock is asserted, the protected resource is guaranteed not to change.

To release a previously asserted read lock, call the lock_done interface.

Notes

You must call lock_init (once only) prior to calling lock_read to initialize the lock structure pointer for the resource. A resource, from the device driver's standpoint, is data that more than one kernel thread can manipulate. You can store the resource in variables (global) and data structure members.

Example

See *Writing Device Drivers: Advanced Topics* for a code example of the `lock_read` interface.

Return Values

None

Related Information

Chapter 14, Header Files Related to Device Drivers: `lock.h`

Section 15.2, Kernel Support Interfaces: `lock_done`, `lock_terminate`, `lock_try_read`, `lock_try_write`, `lock_write`

Chapter 16, Structures Related to Device Drivers: `lock`

Name

lock_terminate – Terminates, using a complex lock

Synopsis

```
#include <kern/lock.h>
void lock_terminate(lock_structptr)
lock_t lock_structptr;
```

Arguments

lock_structptr
> Specifies a pointer to the complex lock structure, lock. The lock structure is an opaque data structure; that is, its associated members are referenced and manipulated by the Digital UNIX operating system and not by the user of the complex lock mechanism.

Description

The lock_terminate interface determines that the driver is done using the complex lock forever. The complex lock must be free (that is, the driver does not hold the lock) before calling lock_terminate. The device driver must not reference the specified complex lock after calling lock_terminate.

Notes

You must call lock_init (once only) prior to calling lock_terminate to initialize the lock structure pointer for the resource. A resource, from the device driver's standpoint, is data that more than one kernel thread can manipulate. You can store the resource in variables (global) and data structure members.

Example

See *Writing Device Drivers: Advanced Topics* for a code example of the lock_terminate interface.

Return Values

None

Related Information

Chapter 14, Header Files Related to Device Drivers: `lock.h`

Section 15.2, Kernel Support Interfaces: `lock_done`, `lock_init`, `lock_try_read`, `lock_try_write`, `lock_write`

Chapter 16, Structures Related to Device Drivers: `lock`

Name

lock_try_read – Tries to assert a complex lock with read-only access

Synopsis

```
#include <kern/lock.h>
boolean_t lock_try_read(lock_structptr)
lock_t lock_structptr;
```

Arguments

lock_structptr
Specifies a pointer to the complex lock structure, lock. This is the
lock structure associated with the resource on which you want to try to
assert a complex lock with read-only access.

The lock structure is an opaque data structure; that is, its associated
members are referenced and manipulated by the Digital UNIX operating
system and not by the user of the complex lock mechanism.

Description

The lock_try_read interface tries to assert a complex lock (without
blocking) with read-only access for the resource associated with the specified
lock structure pointer. To release a complex lock with read-only access
successfully asserted by lock_try_read, call the lock_done interface.

Notes

You must call lock_init (once only) prior to calling lock_try_read
to initialize the lock structure pointer for the resource. A resource, from the
device driver's standpoint, is data that more than one kernel thread can
manipulate. You can store the resource in variables (global) and data
structure members.

Example

See *Writing Device Drivers: Advanced Topics* for a code example of the
lock_try_read interface.

Return Values

The `lock_try_read` interface returns one of the following values:

Value	Meaning
TRUE	The attempt to acquire the read-only complex lock was successful.
FALSE	The attempt to acquire the read-only complex lock was unsuccessful.

Related Information

Chapter 14, Header Files Related to Device Drivers: `lock.h`

Section 15.2, Kernel Support Interfaces: `lock_done`, `lock_terminate`, `lock_try_write`, `lock_write`

Chapter 16, Structures Related to Device Drivers: `lock`

Name

lock_try_write – Tries to assert a complex lock with write access

Synopsis

```
#include <kern/lock.h>
boolean_t lock_try_write(lock_structptr)
lock_t lock_structptr;
```

Arguments

lock_structptr

Specifies a pointer to the complex lock structure, lock. This is the lock structure associated with the resource on which you want to try to assert write access.

The lock structure is an opaque data structure; that is, its associated members are referenced and manipulated by the Digital UNIX operating system and not by the user of the complex lock mechanism.

Description

The lock_try_write interface tries to assert a complex lock (without blocking) with write access for the resource associated with the specified lock structure pointer. To release a complex lock with write access successfully asserted by lock_try_write, call the lock_done interface.

Notes

You must call lock_init (once only) prior to calling lock_try_write to initialize the lock structure pointer for the resource. A resource, from the device driver's standpoint, is data that more than one kernel thread can manipulate. You can store the resource in variables (global) and data structure members.

Example

See *Writing Device Drivers: Advanced Topics* for a code example of the lock_try_write interface.

Return Values

The `lock_try_write` interface returns one of the following values:

Value	Meaning
TRUE	The attempt to acquire the write complex lock was successful.
FALSE	The attempt to acquire the write complex lock was unsuccessful.

Related Information

Chapter 14, Header Files Related to Device Drivers: `lock.h`

Section 15.2, Kernel Support Interfaces: `lock_done`, `lock_terminate`, `lock_try_read`, `lock_write`

Chapter 16, Structures Related to Device Drivers: `lock`

Name

lock_write – Asserts a complex lock with write access

Synopsis

```
#include <kern/lock.h>
void lock_write(lock_structptr)
lock_t lock_structptr;
```

Arguments

lock_structptr
Specifies a pointer to the complex lock structure, lock. This is the lock structure associated with the resource on which you want to assert a complex lock with write access.

The lock structure is an opaque data structure; that is, its associated members are referenced and manipulated by the Digital UNIX operating system and not by the user of the complex lock mechanism.

Description

The lock_write interface asserts a lock with exclusive write access for the resource associated with the specified lock structure pointer. This means that once a write lock is asserted, no other kernel thread can gain read or write access to the resource until it is released.

To release a complex write lock successfully asserted by lock_write, call the lock_done interface.

Notes

You must call lock_init (once only) prior to calling lock_write to initialize the lock structure pointer for the resource. A resource, from the device driver's standpoint, is data that more than one kernel thread can manipulate. You can store the resource in variables (global) and data structure members.

Example

See *Writing Device Drivers: Advanced Topics* for a code example of the
`lock_write` interface.

Return Values

None

Related Information

Chapter 14, Header Files Related to Device Drivers: `lock.h`

Section 15.2, Kernel Support Interfaces: `lock_done`, `lock_read`,
`lock_terminate`, `lock_try_read`, `lock_try_write`

Chapter 16, Structures Related to Device Drivers: `lock`

Name

major – Returns the device major number

Synopsis

```
#include <sys/types.h>
int major(device)
dev_t device;
```

Arguments

device
Specifies the number of the device whose associated major device
number the major interface will obtain.

Description

The major interface returns the device major number associated with the
device specified by the *device* argument. Device driver writers use the
dev_t data type to represent a device's major and minor numbers. This
data type is an abstraction of the internal representations of the major and
minor numbers. It is not necessary for driver writers to know how the system
internally represents the major and minor numbers. To ensure maximum
portability of the device driver, use the major interface to extract the major
number portion of this internal representation.

Example

See Section 9.10.2 for a code example of the major interface.

Return Values

Upon successful completion, major returns the major number portion of the
dev_t passed as the argument.

Related Information

Section 15.2, Kernel Support Interfaces: makedev, minor

Name

makedev – Returns a dev_t

Synopsis

```
#include <sys/types.h>
dev_t makedev(major, minor)
int major;
int minor;
```

Arguments

major
> Specifies the major number for the device.

minor
> Specifies the minor number for the device.

Description

The makedev interface returns a device number of type dev_t based on the numbers specified for the *major* and *minor* arguments.

Return Values

Upon successful completion, makedev returns a dev_t that represents the major and minor device numbers passed as arguments.

Related Information

Section 15.2, Kernel Support Interfaces: major, minor

Name

MALLOC – Allocates a variable-size section of kernel virtual memory

Synopsis

```
#include <sys/malloc.h>
 MALLOC(addr, cast, size, type, flags)
addr;
cast;
u_long size;
int type;
int flags;
```

Arguments

addr
> Specifies the memory pointer that points to the allocated memory. You specify the addr argument's data type in the cast argument.

cast
> Specifies the data type of the addr argument and the type of the memory pointer returned by MALLOC.

size
> Specifies the size of the memory (in bytes) to allocate. You should pass the size as a constant to speed up the memory allocation.

type
> Specifies the purpose for which the memory is being allocated. The memory types are defined in the file malloc.h. Typically, device drivers use the constant M_DEVBUF to indicate that device driver memory is being allocated (or freed).

flags
> Specifies one of the following flag constants defined in /usr/sys/include/sys/malloc.h:

Value	Meaning
M_WAITOK	Allocates memory from the virtual memory subsystem if there is not enough memory in the preallocated pool. This constant signifies that MALLOC can block.
M_NOWAIT	Does not allocate memory from the virtual memory subsystem if there is not enough memory in the preallocated pool. This constant signifies that MALLOC cannot block.

Description

The MALLOC interface allocates at least *size* bytes from the kernel memory and returns the address of the allocated memory. A device driver can allocate the memory in interrupt and process context.

The MALLOC interface maintains a pool of preallocated memory for quick allocation. If there is not enough memory in the pool, MALLOC allocates memory from the virtual memory subsystem by calling kmem_alloc, which can potentially block (sleep). There is a kernel thread that allocates and frees memory to and from the preallocated pool.

The MALLOC interface is actually a wrapper that calls malloc. A device driver should not directly call the malloc interface.

The *type* argument allows the memory allocator to keep track of memory usage by a subsystem.

If the allocation size is greater than 16K, you must pass M_WAITOK to the *flags* argument. You cannot allocate more than 16K bytes of memory in interrupt context.

Notes

In previous versions of the Digital UNIX operating system (formerly known as DEC OSF/1), device drivers could call the following memory allocation-related interfaces:

- kalloc and kfree

  Device drivers called these interfaces to allocate and free a variable-sized section of kernel virtual memory.

- kget

  Device drivers called this interface to perform nonblocking allocation of a variable-sized section of kernel virtual memory.

- `zinit`, `zchange`, `zalloc`, `zfree`, and `zget`

  Device drivers called these interfaces to allocate exact-size sections of kernel virtual memory.

The Digital UNIX operating system still provides backwards compatibility with the `kalloc`, `kfree`, and `kget` interfaces and the `zinit`, `zchange`, `zalloc`, `zfree`, and `zget` interfaces. However, Digital recommends that for new device drivers you use the `MALLOC` and `FREE` interfaces to allocate and to free sections of kernel virtual memory.

A memory corruption can occur if a device driver continues to use the memory after freeing it. The Digital UNIX operating system provides a built-in mechanism to debug such erroneous use of memory. You can enable this debugging feature at boot time by providing the following boot parameter: `kmem_debug=1`. When you enable this debugging feature, the `free` interface stores the following in the last word of freed memory:

- The program counter (pc) of the module that last freed the memory
- The checksum of the memory content

The `malloc` interface checks the checksum of the memory content before reallocating this corrupted memory. If the checksum of the memory content does not match the corrupted memory, `malloc` stores the debug information and then causes the kernel to panic. The `malloc` interface stores the address and size of the corrupted memory and the pc of the interface that last freed it in a `kmem_corrupt_data` structure.

You should consider the following when using this debugging feature:

- This debugging feature does not detect cases where the corruption occurs after `malloc` reallocates the freed memory to some other module.
- There is a small chance that the pc of the interface that freed the memory (stored in the last word of freed memory) may itself get corrupted.

Cautions

A device driver must not call `MALLOC` in interrupt context with the *flags* argument set to `M_WAITOK`. If *flags* is set to `M_WAITOK`, `MALLOC` checks if the kernel thread is in interrupt context. If so, `MALLOC` returns a null pointer and displays a message on the console terminal.

The `M_WAITOK` flag implies that it is valid to allocate memory from the virtual memory subsystem if there is not enough memory in the preallocated pool. To be able to allocate memory from the virtual memory subsystem (which can page fault), the device driver must be in process context.

Example

See Section 9.2.1 for a code example of the MALLOC interface.

Return Values

Upon successful completion, MALLOC returns the address of the allocated memory. The return type associated with this address is the same as that specified for the *addr* argument. If the memory allocation request cannot be fulfilled, MALLOC returns a null pointer in the *addr* argument.

Related Information

Section 15.2, Kernel Support Interfaces: FREE

Name

mb – Performs a memory barrier

Synopsis

void mb *( );*

Arguments

None

Description

The Alpha architecture, unlike traditional CPU architectures, does not guarantee read/write ordering. That is, the memory subsystem is free to complete read and write operations in any order that is optimal, without regard for the order in which they were issued. Read/write ordering is not the same as cache coherency, which is handled separately and is not an issue.

The Alpha architecture also contains a write buffer (as do many high-performance RISC CPUs, including the MIPS R3000). This write buffer can coalesce multiple writes to identical or adjacent addresses into a single write, effectively losing earlier write requests. Similarly, multiple reads to the same identical or adjacent addresses can be coalesced into a single read.

This coalescing has implications for multiprocessor systems, as well as systems with off-board I/O or DMA engines that can read or modify memory asynchronously or that can require multiple writes to actually issue multiple data items. The mb (memory barrier) interface guarantees ordering of operations. The mb interface is derived from the MB instruction, which is described in the *Alpha Architecture Reference Manual.*

The mb interface is a superset of the wbflush interface that MIPS CPUs use. For compatibility, wbflush is aliased to mb on Digital UNIX Alpha systems.

You call mb in a device driver under the following circumstances:

- To force a barrier between load/store operations
- After the CPU has prepared a data buffer in memory and before the device driver tries to perform a DMA out of the buffer
- Before attempting to read any device CSRs after taking a device interrupt
- Between writes

Device drivers and the Digital UNIX operating system are the primary users of the mb interface. However, some user programs, such as a graphics program that directly maps the frame buffer and manipulates registers, might need to call mb. The Digital UNIX operating system does not provide a C library interface for mb. User programs that require use of mb should use the following asm construct:

```
#include <c_asm.h>

asm ("mb");
```

Notes

In most situations that would require a cache flush on other CPU architectures, you should call the mb interface on Digital UNIX Alpha systems. The reason is not that mb is equivalent to a cache flush (as it is not). Rather, a common reason for doing a cache flush is to make data that the host CPU wrote available in main memory for access by the DMA device or to access from the host CPU data that was put in main memory by a DMA device. In each case, on an Alpha CPU you should use a memory barrier to synchronize with that event.

One example of using mb occurs with an ethernet network controller. Each ethernet network controller has a unique ethernet hardware address that is typically contained in a ROM on the ethernet controller board. The ethernet hardware address is a multibyte sequence typically consisting of at least 10 bytes. Frequently this multibyte ethernet hardware address is read from the controller hardware by the driver's probe interface by issuing a sequence of reads to the same controller register. Each successive read returns the next byte of the ethernet hardware address. In such instances, a call to mb should be inserted between each of these read operations to ensure that successive read operations do not get coalesced into fewer actual reads as seen by the ethernet controller.

Example

See Section 2.6.6 for a code example of the mb interface.

Return Values

None

Name

minor – Returns the device minor number

Synopsis

```
#include <sys/types.h>
int minor(device)
dev_t device;
```

Arguments

device

Specifies the number of the device whose associated minor device number the minor interface will obtain.

Description

The minor interface returns the device minor number associated with the device specified by the *device* argument. Device driver writers use the dev_t data type to represent a device's major and minor numbers. This data type is an abstraction of the internal representations of the major and minor numbers. It is not necessary for driver writers to know how the system internally represents the major and minor numbers. To ensure maximum portability of the device driver, use the minor interface to extract the minor number portion of this internal representation.

Example

See Section 9.10.3 for a code example of the minor interface.

Return Values

Upon successful completion, minor returns the minor number portion of the dev_t passed as the argument.

Related Information

Section 15.2, Kernel Support Interfaces: major, makedev

Name

minphys – Bounds the data transfer size

Synopsis

```
void minphys(bp)
struct buf *bp;
```

Arguments

bp

Specifies a pointer to a buf structure.

Description

The minphys interface bounds the data transfer size by checking the b_bcount member of the buf structure pointed to by the *bp* argument. If the b_bcount member is greater than 63 * 1024, minphys sets b_bcount to 63 * 1024.

Return Values

The minphys interface does not return a value. However, it may change the contents of the b_bcount member of the buf structure.

Related Information

Section 15.2, Kernel Support Interfaces: physio

Name

mpsleep – Blocks (puts to sleep) the current kernel thread

Synopsis

```
int mpsleep(channel, pri, wmesg, timo, lockp, flags)
caddr_t channel;
long pri;
char *wmesg;
long timo;
void *lockp;
long flags;
```

Arguments

channel
Specifies an address associated with the calling kernel thread to be put to sleep.

pri
Specifies whether the sleep request is interruptible. Setting this argument to the PCATCH flag causes the process to sleep in an interruptible state. Not setting the PCATCH flag causes the process to sleep in an uninterruptible state. The param.h file defines the different priorities.

wmesg
Specifies the wait message.

timo
Specifies the maximum amount of time the kernel thread should block (sleep). If you pass the value zero (0), mpsleep assumes there is no timeout.

lockp
Specifies a pointer to a simple or complex lock structure. You should replace the void * data type with simple_lock_t or lock_t if you want to acquire the lock. If you do not want to release a lock, pass the value zero (0).

flags

Specifies the lock type. You can pass the bitwise inclusive OR of the following valid lock bits defined in the `param.h` file:

Value	Meaning
MS_LOCK_SIMPLE	Calls mpsleep with a simple lock asserted.
MS_LOCK_READ	Calls mpsleep with a read-only lock asserted on entry.
MS_LOCK_WRITE	Calls mpsleep with a write lock asserted.
MS_LOCK_ON_ERROR	Forces mpsleep to relock the lock on failure.
MS_LOCK_NO_RELOCK	Forces mpsleep not to relock after blocking (sleeping).

Description

The mpsleep interface blocks (puts to sleep) the current kernel thread until a wakeup is issued on the address you specified in the *channel* argument. This interface is the symmetric multiprocessor (SMP) sleep call. The kernel thread blocks (sleeps) a maximum of *timo* divided by *hz* seconds. The value zero (0) means there is no timeout.

If you pass the PCATCH flag to the *pri* argument, mpsleep checks signals before and after blocking (sleeping). Otherwise, mpsleep does not check signals.

The mpsleep interface allows you to specify a pointer to a simple or complex lock structure that is associated with some resource. This interface unlocks this resource prior to blocking (sleeping). The *flags* argument specifies the lock type. The mpsleep interface releases the lock when the current kernel thread successfully performs an assert wait on the specified channel.

Notes

The mpsleep interface cannot be called from within a device driver's ISI because it is illegal to block at interrupt context.

Return Values

The mpsleep interface returns the value zero (0) if awakened (success) and EWOULDBLOCK if the timeout specified in the *timo* argument expires (failure). On success, mpsleep relocks the lock if you did not set MS_LOCK_NO_RELOCK in *flags*. On failure, it leaves the lock unlocked. If you set the *flags* argument to MS_LOCK_ON_ERROR, mpsleep relocks the lock on failures.

Related Information

Section 15.2, Kernel Support Interfaces: `assert_wait_mesg`, `clear_wait`, `thread_block`, `thread_wakeup`, `thread_wakeup_one`

Name

ntohl, ntohs – Convert longword and word values from network-to-host byte order

Synopsis

```
#include <sys/param.h>
unsigned int ntohl(longword)
unsigned int longword;


unsigned short ntohs(word)
unsigned short word;
```

Arguments

longword
    Specifies a 32-bit value to be conditionally byte swapped.

word
    Specifies a 16-bit value to be conditionally byte swapped.

Description

The ntohl interface converts the specified longword value from network-to-host byte order. The ntohs interface converts the specified word value from network-to-host byte order.

The TCP/IP protocols specify the canonical network byte order, which is big endian (meaning that the most significant byte is leftmost in memory).

Return Values

Upon successful completion, the ntohl interface returns the converted longword value in host byte order. Similarly, upon successful completion, the ntohs interface returns the converted word value in host byte order.

Related Information

Section 15.2, Kernel Support Interfaces: htonl

Name

ovbcopy – Copies a byte string with a specified limit

Synopsis

```
void ovbcopy(b1, b2, n)
char *b1;
char *b2;
int n;
```

Arguments

b1

Specifies a pointer to a string of bytes.

b2

Specifies a pointer to a buffer of at least *n* bytes.

n

Specifies the number of bytes to be copied.

Description

The ovbcopy interface copies *n* bytes from string *b1* to buffer *b2*. No
check is made for null bytes.

The address ranges of *b1* and *b2* can overlap.

Notes

In most cases, ovbcopy is not as efficient as bcopy.

Return Values

None

Related Information

Section 15.2, Kernel Support Interfaces: bcopy, blkclr, copystr,
strcpy, strncpy

Name

panic – Causes a system crash

Synopsis

```
void panic(message)
char *message;
```

Arguments

message
Specifies the message you want the panic interface to display on the console terminal.

Description

The panic interface causes a system crash, usually because of fatal errors. It sends to the console terminal and error logger the specified message and, possibly, other system-dependent information (for example, register dumps). It also causes a crash dump to be generated. After displaying the message, panic reboots the system if the console environment variables are set appropriately.

Return Values

None

Related Information

Section 15.2, Kernel Support Interfaces: printf

Name

physio – Implements raw I/O

Synopsis

```
void physio(strategy, bp, device, rwflag, mincnt, uio)
int (*strategy) ();
register struct buf *bp;
dev_t device;
int rwflag;
void (*mincnt) ();
register struct uio *uio;
```

Arguments

strategy
Specifies the device driver's strategy interface for the device.

bp
Specifies a pointer to a buf structure. This structure contains information such as the binary status flags, the major/minor device numbers, and the address of the associated buffer. This buffer is always a special buffer header owned exclusively by the device for handling I/O requests.

device
Specifies the device number.

rwflag
Specifies the read/write flag.

mincnt
Specifies a pointer to a minphys interface.

uio
Specifies a pointer to a uio structure.

Description

The physio interface implements raw I/O. This interface maps the raw I/O request directly into the user buffer, without using bcopy. The memory pages in the user address space are locked while the transfer is processed.

Example

See Section 9.10.4 for a code example of the physio interface.

Return Values

None

Related Information

Section 15.2, Kernel Support Interfaces: minphys

Section 17.2, Block and Character Device Driver Interfaces: xxstrategy

Name

PHYS_TO_KSEG – Converts a physical address to a kernel-unmapped virtual address

Synopsis

vm_offset_t PHYS_TO_KSEG(*addr*)
vm_offset_t *addr*;

Arguments

addr
Specifies the physical address to convert to a kernel-unmapped virtual address.

Description

The PHYS_TO_KSEG interface converts a physical address to a kernel-unmapped virtual address.

Example

The following code fragment shows a call to PHYS_TO_KSEG:

```
      .
      .
      .
caddr_t virt_addr;    1
unsigned phys_addr;   2
      .
      .
      .

        virt_addr = PHYS_TO_KSEG(phys_addr);  3
      .
      .
      .
```

1 Declares a variable to store the virtual address returned by PHYS_TO_KSEG.

2 Declares a variable to store the physical address. This address might have been obtained from a call to KSEG_TO_PHYS.

3 Calls PHYS_TO_KSEG to convert the physical address to a corresponding virtual address.

Return Values

Upon successful completion, PHYS_TO_KSEG returns the virtual address associated with the specified physical address.

Related Information

Section 15.2, Kernel Support Interfaces: IS_KSEG_VA, KSEG_TO_PHYS

Name

`pmap_extract` – Extracts a physical page address

Synopsis

vm_offset_t pmap_extract(*pmap*, *virt_addr*)
pmap_t *pmap*;
vm_offset_t *virt_addr*;

Arguments

pmap
    Specifies the physical map.

virt_addr
    Specifies the virtual address associated with the physical map.

Description

The `pmap_extract` interface extracts the physical page address associated with the specified *pmap* (physical map) and *virt_addr* (virtual address) arguments. The virtual address includes the offset within a page.

Return Values

The `pmap_extract` interface returns the value zero (0) if no valid translation exists for the specified virtual address in the specified physical map.

Related Information

Section 15.2, Kernel Support Interfaces: `pmap_kernel`, `pmap_set_modify`

Name

pmap_kernel – Returns the physical map handle for the kernel

Synopsis

```
pmap_t pmap_kernel ();
```

Arguments

None

Description

The pmap_kernel interface returns the physical map handle for the kernel.

Return Values

The pmap_kernel interface returns the physical map handle for the kernel.

Name

pmap_set_modify – Sets the modify bits of the specified physical page

Synopsis

```
void pmap_set_modify(phys_page)
vm_offset_t phys_page;
```

Arguments

phys_page
> Specifies the physical page that was previously modified.

Description

The pmap_set_modify interface informs the pmap module that the specified physical page was modified through a back-door mechanism.

Return Values

None

Related Information

Section 15.2, Kernel Support Interfaces: pmap_extract, pmap_kernel

Name

printf, uprintf – Write formatted text to some output device

Synopsis

```
void printf(format, var_arglist)
char *format
va_dcl var_arglist;


void uprintf(format, var_arglist)
char *format
va_dcl var_arglist;
```

Arguments

format

Specifies a pointer to a string that contains two types of objects. One object is ordinary characters such as "hello, world", which are copied to the output stream. The other object is a conversion specification such as %d, %o, or %x. Each conversion specification causes the interfaces described here to convert and print for the next argument in the *var_arglist* argument. The printf formats %d and %x will print 32 bits of data. To obtain 64 bits of data, use %ld and %lx.

var_arglist

Specifies the argument list.

Description

The printf and uprintf interfaces are scaled-down versions of the corresponding C library interfaces. The printf interface prints diagnostic information directly on the console terminal and writes ASCII text to the error logger. Because printf is not interrupt driven, all system activities are suspended when you call it.

The uprintf interface prints to the current user's terminal. Interrupt service interfaces should never call uprintf. It does not perform any space checking, so you should not use this interface to print verbose messages. The uprintf interface does not log messages to the error logger.

You introduce conversion specifications by using the percent sign (%). Following the %, you can include:

- Zero or more flags, which modify the meaning of the conversion specification.

- An optional minus sign (–), which specifies left adjustment of the converted value in the indicated field.

- An optional digit string, which specifies a field width. If the converted value has fewer characters than the field width, the printf and uprintf interfaces pad the value with blanks. By default, these interfaces pad the value on the left. If the conversion string that specifies the value is left justified, these interfaces pad the value on the right. If the field width begins with a zero, these interfaces pad the values with zeros instead of blanks.

- The character **h** or **l**, which specifies that a following **d**, **i**, **o**, **u**, **x**, or **X** corresponds to an integer or longword integer argument. You can use an uppercase **L** or a lowercase **l**.

- A character that indicates the type of conversion to be applied.

A field width or precision can be an asterisk (*) instead of a digit string. If you use an asterisk, you can include an argument that supplies the field width or precision.

The flag characters and their meanings are as follows:

–

The result of the conversion is left justified within the field.

+

The result of a signed conversion always begins with a sign (+ or –).

blank

If the first character of a signed conversion is not a sign, the printf and uprintf interfaces pad the value on the left with a blank. If the blank and plus sign (+) flags both appear, these interfaces ignore the blank flag.

#

The result has been converted to a different format. The value is to be converted to an alternative form.

For **c**, **d**, **s**, and **u** conversions, this flag has no effect.

For **x** or **X** conversions, the printf and uprintf interfaces pad a nonzero result on the left with **0x** or **0X**.

These interfaces support the following formats that device driver writers find particularly useful:

b

Allows decoding of error registers.

c

Prints the character argument.

d o x

Converts the integer argument to decimal, octal, or hexadecimal notation, respectively.

s

Prints the character argument. The `printf` and `uprintf` interfaces print the argument until encountering a null character or until printing the number of characters specified by the precision. If the precision is zero or the precision has not been specified, these interfaces print the character argument until encountering a null character.

u

Converts the unsigned integer argument to a decimal value. The result must be in the range of 0 through 4294967295, where the upper bound is defined by `MAXUINT`.

%

Prints a percent sign (%). The interfaces convert no argument.

The following line shows the format of the `printf` interface with the % **b** conversion character:

```
printf("reg=%b\n", regval, "<base><arg>*");
```

In this case, base and arg are defined as:

<base>

The output base expressed as a control character. For example, \10 gives octal and \20 gives hexadecimal.

<arg>

A sequence of characters. The first character gives the bit number to be inspected (origin 1). The second and subsequent characters (up to a control character, that is, a character <=32) give the name of the register.

The following shows a call to `printf`:

```
printf("reg=%b\n", 3, "\10\2BITTWO\1BITONE\n");
```

This example would produce the following output:

```
reg=2<BITTWO,BITONE>
```

The following shows the format of the `printf` interface with the % **r** and % **R** conversion characters:

```
printf("%r R", val, reg_desc);
```

r

Allows formatted printing of bit fields. This code outputs a string of the format:

```
"<bit field descriptions>"
```

R

Allows formatted printing of bit fields. This code outputs a string of the format:

```
"0x%x<bit field descriptions>"
```

You use a `reg_desc` structure to describe the individual bit fields. To describe multiple bit fields within a single word, you can declare multiple `reg_desc` structures. The `reg_desc` structure is defined as follows:

```
struct reg_desc {
  unsigned rd_mask;              /* mask to extract field */
  int rd_shift;                  /* shift for extracted   */
                                 /* value, - >>, + <<     */
  char *rd_name;                 /* field name            */
  char *rd_format;               /* format to print field */
  struct reg_values *rd_values;  /* symbolic names of     */
                                 /* values                */
};
```

`rd_mask`

Specifies an appropriate mask to isolate the bit field within a word ANDed with the *val* argument.

`rd_shift`

Specifies a shift amount to be done to the isolated bit field. The shift is done before printing the isolated bit field with the `rd_format` member and before searching for symbolic value names in the `rd_values` member.

`rd_name`

If non-NULL, specifies a bit field name to label any output from `rd_format` or searching `rd_values`. If neither `rd_format` nor `rd_values` is non-NULL, `rd_name` is printed only if the isolated bit field is non-NULL.

`rd_format`

If non-NULL, specifies that the shifted bit field value is printed using this format.

rd_values
> If non-NULL, specifies a pointer to a table that matches numeric values with symbolic names. The interface searches the rd_values member and prints the symbolic name if it finds a match. If it does not find a match, it prints "???".

The following is a sample reg_desc entry:

```
struct reg_desc dsc[] = {
        /* mask        shift        name    format  values */
        { VPNMASK,     0,           "VA",   "0x%x", NULL },
        { PIDMASK,     PIDSHIFT,    "PID",  "%d",   NULL },
        { 0,           0,           NULL,   NULL,   NULL },
};
```

The printf and uprintf interfaces also accept a field number, zero filling to length. For example:

```
printf(" %8x\n",regval);
```

The maximum field size is 11.

Notes

Some device drivers might have used the tprintf interface to print on a specified terminal or on the system console if no terminal was provided. Digital recommends that you discontinue use of tprintf because it will not be supported in future releases of the Digital UNIX operating system.

Return Values

None

Name

privileged – Checks for proper privileges

Synopsis

```
int privileged(privilege, error_code)
int privilege;
int error_code;
```

Arguments

privilege
Specifies the privilege to check against. This privilege must be one of the constants defined in /usr/sys/include/sys/security.h. For example, you would specify SEC_FILESYS for disk drivers that must manipulate partition tables on disk drives.

error_code
Specifies the value used to control auditing. You can pass one of the following values: –1, 0, 1, or one of the system's error codes. An example of an error code is the constant EPERM.

Description

The privileged interface checks for an appropriate privilege when the security feature is enabled. Use privileged with a privilege number and with the *error_code* argument set to the constant EPERM to emulate the traditional behavior of the suser interface. Set *error_code* to a value of zero (0) if you want to check the privilege but not fail the operation if the user does not have the proper privilege. A value of –1 turns off all auditing as well.

Return Values

The privileged interface returns the value zero (0) if the process does not have privilege. It returns the value 1 if the process does have privilege.

Related Information

Chapter 14, Header Files Related to Device Drivers: `errno.h`, `security.h`

Section 15.2, Kernel Support Interfaces: `suser`

Name

psignal – Sends a signal to a process

Synopsis

```
void psignal(process, signal)
struct proc *process;
int signal;
```

Arguments

process
    Specifies a pointer to a proc structure.

signal
    Specifies the signal that you want to send to the specified process. You can specify any of the signals defined in /usr/sys/include/sys/signal.h.

Description

The psignal interface posts a signal to the specified process. The posting of a signal causes that signal to be added to the set of pending signals for the specified process. Depending on the state of the process and the state of the process's signals, the specified signal may be ignored, masked, caught by a tracing parent, or caught by the actual target process. If the signal is to be delivered to the target process, psignal examines and modifies the process state to prepare the execution of the appropriate signal handler.

Return Values

None

Related Information

Section 15.2, Kernel Support Interfaces: gsignal

Name

queue_init – Initializes the specified queue

Synopsis

void queue_init(*queue_pointer*)
queue_t *queue_pointer;*

Arguments

queue_pointer
Specifies a pointer to a queue_entry structure.

Description

The queue_init interface initializes the specified queue. Device drivers
call this interface prior to calling select_enqueue to initialize a pointer
to a sel_queue data structure.

Return Values

None

Related Information

Chapter 14, Header Files Related to Device Drivers: select.h

Section 15.2, Kernel Support Interfaces: select_enqueue

Chapter 16, Structures Related to Device Drivers: sel_queue

Name

READ_BUS_D8, READ_BUS_D16, READ_BUS_D32, READ_BUS_D64 –
Perform byte, word, longword, and quadword bus I/O read operations

Synopsis

```
unsigned char READ_BUS_D8(dev_addr)
io_handle_t dev_addr;


unsigned short READ_BUS_D16(dev_addr)
io_handle_t dev_addr;


unsigned int READ_BUS_D32(dev_addr)
io_handle_t dev_addr;


unsigned long READ_BUS_D64(dev_addr)
io_handle_t dev_addr;
```

Arguments

dev_addr
> Specifies an I/O handle that you can use to reference a device register or memory located in bus address space (either I/O space or memory space). This I/O handle references a device register in the bus address space where the read operation originates. You can perform standard C mathematical operations on the I/O handle.

Description

The READ_BUS_D8 interface reads a byte (8 bits) from a device register located in the bus I/O address space. The READ_BUS_D16 interface reads a word (16 bits) from a device register located in the bus I/O address space. The READ_BUS_D32 interface reads a longword (32 bits) from a device register located in the bus I/O address space. The READ_BUS_D64 interface reads a quadword (64 bits) from a device register located in the bus I/O address space. These are convenience interfaces that call read_io_port, which is a generic interface that maps to a bus- and machine-specific interface that actually performs the task of reading the byte, word, longword, or quadword. Use of these interfaces to read data from a device register makes the device driver more portable across different bus architectures, different CPU architectures, and different CPU types within the same CPU architecture.

In addition to `dev_addr`, the READ_BUS_D8, READ_BUS_D16, and READ_BUS_D32 interfaces automatically pass values to the `width` and `flags` arguments of read_io_port. The following list identifies these values:

- The READ_BUS_D8, READ_BUS_D16, READ_BUS_D32, and READ_BUS_D64 interfaces set the `width` to the values 1, 2, 4, and 8, respectively.

- The READ_BUS_D8, READ_BUS_D16, READ_BUS_D32, and READ_BUS_D64 interfaces set the `flags` argument to the value zero (0).

Cautions

The I/O handle that you pass to the `dev_addr` argument of the READ_BUS_D8, READ_BUS_D16, READ_BUS_D32, READ_BUS_D64 interfaces must be an I/O handle that references addresses residing in sparse space. All Alpha CPUs support sparse space. As a result, all bus configuration code should supply an I/O handle that references bus address space.

If you pass an I/O handle to the `dev_addr` argument that references addresses residing in some other space (for example, dense space) the results of the read operation are unpredictable.

The Digital UNIX operating system provides the following interfaces that allow device drivers to perform copy operations on and zero blocks of memory on addresses that reside in dense space:

- bcopy

  Copies a series of bytes with a specified limit

- blkclr and bzero

  Zeros a block of memory

- copyin

  Copies data from a user address space to a kernel address space

- copyinstr

  Copies a null-terminated string from a user address space to a kernel address space

- copyout

  Copies data from a kernel address space to a user address space

- `copyoutstr`

  Copies a null-terminated string from a kernel address space to a user address space

Return Values

Upon successful completion, these interfaces return the requested data from the device register located in the bus address space: `READ_BUS_D8` returns a byte (8 bits), `READ_BUS_D16` returns a word (16 bits), `READ_BUS_D32` returns a longword (32 bits), and `READ_BUS_D64` returns a quadword (64 bits).

Related Information

Section 15.2, Kernel Support Interfaces: `read_io_port`

Name

read_io_port – Reads data from a device register

Synopsis

```
#include <io/common/devdriver.h>
long read_io_port(dev_addr, width, flags)
io_handle_t dev_addr;
int width;
int flags;
```

Arguments

dev_addr
> Specifies an I/O handle that you can use to reference a device register or memory located in bus address space (either I/O space or memory space). This I/O handle references a device register in the bus address space where the read operation originates. You can perform standard C mathematical operations on the I/O handle. For example, you can add an offset to or subtract an offset from the I/O handle.

width
> Specifies the width (in bytes) of the data to be read. Valid values are 1, 2, 3, 4, and 8. Not all CPU platforms or bus adapters support all of these values.

flags
> Specifies flags to indicate special processing requests. Currently, no flags are used.

Description

The read_io_port interface reads data of the specified width from a device register located in bus address space. The I/O handle you pass to *dev_addr* identifies where the read operation originates.

Notes

The read_io_port interface is a generic interface that maps to a bus- and machine-specific interface that actually performs the read operation. Using this interface to read data from a device register makes the device driver more portable across different bus architectures, different CPU architectures, and different CPU types within the same CPU architecture.

This interface also must call the `mb` interface under certain circumstances. For discussions and examples of these circumstances, see Section 2.6.6.

Cautions

The I/O handle that you pass to the *dev_addr* argument of the `read_io_port` interface must be an I/O handle that references addresses residing in sparse space. All Alpha CPUs support sparse space. As a result, all bus configuration code should supply an I/O handle that references bus address space.

If you pass an I/O handle to the *dev_addr* argument that references addresses residing in some other space (for example, dense space) the results of the read operation are unpredictable.

The Digital UNIX operating system provides the following interfaces that allow device drivers to perform copy operations on and zero blocks of memory on addresses that reside in dense space:

- `bcopy`

  Copies a series of bytes with a specified limit

- `blkclr` and `bzero`

  Zeros a block of memory

- `copyin`

  Copies data from a user address space to a kernel address spacc

- `copyinstr`

  Copies a null-terminated string from a user address space to a kernel address space

- `copyout`

  Copies data from a kernel address space to a user address space

- `copyoutstr`

  Copies a null-terminated string from a kernel address space to a user address space

Example

See Section 9.8.1.1 for a code example of the `read_io_port` interface.

Return Values

Upon successful completion, `read_io_port` returns the requested data from the device register located in the bus address space: a byte (8 bits), a word (16 bits), a longword (32 bits), or a quadword (64 bits). This interface returns data justified to the low-order byte lane. For example, a byte (8 bits) is always returned in byte lane 0 and a word (16 bits) is always returned in byte lanes 0 and 1.

Related Information

Section 15.2, Kernel Support Interfaces: `write_io_port`

Name

rmalloc – Allocates size units from the given resource map

Synopsis

```
long rmalloc(map_struct, size)
struct map *map_struct;
long size;
```

Arguments

map_struct
:   Specifies a pointer to a map structure that was previously initialized by
    a call to rminit.

size
:   Specifies the size of the units to allocate.

Description

The rmalloc interface allocates size units from the given resource map.
In a map, the addresses are increasing, and the list is terminated by a zero
size. The actual units managed by the map are arbitrary and can be map
registers, bytes, blocks, and so forth.

Notes

The caller is responsible for providing any locking necessary for the map
structure that the system passes to this interface.

Return Values

The rmalloc interface returns the base of the allocated space. The
interface returns an error if no space could be allocated.

Related Information

Section 15.2, Kernel Support Interfaces: rmfree, rmget, rminit

Name

rmfree – Frees space previously allocated into the specified resource map

Synopsis

```
void rmfree(map_struct, size, addr)
struct map *map_struct;
long size;
long addr;
```

Arguments

map_struct
: Specifies a pointer to a map structure that was previously initialized by a call to rminit.

size
: Specifies the size of the units to free.

addr
: Specifies the address at which to free the previously allocated space.

Description

The rmfree interface frees the space previously allocated with a call to rmalloc. The rmfree interface frees a space of the size specified by the *size* argument at the address specified by the *addr* argument.

Notes

The caller is responsible for providing any locking necessary for the map structure that the system passes to this interface.

Return Values

None

Related Information

Section 15.2, Kernel Support Interfaces: rmalloc, rmget, rminit

Name

rmget – Allocates size units from the given resource map

Synopsis

```
int rmget(map_struct, size, addr)
struct map *map_struct;
long size;
long addr;
```

Arguments

map_struct
> Specifies a pointer to a map structure that was previously initialized by a call to rminit.

size
> Specifies the size of the units to allocate.

addr
> Specifies the address at which to allocate the space.

Description

The rmget interface allocates the number of units specified in *size* starting at the address specified in *addr*.

Notes

The caller is responsible for providing any locking necessary for the map structure that the system passes to this interface.

Return Values

Upon successful completion, rmget returns the starting address, *addr*. Otherwise, it returns the value zero (0).

Related Information

Section 15.2, Kernel Support Interfaces: rmalloc, rmfree, rminit

Name

rminit – Initializes a resource map

Synopsis

```
void rminit(map_struct, size, addr, name, mapsize)
struct map *map_struct;
long size;
long addr;
char *name;
int mapsize;
```

Arguments

map_struct
Specifies a pointer to a map structure to be initialized by a call to
rminit.

size
Specifies the size elements used to initialize the resource map.

addr
Specifies the address that identifies the start of the free elements.

name
Specifies the name for the resource map. The rminit interface uses
this name in warning messages when the map overflows.

mapsize
Specifies the maximum number of fragments.

Description

The rminit interface initializes the specified resource map to have
mapsize − 2 segments. The interface also identifies this resource map with
the string passed to the *name* argument. It prints this name if the slots
become so fragmented that space is lost.

The resource map itself is initialized with *size* elements free starting at the
address specified in *addr*.

Notes

The caller is responsible for providing any locking necessary for the `map` structure that the system passes to this interface.

Return Values

None

Related Information

Section 15.2, Kernel Support Interfaces: `rmalloc`, `rmfree`, `rmget`

Name

round_page – Rounds the specified address

Synopsis

```
#include <mach/vm_param.h>
vm_offset_t round_page(address)
vm_offset_t address;
```

Arguments

address
Specifies the address (or byte count) that is being rounded.

Description

The round_page interface rounds the specified address (or byte count) to a multiple of the page size. For example, round_page would round a 1-byte count to be equal to the size of one page. This interface shields the driver writer from having to know the page size of the system, which could vary in different CPU architectures and on different CPU types within the same architecture. Typically, a device driver calls round_page in preparation for doing a DMA operation to a user's buffer. The value returned by this interface is used in the call to the vm_map_pageable interface. To use this interface, the driver writer must include the <mach/vm_param.h> header file in the driver.

Return Values

The round_page interface returns the rounded address or byte count.

Related Information

Section 15.2, Kernel Support Interfaces: current_task, trunc_page, vm_map_pageable

Name

select_dequeue – Removes the last kernel thread waiting for an event

Synopsis

```
void select_dequeue(selq)
sel_queue_t *selq;
```

Arguments

selq
> Specifies a pointer to an sel_queue structure.

Description

The select_dequeue interface removes the last kernel thread waiting for an event to occur on the specified device. This interface is called to terminate a select call. Typically, a driver's *xx*select interface calls select_dequeue when the kernel sets the *scanning* argument (for the driver's *xx*select interface) to the value zero (0). This value causes the kernel to unblock any kernel threads suspended when selecting events for this device.

Return Values

None

Related Information

Chapter 14, Header Files Related to Device Drivers: poll.h, select.h

Section 15.2, Kernel Support Interfaces: select_dequeue_all, select_enqueue, select_wakeup

Chapter 16, Structures Related to Device Drivers: sel_queue

Section 17.2, Block and Character Device Driver Interfaces: *xx*select

Reference Pages Section 2: select

Name

select_dequeue_all – Removes all kernel threads waiting for an event

Synopsis

```
void select_dequeue_all(selq)
sel_queue_t *selq;
```

Arguments

selq
Specifies a pointer to an sel_queue structure.

Description

The select_dequeue_all interface is similar in functionality to the
select_dequeue interface. The difference is that
select_dequeue_all removes all kernel threads (not just the last one)
while waiting for an event on the specified device.

Return Values

None

Related Information

Chapter 14, Header Files Related to Device Drivers: poll.h, select.h

Section 15.2, Kernel Support Interfaces: select_dequeue,
select_enqueue, select_wakeup

Chapter 16, Structures Related to Device Drivers: sel_queue

Section 17.2, Block and Character Device Driver Interfaces: xxselect

Reference Pages Section 2: select

Name

select_enqueue – Adds the current kernel thread

Synopsis

void select_enqueue(*selq*)
sel_queue_t **selq;*

Arguments

selq
　　Specifies a pointer to an sel_queue structure.

Description

The select_enqueue interface adds the current kernel thread to the list of kernel threads waiting for a select event on the specified device. This interface is called when a driver's *xx*select interface has been called and the requested event cannot be immediately satisfied. For example, the requested event cannot be immediately satisfied when *xx*select is called for the following reasons:

- To select on input and there are no characters available
- When *xx*select is called for output and the driver's output buffers are currently full

By calling select_enqueue, the driver's *xx*select interface ensures that the kernel thread issuing the select call will be blocked until the requested event can be satisfied or the select call terminates.

Cautions

You must call the queue_init interface to initialize the sel_queue structure pointer prior to calling select_enqueue. Failure to do so causes the kernel to panic.

Return Values

None

Related Information

Chapter 14, Header Files Related to Device Drivers: `poll.h`, `select.h`

Section 15.2, Kernel Support Interfaces: `queue_init`, `select_dequeue`, `select_dequeue_all`, `select_wakeup`

Chapter 16, Structures Related to Device Drivers: `sel_queue`

Section 17.2, Block and Character Device Driver Interfaces: *xx*`select`

Reference Pages Section 2: `select`

Name

select_wakeup – Wakes up a kernel thread

Synopsis

```
void select_wakeup(selq)
sel_queue_t *selq;
```

Arguments

selq
  Specifies a pointer to an sel_queue structure.

Description

The select_wakeup interface wakes up a kernel thread that is suspended
while waiting for an event on the specified device. A user-level process can
use the select system call to cause the process to be suspended while
waiting for an event to happen on a device. For example, a graphics
application may issue a select call while waiting for mouse or keyboard input
to arrive. In this case the process would issue the select system call,
which would indirectly call the graphics driver's select interface (through
the driver's select entry point in the cdevsw table) to determine if any
input is available. If input is available, the select call may return
immediately. If no input is currently available, the graphics driver would
suspend the process until input arrived.

For this example, when the graphics driver has received input (typically
through its Interrupt Service Interface (ISI)), it causes any processes
suspended from calling select to continue by calling the select_wakeup
interface. This causes any process currently suspended on the select channel
(as specified by the *selq* argument) to resume.

Return Values

None

Related Information

Section 15.2, Kernel Support Interfaces: `select_dequeue`, `select_dequeue_all`, `select_enqueue`

Section 17.2, Block and Character Device Driver Interfaces: `xxselect`

Reference Pages Section 2: `select`

Name

simple_lock – Asserts a simple lock

Synopsis

```
#include <kern/lock.h>
void simple_lock(slock_ptr)
simple_lock_t slock_ptr;
```

Arguments

slock_ptr

Specifies a pointer to a simple lock structure. You can declare this simple lock structure by using the decl_simple_lock_data interface.

Description

The simple_lock interface asserts a lock with exclusive access for the resource associated with the specified slock structure pointer. This means that no other kernel thread can gain access to the locked resource until you call simple_unlock to release it. Because simple locks are spin locks, simple_lock does not return until the lock has been obtained.

Notes

You must call simple_lock_init (once only) prior to calling simple_lock to initialize the simple lock structure for the resource. A resource, from the device driver's standpoint, is data that more than one kernel thread can manipulate. You can store the resource in variables (global) and data structure members.

Example

See *Writing Device Drivers: Advanced Topics* for a code example of the simple_lock interface.

Return Values

None

Related Information

Chapter 14, Header Files Related to Device Drivers: `lock.h`

Section 15.2, Kernel Support Interfaces: `decl_simple_lock_data`, `simple_lock_init`, `simple_lock_terminate`, `simple_lock_try`, `simple_unlock`

Chapter 16, Structures Related to Device Drivers: `slock`

Name

simple_lock_init – Initializes a simple lock structure

Synopsis

```
#include <kern/lock.h>
void simple_lock_init(slock_ptr)
simple_lock_t slock_ptr;
```

Arguments

slock_ptr

    Specifies a pointer to a simple lock structure. You can declare this simple lock structure by using the decl_simple_lock_data interface.

Description

The simple_lock_init interface initializes the simple lock structure that you previously declared with the decl_simple_lock_data interface. You need to initialize the simple lock structure only once. After you initialize the simple lock structure, you can call simple_lock to assert exclusive access on the associated resource.

Example

See *Writing Device Drivers: Advanced Topics* for a code example of the simple_lock_init interface.

Return Values

None

Related Information

Chapter 14, Header Files Related to Device Drivers: lock.h

Section 15.2, Kernel Support Interfaces: decl_simple_lock_data, simple_lock, simple_lock_terminate, simple_lock_try, simple_unlock

Chapter 16, Structures Related to Device Drivers: slock

Name

simple_lock_terminate – Terminates, using a simple lock

Synopsis

```
#include <kern/lock.h>
void simple_lock_terminate(slock_ptr)
simple_lock_t slock_ptr;
```

Arguments

slock_ptr
Specifies a pointer to a simple lock structure. You can declare this simple lock structure by using the decl_simple_lock_data interface.

Description

The simple_lock_terminate interface determines that the driver is done using the simple lock permanently. The simple lock must be free (that is, the driver does not hold the lock) before calling simple_lock_terminate. The device driver must not reference the specified simple lock after calling simple_lock_terminate.

Notes

You must call simple_lock_init (once only) prior to calling simple_lock_terminate to initialize the simple lock structure for the resource. A resource, from the device driver's standpoint, is data that more than one kernel thread can manipulate. You can store the resource in variables (global) and data structure members.

Example

See *Writing Device Drivers: Advanced Topics* for a code example of the simple_lock_terminate interface.

Return Values

None

Related Information

Chapter 14, Header Files Related to Device Drivers: `lock.h`

Section 15.2, Kernel Support Interfaces: `decl_simple_lock_data`, `simple_lock_init`, `simple_lock_try`, `simple_unlock`

Chapter 16, Structures Related to Device Drivers: `slock`

Name

simple_lock_try – Tries to assert a simple lock

Synopsis

```
#include <kern/lock.h>
boolean_t simple_lock_try(slock_ptr)
simple_lock_t slock_ptr;
```

Arguments

slock_ptr
>   Specifies a pointer to a simple lock structure. You can declare this
>   simple lock structure by using the decl_simple_lock_data
>   interface.

Description

The simple_lock_try interface tries to assert a lock with read and write
access for the resource associated with the specified simple lock. The main
difference between this interface and simple_lock is that
simple_lock_try returns immediately if the resource is already locked
while simple_lock spins until the lock has been obtained. Thus, call
simple_lock_try when you need a simple lock but the code cannot spin
until the lock is obtained.

To release a simple lock successfully asserted by simple_lock_try, call
the simple_unlock interface.

Example

See *Writing Device Drivers: Advanced Topics* for a code example of the
simple_lock_try interface.

Return Values

The `simple_lock_try` interface returns one of the following values:

Value	Meaning
TRUE	The `simple_lock_try` interface successfully asserted the simple lock.
FALSE	The `simple_lock_try` interface failed to assert the simple lock.

Related Information

Chapter 14, Header Files Related to Device Drivers: `lock.h`

Section 15.2, Kernel Support Interfaces: `decl_simple_lock_data`, `simple_lock`, `simple_lock_init`, `simple_lock_terminate`, `simple_unlock`

Chapter 16, Structures Related to Device Drivers: `slock`

Name

simple_unlock – Releases a simple lock

Synopsis

```
#include <kern/lock.h>
void simple_unlock(slock_ptr)
simple_lock_t slock_ptr;
```

Arguments

slock_ptr
    Specifies a pointer to a simple lock structure. You passed this pointer in
    a previous call to the simple_lock interface.

Description

The simple_unlock interface releases a simple lock for the resource
associated with the specified simple lock structure pointer. This simple lock
was previously asserted by calling the simple_lock or
simple_lock_try interface.

Example

See *Writing Device Drivers: Advanced Topics* for a code example of the
simple_unlock interface.

Return Values

None

Related Information

Chapter 14, Header Files Related to Device Drivers: lock.h

Section 15.2, Kernel Support Interfaces: decl_simple_lock_data,
simple_lock, simple_lock_terminate, simple_lock_try

Chapter 16, Structures Related to Device Drivers: slock

Name

sleep – Puts a calling process to sleep

Synopsis

void sleep(*channel, pri*)
caddr_t *channel*;
long *pri*;

Arguments

channel
Specifies a unique address associated with the calling kernel thread to be put to sleep.

pri
Specifies whether the sleep request is interruptible. Setting this argument to the PCATCH flag causes the process to sleep in an interruptible state. Not setting the PCATCH flag causes the process to sleep in an uninterruptible state. The param.h file defines the different priorities.

Description

The sleep interface puts a calling process to sleep on the address specified by the *channel* argument. Some common addresses are the *lbolt* argument, a buf structure, and a proc structure. This address should be unique to prevent unexpected wake/sleep cycles, which can occur if different processes are sleeping on the same address accidentally. If you set the PCATCH flag in the *pri* argument, the sleep interface puts signals on the queue and does not wake up the sleeping process.

The sleep and wakeup interfaces block and then wake up a process. Generally, device drivers call these interfaces to wait for the transfer to complete an interrupt from the device. That is, the write interface of the device driver sleeps on the address of a known location, and the device's interrupt service interface wakes the process when the device interrupts. It is the responsibility of the wakened process to check if the condition for which it was sleeping has been removed.

Notes

Digital UNIX provides two ways to put a process to sleep: interruptible and uninterruptible. The `sleep` interface performs an uninterruptible sleep operation if you do not set the PCATCH flag and an interruptible sleep operation if you set the PCATCH flag. This means that device drivers cannot call sleep at interrupt context because at interrupt context there is no calling process to be put to sleep. Thus, a device driver's Interrupt Service Interface (ISI) and those interfaces called from within the ISI must not call the `sleep` interface.

On the Digital UNIX operating system you cannot use *pri* to set the scheduling priority of the calling process.

Example

See Section 9.5.3 for a code example of the `sleep` interface.

Return Values

None

Related Information

Chapter 14, Header Files Related to Device Drivers: `param.h`

Section 15.2, Kernel Support Interfaces: `wakeup`

Name

spl – Sets the processor priority to mask different levels of interrupts

Synopsis

```
#include <machine/cpu.h>
int getspl();

int splbio();

int splclock();

int spldevhigh();

int splextreme();

int splhigh();

int splimp();

int splnet();

int splnone();

int splsched();

int splsoftclock();

int spltty();

int splvm();
```

```
int splx(x)
int x;
```

Arguments

x

Specifies a CPU priority level. This level must be a value returned by a previous call to one of the spl interfaces.

Description

The spl interfaces set the CPU priority to various interrupt levels. The current CPU priority level determines which types of interrupts are masked (disabled) and which are unmasked (enabled). Historically, seven levels of interrupts were supported, with eight different spl interfaces to handle the possible cases. For example, calling spl0 would unmask all interrupts and calling spl7 would mask all interrupts. Calling an spl interface between 0 and 7 would mask out all interrupts at that level and at all lower levels.

Specific interrupt levels were assigned for different device types. For example, before handling a given interrupt, a device driver would set the CPU priority level to mask all other interrupts of the same level or lower. This setting meant that the device driver could be interrupted only by interrupt requests from devices of a higher priority.

Digital UNIX currently supports the naming of spl interfaces to indicate the associated device types. Named spl interfaces make it easier to determine which interface you should use to set the priority level for a given device type. The following table summarizes the uses for the different spl interfaces:

spl Interface	Meaning
getspl	Gets the spl value.
splbio	Masks all disk and tape controller interrupts.
splclock	Masks all hardware clock interrupts.
spldevhigh	Masks all device and software interrupts.
splextreme	Blocks against all but halt interrupts.
splhigh	Masks all interrupts except for realtime devices, machine checks, and halt interrupts.
splimp	Masks all Ethernet hardware interrupts.
splnet	Masks all network software interrupts.

spl Interface	Meaning
splnone	Unmasks (enables) all interrupts.
splsched	Masks all scheduling interrupts (usually hardware clock).
splsoftclock	Masks all software clock interrupts.
spltty	Masks all tty (terminal device) interrupts.
splvm	Masks all virtual memory clock interrupts.
splx	Resets the CPU priority to the level specified by the argument.

Notes

The binding of any spl interface with a specific CPU priority level is highly machine dependent. With the exceptions of the splhigh and splnone interfaces, knowledge of the explicit bindings is not required to create new device drivers. You always use splhigh to mask (disable) all interrupts and splnone to unmask (enable) all interrupts.

Example

The following code fragment shows the use of spl interfaces as part of a disk strategy interface:

```
int s;
 .
 .
 .
s = splbio(); /* Mask (disable) all disk interrupts */
 .
 .
 .
[Code to deal with data that can be modified by the disk interrupt
code]
 .
 .
 .
splx(s); /* Restore CPU priority to what it was */
```

Return Values

Upon successful completion, each spl interface returns an integer value that represents the CPU priority level that existed before it was changed by a call to the specified spl interface.

Name

`strcmp` – Compares two null-terminated character strings

Synopsis

```
int strcmp(s1, s2)
char *s1;
char *s2;
```

Arguments

s1

Specifies a pointer to a string (an array of characters terminated by a null character).

s2

Specifies a pointer to a string (an array of characters terminated by a null character).

Description

The `strcmp` interface lexicographically compares string *s1* to string *s2*. The interface does not continue the comparison beyond the first null character it finds. A fatal error occurs if you call `strcmp` with strings that are not null terminated.

Example

See Section 9.1.1 for a code example of the `strcmp` interface.

Return Values

If string *s1* is less than string *s2*, `strcmp` returns an integer less than zero. If *s1* and *s2* are equal, the interface returns the value zero (0). If *s1* is greater than *s2*, it returns an integer greater than zero.

Related Information

Section 15.2, Kernel Support Interfaces: `bcmp`

Name

strcpy – Copies a null-terminated character string

Synopsis

```
char * strcpy(s1, s2)
char *s1;
char *s2;
```

Arguments

s1

Specifies a pointer to a buffer large enough to hold the string s2.

s2

Specifies a pointer to a string (an array of characters terminated by a null character).

Description

The strcpy interface copies string s2 to buffer s1. The interface stops copying after it copies a null character. Note that the character size is 1 byte.

Example

See Section 9.1.3 for a code example of the strcpy interface.

Return Values

The interface returns a pointer to the location following the end of the destination buffer, s1.

Related Information

Section 15.2, Kernel Support Interfaces: bcopy, blkclr, copystr, ovbcopy, strncpy

Name

strlen – Returns the number of characters in a null-terminated string

Synopsis

```
int strlen(s)
char *s;
```

Arguments

s

Specifies a pointer to a string (an array of characters terminated by a null character).

Description

The strlen interface returns the number of characters in s. The count does not include the terminating null character.

Note that the character size is 1 byte.

Example

See Section 9.1.5 for a code example of the strlen interface.

Return Values

The strlen interface returns the number of characters in s, not counting the terminating null character.

Name

`strncmp` – Compares two strings, using a specified number of characters

Synopsis

```
int strncmp(s1, s2, n)
char *s1;
char *s2;
int n;
```

Arguments

s1

Specifies a pointer to a string (an array of characters terminated by a null character).

s2

Specifies a pointer to a string (an array of characters terminated by a null character).

n

Specifies the number of bytes to be compared.

Description

The `strncmp` interface compares string *s1* to string *s2*, using the number of characters specified in *n*.

Example

See Section 9.1.2 for a code example of the `strncmp` interface.

Return Values

If string *s1* is equal to the null character (´\0´), `strncmp` returns the value zero (0). Otherwise, it returns the difference between the number of characters in *s1* and *s2*.

Related Information

Section 15.2, Kernel Support Interfaces: `strcmp`

Name

strncpy – Copies a null-terminated character string with a specified limit

Synopsis

```
char * strncpy(s1, s2, n)
char *s1;
char *s2;
int n;
```

Arguments

s1

Specifies a pointer to a buffer of at least n bytes.

s2

Specifies a pointer to a string (an array of characters terminated by a null character).

n

Specifies the number of characters to be copied.

Description

The strncpy interface copies string $s2$ to buffer $s1$. The interface stops copying after it copies a null character or n characters, whichever comes first. If the length of $s2$ as determined by the null character is less than n, the interface pads $s1$ with null characters.

Example

See Section 9.1.4 for a code example of the strncpy interface.

Return Values

The strncpy interface returns a pointer to /NULL at the end of the first string (or to the location following the last copied character if there is no NULL). The copied string will not be null terminated if the length of $s2$ is n characters or more.

Related Information

Section 15.2, Kernel Support Interfaces: `bcopy`, `blkclr`, `copystr`, `ovbcopy`, `strcpy`

Name

subyte – Writes a byte into user address space

Synopsis

```
int subyte(user_dest, byte)
char *user_dest;
char byte;
```

Arguments

user_dest
    Specifies the address in user space to write the byte.

byte
    Specifies the byte to be written.

Description

The subyte interface copies 1 byte from the protected kernel address space to the unprotected user address space.

Return Values

Upon successful completion, subyte returns the value zero (0). Otherwise, it returns a –1, indicating that the user address specified in user_dest could not be accessed.

Related Information

Section 15.2, Kernel Support Interfaces: copyout, copyoutstr, fubyte, fuword, suword

Name

suibyte – Writes a byte into user instruction address space

Notes

The suibyte interface is for use on machines that have separate address spaces for code and data. Because the Alpha architecture does not have separate address spaces for code and data, suibyte is mapped to subyte. The suibyte interface is provided for compatibility reasons. See the interface description for subyte for a complete description of suibyte.

Name

`suiword` – Writes a word into user instruction address space

Notes

The `suiword` interface is for use on machines that have separate address spaces for code and data. Because the Alpha architecture does not have separate address spaces for code and data, `suiword` is mapped to `suword`. The `suiword` interface is provided for compatibility reasons. See the interface description for `suword` for a complete description of `suiword`.

Name

suser – Checks whether the current user is the superuser

Synopsis

```
#include <sys/proc.h>
#include <sys/acct.h>
int suser(cred, ac_flag)
struct u_cred *cred;
struct flag_field *ac_flag;
```

Arguments

cred
> Specifies a pointer to the credentials for the current process.

ac_flag
> Specifies a pointer to a flag_field structure that contains accounting flags.

Description

The suser interface checks whether the current user is the superuser. If the test succeeds and ac_flag is not a null pointer, the ASU flag is set in the flag_field structure pointed to by ac_flag. The most common value for ac_flag is as follows:

&u.u_acflag

Notes

You use the suser interface only if the security feature is not enabled. If the security feature is enabled, use the privileged interface to determine if the current process has the appropriate privilege.

Errors

EPERM
> The current user is not the superuser.

Return Values

If the current user is the superuser, the `suser` interface returns the value zero (0). Otherwise, it returns an error.

Related Information

Section 15.2, Kernel Support Interfaces: `privileged`

Name

suword – Writes a word into user address space

Synopsis

```
int suword(user_dest, word)
char *user_dest;
int word;
```

Arguments

user_dest
  Specifies the address in user space to write the word.

word
  Specifies the word to be written.

Description

The suword interface copies one word from the protected kernel address space to the unprotected user address space.

Return Values

Upon successful completion, suword returns the value zero (0). Otherwise, it returns a –1, indicating that the user address specified in *user_dest* could not be accessed.

Related Information

Section 15.2, Kernel Support Interfaces: copyout, copyoutstr, fubyte, fuword, subyte

Name

svatophys – Converts a system virtual address to a physical address

Synopsis

kern_return_t svatophys(*kern_addr, phys_addr*)
vm_offset_t *kern_addr;*
vm_offset_t **phys_addr;*

Arguments

kern_addr
 Specifies the kernel virtual address.

phys_addr
 Specifies a pointer to the physical address to be filled in.

Description

The svatophys interface converts a system virtual address to the corresponding physical address. All address and data structure manipulation done within the kernel is performed using system virtual addresses. Typically, system virtual addresses are a means of mapping physical memory and I/O space, which often consists of device registers and DMA buffers. In contrast to this, devices are usually unaware of any virtual addressing and for this reason utilize physical addresses. You use the svatophys interface to perform this address translation.

As an example of where you can use this address translation, a disk device driver can utilize DMA buffers to transfer blocks of data to the disk (for the case of a write operation). The data to be written to disk is present in system memory at a system virtual address known to the driver. To initiate the DMA operation, the disk driver can set up a command packet to specify a write operation to the underlying disk controller hardware. This write command packet contains (among other things) the location of the DMA buffer as a physical address and the length of the buffer. Here, the driver calls the svatophys interface to translate the system virtual address of the DMA buffer to a physical address in the command packet issued to the disk driver.

Return Values

The `svatophys` interface returns the following:

KERN_SUCCESS
   The address translation has been completed successfully.

KERN_INVALID_ADDRESS
   Unable to perform address translation. This value indicates that the address specified by the *kern_addr* argument is not a valid kernel or system virtual address.

Name

swap_lw_bytes, swap_word_bytes, swap_words – Perform byte-swapping operations

Synopsis

```
unsigned int swap_lw_bytes(buffer)
unsigned int buffer;


unsigned int swap_word_bytes(buffer)
unsigned int buffer;


unsigned int swap_words(buffer)
unsigned int buffer;
```

Arguments

buffer
  Specifies a 32-bit (4 bytes) quantity.

Description

The swap_lw_bytes interface performs a longword byte swap. The swap_word_bytes interface performs a short word byte swap. The swap_words interface performs a word byte swap. Many computer vendors support devices that use a big endian model of byte ordering. Because Digital devices support the little endian model of byte ordering, there is a need for these byte-swapping interfaces. In addition, some buses (for example, the VMEbus) can have specific or implied byte ordering that may require the use of these interfaces.

Figure 15-1 compares the byte swapping performed by these interfaces. For the purposes of the following discussion, a longword is equal to 4 bytes; a short word is equal to 2 bytes; and 1 byte is equal to 8 bits. The swap_lw_bytes interface takes the 32-bit quantity specified by the *buffer* argument and swaps all 4 bytes. The swap_word_bytes interface takes the 32-bit quantity specified by the *buffer* argument and swaps the individual bytes that make up each word of the 32-bit quantity. The swap_words interface takes the 32-bit quantity specified by the *buffer* argument and swaps the two 16-bit words.

Figure 15-1: Byte Swapping

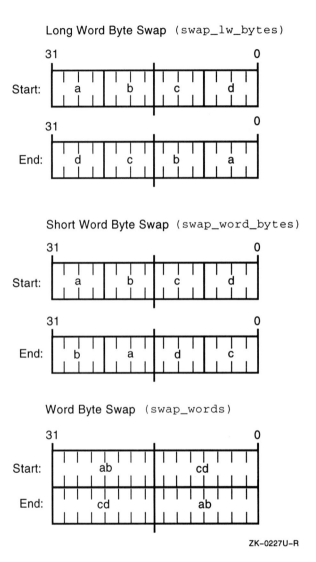

ZK-0227U-R

Return Values

Upon successful completion, these interfaces return the result of the byte swapping.

Name

`thread_block` – Blocks (puts to sleep) the current kernel thread

Synopsis

`void thread_block();`

Arguments

None

Description

The `thread_block` interface blocks (puts to sleep) the current kernel thread and selects the next kernel thread to start (run). The interface schedules the next kernel thread onto this CPU.

When a kernel thread is waiting for an event, it should block. In general, a kernel thread is blocked when the thread wait bit in the `thread` structure pointer associated with the current kernel thread is set. This bit signifies that this kernel thread is on the appropriate wait hash queue, waiting for a wakeup call. This allows the CPU to execute another kernel thread while this kernel thread is blocked.

Example

See *Writing Device Drivers: Advanced Topics* for a code example of the `thread_block` interface.

Return Values

None

Related Information

Section 15.2, Kernel Support Interfaces: `assert_wait_mesg`

Name

thread_halt_self – Handles asynchronous traps for self-terminating kernel threads

Synopsis

```
void thread_halt_self ();
```

Arguments

None

Description

The thread_halt_self interface performs the work associated with a variety of asynchronous traps (ASTs) for a kernel thread that terminates itself. A kernel thread terminates itself (or one kernel thread terminates another kernel thread) by calling the thread_terminate interface.

The thread_halt_self interface examines the AST-related member of the thread structure pointer associated with the kernel thread that wants to terminate itself. This thread structure pointer was returned in a previous call to kernel_isrthread or kernel_thread_w_arg and passed by you to the thread_terminate interface. This AST-related member is set to a bit that identifies the specific AST trap associated with this kernel thread. Based on the AST bit set in this member, thread_halt_self does the appropriate cleanup work before the kernel thread exits from the kernel.

Notes

A kernel thread that terminates itself must call thread_halt_self immediately after the call to thread_terminate.

Return Values

None

Related Information

Section 15.2, Kernel Support Interfaces: thread_terminate

Name

`thread_set_timeout` – Sets a timer for the current kernel thread

Synopsis

```
void thread_set_timeout(timeout_interval)
int timeout_interval;
```

Arguments

timeout_interval
Specfies the amount of time to wait for an event. The time is used in conjunction with the `assert_wait` interface.

Description

The `thread_set_timeout` interface must be called as follows:

1. Lock the resource.
2. Call `assert_wait_mesg` to assert that the current kernel thread is about to block.
3. Unlock the resource.
4. Call `thread_set_timeout` to set the time of delay for the current kernel thread.
5. Call `thread_block` to block (put to sleep) the current kernel thread.

Example

See *Writing Device Drivers: Advanced Topics* for a code example of the `thread_set_timeout` interface.

Return Values

None

Related Information

Section 15.2, Kernel Support Interfaces: `assert_wait_mesg`, `thread_block`

Name

thread_terminate – Stops execution of the specified kernel thread

Synopsis

kern_return_t thread_terminate(*thread_to_terminate*)
thread_t *thread_to_terminate*;

Arguments

thread_to_terminate
Specifies a pointer to the thread structure associated with the kernel thread that you want to terminate. This pointer was returned in a previous call to the kernel_isrthread or kernel_thread_w_arg interface.

Description

The thread_terminate interface permanently stops execution of the specified kernel thread. You created and started this kernel thread in a previous call to the kernel_isrthread or kernel_thread_w_arg interface. These interfaces return a pointer to the thread structure associated with the newly created and started kernel thread. Device drivers use this pointer as a handle to identify the specific kernel thread that thread_terminate stops executing.

Typically, a kernel thread terminates itself. However, it is possible for one kernel thread to terminate another kernel thread. A kernel thread that terminates itself must call thread_halt_self immediately after the call to thread_terminate.

Notes

You do not need to terminate every kernel thread that you create. The basic rule is that you should terminate those kernel threads that you do not need anymore. For example, if your loadable device driver uses kernel threads, you need to terminate these kernel threads in the unconfigure section of the loadable driver's *xx*configure interface. The kernel threads are no longer needed after the driver is unconfigured.

Note that the thread_terminate interface not only permanently stops execution of the specified kernel thread, but it also frees any resources associated with that kernel thread. Thus, this kernel thread can no longer be used. Specifically, the `thread_terminate` interface works as follows:

- For terminating other kernel threads

  The `thread_terminate` interface stops execution of the specified
  kernel thread, frees any resources associated with that kernel thread, and
  thus makes the kernel thread unavailable. To make this kernel thread
  available again, you need to create it by calling `kernel_isrthread`
  or `kernel_thread_w_arg`.

- A kernel thread terminates itself

  The `thread_terminate` interface stops execution of the kernel thread
  that wants to terminate itself. It also frees any resources associated with
  that self-terminating kernel thread. However, the self-terminating kernel
  thread does not become unavailable until after you immediatedly call
  `thread_halt_self`. After you call `thread_halt_self` the self-
  terminating kernel thread becomes unavailable until you create it again by
  calling `kernel_isrthread` or `kernel_thread_w_arg`.

Return Values

Upon successfully terminating the specified kernel thread,
`thread_terminate` returns the constant KERN_SUCCESS. If the
`thread` structure pointer passed to the *thread_to_terminate*
argument does not identify a valid kernel thread, `thread_terminate`
returns the constant KERN_INVALID_ARGUMENT. On any other error,
`thread_terminate` returns the constant KERN_FAILURE.

Related Information

Section 15.2, Kernel Support Interfaces: `kernel_isrthread`,
`kernel_thread_w_arg`, `thread_halt_self`

Chapter 16, Structures Related to Device Drivers: `thread`

Name

thread_wakeup – Wakes up all kernel threads waiting for the specified event

Synopsis

```
void thread_wakeup(event)
vm_offset_t event;
```

Arguments

event
Specifies the event associated with the current kernel thread.

Description

The thread_wakeup interface wakes up all kernel threads waiting for the event specified in the event argument. This interface is actually a convenience wrapper for the thread_wakeup_prim interface with the one_thread argument set to FALSE (wake up all kernel threads) and the result argument set to THREAD_AWAKENED (wakeup is normal).

Example

See *Writing Device Drivers: Advanced Topics* for a code example of the thread_wakeup interface.

Return Values

None

Related Information

Section 15.2, Kernel Support Interfaces: assert_wait_mesg, clear_wait, thread_block, thread_wakeup_one

Name

thread_wakeup_one – Wakes up the first kernel thread waiting on a channel

Synopsis

```
void thread_wakeup_one(event)
vm_offset_t event;
```

Arguments

event
Specifies the event associated with the current kernel thread.

Description

The thread_wakeup_one interface wakes up only the first kernel thread in the hash chain waiting for the event specified in the *event* argument. This interface is actually a convenience wrapper for the thread_wakeup_prim interface with the *one_thread* argument set to TRUE (wake up only the first kernel thread) and the *result* argument set to THREAD_AWAKENED (wakeup is normal).

Example

See *Writing Device Drivers: Advanced Topics* for a code example of the thread_wakeup_one interface.

Return Values

None

Related Information

Section 15.2, Kernel Support Interfaces: assert_wait_mesg, clear_wait, thread_block, thread_wakeup

Name

timeout – Initializes a callout queue element

Synopsis

```
void timeout(function, argument, time)
int (*function) ();
caddr_t argument;
register int time;
```

Arguments

function
> Specifies a pointer to the interface to be called.

argument
> Specifies a single argument to be passed to the called interface.

time
> Specifies the amount of time to delay before calling the specified
> interface. You express time as time (in seconds) * hz.

Description

The timeout interface initializes a callout queue element to make it easy to
execute the specified interface at the time specified in the *time* argument.
You often use callout interfaces for infrequent polling or error handling. The
interface you specify will be called on the interrupt stack (not in processor
context) as dispatched from the softclock interface.

The granularity of the time delay is dependent on the hardware. For
example, the granularity of Alpha CPUs is 1024/second.

The global variable *hz* contains the number of clock ticks per second. This
variable is a second's worth of clock ticks. Thus, if you wanted a 4-minute
timeout, you would pass 4 * 60 * hz as the third argument to the timeout
interface as follows:

```
/* A 4-minute timeout */
    .
    .
    .
timeout(lptout, (caddr_t)dev, 4 * 60 * hz);
```

Example

See Section 9.5.5 for a code example of the `timeout` interface.

Return Values

None

Related Information

Section 15.2, Kernel Support Interfaces: `untimeout`

Name

trunc_page – Truncates the specified address

Synopsis

```
#include <mach/vm_param.h>
vm_offset_t trunc_page(address)
vm_offset_t address;
```

Arguments

address
: Specifies the address that is being truncated to a page boundary.

Description

The trunc_page interface truncates the specified address to be aligned on a page boundary. This interface shields the driver writer from having to know the page size of the system, which could vary in different CPU architectures and on different CPU types within the same architecture. Typically, a device driver calls trunc_page in preparation for doing a DMA operation on a user's buffer. The value returned by this interface is used in the call to the vm_map_pageable interface. To use this interface, the driver writer must include the <mach/vm_param.h> header file in the driver.

Return Values

The trunc_page interface returns an address truncated to a page boundary.

Related Information

Section 15.2, Kernel Support Interfaces: current_task, round_page, vm_map_pageable

Name

uiomove – Moves data between user and system virtual space

Synopsis

```
#include <sys/uio.h>
int uiomove(kern_buf, nbytes, uio)
caddr_t kern_buf;
int nbytes;
struct uio *uio;
```

Arguments

kern_buf
Specifies a pointer to the kernel buffer in system virtual space.

nbytes
Specifies the number of bytes of data to be moved.

uio
Specifies a pointer to a uio structure. This structure describes the current position within a logical user buffer in user virtual space.

Description

The uiomove interface moves data between user and system virtual space. Data can be moved in either direction. Accessibility to the logical user buffer is verified before the move is made. Accessibility to the kernel buffer is always assumed.

The kernel buffer must always be of sufficient size to accommodate the data. It cannot be less than the number of bytes requested to be moved. Data corruption or a system panic may result if this condition occurs.

The size of the logical user buffer, as described by the uio structure, may be less than, equal to, or greater than the number of bytes requested. The number of bytes actually moved is truncated whenever this size is not sufficient to fulfill a request. In all other cases, only the bytes requested are moved.

Normally there is no need for device drivers to set up uio structures or worry about their composition or content. The uio structures are usually set up externally to drivers. Their addresses are passed in through the cdevsw table as arguments to driver read and write interfaces. The user logical buffers they describe are accessed only by kernel interfaces external to the driver, for example, uiomove. The external uio structures are quite often updated by such accesses.

The uiomove interface always updates the uio structure to reflect the number of bytes actually moved. The structure continues to describe the current position within the logical user buffer. The structure members that are subject to change are listed in the Side Effects section.

Notes

You can also use the uiomove interface to move data only within system virtual space. In such cases, you still specify a pointer to a uio structure. However, in these cases, the structure describes a logical buffer in system virtual space.

Example

See Section 9.3.5 for a code example of the uiomove interface.

Side Effects

The uiomove interface can update the following members of the uio structure:

uio_iov
Specifies the address of the current logical buffer segment.

uio_iovcnt
Specifies the number of remaining logical buffer segments.

uio_resid
Specifies the size of the remaining logical buffer.

uio_offset
Specifies the current offset into the full logical buffer.

The uiomove interface can update the following members of uio_iov (the logical buffer segment descriptor vector):

iov_base
Specifies the address of the current byte within the current logical buffer segment.

iov_len
Specifies the remaining size of the current segment.

Return Values

A zero (0) value is returned whenever the user virtual space described by the `uio` structure is accessible and the data is successfully moved. Otherwise, an `EFAULT` error value is returned, indicating an inability to fully access the user virtual space from within the context of the current process. A partial move may have occurred before the logical user buffer became inaccessible. The `uio` structure is appropriately updated to reflect such partial moves.

The `EFAULT` return value is suitable for placement in the `u_error` member of the `user` structure. Following failure of a system call, this member contains the error code automatically returned in *errno* to the current process. Device driver writers should explicitly set this value when it is returned and disallow the requested operation. This setting lets the current process determine the appropriate reason ("bad address") why its request could not be satisfied.

Related Information

Section 15.2, Kernel Support Interfaces: `copyin`, `copyout`, `fubyte`, `subyte`

Chapter 16, Structures Related to Device Drivers: `uio`

Name

unix_master – Forces execution onto the master CPU

Synopsis

```
void unix_master ();
```

Arguments

None

Description

The unix_master interface forces execution of the kernel thread onto the master CPU (also called the boot CPU). In other words, unix_master binds the kernel thread to the master CPU. To release the kernel thread from the bind to the master CPU, call the unix_release interface. You can make recursive calls to unix_master as long as you make an equal number of calls to unix_release.

The unix_master interface provides another way besides the simple and complex lock interfaces to make a device driver symmetric multiprocessing (SMP) safe. Although calling unix_master is not optimal for performance on an SMP CPU, it does provide third-party device driver writers with an easy way to make their drivers SMP safe without using the lock interfaces.

Notes

Device drivers should not directly call the unix_master and unix_release interfaces. One exception to this recommendation is when you want a device driver's kernel threads to run only on the master CPU. This situation occurs when your driver creates and starts its own kernel threads and you set the d_funnel member of the bdevsw or cdevsw table to the value DEV_FUNNEL. In this case, each kernel thread must call unix_master once to ensure that the kernel thread runs only on the master CPU. Remember to make a corresponding call to unix_release.

Cautions

To avoid deadlock, do not call the `unix_master` interface under the following circumstances:

- When holding a simple lock
- In the driver's interrupt service interface

Return Values

None

Related Information

Section 15.2, Kernel Support Interfaces: `unix_release`

Name

unix_release – Releases binding of the kernel thread

Synopsis

```
void unix_release();
```

Arguments

None

Description

The unix_release interface releases a kernel thread from being bound to
the master CPU. This binding was enforced in a previous call to the
unix_master interface.

Cautions

You can make recursive calls to unix_master as long as you make an
equal number of calls to unix_release.

Return Values

None

Related Information

Section 15.2, Kernel Support Interfaces: unix_master

Name

untimeout – Removes the scheduled interface from the callout queues

Synopsis

```
boolean_t untimeout(function, argument)
int (*function) ();
caddr_t argument;
```

Arguments

function
Specifies a pointer to the interface to be removed from the callout queues.

argument
Specifies a single argument to be passed to the called interface.

Description

The untimeout interface removes the scheduled interface from the callout queue. The specified interface was placed on the callout queue in a previous call to the timeout interface. The *argument* formal parameter must match the *argument* parameter you specified in the previous call to timeout.

If the specified interface is not in the callout queue, untimeout returns without removing any scheduled interfaces.

Example

See Section 9.5.6 for a code example of the untimeout interface.

Return Values

The untimeout interface returns the value TRUE on success and the value FALSE on failure.

Related Information

Section 15.2, Kernel Support Interfaces: `timeout`

Name

vm_map_pageable – Sets pageability of the specified address range

Synopsis

```
kern_return_t vm_map_pageable(map, start, end, access_type)
vm_map_t map;
vm_offset_t start;
vm_offset_t end;
vm_prot_t access_type;
```

Arguments

map
> Specifies the address map associated with an individual process.

start
> Specifies the starting address of an address range. Typically, this is the address of the user's buffer where the DMA operation occurs.

end
> Specifies the ending address of a consecutive range of addresses beginning with the start argument.

access_type
> Specifies the access mode to be set for memory specified by the start and end arguments. You can set this argument to VM_PROT_NONE or to the bitwise inclusive OR of the protection bits VM_PROT_READ and VM_PROT_WRITE. These bits are defined in the file <mach/vm_prot.h> and have the following meanings:

Value	Meaning
VM_PROT_NONE	Modifies the memory attributes so that the specified range of addresses is no longer locked. This should be done after the DMA operation has completed.
VM_PROT_READ	Verifies that the specifed range of addresses are readable by the specified process. If so, the range of addresses are locked in memory to remain stable throughout the DMA operation.
VM_PROT_WRITE	Verifies that the specifed range of addresses is writeable by the specified process. If so, the range of addresses are locked in memory to remain stable throughout the DMA operation.

Value	Meaning
VM_PROT_READ | VM_PROT_WRITE	Verifies that the specifed range of addresses is readable and writeable by the specified process. If so, the range of addresses are locked in memory to remain stable throughout the DMA operation.

Description

The vm_map_pageable interface ensures that the address range you specified in the *start* and *end* arguments is accessible. If the address range is accessible by the specified process, the memory associated with this address range will have its locked attributes modified as specified by the *access_type* argument. A device driver can call this interface prior to performing a DMA operation to ensure that:

- The currently running process has read or write access permission to the user's buffer

- The memory representing the user's buffer is locked so that it remains available throughout the DMA operation.

Notes

Historically, some ULTRIX device drivers used the useracc kernel interface to perform tasks similar to those performed by vm_map_pageable. For example, both useracc and vm_map_pageable verify that the currently running process has access permissions to the specified memory. However, vm_map_pageable locks the associated memory so that it remains available throughout the DMA operation. In contrast, useracc does not lock the corresponding memory. This leaves the memory vulnerable to having its access permissions changed, which could result in a system panic during the DMA operation.

Example

The following code fragment shows how the vm_map_pageable interface ensures that the user's buffer is accessible to cause the corresponding memory to be locked:

```
if (vm_map_pageable(current_task()->map,
        trunc_page(bp->b_un.b_addr),
        round_page(bp->b_un.b_addr + (int)bp->b_bcount),
        (bp->b_flags == B_READ ? VM_PROT_READ : VM_PROT_WRITE))) {
/*****************************************************
 * Here you implement the code to perform the       *
 * actual DMA operation.  Upon conclusion of the    *
 * DMA operation, add the following code to         *
 * release the locked attribute.                    *
 *****************************************************/

        if (vm_map_pageable(current_task()->map,
                trunc_page(bp->b_un.b_addr),
                round_page(bp->b_un.b_addr + (int)bp->b_bcount),
                VM_PROT_NONE)) {
```

The following example shows a comparable use of a call to useracc. The
Notes section provides reasons for not using this call on Digital UNIX
systems.

```
if (useracc(bp->b_un.b_addr, (int)bp->b_bcount,
        (bp->b_flags & B_READ))) {
```

Return Values

Upon successful completion, the vm_map_pageable interface returns the
value zero (0). Otherwise, it returns a nonzero value to indicate an error.

Related Information

Section 15.2, Kernel Support Interfaces: current_task, round_page,
trunc_page

Name

vtop – Converts any virtual address to a physical address

Synopsis

```
vm_offset_t vtop(proc_p, virt_addr)
struct proc *proc_p;
vm_offset_t virt_addr;
```

Arguments

proc_p
: Specifies a pointer to a proc structure. The vtop interface uses the proc structure pointer to obtain the pmap.

virt_addr
: Specifies the virtual address that vtop converts to a physical address.

Description

The vtop interface converts a specified virtual address to a physical address.

Cautions

The vtop interface panics and displays the following message on the console terminal if the proc structure pointer you pass is NULL and the virtual address is in user space:

```
vtop: user address passed with null proc pointer
```

Return Values

Upon successful completion, vtop returns the physical address associated with the specified virtual address.

Name

wakeup – Wakes up all processes sleeping on a specified address

Synopsis

void wakeup(*channel*)
caddr_t *channel*;

Arguments

channel
Specifies the address on which the wakeup is to be issued.

Description

The wakeup interface wakes up all processes sleeping on the address specified by the *channel* argument. All processes sleeping on this address are awakened and made scheduable according to the priorities they specified when they went to sleep. It is possible that there are no processes sleeping on the channel at the time the wakeup is issued. This situation can occur for a variety of reasons and does not represent an error condition.

The sleep and wakeup interfaces block and unblock a process. Generally, a device driver issues these interfaces on behalf of a process requesting I/O while a transfer is in progress. That is, a process requesting I/O is put to sleep on an address associated with the request by the appropriate device driver interface. When the transfer has asynchronously completed, the device driver interrupt service interface issues a wakeup on the address associated with the completed request. This action makes the relevant process scheduable.

The process resumes execution within the relevant device driver interface at the point immediately following the request to sleep. The driver, on behalf of the process, can then determine whether the condition for which it was sleeping (in this example completion of an I/O request) has been removed. If so, it can continue on to complete the I/O request. Otherwise, the appropriate driver interface can decide to put the process back to sleep to await removal of the indicated condition.

Example

See Section 9.5.4 for a code example of the `wakeup` interface.

Return Values

None

Related Information

Section 15.2, Kernel Support Interfaces: `mpsleep`, `sleep`

Section 15.4, Global Variables: *lbolt*

Name

WRITE_BUS_D8, WRITE_BUS_D16, WRITE_BUS_D32,
WRITE_BUS_D64 – Perform byte, word, longword, and quadword bus I/O
write operations

Synopsis

```
void WRITE_BUS_D8(dev_addr, data)
io_handle_t dev_addr;
long data;


void WRITE_BUS_D16(dev_addr, data)
io_handle_t dev_addr;
long data;


void WRITE_BUS_D32(dev_addr, data)
io_handle_t dev_addr;
long data;


void WRITE_BUS_D64(dev_addr, data)
io_handle_t dev_addr;
long data;
```

Arguments

dev_addr
>   Specifies an I/O handle that you can use to reference a device register or
>   memory located in bus address space (either I/O space or memory
>   space). This I/O handle references a device register in the bus address
>   space where the write operation occurs.

data
>   Specifies the data to be written to the specified device register in bus
>   address space.

Description

The WRITE_BUS_D8 interface writes a byte (8 bits) to a device register
located in the bus I/O address space. The WRITE_BUS_D16 interface
writes a word (16 bits) to a device register located in the bus I/O address
space. The WRITE_BUS_D32 interface writes a longword (32 bits) to a

device register located in the bus I/O address space. The `WRITE_BUS_D64` interface writes a quadword (64 bits) to a device register located in the bus I/O address space. These are convenience interfaces that call `write_io_port`, which is a generic interface that maps to a bus- and machine-specific interface that actually performs the task of writing the byte, word, longword, or quadword to a device register. Use of these interfaces to write data to a device register makes the device driver more portable across different bus architectures, different CPU architectures, and different CPU types within the same CPU architecture.

The `WRITE_BUS_D8`, `WRITE_BUS_D16`, `WRITE_BUS_D32`, and `WRITE_BUS_D64` interfaces automatically pass values to the *width* and *flags* arguments of `write_io_port`. The following list identifies these values:

- The `WRITE_BUS_D8`, `WRITE_BUS_D16`, `WRITE_BUS_D32`, and `WRITE_BUS_D64` interfaces set *width* to the values 1, 2, 4, and 8, respectively.

- The `WRITE_BUS_D8`, `WRITE_BUS_D16`, `WRITE_BUS_D32`, and `WRITE_BUS_D64` interfaces set *flags* to the value zero (0).

Cautions

The I/O handle that you pass to the *dev_addr* argument of the `WRITE_BUS_D8`, `WRITE_BUS_D16`, `WRITE_BUS_D32`, `WRITE_BUS_D64` interfaces must be an I/O handle that references addresses residing in sparse space. All Alpha CPUs support sparse space. As a result, all bus configuration code should supply an I/O handle that references bus address space.

If you pass an I/O handle to the *dev_addr* argument that references addresses residing in some other space (for example, dense space) the results of the copy operation are unpredictable.

The Digital UNIX operating system provides the following interfaces that allow device drivers to perform copy operations on and zero blocks of memory on addresses that reside in dense space:

- `bcopy`

  Copies a series of bytes with a specified limit

- `blkclr` and `bzero`

  Zeros a block of memory

- `copyin`

  Copies data from a user address space to a kernel address space

- `copyinstr`

  Copies a null-terminated string from a user address space to a kernel address space

- `copyout`

  Copies data from a kernel address space to a user address space

- `copyoutstr`

  Copies a null-terminated string from a kernel address space to a user address space

Return Values

None

Related Information

Section 15.2, Kernel Support Interfaces: `write_io_port`

Name

write_io_port – Writes data to a device register

Synopsis

```
#include <io/common/devdriver.h>
void write_io_port(dev_addr, width, flags, data)
io_handle_t dev_addr;
int width;
int flags;
long data;
```

Arguments

dev_addr
Specifies an I/O handle that you can use to reference a device register or memory located in bus address space (either I/O space or memory space). This I/O handle references a device register in the bus address space where the write operation occurs. You can perform standard C mathematical operations on the I/O handle. For example, you can add an offset to or subtract an offset from the I/O handle.

width
Specifies the width (in bytes) of the data to be written. Valid values are 1, 2, 3, 4, and 8. Not all CPU platforms or bus adapters support all of these values.

flags
Specifies flags to indicate special processing requests. Currently, no flags are used.

data
Specifies the data to be written to the specified device register in bus address space.

Description

The write_io_port interface writes the data of the specified width to the specified device register in bus address space. This interface shifts the data to the appropriate byte lanes before performing the write to bus address space. The I/O handle you pass to dev_addr identifies where the write operation occurs.

Notes

The write_io_port interface is a generic interface that maps to a bus- and machine-specific interface that actually performs the write operation. Using this interface to write data to a device register makes the device driver more portable across different bus architectures, different CPU architectures, and different CPU types within the same CPU architecture.

This interface also must call the mb interface under certain circumstances. For discussions and examples of these circumstances, see Section 2.6.6.

Cautions

The I/O handle that you pass to the *dev_addr* argument of the write_io_port interface must be an I/O handle that references addresses residing in sparse space. All Alpha CPUs support sparse space. As a result, all bus configuration code should supply an I/O handle that references bus address space.

If you pass an I/O handle to the *dev_addr* argument that references addresses residing in some other space (for example, dense space) the results of the write operation are unpredictable.

The Digital UNIX operating system provides the following interfaces that allow device drivers to perform copy operations on and zero blocks of memory on addresses that reside in dense space:

- bcopy

  Copies a series of bytes with a specified limit

- blkclr and bzero

  Zeros a block of memory

- copyin

  Copies data from a user address space to a kernel address space

- copyinstr

  Copies a null-terminated string from a user address space to a kernel address space

- copyout

  Copies data from a kernel address space to a user address space

- copyoutstr

  Copies a null-terminated string from a kernel address space to a user address space

Example

See Section 9.8.1.2 for a code example of the `write_io_port` interface.

Return Values

None

Related Information

Section 15.2, Kernel Support Interfaces: `read_io_port`

Name

zalloc – Returns an element from the specified zone

Synopsis

vm_offset_t zalloc(*zone*)
zone_t *zone*;

Arguments

zone
> Specifies a pointer to the zone structure for the element specified in a previous call to zinit. This is the zone structure pointer returned by zinit.

Description

The zalloc interface returns an element from the specified zone.

Notes

In previous versions of the Digital UNIX operating system (formerly known as DEC OSF/1), device drivers could call the following memory allocation-related interfaces:

- kalloc and kfree

  Device drivers called these interfaces to allocate and free a variable-sized section of kernel virtual memory.

- kget

  Device drivers called this interface to perform nonblocking allocation of a variable-sized section of kernel virtual memory.

- zinit, zchange, zalloc, zfree, and zget

  Device drivers called these interfaces to allocate exact-size sections of kernel virtual memory.

The Digital UNIX operating system still provides backwards compatibility with the kalloc, kfree, and kget interfaces and the zinit, zchange, zalloc, zfree, and zget interfaces. However, Digital recommends that for new device drivers you use the MALLOC and FREE interfaces to allocate and to free sections of kernel virtual memory.

Return Values

Upon successful completion, `zalloc` returns an element from the specified zone.

Related Information

Section 15.2, Kernel Support Interfaces: `MALLOC`, `zfree`, `zget`, `zinit`

Name

zchange – Changes a zone's flags

Synopsis

```
void zchange(zone, pageable, sleepable, exhaustible,
collectable)
zone_t zone;
boolean_t pageable;
boolean_t sleepable;
boolean_t exhaustible;
boolean_t collectable;
```

Arguments

zone

Specifies the zone whose associated flags you want to change. You must have previously initialized this zone by calling the zinit interface.

pageable

Specifies a pageable/nonpageable flag. You can pass the constants TRUE or FALSE to this argument. The following value table describes the meaning of these constants:

Value	Meaning
TRUE	zchange sets the Z_PAGEABLE flag. The zone allocates pageable memory.
FALSE	zchange does not set the Z_PAGEABLE flag. The zone cannot allocate pageable memory.

sleepable

Specifies a sleepable/nonsleepable flag. You can pass the constants TRUE or FALSE to this argument.

The following value table describes the meaning of these constants:

Value	Meaning
TRUE	Allows the calling interface to block (sleep).
FALSE	Does not allow the calling interface to block (sleep).

exhaustible

Specifies a panic disable/enable flag. You can pass the constants TRUE or FALSE to this argument. The following value table describes the meaning of these constants:

Value	Meaning
TRUE	zchange sets the Z_EXHAUST flag. It is okay to expand the zone beyond its maximum size.
FALSE	zchange does not set the Z_EXHAUST flag. It is not okay to expand the zone beyond its maximum size.

collectable

Specifies a garbage collector flag. You can pass the constants TRUE or FALSE to this argument. The following value table describes the meaning of these constants:

Value	Meaning
TRUE	zchange sets the Z_COLLECT flag. The system garbage collects the specified zone.
FALSE	zchange does not set the Z_COLLECT flag. The system does not garbage collect the specified zone.

Description

The zchange interface sets the flags for *zone* to the specified values. A zone is a collection of fixed-size elements for which there is fast allocation/deallocation access. Each fixed-size element has an associated zone structure that contains such things as the sizes of the element and the zone.

Device drivers use zones to dynamically allocate fixed-size memory for data structures (elements) on an individual basis. In this case, the zone interfaces maintain a linked list of `zone` structures. You must call `zchange` immediately after calling `zinit`.

The `zchange` interface sets the `Z_PAGEABLE`, `Z_EXHAUST`, and `Z_COLLECT` flags for the specified zone when you pass the value `TRUE` to the *pageable*, *exhaustible*, and *collectable* arguments. You can also block (sleep) on the change operation by passing the value `TRUE` to the *sleepable* argument.

Notes

In previous versions of the Digital UNIX operating system (formerly known as DEC OSF/1), device drivers could call the following memory allocation-related interfaces:

- `kalloc` and `kfree`

  Device drivers called these interfaces to allocate and free a variable-sized section of kernel virtual memory.

- `kget`

  Device drivers called this interface to perform nonblocking allocation of a variable-sized section of kernel virtual memory.

- `zinit`, `zchange`, `zalloc`, `zfree`, and `zget`

  Device drivers called these interfaces to allocate exact-size sections of kernel virtual memory.

The Digital UNIX operating system still provides backwards compatibility with the `kalloc`, `kfree`, and `kget` interfaces and the `zinit`, `zchange`, `zalloc`, `zfree`, and `zget` interfaces. However, Digital recommends that for new device drivers you use the `MALLOC` and `FREE` interfaces to allocate and to free sections of kernel virtual memory.

The `zchange` interface allows device drivers to add or remove zone flags without modifying the `zinit` parameters. The `zchange` interface does not lock the zone when it is altering the flag values.

Return Values

None

Related Information

Chapter 14, Header Files Related to Device Drivers: `zalloc.h`

Section 15.2, Kernel Support Interfaces: `MALLOC`, `zinit`

Chapter 16, Structures Related to Device Drivers: `zone`

Name

zfree – Frees (deallocates) an element

Synopsis

```
void zfree(zone, elem)
zone_t zone;
vm_offset_t elem;
```

Arguments

zone

Specifies a pointer to the zone structure for the element specified in previous calls to zinit and zalloc. This is the zone structure pointer returned by zinit and passed by the driver to zalloc.

elem

Specifies the element to be freed.

Description

The zfree interface deallocates (frees) an element back to a zone. This element was returned to the caller in a previous call to zalloc.

Notes

In previous versions of the Digital UNIX operating system (formerly known as DEC OSF/1), device drivers could call the following memory allocation-related interfaces:

- kalloc and kfree

  Device drivers called these interfaces to allocate and free a variable-sized section of kernel virtual memory.

- kget

  Device drivers called this interface to perform nonblocking allocation of a variable-sized section of kernel virtual memory.

- zinit, zchange, zalloc, zfree, and zget

  Device drivers called these interfaces to allocate exact-size sections of kernel virtual memory.

The Digital UNIX operating system still provides backwards compatibility with the `kalloc`, `kfree`, and `kget` interfaces and the `zinit`, `zchange`, `zalloc`, `zfree`, and `zget` interfaces. However, Digital recommends that for new device drivers you use the `MALLOC` and `FREE` interfaces to allocate and to free sections of kernel virtual memory.

Return Values

None

Related Information

Section 15.2, Kernel Support Interfaces: `MALLOC`, `zalloc`, `zget`, `zinit`

Name

zget – Returns an element from the specified zone

Synopsis

```
vm_offset_t zget(zone)
zone_t zone;
```

Arguments

zone
Specifies a pointer to the zone structure for the element specified in a previous call to zinit.

Description

The zget interface returns an element from the specified zone and immediately returns nothing if there is no element. A device driver calls this interface when it cannot block (sleep), for example, when processing an interrupt.

Notes

In previous versions of the Digital UNIX operating system (formerly known as DEC OSF/1), device drivers could call the following memory allocation-related interfaces:

- kalloc and kfree

  Device drivers called these interfaces to allocate and free a variable-sized section of kernel virtual memory.

- kget

  Device drivers called this interface to perform nonblocking allocation of a variable-sized section of kernel virtual memory.

- zinit, zchange, zalloc, zfree, and zget

  Device drivers called these interfaces to allocate exact-size sections of kernel virtual memory.

The Digital UNIX operating system still provides backwards compatibility with the kalloc, kfree, and kget interfaces and the zinit, zchange, zalloc, zfree, and zget interfaces. However, Digital recommends that for new device drivers you use the MALLOC and FREE interfaces to allocate and to free sections of kernel virtual memory.

Return Values

Upon successful completion, `zget` returns an element from the specified zone and immediately returns nothing if there is no element.

Related Information

Section 15.2, Kernel Support Interfaces: `MALLOC`, `zalloc`, `zfree`, `zinit`

Name

zinit – Initializes a new zone

Synopsis

```
zone_t zinit(size, max, alloc, name)
vm_size_t size;
vm_size_t max;
vm_size_t alloc;
char *name;
```

Arguments

size
  Specifies the size of an element.

max
  Specifies the maximum memory size of the zone.

alloc
  Specifies the size of the memory to allocate. If you specify the value zero (0), zinit sets *alloc* to be equal to the value stored in *size*. This stored value is based on the value you passed and a rounding operation performed by zinit.

name
  Specifies a pointer to the name for the zone.

Description

The zinit interface initializes a new zone. A zone is a collection of fixed-size elements for which there is fast allocation/deallocation access. Each fixed-size element has an associated zone structure that contains such things as the sizes of the element and the zone.

Device drivers use zones to dynamically allocate fixed-size memory for data structures (elements) on an individual basis. In this case, the zone interfaces maintain a linked list of zone structures. The zinit interface checks the values you passed to the *size* (size of the element), *max* (maximum memory size of the zone), and *alloc* (the size of the memory to allocate) arguments and performs the following tasks:

- Rounds the size of the element to a longword multiple. This ensures that element addresses are always on longword boundaries.

- Rounds the maximum memory size of the zone to the next page boundary.

- Rounds the size of the memory to allocate to the next page boundary. If the maximum memory size of the zone is less than the size of the memory to allocate, `zinit` sets *max* to the rounded value now stored in *alloc*.

The `zinit` interface then initializes the members of the `zone` structure pointer associated with *name*.

Notes

In previous versions of the Digital UNIX operating system (formerly known as DEC OSF/1), device drivers could call the following memory allocation-related interfaces:

- `kalloc` and `kfree`

  Device drivers called these interfaces to allocate and free a variable-sized section of kernel virtual memory.

- `kget`

  Device drivers called this interface to perform nonblocking allocation of a variable-sized section of kernel virtual memory.

- `zinit`, `zchange`, `zalloc`, `zfree`, and `zget`

  Device drivers called these interfaces to allocate exact-size sections of kernel virtual memory.

The Digital UNIX operating system still provides backwards compatibility with the `kalloc`, `kfree`, and `kget` interfaces and the `zinit`, `zchange`, `zalloc`, `zfree`, and `zget` interfaces. However, Digital recommends that for new device drivers you use the `MALLOC` and `FREE` interfaces to allocate and to free sections of kernel virtual memory.

Return Values

Upon successful completion, `zinit` returns a pointer to the initialized `zone` structure. If there is no more space in the zone that contains all other zones for the element, `zinit` returns the value zero (0).

Related Information

Chapter 14, Header Files Related to Device Drivers: `zalloc.h`

Section 15.2, Kernel Support Interfaces: `MALLOC`, `zalloc`, `zfree`, `zget`

Chapter 16, Structures Related to Device Drivers: `zone`

15.3 ioctl Commands

When defining `ioctl` commands that your driver supports, use a set of macros defined in `/usr/sys/include/sys/ioctl.h` to construct these definitions. These macros instruct the kernel on how much data, if any, is transferred between the application program making the `ioctl` system call and the device driver. Table 15-2 describes the macros defined in `/usr/sys/include/sys/ioctl.h` as well as the DEVIOCGET `ioctl` command defined in `/usr/sys/include/sys/ioctl_compat.h`.

Table 15-2: Summary Descriptions of ioctl Commands

ioctl Macro/Command	Summary Description
DEVGETGEOM	Obtains device geometry information.
DEVIOCGET	Obtains information about a device.
_IO	Defines `ioctl` types for device control operations.
_IOR	Defines `ioctl` types for device control operations.
_IOW	Defines `ioctl` types for device control operations.
_IOWR	Defines `ioctl` types for device control operations.

Name

DEVGETGEOM – Obtains device geometry information

Synopsis

```
#include <io/common/devio.h>
#include <sys/ioctl.h>
```

Description

The DEVGETGEOM ioctl request obtains generic device geometry information by polling the underlying device driver. DEVGETGEOM uses the following union defined in the file /usr/sys/include/io/common/devio.h:

```
typedef union devgeom {
 struct {
     unsigned long    dev_size;
     unsigned short   ntracks;
     unsigned short   nsectors;
     unsigned short   ncylinders;
     unsigned long    attributes;
     unsigned long    sector_size;
     unsigned long    min_trans;
     unsigned long    max_trans;
     unsigned long    prefer_trans;
     } geom_info;
     unsigned char        pad[108];
} DEVGEOMST;
```

This union contains two members: a geom_info data structure and a pad array that allocates space to allow for future expansion. The following list describes the members of the geom_info structure:

dev_size
    Specifies the total number of sectors/blocks on the device available for use.

ntracks
    Specifies the number of tracks per cylinder. This number may not actually reflect the number of tracks per cylinder but is an estimate (RAID devices).

nsectors
    Specifies an average number of sectors per track.

ncylinders
    Specifies an average number of cylinders per track.

attributes
Specifies device attributes. You can set this member to one of the following constants: DEVGEOM_REMOVE (a removable device) or DEVGEOM_DYNAMIC (a dynamic geometry device).

sector_size
Specifies the number of bytes in the sector.

min_trans
Specifies the minimum number of bytes for the transfer size.

max_trans
Specifies the maximum number of bytes for the transfer size.

prefer_trans
Specifies the preferred number of bytes for the transfer size.

Example

The following code example shows how a disk device driver can use the DEVGETGEOM ioctl command. The example uses the attributes, dev_size, and sector_size members of the geom_info structure.

```
      .
      .
      .
cdisk_ioctl(dev, cmd, data, flag)
dev_t dev; /* major/minor number */
register int cmd; /* Ioctl command */
caddr_t data; /* User data buffer - already copied in */
int flag; /* unused */
      .
      .
      .
        switch (cmd) {
      .
      .
      .
            /*
             * Disk geometry info.
             */
case DEVGETGEOM:
    {
        DEVGEOMST *devgeom = (DEVGEOMST *)data;
      .
      .
      .
        bzero((caddr_t)devgeom, sizeof(DEVGEOMST));

        if(inqp->rmb)
            devgeom->geom_info.attributes |= DEVGEOM_REMOVE;

        /*
         * HSX00 and HSX01 FIB RAID devices are flagged
         * as having "dynamic geometry" because the
         * geometry of the underlying device can change
         * depending on the configuration of units.
```

```
 */
if ( dd->dd_flags & SZ_DYNAMIC_GEOM != 0)
    devgeom->geom_info.attributes |= DEVGEOM_DYNAMIC;

/*
 * Get disk size via read capacity command.
 */
read_cap_data = (DIR_READ_CAP_DATA *)
      ccmn_get_dbuf((U32)sizeof(DIR_READ_CAP_DATA));
if(cdisk_read_capacity(pd, read_cap_data) == 0) {
      BTOL(&read_cap_data->lbn3, nblocks);
      /*
       * RDCAP returns the address of the last LBN.
       * Add one to get the number of LBNs.
       */
      devgeom->geom_info.dev_size = ++nblocks;

      /*
       * Get the sector size.
       */
      BTOL(&read_cap_data->block_len3, blk_len);
      devgeom->geom_info.sector_size = blk_len ;
```
.
.
.

Name

DEVIOCGET – Obtains information about a device

Synopsis

```
#include <io/common/devio.h>
#include <sys/ioctl.h>
```

Description

The DEVIOCGET ioctl request obtains information about a device. This request obtains generic device information by polling the underlying device driver. DEVIOCGET uses the following structure defined in the file /usr/sys/include/io/common/devio.h:

```
struct  devget  {
        short       category;
        short       bus;
        char        interface[DEV_SIZE];
        char        device[DEV_SIZE];
        short       adpt_num;
        short       nexus_num;
        short       bus_num;
        short       ctlr_num;
        short       rctlr_num;
        short       slave_num;
        char        dev_name[DEV_SIZE];
        short       unit_num;
        unsigned    soft_count;
        unsigned    hard_count;
        long        stat;
        long        category_stat;
};
```

The following list describes the members of this structure:

category
>   Specifies the general class of the device. This member can be set to one of the following values: DEV_TAPE (tape category), DEV_DISK (disk category), DEV_TERMINAL (terminal category), DEV_PRINTER (printer category), or DEV_SPECIAL (special category).

bus
>   Specifies the communications bus type. For example, this member would be set to the value DEV_SCSI for SCSI devices.

interface
>   Specifies a string of up to eight characters that identifies the controller

interface type.

`device`
> This member is set to the device string.

`adpt_num`
> This member is set to the adapter number.

`nexus_num`
> This member is set to the nexus, or node, on the adapter number.

`bus_num`
> This member is set to the bus number that the device controller resides on.

`ctlr_num`
> This member is set to the specific controller number for the controller of this device. This number is the specific controller number on this bus.

`rctlr_num`
> This member is set to the remote controller number.

`slave_num`
> This member is set to the device unit number. For a disk device, this unit number is the physical device unit number. For a terminal device, this number is the terminal line number.

`dev_name`
> This member is set to the device name type, which is a string of up to eight characters. For example, Digital defines the strings `rz` and `tz` to represent disk and tape devices.

`unit_num`
> This member is set to the kernel configuration representation of a device unit number. The value in this member is frequently the same as the `slave_num` member. The difference is that `slave_num` represents the physical unit number, while the `unit_num` member represents a logical unit number for the device.

`soft_count`
> This member is set to a driver counter of soft (noncritical) errors.

`hard_count`
> This member is set to a driver counter of hardware errors.

`stat`
> This member is set to the device status. This member is used primarily to represent drive status for tape devices. Some examples of drive status include: the drive is at the bottom or end of tape, or the drive is write-protected.

`category_stat`

> This member is set to generic device status values, which are defined in
> `/usr/sys/include/io/common/devio.h`. The values are
> organized according to the following device types: tapes, disks, and
> communications devices.

Example

The following example prints out the device type and unit number:

```
 .
 .
 .
struct devget dev_st; 1
if (ioctl (fd, DEVIOCGET, &dev_st) < 0) {
        printf ("DEVIOCGET failed\n");
        exit(1);
} 2
printf ("Device type = %s\n",dev_st.device); 3
printf ("Unit number = %d\n",dev_st.unit_num); 4
```

1 Declares a structure of type `devget`.

2 Determines whether the call to `ioctl` succeeds or fails. Note that `fd` is
an open file descriptor for the associated device special file.

3 Obtains the device type.

4 Obtains the unit number.

Name

_IO – Defines ioctl types for device control operations

Synopsis

```
#include <sys/ioctl.h>
```

_IO(*g*, *n*)

Arguments

g

Specifies the group that this ioctl type belongs to. This argument must be a nonnegative 8-bit number (that is, in the range 0–255 inclusive). You can pass the value zero (0) to this argument if a new ioctl group is not being defined.

n

Specifies the specific ioctl type within the group. These types should be sequentially assigned numbers for each different ioctl operation the driver supports. This argument must be a nonnegative 8-bit number (that is, in the range 0–255 inclusive).

Description

The _IO macro defines ioctl types for situations where no data is actually transferred between the application program and the kernel. For example, this could occur in a device control operation.

Example

The following example uses the _IO macro to construct an ioctl called DN_OPERATION1. Note that DN_OPERATION1 passes the value zero (0) for the group that this ioctl belongs to and the value 1 to identify the specific ioctl type within the group.

```
#define DN_OPERATION1    _IO(0,1)
```

Related Information

Section 15.3, ioctl Commands: _IOR, _IOW, _IOWR

Name

_IOR – Defines ioctl types for device control operations

Synopsis

```
#include <sys/ioctl.h>
_IOR(g, n, t)
```

Arguments

g

Specifies the group that this ioctl type belongs to. This argument must be a nonnegative 8-bit number (that is, in the range 0–255 inclusive). You can pass the value zero (0) to this argument if a new ioctl group is not being defined.

n

Specifies the specific ioctl type within the group. These types should be sequentially assigned numbers for each different ioctl operation the driver supports. This argument must be a nonnegative 8-bit number (that is, in the range 0–255 inclusive).

t

Specifies the data structure size, which cannot exceed 128 bytes. You use this argument to size how much data is passed from the kernel back to the user application. The kernel determines the number of bytes to transfer by passing the value in this argument to the sizeof operator.

Description

The _IOR macro defines ioctl types for situations where data is transferred from the kernel into the user's buffer. Typically, this data consists of device control or status information returned to the application program.

Example

The following example uses the _IOR macro to construct an ioctl called DN_GETCOUNT. Note that DN_GETCOUNT passes the value zero (0) for the group that this ioctl belongs to and the value 2 to identify the specific ioctl type within the group. The DN_GETCOUNT ioctl also passes the data type int, which the kernel passes to the sizeof operator to determine how much data is passed from the kernel back to the user application.

```
#define DN_GETCOUNT    _IOR(0,2,int)
```

Related Information

Section 15.3, ioctl Commands: DEVIOCGET, _IO, _IOW, _IOWR

Name

_IOW – Defines ioctl types for device control operations

Synopsis

```
#include <sys/ioctl.h>
_IOW(g, n, t)
```

Arguments

g

Specifies the group that this ioctl type belongs to. This argument must be a nonnegative 8-bit number (that is, in the range 0–255 inclusive). You can pass the value zero (0) to this argument if a new ioctl group is not being defined.

n

Specifies the specific ioctl type within the group. These types should be sequentially assigned numbers for each different ioctl operation the driver supports. This argument must be a nonnegative 8-bit number (that is, in the range 0–255 inclusive).

t

Specifies the size of the data passed from the user application back to the kernel. The kernel determines the number of bytes to transfer by passing the value in this argument to the sizeof operator.

Description

The _IOW macro defines ioctl types for situations where data is transferred from the user's buffer into the kernel. Typically, this data consists of device control or status information passed to the driver from the application program.

Example

The following example uses the _IOW macro to construct an ioctl called DN_SETCOUNT. Note that DN_SETCOUNT passes the value zero (0) for the group that this ioctl belongs to and the value 3 to identify the specific ioctl type within the group. The DN_SETCOUNT ioctl also passes the data type int, which the kernel passes to the sizeof operator to determine how much data is passed from the user application back to the kernel.

```
#define DN_SETCOUNT    _IOR(0,3,int)
```

Related Information

Section 15.3, ioctl Commands: _IO, _IOR, _IOWR

Name

_IOWR – Defines ioctl types for device control operations

Synopsis

```
#include <sys/ioctl.h>

_IOWR(g, n, t)
```

Arguments

g

Specifies the group that this ioctl type belongs to. This argument must be a nonnegative 8-bit number (that is, in the range 0–255 inclusive). You can pass the value zero (0) to this argument if a new ioctl group is not being defined.

n

Specifies the specific ioctl type within the group. These types should be sequentially assigned numbers for each different ioctl operation the driver supports. This argument must be a nonnegative 8-bit number (that is, in the range 0–255 inclusive).

t

Specifies the size of the data passed from the user application back to the kernel. The kernel determines the number of bytes to transfer by passing the value in this argument to the sizeof operator. Upon completion of the ioctl operation, this same data structure contains the data returned from the driver back to the user level application.

Description

The _IOWR macro defines ioctl types for situations where data is transferred from the user's buffer into the kernel. The driver then performs the appropriate ioctl operation and returns data of the same size back up to the user-level application. Typically, this data consists of device control or status information passed to the driver from the application program.

Example

The following example uses the _IOWR macro to construct an ioctl called DN_SETVERIFY. Note that DN_SETVERIFY passes the value zero (0) for the group that this ioctl belongs to and the value 4 to identify the specific ioctl type within the group. The DN_SETVERIFY ioctl also passes the data type int, which the kernel passes to the sizeof operator to determine how much data is passed from the user application back to the kernel.

```
#define DN_SETVERIFY    _IOWR(0,4,int)
```

Related Information

Section 15.3, ioctl Commands: _IO, _IOR, _IOW

15.4 Global Variables

Table 15-3 summarizes the global variables that device drivers use.

Table 15-3: Summary Descriptions of Global Variables

Global Variable	Summary Description
cpu	Provides a unique logical processor-type family identifier.
hz	Stores the number of clock ticks per second.
lbolt	Is a periodic wakeup mechanism.
page_size	Is the virtual page size.

Name

cpu – Provides a unique logical processor-type family identifier

Synopsis

```
extern int cpu;
```

Description

The cpu global variable provides a unique logical family identifier of the
processor type of the running system. The logical system name can represent
a single processor or a family of processor types. For example, the constant
DEC_3000_500 represents the DEC 3000 Model 500 AXP Workstation.
The defined processor names appear in the following file:
/usr/sys/include/arch/alpha/hal/cpuconf.h.

You use the cpu global variable to conditionally execute processor-specific
code. For example, the following code fragment calls a system-specific
initialization interface for the DEC 3000 Model 500 AXP Workstation:

```
    .
    .
    .
if (cpu == DEC_3000_500) {
        init_3000_500();
}
    .
    .
    .
```

Name

hz – Stores the number of clock ticks per second

Synopsis

```
extern int hz;
```

Location

/usr/sys/include/sys/kernel.h

Description

The hz global variable is set to the number of clock ticks per second. The value is useful for timing purposes. For example, if a device driver wants to schedule an interface to be run in 2 seconds, you could use the following call:

```
   .
   .
   .
timeout(lptout, (caddr_t)dev, 2*hz);
   .
   .
   .
```

Name

lbolt – Is a periodic wakeup mechanism

Synopsis

```
extern time_t lbolt;
```

Location

```
/usr/sys/include/sys/kernel.h
```

Description

You use the lbolt global variable as a periodic wakeup mechanism.
Wakeups are done on the lbolt variable once per second. For example, if
a driver was polling for an event once per second, you could use the
following code:

```
 .
 .
 .
sleep((caddr_t) &lbolt, PZERO);
 .
 .
 .
```

Name

`page_size` – Is the virtual page size

Synopsis

`extern vm_size_t page_size;`

Location

`/usr/sys/include/mach/vm_param.h`

Description

The `page_size` global variable is the size of a virtual page on a CPU. A device driver can use this global variable to partition I/O transfers so that they never cross a virtual page boundary. You should use this global variable only when:

- A subsystem cannot use the DMA mapping interfaces (such as, `dma_map_alloc`, `dma_map_load`, and so forth)

- There is a one-to-one correspondence between the system memory map and the I/O's view of the system memory space

Structures Related to Device Drivers 16

This chapter describes:

- Conventions for structures that device drivers use
- Structures that device drivers use

16.1 Conventions for Data Structures

The descriptions of the structures related to device drivers are presented in alphabetical order and in reference (man) page style. The descriptions can include the following sections.

Name

This section lists the name of the structure along with a summary description of its purpose.

Include File

This section lists the header file, including the path, where the structure is defined.

Synopsis

This section takes the following approaches when describing structures:

- The C structure definition is shown

    This occurs when the driver writer needs to understand or needs to initialize all of the members of a structure. For example, the declaration of the `driver` structure is shown because driver writers initialize this structure in their device drivers.

- The structure members are shown in a table

    This occurs when the driver writer needs to understand or needs to reference some of the members of a particular structure. For example, the members of the `buf` structure are shown in a table because the driver writer references only some of its members.

- No structure declaration or structure table is shown

  This occurs when the data structure is opaque. This means the members of the structure are manipulated by the Digital UNIX operating system. The driver writer does not manipulate or reference any of the members.

Members

This section provides a short description of each member of the structure.

Description

This section gives more details about the purpose of the structure.

Related Information

This section lists related kernel interfaces, structures, system calls, and so forth.

16.2 Data Structures

Table 16-1 summarizes the structures that device drivers use.

Table 16-1: Summary Descriptions of Data Structures

Structure Name	Meaning
bdevsw	Defines a device driver's entry points in the block device switch table.
buf	Describes arbitrary I/O.
bus	Represents an instance of a bus entity to which other buses or controllers are logically attached.
cdevsw	Defines a device driver's entry points in the character device switch table.
cfg_attr_t	Contains information for managing the loading and unloading of loadable drivers.
cfg_subsys_attr_t	Contains attribute information for loadable drivers.
controller	Contains members that store information about hardware resources and store data for communication between the kernel and the device driver.

Table 16-1: (continued)

Structure Name	Meaning
device	Contains information that identifies the device. There is one device data structure for each device connected to the controller.
driver	Defines driver entry points and other driver-specific information. You initialize this data structure in the device driver.
handler_intr_info	Contains interrupt handler information.
ihandler_t	Contains information associated with device driver interrupt handling.
item_list	Contains hardware platform-specific information.
lock	Contains complex lock-specific information.
port	Contains information about a port.
sel_queue	Defines a queue of select events.
sg_entry	Contains bus address/byte count pairs.
slock	Contains simple lock-specific information.
task	Contains task-specific information.
thread	Contains kernel threads-related information.
uio	Describes I/O, either single vector or multiple vectors.
zone	Contains zone-related information.

Name

bdevsw – Defines a device driver's entry points in the block device switch table

Include File

/usr/sys/include/sys/conf.h

Synopsis

```
struct bdevsw
{
    int       (*d_open)();
    int       (*d_close)();
    int       (*d_strategy)();
    int       (*d_dump)();
    int       (*d_psize)();
    int       d_flags;
    int       (*d_ioctl)();
    int       d_funnel; /* serial code compatibility */
};
```

Members

d_open
>   Specifies a pointer to an entry point for the driver's open interface, which opens a device.

d_close
>   Specifies a pointer to an entry point for the driver's close interface, which closes a device.

d_strategy
>   Specifies a pointer to an entry point for the driver's strategy interface, which reads and writes block data.

d_dump
>   Specifies a pointer to an entry point for the driver's dump interface, which is used for panic dumps of the system image.

d_psize
>   Specifies a pointer to an entry point for the driver's psize interface, which returns the size in physical blocks of a device (disk partition).

d_flags
>   Specifies device-related and other flags. You set this member to the bitwise inclusive OR of the device-related and other flags. One example

of a device-related flag is B_TAPE. This flag is set in the b_flags member of the buf structure. The B_TAPE flag determines whether to use delayed writes, which are not allowed for tape devices. For all other drivers, this member is set to the value zero (0).

Another flag specifies whether this is an SVR4 DDI/DKI-compliant device driver. You set this member to the B_DDIDKI flag to indicate that this is an SVR4 DDI/DKI-compliant device driver.

d_ioctl
Specifies a pointer to an entry point for the driver's ioctl interface, which performs special functions or I/O control.

d_funnel
Schedules a device driver onto a CPU in a multiprocessor configuration. You set this member to one of the following constants:

Value	Meaning
DEV_FUNNEL	Specifies that you want to funnel the device driver because you have not made it SMP safe. This means that the driver is forced to execute on a single (the master) CPU.
	Even if you funnel your device driver, you must follow the SMP locking conventions when accessing kernel data structures external to the driver. Typically, you use kernel interfaces that Digital supplies to indirectly access kernel data structures outside the driver.
DEV_FUNNEL_NULL	Specifies that you do not want to funnel the device driver because you have made it SMP safe. This means that the driver can execute on multiple CPUs. You make a device driver SMP safe by using the simple or complex lock mechanism.

Description

The block device switch, or bdevsw, table is an array of data structures that contains pointers to device driver entry points for each block mode device supported by the system. In addition, the table can contain stubs for device driver entry points for block mode devices that do not exist or entry points not used by a device driver.

Related Information

Section 15.2, Kernel Support Interfaces: `bdevsw_add`

Chapter 16, Structures Related to Device Drivers: `cdevsw`

Name

buf – Describes arbitrary I/O

Include File

/usr/sys/include/sys/buf.h

Synopsis

Member Name	Data Type
b_flags	int
b_forw	struct buf *
b_back	struct buf *
av_forw	struct buf *
av_back	struct buf *
b_bcount	int
b_error	short
b_dev	dev_t
b_un.b_addr	caddr_t
b_lblkno	daddr_t
b_blkno	daddr_t
b_resid	int
b_iodone	void (*b_iodone) ()
b_proc	struct proc *

Members

b_flags
>   Specifies binary status flags. These flags indicate how a request is to be
>   handled and the current status of the request.

The following flags are applicable to device drivers:

Flag	Meaning
B_READ	This flag is set if the operation is read and cleared if the operation is write.
B_DONE	This flag is cleared when a request is passed to a driver strategy interface. The device driver writer must call iodone to mark a buffer as completed.
B_ERROR	This flag specifies that an error occurred on this data transfer. Device drivers set this flag if an error occurs.
B_BUSY	This flag indicates that the buffer is in use.
B_PHYS	This flag indicates that the associated data is in user address space.

b_forw
    Specifies a hash chain. Only the entity (driver, buffer cache) that owns the buf structure can use or reference this member. A driver receiving a buf structure from the buffer cache through the strategy interface must not use this member.

b_back
    Specifies a hash chain. Only the entity (driver, buffer cache) that owns the buf structure can use or reference this member. A driver receiving a buf structure from the buffer cache through the strategy interface must not use this member.

av_forw
    Specifies the position on the free list if the b_flags member is not set to B_BUSY.

av_back
    Specifies the position on the free list if the b_flags member is not set to B_BUSY.

b_bcount
    Specifies the size of the requested transfer (in bytes).

b_error

> Specifies that an error occurred on this data transfer. This member is set to an error code if the b_flags member bit was set.

b_dev

> Specifies the special device to which the transfer is directed.

b_un.b_addr

> Specifies the address at which to pull or push the data.

b_lblkno

> Specifies the logical block number.

b_blkno

> Specifies the block number on the partition of a disk or on the file system.

b_resid

> Specifies (in bytes) the data not transferred because of some error.

b_iodone

> Specifies the interface called by iodone. The device driver calls iodone at the completion of an I/O operation.

b_proc

> Specifies a pointer to the proc structure that represents the process performing the I/O.

Description

The buf structures describe arbitrary I/O, but are usually associated with block I/O and physio. A systemwide pool of buf structures exists for block I/O; however, many device drivers also include locally defined buf structures.

Notes

Device drivers written for the ULTRIX operating system set the B_CALL flag in the b_flags member and a completion interface in the b_iodone member. At the completion of an I/O operation, the device driver on the ULTRIX operating system calls the iodone interface, which clears the B_CALL flag and then calls the completion interface set in the b_iodone member.

The Digital UNIX operating system does not define a B_CALL flag. The iodone interface checks the b_iodone member to determine if you specified a completion interface. If so, iodone clears b_iodone and then calls the specified completion interface. If you want to reuse this buf structure, you must reset the b_iodone member to a completion interface.

In fact, it is good programming practice to reset all of the referenced members of a `buf` structure that you plan to reuse.

Related Information

Section 15.2, Kernel Support Interfaces: `iodone`

Section 17.2, Block and Character Device Driver Interfaces: *xxstrategy*

Name

bus – Represents an instance of a bus entity to which other buses or controllers are logically attached

Include File

/usr/sys/include/io/common/devdriver.h

Synopsis

Member Name	Data Type
bus_mbox	u_long *
bus_hd	struct bus *
nxt_bus	struct bus *
ctlr_list	struct controller *
bus_list	struct bus *
bus_type	int
bus_name	char *
bus_num	int
slot	int
connect_bus	char *
connect_num	int
confl1	int (*confl1)()
confl2	int (*confl2)()
pname	char *
port	struct port *
intr	int (**intr)()
alive	int
framework	struct bus_framework *
driver_name	char *
bus_bridge_dma	void *
private	void * [8]
conn_priv	void * [8]
rsvd	

Members

bus_mbox
: Specifies a pointer to the mailbox data structure for hardware platforms that access I/O space through hardware mailboxes. The bus adapter code sets this member.

bus_hd
: Specifies a pointer to the bus structure that this bus is connected to.

nxt_bus
: Specifies a pointer to the next bus at this level.

ctlr_list
: Specifies a linked list of controllers connected to this bus.

bus_list
: Specifies a linked list of buses connected to this bus.

bus_type
: Specifies the type of bus.

bus_name
: Specifies the bus name.

bus_num
: Specifies the bus number of this bus.

slot
: Specifies the bus slot or node number.

connect_bus
: Specifies the name of the bus that this bus is connected to.

connect_num
: Specifies the number of the bus that this bus is connected to.

confl1
: Specifies a pointer to an entry point of the level 1 bus configuration interface. This interface is not typically used by device driver writers, but by systems engineers who want to implement a configuration procedure for a specific bus.

confl2
: Specifies a pointer to an entry point of the level 2 bus configuration interface. This interface is not typically used by device driver writers, but by systems engineers who want to implement a configuration procedure for a specific bus.

pname
: Specifies a pointer to the port name for this bus, if applicable.

port
   Specifies a pointer to the `port` structure for this bus, if applicable.

intr
   Specifies an array that contains an entry point or points for the bus
   interrupt interfaces.

alive
   Specifies a flag word to indicate the current status of the bus. The
   system sets this member to the bitwise inclusive OR of the valid alive
   bits defined in `devdriver.h`.

framework
   Specifies a pointer to the `bus_framework` structure. This structure
   contains pointers to bus interfaces for loadable device drivers. These
   interfaces provide dynamic extensions to bus functionality. They are
   used in the autoconfiguration of loadable drivers to perform bus-specific
   tasks, such as the registration of interrupt handlers.

driver_name
   Specifies the name of the controlling device driver.

bus_bridge_dma
   Signifies that the bus adapter has direct memory access (DMA) mapping
   support.

private
   Specifies private storage for use by this bus or bus class.

conn_priv
   Specifies private storage for use by the bus that this bus is connected to.

rsvd
   This member is reserved for future expansion of the data structure.

Description

The `bus` structure represents an instance of a bus entity. A bus is a real or
imagined entity to which other buses or controllers are logically attached.
All systems have at least one bus, the system bus, even though the bus may
not actually exist physically. The term *controller* here refers both to
devices that control slave devices (for example, disk or tape controllers) and
to devices that stand alone (for example, terminal or network controllers).

Related Information

Section 15.2, Kernel Support Interfaces: `handler_disable`, `handler_enable`

Chapter 16, Structures Related to Device Drivers: `controller`, `device`, `driver`

Name

cdevsw – Defines a device driver's entry points in the character device switch table

Include File

/usr/sys/include/sys/conf.h

Synopsis

```
struct cdevsw
{
  int     (*d_open)();
  int     (*d_close)();
  int     (*d_read)();
  int     (*d_write)();
  int     (*d_ioctl)();
  int     (*d_stop)();
  int     (*d_reset)();
  struct tty *d_ttys;
  int     (*d_select)();
  int     (*d_mmap)();
  int     d_funnel; /* serial code compatibility */
  int     (*d_segmap)(); /* xxx_segmap() entry point */
  int     d_flags; /* if (C_DDIDKI), driver follows
                   SVR4 DDI/DKI interfaces*/
};
```

Members

d_open
> Specifies a pointer to an entry point for the driver's open interface, which opens a device.

d_close
> Specifies a pointer to an entry point for the driver's close interface, which closes a device.

d_read
> Specifies a pointer to an entry point for the driver's read interface, which reads characters or raw data.

d_write
> Specifies a pointer to an entry point for the driver's write interface, which writes characters or raw data.

d_ioctl
> Specifies a pointer to an entry point for the driver's ioctl interface,

which performs special functions or I/O control.

d_stop

Specifies a pointer to an entry point for the driver's stop interface, which suspends other processing on behalf of the current process. You typically use the d_stop member only for terminal drivers.

d_reset

Specifies a pointer to an entry point for the driver's reset interface, which stops all current work and places the device connected to the controller in a known, quiescent state.

d_ttys

Specifies a pointer to driver private data.

d_select

Specifies a pointer to an entry point for the driver's select interface, which determines if a call to a read or write interface will block.

d_mmap

Specifies a pointer to an entry point for the driver's mmap interface, which maps kernel memory to user address space.

d_funnel

Schedules a device driver onto a CPU in a multiprocessor configuration. You set this member to one of the following constants:

Value	Meaning
DEV_FUNNEL	Specifies that you want to funnel the device driver because you have not made it SMP safe. This means that the driver is forced to execute on a single (the master) CPU.
	Even if you funnel your device driver, you must follow the SMP locking conventions when accessing kernel data structures external to the driver. Typically, you use kernel interfaces that Digital supplies to indirectly access kernel data structures outside the driver.
DEV_FUNNEL_NULL	Specifies that you do not want to funnel the device driver because you have made it SMP safe. This means that the driver can execute on multiple CPUs. You make a device driver SMP safe by using the simple or complex lock mechanism.

d_segmap

Specifies the segmap entry point.

d_flags

Specifies whether this is an SVR4 DDI/DKI-compliant device driver.

Set this member to the C_DDIDKI constant to indicate that this is an SVR4 DDI/DKI-compliant device driver.

Description

The character device switch, or cdevsw, table is an array of data structures that contains pointers to device driver entry points for each character device the system supports. In addition, the table can contain stubs for device driver entry points for character mode devices that do not exist or for entry points not used by a device driver.

Related Information

Section 15.2, Kernel Support Interfaces: cdevsw_add, cdevsw_del

Chapter 16, Structures Related to Device Drivers: bdevsw

Name

cfg_attr_t – Contains information for managing the loading and unloading of loadable drivers

Include File

/usr/sys/include/sys/sysconfig.h

Synopsis

```
typedef struct cfg_attr {
    char                name[CFG_ATTR_NAME_SZ];
    uchar               type;
    uchar               operation;
    uint                status;
    long                index;
    union {
        struct {
            caddr_t     val;
            ulong       min_size;
            ulong       max_size;
            void        (*disposal)();
            ulong       val_size;
        } bin;

        struct {
            caddr_t     val;
            ulong       min_len;
            ulong       max_len;
            void        (*disposal)();
        } str;

        struct {
            ulong       val;
            ulong       min_val;
            ulong       max_val;
        } num;
    } attr;
} cfg_attr_t;
```

Members

name
> Specifies the ASCII name of the attribute. The name must be between 2 and CFG_ATTR_NAME_SZ characters in length, including the terminating null character.

type

Specifies the data type associated with the name attribute. You must set the type member to one of the following constants:

Value	Meaning
CFG_ATTR_STRTYPE	Data type is a null-terminated array of characters.
CFG_ATTR_INTTYPE	Data type is a 32-bit signed integer.
CFG_ATTR_UINTTYPE	Data type is a 32-bit unsigned integer.
CFG_ATTR_LONGTYPE	Data type is a 64-bit signed integer.
CFG_ATTR_ULONGTYPE	Data type is a 64-bit unsigned integer.
CFG_ATTR_BINTYPE	Data type is an array of bytes.

operation

Specifies the operations that the device driver method of cfgmgr can perform on the attribute. You can set this member to one of the following constants:

Value	Meaning
CFG_OP_CONFIGURE	Configures a loadable device driver.
CFG_OP_UNCONFIGURE	Unconfigures a loadable device driver.
CFG_OP_QUERY	Queries the device driver for configuration information.
CFG_OP_RECONFIGURE	The device driver method of cfgmgr allows a user to modify the attribute.

status

Stores the return code (configure, unconfigure, query) from operations performed by the cfgmgr daemon. The device driver method of cfgmgr can return one of the following operation codes:

Value	Meaning
CFG_ATTR_SUCCESS	Successful operation.
CFG_ATTR_EEXISTS	The attribute you specified in the name member does not exist.
CFG_ATTR_EOP	The attribute you specified in the name member does support the operation.

Value	Meaning
CFG_ATTR_ESUBSYS	The device driver method subsystem failed.
CFG_ATTR_ESMALL	The value or size of the attribute you specified in the name member is too small.
CFG_ATTR_ELARGE	The value or size of the attribute you specified in the name member is too large.
CFG_ATTR_ETYPE	The data type that you specified for the attribute you specified in the name member is invalid or is a mismatch.
CFG_ATTR_EINDEX	The index associated with the attribute that you specified in the name member is invalid.
CFG_ATTR_EMEM	The device driver method subsystem could not allocate memory for the specified attribute.

index
Stores a value that scopes the target for indexed attributes.

attr
Specifies a union of the possible attribute types used for storing values, kernel locations, validation criteria, and disposal interfaces. The cfgmgr daemon uses the appropriate union element according to the attribute type. For example, attributes of type CFG_ATTR_ULONGTYPE use the union element num.

Description

The cfg_attr_t data structure contains information for managing the loading and unloading of loadable device drivers. The cfgmgr daemon passes a pointer to this data structure to the device driver's xxconfigure interface. The device driver can parse this structure pointer to check the validity of the values associated with the driver's associated stanza.loadable file fragment and the /etc/sysconfigtab database.

Related Information

Chapter 14, Header Files Related to Device Drivers: sysconfig.h

Section 17.2, Block and Character Device Driver Interfaces: xxconfigure

Name

cfg_subsys_attr_t – Contains attribute information for loadable
drivers

Include File

/usr/sys/include/sys/sysconfig.h

Synopsis

```
typedef struct {
    char    name[CFG_ATTR_NAME_SZ]; /* attribute name */
    uchar   type;                   /* attribute type */
    uchar   operation;              /* supported operations */
    caddr_t addr;                   /* address of data value */
    ulong   min_val;                /* min size/length/value */
    ulong   max_val;                /* max size/length/value */
    ulong   val_size;               /* binary data size */
} cfg_subsys_attr_t;
```

Members

name
> Specifies the ASCII name of the attribute. The name must be between 2
> and CFG_ATTR_NAME_SZ characters in length, including the
> terminating null character.

type
> Specifies the data type associated with the name attribute. You must
> set the type member to one of the following constants:

Value	Meaning
CFG_ATTR_STRTYPE	Data type is a null-terminated array of characters.
CFG_ATTR_INTTYPE	Data type is a 32-bit signed integer.
CFG_ATTR_UINTTYPE	Data type is a 32-bit unsigned integer.
CFG_ATTR_LONGTYPE	Data type is a 64-bit signed integer.
CFG_ATTR_ULONGTYPE	Data type is a 64-bit unsigned integer.
CFG_ATTR_BINTYPE	Data type is an array of bytes.

operation
> Specifies the operations that the device driver method of cfgmgr can

perform on the attribute. You can set this member to one of the following constants:

Value	Meaning
CFG_OP_CONFIGURE	Configures a loadable device driver.
CFG_OP_UNCONFIGURE	Unconfigures a loadable device driver.
CFG_OP_QUERY	Queries the device driver for configuration information.
CFG_OP_RECONFIGURE	The device driver method of cfgmgr allows a user to modify the attribute.

addr
> Specifies the address of the data value associated with the attribute. The cfgmgr daemon obtains the data value for this attribute from the /etc/sysconfigtab database and stores it at this address. The cfgmgr daemon performs this storage operation if the attribute appears in the array with an operation code of CFG_OP_CONFIGURE.
>
> In addition, the device driver's configure interface initializes (when the driver is dynamically configured) other attributes that appear in the array with an operation code of CFG_OP_CONFIGURE.

min_val
> Specifies the minimum length of the data value.

max_val
> Specifies the maximum length of the data value.

val_size
> Specifies the binary data size.

Description

The cfg_attr_t data structure contains information for managing the loading and unloading of loadable device drivers. The cfgmgr daemon passes a pointer to this data structure to the device driver's xxconfigure interface. The device driver can parse this structure pointer to check the validity of the values associated with the driver's associated stanza.loadable file fragment and the /etc/sysconfigtab database.

Related Information

Section 17.2, Block and Character Device Driver Interfaces: *xx*configure

Name

controller – Contains members that store information about hardware resources and store data for communication between the kernel and the device driver

Include File

/usr/sys/include/io/common/devdriver.h

Synopsis

Member Name	Data Type
ctlr_mbox	u_long *
bus_hd	struct bus *
nxt_ctlr	struct controller *
dev_list	struct device *
driver	struct driver *
ctlr_type	int
ctlr_name	char *
ctlr_num	int
bus_name	char *
bus_num	int
rctlr	int
slot	int
alive	int
pname	char *
port	struct port *
intr	int (**intr)()
addr	caddr_t
addr2	caddr_t
flags	int
bus_priority	int
ivnum	int
priority	int
cmd	int
physaddr	caddr_t

Member Name	Data Type
physaddr2	caddr_t
private	void * [8]
conn_priv	void * [8]
rsvd	void * [8]

Members

ctlr_mbox

> Specifies a pointer to the mailbox data structure for hardware platforms that access I/O space through hardware mailboxes. The bus adapter code sets this member.

bus_hd

> Specifies a pointer to the bus structure that this controller is connected to.

nxt_ctlr

> Specifies a pointer to the next controller at this level.

dev_list

> Specifies a linked list of devices connected to this controller.

driver

> Specifies a pointer to the driver structure for this controller.

ctlr_type

> Specifies the controller type.

ctlr_name

> Specifies the controller name.

ctlr_num

> Specifies the controller number.

bus_name

> Specifies the name of the bus to which this controller is connected.

bus_num

> Specifies the number of the bus to which the controller is connected.

rctlr

> Specifies the remote controller number (for example, the SCSI ID).

slot

> Specifies the bus slot or node number.

`alive`
> Specifies a flag word to indicate the current status of the controller.

`pname`
> Specifies a pointer to the port name for this controller, if applicable.

`port`
> Specifies a pointer to the `port` structure for this controller, if applicable.

`intr`
> Specifies an array that contains one or more entry points for the controller interrupt service interfaces.

`addr`
> Specifies the address of the device registers or memory.

`addr2`
> Specifies an optional second virtual address for this controller. This member is set if there are two CSR spaces.

`flags`
> Specifies controller-specific flags.

`bus_priority`
> Specifies the configured VMEbus priority level of the device. Only drivers operating on the VMEbus use this member.

`ivnum`
> Specifies an interrupt vector number. Only drivers operating on the VMEbus use this member.

`priority`
> Specifies the system priority level (spl) to block interrupts from this device. Only drivers operating on the VMEbus use this member.

`cmd`
> Specifies a field that is not currently used.

`physaddr`
> Specifies the physical address that corresponds to the virtual address set in the `addr` member.

`physaddr2`
> Specifies the physical address that corresponds to the virtual address set in the `addr2` member.

`private`
> Specifies private storage for use by this controller or controller type.

`conn_priv`
    Specifies private storage for use by the bus that this controller is
    connected to.

`rsvd`
    This member is reserved for future expansion of the data structure.

Description

The `controller` structure represents an instance of a controller entity, one
that connects logically to a bus. A controller can control devices that are
directly connected or can perform some other controlling operation, such as a
network interface or terminal controller operation.

Related Information

Chapter 16, Structures Related to Device Drivers: `bus, device, driver`

Name

device – Contains information that identifies the device. There is one device data structure for each device connected to the controller.

Include File

/usr/sys/include/io/common/devdriver.h

Synopsis

Member Name	Data Type
nxt_dev	struct device *
ctlr_hd	struct controller *
dev_type	char *
dev_name	char *
logunit	int
unit	int
ctlr_name	char *
ctlr_num	int
alive	int
private	void * [8]
conn_priv	void * [8]
rsvd	void * [8]

Members

nxt_dev
Specifies a pointer to the next device at this level.

ctlr_hd
Specifies a pointer to the controller structure that this device is connected to.

dev_type
Specifies the device type (for example, disk or tape).

dev_name
This member is set to the device name type, which is a string of up to

eight characters. For example, Digital defines the strings `rz` and `tz` to represent disk and tape devices.

`logunit`
Specifies the device logical unit number.

`unit`
Specifies the device physical unit number.

`ctlr_name`
Specifies the name of the controller that this device is connected to.

`ctlr_num`
Specifies the number of the controller that this device is connected to.

`alive`
Specifies a flag word to indicate the current status of the device.

`private`
Specifies private storage for use by this device or device class.

`conn_priv`
Specifies private storage for use by the controller that this device is connected to.

`rsvd`
This member is reserved for future expansion of the data structure.

Description

The `device` structure represents an instance of a device entity. A device is an entity that connects to and is controlled by a controller. A device does not connect directly to a bus.

Related Information

Chapter 16, Structures Related to Device Drivers: `bus`, `controller`, `driver`

Name

driver – Defines driver entry points and other driver-specific information

Include File

/usr/sys/include/io/common/devdriver.h

Synopsis

```
struct driver {
  int      (*probe)();
  int      (*slave)();
  int      (*cattach)();
  int      (*dattach)();
  int      (*go)();
  caddr_t *addr_list;
  char    *dev_name;
  struct  device **dev_list;
  char    *ctlr_name;
  struct  controller **ctlr_list;
  short   xclu;
  int     addr1_size;
  int     addr1_atype;
  int     addr2_size;
  int     addr2_atype;
  int     (*ctlr_unattach)();
  int     (*dev_unattach)();
};
```

Members

probe
> Specifies a pointer to the driver's probe interface, which is called to verify that the controller exists.

slave
> Specifies a pointer to the driver's slave interface, which is called once for each device connected to the controller.

cattach
> Specifies a pointer to the driver's cattach interface, which is called to allow controller-specific initialization. You can set this pointer to NULL.

dattach
> Specifies a pointer to the driver's dattach interface, which is called once for each slave call that returns success. You use the dattach

interface for device-specific initialization. You can set this pointer to NULL.

go
> Specifies a pointer to the driver's `go` interface, which is not currently used.

addr_list
> Specifies a list of optional CSR addresses.

dev_name
> Specifies the name of the device connected to this controller.

dev_list
> Specifies an array of pointers to device structures currently connected to this controller. This member is indexed through the `logunit` member of the `device` structure associated with this device.

ctlr_name
> Specifies the controller name.

ctlr_list
> Specifies an array of pointers to `controller` structures. The system uses this member when multiple controllers are controlled by a single device driver. This member is indexed through the `ctlr_num` member of the `controller` structure associated with this device.

xclu
> Specifies a field that is not currently used.

addr1_size
> Specifies the size (in bytes) of the first CSR area. This area is usually the control status register of the device. Only drivers operating on the VMEbus use this member.

addr1_atype
> Specifies the address space, access mode, transfer size, and swap mode of the first CSR area. Note that not all bus adapters use the transfer size. Only drivers operating on the VMEbus use this member.

addr2_size
> Specifies the size (in bytes) of the second CSR area. This area is usually the data area that the system uses with devices that have two separate CSR areas. Only drivers operating on the VMEbus use this member.

addr2_atype
> Specifies the address space, access mode, transfer size, and swap mode of the second CSR area. Note that not all bus adapters use the transfer size. Only drivers operating on the VMEbus use this member.

```
ctlr_unattach
```
Specifies a pointer to the controller's `unattach` interface. Loadable
drivers use the controller `unattach` interface.

```
dev_unattach
```
Specifies a pointer to the device's `unattach` interface. Loadable
drivers use the device `unattach` interface.

Description

The `driver` structure defines driver entry points and other driver-specific
information. You declare and initialize an instance of this structure in the
device driver. The bus configuration code uses the entry points defined in
this structure during system configuration. The bus configuration code fills
in the `dev_list` and `ctlr_list` arrays. The driver interfaces use these
arrays (members of the `device` and `controller` structures) to get the
structures for specific devices or controllers.

Related Information

Chapter 16, Structures Related to Device Drivers: `bus`, `controller`,
`device`

Name

handler_intr_info – Contains interrupt handler information

Include File

/usr/sys/include/io/common/handler.h

Synopsis

Member Name	Data Type
configuration_st	caddr_t
intr	int (*intr) ()
param	caddr_t
config_type	unsigned int

Members

configuration_st
> Specifies a pointer to the bus or controller structure for which an associated interrupt handler is written.

intr
> Specifies a pointer to the interrupt handler for the specified bus or controller.

param
> Specifies a member whose contents are passed to the interrupt service interface.

config_type
> Specifies the driver type. You can set this member to one of the following constants defined in handler.h:
> CONTROLLER_CONFIG_TYPE (controller) or
> ADAPTER_CONFIG_TYPE (bus adapter).

Description

The handler_intr_info structure contains interrupt handler information for device controllers connected to a bus. This generic structure makes device drivers more portable across different buses because it contains all of the necessary information to add an interrupt handler for any bus. Device drivers set the `ih_bus_info` member of the `ihandler_t` structure to the filled-in `handler_intr_info` structure, usually in the driver's `probe` interface.

Both static and loadable device drivers can use the `handler_intr_info` structure and the `handler_add` interfaces to register a device driver's interrupt service interface. The `bus` and `controller` structures contain the bus- and controller-specific information that is not provided in `handler_intr_info`.

Notes

The `handler_intr_info` data structure is a direct copy of the `tc_intr_info` data structure that TURBOchannel bus device drivers use. The `handler_intr_info` structure provides binary compatibility with previously written TURBOchannel device drivers and source code compatibility across device drivers that operate on a variety of buses including TURBOchannel, PCI, EISA, and ISA buses.

Related Information

Section 15.2, Kernel Support Interfaces: `handler_add`, `handler_del`, `handler_disable`, `handler_enable`

Chapter 16, Structures Related to Device Drivers: `ihandler_t`

Name

`ihandler_t` – Contains information associated with device driver interrupt handling

Include File

`/usr/sys/include/io/common/handler.h`

Synopsis

Member Name	Data Type
ih_id	ihandler_id_t
ih_bus	struct bus *
ih_bus_info	char *

Members

`ih_id`
  Specifies a unique ID.

`ih_bus`
  Specifies a pointer to the `bus` structure associated with this device driver. This member is needed because the interrupt dispatching methodology requires that the bus be responsible for dispatching interrupts in a bus-specific manner.

`ih_bus_info`
  Specifies bus registration information.

Description

The `ihandler_t` structure contains information associated with device driver interrupt handling. In previous versions of the Digital UNIX operating system (formerly known as DEC OSF/1), only loadable drivers used this data structure. Digital recommends that both static and loadable drivers use the `ihandler_t` structure and the `handler` interfaces to dynamically register ISIs. See the bus-specific book for the registration methods supported by the bus on which your driver operates.

This model of interrupt dispatching uses the bus as the means of interrupt dispatching for all drivers. For this reason, all of the information needed to register an interrupt is considered to be bus specific. As a result, no attempt is made to represent all the possible permutations within the ihandler_t data structure.

Device driver writers pass the ihandler_t structure to the handler_add interface to specify how interrupt handlers are to be registered with the bus-specific interrupt dispatcher. This task is usually done within the driver's probe interface.

Related Information

Section 15.2, Kernel Support Interfaces: handler_add

Chapter 16, Structures Related to Device Drivers: bus

Name

item_list – Contains hardware platform-specific information

Include File

/usr/sys/include/io/common/devdriver.h

Synopsis

Member Name	Data Type
function	u_long
out_flags	u_int
in_flags	u_int
rtn_status	u_long
next_function	struct item_list *
input_data	u_long
output_data	u_long

Members

function

Stores the function code that represents the system item for which you
want to obtain specific information. You can pass one of the following
constants defined in devdriver.h to the function member:

Constant	Meaning
GET_TC_SPEED	Requests that get_info return the TURBOchannel bus clock speed (in kilohertz) for this system. For example, get_info returns 250 for a 25-megahertz clock speed. You pass this constant only if a TURBOchannel bus is hardwired to the hardware platform.
MOP_SYSID	Requests that get_info return the MOP system ID for the system that the drivier operates on.

Constant	Meaning
CONSOLE_2_DEV	Requests that get_info return the controller number associated with the controller that the system booted from. The get_info interface locates this controller by traversing the array of bus structures.
DEV_2_CONSOLE	Requests that get_info return the boot device string for the console. The get_info interface constructs the boot device string from information contained in the devget structure.
DEV_2_USER	Requests that get_info return the string that a user enters at the console terminal to boot the system.

out_flags
    Stores flags for output data. This member is for future use.

in_flags
    Stores flags for input data. This member is for future use.

rtn_status
    Stores the status code for the function code you passed to the function member. The get_info interface can set this member to one of the following status codes:

Status Code	Meaning
INFO_RETURNED	The CPU platform that the driver operates on supports the system item associated with the function code you passed to the function member. This value indicates that the system item returned by get_info to the output_data member is valid.
NOT_SUPPORTED	The CPU platform that the driver operates on does not support the system item associated with the function code you passed to the function member; or, the CPU platform does not support the get_info interface.

next_function
    Specifies a pointer to the next item_list structure in the linked list. This item_list structure stores the function code that represents the next system item for which you want to obtain specific information. You set this member to the value NULL to indicate the last item_list structure in the linked list.

`input_data`
> Specifies a pointer to input data for the function associated with the function code that you specified in the `function` member.

`output_data`
> Stores the specific information for the system item associated with the function code that you passed to the `function` member. The `get_info` interface returns CPU-specific values to the `output_data` member. These values are for the function associated with the function code that you specified in the `function` member.

Description

The `item_list` data structure contains platform-specific information. Device drivers obtain this platform-specific information by calling the `get_info` interface.

Related Information

Section 15.2, Kernel Support Interfaces: `get_info`

Name

lock – Contains complex lock-specific information

Include File

/usr/sys/include/kern/lock.h

Synopsis

The lock structure is an opaque data structure; that is, its associated
members are referenced and manipulated by the Digital UNIX operating
system and not by the user of the complex lock mechanism. Therefore, this
reference page omits a description of the lock structure's associated
members.

Description

The lock data structure is the complex lock structure that contains complex
lock-specific information. A device driver writer using the complex lock
method declares a pointer to a lock structure and passes its address to the
associated lock interfaces.

Notes

The header file lock.h shows typedef statements that assign the alternate
name lock_data_t for the complex lock structure and lock_t for a
pointer to the complex lock structure.

Related Information

Chapter 14, Header Files Related to Device Drivers: lock.h

Section 15.2, Kernel Support Interfaces: lock_done, lock_init,
lock_read, lock_terminate, lock_try_read,
lock_try_write, lock_write

Chapter 16, Structures Related to Device Drivers: slock

Name

port – Contains information about a port

Include File

/usr/sys/include/io/common/devdriver.h

Synopsis

Member Name	Data Type
conf	int (*conf) ()

Members

conf
> Specifies a pointer to the configuration interface for this port.

Description

The port structure contains information about a port.

Related Information

Chapter 16, Structures Related to Device Drivers: bus, controller

Name

sel_queue – Defines a queue of select events

Include File

/usr/sys/include/sys/select.h

Synopsis

Member Name	Data Type
links	struct queue_entry
event	struct event *

Members

links

Specifies a queue_entry structure. This structure contains a generic doubly linked list (queue).

event

Specifies a pointer to an event structure. This structure is an opaque structure. That is, you do not reference it in your device driver.

Description

The sel_queue data structure provides device driver writers with a generic queue of select events. You must initialize the links member prior to using the select_enqueue and select_dequeue interfaces.

Related Information

Chapter 14, Header Files Related to Device Drivers: select.h

Section 15.2, Kernel Support Interfaces: select_dequeue, select_enqueue

Name

sg_entry – Contains bus address/byte count pairs

Include File

/usr/sys/include/io/common/devdriver.h

Synopsis

Member Name	Data Type
ba	bus_addr_t
bc	long

Members

ba

Stores an I/O bus address.

bc

Stores the byte count associated with the I/O bus address. This byte count indicates the contiguous addresses that are valid on this bus.

Description

The sg_entry data structure contains two members: ba and bc. These members represent a bus address/byte count pair for a contiguous block of an I/O buffer mapped onto a controller's bus memory space. The byte count indicates the number of bytes that the address is contiguously valid for on the controller's bus address space. Consider a list entry that has its ba member set to aaaa and its bc member set to nnnn. In this case, the device can perform a contiguous DMA data transfer starting at bus address aaaa and ending at bus address aaaa+nnnn-1.

Notes

The header file devdriver.h shows a typedef statement that assigns the alternate name sg_entry_t for a pointer to the sg_entry structure.

Related Information

Section 15.2, Kernel Support Interfaces: `dma_get_curr_sgentry`, `dma_get_next_sgentry`, `dma_put_curr_sgentry`, `dma_put_prev_sgentry`

Name

`slock` – Contains simple lock-specific information

Include File

`/usr/sys/include/kern/lock.h`

Synopsis

The `slock` structure is an opaque data structure; that is, its associated members are referenced and manipulated by the Digital UNIX operating system and not by the user of the simple lock method. Therefore, this reference page omits a description of the `slock` structure's associated members.

Description

The `slock` data structure is the simple spin lock structure that contains simple lock-specific information. The user of the simple lock method declares a `slock` structure by calling the `decl_simple_lock_data` interface. In subsequent calls to `simple_lock`, `simple_lock_init`, `simple_lock_try`, and `simple_unlock`, the caller passes the address of the previously declared `slock` structure.

Notes

The header file `lock.h` shows `typedef` statements that assign the alternate name `simple_lock_data_t` for the simple spin lock structure and `simple_lock_t` for a pointer to the simple spin lock structure.

Related Information

Chapter 14, Header Files Related to Device Drivers: `lock.h`

Section 15.2, Kernel Support Interfaces: `decl_simple_lock_data`, `simple_lock`, `simple_lock_init`, `simple_lock_terminate`, `simple_lock_try`, `simple_unlock`

Chapter 16, Structures Related to Device Drivers: `lock`

Name

task – Contains task-specific information

Include File

/usr/sys/include/kern/task.h

Synopsis

The task structure is an opaque data structure; that is, all of its associated members are referenced and manipulated by the Digital UNIX operating system and not by the user of kernel threads. Therefore, this reference page omits a description of the task structure's associated members.

Description

The task data structure contains task-related information.

Notes

The header file task.h shows a typedef statement that assigns the alternate name task_t for a pointer to the task structure. Some of the kernel threads-related interfaces require that you pass a pointer to the task structure.

Related Information

Chapter 14, Header Files Related to Device Drivers: task.h

Section 15.2, Kernel Support Interfaces: kernel_thread_w_arg

Name

`thread` – Contains kernel threads-related information

Include File

`/usr/sys/include/kern/thread.h`

Synopsis

The `thread` structure is an opaque data structure; that is, all of its associated members are referenced and manipulated by the Digital UNIX operating system and not by the user of kernel threads. Therefore, this reference page omits a description of the `thread` structure's associated members.

Description

The `thread` data structure contains kernel threads-related information.

Notes

The header file `thread.h` shows a `typedef` statement that assigns the alternate name `thread_t` for a pointer to the `thread` structure. Many of the kernel threads-related interfaces operate on these pointers to `thread` structures.

Related Information

Chapter 14, Header Files Related to Device Drivers: `thread.h`

Section 15.2, Kernel Support Interfaces: `thread_block`, `thread_set_timeout`, `thread_wakeup`, `thread_wakeup_one`

Name

uio – Describes I/O, either single vector or multiple vectors

Include File

/usr/sys/include/sys/uio.h

Synopsis

Member Name	Data Type
uio_iov	struct iovec *
uio_iovcnt	int
uio_offset	off_t
uio_segflg	enum uio_seg
uio_resid	int
uio_rw	enum uio_rw

Members

uio_iov
> Specifies a pointer to the first iovec structure. The iovec structure has two members: one that specifies the address of the segment and another that specifies the size of the segment. The system allocates contiguous iovec structures for a given transfer.

uio_iovcnt
> Specifies the number of iovec structures for this transfer.

uio_offset
> Specifies the offset within the file.

uio_segflg
> Specifies the segment type. This member can be set to one of the following values: UIO_USERSPACE (the segment is from the user data space), UIO_SYSSPACE (the segment is from the system space), or UIO_USERISPACE (the segment is from the user I space).

uio_resid
> Specifies the number of bytes that still need to be transferred.

```
uio_rw
```
Specifies whether the transfer is a read or a write. This member is set by `read` and `write` system calls according to the corresponding field in the file descriptor. This member can be set to one of the following values: `UIO_READ` (read transfer) or `UIO_WRITE` (write transfer).

Description

The `uio` structure describes I/O, either single vector or multiple vectors. Typically, device drivers do not manipulate the members of this structure. However, the structure is presented here for the purpose of understanding the `uiomove` kernel interface, which operates on the members of the `uio` structure.

Related Information

Section 15.2, Kernel Support Interfaces: `uiomove`

Name

zone – Contains zone-related information

Include File

/usr/sys/kernel/kern/zalloc.h

Synopsis

The zone structure is an opaque data structure; that is, its associated members are referenced and manipulated by the Digital UNIX operating system and not by the user of the zone memory allocator. Therefore, this reference page omits a description of the zone structure's associated members.

Description

A zone is a collection of fixed-size elements for which there is fast allocation/deallocation access. Each fixed-size element has an associated zone structure that contains such things as the sizes of the element and the zone.

Device drivers use zones to dynamically allocate fixed-size memory for data structures (elements) on an individual basis. In this case, the zone interfaces maintain a linked list of zone structures. You do not reference any of the members of the zone data structure. Instead, you call zinit to initialize a zone for an associated element. The zinit interface returns a pointer to the element's zone structure. You pass this zone structure pointer in subsequent calls to zalloc, zfree, and zget.

Notes

The header file zalloc.h shows a typedef statement that assigns the alternate name zone_t for a pointer to the zone structure.

Related Information

Chapter 14, Header Files Related to Device Drivers: zalloc.h

Section 15.2, Kernel Support Interfaces: zalloc, zfree, zget, zinit

Device Driver and Bus Configuration Interfaces 17

This chapter describes:

- Conventions for driver and bus configuration interfaces
- Block and character device driver interfaces
- Bus configuration interfaces

17.1 Conventions for Device Driver and Bus Configuration Interfaces

The descriptions of the device driver interfaces are presented in alphabetical order and in reference (man) page style. The bus configuration interfaces are presented in a separate section and they, too, appear in reference (man) page style. The descriptions can include the following sections.

Name

This section lists the name of the driver or bus configuration interface along with a summary description of its purpose. In general, there is one interface described for each reference page. However, in some cases it makes sense to describe more than one interface on the same page if the interfaces are related. When this occurs, this section lists the names of all the interfaces it describes.

Entry Point

This section lists the structure or file where the driver writer specifies the entry for the device driver interface. This section is not applicable to the bus configuration interfaces.

Synopsis

This section shows the device driver or bus configuration interface function definition. The style used is that of the function definition, not the function call. This book assumes that you understand how to interpret the function definition and how to write an appropriate call for a specific interface.

The presentation shown in the following example is of the function definitions for all the block and character driver interfaces and for the *xx*confl1 and *xx*confl2 bus configuration interfaces:

```
int xxopen(dev, flag, format)
dev_t dev;
int flag;
int format;
```

The presentation shown in the following example is of the function definitions for the bus configuration interfaces that obtain the interface name through the bus structure's framework member:

```
int (*bus->framework->adp_handler_disable)(id)
ihandler_id_t id;
```

The presentation shown in the following example is of the function definitions for the bus configuration interfaces that do not obtain the interface name through the bus structure's framework member:

```
void conn_dev(ctlr, device)
struct controller *ctlr
struct device *device
```

These interface function definitions give you the following information:

- Return type

  Gives the data type of the return value, if the interface returns data. If the interface does not return a value, uses the void data type.

- Interface name

  Gives the driver or bus configuration interface name. In the first example, *xx*open is the name of the block or character driver interface. The prefix *xx* indicates that this part of the name is variable. Replace it with the character prefix that represents the name of the device for which the driver is being written.

  In the second example, the name of the bus configuration interface is obtained through the bus structure's framework member. This member is a pointer to a bus_framework structure, which contains a pointer to the actual interface. The example shows that the disable interrupt member contains a pointer to the actual adp_handler_disable interface.

  In the third example, the name of the bus configuration interface is as specified, for example, conn_device.

- Argument names

  Gives the name of each driver or bus configuration interface argument. In the first example, the argument names are *dev*, *flag*, and *format*. In some cases, the driver interface function definition will have different arguments based on the bus on which the driver operates. For example, the *xxprobe* interface has different arguments for the TURBOchannel and the VMEbus.

- Argument types

  Gives the types for each of the arguments. In the first example, these types are dev_t and int. Note that the term *driver interface* or *bus configuration interface* is used, instead of the term *driver routine* or *bus configuration routine* to establish consistent terminology with that used for the kernel interfaces.

Arguments

This section provides descriptions for the arguments associated with a given driver or bus configuration interface. In most cases, argument descriptions begin with the word *specifies* to indicate that the driver writer passes the argument (with some specified value) to the driver or bus configuration interface.

Description

This section contains explanations of the tasks performed by the driver or bus configuration interface.

Notes

This section contains information about the driver or bus configuration interface pertinent to the device driver writer. For example, this section could point out that the interface is specific to loadable device drivers.

Return Values

This section describes the values that a given driver or bus configuration interface can return.

Related Information

This section lists related kernel interfaces, structures, system calls, and so forth.

17.2 Block and Character Device Driver Interfaces

Table 17-1 summarizes the interfaces that device drivers use. The table has the following columns:

- Interface

  This column lists the driver interface name.

- Entry point

  This column lists the structure (or file) where the driver writer defines the entry point for the device driver interface.

- Character

  A Yes appears in this column if the interface is applicable to a character device. Otherwise, N/A (not applicable) appears.

- Block

  A Yes appears in this column if the interface is applicable to a block device. Otherwise, N/A (not applicable) appears.

Table 17-1: Summary of Block and Character Device Driver Interfaces

Interface	Entry Point	Character	Block
cattach	driver	Yes	Yes
dattach	driver	Yes	Yes
close	bdevsw, cdevsw	Yes	Yes
configure	N/A	Yes	Yes
ctrl_unattach	driver	Yes	Yes
dev_unattach	driver	Yes	Yes
dump	bdevsw	N/A	Yes
intr	Use the handler_add and handler_enable interfaces for dynamic registration of interrupt handlers for loadable and static drivers	Yes	Yes

Table 17-1: (continued)

Interface	Entry Point	Character	Block
ioctl	bdevsw, cdevsw	Yes	Yes
mmap	cdevsw	Yes	N/A
open	bdevsw, cdevsw	Yes	Yes
probe	driver	Yes	Yes
psize	bdevsw	N/A	Yes
read	cdevsw	Yes	N/A
reset	cdevsw	Yes	N/A
select	cdevsw	Yes	N/A
slave	driver	Yes	Yes
stop	cdevsw	Yes	N/A
strategy	bdevsw	N/A	Yes
write	cdevsw	Yes	N/A

Name

*xxc*attach, *xxd*attach – Perform controller- or device-specific initialization

Entry Point

The driver structure

Synopsis

```
void xxcattach(ctlr)
struct controller *ctlr

void xxdattach(device)
struct device *device
```

Arguments

ctlr
Specifies a pointer to the controller structure for this controller. This structure contains such information as the controller type, the controller name, and the current status of the controller.

device
Specifies a pointer to a device structure for this device. This structure contains such information as the logical unit number of the device, whether the device is functional, and the bus number the device resides on.

Description

The *xxc*attach and *xxd*attach interfaces perform controller- or device-specific initialization. These interfaces usually perform the tasks necessary to establish communication with the actual device. These tasks might include, for a device attach interface, initializing a tape drive or putting a disk drive on line. In addition, *xxc*attach and *xxd*attach initialize any global data structures that the device driver uses.

At boot time, the autoconfiguration software calls these interfaces under the following conditions:

- If the device is connected to a controller, the *xx*dattach interface is called if the controller's slave interface returns a nonzero value, indicating that the device exists.

- If the device is not connected to a controller, the *xx*cattach interface is called if the probe interface returns a nonzero value, indicating that the device exists.

If you set the cattach or dattach member of the driver structure to NULL, no call is made to the *xx*cattach or *xx*dattach interface. The *xx*cattach interface is passed a controller structure and the *xx*dattach interface is passed a device structure for this device.

For loadable drivers, the *xx*cattach or *xx*dattach interface is called indirectly when the system manager issues a command to dynamically load the driver.

Return Values

None

Related Information

Chapter 16, Structures Related to Device Drivers: controller, device

Name

*xx*close – Closes a device

Entry Point

The bdevsw for block device drivers and the cdevsw for character device drivers

Synopsis

```
int xxclose(dev, flag, format)
dev_t dev;
int flag;
int format;
```

Arguments

dev
> Specifies the major and minor device numbers for this device. The minor device number is used to determine the logical unit number for the device that is to be closed.

flag
> Specifies the access mode of the device. The access modes are represented by a bit mask of flags defined in the file /usr/sys/include/sys/fcntl.h. Typically, the *xx*close interface does not use this argument.

format
> Specifies the format of the special device to be closed. The *format* argument is used by a driver that has both block and character interfaces and uses the same *xx*close interface in both the bdevsw and cdevsw tables. The driver uses this argument to distinguish the type of device being closed. Typically, the *xx*close interface does not use this argument.

Description

A device driver's *xx*close interface is called when a process closes the special device file that corresponds to this driver. This action occurs when the last file descriptor that is open and associated with this device is closed by means of the close system call.

A block device driver's *xxclose* interface closes a device that was previously opened by the *xxopen* interface. The *xxclose* interface is called only after making the final open reference to the device.

A character and block device driver's *xxclose* interfaces perform similar tasks. If the character device provides raw access to a block device, the *xxclose* interface is usually the same. Almost all character device drivers provide an *xxclose* interface; however, some block devices do not require this interface.

The *xxclose* interface for a block or character device driver also performs the following tasks:

- Determines the logical unit number from the minor device number
- Turns off interrupts for the device
- Cleans up the software state and flag
- Flushes any remaining buffers

Return Values

The return status of the *xxclose* interface will eventually be the return status from the close system call.

Related Information

Chapter 14, Header Files Related to Device Drivers: fcntl.h, sysconfig.h

Chapter 16, Structures Related to Device Drivers: bdevsw, cdevsw

Section 17.2, Block and Character Device Driver Interfaces: *xxopen*

Name

xxconfigure – Configuration call for loadable drivers

Entry Point

None

Synopsis

```
int xx_configure(optype, indata, indatalen, outdata, outdatalen)
cfg_op_t optype;
cfg_attr_t *indata;
size_t indatalen;
cfg_attr_t *outdata;
size_t outdatalen;
```

Arguments

optype
> Specifies the configuration operation to be performed on the loadable module. The supported operation types you can pass to this argument include:

Value	Meaning
CFG_OP_CONFIGURE	Configures (loads) the device driver.
CFG_OP_UNCONFIGURE	Unconfigures (unloads) the device driver.
CFG_OP_QUERY	Queries the driver for configuration information.

indata
> Specifies a pointer to a cfg_attr_t data structure that contains information for managing the loading and unloading of loadable device drivers. The cfgmgr daemon fills in this data structure with information contained in the /etc/sysconfigtab database for the device driver that the user wants to dynamically load or unload. You specify this information in the file fragment associated with the loadable driver.

indatalen
> Specifies the number of elements in the cfg_attr_t data structure.

outdata
>Specifies a formal parameter that is not currently used.

outdatalen
>Specifies a formal parameter that is not currently used.

Description

The *xx_configure* interface is called indirectly from cfgmgr in response to system manager commands. These commands include loading (configuring), unloading (unconfiguring), and querying a driver.

Your *xx_configure* interface must use an underscore (_) in the name. For example, a fax device driver could have a configure interface called fax_configure.

Return Values

The *xx_configure* interface returns one of the following values:

The value zero (0)
>Success.

EINVAL
>The *optype* parameter contains an invalid parameter or the call is unable to configure the loadable driver.

ENOPEN
>The call to bdevsw_add or cdevsw_add failed.

EBUSY
>The interface cannot be configured because the driver is currently active.

ESRCH
>The interface cannot be unconfigured because the call to bdevsw_del or cdevsw_del failed.

Related Information

Chapter 16, Structures Related to Device Drivers: cfg_attr_t

Name

xxctrl_unattach – Removes the specified controller

Entry Point

The driver structure

Synopsis

```
int xxctrl_unattach(bus_struct, ctlr_struct)
struct bus *bus_struct;
struct controller *ctlr_struct;
```

Arguments

bus_struct
    Specifies a pointer to a bus structure.

ctlr_struct
    Specifies a pointer to the controller structure you want to remove from the list of controllers that this device driver handles.

Description

A device driver's *xxctrl_unattach* interface removes the specified controller structure from the list of controllers it handles. This interface should clean up any in-memory data structures and remove any interrupt handlers the driver may have established.

Because this interface is called indirectly from the unconfigure portion of the driver's configure interface, the driver has already determined that the controller is in a quiescent state. Thus, *xxctrl_unattach* need not check this condition.

Notes

Because you cannot unconfigure static device drivers, the *xxctrl_unattach* interface is specific to loadable device drivers.

Return Values

The *xxctrl_unattach* interface can return one of the following values:

ESUCCESS
> The controller was successfully unattached.

ENODEV
> There is no such controller.

Related Information

Chapter 16, Structures Related to Device Drivers: `bus`, `controller`

Section 17.2, Block and Character Device Driver Interfaces: *xx*dev_unattach

Section 17.3, Bus Configuration Interfaces: ctlr_unconfigure

Name

*xx*dev_unattach – Removes the specified device

Entry Point

The driver structure

Synopsis

```
int xxdev_unattach(ctlr_struct, dev_struct)
struct controller *ctlr_struct;
struct device *dev_struct;
```

Arguments

ctlr_struct
> Specifies a pointer to a controller structure for the controller to which the device is connected.

dev_struct
> Specifies a pointer to the device structure you want to remove from the list of devices that this device driver handles.

Description

A device driver's *xx*dev_unattach interface removes the specified device structure from the list of devices it handles. This interface should free any in-memory data structures that were dynamically allocated in the driver's attach interface. You can write this interface so that it removes a single device, or you can write the interface as part of a calling sequence to remove a controller structure.

Notes

Because you cannot unconfigure static device drivers, the *xx*dev_unattach interface is specific to loadable device drivers.

Return Values

The *xxdev_unattach* interface can return one of the following values:

ESUCCESS
>   The device was successfully unattached.

ENODEV
>   There is no such device.

Related Information

Chapter 16, Structures Related to Device Drivers: `controller, device`

Section 17.2, Block and Character Device Driver Interfaces:
xxctrl_unattach

Name

xxdump – Copy system memory to the dump device

Entry Point

The bdevsw table

Synopsis

```
int xxdump(dumpdev)
dev_t dumpdev;
```

Arguments

dumpdev
Specifies the device on which the dump operation should be performed. The values in this argument are passed to the driver's xxdump interface. Typically, these values specify the disk unit number and partition. The dump device is often specified explicitly in the system configuration file. If the dump device is not explicitly specified in the system configuration file, the default is to dump to the dump partition of the system's boot device.

Description

The xxdump interface copies the contents of system memory to the specified device. Usually, xxdump is called when a system panic occurs. By copying the contents of memory to the dump device, you can investigate what is called a ''core dump'' to determine the cause of the panic. After the system panic, the next time the system is booted, the system startup software looks on the swap device for the existence of a core dump. If the core dump exists, it will be formatted and copied to the specified location in the file system, thereby freeing up the dump device for subsequent dumps.

Because the xxdump interface is usually called only when a system panic occurs, the exact state and sanity of the operating system are compromised. It could be possible that the panic is the result of an error in the device driver that contains the xxdump interface. In an effort to have a known stable means of dumping system memory to the dump device, there are some hardware platforms that utilize console firmware callbacks to implement the actual dump functions.

A device driver is required to implement an *xx*dump interface only if the associated device is capable of accepting the contents of system memory. Typically, only disk device drivers, which are candidates for being dump devices, implement the *xx*dump interface. If the driver does not implement the *xx*dump interface, you specify the `nodev` interface in the `bdevsw` table.

Notes

The Digital UNIX operating system does not currently support an *xx*dump interface's ability to copy the contents of system memory to the specified device. Device driver writers should not provide an *xx*dump interface for this version of Digital UNIX.

Return Values

The *xx*dump interface can return one of the following values:

`ENXIO`
> The specified dump device does not exist.

`EIO`
> An error occurred in copying the contents of system memory to the dump device.

`ENOSPC`
> The dump device is not large enough to accommodate all of the requested system memory contents to be dumped.

The value zero (0)
> Success; the dump was completed without error.

Related Information

Section 17.2, Block and Character Device Driver Interfaces: `xxpsize`

Name

xxintr – Handles hardware interrupts

Entry Point

For static and loadable drivers, through the `handler_add` and `handler_enable` interfaces

Synopsis

int *xxintr*(*parameter*)
caddr_t *parameter*;

Arguments

parameter
> If you register a device's interrupt service interface in the system configuration or `stanza.static` file fragment, this argument specifies the logical controller number (the `ctlr_num` member of the `controller` structure).

> If you call the `handler` interfaces to dynamically register a device's interrupt service interface, this argument specifies any parameter that the driver needs to control operation of the interrupt service interface.

> Typically, you pass the logical controller number, which is used to specify the instance of the controller the interrupt corresponds to. For device drivers that operate on the TURBOchannel bus, you can set the logical controller number in the `param` member of the `tc_intr_info` data structure.

Description

The *xxintr* interface is called as a result of a hardware interrupt. The way in which interrupts are dispatched is bus specific.

Return Values

None

Related Information

Section 15.2, Kernel Support Interfaces: `handler_add`

Chapter 16, Structures Related to Device Drivers: `controller`, `handler_intr_info`

Name

xxioctl – General-purpose I/O control

Entry Point

The bdevsw for block device drivers and the cdevsw for character device drivers

Synopsis

```
int xxioctl(dev, cmd, data, flag)
dev_t dev;
unsigned int cmd;
caddr_t data;
int flag;
```

Arguments

dev

Specifies the device for the ioctl command.

cmd

Specifies the ioctl command in the file /usr/sys/include/sys/ioctl.h or in another include file that the device driver writer defines. There are two types of ioctl commands. One type is supported by all drivers of a given class. Another type is specific to a given device. The values of the cmd argument are defined by using the _IO, _IOR, _IOW, and _IOWR macros.

Many ioctl commands are handled by the I/O system and do not result in a call to the device driver's xxioctl interface. However, when a command requires a device-specific action, this information is passed to the driver's xxioctl interface. One of the values you can pass to this argument is DEVIOCGET.

data

Specifies a pointer to ioctl command-specific data that is to be passed to the device driver or filled in by the device driver. This argument is a kernel address. The size of the data cannot exceed the size of a page (currently 8 kilobytes (KB) on Alpha systems). At least 128 bytes are guaranteed. Any size between 128 bytes and the page size may fail if memory cannot be allocated. The particular ioctl command implicitly determines the action to be taken. The ioctl system call

performs all the necessary copy operations to move data to and from
user space.

flag

Specifies the access mode of the device. The access modes are
represented by a bit mask of flags defined in the file
/usr/sys/include/sys/fcntl.h. The following table describes
the access mode flag bit masks:

Value	Meaning
FREAD	The device is open for reading.
FWRITE	The device is open for reading and writing.
FAPPEND	The device is open for writing at the end of the file.

Description

The *xxioctl* interface typically performs all device-related operations other
than read or write operations. A device driver's *xxioctl* interface is called
as a result of an ioctl system call. Only those ioctl commands that are
device specific or that require action on the part of the device driver result in
a call to the driver's *xxioctl* interface.

Some of the device-related operations performed by the *xxioctl* interface
are:

- Returns device attributes and parameters in response to queries by user
  programs

  In general, all device drivers have an *xxioctl* interface that identifies
  the device type, controller name, and other related parameters. For
  example, user programs may request information about disks, in which
  case the *xxioctl* interface returns disk geometry information. For user
  program requests about terminal devices, the *xxioctl* interface might
  return the current values of the terminal line attributes. User program
  requests about tape drives can result in the return of such attributes as
  tape density.

- Returns the status of a device

  The device status for a tape drive, for example, might consist of the tape
  mark encountered, end of media encountered, positioning at the bottom of
  the tape, or device is write protected.

- Allows for the setting of device-related parameters

  The device settings for a terminal device, for example, might consist of baud rate or parity. For disk drives, the partition-related information might be specified by the ioctl interface. For tape drives, the xxioctl interface performs tape repositioning commands, such as rewinding and forward or backward skipping of tape marks and tape records.

Return Values

The xxioctl interface returns an error number if there is a failure; otherwise, it returns the value zero (0). The return value is also used as the return value for the ioctl system call.

Related Information

Section 15.3, ioctl Commands: DEVIOCGET, _IO, _IOR, _IOW, _IOWR

Reference Pages Section 4: devio

Name

xxmmap – Maps kernel space to user space

Entry Point

The cdevsw table

Synopsis

```
caddr_t xxmmap(dev, offset, prot)
dev_t dev;
off_t offset;
int prot;
```

Arguments

dev

Specifies the major and minor device numbers for this device. The minor device number is used to determine the logical unit number for the character device whose memory is to be mapped.

offset

Specifies the offset (in bytes) into the character device's memory. The offset must be a valid offset into device memory.

prot

Specifies the protection flag for the mapping. The protection flag is the bitwise inclusive OR of the following valid protection flag bits defined in /usr/sys/include/sys/mman.h:

Flag	Meaning
PROT_READ	Pages can be read.
PROT_WRITE	Pages can be written.

Description

The xxmmap interface is invoked by the kernel as a result of an application calling the mmap system call. The xxmmap interface verifies that the requested offset is valid for this device and returns the page frame number that corresponds to the offset. In conjunction with the mmap system call, this interface allows a user process to map device memory into the user process address space.

Notes

Some Alpha CPUs do not support an application's use of the mmap system call.

Return Values

The *xx*mmap interface, if successful, returns the page frame number that corresponds to the page at the byte offset specified by the *offset* argument. Otherwise, *xx*mmap returns −1.

Related Information

Chapter 14, Header Files Related to Device Drivers: mman.h

Chapter 16, Structures Related to Device Drivers: cdevsw

Reference Pages Section 2: mmap, munmap

Name

xxopen – Opens a device

Entry Point

The bdevsw for block device drivers and the cdevsw for character device drivers

Synopsis

```
int xxopen(dev, flag, format)
dev_t dev;
int flag;
int format;
```

Arguments

dev

Specifies the major and minor device numbers for this device. The minor device number is used to determine the logical unit number for the device that is to be opened.

flag

Specifies the access mode of the device. The access modes are represented by a bit mask of flags defined in the file /usr/sys/include/sys/fcntl.h. The following table describes the access mode flag bit masks:

Value	Meaning
FREAD	The device is open for reading.
FWRITE	The device is open for reading and writing.
FAPPEND	The device is open for writing at the end of the file.

format

Specifies the format of the special device to be opened. The *format* argument is used by a driver that has both block and character interfaces and uses the same *xx*open interface in both the bdevsw and cdevsw tables. The driver uses this argument to distinguish the type of device being opened. Possible values for this argument, defined in mode.h, are:

Value	Meaning
S_IFCHR	Character device
S_IFBLK	Block device

Description

A device driver's *xx*open interface is called when a process opens the special device file that corresponds to this driver. This correspondence is made by the open system call through the major device number, which serves as an index into either the cdevsw or bdevsw table.

A block device driver's *xx*open interface opens a device to prepare it for I/O operations. This interface usually verifies that the device was identified during autoconfiguration. For tape devices, this identification may consist of bringing the device on line and selecting the appropriate density.

A character device driver's *xx*open interface performs tasks similar to those performed by the block device driver. If the character device provides raw access to a block device, the *xx*open interface is usually the same. Almost all character device drivers provide an *xx*open interface; however, some block devices do not require this interface. For terminal devices, the *xx*open interface may block waiting for the necessary modem signals, for example, carrier detect.

The *xx*open interface for a block or character device driver also performs the following tasks:

- Determines the logical unit number from the minor device number
- Checks the logical unit number to determine if it is a valid device that is functional
- Checks the state of the device or the *flag* argument if the device is to be an exclusive open, that is, nonblocking open, read-only, or write-only
- Starts any device bookkeeping activities, for example, by setting any software flags and state variables

Return Values

The return value of the *xxopen* interface will eventually be the return value for the open system call.

Related Information

Chapter 14, Header Files Related to Device Drivers: fcntl.h, mode.h

Chapter 16, Structures Related to Device Drivers: bdevsw, cdevsw

Section 17.2, Block and Character Device Driver Interfaces: *xxclose*

Name

xxprobe – Determines whether the device exists

Entry Point

The `driver` structure

Synopsis

```
int xxprobe(bus_io_handle, ctlr)
io_handle_t bus_io_handle;
struct controller *ctlr;
```

Arguments

bus_io_handle
> Specifies an I/O handle that you can use to reference a device register located in the TURBOchannel bus address space. The TURBOchannel bus configuration code passes this I/O handle to the driver's xxprobe interface during device autoconfiguration. You can perform standard C mathematical operations on the I/O handle. For example, you can add an offset to or subtract an offset from the I/O handle.

ctlr
> Specifies a pointer to the `controller` structure for this controller. This structure contains such information as the controller type, the controller name, and the current status of the controller.

Description

A device driver's xxprobe interface performs tasks necessary to determine if the device exists and is functional on a given system.

Some tasks performed by the xxprobe interface vary, depending on whether the device driver is configured as static or loadable:

- For static drivers

  The xxprobe interface typically checks some device control status register (CSR) to determine whether the physical device is present. If the device is not present, the device is not initialized and not available for use. The kernel calls the xxprobe interface for each device that you defined in the system configuration file or `config.file` file fragment.

In previous versions of the Digital UNIX operating system (formerly known as DEC OSF/1), you defined the device interrupt handlers for static device drivers in the system configuration file or the `stanza.static` file fragment. At system configuration time, the `config` program registered the defined device interrupt handlers. For the Digital UNIX, Digital recommends that you register the device interrupt handlers for static device drivers in the same way that you register them for loadable device drivers: by calling the `handler_add` and `handler_enable` interfaces.

- For loadable drivers

  For loadable drivers, the *xxprobe* interface is called indirectly during the driver loading process. You specify loadable driver configuration information in the `stanza.loadable` file fragment. This information includes the driver's name, location of the loadable object, device connectivity information, and device special file information. When the system manager requests that the driver be dynamically loaded, the system accesses the information in the `stanza.loadable` file fragment from the `/etc/sysconfigtab` data base. The *xx_configure* interface calls the `ldbl_stanza_resolver` interface to merge the driver's connectivity information into the hardware topology tree, which consists of `bus`, `controller`, and `device` structures. Next, the `ldbl_ctlr_configure` interface is called, which results in the system calling *xxprobe* for each instance of the controller present on the bus.

  When device drivers are dynamically loaded, the loadable subsystem checks for the existence of the device before calling *xxprobe*.

  For loadable device drivers, the *xxprobe* interface registers the device interrupt handlers by calling `handler_add` and `handler_enable`.

The Synopsis section shows the arguments associated with a `probe` interface for device drivers that operate on the TURBOchannel bus. See the bus-specific device driver manual, which describes the `probe` interface as it applies to the specific bus.

Return Values

The *xxprobe* interface returns a nonzero value if the probe operation is successful. It returns the value zero (0) to indicate that the driver did not complete the probe operation.

Related Information

Chapter 16, Structures Related to Device Drivers: `controller, driver`

Name

xxpsize – Returns the size of a disk partition.

Entry Point

The bdevsw table

Synopsis

```
int xxpsize(dev)
dev_t dev;
```

Arguments

dev
    Specifies the device and partition for which the size is being requested.

Description

The *xxpsize* interface is a means for the upper layer of kernel interfaces to determine the size of a disk partition. The driver returns the size of the specified partition, which is initially specified in the device's partition table or disk label.

The *xxpsize* interface could be called during system startup in configuring the swapping functions. These functions need to know the size of the disk (in units) of the disk blocks (typically 512-byte disk blocks).

The *xxpsize* interface is usually implemented only in disk device drivers. Other types of device drivers that do not implement this interface should specify a value of zero (0) in the bdevsw table.

Return Values

The *xxpsize* interface returns the size of the device partition in units of the disk blocks. If the specified device or partition does not exist, *xxpsize* returns the value −1.

Related Information

Section 17.2, Block and Character Device Driver Interfaces: *xx*dump

Name

xxread – Reads data from a device

Entry Point

The cdevsw table

Although raw block devices require a read and write device section, their driver entry points are specified through the cdevsw, not the bdevsw table. In other words, the device driver for the raw block device is both a block and a character driver. When accessed as a block device, the system uses the driver's strategy interface as the entry point. When accessed as a character device, the driver's read and write interfaces are used as the entry points.

Synopsis

```
int xxread(dev, uio, flag)
dev_t dev;
register struct uio *uio;
int flag;
```

Arguments

dev

Specifies the major and minor device numbers for this device. The system uses the minor device number to determine the logical unit number for the device on which the read operation will be performed.

uio

Specifies a pointer to a uio structure. This structure describes the read operation to be performed. You typically pass this pointer unmodified to the uiomove or physio kernel interface.

flag

Specifies the access mode of the device. The access modes are represented by a bit mask of flags defined in the file /usr/sys/include/sys/fcntl.h.

Description

The xxread interface is called from the I/O system as the result of a read system call. The driver's xxread interface reads data from a device. If there is no data available, the xxread interface puts the calling process to sleep until data is available. If data is available, xxread calls the uiomove interface to copy it from the private kernel buffer to the user's process.

In the case of raw block devices, the xxread interface calls the physio kernel interface, passing to it the device-specific parameters. For terminal-oriented devices, the driver passes the read request to the generic terminal read interface.

Return Values

The xxread interface returns an error number to the process's read system call if there is a failure. Otherwise, it returns the number of bytes actually read.

Related Information

Chapter 14, Header Files Related to Device Drivers: fcntl.h

Section 15.2, Kernel Support Interfaces: physio, uiomove

Chapter 16, Structures Related to Device Drivers: cdevsw, uio

Section 17.2, Block and Character Device Driver Interfaces: xxwrite

Reference Pages Section 2: read

Name

xxreset – Resets the device

Entry Point

The `cdevsw` table

Synopsis

void *xxreset(busnum)*
int *busnum;*

Arguments

busnum
Specifies the logical unit number of the bus on which the bus reset occurred.

Description

The *xxreset* interface is used to force a device reset to place the device in a known state after a bus reset. The bus adapter support interfaces call the *xxreset* interface after completion of a bus reset. Note that not all buses support the reset functionality.

For a terminal device driver, the *xxreset* interface can consist of reenabling interrupts on all open lines and resetting the line parameters for each open line. Following a reset of terminal state and line attributes, transmission can resume on the terminal lines.

Return Values

None

Related Information

Chapter 16, Structures Related to Device Drivers: `cdevsw`

Name

xxselect – Determines whether read/write will block

Entry Point

The cdevsw table

Synopsis

```
int xxselect(dev, events, revents, scanning)
dev_t dev;
short events;
short revents;
int scanning;
```

Arguments

dev
> Specifies the major and minor device numbers for this device. The minor device number is used to determine the logical unit number for the device on which the select operation will be performed.

events
> Specifies the events to be polled. This argument is an input to the device driver. The kernel can set this argument to the bitwise inclusive OR of one or more of the polling bit masks defined in the file /usr/sys/include/sys/poll.h:

> - POLLNORM
>
>   Read input select — The caller of select wants to know if input data is available on this device. A user-level process issues a select system call. The select system call then calls the driver's xxselect interface.
>
> - POLLOUT
>
>   Write output select — The caller of select wants to know if the device is ready to accept data to be output.
>
> - POLLPRI
>
>   Exception event select — The caller of select wants to know if an exception event has occurred on the device. This is rarely used on device drivers. It is used on pseudoterminal devices to indicate the presence of control status information.

revents

Specifies the events that are ready. The driver writer sets this value in the driver's *xxselect* interface. The driver writer can set this argument to the bitwise inclusive OR of one or more of the polling bit masks defined in /usr/sys/include/sys/poll.h:

- POLLNVAL

  It is an error to issue a select on this device. Driver writers can use this bit mask to indicate a select on input to an output-only device or a select on output to an input-only device.

- POLLHUP

  Indicates that the device has entered a state where it cannot perform input or output. Driver writers might set this bit mask when selecting on a terminal device and the modem connection has disconnected.

- POLLNORM

  Indicates that the device is readable.

- POLLOUT

  Indicates that the device is writable.

scanning

Specifies the initiation and termination of a select call. The kernel sets this argument to the value 1 to indicate initiation of a select call. A user-level process issues a select system call. The select system call then calls the driver's *xxselect* interface. The driver should determine if input is available or the device is ready to accept output, as specified by the bit mask setting in the *events* argument. If the device is not ready, the driver should register this select call for this instance of the device by calling the select_enqueue interface.

The kernel sets this argument to the value zero (0) to indicate the termination of a select call. In response to this setting, the driver should call the select_dequeue interface to remove all instances for this device that are waiting for input or output notification.

Description

A device driver's *xxselect* interface is called to determine whether the device is ready to perform an I/O operation without blocking. The *xxselect* interface is called as a result of the select system call.

A typical use of the select system call is when an application might be performing I/O to more than one file descriptor. One such example is a graphics server that receives input from the mouse and keyboard. When this graphics server is ready to accept input, it issues a `select` system call on the file descriptors associated with the mouse and keyboard to determine if input is available from either of them. In this way, the `select` system call is a form of polling to see if the device has input data that could be received by subsequent read calls or written by subsequent write calls.

The *xxselect* interface is called to determine if the specified device is ready to perform an I/O operation. The *xxselect* interface can be called to determine if input data is available to be read without blocking or if the device is ready to output data without blocking.

Return Values

The return value of the *xxselect* interface will eventually be the return value for the `select` system call. The *xxselect* interface can return one of the following values:

The value zero (0)
> The interface has successfully completed. This value does not indicate if data is available. The driver writer indicates that data is available for reading or writing by setting the appropriate polling bit masks in the *revents* argument.

EACCESS
> An error status is returned if a request is made to select on input for a device that is an output-only device or if a request is made to select on output for an input-only device.

Related Information

Chapter 14, Header Files Related to Device Drivers: `poll.h`

Section 15.2, Kernel Support Interfaces: `select_dequeue`, `select_dequeue_all`, `select_enqueue`, `select_wakeup`

Chapter 16, Structures Related to Device Drivers: `cdevsw`

Reference Pages Section 2: `select`

Name

*xx*slave – Checks that the device is valid for this controller

Entry Point

The driver structure

Synopsis

```
int xxslave(device, bus_io_handle)
struct device *device;
io_handle_t bus_io_handle;
```

Arguments

device

Specifies a pointer to a device structure for this device. The bus configuration code passes this pointer to the driver's *xx*slave interface. The device driver can reference such information as the logical unit number of the device, whether the device is functional, and the bus number the device resides on.

bus_io_handle

Specifies an I/O handle that you can use to reference a device register located in the TURBOchannel bus address space. The TURBOchannel bus configuration code passes this I/O handle to the driver's *xx*slave interface during device autoconfiguration. You can perform standard C mathematical operations on the I/O handle. For example, you can add an offset to or subtract an offset from the I/O handle.

Description

A device driver's *xx*slave interface is called only for a controller that has slave devices connected to it. This interface is called once for each slave attached to the controller. You (or the system manager) specify the attachments of these slave devices as follows:

- For the static version of your driver, in the system configuration file or stanza.static file fragment

- For the loadable version of your driver, in the stanza.loadable file fragment

The arguments you pass to the slave interface differ according to the bus on which the driver operates. The Synopsis section shows the arguments associated with a slave interface for a TURBOchannel bus. See the bus-specific device driver manual, which describes the slave interface as it applies to the specific bus.

Return Values

The xxslave interface returns a nonzero value if the device is present.

Related Information

Chapter 16, Structures Related to Device Drivers: device, driver

Name

*xx*stop – Stops data transmission

Entry Point

The cdevsw table

Synopsis

```
void xxstop(tp, flag)
struct tty *tp;
int flag;
```

Arguments

tp

Specifies a pointer to a tty structure. This structure contains data such as state information about the hardware terminal line, input and output queues, and the line discipline number.

flag

Specifies whether the output is to be flushed or suspended. Some device drivers do not use this argument. The argument is included here for use in terminal drivers.

Description

Terminal device drivers use the *xx*stop interface to suspend transmission on a specified line. The *xx*stop interface is called when the terminal driver has recognized a stop character such as ^S. There are also specific ioctl calls that request that output on a terminal line be suspended. These ioctl calls result in the general terminal driver interface calling the associated device driver's *xx*stop interface.

Typically, the *xx*stop interface sets the terminal's state to stopped. This action causes output to be suspended until the stopped state is cleared. For example, the stopped state may be cleared upon receipt of a start character such as ^Q.

Return Values

None

Related Information

Chapter 16, Structures Related to Device Drivers: `cdevsw`

Name

xxstrategy – Performs block I/O for block devices and initiates read and write operations for character devices

Entry Point

The bdevsw table

Synopsis

```
int xxstrategy(bp)
struct buf *bp;
```

Arguments

bp

Specifies a pointer to a buf structure. This structure describes the I/O operation to be performed.

Description

The *xxstrategy* interface performs block I/O for block devices and initiates read and write operations for character devices.

Typically, this interface is not called directly from user-level programs; instead, the interface is called from different interfaces within the kernel. For the block driver, it is the *xxstrategy* interface that implements the concept of disk partitions. Disk partitions involve subdividing the physical disk into smaller logical disk partitions. Through the use of partition tables that define partition boundaries, the *xxstrategy* interface maps read and write requests to the correct disk offset.

The main user of the block device is the file system. File system reads and writes are usually handled through kernel interfaces. Through these interfaces and the interfaces that they call, the data is read from or written to the data cache. When the data being read is not present in the data cache, the system calls the block device *xxstrategy* interface to initiate a data transfer to read in the data from the disk. When a decision is made to flush the written data out of the data cache to the disk media, the system calls the block driver *xxstrategy* interface to initiate the transfer.

Return Values

None

Related Information

Chapter 16, Structures Related to Device Drivers: `bdevsw`, `buf`

Name

*xx*write – Writes data to a device

Entry Point

The cdevsw table

Although raw block devices require a read and write device section, their driver entry points are specified through the cdevsw, not the bdevsw table. In other words, the device driver for the raw block device is both a block and a character driver. When accessed as a block device, the system uses the driver's strategy interface as the entry point. When accessed as a character device, the driver's read and write interfaces are used as the entry points.

Synopsis

```
int xxwrite(dev, uio, flag)
dev_t dev;
register struct uio *uio;
int flag;
```

Arguments

dev
> Specifies the major and minor device numbers for this device. The minor device number is used to determine the logical unit number for the device on which the write operation will be performed.

uio
> Specifies a pointer to a uio structure. This structure describes the write operation to be performed. You typically pass this pointer unmodified to the uiomove or physio kernel interface.

flag
> Specifies the access mode of the device. The access modes are represented by a bit mask of flags defined in the file /usr/sys/include/sys/fcntl.h.

Description

The *xxwrite* interface is called from the I/O system as the result of a `write` system call. The *xxwrite* interface checks the software state of the device to determine if the device is in a state that permits the write operation. If not, *xxwrite* places the device into a writable state and writes data to the device. (Note that read/write permission is checked at the file system level, not in the device driver.)

If necessary, *xxwrite* allocates a private kernel buffer. It uses the `uiomove` kernel interface to copy the data of the user process into the private kernel buffer. It then sets up the software state of the device for the current output transfer and starts the hardware transferring the data. Following this action, *xxwrite* puts the process to sleep and wakes it after all of the data in the current transfer has been sent to the device.

If the device is a raw block device, the *xxwrite* interface calls the `physio` kernel interface to accomplish the write. For terminal-oriented devices, the device driver passes the write request to the generic terminal interface.

Return Values

The *xxwrite* interface returns an error number to the process's `write` system call if there is a failure. Otherwise, it returns the number of bytes actually written.

Related Information

Chapter 14, Header Files Related to Device Drivers: `fcntl.h`

Section 15.2, Kernel Support Interfaces: `physio`, `uiomove`

Chapter 16, Structures Related to Device Drivers: `cdevsw`, `uio`

Section 17.2, Block and Character Device Driver Interfaces: *xxread*

Reference Pages Section 2: `write`

17.3 Bus Configuration Interfaces

Table 17-2 summarizes the bus configuration interfaces related to device drivers. Following the table are descriptions of each interface, presented in alphabetical order.

Table 17-2: Summary Descriptions of Bus Configuration Interfaces

Bus Interface	Summary Description
adp_handler_add	Registers a driver's interrupt service interface.
adp_handler_del	Deregisters a driver's interrupt service interface.
adp_handler_disable	Signifies that the driver's interrupt service interface is not callable.
adp_handler_enable	Signifies that the driver's interrupt service interface is now callable.
adp_unattach	Cleans up any in-memory data structures.
bus_search	Searches a bus structure for specified values.
config_resolver	Configures buses.
conn_bus	Connects bus structures.
conn_ctlr	Connects a controller structure to a bus structure.
conn_device	Connects a device structure to a controller structure.
ctlr_configure	Performs the tasks necessary to make the controller available.
ctlr_search	Searches for a controller structure connected to a specific bus.
ctlr_unconfigure	Performs the tasks necessary to unload a loadable controller.
get_bus	Searches the static bus_list array for a bus structure.
get_ctlr	Searches the static ctlr_list array for a controller structure.
get_ctlr_num	Gets a controller structure that matches the specified controller name and number.
get_device	Searches for the next device in a controller structure.
get_sys_bus	Returns a pointer to a system bus structure.
perf_init	Initializes the performance structure for a disk device.
xxconfl1	Configures the specified bus.
xxconfl2	Configures the specified bus.

Name

`adp_handler_add` – Registers a driver's interrupt service interface

Synopsis

```
ihandler_id_t (*bus->framework->adp_handler_add)(handler)
ihandler_t *handler;
```

Arguments

handler
> Specifies a pointer to an `ihandler_t` data structure.

Description

The `adp_handler_add` interface registers a driver's interrupt service
interface with the appropriate parameters into the bus-specific interrupt
dispatching algorithm. The `ihandler_t` data structure contains all of the
information needed to register the interrupt handler. This information
includes the interrupt service interface name and its associated formal
parameter.

The Synopsis section shows that the name of the `adp_handler_add`
interface is obtained through the `bus` structure's `framework` member. This
member is a pointer to a `bus_framework` structure, which contains a
pointer to the actual `adp_handler_add` interface.

Return Values

The return value of `adp_handler_add` is a bus-specific "key" that can
later be passed to the other `adp_handler` interfaces to identify the
interrupt service interfaces to act upon. If `adp_handler_add` returns an
error status, the return value for this "key" is –1. When
`adp_handler_add` returns to the generic `handler_add` interface a
value of –1, `handler_add` returns an error status to its caller indicating
that the handler add operation failed.

Related Information

Chapter 16, Structures Related to Device Drivers: `bus`, `ihandler_t`

Section 17.3, Bus Configuration Interfaces: `adp_handler_del`,
`adp_handler_disable`, `adp_handler_enable`

Name

adp_handler_del – Deregisters a driver's interrupt service interface

Synopsis

```
int (*bus->framework->adp_handler_del)(id)
ihandler_id_t id;
```

Arguments

id
Specifies which interrupt service interface to delete.

Description

The adp_handler_del interface deregisters a driver's interrupt service interface. One task this interface might perform consists of replacing the driver's interrupt service interface with the stray interface. The adp_handler_del interface fails if adp_handler_disable was not previously called.

The Synopsis section shows that the name of the adp_handler_del interface is obtained through the bus structure's framework member. This member is a pointer to a bus_framework structure, which contains a pointer to the actual adp_handler_del interface.

Return Values

The adp_handler_del interface returns the value zero (0) on success and the value –1 on an error.

Related Information

Chapter 16, Structures Related to Device Drivers: bus

Section 17.3, Bus Configuration Interfaces: adp_handler_add, adp_handler_disable, adp_handler_enable

Name

adp_handler_disable – Signifies that the driver's interrupt service
interface is not callable

Synopsis

```
int (*bus->framework->adp_handler_disable)(id)
ihandler_id_t id;
```

Arguments

id
Specifies which interrupt service interface to disable.

Description

The adp_handler_disable interface specifies that the driver's interrupt
service interface should not be called through the bus-specific interrupt
dispatching algorithm. The adp_handler_disable interface must be
called to disable the device's interrupt service interface prior to calling the
adp_handler_del interface.

The Synopsis section shows that the name of the adp_handler_disable
interface is obtained through the bus structure's framework member. This
member is a pointer to a bus_framework structure, which contains a
pointer to the actual adp_handler_disable interface.

Return Values

The adp_handler_disable interface returns the value zero (0) on
success and the value –1 on an error.

Related Information

Chapter 16, Structures Related to Device Drivers: bus

Section 17.3, Bus Configuration Interfaces: adp_handler_add,
adp_handler_del, adp_handler_enable

Name

adp_handler_enable – Signifies that the driver's interrupt service
interface is now callable

Synopsis

```
int (*bus->framework->adp_handler_enable)(id)
ihandler_id_t id;
```

Arguments

id
    Specifies which interrupt service interface to enable.

Description

The adp_handler_enable interface signifies that the driver's interrupt
service interface is now callable by the bus-specific interrupt dispatching
algorithm. This interface fails if adp_handler_add was not previously
called.

The Synopsis section shows that the name of the adp_handler_enable
interface is obtained through the bus structure's framework member. This
member is a pointer to a bus_framework structure, which contains a
pointer to the actual adp_handler_enable interface.

Return Values

The adp_handler_enable interface returns the value zero (0) on success
and the value –1 on an error.

Related Information

Chapter 16, Structures Related to Device Drivers: bus

Section 17.3, Bus Configuration Interfaces: adp_handler_add,
adp_handler_del, adp_handler_disable

Name

adp_unattach – Cleans up any in-memory data structures

Synopsis

```
int (*bus->framework->adp_unattach)(bus_struct)
struct bus *bus_struct;
```

Arguments

bus_struct
Specifies a pointer to a bus structure.

Description

The adp_unattach interface is called whenever an adapter is being
removed from the configuration. All controllers that might be present on it
have already been disabled. This interface is responsible for cleaning up any
in-memory data structures that may exist as well as any interrupt service
interfaces that might have been connected.

The Synopsis section shows that the name of the adp_unattach interface
is obtained through the bus structure's framework member. This member
is a pointer to a bus_framework structure, which contains a pointer to the
actual adp_unattach interface for this adapter.

Return Values

The adp_unattach interface returns the value zero (0) on success and the
value –1 on an error.

Related Information

Section 17.3, Bus Configuration Interfaces: adp_handler_add,
adp_handler_del, adp_handler_disable,
adp_handler_enable

Name

bus_search – Searches a bus structure for specified values

Synopsis

```
struct bus * bus_search(bus_name, slot)
char *bus_name;
int slot;
```

Arguments

bus_name
    Specifies the bus name to search for.

slot
    Specifies the bus slot or node number.

Description

The bus_search interface searches the bus_list array for a bus structure with values that match the parameters you specify. You use this interface with buses that have autoconfiguration capability.

Return Values

The interface returns a zero (0) when no values match. If the *bus_name* argument matches the name of a bus in the bus_list array, the interface returns a pointer to the bus's associated bus structure.

Related Information

Chapter 16, Structures Related to Device Drivers: bus

Section 17.3, Bus Configuration Interfaces: get_bus

Name

config_resolver – Configures buses

Synopsis

```
int (*bus->framework->config_resolver)(bus_struct, parameter)
struct bus *bus_struct;
caddr_t *parameter;
```

Arguments

bus_struct
Specifies a pointer to a bus structure.

parameter
Specifies a bus-specific parameter.

Description

The config_resolver interface configures buses. Examples of buses that this interface configures are the VMEbus, EISA bus, and TURBOchannel bus. The system typically calls this interface from the driver's configure interface for loadable drivers. For these types of buses, a mechanism is needed to search for adapters or controllers that the device driver can handle. If they are found, bus or controller structures need to be created (if they are not already) and connected to the hardware topology tree.

For example, the current TURBOchannel code does not create bus or controller structures for modules that are not defined in the tc_option table. Because the modules cannot be autoconfigured without a preexisting bus or controller structure, some method is needed to create the structures without requiring an explicit statement in the configuration section of the stanza.loadable file fragment.

To handle this situation, the TURBOchannel config_resolver interface scans the tc_slot structure looking for module name matches as supplied in the parameter tc_option_snippet (a smaller tc_option table supplied by the driver that contains only the modules this driver supports). If found, the match validates that the appropriate bus or controller structures have been created. If these structures do not exist, this interface causes them to be created.

The ldbl_stanza_resolver interface can call this interface multiple times, once for each instance of the bus found in the hardware topology tree.

The Synopsis section shows that the name of the `config_resolver`
interface is obtained through the `bus` structure's `framework` member. This
member is a pointer to a `bus_framework` structure, which contains a
pointer to the actual `config_resolver` interface for this bus.

Return Values

The `config_resolver` interface can return the following value:

ESUCCESS
> The bus is successfully resolved.

Related Information

Section 15.2, Kernel Support Interfaces: `ldbl_stanza_resolver`

Chapter 16, Structures Related to Device Drivers: `bus`, `controller`

Section 17.2, Block and Character Device Driver Interfaces: `xxconfigure`

Section 17.3, Bus Configuration Interfaces: `ctlr_configure`,
`ctlr_unconfigure`

Name

conn_bus – Connects bus structures

Synopsis

```
void conn_bus(hdbus, bus)
struct bus *hdbus;
struct bus *bus;
```

Arguments

hdbus
> Specifies a pointer to the bus structure for connection.

bus
> Specifies a pointer to the bus structure to be connected to hdbus.

Description

The conn_bus interface logically connects the second bus structure you pass to the first bus structure you pass. Specifically, the bus_hd member in the second bus structure is set to the first bus structure you pass, and the second bus structure is added to the list of buses connected to the first (the bus_list member in the first bus structure).

Return Values

None

Related Information

Chapter 16, Structures Related to Device Drivers: bus

Section 17.3, Bus Configuration Interfaces: get_bus

Name

conn_ctlr – Connects a `controller` structure to a `bus` structure

Synopsis

```
void conn_ctlr(bus, ctlr)
struct bus *bus;
struct controller *ctlr;
```

Arguments

bus
   Specifies a pointer to the `bus` structure for connection.

ctlr
   Specifies a pointer to the `controller` structure to be connected to the specified `bus` structure.

Description

The `conn_ctlr` interface logically connects the `controller` structure you pass to the `bus` structure you pass. Specifically, the bus pointer becomes the `bus_hd` member in the `controller` structure; the pointer to the next controller on the bus (the `nxt_ctlr` member in the `controller` structure) is added to the `ctlr_list` (the list of controllers) member in the bus structure.

Return Values

None

Related Information

Chapter 16, Structures Related to Device Drivers: `bus`, `controller`

Section 17.3, Bus Configuration Interfaces: `bus_search`, `ctlr_search`, `get_bus`, `get_ctlr`

Name

conn_device – Connects a device structure to a controller structure

Synopsis

```
void conn_device(ctlr, device)
struct controller *ctlr;
struct device *device;
```

Arguments

ctlr
: Specifies a pointer to the controller structure for connection.

device
: Specifies a pointer to the device structure to be connected to the controller structure that the ctlr argument specifies.

Description

The conn_device interface logically connects the device structure you pass to the controller structure you pass. Specifically, the controller structure pointer you pass (the *ctlr* argument) becomes the ctlr_hd pointer in the device structure; the device pointer is added to the list of devices on the controller (the dev_list member) in the controller structure.

Return Values

None

Related Information

Chapter 16, Structures Related to Device Drivers: controller, device

Section 17.3, Bus Configuration Interfaces: ctlr_search, get_ctlr, get_device

Name

ctlr_configure – Performs the tasks necessary to make the controller available

Synopsis

```
int (*bus->framework->ctlr_configure)(driver_name, bus_struct,
ctlr_struct, flags)
char *driver_name;
struct bus *bus_struct;
struct controller *ctlr_struct;
int flags;
```

Arguments

driver_name
> Specifies the name of the controlling driver.

bus_struct
> Specifies a pointer to a bus structure.

ctlr_struct
> Specifies a pointer to a controller structure.

flags
> Specifies miscellaneous flags contained in the file
> /usr/sys/include/io/common/devdriver_loadable.h.

Description

The ctlr_configure interface performs the tasks necessary to make the controller available. One of these tasks is mapping the CSRs. After this task, ctlr_configure should call the driver's probe interface to verify that the controller exists. Then, ctlr_configure calls the driver's slave and dattach interfaces for each device found for this controller in the loadable_device list.

If the controller supports autoconfiguration of devices (that is, the LDBL_AUTOCONFIG bit is set), a wildcard device structure is found, and the slave and dattach interfaces are called at the end with a null device structure until the slave interface returns an error (no more devices).

The Synopsis section shows that name of the ctlr_configure interface is obtained through the bus structure's framework member. This member is a pointer to a bus_framework structure, which contains a pointer to the actual ctlr_configure interface for this controller.

Return Values

The `ctlr_configure` interface can return the following values:

ESUCCESS
: The controller has been configured successfully.

ENODEV
: There is no such controller.

Related Information

Chapter 14, Header Files Related to Device Drivers: `devdriver_loadable.h`

Chapter 16, Structures Related to Device Drivers: `bus`, `controller`, `driver`

Section 17.3, Bus Configuration Interfaces: `config_resolver`, `ctlr_unconfigure`

Name

ctlr_search – Searches for a controller structure connected to a specific bus

Synopsis

```
struct controller * ctlr_search(num, name)
int num;
char *name;
```

Arguments

num
> Specifies the bus number to which the device is connected.

name
> Specifies the bus name.

Description

The ctlr_search interface searches for a controller structure connected to a specific bus. Buses without autoconfiguration capabilities use this interface. You call this interface repeatedly until all controllers connected to the specified bus are found.

Return Values

The interface returns the value zero (0) when no (or the last) controllers are connected to the bus you specify. Otherwise, it returns a pointer to the controller structure connected to this bus.

Related Information

Chapter 16, Structures Related to Device Drivers: bus, controller

Section 17.3, Bus Configuration Interfaces: conn_ctlr, get_ctlr

Name

ctlr_unconfigure – Performs the tasks necessary to unload a loadable controller

Synopsis

```
int (*bus->framework->ctlr_unconfigure)(bus_struct, driver_struct,
ctlr_struct)
struct bus *bus_struct;
struct driver *driver_struct;
struct controller *ctlr_struct;
```

Arguments

bus_struct
Specifies a pointer to a bus structure.

driver_struct
Specifies a pointer to the driver structure for the controlling device driver.

ctlr_struct
Specifies a pointer to a controller structure.

Description

The ctlr_unconfigure interface performs the tasks necessary to unload a loadable controller from the Digital UNIX operating system. These tasks include undoing anything that the ctlr_configure interface may have done to set up the controller. Two of these tasks are unmapping any CSRs and cleaning up any interrupt dispatching tables the bus might control.

This interface is called after the driver's xxctrl_unattach and xxdev_unattach interfaces have been called. Therefore, the bus interface writer can assume that the controller is fully disabled.

The Synopsis section shows that the name of the ctlr_unconfigure interface is obtained through the bus structure's framework member. This member is a pointer to a bus_framework structure, which contains a pointer to the actual ctlr_unconfigure interface for this controller.

Return Values

The `ctlr_unconfigure` interface can return the following values:

ESUCCESS
> The controller has been configured successfully.

ENODEV
> There is no such controller.

Related Information

Chapter 16, Structures Related to Device Drivers: `bus`, `controller`, `driver`

Section 17.2, Block and Character Device Driver Interfaces: *xx*`ctrl_unattach`, *xx*`dev_unattach`

Section 17.3, Bus Configuration Interfaces: `config_resolver`, `ctlr_configure`

Name

get_bus – Searches the static bus_list array for a bus structure

Synopsis

```
struct bus * get_bus(name, slot, bus_name, num)
char *name;
int slot;
char *bus_name;
int num;
```

Arguments

name
> Specifies the device name.

slot
> Specifies the bus slot or node number.

bus_name
> Specifies the name of the bus to which the controller is connected.

num
> Specifies the bus number to which the device is connected.

Description

The get_bus interface searches the static bus_list array for a bus structure that matches values you pass. Buses that can automatically configure themselves use this interface.

Return Values

The interface returns the value zero (0) if none of the values you pass matches. Otherwise, the interface returns a pointer to the bus structure associated with the bus in bus_list whose values match those you passed.

Related Information

Chapter 16, Structures Related to Device Drivers: bus

Section 17.3, Bus Configuration Interfaces: get_ctlr, get_sys_bus

Name

get_ctlr – Searches the static ctlr_list array for a controller structure

Synopsis

```
struct controller * get_ctlr(ctlr_name, slot, bus_name, bus_num)
char *ctlr_name;
int slot;
char *bus_name;
int bus_num;
```

Arguments

ctlr_name
Specifies the controller name.

slot
Specifies the bus slot or node number.

bus_name
Specifies the name of the bus to which the controller is connected.

bus_num
Specifies the number of the bus to which the controller is connected.

Description

The get_ctlr interface searches the static ctlr_list array for a controller structure whose values match the ones you pass. Buses that can automatically configure the bus use this interface.

Return Values

The get_ctlr interface returns the value zero (0) if the values you pass do not match those in the associated members in the controller structures residing in ctlr_list. Otherwise, the interface returns a pointer to the controller structure that matches the values you passed.

Related Information

Chapter 16, Structures Related to Device Drivers: controller

Section 17.3, Bus Configuration Interfaces: ctlr_search

Name

get_ctlr_num – Gets a controller structure that matches the specified controller name and number

Synopsis

struct controller * get_ctlr_num(*ctlr_name*, *ctlr_num*)
char **ctlr_name;*
int *ctlr_num;*

Arguments

ctlr_name
    Specifies the controller name.

ctlr_num
    Specifies the controller number.

Description

The get_ctlr_num interface searches the static ctlr_list array for a controller structure with values that match the passed parameters. Specifically, get_ctlr_num compares the values passed to the *ctlr_name* and *ctlr_num* arguments to the ctlr_name and ctlr_num members for each controller structure in the ctlr_list array.

Graphics device drivers use this interface to gain access to a specific controller data structure, for example, fb0. This action occurs during console initialization when the controller structures are not connected to devices.

Return Values

The get_ctlr_num interface returns the value zero (0) if the values you pass do not match any of the controller structures in ctlr_list. Otherwise, the interface returns a pointer to the controller structure that matches the values you passed.

Related Information

Chapter 16, Structures Related to Device Drivers: `controller`

Section 17.3, Bus Configuration Interfaces: `ctlr_search`, `get_ctlr`, `get_device`

Name

get_device – Searches for the next device in a controller structure

Synopsis

```
struct device * get_device(ctlr)
struct controller *ctlr;
```

Arguments

ctlr
Specifies a pointer to a specific controller structure in the controller_list array.

Description

The get_device interface returns a pointer to the device structure associated with the next device that was connected to the controller in the system configuration file.

Return Values

The get_device interface returns the value zero (0) if there was no device connected to the controller associated with the specified controller structure. Otherwise, it returns a pointer to the device structure associated with the next device that was connected to the controller in the system configuration file.

Related Information

Chapter 16, Structures Related to Device Drivers: controller, device

Section 17.3, Bus Configuration Interfaces: ctlr_search, get_ctlr

Name

get_sys_bus – Returns a pointer to a system bus structure

Synopsis

```
struct bus * get_sys_bus(bus_name)
char *bus_name;
```

Arguments

bus_name
    Specifies the bus name to search for.

Description

The get_sys_bus interface searches the bus_list array for the system
bus structure that matches the name you specified in the *bus_name*
argument. A system bus structure is one whose connect_num member is
set to the value –1. The system bus structure is sometimes referred to as
nexus.

Return Values

The get_sys_bus interface causes the following system panic message if
the *bus_name* argument you specified does not match the bus_name
member of any system bus structure in the bus_list array:

No system bus structure

If the name matches, however, the interface returns a pointer to the associated
system bus structure.

Related Information

Chapter 16, Structures Related to Device Drivers: bus

Section 17.3, Bus Configuration Interfaces: get_bus

Name

perf_init – Initializes the performance structure for a disk device

Synopsis

```
void perf_init(device)
struct device *device;
```

Arguments

device
Specifies a pointer to a device structure.

Description

The perf_init interface initializes the performance structure for a disk device. This interface sets the private member of the device structure associated with this disk device to the value –1 if the dev_type member of the specified device structure points to the string disk and the number of disk units on the system is less than 256.

Return Values

None

Related Information

Chapter 16, Structures Related to Device Drivers: device

Name

xxconf11, xxconf12 – Configure the specified bus

Synopsis

void *xxconf11*(*bus_type, bus_info, bus*)
int *bus_type;*
caddr_t *bus_info;*
struct bus **bus*

void *xxconf12*(*bus_type, bus_info, bus*)
int *bus_type;*
caddr_t *bus_info;*
struct bus **bus*

Arguments

bus_type
  Specifies the type of the calling bus. You pass the value –1 to indicate that this bus is the system bus (that is, the bus being called from the system startup code).

bus_info
  Specifies a bus-specific data structure that contains information needed to configure the bus. This structure is specific to the calling bus. You use the *bus_type* argument to determine how to cast this structure.

bus
  Specifies a pointer to the bus structure for this bus.

Description

The *xxconf11* and the *xxconf12* interfaces perform configuration tasks for the bus. The system first calls *xxconf11* interfaces for all buses and then calls *xxconf12* interfaces for all buses.

Return Values

None

Related Information

Chapter 16, Structures Related to Device Drivers: bus

Part 8

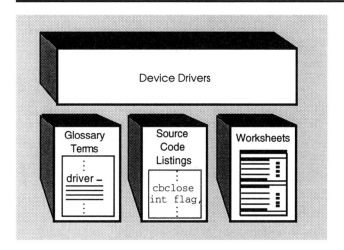

Device Drivers

Glossary Terms

driver —

Source Code Listings

cbclose
int flag,

Worksheets

Device Driver Example Source Listings

This appendix contains source listings for the following:

- The `/dev/none` device driver
- The `/dev/cb` device driver

A.1   Source Listing for the /dev/none Device Driver

```
/*****************************************************
 *                                                   *
 *           Copyright (c) 1994 by                   *
 *   Digital Equipment Corporation, Maynard, MA      *
 *           All rights reserved.                    *
 *                                                   *
 * This software is furnished under the terms and    *
 * conditions of the TURBOchannel Technology         *
 * license and may be used and copied only in        *
 * accordance with the terms of such license and     *
 * with the inclusion of the above copyright         *
 * notice.  No title to and ownership of the         *
 * software is hereby transferred.                   *
 *                                                   *
 * The information in this software is subject to    *
 * change without notice and should not be           *
 * construed as a commitment by Digital Equipment    *
 * Corporation.                                      *
 *                                                   *
 * Digital assumes no responsibility for the use     *
 * or reliability of its software on equipment       *
 * which is not supplied by Digital.                 *
 *****************************************************/


/*****************************************************
 * nonereg.h   Header file for none.c 13-Apr-1994    *
 *                                                   *
 *                                                   *
 * Define ioctl macros for the none driver.          *
 *****************************************************/


#define DN_GETCOUNT   _IOR(0,1,int)
#define DN_CLRCOUNT   _IO(0,2)
```

```
/*******************************************************
 *                                                     *
 * Device register offset definition for a none        *
 * device.                                             *
 *                                                     *
 *******************************************************/

#define NONE_CSR 0 /* 64-bit read/write CSR/LED register */


/*******************************************************
 * none.c  Driver for none device     13-Apr-1994      *
 *                                                     *
 * The /dev/none device driver is an example           *
 * driver that supports a fictitious ''none''          *
 * device.  The /dev/none device driver shows you      *
 * how to write a static and loadable device           *
 * driver.  In addition, the /dev/none driver          *
 * shows you how to write a driver that operates        *
 * on multiple buses.  The /dev/none driver is          *
 * implemented to operate on the following buses:       *
 * EISA, PCI, and TURBOchannel.  To help you more       *
 * easily locate sections in the driver that need       *
 * to deal with multiple bus issues, the following      *
 * words appear in the comment line:                   *
 *                                                     *
 *        !!* BUS-SPECIFIC CHANGE *!!                  *
 *                                                     *
 * The comments following the above words provide       *
 * information on what changes you need to make         *
 * to a device driver to support more than one          *
 * bus.                                                *
 *******************************************************/
/*******************************************************
 * Tim Burke, Karl Ebner, Mark Parenti, and            *
 * Al Wojtas                                           *
 *                                                     *
 * Digital Device Driver Project                       *
 *                                                     *
 *******************************************************/
/*******************************************************
 *              Include Files Section                  *
 *******************************************************/


/*******************************************************
 * Common driver header files                          *
 *******************************************************/
#include <sys/param.h>
#include <sys/systm.h>
#include <sys/ioctl.h>
#include <sys/tty.h>
#include <sys/user.h>
#include <sys/proc.h>
#include <sys/map.h>
```

```
#include <sys/buf.h>
#include <sys/vm.h>
#include <sys/file.h>
#include <sys/uio.h>
#include <sys/types.h>
#include <sys/errno.h>
#include <sys/conf.h>
#include <sys/kernel.h>
#include <sys/devio.h>
#include <hal/cpuconf.h>
#include <sys/exec.h>
#include <io/common/devdriver.h>
#include <sys/sysconfig.h>

/******************************************************
 *          !!* BUS-SPECIFIC CHANGE *!!               *
 ******************************************************
 * If you are writing this device driver to          *
 * operate on more than one bus, you must include     *
 * the correct bus-specific header file.  The         *
 * following list shows the correct header files      *
 * for the EISA, PCI, and TURBOchannel buses.         *
 *                                                    *
 *    #include <io/dec/eisa/eisa.h>            *
 *    #include <io/dec/pci/pci.h>              *
 *    #include <io/dec/tc/tc.h>                *
 *                                                    *
 ******************************************************/
#include <io/dec/tc/tc.h>

#include <machine/cpu.h>
#include <io/ESA100/nonereg.h>   /* Device register header file */


/******************************************************
 *       Data structure sizing approach               *
 ******************************************************
 *                                                    *
 * The following define will be used to allocate      *
 * data structures needed by the /dev/none driver.    *
 * There can be at most 4 instances of the none       *
 * controller on the system.  This is a small         *
 * number of instances of the driver and the data     *
 * structures themselves are not large, so it is      *
 * acceptable to allocate for the maximum             *
 * configuration.                                     *
 ******************************************************/


#define NNONE 4
```

```
/****************************************************
 * Autoconfiguration Support Declarations and      *
 * Definitions Section                             *
 ****************************************************/


/****************************************************
 *           Bits for csr member                   *
 ****************************************************/

#define DN_RESET 0001 /* Device ready for data transfer */
#define DN_ERROR 0002 /* Indicate error */

/****************************************************
 *          Defines for softc structure            *
 ****************************************************/


#define DN_OPEN  1 /* Device open bit */
#define DN_CLOSE 0 /* Device close bit */

/****************************************************
 *      Forward declarations of driver interfaces  *
 ****************************************************/


int noneprobe(), nonecattach(), noneintr();
int noneopen(),  noneclose(),   noneread(), nonewrite();
int noneioctl(), none_ctlr_unattach();


/****************************************************
 *      controller and driver Structures           *
 ****************************************************/

/****************************************************
 * Declare an array of pointers to controller      *
 * structures                                      *
 ****************************************************/

struct controller *noneinfo[NNONE];

/****************************************************
 * Declare and initialize driver structure         *
 ****************************************************/

struct driver nonedriver = {
        noneprobe,              /* probe */
        0,                      /* slave */
        nonecattach,            /* cattach */
        0,                      /* dattach */
        0,                      /* go */
        0,                      /* addr_list */
        0,                      /* dev_name */
```

```
                0,                      /* dev_list */
        "none",                 /* ctlr_name */
        noneinfo,               /* ctlr_list */
        0,                      /* xclu */
        0,                      /* addr1_size */
        0,                      /* addr1_atype */
        0,                      /* addr2_size */
        0,                      /* addr2_atype */
        none_ctlr_unattach,     /* ctlr_unattach */
        0                       /* dev_unattach */
};

/**************************************************
 * Declare softc structure                       *
 **************************************************/

struct none_softc {
    int sc_openf; /* Open flag */
    int sc_count; /* Count of characters written to device */
    int sc_state; /* Device state, not currently used */
} none_softc[NNONE];


/**************************************************
 * Loadable Driver Configuration Support         *
 * Declarations and Definitions Section          *
 **************************************************/

static int cmajnum = 0;
static int bmajnum = 0;
static int begunit = 0;
static int numunit = 0;
static int dsflags = 0;
static int noneversion = 0;
static unsigned char mcfgname[CFG_ATTR_NAME_SZ] = "";
static unsigned char modtype[CFG_ATTR_NAME_SZ] = "";
static unsigned char devcmajor[CFG_ATTR_NAME_SZ] = "";
static unsigned char devmgrreq[CFG_ATTR_NAME_SZ] = "";
static unsigned char devblkmaj[CFG_ATTR_NAME_SZ] = "";
static unsigned char devblkminor[CFG_ATTR_NAME_SZ] = "";
static unsigned char devblkfiles[CFG_ATTR_NAME_SZ] = "";
static unsigned char devcminor[CFG_ATTR_NAME_SZ] = "";
static unsigned char devcfiles[CFG_ATTR_NAME_SZ] = "";
static unsigned char devuser[CFG_ATTR_NAME_SZ] = "";
static unsigned char devgroup[CFG_ATTR_NAME_SZ] = "";
static unsigned char devmode[CFG_ATTR_NAME_SZ] = "";

cfg_subsys_attr_t none_attributes[] = {

/**************************************************
 * Declares an array of cfg_subsys_attr_t        *
 * structures and calls it none_attributes.      *
 * The device driver method of cfgmgr fills in   *
 * the elements in none_attributes because       *
```

```
 * the operation types designated by these      *
 * are CFG_OP_CONFIGURE.  The device driver      *
 * method of cfgmgr reads the entries for the    *
 * /dev/none driver from the sysconfigtab        *
 * database.  (A stanza.loadable file            *
 * fragment was created for the /dev/none        *
 * driver.  The sysconfigdb utility appends      *
 * this stanza.loadable file fragment to the     *
 * sysconfig database.)                          *
 *                                               *
 * To determine if any of these element reads    *
 * failed, the /dev/none driver verifies each    *
 * from the cfg_attr_t structure passed into     *
 * the none_configure interface.                 *
 *                                               *
 * Several of the following fields are used      *
 * in the /dev/none device driver while other    *
 * fields exist to illustrate what can be        *
 * loaded by cfgmgr into the driver attributes   *
 * table.                                        *
 ************************************************/

/* Fields used in this driver. */
{"Module_Config_Name",    CFG_ATTR_STRTYPE, CFG_OP_CONFIGURE,
                          (caddr_t)mcfgname,2,CFG_ATTR_NAME_SZ,0},
{"Module_Type",           CFG_ATTR_STRTYPE, CFG_OP_CONFIGURE,
                          (caddr_t)modtype,2,CFG_ATTR_NAME_SZ,0},
{"Device_Char_Major",     CFG_ATTR_STRTYPE, CFG_OP_CONFIGURE,
                          (caddr_t)devcmajor,0,CFG_ATTR_NAME_SZ,0},


/* Fields the device driver can request the cfgmgr load */
{"Device_Major_Req",      CFG_ATTR_STRTYPE, CFG_OP_CONFIGURE,
                          (caddr_t)devmgrreq,0,CFG_ATTR_NAME_SZ,0},
{"Device_Block_Major",    CFG_ATTR_STRTYPE, CFG_OP_CONFIGURE,
                          (caddr_t)devblkmaj,0,CFG_ATTR_NAME_SZ,0},
{"Device_Block_Minor",    CFG_ATTR_STRTYPE, CFG_OP_CONFIGURE,
                          (caddr_t)devblkminor,0,CFG_ATTR_NAME_SZ,0},
{"Device_Block_Files",    CFG_ATTR_STRTYPE, CFG_OP_CONFIGURE,
                          (caddr_t)devblkfiles,0,CFG_ATTR_NAME_SZ,0},
{"Device_Char_Minor",     CFG_ATTR_STRTYPE, CFG_OP_CONFIGURE,
                          (caddr_t)devcminor,0,CFG_ATTR_NAME_SZ,0},
{"Device_Char_Files",     CFG_ATTR_STRTYPE, CFG_OP_CONFIGURE,
                          (caddr_t)devcfiles,0,CFG_ATTR_NAME_SZ,0},
{"Device_User",           CFG_ATTR_STRTYPE, CFG_OP_CONFIGURE,
                          (caddr_t)devuser,0,CFG_ATTR_NAME_SZ,0},
{"Device_Group",          CFG_ATTR_STRTYPE, CFG_OP_CONFIGURE,
                          (caddr_t)devgroup,0,CFG_ATTR_NAME_SZ,0},
{"Device_Mode",           CFG_ATTR_STRTYPE, CFG_OP_CONFIGURE,
                          (caddr_t)devmode,0,CFG_ATTR_NAME_SZ,0},


/************************************************
 * The /dev/none device driver modifies the     *
 * following attributes during a configure       *
 * or unconfigure operation.  The device         *
```

```
 * driver method of cfgmgr uses these        *
 * attributes to provide the special files   *
 * needed by loadable device drivers.        *
 ************************************************/

{"cmajnum",            CFG_ATTR_INTTYPE, CFG_OP_QUERY,
                       (caddr_t)&cmajnum,0,99,0},
{"bmajnum",            CFG_ATTR_INTTYPE, CFG_OP_QUERY,
                       (caddr_t)&bmajnum,0,99,0},
{"begunit",            CFG_ATTR_INTTYPE, CFG_OP_QUERY,
                       (caddr_t)&begunit,0,8,0},
{"numunit",            CFG_ATTR_INTTYPE, CFG_OP_QUERY,
                       (caddr_t)&numunit,0,8,0},
{"dsflags",            CFG_ATTR_INTTYPE, CFG_OP_QUERY,
                       (caddr_t)&dsflags,0,8,0},
{"version",            CFG_ATTR_INTTYPE, CFG_OP_QUERY,
                       (caddr_t)&noneversion,0,9999999,0},
{"",0,0,0,0,0,0}
};


/*****************************************************
 * External function references.  These are needed *
 * for the cdevsw declaration.  The handler_add    *
 * interface is used to register the interrupt     *
 * service interface for the loadable driver.  The *
 * none_id_t array contains "id's" that are used   *
 * to deregister the interrupt handlers.           *
 *****************************************************/

extern int nodev(), nulldev();
ihandler_id_t *none_id_t[NNONE];

/*****************************************************
 *         !!* BUS-SPECIFIC CHANGE *!!             *
 *****************************************************
 * This device driver may be configured for any   *
 * of the busses listed below:                     *
 *                                                 *
 *      #define DN_BUSNAME    "tc"   TURBOchannel  *
 *      #define DN_BUSNAME    "isa"  isa bus       *
 *      #define DN_BUSNAME    "eisa" eisa bus      *
 *      #define DN_BUSNAME    "pci"  pci bus       *
 *                                                 *
 *      If you are writing this device             *
 *      driver to work on any additional           *
 *      buses The correct  bus names will          *
 *      need to be defined for later use.          *
 *****************************************************/


#define DN_BUSNAME      "tc" /* This is a TURBOchannel driver */
```

```
/********************************************************
 * The variable none_is_dynamic will be used to        *
 * control any differences in functions performed      *
 * by the static and loadable versions of the          *
 * driver.  In this manner any differences are         *
 * made on a run-time basis and not on a               *
 * compile-time basis.                                  *
 ********************************************************/

int none_is_dynamic = 0;


/********************************************************
/********************************************************
 *          !!* BUS-SPECIFIC CHANGE *!!                 *
 ********************************************************
 * When the driver is loadable it may not have an      *
 * entry in the following statically built tables:     *
 *                                                      *
 *    o eisa - eisa_option                              *
 *    o isa -  isa_option                               *
 *    o pci -  pci_option                               *
 *    o tc -   tc_option                                *
 *                                                      *
 * These tables are declared and initialized in        *
 * the following files:                                 *
 *                                                      *
 *    o eisa - eisa_option_data.c                       *
 *    o isa -  isa_option_data.c                        *
 *    o pci -  pci_option_data.c                        *
 *    o tc -   tc_option_data.c                         *
 *                                                      *
 * These tables contain the bus-specific ROM           *
 * module name for the driver.  This information       *
 * forms the bus-specific parameter that the           *
 * driver passes to the ldbl_stanza_resolver           *
 * interface to look for matches in the eisa_slot,     *
 * isa_slot, pci_slot, or tc_slot table.               *
 *                                                      *
 * It is not an error if this entry already            *
 * exists in the table(s).  The entry in               *
 * eisa_option, isa_option, pci_option, or             *
 * tc_option is only used when the driver is           *
 * configured statically; the entry below is only      *
 * used when the driver is configured dynamically.     *
 *                                                      *
 ********************************************************/


struct tc_option none_option_snippet [] =
/********************************************************/
{
/*  module          driver  intr_b4 itr_aft         adpt   */
/*  name            name    probe   attach  type    config */
/*  ------          ------  ------- ------- ----    ------  */
```

```
{    "NONE    ",   "none",     0,      1,     'C',    0},
{    "",            ""        } /* Null terminator in the */
                               /* table */
};
int num_none = 0;    /* Count on the number of controllers probed */


/*****************************************************
 * Loadable Driver Local Structure and Variable     *
 * Definitions Section                              *
 *****************************************************/


int none_config = FALSE;  /* State flags indicating driver configured */
dev_t none_devno = NODEV; /* No major number assigned yet. */


/*****************************************************
 * Device switch structure for dynamic              *
 * configuration.  The following is a definition    *
 * of the cdevsw entry that will be dynamically     *
 * added for the loadable driver.  For this reason  *
 * the loadable driver does not need to have its    *
 * entry points statically configured into conf.c.  *
 *****************************************************/


struct cdevsw none_cdevsw_entry = {
        noneopen,           /* d_open */
        noneclose,          /* d_close */
        noneread,           /* d_read */
        nonewrite,          /* d_write */
        noneioctl,          /* d_ioctl */
        nodev,              /* d_stop */
        nodev,              /* d_reset */
        0,                  /* d_ttys */
        nodev,              /* d_select */
        0,                  /* d_mmap */
        DEV_FUNNEL_NULL,    /* d_funnel */
        0,                  /* xxx_segmap */
        0,                  /* SVR4 DDI/DKI */
};


/*****************************************************
 *          Autoconfiguration Support Section       *
 *****************************************************/
/*****************************************************
 *                                                  *
 *                                                  *
 *-------------- noneprobe ----------------------*
 *****************************************************/


/*****************************************************
 *           Probe Interface                        *
```

```
/********************************************************
*            !!* BUS-SPECIFIC CHANGE *!!                *
*********************************************************
*                                                      *
* The noneprobe interface is called from the           *
* operating system configuration code during boot      *
* time.  The noneprobe interface calls the             *
* BADADDR interface to determine if the device is      *
* present.  If the device is present, noneprobe        *
* returns a nonzero value.  If the device is not       *
* is not present, noneprobe returns 0.                 *
*********************************************************/

noneprobe(addr1, ctlr)
io_handle_t addr1; /* I/O handle passed to the /dev/none *
                          * driver's probe interface */
struct controller *ctlr; /* Pointer to controller structure */

{

/********************************************************
*                                                      *
* These data structures will be used to register       *
* the interrupt handler for the loadable and           *
* static driver.                                       *
*                                                      *
*********************************************************/

        ihandler_t handler;
        struct handler_intr_info info;
        int unit = ctlr->ctlr_num;
        register io_handle_t reg = addr1;

/********************************************************
* Dynamically register the interrupt handlers          *
* for the static and loadable versions of the          *
* /dev/none device driver.                             *
*********************************************************/



/********************************************************
* Increment the num_none variable to indicate          *
* that noneprobe probed at least one controller.        *
* Return the value zero (0) to indicate that            *
* noneprobe did not complete the probe operation.       *
*********************************************************/

        num_none++;
        return(0);

/********************************************************
* Specify the bus that this controller is              *
* attached to.                                         *
*********************************************************/

        handler.ih_bus = ctlr->bus_hd;
```

```
/*****************************************************
 * Set up the fields of the TC-specific bus info    *
 * structure and specify the controller number.     *
 *****************************************************/

    info.configuration_st = (caddr_t)ctlr;

/*****************************************************
 * Specifies the driver type as a controller.       *
 *****************************************************/

    info.config_type = CONTROLLER_CONFIG_TYPE;

/*****************************************************
 * Specifies the interrupt service interface (ISI). *
 *****************************************************/

    info.intr = noneintr;

/*****************************************************
 * This parameter will be passed to the ISI.        *
 *****************************************************/

    info.param = (caddr_t)unit;

/*****************************************************
 * The address of the bus-specific info structure.  *
 *****************************************************/

    handler.ih_bus_info = (char *)&info;

/*****************************************************
 * Save off the return id from handler_add.  This   *
 * id will be used later to deregister the           *
 * handler.                                          *
 *****************************************************/

    none_id_t[unit] = handler_add(&handler);
    if (none_id_t[unit] == NULL) {
            return(0); /* Return failure status */
            }
            if (handler_enable(none_id_t[unit]) != 0) {
                    handler_del(none_id_t[unit]);
                    return(0); /* Return failure status */
            }


/*****************************************************
 * Increment the num_none variable to indicate      *
 * that noneprobe probed at least one controller.   *
 * Return the value zero (0) to indicate that       *
 * noneprobe did not complete the probe operation.  *
 *****************************************************/
```

```
        num_none++;
        return(0);
/***************************************************
 * Determine if the device is present by calling   *
 * the BADADDR interface.  If the device is         *
 * present, return 0.  Otherwise, reset the         *
 * device and assure that a write to I/O            *
 * space completes.                                 *
 ***************************************************/

        if (!none_is_dynamic) {
            if (BADADDR( (caddr_t) reg + NONE_CSR, sizeof(long), NULL) !=0)
            {
                    return (0);
            }
               }
        write_io_port(reg + NONE_CSR, 8, 0, DN_RESET); /* Reset the device */
        mb();                    /* Ensure a write to I/O space completes */
/***************************************************
 * If the error bit is set, noneprobe returns 0 to *
 * the configuration code.  Otherwise, it           *
 * calls write_io_port and calls wbflush to assure  *
 * that a write to I/O space completes.             *
 ***************************************************/
        if(read_io_port(reg + NONE_CSR, 8, 0) & DN_ERROR)
        {
            return (0);
        }

        write_io_port(reg + NONE_CSR, 8, 0, 0); /* Write to the CSR/LED register */
        mb();     /* Ensure a write to I/O space completes */
/***************************************************
 * Return a nonzero value.  The device is present. *
 ***************************************************/
        return (1);
}



/***************************************************
 *              Attach Interface                   *
 ***************************************************/
/***************************************************
 *                                                 *
 *                                                 *
 *-------------- nonecattach --------------------*
 *                                                 *
 *                                                 *
 * The nonecattach interface does not currently    *
 * perform any tasks.  It is provided here as a     *
 * stub for future development.                     *
 ***************************************************/

nonecattach(ctlr)
struct controller *ctlr; /* Pointer to controller struct */
{
        /* Attach interface goes here. */
        return;
}
```

```
/*****************************************************
 *------------ none_ctlr_unattach ---------------- *
 *                                                 *
 * Loadable driver-specific interface called       *
 * indirectly from the bus code when a driver is   *
 * being unloaded.                                 *
 *                                                 *
 * Returns 0 on success, nonzero (1) on error.     *
 *****************************************************/

int none_ctlr_unattach(bus, ctlr)
    struct bus *bus;        /* Pointer to bus structure */
    struct controller *ctlr; /* Pointer to controller structure */
{
        register int unit = ctlr->ctlr_num;


/*****************************************************
 * Validate the unit number.                       *
 *****************************************************/

        if ((unit > num_none) || (unit < 0)) {
                return(1); /* Return error status */
        }


/*****************************************************
 * This interface should never be called for a     *
 * static driver.  The reason is that the static   *
 * driver does not do a handler_add in the first   *
 * place.                                          *
 *****************************************************/

        if (none_is_dynamic == 0) {
                return(1); /* Return error status */
        }


/*****************************************************
 * The deregistration of interrupt handlers        *
 * consists of a call to handler_disable to        *
 * disable any further interrupts.  Then, call     *
 * handler_del to remove the ISI.                  *
 *****************************************************/

        if (handler_disable(none_id_t[unit]) != 0) {
                return(1); /* Return error status */
        }
        if (handler_del(none_id_t[unit]) != 0) {
                return(1); /* Return error status */
        }
        return(0); /* Return success status */
```

```
}


/*****************************************************
 * Loadable Device Driver Section                    *
 *****************************************************/
/*****************************************************
 *------------------ none_configure ----------------*
 *****************************************************/
/*****************************************************
 * The none_configure interface is called to        *
 * configure a loadable driver.  This interface is   *
 * also called to configure, unconfigure, and        *
 * query the driver.  These operations are           *
 * differentiated by the "op" parameter.             *
 *****************************************************/

none_configure(op,indata,indatalen,outdata,outdatalen)
    cfg_op_t op;            /* Configure operation */
    cfg_attr_t *indata;         /* Input data structure, cfg_attr_t */
    size_t indatalen;           /* Size of input data structure */
    cfg_attr_t *outdata;        /* Formal parameter not used */
    size_t outdatalen;          /* Formal parameter not used */
{
        dev_t   cdevno;
        int     retval;
        int     i;
/*****************************************************
 *                                                   *
 * MAX_DEVICE_CFG_ENTRIES represents the number of   *
 * config lines in the stanza.loadable fragment      *
 * for this driver.                                  *
 *                                                   *
 *****************************************************/
#define MAX_DEVICE_CFG_ENTRIES 18
/*****************************************************
 * The cfg_attr_t list passed into the              *
 * none_configure routine (indata) contains the     *
 * strings that are stored in the sysconfigtab      *
 * database for this subsystem.                     *
 *****************************************************/
#define NONE_DEBUG
#ifdef NONE_DEBUG
        cfg_attr_t cfg_buf[MAX_DEVICE_CFG_ENTRIES];
#endif /* NONE_DEBUG */
```

```
        switch (op) {

/*******************************************************
*              Configure (load) the driver.           *
*                                                      *
*******************************************************/

            case CFG_OP_CONFIGURE:
#ifdef NONE_DEBUG
printf("none_configure: CFG_OP_CONFIGURE.\n");
#endif /* NONE_DEBUG */

#ifdef NONE_DEBUG

/*******************************************************
*       Pass Attributes Verification                  *
*                                                      *
* Attributes passed through the none_attributes        *
* structure are not known to be valid until the        *
* /dev/none driver can check their status in the       *
* indata argument.  A status other than                *
* CFG_FRAME_SUCCESS is an error condition.  You        *
* can use this debug code to:                          *
*                                                      *
*  o Debug cfgmgr loading problems with the            *
*    none_attributes structure                         *
*                                                      *
*  o Display the contents and status of the            *
*    attributes in the sysconfigtab database for       *
*    the /dev/none driver                              *
*                                                      *
*  o Report cfgmgr's status that indicates a           *
*    failure to load any of the attribute fields       *
*    into the none_attributes structure.               *
*******************************************************/

                bcopy(indata, cfg_buf[0].name,
                    indatalen*(sizeof(cfg_attr_t)));
                printf(" The none_configure routine was called.  op = %x\n",op);
                for( i=0; i < indatalen; i++){
                    printf("%s: ",cfg_buf[i].name);
                    switch(cfg_buf[i].type){
                        case CFG_ATTR_STRTYPE:
                            printf("%s\n",cfg_buf[i].attr.str.val);
                            break;

                        default:
                          switch(cfg_buf[i].status){
                            case CFG_ATTR_EEXISTS:
                                printf("**Attribute does not exist\n");
                                break;

                            case CFG_ATTR_EOP:
                                printf("**Attribute does not support operation\n");
                                break;

                            case CFG_ATTR_ESUBSYS:
                                printf("**Subsystem Failure\n");
```

```
                              break;

                    case CFG_ATTR_ESMALL:
                       printf("**Attribute size/value too small\n");
                       break;

                    case CFG_ATTR_ELARGE:
                       printf("**Attribute size/value too large\n");
                       break;

                    case CFG_ATTR_ETYPE:
                       printf("**Attribute invalid type\n");
                       break;

                    case CFG_ATTR_EINDEX:
                       printf("**Attribute invalid index\n");
                      break;

                    case CFG_ATTR_EMEM:
                       printf("**Attribute memory allocation error\n");
                       break;

                    default:
                       printf("**Unknown attribute: ");
                       printf("%x\n", cfg_buf[i].status);
                       break;
                       }
                  break;
                  }
              }
#endif

/****************************************************
 *          The configure interface could be        *
 *          called for either a static or loadable   *
 *          driver.  For this reason it is not        *
 *          possible to conclude that the driver      *
 *          is being dynamically loaded merely        *
 *          because the configure interface has       *
 *          been entered.  To see if the driver       *
 *          is dynamically configured check the       *
 *          flags field.  If this is set, then        *
 *          set a driver global variable to           *
 *          indicate the driver is loaded.            *
 ****************************************************/

                 if(strcmp(modtype,"Dynamic")==0) {
                       none_is_dynamic = 1;
                       }

                 if (none_is_dynamic) {

/****************************************************
 *          Sanity check on the config name.         *
 *          If it is null the resolver and           *
 *          configure code won't know what to         *
 *          look for.                                 *
 ****************************************************/

                    if(strcmp(mcfgname,"")==0) {
```

```
                                        printf("none_configure, null config name.\n");
                                        return(EINVAL);
                                        }

/******************************************************
 *          Call the resolver to look for          *
 *          matches to the module's rom name        *
 *          in the pci_slot table.  This will       *
 *          add the controller data structure       *
 *          into the topology tree.                 *
 ******************************************************/

                if (ldbl_stanza_resolver(mcfgname, DN_BUSNAME,
                        &nonedriver,
                        (caddr_t *)none_option_snippet) != 0) {
                        return(EINVAL);
                        }

/******************************************************
 *          Call the configuration code to          *
 *          cause the driver's probe interface      *
 *          to be called once for each instance     *
 *          of the controller found on the          *
 *          system.                                 *
 ******************************************************/

                if (ldbl_ctlr_configure(DN_BUSNAME,
                                LDBL_WILDNUM, mcfgname,
                                &nonedriver, 0)) {
                                return(EINVAL);
                        }

/******************************************************
 *          The above call should have called       *
 *          the driver's probe interface for        *
 *          each instance of the controller.        *
 *          If there were no controllers found      *
 *          then fail the driver configure          *
 *          operation.                              *
 ******************************************************/

                num_none++;
                if (num_none == 0) {
                        return(EINVAL);
                }
        }

/******************************************************
 *          Perform the driver configuration        *
 *          above prior to getting the major        *
 *          number so that user-level programs do   *
 *          not have access to the driver's         *
 *          entry points in cdevsw prior to the     *
 *          completion of the topology and          *
 *          interrupt configuration.                *
 *                                                  *
 *          Register the driver's cdevsw entry      *
 *          points and obtain the major number      *
 ******************************************************/
```

```
                if(strcmp(devcmajor,"")!=0) {
                        if((strcmp(devcmajor,"-1")==0) ||
                           (strcmp(devcmajor,"?")==0) ||
                           (strcmp(devcmajor,"any")==0) ||
                           (strcmp(devcmajor,"ANY")==0)){
                            cdevno = NODEV;
                            }
                        else {
                            cdevno = atoi(devcmajor);
                            cdevno = makedev(cdevno,0);
                            }
                    }
                else
                        return EINVAL;
                    cdevno = cdevsw_add(cdevno,&none_cdevsw_entry);
                    if (cdevno == NODEV) {

/**************************************************
 *          The call to cdevsw_add could fail if *
 *          the driver is requesting a specific  *
 *          major number and that number is      *
 *          currently in use, or if the cdevsw   *
 *          table is currently full.             *
 **************************************************/

                            return(ENODEV);
                    }

/**************************************************
 *          Stash away the dev_t so that it can  *
 *          be used later to unconfigure the     *
 *          device.  Save off the minor number   *
 *          information.  This will be returned   *
 *          by the query call.                   *
 **************************************************/

                none_devno = cdevno;

/**************************************************
 *                                               *
 *          Set up the none_attribute list with  *
 *          the none-specific information that    *
 *          can be queried.                      *
 *                                               *
 *          This member specifies the major      *
 *          number that was assigned to this     *
 *          driver.                              *
 **************************************************/

                cmajnum = major(none_devno);

/**************************************************
 *          This member indicates that the       *
 *          beginning minor number will be       *
 *          zero (0).                            *
 **************************************************/
```

```
            begunit = 0;


/*****************************************************
 *            Specifies the number of instances of *
 *            the controller that were located.    *
 *****************************************************/

            numunit = num_none;


/*****************************************************
 *            This is a character driver.  For this *
 *            reason no block major number is       *
 *            assigned.                             *
 *****************************************************/

            bmajnum = NODEV;


/*****************************************************
 *            Set this state field to indicate that *
 *            the driver has successfully           *
 *            configured.                           *
 *****************************************************/

            none_config = TRUE;
            break;



/*****************************************************
 * Unconfigure (unload) the driver.                 *
 *****************************************************/

            case CFG_OP_UNCONFIGURE:


/*****************************************************
 *            DEBUG STATEMENT                        *
 *****************************************************/
#ifdef NONE_DEBUG
printf("none_configure: CFG_OP_UNCONFIGURE.\n");
#endif /* NONE_DEBUG */
/*****************************************************
 *            Fail the unconfiguration if the driver *
 *            is not currently configured.          *
 *****************************************************/

            if (none_config != TRUE) {
                    return(EINVAL);
            }


/*****************************************************
 *            Do not allow the driver to be unloaded *
 *            if it is currently active.  To see if  *
 *            the driver is active look to see if    *
 *            any users have the device open.        *
 *****************************************************/
```

```
                    for (i = 0; i < num_none; i++) {
                            if (none_softc[i].sc_openf != 0) {
                                    return(EBUSY);
                            }
                    }


/*****************************************************
 *         Call cdevsw_del to remove the driver       *
 *         entry points from the in-memory resident   *
 *         cdevsw table.  This is done prior to       *
 *         deleting the loadable configuration        *
 *         and handlers to prevent users from         *
 *         accessing the device in the middle of      *
 *         deconfigure operation.                     *
 *****************************************************/

                    retval = cdevsw_del(none_devno);
                    if (retval) {
                            return(ESRCH);
                    }


/*****************************************************
 *         Deregister the driver's configuration      *
 *         data structures from the hardware          *
 *         topology and cause the interrupt handlers  *
 *         to be deleted.                             *
 *****************************************************/

                    if (none_is_dynamic) {


/*****************************************************
 *         The bus number is wildcarded to            *
 *         deregister on all instances of the tc      *
 *         bus.  The controller name and number are   *
 *         wildcarded.  This causes all instances     *
 *         that match the specified driver structure  *
 *         to be deregistered.  Through the           *
 *         bus-specific code, this interface results  *
 *         in a call to the none_ctlr_unattach        *
 *         interface for each instance of the         *
 *         controller.                                *
 *****************************************************/

                            if (ldbl_ctlr_unconfigure(DN_BUSNAME,
                                    LDBL_WILDNUM, &nonedriver,
                                    LDBL_WILDNAME, LDBL_WILDNUM) != 0) {


/*****************************************************
 *                   DEBUG STATEMENT                  *
 *****************************************************/
#ifdef NONE_DEBUG
printf("none_configure:ldbl_ctlr_unconfigure failed.\n");
#endif /* NONE_DEBUG */


                                    return(ESRCH);
                            }
```

```
                }
                none_config = FALSE;
                break;


/*****************************************************
 *   Requests to query a loadable subsystem will   *
 *   only succeed if the  CFG_OP_QUERY: entry      *
 *   returns success.                              *
 *****************************************************/

                case CFG_OP_QUERY:
                break;

                default: /* Unknown operation type */
                    return(EINVAL);
        }


/*****************************************************
 *        The driver's configure interface has      *
 *        completed successfully.  Return a success *
 *        status.                                   *
 *****************************************************/


        return(0);
}


/*****************************************************
 *            Open and Close Device Section         *
 *****************************************************/
/*****************************************************
 *                                                  *
 *                                                  *
 *                                                  *
 *---------------- noneopen --------------------    *
 *                                                  *
 *                                                  *
 *                                                  *
 * The noneopen interface is called as the result  *
 * of an open system call.  The noneopen interface  *
 * checks to ensure that the open is unique,        *
 * marks the device as open, and returns the        *
 * value zero (0) to the open system call to        *
 * indicate success.                                *
 *****************************************************/

noneopen(dev, flag, format)
dev_t dev;  /* Major/minor device number */
int flag;   /* Flags from /usr/sys/h/file.h */
int format; /* Format of special device */
{
```

```
/*******************************************************
 * Perform the following initializations:              *
 *                                                     *
 *   (1) Initialize unit to the minor device number    *
 *   (2) Initialize the pointer to the controller      *
 *       structure associated with this none device    *
 *   (3) Initialize the pointer to the none_softc       *
 *       structure associated with this none           *
 *       device                                        *
 *******************************************************/
      register int unit = minor(dev);
      struct controller *ctlr = noneinfo[unit];
      struct none_softc *sc = &none_softc[unit];
/*******************************************************
 * If the device does not exist, return no such        *
 * device.                                             *
 *******************************************************/
      if(unit >= NNONE)
          return ENODEV;
/*******************************************************
 * Make sure the open is unique.                       *
 *******************************************************/
      if (sc->sc_openf == DN_OPEN)
          return (EBUSY);
/*******************************************************
 * If device is initialized, set sc_openf and          *
 * return 0 to indicate success.  Otherwise, the       *
 * device does not exist.  Return an error code.       *
 *******************************************************/
      if ((ctlr !=0) && (ctlr->alive & ALV_ALIVE))
      {
          sc->sc_openf = DN_OPEN;
          return(0);
      }
/*******************************************************
 * Return an error code to indicate device does        *
 * not exist.                                          *
 *******************************************************/
      else return(ENXIO);
}


/*******************************************************
 * Close Interface                                     *
 *******************************************************/
/*******************************************************
 *                                                     *
 *                                                     *
 *-------------- noneclose ----------------------*
 *                                                     *
 *                                                     *
 *                                                     *
```

```
/*****************************************************
 * The noneclose interface uses the same arguments  *
 * as noneopen; gets the device minor number in     *
 * the same way; and initializes the device and     *
 * none_softc structures identically. The purpose   *
 * of noneclose is to turn off the open flag for    *
 * the specified none device.                       *
 *****************************************************/

noneclose(dev, flag, format)
dev_t dev;   /* Major/minor device number */
int flag;    /* Flags from /usr/sys/h/file.h */
int format;  /* Format of special device */
{

/*****************************************************
 * Perform the following initializations:           *
 *                                                  *
 *   (1) Initialize unit to the minor device number *
 *   (2) Initialize the pointer to the controller   *
 *       structure associated with this none device *
 *   (3) Initialize the pointer to the none_softc   *
 *       structure associated with this none        *
 *       device                                     *
 *   (4) Initialize the pointer to the device       *
 *       register structure.                        *
 *****************************************************/

    register int unit = minor(dev);

    struct controller *ctlr = noneinfo[unit];

    struct none_softc *sc = &none_softc[unit];

        register io_handle_t reg =
        (io_handle_t) ctlr->addr;
/*****************************************************
 * Turn off the open flag for the specified device. *
 *****************************************************/

    sc->sc_openf = DN_CLOSE;
/*****************************************************
 * Turn off interrupts.                             *
 *****************************************************/

        write_io_port(reg + NONE_CSR, 8, 0, 0);
/*****************************************************
 * Assure that write to I/O space completes.        *
 *****************************************************/

    mb();
/*****************************************************
 * Return success.                                  *
 *****************************************************/

    return(0);
}
```

```
/********************************************************
 *              Read and Write Device Section           *
 ********************************************************/
/********************************************************
 *                                                      *
 *                                                      *
 *-------------- noneread -----------------------*
 *                                                      *
 *                                                      *
 *                                                      *
 * The noneread interface simply returns success        *
 * to the read system call because the /dev/none        *
 * driver always returns EOF on read operations.        *
 ********************************************************/

noneread(dev, uio, flag)
dev_t dev;        /* Major/minor device number */
struct uio *uio; /* Pointer to uio structure  */
int flag; /* Access mode of device */
{
     return (0); /* Return success */
}


/********************************************************
 *              Write Interface                         *
 *                                                      *
 *                                                      *
 *-------------- nonewrite -----------------------*
 *                                                      *
 *                                                      *
 *                                                      *
 * The nonewrite interface takes the same formal        *
 * parameters as the noneread interface.  The           *
 * nonewrite interface, however, copies data from       *
 * the address space pointed to by the uio              *
 * structure to the device.  Upon a successful          *
 * write, nonewrite returns the value zero (0) to       *
 * the write system call.                               *
 ********************************************************/

nonewrite(dev, uio, flag)
dev_t dev;        /* Major/minor device number */
struct uio *uio;  /* Pointer to uio structure  */
int flag; /* Access mode of device */

{
/********************************************************
 * Perform the following initializations and           *
 * declarations:                                        *
 *                                                      *
 *   (1) Initialize unit to the minor device number    *
 *   (2) Initialize the pointer to the controller      *
```

```
 *       structure associated with this none device *
 *   (3) Initialize the pointer to the none_softc   *
 *       structure associated with this none device *
 *   (4) Declare a count variable to store the       *
 *       size of the write request                   *
 *   (5) Declare a pointer to an iovec structure     *
 ****************************************************/

     int unit = minor(dev);

     struct controller *ctlr = noneinfo[unit];

     struct none_softc *sc = &none_softc[unit];

     unsigned int count;

     struct iovec *iov;

/****************************************************
 * While true, get the next I/O vector.            *
 ****************************************************/

     while(uio->uio_resid > 0) {
          iov = uio->uio_iov;
          if(iov->iov_len == 0) {
               uio->uio_iov++;
               uio->uio_iovcnt--;
               if(uio->uio_iovcnt < 0)
                    panic("none write");
               continue;
          }

/****************************************************
 * Figure out how big the write request is.        *
 ****************************************************/

     count = iov->iov_len;

/****************************************************
 * Note that the data is consumed.                 *
 ****************************************************/

     iov->iov_base += count;
     iov->iov_len -= count;
     uio->uio_offset += count;
     uio->uio_resid -= count;

/****************************************************
 * Count the bytes written.                        *
 ****************************************************/

     sc->sc_count +=count;
     }
     return (0);
}
```

```
/*****************************************************
 *              Interrupt Section                    *
 *                                                   *
 *                                                   *
 *-------------- noneintr ---------------------*
 *                                                   *
 *                                                   *
 *                                                   *
 * The noneintr interface does not currently         *
 * perform any tasks.  It is provided here as a      *
 * stub for future development.  The noneintr        *
 * interface does nothing because there is no        *
 * real physical device to generate an interrupt.    *
 *****************************************************/

noneintr(ctlr_num)
int ctlr_num; /* Controller number for device */

{
/*****************************************************
 * Declare and initialize structures                 *
 *****************************************************/

     struct controller *ctlr = noneinfo[ctlr_num];
     struct none_softc *sc = &none_softc[ctlr_num];

/* Code to perform the interrupt processing */

}


/*****************************************************
 *                ioctl Section                      *
 *                                                   *
 *                                                   *
 *-------------- noneioctl ---------------------*
 *                                                   *
 *                                                   *
 *                                                   *
 * The noneioctl interface obtains and clears the    *
 * count of bytes that was previously written by     *
 * nonewrite.  When a user program issues the        *
 * command to obtain the count, the /dev/none        *
 * driver returns the count through the data         *
 * pointer passed to the noneioctl interface.        *
 * When a user program asks to clear the count,      *
 * the /dev/none driver does so.                     *
 *****************************************************/

noneioctl(dev, cmd, data, flag)
dev_t dev;                /* Major/minor device number */
unsigned int cmd;         /* The ioctl command */
caddr_t data;             /* ioctl command-specified data */
int flag;                 /* Access mode of the device */

{
```

```
/*****************************************************
 * Perform the following initializations and        *
 * declarations:                                     *
 *   (1) Initialize unit to the minor device number  *
 *   (2) Declare a pointer to variable that stores    *
 *       the character count                         *
 *   (3) Initialize the pointer to the none_softc    *
 *       structure associated with this none device  *
 *****************************************************/

     int unit = minor(dev);

     int *res;

     struct none_softc *sc = &none_softc[unit];

/*****************************************************
 * For GETCOUNT operations, set the res variable     *
 * to point to the kernel memory allocated by the    *
 * ioctl system call.  The ioctl system call          *
 * copies the data to and from user address space.   *
 *****************************************************/

     res = (int *) data;

/*****************************************************
 * Save the count, if necessary.                     *
 *****************************************************/

     if(cmd == DN_GETCOUNT)
          *res = sc->sc_count;

/*****************************************************
 * Clear the count, if necessary.                    *
 *****************************************************/

     if(cmd == DN_CLRCOUNT)
          sc->sc_count = 0;

/*****************************************************
 * Success                                           *
 *****************************************************/

     return (0);
}
```

A.2 Source Listing for the /dev/cb Device Driver

```
/*****************************************************
 * cbreg.h   Header file for cb.c 17-Nov-1993       *
 *                                                   *
 *****************************************************/
/*****************************************************
 *                                                   *
 *            Copyright (c) 1994 by                  *
 *   Digital Equipment Corporation, Maynard, MA      *
 *              All rights reserved.                 *
 *                                                   *
 * This software is furnished under the terms and    *
 * conditions of the TURBOchannel Technology         *
 * license and may be used and copied only in        *
 * accordance with the terms of such license and     *
 * with the inclusion of the above copyright         *
 * notice.  No title to and ownership of the         *
 * software is hereby transferred.                   *
 *                                                   *
 * The information in this software is subject to    *
 * change without notice and should not be           *
 * construed as a commitment by Digital Equipment    *
 * Corporation.                                      *
 *                                                   *
 * Digital assumes no responsibility for the use     *
 * or reliability of its software on equipment       *
 * which is not supplied by Digital.                 *
 *****************************************************/


/*****************************************************
 *                                                   *
 * Define an offset of registers from base address   *
 * of option; a macro to convert register offset     *
 * to kernel virtual address; and a macro to         *
 * scramble physical address to TC DMA address.      *
 *****************************************************/


#define CB_REL_LOC 0x00040000
#define CB_ADR(n) ((io_handle_t)(n + CB_REL_LOC))
#define CB_SCRAMBLE(x) (((unsigned)x<<3)&~(0x1f))|(((unsigned)x>>29)&0x1f)


/*****************************************************
 * TURBOchannel test board CSR Enable and Status     *
 * bits                                              *
 *                                                   *
 *****************************************************/


#define CB_INTERUPT 0x0e00 /* Bits: 8 = 0; 9, 10 & 11 = 1 */
#define CB_CONFLICT 0x0d00 /* Bits: 9 = 0; 8, 10 & 11 = 1 */
#define CB_DMA_RD   0x0b00 /* Bits: 10 = 0; 8, 9 & 11 = 1 */
#define CB_DMA_WR   0x0700 /* Bits: 11 = 0; 8, 9 & 10 = 1 */
#define CB_DMA_DONE 0x0010 /* Use in timeout loop */


/*****************************************************
 * Define ioctl macros for the cb driver.            *
 *                                                   *
```

```
**********************************************/

#define CBPIO _IO('v',0) /* Set Read/Write mode to PIO */
#define CBDMA _IO('v',1) /* Set Read/Write mode to DMA */
#define CBINT _IO('v',2) /* Perform Interrupt test */

#define CBROM _IOWR('v',3,int) /* Return specified word */
#define CBCSR _IOR('v',4,int)  /* Update & return CSR word */

#define CBINC _IO('v',5) /* Start incrementing lights */
#define CBSTP _IO('v',6) /* Stop incrementing lights */


/****************************************************
 * Register offset definitions for a CB device.    *
 * The registers are aligned on longword (32-bit)   *
 * boundaries, even when they are implemented with  *
 * less than 32 bits.                               *
 *                                                  *
 ****************************************************/


#define CB_ADDER    0x0 /* 32-bit read/write DMA address register */
#define CB_DATA     0x4 /* 32-bit read/write data register */
#define CB_CSR      0x8 /* 16-bit read/write CSR/LED register */
#define CB_TEST     0xC /* Go bit: Write sets and Read Clears */

/****************************************************
 *                                                  *
 *          Copyright (c) 1994 by                   *
 *    Digital Equipment Corporation, Maynard, MA    *
 *             All rights reserved.                 *
 *                                                  *
 * This software is furnished under the terms and   *
 * conditions of the TURBOchannel Technology        *
 * license and may be used and copied only in       *
 * accordance with the terms of such license and    *
 * with the inclusion of the above copyright        *
 * notice.  No title to and ownership of the        *
 * software is hereby transferred.                  *
 *                                                  *
 * The information in this software is subject to   *
 * change without notice and should not be          *
 * construed as a commitment by Digital Equipment   *
 * Corporation.                                     *
 *                                                  *
 * Digital assumes no responsibility for the use    *
 * or reliability of its software on equipment      *
 * which is not supplied by Digital.                *
 ****************************************************/
/****************************************************
 *                                                  *
 * The /dev/cb device driver operates on a          *
 * TURBOchannel (TC) bus.  The device it controls   *
 * is called a TURBOchannel test board.  The        *
 * TURBOchannel test board is a minimal             *
 * implementation of all TURBOchannel hardware      *
 * functions:                                       *
 *                                                  *
 *    o Programmed I/O (PIO)                        *
 *    o Direct Memory Access (DMA) read             *
```

```
*       o DMA write                                      *
*       o Input/Output (I/O) read/write conflict         *
*         testing                                        *
*                                                        *
* The software view of the board consists of:            *
*                                                        *
*       o An EPROM address space                         *
*       o A 32-bit ADDRESS register with bits            *
*         scrambled for direct use as a TC               *
*         DMA address                                    *
*       o A 32-bit DATA register used for                *
*         programmed I/O and as the holding              *
*         register for DMA                               *
*       o A 16-bit Light Emitting Diode (LED)/           *
*         Control Status Register (CSR)                  *
*       o A 1-bit TEST register                          *
*                                                        *
* All registers MUST be accessed as 32-bit               *
* longwords, even when they are not implemented          *
* as 32 bits.  The CSR contains bits to enable           *
* option DMA read testing, conflict signal               *
* testing, I/O interrupt testing, and option             *
* DMA write testing.  It also contains a bit to          *
* indicate that one or more of the tests are             *
* enabled, 4-byte mask flag bits, and a DMA              *
* done bit.                                              *
**********************************************************/
/*********************************************************
* This example Digital UNIX driver provides a            *
* simple interface to the TURBOchannel test              *
* board.  It:                                            *
*                                                        *
*       (1) Reads from the data register on the          *
*           test board to words in system memory         *
*       (2) Writes to the data register on the test      *
*           board from words in system memory            *
*       (3) Tests the interrupt logic on the             *
*           test board                                   *
*       (4) Reads one 32-bit word from the test          *
*           board address (ROM/register) space into      *
*           system memory                                *
*       (5) Updates, reads, and returns the 32-bit       *
*           CSR value                                    *
*       (6) Starts and stops clock-driven                *
*           incrementing of the four spare LEDs on       *
*           the board.                                   *
*                                                        *
* ioctl calls are used to:                               *
*                                                        *
*       (1) Set the I/O mode to Programmed I/O           *
*           (the default)                                *
*       (2) Set the I/O mode to DMA I/O                  *
*       (3) Enable a single interrupt test               *
*       (4) Read one 32-bit word from the test           *
*           board address (ROM/register) space           *
*       (5) Start clock-driven incrementing of the       *
*           4 spare LEDs on the board or                 *
*       (6) Stop clock-driven incrementing of the 4      *
*           spare LEDs on the board.                     *
*                                                        *
```

```
 * Standard read and write calls are used to       *
 * perform the data register reads and writes.      *
 ***************************************************/

/***************************************************
 * Larry Robinson and Jim Crapuchettes, Digital    *
 * TRIADD Program.  Ported to Digital UNIX by Mark *
 * Parenti, Digital.  Made loadable on Digital UNIX*
 * by Tim Burke, Digital, and Jeff Anuszczyk,      *
 * formerly of Digital.                            *
 ***************************************************/

/***************************************************
 *              Include Files Section              *
 *                                                 *
 ***************************************************/

/***************************************************
 * Define a constant called NCB that is used to    *
 * allocate the data structures needed by the      *
 * /dev/cb driver.  Note that the define uses the  *
 * TC_OPTION_SLOTS constant, which is defined in    *
 * tc.h.  There can be at most three instances of   *
 * the CB controller on the system.  This is a     *
 * small number of instances of the device on the  *
 * system and the data structures themselves are    *
 * not large, so it is acceptable to allocate for   *
 * the maximum configuration.  This is an example  *
 * of the static allocation technique model 2.      *
 ***************************************************/


/***************************************************
 * The following include files assume that the     *
 * current directory is a subdirectory of          *
 * /usr/sys.                                        *

 ***************************************************/
#include <sys/param.h>
#include <kern/lock.h>
#include <sys/ioctl.h>
#include <sys/user.h>
#include <sys/proc.h>
#include <hal/cpuconf.h>
#include <io/common/handler.h>
#include <sys/vm.h>
#include <sys/buf.h>
#include <sys/errno.h>
#include <sys/conf.h>
#include <sys/file.h>
#include <sys/uio.h>
#include <sys/types.h>

#include <io/common/devdriver.h>
#include <sys/sysconfig.h>
#include <io/dec/tc/tc.h>

#include <io/ESB100/cbreg.h> /* Device register header file */

#define NCB TC_OPTION_SLOTS
```

```
/*******************************************************
 * Autoconfiguration Support Declarations and          *
 * Definitions Section                                 *
 *******************************************************/


extern   int hz; /* System clock ticks per second */


/*******************************************************
 * Do forward declaration of driver entry points       *
 * and define information structures for driver         *
 * structure definition and initialization below.       *
 *******************************************************/


int cbprobe(), cbattach(), cbintr(), cbopen(), cbclose();
int cbread(), cbwrite(), cbioctl(), cbstart(), cbminphys();
int cbincled(), cb_ctlr_unattach(), cbstrategy();


/*******************************************************
 * Declare an array of pointers to controller           *
 * structures                                           *
 *******************************************************/


struct controller *cbinfo[NCB];


/*******************************************************
 * Define and initialize the driver structure for       *
 * this driver.  It is used to connect the driver        *
 * entry points and other information to the             *
 * Digital UNIX code.  The driver structure is           *
 * used primarily during Autoconfiguration.  Note        *
 * that the "slave" and "go" entry points do not         *
 * exist in this driver and that a number of the         *
 * members of the structure are not used because         *
 * this is a driver that operates on the                 *
 * TURBOchannel bus (not on the VMEbus or some           *
 * other bus).                                           *
 *******************************************************/


struct   driver cbdriver = {
        cbprobe,                /* probe */
        0,                      /* slave */
        cbattach,               /* cattach */
        0,                      /* dattach */
        0,                      /* go */
        0,                      /* addr_list */
        0,                      /* dev_name */
        0,                      /* dev_list */
        "cb",                   /* ctlr_name */
        cbinfo,                 /* ctlr_list */
        0,                      /* xclu */
        0,                      /* addr1_size */
        0,                      /* addr1_atype */
        0,                      /* addr2_size */
        0,                      /* addr2_atype */
        cb_ctlr_unattach,       /* ctlr_unattach */
        0                       /* dev_unattach */
};
```

A–32 Device Driver Example Source Listings

```
/********************************************************
 * Loadable Driver Configuration Support               *
 * Declarations and Definitions Section                *
 *                                                     *
 ********************************************************/


/********************************************************
 * The following code is an example of the array of    *
 * cfg_subsys_attr_t data structures that the          *
 * /dev/cb driver passes to the cb_configure           *
 * interface.  The attributes for the array of         *
 * cfg_subsys_attr_t structures map to the following   *
 * stanza fields that you specify in the               *
 * stanza.loadable file fragment for the               *
 * /dev/cb driver:                                     *
 *                                                     *
 *   Subsystem_Description = cb device driver          *
 *   Module_Type = Dynamic                             *
 *   Module_Config_Name = cb                           *
 *   Module_Config1 = controller cb0 at tc*            *
 *   Device_Dir = /dev                                 *
 *   Device_Char_Major = Any                           *
 *   Device_Char_Minor = 0                             *
 *   Device_Char_Files = cb                            *
 *   Device_User = root                                *
 *   Device_Group = 0                                  *
 *   Device_Mode = 666                                 *
 *                                                     *
 * The attributes array holds driver-specific kernel   *
 * information relating to the configuring of a        *
 * loadable device driver.                             *
 *                                                     *
 * The /dev/cb device driver keeps information in the  *
 * attributes array that relates to the major device   *
 * information allocated during the loadable driver    *
 * configuration process.                              *
 *                                                     *
 * It is possible to create an attributes array that   *
 * completly mirrors the entries specified for the     *
 * stanza.loadable file fragment.  The attribute       *
 * array in a driver supercedes the stanza.loadable    *
 * file fragment when a user requests a query.         *
 * Variables not found in the cb_attributes array      *
 *  will be checked for in the sysconfigtab database.  *
 *                                                     *
 *                                                     *
 ********************************************************/

static int cmajnum = 0;
static int bmajnum = 0;
static int begunit = 0;
static int numunit = 0;
static int cbversion = 0;

static unsigned char mcfgname[CFG_ATTR_NAME_SZ] = "";
static unsigned char modtype[CFG_ATTR_NAME_SZ] = "";
```

```
static unsigned char devcmajor[CFG_ATTR_NAME_SZ] = "";

cfg_subsys_attr_t cb_attributes[] = {
{"Module_Config_Name", CFG_ATTR_STRTYPE, CFG_OP_CONFIGURE,
                    (caddr_t)mcfgname,2,CFG_ATTR_NAME_SZ,0},
{"Module_Type",            CFG_ATTR_STRTYPE, CFG_OP_CONFIGURE,
                    (caddr_t)modtype,2,CFG_ATTR_NAME_SZ,0},
{"Device_Char_Major",      CFG_ATTR_STRTYPE, CFG_OP_CONFIGURE,
                    (caddr_t)devcmajor,0,CFG_ATTR_NAME_SZ,0},
{"cmajnum",                CFG_ATTR_INTTYPE, CFG_OP_QUERY,
                    (caddr_t)&cmajnum,0,99,0},
{"bmajnum",                CFG_ATTR_INTTYPE, CFG_OP_QUERY,
                    (caddr_t)&bmajnum,0,99,0},
{"begunit",                CFG_ATTR_INTTYPE, CFG_OP_QUERY,
                    (caddr_t)&begunit,0,8,0},
{"numunit",                CFG_ATTR_INTTYPE, CFG_OP_QUERY,
                    (caddr_t)&numunit,0,8,0},
{"version",                CFG_ATTR_INTTYPE, CFG_OP_QUERY,
                    (caddr_t)&cbversion,0,9999999,0},
{"",0,0,0,0,0,0}
};


/*****************************************************
 * External function references.  These are needed  *
 * for the cdevsw declaration. The pointer to an     *
 * array of cb_id_t contains "id's" that the         *
 * interrupt handler interfaces use to deregister    *
 * the interrupt handlers.                           *
 *****************************************************/

extern int nodev(), nulldev();
ihandler_id_t *cb_id_t[NCB];

#define CB_BUSNAME      "tc" /* This is a TURBOchannel driver */


/*****************************************************
 * The variable cb_is_dynamic will be used to        *
 * control any differences in functions performed    *
 * by the static and loadable versions of the        *
 * driver.  In this manner any differences are       *
 * made on a run-time basis and not on a             *
 * compile-time basis.                               *
 *****************************************************/


int cb_is_dynamic = 0;


/*****************************************************
 * When the driver is loadable it may not have an    *
 * entry in the statically built tc_option           *
 * table (located in tc_option_data.c).  It is not   *
 * an error if this entry already existed in the     *
 * table.  The entry in tc_option_data.c is used     *
 * only when the driver is configured statically.    *
 * The entry below is used only when the driver is   *
 * configured dynamically.                           *
 *                                                   *
 * This table contains the bus-specific ROM module   *
 * name for the driver.  This information forms      *
```

```
 * the bus-specific parameter that is passed to    *
 * the ldbl_stanza_resolver interface to look for  *
 * matches in the tc_slot table.                   *
 ***************************************************/

struct tc_option cb_option_snippet [] =
{
    /*  module           driver  intr_b4 itr_aft        adpt    */
    /*  name             name    probe   attach  type   config  */
    /*  ------           ------  ------- ------- ----   ------  */
    {   "CB       ",     "cb",     0,       1,    'C',    0},
    {   "",              ""       } /* Null terminator in the table */
};
int num_cb = 0;    /* Count on the number of controllers probed */


/****************************************************
 * Local Structure and Variable Definitions        *
 * Section                                          *
 ***************************************************/

/****************************************************
 * Declare an array of buffer headers, 1 per        *
 * CB unit.                                         *
 ***************************************************/

struct buf cbbuf[NCB];
unsigned tmpbuffer; /* Temporary one-word buffer for cbstart */


/****************************************************
 * Structure declaration for a CB unit. It          *
 * contains status, pointers, and I/O mode for a    *
 * single CB device.                                *
 ***************************************************/

struct cb_unit { /* All items are "for this unit": */
    int  attached;       /* An attach was done */
    int  opened;         /* An open was done */
    int  iomode;         /* Read/write mode (PIO/DMA) */
    int  intrflag;       /* Flag for interrupt test */
    int  ledflag;        /* Flag for LED increment function */
    int  adapter;        /* TC slot number */
    caddr_t cbad;        /* ROM base address */
    io_handle_t cbr;   /* I/O handle for device registers */
    struct buf  *cbbuf; /* Buffer structure address */
} cb_unit[NCB];
#define MAX_XFR 4 /* Maximum transfer chunk in bytes */


/****************************************************
 * Loadable Driver Local Structure and Variable     *
 * Definitions Section                              *
 ***************************************************/


int cb_config = FALSE;  /* State flags indicating driver configured */
dev_t cb_devno = NODEV; /* No major number assigned yet. */
```

```
/******************************************************
 * Device switch structure for dynamic                *
 * configuration. The following is a definition of    *
 * the cdevsw entry that will be dynamically added    *
 * for the loadable driver.  For this reason the      *
 * loadable driver does not need to have its entry    *
 * points statically configured into conf.c.          *
 ******************************************************/

struct cdevsw cb_cdevsw_entry = {
        cbopen,                 /* d_open */
        cbclose,                /* d_close */
        cbread,                 /* d_read */
        cbwrite,                /* d_write */
        cbioctl,                /* d_ioctl */
        nodev,                  /* d_stop */
        nodev,                  /* d_reset */
        0,                      /* d_ttys */
        nodev,                  /* d_select */
        nodev,                  /* d_mmap */
        DEV_FUNNEL_NULL,        /* d_funnel */
        0,                      /* d_segmap */
        0                       /* d_flags */
};


/******************************************************
 * WARNING ON USE OF printf FOR DEBUGGING             *
 *                                                    *
 * Only a limited number of characters                *
 * (system-release dependent; currently, seems to     *
 * be 128) can be sent to the "console" display       *
 * during each call to any section of a driver.       *
 * This is because the characters are buffered        *
 * until the driver returns to the kernel, at         *
 * which time they are actually sent to the           *
 * "console."  If more than this number of            *
 * characters are sent to the "console," the          *
 * storage pointer may wrap around, discarding all    *
 * previous characters, or it may discard all         *
 * following characters! (Also system-release         *
 * dependent.)  Limit "console" output from within    *
 * the driver if you need to see the results in       *
 * the console window.  However, 'printf' from        *
 * within a driver also puts the messages into the    *
 * error log file.  The text can be viewed with       *
 * 'uerf.'  See the 'uerf' man page for more          *
 * information.  The "-o terse" option makes the      *
 * messages easier to read by removing the time       *
 * stamp information.                                 *
 *                                                    *
 * WARNING ON USE OF printf FOR DEBUGGING             *
 ******************************************************/

#define CB_DEBUG /* Define debug constants */
#undef CB_DEBUGx /* Disable xtra debug */
```

```
/******************************************************
 * Autoconfiguration Support Section                  *
 ******************************************************/
/******************************************************
 *                                                    *
 *                                                    *
 *-------------- cbprobe ----------------------*
 ******************************************************/

cbprobe(addr, ctlr)
io_handle_t addr;            /* I/O handle passed to cbprobe */
struct controller *ctlr;     /* controller structure for this unit */
{

/******************************************************
 *                                                    *
 * These data structures will be used to register     *
 * the interrupt handler for the loadable and         *
 * static driver.                                      *
 *                                                    *
 ******************************************************/


        ihandler_t handler;
        struct handler_intr_info info;
        int unit = ctlr->ctlr_num;

/******************************************************
 * Call printf during debug                           *
 ******************************************************/


/******************************************************
 *              DEBUG STATEMENT                        *
 ******************************************************/
#ifdef CB_DEBUG
printf("CBprobe @ %8x, addr = %8x, ctlr = %8x\n",cbprobe,addr,ctlr);
#endif /* CB_DEBUG */


/******************************************************
 * Dynamically register the interrupt handlers        *
 * for the static and loadable versions of the        *
 * /dev/cb device driver.                              *
 ******************************************************/


/******************************************************
 *   DEBUG STATEMENT                                   *
 ******************************************************/
#ifdef CB_DEBUG
printf("CBprobe: perform loadable driver config of unit %d\n",unit);
#endif /* CB_DEBUG */


/******************************************************
 * Specify the bus that this controller is            *
 * attached to.                                        *
 ******************************************************/
```

```
                handler.ih_bus = ctlr->bus_hd;

/*****************************************************
 * Set up the fields of the TC-specific bus info    *
 * structure and specify the controller number.     *
 *****************************************************/

                info.configuration_st = (caddr_t)ctlr;

/*****************************************************
 * Specifies the driver type as a controller.       *
 *****************************************************/

                info.config_type = CONTROLLER_CONFIG_TYPE;

/*****************************************************
 * Specifies the interrupt service interface (ISI). *
 *****************************************************/

                info.intr = cbintr;

/*****************************************************
 * This parameter will be passed to the ISI.        *
 *****************************************************/

                info.param = (caddr_t)unit;

/*****************************************************
 * The address of the bus-specific info structure.  *
 *****************************************************/

                handler.ih_bus_info = (char *)&info;

/*****************************************************
 * Save off the return id from handler_add.  This   *
 * id will be used later to deregister the           *
 * handler.                                          *
 *****************************************************/

                cb_id_t[unit] = handler_add(&handler);
                if (cb_id_t[unit] == NULL) {

/*****************************************************
 *                DEBUG STATEMENT                    *
 *****************************************************/
#ifdef CB_DEBUG
printf("CBprobe: handler_add failed.\n");
#endif /* CB_DEBUG */

                        return(0); /* Return failure status */
                }
                if (handler_enable(cb_id_t[unit]) != 0) {
                        handler_del(cb_id_t[unit]);
```

```
/******************************************************
 *                 DEBUG STATEMENT                    *
 ******************************************************/
#ifdef CB_DEBUG
printf("CBprobe: handler_enable failed.\n");
#endif /* CB_DEBUG */


                        return(0); /* Return failure status */
              }


/******************************************************
 * Increment the number of instances of this          *
 * controller.                                         *
 ******************************************************/

        num_cb++;


/******************************************************
 *                 DEBUG STATEMENT                    *
 ******************************************************/
#ifdef CB_DEBUG
printf("CBprobe: return success.\n");
#endif /* CB_DEBUG */


        return(1); /* Assume ok since TC ROM probe worked */
}




/******************************************************
 *-------------- cbattach ------------------------*
 ******************************************************/


cbattach(ctlr)
struct controller *ctlr; /* controller structure for this unit */
{
     struct cb_unit *cb; /* Pointer to unit data structure */
/******************************************************
 * Set up per-unit data structure for this device  *
 ******************************************************/
     cb = &cb_unit[ctlr->ctlr_num]; /* Point to this device's
                                    structure */
     cb->attached = 1; /* Indicate device is attached */
     cb->adapter = ctlr->slot; /* Set the adapter (slot) number */
     cb->cbad = ctlr->addr; /* Set base of device ROM */
     cb->cbr = (io_handle_t)CB_ADR(ctlr->addr); /* Point to device's
                                                registers */
     cb->cbbuf = &cbbuf[ctlr->ctlr_num]; /* Point to device's
                                        buffer header */
     cb->iomode = CBPIO; /* Start in PIO mode */
}
```

```
/******************************************************
 *------------ cb_ctlr_unattach -------------------*
 *                                                 *
 * Loadable driver-specific interface called       *
 * indirectly from the bus code when a driver is   *
 * being unloaded.                                 *
 *                                                 *
 * Returns 0 on success, nonzero (1) on error.     *
 ******************************************************/

int cb_ctlr_unattach(bus, ctlr)
    struct bus *bus;          /* Pointer to bus structure */
    struct controller *ctlr; /* Pointer to controller structure */
{

        register int unit = ctlr->ctlr_num;

/******************************************************
 * Validate the unit number.                       *
 ******************************************************/

        if ((unit > num_cb) || (unit < 0)) {
                return(1); /* Return error status */
        }

/******************************************************
 * This interface should never be called for a     *
 * static driver.  The reason is that the static   *
 * driver does not do a handler_add in the first   *
 * place.                                          *
 ******************************************************/

        if (cb_is_dynamic == 0) {
                return(1); /* Return error status */
        }

/******************************************************
 * The deregistration of interrupt handlers        *
 * consists of a call to handler_disable to        *
 * disable any further interrupts.  Then, call     *
 * handler_del to remove the ISI.                  *
 ******************************************************/

        if (handler_disable(cb_id_t[unit]) != 0) {
                return(1); /* Return error status */
        }
        if (handler_del(cb_id_t[unit]) != 0) {
                return(1); /* Return error status */
        }
        return(0); /* Return success status */
}
```

```
/*****************************************************
 * Loadable Device Driver Section                    *
 *****************************************************/
/*****************************************************
 *------------------ cb_configure -----------------*
 *****************************************************/
/*****************************************************
 * The cb_configure interface is called to           *
 * configure a loadable driver.  This interface      *
 * is also called to configure and unconfigure       *
 * the driver.  These operations are                 *
 * differentiated by the "op" parameter.             *
 *****************************************************/

cb_configure(op,indata,indatalen,outdata,outdatalen)
    cfg_op_t op;    /* Configure operation */
    cfg_attr_t *indata;  /* Input data structure, cfg_attr_t */
    size_t indatalen;    /* Size of input data structure */
    cfg_attr_t *outdata; /* Formal parameter not used */
    size_t outdatalen;   /* Formal parameter not used */
{
        dev_t    cdevno;
        int      retval;
        int      i;
        struct cb_unit *cb; /* Pointer to unit data structure */
        int cbincled();      /* Forward reference function */

/*****************************************************
 *                                                   *
 * MAX_DEVICE_CFG_ENTRIES represents the number of   *
 * config lines in the stanza.loadable file          *
 * fragment for this driver.                         *
 *                                                   *
 *****************************************************/

#define MAX_DEVICE_CFG_ENTRIES 18

/*****************************************************
 * The cfg_attr_t list passed into the               *
 * cb_configure interface's indata parameter         *
 * contains the strings that are stored in the       *
 * sysconfigtab database for this subsystem (the     *
 * /dev/cb device driver).                           *
 *****************************************************/

#ifdef CB_DEBUG
        cfg_attr_t cfg_buf[MAX_DEVICE_CFG_ENTRIES];
#endif


/*****************************************************
 *      Execute the directed Operation Code          *
 *           (Configure/Unconfigure)                 *
 *****************************************************/

        switch (op) {

/*****************************************************
```

```
*              Configure (load) the driver.                *
*                                                          *
*********************************************************/


              case CFG_OP_CONFIGURE:
/*********************************************************
*                DEBUG STATEMENT                         *
*********************************************************/
#ifdef CB_DEBUG
printf("cb_configure: CFG_OP_CONFIGURE.\n");
#endif /* CB_DEBUG */
#ifdef CB_DEBUG
/*********************************************************
*  Copy the data into a local cfg_attr_t                *
*  array.                                                *
*                                                        *
*********************************************************/


/*********************************************************
*       Pass Parameter Verification                     *
*                                                        *
* Parameters passed via the cb_attribute                *
* structure will not be known to be correct/valid       *
* their status in the indata list can be checked.       *
* A status other CFG_FRAME_SUCCESS is an error           *
* condition.                                            *
*********************************************************/

                bcopy(indata, cfg_buf[0].name,
                    indatalen*(sizeof(cfg_attr_t)));
                  printf(" The cb_configure routine was called.  op = %x\n",op);
                  for( i=0; i < indatalen; i++){
                      printf("%s: ",cfg_buf[i].name);
                      switch(cfg_buf[i].type){
                          case CFG_ATTR_STRTYPE:
                              printf("%s\n",cfg_buf[i].attr.str.val);
                              break;
                          default:
                            switch(cfg_buf[i].status){
                            case CFG_ATTR_EEXISTS:
                                printf("**Attribute does not exist\n");
                                break;
                            case CFG_ATTR_EOP:
                                printf("**Attribute does not support operation\n");
                                break;
                            case CFG_ATTR_ESUBSYS:
                                printf("**Subsystem Failure\n");
                                break;
                            case CFG_ATTR_ESMALL:
                                printf("**Attribute size/value too small\n");
                                break;
                            case CFG_ATTR_ELARGE:
                                printf("**Attribute size/value too large\n");
                                break;
                            case CFG_ATTR_ETYPE:
                                printf("**Attribute invalid type\n");
                                break;
                            case CFG_ATTR_EINDEX:
                                printf("**Attribute invalid index\n");
                                break;
```

```
                              case CFG_ATTR_EMEM:
                                 printf("**Attribute memory allocation error\n");
                                 break;
                              default:
                                 printf("**Unknown attribute: ");
                                 printf("%x\n", cfg_buf[i].status);
                                 break;
                                 }
                        break;
                        }
                 }
#endif


/****************************************************
 *           The configure interface could be      *
 *           called for either a static or loadable *
 *           driver.  For this reason it is not     *
 *           possible to conclude that the driver   *
 *           is being dynamically loaded merely     *
 *           because the configure interface has    *
 *           been entered.  To see if the driver    *
 *           is dynamically configured check the    *
 *           flags field.  If this is set, then     *
 *           set a driver global variable to        *
 *           indicate the driver is loaded.         *
 ****************************************************/

              if(strcmp(modtype,"Dynamic")==0) {
                 cb_is_dynamic = 1;
                 }
              if (cb_is_dynamic) {


/****************************************************
 *           Sanity check on the config name.       *
 *           If it is null the resolver and         *
 *           configure code won't know what to      *
 *           look for.                              *
 ****************************************************/

              if(strcmp(mcfgname,"")==0) {
                 printf("cb_configure, null config name.\n");
                 return(EINVAL);
                 }


/****************************************************
 *           Call the resolver to look for          *
 *           matches to the module's rom name       *
 *           in the tc_slot table.  This will       *
 *           add the controller data structure      *
 *           into the topology tree.                *
 ****************************************************/

              if (ldbl_stanza_resolver(mcfgname,
                  CB_BUSNAME, &cbdriver,
                  (caddr_t *)cb_option_snippet) != 0) {
```

```
                    return(EINVAL);
                    }


/*******************************************************
 *              Call the configuration code to         *
 *              cause the driver's probe interface     *
 *              to be called once for each instance    *
 *              of the controller found on the         *
 *              system.                                *
 *******************************************************/

                if (ldbl_ctlr_configure(CB_BUSNAME,
                    LDBL_WILDNUM, mcfgname,
                    &cbdriver, 0)) {
                    return(EINVAL);
                    }


/*******************************************************
 *              The above call should have called      *
 *              the driver's probe interface for       *
 *              each instance of the controller.       *
 *              If there were no controllers found     *
 *              then fail the driver configure          *
 *              operation.                             *
 *******************************************************/

                if (num_cb == 0) {

/*******************************************************
 *              DEBUG STATEMENT                        *
 *******************************************************/
#ifdef CB_DEBUG
printf("cb_configure: no controllers found.\n");
#endif /* CB_DEBUG */

                    return(EINVAL);
                    }
                }


/*******************************************************
 *              Perform the driver configuration       *
 *              above prior to getting the major       *
 *              number so that user-level programs do  *
 *              not have access to the driver's        *
 *              entry points in cdevsw prior to the    *
 *              completion of the topology and         *
 *              interrupt configuration.               *
 *                                                     *
 *              Register the driver's cdevsw entry     *
 *              points and obtain the major number.    *
 *******************************************************/

                if(strcmp(devcmajor,"")!=0) {
                        if((strcmp(devcmajor,"-1")==0) ||
                            (strcmp(devcmajor,"?")==0) ||
```

```
                          (strcmp(devcmajor,"any")==0) ||
                          (strcmp(devcmajor,"ANY")==0)){
                             cdevno = NODEV;
                          }
                   else {
                             cdevno = atoi(devcmajor);
                             cdevno = makedev(cdevno,0);
                          }
               }
          else
                   return EINVAL;

          cdevno = cdevsw_add(cdevno,&cb_cdevsw_entry);
          if (cdevno == NODEV) {

/***************************************************
 *                                               *
 *        The call to cdevsw_add could fail if   *
 *        the driver is requesting a specific    *
 *        major number and that number is        *
 *        currently in use, or if the cdevsw     *
 *        table is currently full.               *
 ***************************************************/

                   return(ENODEV);
          }

/***************************************************
 *                                               *
 *        Stash away the dev_t so that it can    *
 *        be used later to unconfigure the       *
 *        device.  Save off the minor number     *
 *        information.  This will be returned     *
 *        by the query call.                     *
 ***************************************************/

          cb_devno = cdevno;

/***************************************************
 *                                               *
 *        Set up the cb_attribute list with      *
 *        the cb-specific information that        *
 *        that can be queried.                   *
 *                                               *
 *        This member specifies the major        *
 *        number that was assigned to this       *
 *        driver.                                *
 ***************************************************/

          cmajnum = major(cb_devno);

/***************************************************
 *                                               *
 *        This member indicates that the         *
 *        beginning minor number will be         *
 *        zero (0).                              *
 ***************************************************/

          begunit = 0;
```

```
/*********************************************************
 *          Specifies the number of instances of *
 *          the controller that were located.    *
 *********************************************************/

          numunit = num_cb;


/*********************************************************
 *          This is a character driver.  For this *
 *          reason no block major number is       *
 *          assigned.                             *
 *********************************************************/

          bmajnum = NODEV;


/*********************************************************
 *          Set this state field to indicate that *
 *          the driver has successfully            *
 *          configured.                            *
 *********************************************************/

          cb_config = TRUE;
          break;



/*********************************************************
 * Unconfigure (unload) the driver.                      *
 *********************************************************/

          case CFG_OP_UNCONFIGURE:


/*********************************************************
 *          DEBUG STATEMENT                        *
 *********************************************************/
#ifdef CB_DEBUG
printf("cb_configure: CFG_OP_UNCONFIGURE.\n");
#endif /* CB_DEBUG */
/*********************************************************
 *          Fail the unconfiguration if the driver *
 *          is not currently configured.          *
 *********************************************************/

          if (cb_config != TRUE) {
                  return(EINVAL);
          }


/*********************************************************
 *          Do not allow the driver to be unloaded *
 *          if it is currently active.  To see if  *
 *          the driver is active look to see if any *
 *          users have the device open.            *
 *********************************************************/

          for (i = 0; i < num_cb; i++) {
```

```
                        if (cb_unit[i].opened != 0) {
                                return(EBUSY);
                        }
                }


/*****************************************************
 *        Turn off the LED increment function.      *
 *        This is needed to ensure that the driver  *
 *        is quiescent.  If this was not done, the   *
 *        cbincled interface could be called later  *
 *        after its interval timeout had expired.    *
 *        This could then try to execute an          *
 *        interface of this driver which had         *
 *        already been unloaded, resulting in a      *
 *        system panic.                              *
 *****************************************************/

                for (i = 0; i < num_cb; i++) {
                        cb = &cb_unit[i];
                        cb->ledflag = 0;
                        untimeout(cbincled, (caddr_t)cb);
                }


/*****************************************************
 *        Call cdevsw_del to remove the driver      *
 *        entry points from the in-memory resident  *
 *        cdevsw table.  This is done prior to       *
 *        deleting the loadable configuration        *
 *        and handlers to prevent users from         *
 *        accessing the device in the middle of      *
 *        deconfigure operation.                     *
 *****************************************************/

                        retval = cdevsw_del(cb_devno);
                        if (retval) {
                        return(ESRCH);
                        }


/*****************************************************
 *        Deregister the driver's configuration     *
 *        data structures from the hardware          *
 *        topology and cause the interrupt handlers *
 *        to be deleted.                             *
 *****************************************************/

                if (cb_is_dynamic) {


/*****************************************************
 *        The bus number is wildcarded to           *
 *        deregister on all instances of the tc      *
 *        bus.  The controller name and number is    *
 *        wildcarded.  This causes all instances     *
 *        that match the specified driver structure *
 *        to be deregistered.  Through the           *
 *        bus-specific code, this interface call     *
 *        will result in a call to the               *
```

```
*           cb_ctlr_unattach interface for each        *
*           instance of the controller.               *
********************************************************/

                    if (ldbl_ctlr_unconfigure(CB_BUSNAME,
                           LDBL_WILDNUM, &cbdriver,
                           LDBL_WILDNAME, LDBL_WILDNUM) != 0) {

/*******************************************************
*              DEBUG STATEMENT                      *
********************************************************/
#ifdef CB_DEBUG
printf("cb_configure:ldbl_ctlr_unconfigure failed.\n");
#endif /* CB_DEBUG */

                            return(ESRCH);
                    }
               }
               cb_config = FALSE;
               break;


/*******************************************************
*  Requests to query a loadable subsystem will      *
*  only succeed if the   CFG_OP_QUERY: entry        *
*  returns success.                                 *
********************************************************/

            case CFG_OP_QUERY:
              break;

            default: /* Unknown operation type */
              return(EINVAL);
              break;
       }

/*******************************************************
*      The driver's configure interface has         *
*      completed successfully.  Return a success    *
*      status.                                      *
********************************************************/


       return(0);
}


/*******************************************************
* Open and Close Device Section                     *
********************************************************/
/*******************************************************
*-------------- cbopen --------------------*
********************************************************/

cbopen(dev, flag, format)
dev_t dev;   /* Major/minor device number */
int flag;    /* Flags from /usr/sys/h/file.h */
```

```
int format;  /* Format of special device */
{
/******************************************************
 *         Get device (unit) number                  *
 ******************************************************/
        int unit = minor(dev);
/******************************************************
 *       Error if unit number too big or if unit     *
 *       not attached                                *
 ******************************************************/
        if ((unit > NCB) || !cb_unit[unit].attached)
                return(ENXIO);
        cb_unit[unit].opened = 1; /* All ok, indicate device opened */
        return(0);                /* Return success! */
}



/******************************************************
 *---------------- cbclose ------------------------*
 ******************************************************/


cbclose(dev, flag, format)
dev_t dev;  /* Major/minor device number */
int flag;   /* Flags from /usr/sys/h/file.h */
int format; /* Format of special device */
{
        int unit = minor(dev);    /* Get device (unit) number */
        cb_unit[unit].opened = 0; /* Indicate device closed */
        return(0);                /* Return success! */
}


/******************************************************
 * Read and Write Device Section                     *
 ******************************************************/
/******************************************************
 *---------------- cbread -------------------------*
 ******************************************************/


cbread(dev, uio, flag)
dev_t dev;        /* Major/minor device numbers */
struct uio *uio; /* I/O descriptor structure */
int flag; /* Access mode of device */
{
        unsigned tmp;
        int cnt, err;
        int unit = minor(dev); /* Get device (unit) number */
        struct cb_unit *cb;    /* Pointer to unit data structure */


/******************************************************
 * To do the read, the device index (unit number)   *
 * is used to select the TC test board to be         *
 * accessed and the mode setting within the          *
 * controller structure for that unit is tested      *
 * to determine whether to do a programmed read or   *
 * a DMA read.  For a programmed read, the           *
 * contents of the data register on the test board   *
 * are read into a 32-bit local variable and then    *
```

```
* the contents of that variable are moved into      *
* the buffer in the user's virtual address space    *
* with the uiomove interface.                        *
*                                                    *
* For a DMA read, the system's physio interface      *
* and the driver's strategy and minphys              *
* interfaces are used to transfer the contents of  *
* the data register on the test board into the      *
* buffer in the user's virtual address space.        *
*                                                    *
* Note that since only a single word of 4            *
* (the constant MAX_XFR) bytes can be transferred *
* at a time, both modes of reading include code      *
* to limit the read to chunks with a maximum of      *
* MAX_XFR bytes each and that reading more than      *
* MAX_XFR bytes will propagate the contents of      *
* the data register throughout the words of the      *
* user's buffer.                                     *
*****************************************************/

        err = 0;                    /* Initialize for no error (yet) */
        cb = &cb_unit[unit];        /* Set pointer to unit's structure */
        if(cb->iomode == CBPIO) { /* Programmed I/O read code */


/*****************************************************
* Transfer bytes from the test board data            *
* register to the user's buffer until all            *
* requested bytes are moved or an error occurs.      *
* This must be done as a loop because the source    *
* (the board data register) can supply only          *
* MAX_XFR bytes at a time.  The loop may not be      *
* required for other devices.                        *
*****************************************************/

            while((cnt = uio->uio_resid) && (err == 0)) {


/*****************************************************
* Force count for THIS "section" to be less than    *
* or equal to MAX_XFR bytes (the size of the data  *
* buffer on the test board).  This causes a read   *
* of more than MAX_XFR bytes to be chopped up      *
* into a number MAX_XFR-byte transfers with a      *
* final transfer of MAX_XFR bytes or less.          *
*****************************************************/

                if(cnt > MAX_XFR)cnt = MAX_XFR;
                tmp = read_io_port(cb->cbr | CB_DATA,
                                   4,
                                   0);/* Read data */
                                      /* register */


/*****************************************************
* Move bytes read from the data register to the      *
* user's buffer. Note that:                          *
*                                                    *
*       (1) The maximum number of bytes moved is    *
*           MAX_XFR for each call due to the code    *
```

```
*        above.                                    *
*    (2) The uio structure is updated as each     *
*        move is done.                            *
*                                                  *
* Thus, uio->uio_resid will be updated for the    *
* "while" statement above.                        *
***************************************************/

                        err = uiomove(&tmp,cnt,uio);
                        }
                return(err);
                }
        else if(cb->iomode == CBDMA) /* DMA I/O read code */

/***************************************************
* Transfer bytes from the test board data         *
* register to the user's buffer until all         *
* requested bytes are moved or an error occurs.   *
* The driver's strategy and minphys interfaces    *
* account for the fact that the source (the board *
* data register) can supply only 4 bytes at a     *
* time and the physio interface loops as required *
* to transfer all requested bytes.                *
***************************************************/

        return(physio(cbstrategy,cb->cbbuf,dev,
                      B_READ,cbminphys,uio));
}


/***************************************************
*--------------- cbwrite ----------------------*
***************************************************/


cbwrite(dev, uio, flag)
dev_t dev;         /* Major/minor device numbers */
struct uio *uio;   /* I/O descriptor structure */
int flag; /* Access mode of device */
{
        unsigned tmp;
        int cnt, err;
        int unit = minor(dev); /* Get device (unit) number */
        struct cb_unit *cb;    /* Pointer to unit data structure */

/***************************************************
* To do the write, the device index (unit number) *
* is used  to select the TC test board to be      *
* accessed and the mode setting within the        *
* controller structure for that unit is tested to *
* determine whether to do a programmed write or a *
* DMA write.                                       *
*                                                  *
* For a programmed write, the contents of one     *
* word from the buffer in the user's virtual      *
* address space are moved to a 32-bit local       *
* variable with the uiomove interface and the     *
* contents of that variable are moved to the data *
```

```
* register on the test board.                          *
*                                                        *
* For a DMA write, the  system's physio interface *
* and the driver's strategy and minphys           *
* interfaces are used to transfer the contents of *
* the buffer in the user's virtual address space  *
* to the data register on the test board.          *
*                                                        *
* Note that since only a single word of 4          *
* (MAX_XFR) bytes can be transferred at a time,   *
* both modes of reading include code to limit the *
* write to chunks with a maximum of MAX_XFR        *
* bytes.  Note that writing more than MAX_XFR      *
* bytes has limited usefulness since all the       *
* words of the user's buffer will be written into *
* the single data register on the test board.      *
************************************************/

        err = 0;                    /* Initialize for no error (yet) */
        cb = &cb_unit[unit];        /* Set pointer to unit's structure */
        if(cb->iomode == CBPIO) { /* Programmed I/O write code */


/*****************************************************
* Transfer bytes from the user's buffer to the    *
* test board data register until all requested    *
* bytes are moved or an error occurs.  This must  *
* be done as a loop because the destination        *
* (the board data register) can accept only 4     *
* bytes at a time.  The loop may not be required  *
* for other devices.                               *
*****************************************************/

            while((cnt = uio->uio_resid) && (err == 0)) {
                    if(cnt > MAX_XFR)cnt = MAX_XFR; /* Copy data
                                                      register */


/*****************************************************
* Move bytes to write from the user's buffer to   *
* the local variable. Note that:                   *
*                                                    *
*   (1) The maximum number of bytes moved is      *
*        MAX_XFR for each call due to the above    *
*        code.                                       *
*   (2) The uio structure is updated as each move *
*        is done.  Thus, uio->uio_resid will be   *
*        updated for the above "while" statement.  *
*****************************************************/

                    err = uiomove(&tmp,cnt,uio);
                    write_io_port(cb->cbr | CB_DATA,
                                    4,
                                    0,
                                    tmp); /* Write data
                                            to register */
            }
        return(err);
        }
```

```
          else if(cb->iomode == CBDMA) /* DMA I/O write code */


/****************************************************
 * Transfer bytes from the user's buffer to the    *
 * test board data register until all requested    *
 * bytes are moved or an error occurs.  The        *
 * driver's strategy and minphys interfaces        *
 * account for the fact that the destination       *
 * (the board data register) can take only MAX_XFR *
 * bytes at a time and the physio interface loops  *
 * as required to transfer all requested bytes.    *
 ****************************************************/

            return(physio(cbstrategy,cb->cbbuf,dev,
                          B_WRITE,cbminphys,uio));
}



/****************************************************
 *               Strategy  Section                 *
 ****************************************************/
/****************************************************
 *--------------- cbminphys ---------------------*
 ****************************************************/


cbminphys(bp)
register struct buf *bp; /* Pointer to buf structure */
{
        if (bp->b_bcount > MAX_XFR)
                bp->b_bcount = MAX_XFR; /* Maximum transfer
                                         is 4 bytes */
        return;
}



/****************************************************
 *--------------- cbstrategy ---------------------*
 ****************************************************/


cbstrategy(bp)
register struct buf *bp; /* Pointer to buf structure */
{
        register int unit = minor(bp->b_dev); /* Get device
                                         (unit) number */

        register struct controller *ctlr; /* Pointer to
                                         controller struct */
        struct cb_unit *cb;     /* Pointer to unit data structure */
        caddr_t buff_addr;      /* User buffer's virtual address */
        caddr_t virt_addr;      /* User buffer's virtual address */
        unsigned phys_addr;     /* User buffer's physical address */
        int cmd;                /* Current command for test board */
        int err;                /* Error status from uiomove */
        int status;             /* CSR contents for status checking */
        unsigned lowbits;       /* Low 2 virtual address bits */
        unsigned tmp;           /* Temporary holding variable */
        int s;                  /* Temporary holding variable */
```

```
#ifdef CB_DEBUG
        char *vtype;      /* String pointer for debug */
#endif /* CB_DEBUG */


        ctlr = cbinfo[unit]; /* Set pointer to unit's structure */


/*****************************************************
 * The buffer is accessible, initialize buffer      *
 * structure for transfer.                          *
 *****************************************************/

        bp->b_resid = bp->b_bcount; /* Initialize bytes not xferred */
        bp->av_forw = 0;            /* Clear buffer queue forward link */

        cb = &cb_unit[unit];        /* Set pointer to unit's structure */

        virt_addr = bp->b_un.b_addr; /* Get buffer's virtual address */
        buff_addr = virt_addr;       /* and copy it for internal use */


/*****************************************************
 *                DEBUG STATEMENT                   *
 *****************************************************/
#ifdef CB_DEBUG
printf("\n"); /* Line between */
              /* cbstrategy calls */
#endif /* CB_DEBUG */


/*****************************************************
 *                    NOTE                          *
 *****************************************************/
 * TURBOchannel DMA can ONLY be done with FULL      *
 * WORDS and MUST be aligned on WORD boundaries!    *
 * Since the user's buffer can be aligned on any    *
 * byte boundary, the driver code MUST check for    *
 * and handle the cases where the buffer is NOT     *
 * word aligned (unless, of course, the            *
 * TURBOchannel interface hardware includes        *
 * special hardware to handle non-word-aligned     *
 * transfers.  The test board does NOT have any    *
 * such hardware).  If the user's buffer is NOT    *
 * word-aligned, the driver can:                   *
 *                                                  *
 *    (1) Exit with an error or                     *
 *    (2) Take some action to word-align the        *
 *        transfer.                                 *
 *                                                  *
 * Since virtual to physical mapping is done on a   *
 * page basis, the low 2 bits of the virtual        *
 * address of the user's buffer are also the low 2  *
 * bits of the physical address of the user's       *
 * buffer and the buffer alignment can be           *
 * determined by examining the low 2 bits of the    *
 * virtual buffer address.  If these 2 bits are     *
 * nonzero, the buffer is not word-aligned and the  *
 * driver must take the desired action.             *
 *****************************************************/
```

```
/*******************************************************
 * Use the low-order 2 bits of the buffer virtual      *
 * address as the word-aligned indicator for this      *
 * transfer.  If they are nonzero, the user's          *
 * buffer is not word-aligned and an internal          *
 * buffer must be used, so replace the current         *
 * user buffer virtual address (it is updated by       *
 * physio as each word is transferred) with the        *
 * internal buffer virtual address.  Since DMA to      *
 * the board can only be done a word at a time,        *
 * the internal buffer only needs to be a single       *
 * word.                                               *
 *******************************************************/

        if ((lowbits = (unsigned)virt_addr & 3) != 0) { /* Test low
                                                           2 bits */
                virt_addr = (caddr_t)(&tmpbuffer);  /* Use internal
                                                           buffer */


/*******************************************************
 *               DEBUG STATEMENT                       *
 *******************************************************/
#ifdef CB_DEBUG
printf("Bd %8x (%d)\n",buff_addr,bp->b_resid);
#endif /* CB_DEBUG */



/*******************************************************
 * If the transfer type is a "write"                   *
 * (program => device), then clear the local           *
 * one-word temporary buffer (in case less             *
 * than 4 bytes), move the user's data bytes to        *
 * the local temporary buffer, and return error        *
 * status if an error occurs.  The DMA "write"         *
 * will be done from the temporary buffer.             *
 *                                                     *
 *                  NOTE                               *
 *******************************************************
 * Don't use  B_WRITE to test for a write.  It is      *
 * defined as 0 (zero).  You MUST use the              *
 * complement of test for B_READ!                      *
 *******************************************************/

        if ( !(bp->b_flags&B_READ) ) { /* Move now for "write" */
                tmpbuffer = 0 ;        /* Clear the whole word */


/*******************************************************
 *               DEBUG STATEMENT                       *
 *******************************************************/
#ifdef CB_DEBUG
printf("Ci\n");
#endif /* CB_DEBUG */
```

```
                              if (err = copyin(buff_addr,virt_addr,
                                       bp->b_resid)) {
                                   bp->b_error = err;      /* See cbwrite */
                                   bp->b_flags |= B_ERROR; /* error code */
                                   iodone(bp);             /* Signal
                                                             I/O done */
                                   return;                 /* Return
                                                             error */
                              }
                         }
                  }


/******************************************************
 * Convert the buffer virtual address to a            *
 * physical address for DMA by calling the vtop       *
 * interface.                                         *
 ******************************************************/

    phys_addr = vtop(bp->b_proc, virt_addr);


/******************************************************
 * Convert the 32-bit physical address (actually      *
 * the low 32 bits of the 34-bit physical address)    *
 * from the linear form to the condensed form         *
 * used by DMA to pack 34 address bits onto 32        *
 * board lines.                                       *
 *                                                    *
 ******************************************************/
/******************************************************
 *                 WARNING NOTE                       *
 ******************************************************
 *                                                    *
 * TURBOchannel DMA can ONLY be done with FULL        *
 * WORDS and MUST be aligned on WORD boundaries!      *
 * The CB_SCRAMBLE macro DISCARDS the low-order       *
 * 2 bits of the physical address while scrambling    *
 * the rest of the address! Therefore, anything       *
 * that is going to be done to resolve this issue     *
 * must be done BEFORE CB_SCRAMBLE is used.           *
 ******************************************************/

        tmp = CB_SCRAMBLE(phys_addr);
        write_io_port(cb->cbr | CB_ADDER,
                      4,
                      0,
                      tmp);


/******************************************************
 *                 DEBUG STATEMENT                    *
 ******************************************************/
#ifdef CB_DEBUG
printf("%s %8x= %4s\n",vtype,virt_addr,virt_addr);
printf("ph %8x sc %8x Pr %8x\n",phys_addr,tmp,bp->b_proc);
#endif /* CB_DEBUG */
```

```
        if(bp->b_flags&B_READ)      /* Set up the DMA enable bits: */
                cmd = CB_DMA_WR;     /* Read = "Write to memory" */
        else
                cmd = CB_DMA_RD;     /* Write = "Read from memory" */
        s = splbio();               /* Raise priority */


/****************************************************
 * Although not required in this driver since it   *
 * is only called from the following line, the     *
 * "start I/O" interface is called as a function   *
 * to separate its functionality from the strategy *
 * interface.  This is the typical form it will    *
 * have in other drivers.                          *
 ****************************************************/

        err = cbstart(cmd,cb);      /* Start I/O operation */
        splx(s);                    /* Restore priority */


/****************************************************
 * If the cbstart "timed out" ("err" count not     *
 * positive), return error.  If the loop did not   *
 * "time out," set the bytes remaining to zero (0) *
 * to return with success.                         *
 ****************************************************/

        if(err <= 0) { /* Check return value from cbstart */


/****************************************************
 *              DEBUG STATEMENT                     *
 ****************************************************/
#ifdef CB_DEBUG
printf("err %2d CSR %4x\n",err,
       (read_io_port(cb->cbr | CB_CSR, 4, 0))&0xffff);
#endif /* CB_DEBUG */

                bp->b_error = EIO;      /* Set "I/O error
                                           on device" */
                bp->b_flags |= B_ERROR; /* return access
                                           & error flag */
                iodone(bp);             /* Signal I/O done */
                return;                 /* Return with error. */
                }
        else {


/****************************************************
 *              DEBUG STATEMENT                     *
 ****************************************************/
#ifdef CB_DEBUG
                tmp = read_io_port(cb->cbr | CB_DATA, /* Get data */
                                   4,             /* register */
                                   0);            /* to display */
                status = read_io_port(cb->cbr |  CB_CSR, /* Get */
                                      4,              /* status */
                                      0);             /* from */
                                                      /* CSR */
```

```
                  printf("%2d CSR %4x d %8x= %4s\n",err,
                          status&0xffff,tmp,&tmp);
#endif /* CB_DEBUG */


/*****************************************************
 * Did not time out: DMA transfer worked. Test the  *
 * low-order 2 bits of the buffer virtual address   *
 * and the transfer mode gain.  If the low 2 bits   *
 * are nonzero, then the user's buffer was not      *
 * word-aligned and the internal buffer was used.   *
 * If the tranfer type is a "read"                  *
 * (device => program), then move the user's data   *
 * from the local one-word temporary buffer and     *
 * return error status if an error occurs.  The     *
 * DMA "read" has been done into the temporary      *
 * buffer.                                          *
 *****************************************************/

            if ( (lowbits)!=0 && bp->b_flags&B_READ) { /* Move if
                                                          "read" */


/*****************************************************
 *              DEBUG STATEMENT                      *
 *****************************************************/
#ifdef CB_DEBUG
                      printf("Co\n");
#endif /* CB_DEBUG */

                 if (err = copyout(virt_addr,buff_addr,
                                  bp->b_resid)) {
                         bp->b_error = err;       /* See cbread */
                         bp->b_flags |= B_ERROR;  /* error code */
                 }
            }
            bp->b_resid = 0;   /* DMA complete, clear remainder */
       }
    iodone(bp);                     /* Indicate done on this buffer */
    return;
}



/*****************************************************
 *                Start  Section                     *
 *****************************************************/
/*****************************************************
 *--------------- cbstart ----------------------*
 *                                                  *
 * NOTE on CSR usage: cbstart, cbioctl, and         *
 * cbincled are the only interfaces that load the   *
 * CSR register of the board.  Since cbincled       *
 * increments the LEDs in the high 4 bits of the    *
 * 16-bit CSR register, cbstart and cbioctl always  *
 * load the 4 bits into whatever value they will    *
 * be storing into the CSR before they do the       *
 * actual store.  Note also that cbstart is called  *
```

```
* with system interrupts disabled, so cbincled    *
* should not be called while cbstart is           *
* incrementing.                                    *
****************************************************/


int cbstart(cmd,cb)
int cmd;                /* Current command for test board */
struct cb_unit *cb;    /* Pointer to unit data structure */
{
        int timecnt; /* Timeout loop count */
        int status;  /* CSR contents for status checking */


/****************************************************
 *              DEBUG STATEMENT                     *
 ****************************************************/
#ifdef CB_DEBUGx
        printf("\n"); /* Blank line */
                      /* between cbstart */
                      /* calls */
#endif CB_DEBUGx


        cmd = (read_io_port(cb->cbr | CB_CSR,
                            4,
                            0)&0xf000)|(cmd&0xfff); /* High 4 LED bits */
                                                    /* into cmd */
        status = read_io_port(cb->cbr | CB_TEST,
                              4,
                              0); /* Read "test" reg to */
                                  /* clear "go" bit */

        write_io_port(cb->cbr | CB_CSR,
                      4,
                      0,
                      cmd); /* Load CSR with enable bit(s) */
        mb();             /* Synchronize with CSR write */


/****************************************************
 *              DEBUG STATEMENT                     *
 ****************************************************/
#ifdef CB_DEBUGx
        printf("Chk CSR %4x\n",(read_io_port(cb->cbr | CB_CSR,
                                             4,
                                             0))&0xffff);
#endif CB_DEBUGx


        write_io_port(cb->cbr | CB_TEST,
                      4,
                      0,
                      0); /* Write "test" reg */
                          /* to set "go" bit */
        mb();                   /* Synchronize with test */
                                    reg write */
        timecnt = 10;               /* Initialize timeout */
                                    loop counter */
        status = read_io_port(cb->cbr | CB_CSR,
                              4,
                              0); /* Get status from CSR */
```

```
/*********************************************************
*               DEBUG STATEMENT                         *
*********************************************************/
#ifdef CB_DEBUG
        printf("%2d CSR %4x\n",timecnt,
                (read_io_port(cb->cbr | CB_CSR, 4, 0))&0xffff);
#endif /* CB_DEBUG */




/*********************************************************
* Wait for DMA done bit set or timeout loop             *
* counter to expire.  This driver has a very            *
* short timeout period because the board                *
* should respond within a few machine cycles if         *
* it is not broken.  Thus, the simple timeout           *
* loop below takes less time than calling a             *
* system interface.  In most drivers, where             *
* timeout periods are greater than a few cycles,        *
* timeout is done using the sleep, wakeup,              *
* timeout, and untimeout kernel interfaces.  See        *
* the CBINC (increment LED) code in cbioctl and         *
* cbincled below for an example of using timeout        *
* for repetitive timing.                                *
*********************************************************/

        while((!(status & CB_DMA_DONE)) && timecnt > 0) {
                write_io_port(cb->cbr | CB_CSR,
                              4,
                              0,
                              cmd); /* Write to */
                                    /* update status */
                mb();               /* Synchronize with
                                          CSR write */
                status = read_io_port(cb->cbr | CB_CSR,
                                      4,
                                      0); /* Get status from CSR again */
                timecnt --;             /* Decrement counter */
                }


/*********************************************************
* Return "timeout" count as function result.            *
*********************************************************/

        return(timecnt);
}


/*********************************************************
*               ioctl Section                           *
*********************************************************/
/*********************************************************
*--------------- cbioctl ---------------------*
*********************************************************/


/*********************************************************
* See NOTE on CSR usage at beginning of cbstart.        *
*********************************************************/
```

```
#define CBIncSec  1   /* Number of seconds between
                          increments of lights */
cbioctl(dev, cmd, data, flag)
dev_t dev;              /* Major/minor device number */
unsigned int cmd;       /* The ioctl command */
int *data;              /* ioctl command-specified data */
int flag;               /* Access mode of the device */
{
        int tmp;                 /* A destination word for throw-aways */
        int *addr;               /* Pointer for word access to board */
        int timecnt;             /* Timeout loop count */
        int unit = minor(dev);   /* Get device (unit) number */
        struct cb_unit *cb;      /* Pointer to unit data structure */
        int cbincled();          /* Forward reference interface */

        cb = &cb_unit[unit];     /* Set pointer to unit's structure */


        switch(cmd&0xFF) {        /* Determine operation to do: */
              case CBINC&0xFF:          /* Start incrementing lights */

/*****************************************************
 *            DEBUG STATEMENT                        *
 *****************************************************/
#ifdef CB_DEBUG
printf("\nCBioctl: CBINC ledflag = %d\n",cb->ledflag);
#endif /* CB_DEBUG */

                   if(cb->ledflag == 0) {  /* If not started, */
                        cb->ledflag++;  /* Set flag & start timer */
                        timeout(cbincled, (caddr_t)cb, CBIncSec*hz);
                   }
                   break;

              case CBPIO&0xFF: /* Set mode: programmed I/O */
                   cb->iomode = CBPIO; /* Just set I/O
                                           mode for unit */
                   break;
              case CBDMA&0xFF: /* Set mode: DMA I/O */
                   cb->iomode = CBDMA; /* Just set I/O
                                           mode for unit */
                   break;

            case CBINT&0xFF: /* Do interrupt test */
                 timecnt = 10; /* Initialize timeout
                                   counter */
                 cb->intrflag = 0; /* Clear interrupt flag */
                 tmp = read_io_port(cb->cbr | CB_TEST,
                                    4,
                                    0); /* Clear "go" bit */
                 tmp = CB_INTERUPT|(read_io_port(cb->cbr | CB_CSR,
                                    4,
                                    0)&0xf000); /* New value */
                 write_io_port(cb->cbr | CB_CSR,
                               4,
                               0,
                               tmp); /* Load enables & LEDs */
                   mb();                /* Synch. with CSR write */
```

```
                write_io_port(cb->cbr | CB_TEST,
                              4,
                              0,
                              1); /* Set the "go" bit */
                mb();              /* Synch. with test write */
/*********************************************************
 *              Wait for interrupt flag     *
 *              to set or timeout loop      *
 *              counter to expire.          *
 *              Call write_io_port to       *
 *              update status. Call wbflush *
 *              to synchronize with CSR     *
 *              write.  Then decrement the  *
 *              counter.                    *
 *********************************************************/
                while ((cb->intrflag == 0) && (timecnt > 0)) {
                        write_io_port(cb->cbr | CB_CSR,
                                      4,
                                      0,
                                      tmp);
                        mb();
                        timecnt --;
                }
                tmp = read_io_port(cb->cbr | CB_TEST,
                                   4,
                                   0); /* Be sure "go"
                                         is clear */


/*********************************************************
 *          DEBUG STATEMENT                      *
 *********************************************************/
#ifdef CB_DEBUG
                printf("\nCBioctl: CBINT timecnt = %d\n",timecnt);
#endif /* CB_DEBUG */


                return(timecnt == 0);    /* Success if
                                            nonzero count */

        case CBROM&0xFF:              /* Return a ROM word */
                tmp = *data;          /* Get specified byte offset */
                if(tmp < 0 || tmp >= 32768*4+4*4) /* 32k wrds
                                                     + 4 regs */
                        return(-tmp);  /* Offset is out of range */
                tmp <<= 1; /* Double address offset */
                addr = (int *)&(cb->cbad[tmp]); /* Get byte
                                                   address */
                *data = *addr;        /* Return word from board */
                break;
        case CBCSR&0xFF: /* Update and return CSR */
                write_io_port(cb->cbr | CB_CSR,
                              4,
                              0,
                              read_io_port(cb->cbr | CB_CSR,
                                           4,
                                           0)); /* Read/write
                                                   to update */
                mb();                 /* Synch. with
```

```
                                              CSR write */
                   *data = read_io_port(cb->cbr | CB_CSR,
                                        4,
                                        0); /* Return CSR
                                              from board */
                   break;
            case CBSTP&0xFF: /* Stop incrementing lights */

/*****************************************************
 *               DEBUG STATEMENT                     *
 *****************************************************/
#ifdef CB_DEBUG
                        printf("\nCBioctl: CBSTP called\n");
#endif /* CB_DEBUG */

                   cb->ledflag = 0;         /* Stop on next timeout */
                   break;
            default: /* Default is error case */
                   return(EINVAL);
            }
      return(0);
}


/*****************************************************
 *                Increment LED  Section             *
 *****************************************************/
/*****************************************************
 *                                                   *
 *--------------- cbincled ----------------------*
 *****************************************************/



/*****************************************************
 * This interface is called by the system           *
 * softclock interface CBIncSec seconds after the    *
 * last call to the timeout interface.  If the       *
 * increment flag is still set, increment the        *
 * pattern in the high 4 LEDs of the LED/CSR         *
 * register and restart the timeout to recall        *
 * later.                                            *
 *                                                   *
 *               NOTE                                *
 *****************************************************
 * Because the LEDs are on when a bit is 0, use a    *
 * subtract to do the increment.                     *
 *                                                   *
 * Also, see NOTE on CSR usage at the                *
 * beginning of cbstart.                             *
 *****************************************************/


cbincled(cb)
struct cb_unit *cb; /* Pointer to unit data structure */
{
            int tmp;

            tmp = read_io_port(cb->cbr | CB_CSR,
                               4,
```

```
                                         0);
                                         tmp -= 0x1000;
                        write_io_port(cb->cbr | CB_CSR,
                                      4,
                                      0,
                                      tmp); /* "Increment" lights */
      if(cb->ledflag != 0) {    /* If still set, */
              timeout(cbincled, (caddr_t)cb, CBIncSec*hz); /* restart
                                                              timer */
              }
      return;
}


/********************************************************
 *        Device Interrupt Handler Section             *
 ********************************************************/
/********************************************************
 *--------------- cbintr -----------------------*
 ********************************************************/


cbintr(ctlr)
int ctlr; /* Index for controller structure */
{
        int tmp;
        struct cb_unit *cb;    /* Pointer to unit data structure */
        cb = &cb_unit[ctlr];   /* Point to this device's structure */
        tmp = read_io_port(cb->cbr | CB_TEST,
                           4,
                           0); /* Read test reg to clear "go" bit */
        cb->intrflag++;        /* Set flag to tell it happened */


/********************************************************
 *              DEBUG STATEMENT                         *
 ********************************************************/
#ifdef CB_DEBUG
printf("\nCBintr interrupt, ctlr = %d\n",ctlr); /* Show interrupt */
#endif /* CB_DEBUG */


        return;
}
```

Device Driver Development
Worksheets

B

This appendix provides worksheets that you can use to help you gather information about designing, coding, installing, and testing a device driver. Chapter 2 explains how to fill out these worksheets. You may make copies of these worksheets.

HOST SYSTEM WORKSHEET

Specify the Host CPU

Alpha–based CPUs:

DEC 3000 Model 400 AXP Workstation ☐

DEC 3000 Model 500 AXP Workstation ☐

DEC 4000 Model 600 AXP Distributed/ ☐
    Departmental Server

DEC 7000 Model 600 AXP Server ☐

DEC 10000 Model 600 AXP Server ☐

Other Alpha–based CPUs: _____

Other CPUs: _____

HOST SYSTEM WORKSHEET (Cont.)

Other CPU Architectures:

_____ ☐

_____ ☐

_____ ☐

_____ ☐

_____ ☐

Specify the host operating system:

Digital UNIX   ☐

DEC OSF/1   ☐

ULTRIX   ☐

Other operating systems _____

_____

Specify the bus or buses you plan to connect to the driver:

TURBOchannel   ☐

VMEbus   ☐

EISA bus   ☐

PCI bus   ☐

SCSI   ☐

Pseudodevice drivers ☐

Other buses _____

_____

DEVICE DRIVER CONVENTIONS WORKSHEET

Describe the naming scheme you are following for

Device driver interfaces:

_____

_____

_____

_____

Device driver structures:

_____

_____

_____

_____

_____

Device driver constants:

_____

_____

_____

_____

Device connectivity information:

_____

_____

_____

_____

Describe the approach to writing comments in the device driver:

_____

_____

_____

_____

_____

_____

_____

Describe the approach to writing device driver documentation:

_____

_____

_____

_____

_____

_____

_____

_____

DEVICE CHARACTERISTICS WORKSHEET

Specify the following about the device:

		YES	NO
1.	The device is capable of block I/O	☐	☐
2.	The device supports a file system	☐	☐
3.	The device supports byte stream access	☐	☐

Specify the actions that need to be taken if the device generates interrupts:

_____

_____

_____

_____

_____

_____

_____

Specify how the device should be reset:

_____

_____

_____

_____

_____

Use the remainder of the worksheet to specify any other device characteristics:

_____

_____

_____

_____

_____

_____

DEVICE USAGE WORKSHEET

List the documentation you have on the device (the device documentation can help you answer subsequent questions):

_____   _____

_____   _____

_____   _____

_____   _____

_____   _____

Answer the following questions about the usage of the device:

1. How many of this device type can reside on the system?

2. What will the device be used for?

Describe or sketch the layout of the device registers. Include a short description of the purpose of each register:

DEVICE REGISTER WORKSHEET   (Cont.)

Specify which memory address the registers are associated with:

Device Register	Memory Address

HOST SYSTEM WORKSHEET

Specify the Host CPU

Alpha–based CPUs:

DEC 3000 Model 400 AXP Workstation ☐
DEC 3000 Model 500 AXP Workstation ☐
DEC 4000 Model 600 AXP Distributed/ ☐
    Departmental Server
DEC 7000 Model 600 AXP Server ☐
DEC 10000 Model 600 AXP Server ☐

Other Alpha–based CPUs: _____

Other CPUs: _____

DEVICE DRIVER SUPPORT WORKSHEET

Specify one of the following about the device driver:

		YES	NO
1.	There is no driver for this device. You are going to write it from scratch.	☐	☐
2.	The driver for this device was previously written for an ULTRIX system and the code is available.	☐	☐
3.	The driver for this device was previously written for a UNIX system and the code is available.	☐	☐
4.	The driver for this device was previously written for another operating system and the code is available.	☐	☐
5.	The existing device driver has documentation.	☐	☐

If the answer is yes, specify the title
and location of documentation:

Title: _____

Location: _____

6. If the source code is available,
specify the location:

Location: _____

7. Identify any experts available whose
experience you can draw on for: **Expert's Name, Number, Location:**

The device: _____
The design: _____
The coding: _____
The installation: _____
The debugging: _____
The testing: _____

Specify the type of driver:

Character ☐

Block ☐

Character and Block ☐

Network ☐

Loadable ☐

Static ☐

DEVICE DRIVER ENTRY POINTS WORKSHEET

Block driver entry points:

Entry point:	Name:
probe	_____
slave	_____
cattach	_____
dattach	_____
configure	_____
open	_____
close	_____
strategy	_____
ioctl	_____
interrupt	_____
psize	_____
dump	_____

Character driver entry points:

Entry point:	Name:
probe	_____
slave	_____
cattach	_____
dattach	_____
configure	_____
open	_____
close	_____
strategy	_____
ioctl	_____
stop	_____
reset	_____
read	_____
write	_____
mmap	_____
interrupt	_____

DEVICE DRIVER TESTING WORKSHEET

Specify the scope of the driver test program:

		YES	NO
1.	The test program checks all entry points	☐	☐
2.	The test program checks all ioctl requests separately	☐	☐
3.	The test program checks multiple devices	☐	☐
4.	The test program was run with multiple users using the device	☐	☐
5.	The test program includes debug code to check for impossible situations	☐	☐
6.	The test program tests which entry points are available through the system call interface	☐	☐

DEVICE DRIVER LOCKING METHOD WORKSHEET

Specify the locking method for SMP–safe drivers:

Simple lock method   ☐

Complex lock method   ☐

Funneling method   ☐

Glossary

autoconfiguration
Autoconfiguration is a process that determines what hardware actually exists during the current instance of the running kernel.

autoconfiguration software
The autoconfiguration software consists of the programs that accomplish the tasks associated with the events that occur during the autoconfiguration of devices. In most cases, it is not necessary for device driver writers to know the specific programs that execute during autoconfiguration.

bdevsw table
The block device switch, or bdevsw, table is an array of data structures that contains pointers to device driver entry points for each block mode device supported by the system. In addition, the table can contain stubs for device driver entry points for block mode devices that do not exist or entry points not used by a device driver. See also **cdevsw table** and **device switch table**.

block device
A block device is a device that is designed to operate in terms of the block I/O supported by Digital UNIX. It is accessed through the buffer cache. A block device has a block device driver associated with it.

block device driver
A block device driver is a driver that performs I/O by using file system block-sized buffers from a buffer cache supplied by the kernel. Block device drivers are particularly well-suited for disk drives, the most common block devices.

buffer cache
A buffer cache is supplied by the kernel and contains file system block-sized buffers. Block device drivers use these buffers in I/O operations.

buf structure
The buf structure describes arbitrary I/O, but is usually associated with block I/O and physio.

bus

A bus is a physical communication path and an access protocol between a processor and its peripherals. A bus standard, with a predefined set of logic signals, timings, and connectors, provides a means by which many types of device interfaces (controllers) can be built and easily combined within a computer system. See also **OPENbus**.

bus physical address

A bus physical address is an address that the device driver can pass to another device on the bus. A device driver can use a bus physical address to reference the I/O or memory space of other cards that reside on the same bus as the card that the device driver controls.

bus structure

The bus structure represents an instance of a bus entity. A bus is a real or imagined entity to which other buses or controllers are logically attached. All systems have at least one bus, the system bus, even though the bus may not actually exist physically. The term *controller* here refers both to devices that control slave devices (for example, disk or tape controllers) and to devices that stand alone (for example, terminal or network controllers).

bus support subsystem

The bus support subsystem contains all of the bus adapter-specific code. Isolating the bus-specific code and data structures into a bus support subsystem makes it easier for independent software vendors to implement different bus adapters.

The bus support subsystem communicates with the hardware-dependent and device driver subsystems of the hardware-independent model.

busy wait time

Busy wait time is the amount of CPU time expended on waiting for a simple lock to become free.

cdevsw table

The character device switch, or cdevsw, table is an array of data structures that contains pointers to device driver entry points for each character device the system supports. In addition, the table can contain stubs for device driver entry points for character mode devices that do not exist or for entry points not used by a device driver. See also **bdevsw table** and **device switch table**.

central processing unit (CPU)

The central processing unit (CPU) is the main computational unit in a computer and the one that executes instructions. The CPU is of interest to device driver writers because its associated architecture influences the design of the driver. For example, CPUs can have different mechanisms for handling memory mapping.

cfgmgr daemon

The cfgmgr daemon is a system management process that works with kloadsrv, the kernel load server, to manage loadable device drivers.

character device

A character device is any device that can have streams of characters read from or written to it. A character device has a character device driver associated with it.

character device driver

A character device driver is a driver that can use a variety of approaches to handle I/O. A character device driver can accept or supply a stream of data based on a request from a user process. You can use a character device driver for a device such as a line printer that handles one character at a time. However, character drivers are not limited to performing I/O one character at a time (despite the name "character" driver). For example, tape drivers frequently perform I/O in 10K chunks. You can also use a character device driver when it is necessary to copy data directly to or from a user process.

Because of their flexibility in handling I/O, many drivers are character drivers. Line printers, interactive terminals, and graphics displays are examples of devices that require character device drivers.

compile time variable

The compile time variable defines how many devices exist on the system and is created by the config program for use by static device drivers.

config.file file fragment

The config.file file fragment can be viewed as a "mini" system configuration file. It is the mechanism by which third-party driver writers supply device connectivity, callout keywords, and other information related to their static device driver product and needed by their customers.

config program

The config program is a system management tool that doconfig calls. The config program either creates a new or modifies an existing system configuration file, copies .products.list to *NAME*.list, creates the device special files for static drivers, and builds a new Digital UNIX kernel.

control status register (CSR)

See **device register**.

controller

A device controller is the hardware interface between the computer and a peripheral device. Sometimes a controller handles several devices. In other cases, a controller is integral to the device.

controller structure

The `controller` structure represents an instance of a controller entity, one that connects logically to a bus. A controller can control devices that are directly connected or can perform some other controlling operation, such as a network interface or terminal controller operation.

CPU

See **central processing unit**.

daemon

A daemon is a system management process that controls a variety of kernel tasks.

See also **cfgmgr daemon**.

data structure

Data structures are the mechanism used to pass information between the Digital UNIX kernel and device driver interfaces.

dense space address

A dense space address is an address that resides in dense space. Dense space is an area of I/O space or memory space that device drivers can access as if it were memory. Not all Alpha CPUs support dense space.

See also **sparse space address**.

device autoconfiguration

See **autoconfiguration**.

device controller

See **controller**.

device driver

A device driver is a software module that resides within the Digital UNIX kernel and is the software interface to a hardware device or devices. The purpose of a device driver is to handle requests made by the kernel with regard to a particular type of device. See also **block device driver**, **character device driver**, and **network device driver**.

device driver configuration

Device driver configuration is the process of incorporating device drivers into the kernel and making them available to system management and other utilities. There are two configuration models: the third-party and the traditional device driver configuration models.

See also **third-party device driver configuration model** and **traditional device driver configuration model**.

device driver header file

The device driver header file contains #define statements for as many devices as are configured into the system. This file is generated by the config program during static configuration of the device driver. This file need not be included if you configure the driver as a loadable driver.

device driver kit

The device driver kit contains the files associated with a device driver product. These files contain information necessary for system managers (customers) to configure loadable or static drivers into their systems.

device driver subsystem

The device driver subsystem contains all of the driver-specific code. The device driver subsystem communicates with the hardware-dependent, bus support, and hardware-independent subsystems of the hardware-independent model.

See also **bus support subsystem, hardware-dependent subsystem,** and **hardware-independent subsystem.**

device register

A device register is commonly referred to as a control status register, or CSR. The device register can be used to:

- Control what a device does

- Report the status of a device

- Transfer data to or from the device

device register header file

The device register header file contains any public declarations that the device driver uses. This file usually contains the device register structure associated with the device.

device register structure

A device register structure is a C structure whose members map to the registers of some device. These registers are often referred to as the device's control status register (or CSR) addresses. The device register structure is usually defined in the device register header file.

device structure

The `device` structure represents an instance of a device entity. A device is an entity that connects to and is controlled by a controller. A device does not connect directly to a bus.

device switch table

The device switch tables, `bdevsw` for block devices and `cdevsw` for character devices, have the following characteristics:

- They are arrays of structures that contain device driver entry points. These entry points are actually the addresses of the specific interfaces within the drivers.

- They may contain stubs for device driver entry points for devices that do not exist on a specific machine.

- The location in the table corresponds to the device major number.

See also **bdevsw table** and **cdevsw table**.

direct memory access (DMA)

Direct memory access (DMA) describes the ability of a device to directly access (read from and write to) CPU memory, without CPU intervention.

direct memory access (DMA) device

A direct memory access (DMA) device is one that can directly access (read from and write to) CPU memory, without CPU intervention. Non-DMA devices cannot directly access CPU memory.

DMA handle

Specifies a handle to DMA resources associated with the mapping of an in-memory I/O buffer onto a controller's I/O bus. This handle provides the information to access bus address/byte count pairs. A bus address/byte count pair is represented by the ba and bc members of an sg_entry structure pointer. Device driver writers can view the DMA handle as the tag to the allocated system resources needed to perform a DMA operation.

DMA

See **direct memory access**.

doconfig

The doconfig program is a system management tool that calls config. See **config program**.

driver structure

The driver structure defines driver entry points and other driver-specific information. You declare and initialize an instance of this structure in the device driver.

GENERIC system configuration file

The GENERIC system configuration file supplied by Digital contains all the possible software and hardware options available to Digital UNIX systems and includes all supported Digital devices. The GENERIC system configuration file is used to build a kernel that represents all possible combinations of statically configured drivers that Digital supports.

handler_intr_info structure

The handler_intr_info structure contains interrupt handler information for device controllers connected to a bus. This generic structure makes device drivers more portable across different buses because it contains all of the necessary information to add an interrupt handler for any bus. Device drivers set the ih_bus_info member of the ihandler_t structure to the filled-in handler_intr_info structure, usually in the driver's `probe` interface.

hardware device
> See **peripheral device**.

hardware-dependent subsystem
> The hardware-dependent subsystem contains all of the hardware-dependent pieces of an operating system with the exception of device drivers. This subsystem provides the code that supports a specific CPU platform and, therefore, is implemented by specific vendors.
>
> The hardware-dependent subsystem communicates with the hardware-independent subsystem, device driver subsystem, and bus support subsystem of the hardware-independent model.

hardware-independent model
> The hardware-independent model describes the hardware and software components that make up an open systems environment. Specifically, these hardware and software components are contained in a hardware-independent subsystem, hardware-dependent subsystem, bus support subsystem, and device driver subsystem.

hardware-independent subsystem
> The hardware-independent subsystem contains all of the hardware-independent pieces of an operating system, including the hardware-independent kernel interfaces, user programs, shells, and utilities. This subsystem can contain extensions and enhancements made by vendor companies, including Digital Equipment Corporation.
>
> The hardware-independent subsystem communicates with the hardware-dependent subsystem, bus support subsystem, and device driver subsystem of the hardware-independent model.

ihandler_id_t key
> The `ihandler_id_t` key is a unique number used to identify interrupt service interfaces to be acted on by subsequent calls to the `handler_enable`, `handler_disable`, and `handler_del` kernel interfaces.

ihandler_t structure
> The `ihandler_t` structure contains information associated with device driver interrupt handling. In previous versions of the Digital UNIX operating system (formerly known as DEC OSF/1), only loadable drivers used this data structure. Digital recommends that both static and loadable drivers use the `ihandler_t` structure and the `handler` interfaces to dynamically register ISIs.

interrupt service interface (ISI)
> An interrupt service interface (ISI) is a device driver routine (sometimes called an interrupt handler) that handles hardware interrupts.

ioconf.c file

> The `ioconf.c` file contains the `bus_list`, `controller_list`, and `device_list` arrays created by the `config` program for static device drivers during the autoconfiguration process.

I/O address

> An I/O address is either a sparse space or dense space address that performs an I/O cycle on a specific bus.

> See also **dense space address** and **sparse space address**.

I/O handle

> An I/O handle is a data entity that is of type `io_handle_t`. This I/O handle provides device drivers with bus address information. The bus configuration code passes the I/O handle to the device driver's `xxprobe` interface during device autoconfiguration.

ISI

> See **interrupt service interface**.

kernel

> The kernel is a software entity that runs in supervisor mode and does not communicate with a device except through calls to a device driver.

kernel framework

> See **subsystem**.

kernel physical address

> A kernel physical address is an address that resides in kernel space but does not use the virtual memory (VM) mapping registers.

> See also **kernel-unmapped virtual address**.

kernel-unmapped virtual address

> A kernel-unmapped virtual address is an address that resides in kernel space. This address is sometimes referred to as a kseg address. A kernel-unmapped virtual address makes use of the virtual memory (VM) mapping registers.

> See also **kernel physical address**.

kloadsrv

> The kernel loader daemon is used with the `cfgmgr` daemon to load the specified loadable device driver into the kernel address space and to resolve external references. See also **cfgmgr daemon**.

kmknod

> The `kmknod` utility is a system management tool that uses the information from the `stanza.static` file fragment to dynamically create device special files for static device drivers at boot time.

kreg utility

The `kreg` utility is a system management tool that maintains the `/sys/conf/.product.list` system file, which registers static device driver products.

KSEG address

See **kernel-unmapped virtual address**.

loadable device driver

A loadable device driver is a driver (block or character) that is linked dynamically into the kernel. This type of device driver is installed without having to rebuild the kernel, shut down the system, and reboot. See also **static device driver**.

load module

A load module is the executable image of a loadable device driver.

memory address

A memory address is either a sparse space or dense space address that performs a memory cycle on a specific bus.

See also **dense space address** and **sparse space address**.

method

A method is a subsystem specific portion of the `cfgmgr` daemon. For example, the device method is the portion of the `cfgmgr` daemon that handles loadable device drivers.

name_data.c file

The `name_data.c` file provides a convenient place to size the data structures and data structure arrays that device drivers use. In addition, the file can contain definitions that third-party driver writers might want their customers to change. This file is particularly convenient for third-party driver writers who do not want to ship device driver sources.

NAME.list file

The `NAME.list` file is a copy of the `.products.list` file that is created when the system manager installs the device driver kit supplied by a third-party vendor.

network device

A network device is any device associated with network activities and is responsible for both transmitting and receiving frames to and from the network medium. Network devices have network device drivers associated with them.

network device driver

A network device driver attaches a network subsystem to a network interface, prepares the network interface for operation, and governs the transmission and reception of network frames over the network interface.

nexus

The `nexus` keyword indicates the top of the system configuration tree.

OPENbus

The term *OPENbus* refers to those buses whose architectures and interfaces are publicly documented, allowing a vendor to easily plug in hardware and software components. The TURBOchannel bus the EISA bus, the PCI bus, and the VMEbus, for example, can be classified as having OPENbus architectures.

open systems

The term *open systems* refers to an environment with hardware and software platforms that promote the use of standards. By adhering to a set of standard interfaces, these platforms make it easier for third-party programmers to write applications that can run on a variety of operating systems and hardware. This open systems environment can also make it easier for systems engineers to write device drivers for numerous peripheral devices that operate on this same variety of operating systems and hardware.

peripheral device

A peripheral device is hardware, such as a disk controller, that connects to a computer system. It can be controlled by commands from the computer and can send data to the computer and receive data from it.

port structure

The `port` structure contains information about a port.

.products.list file

The `/usr/sys/conf/.products.list` file (for static drivers) stores information about static device driver products.

pseudodevice driver

A pseudodevice driver, such as the `pty` terminal driver, is structured like any other driver. The difference is that a pseudodevice driver does not operate on a bus.

SCP

See **subset control program**.

setld

The `setld` utility allows the transfer of the contents of the device driver kit to a customer's system on Digital UNIX.

sparse space address

A sparse space address is an address that resides in sparse space. Sparse space contains addresses that reside in bus address space (either I/O space or memory space). All Alpha CPUs support sparse space. As a result, all bus configuration code should supply an I/O handle that references bus address space.

See also **dense space address**.

stanza.loadable file fragment

The `stanza.loadable` file fragment can be viewed as a "mini" `sysconfigtab` database because it contains some of the same information. The `stanza.loadable` file fragment contains an entry for each device driver, providing such information as the driver's name, location of the loadable object, device connectivity information, and device special file information. Parts of the `stanza.loadable` file fragment are functionally similar to the system configuration file in that the fragment uses a subset of the syntaxes that the system configuration file uses to specify each current or planned device on the system.

stanza.static file fragment

The `stanza.static` file fragment (for static drivers) contains such items as the driver's major number requirements, the names and minor numbers of the device special files, the permissions and directory name where the device special files reside, and the driver interface names to be added to the `bdevsw` and `cdevsw` tables.

static device driver

A static device driver is a driver (block, character, or network) that is linked directly into the kernel. This type of device driver must be installed by completing tasks that include rebuilding the kernel, shutting down the system, and rebooting. See also **loadable device driver**.

subset control program (SCP)

A subset control program (SCP) is a program written by the kit developer that contains path specifications for all of the files related to the driver product. The SCP is invoked by `setld` during the installation of the device driver kit.

subsystem

A subsystem is a kernel module that defines a set of kernel framework interfaces that allow for the dynamic configuration and unconfiguration (adding and removal) of subsystem functionality. Examples of subsystems include (but are not restricted to) device drivers, file systems, and network protocols. The ability to dynamically add subsystem functionality is utilized by loadable drivers to allow the driver to be configured and unconfigured without the need for kernel rebuilds and reboots.

sysconfig

The `sysconfig` utility is a system management tool that modifies the loadable subsystem configuration. The `sysconfig` utility provides a user interface to the `cfgmgr` daemon.

sysconfigdb

The `sysconfigdb` utility is a system management tool that maintains the `sysconfigtab` database. The driver stanza entries in the `stanza.loadable` file fragment are appended to this database.

sysconfigtab database

The `sysconfigtab` database contains the information provided in the `stanza.loadable` file fragments. This information is appended to the `sysconfigtab` database when the system manager runs the `sysconfigdb` utility during the installation of the device driver kit.

system configuration file

The system configuration file is an ASCII text file that defines the components of the system. These components are described using valid keywords such as those that identify device definitions, callout definitions, and pseudodevice definitions.

system configuration tree

The system configuration tree represents the result of the autoconfiguration process, after the autoconfiguration software reads the entries in the system configuration file (for static drivers) and the `sysconfigtab` database (for loadable drivers). For static drivers, the result is a correctly linked list of `bus`, `controller`, and `device` structures. As loadable drivers are dynamically loaded, their `bus`, `controller`, and `device` structures are linked into the system configuration tree.

tc_intr_info structure

The `tc_intr_info` structure contains interrupt handler information for device controllers connected to the TURBOchannel bus. TURBOchannel bus device drivers (loadable and static) use this structure with the `handler_add` and `handler_enable` interfaces to dynamically register interrupt handlers. The Digital UNIX operating system supports dynamic registration of interrupt handlers on the TURBOchannel bus for loadable and static device drivers.

See also **handler_intr_info structure**.

terminal device

A terminal device is a special type of character device that can have streams of characters read from or written to it. Terminal devices have terminal (character) device drivers associated with them.

terminal device driver

A terminal device driver is actually a character device driver that handles I/O character processing for a variety of terminal devices. Like any character device, a terminal device can accept or supply a stream of data based on a request from a user process. It cannot be mounted as a file system and, therefore, does not use data caching.

third-party device driver configuration model

This model is recommended for third-party device driver writers who want to ship loadable and static drivers to customers running the Digital UNIX operating system. The third-party device driver configuration model provides tools that customers use to automate the installation of third-party device drivers. This model requires that third-party driver writers provide a device driver kit to their customers.

traditional device driver configuration model
The traditional device driver configuration model provides a manual mechanism for driver writers or system managers to configure device drivers into the kernel. One advantage of the traditional model is that no device driver kit is needed. The disadvantage is that the traditional model is not automated and is potentially error prone.

TURBOchannel test board
The TURBOchannel test board is a minimal implementation of all the TURBOchannel hardware functions: programmed I/O, direct memory access (DMA) read, DMA write, and I/O read/write conflict testing. The /dev/cb device driver provides a simple interface to the functions provided by the TURBOchannel test board.

uio structure
The uio structure describes I/O, either single vector or multiple vectors. Typically, device drivers do not manipulate the members of this structure.

user program
A user program is a software module that allows a user of the Digital UNIX operating system to perform some task. For example, the ls user program allows users to list the files contained in a specific directory. User programs make system calls to the kernel that result in the kernel making requests of a device driver. A user program never directly calls a device driver.

Index

B

b_back member

formal description of buf structure field, 8–4

summary description of buf structure field, 16–8

b_bcount member

buf structure field used by cbminphys, 10–54

buf structure field used by cbstrategy to initialize b_resid member, 10–57

formal description of buf structure field, 8–4

summary description of buf structure field, 16–9

b_blkno member

formal description of buf structure field, 8–5

summary description of buf structure field, 16–9

B_BUSY constant

formal description of binary status flag for b_flags member of buf structure, 8–4

relationship to av_forw and av_back buf structure members, 8–4

b_dev member

buf structure field used by cbstrategy, 10–55

formal description of buf structure field, 8–5

summary description of buf structure field, 16–9

B_DONE constant

formal description of binary status flag for b_flags member of buf structure, 8–4

B_ERROR constant

formal description of binary status flag for b_flags member of buf structure, 8–4

b_error member

buf structure field set by cbstrategy, 10–59

formal description of buf structure field, 8–5

summary description of buf structure field, 16–9

b_flags member

buf structure field set by cbstrategy, 10–59

discussion of B_TAPE flag, 8–18

formal description of buf structure field, 8–3

summary description of buf structure field, 16–8

b_forw member

formal description of buf structure field, 8–4

summary description of buf structure field, 16–8

b_iodone member

formal description of buf structure field, 8–5

summary description of buf structure field, 16–9

b_lblkno member

formal description of buf structure field, 8–5

summary description of buf structure field, 16–9

B_PHYS constant

formal description of binary status flag for b_flags member of buf structure, 8–4

b_proc member

formal description of buf structure field, 8–6

summary description of buf structure field, 16–9

B_READ constant

formal description of binary status flag for b_flags member of buf structure, 8–4

b_resid member

buf structure field initialized by cbstrategy, 10–57

formal description of buf structure field, 8–5

summary description of buf structure field, 16–9

use as argument with copyin kernel interface, 9–14

drvr_register_shutdown kernel interface

description, 15–76

function definition, 15–76

dualdevsw_add kernel interface

description, 15–78

function definition, 15–78

dualdevsw_del kernel interface

description, 15–80

function definition, 15–80

dump interface

relationship to d_dump member of bdevsw structure, 8–17

setting up xxdump in dump section, 3–27

dump section

description, 3–27

E

EBUSY error code

to indicate cb driver not currently configured as loadable, 10–37

EFAULT error code

possible value returned by copyin, 10–59

possible value returned by uiomove, 10–48, 10–52

EINVAL error code

description, 3–5

to indicate cb driver not currently configured as loadable, 10–37

to indicate invalid argument in cb_configure, 10–33

used by cb_configure to define unknown operation type, 10–40

EIO error code

description, 3–5

enable_option kernel interface

description, 15–81

enable_option kernel interface (cont.)

function definition, 15–81

ENODEV constant

use by cb_configure, 10–36

ENODEV error code

description, 3–5

ENXIO error code

used by cbopen to indicate no such device, 10–42

err variable

declared by cbread to store return value from uiomove, 10–46

declared by cbstrategy to store return value from uiomove, 10–56

declared by cbwrite to store return value from uiomove, 10–50

errno.h file

defines error codes returned to user process by device driver, 3–5

defines error codes used for b_error member, 8–5

defining ENXIO error code used by cbopen, 10–42

defining error codes, 10–33

ESRCH error code

use by cdevsw_del, 10–38

event member

summary description of sel_queue structure field, 16–42

F

ffs kernel interface

description, 15–82

function definition, 15–82

file.h file

defining flag bits used by cbopen, 10–42

header files

description of code example for cb driver, 10–7 to 10–8

discussion of common driver, 3–4

discussion of conf.h, 3–5

discussion of cpu.h, 3–5

discussion of devdriver.h, 3–5

discussion of device driver, 3–3

discussion of device register, 3–6

discussion of errno.h, 3–5

discussion of loadable driver, 3–5

discussion of name_data.c, 3–7

discussion of number and types included in device driver, 3–3

discussion of sysconfig.h, 3–6

discussion of uio.h, 3–5

example for /dev/none driver, 4–4

example of commonly used by device drivers, 3–4

list of with summary descriptions, 14–2t

recommendations on using angle brackets (< and >) in explicit pathnames, 3–4

relationship to third-party configuration model, 11–15

relationship to traditional configuration model, 11–28

host CPU

See central processing unit

htonl kernel interface

description, 15–103

function definition, 15–103

htons kernel interface

description, 15–103

function definition, 15–103

hz global variable

external declaration in cb device driver, 10–8

I

I/O address

defined, 2–32

description of address type that device drivers use, 2–32

I/O handle

See also io_handle_t data type

defined, 2–29

description, 9–41

ih_bus member

formal description of ihandler_t structure field, 7–89

summary description of ihandler_t structure field, 16–35

ih_bus_info member

formal description of ihandler_t structure field, 7–90

summary description of ihandler_t structure field, 16–35

ih_id member

formal description of ihandler_t structure field, 7–89

summary description of ihandler_t structure field, 16–35

ihandler_t structure

associated include file, 16–35

code fragment example, 7–90

declaration in cbprobe interface, 10–20

initializing ih_bus member in cbprobe interface, 10–21

list of member names and data types, 7–89t, 16–35

passed as an argument to handler_add kernel interface, 9–27

setting of ih_bus_info member in cbprobe interface, 10–22

M

major kernel interface

description, 15–151

explanation of code fragment, 9–70

function definition, 15–151

makedev kernel interface

arguments as related to call by cb_configure, 10–35

description, 15–152

function definition, 15–152

makefile

completed by config program, 11–20

MALLOC kernel interface

description, 15–153

explanation of code fragment, 9–9

function definition, 15–153

to dynamically allocate memory, 2–38

max_val member

summary description of cfg_subsys_attr_t structure field, 16–22

MAX_XFR constant

definition in cb device driver, 10–16

used by cbread to transfer maximum bytes, 10–47

used by cbwrite to transfer maximum bytes, 10–51

mb kernel interface

called by cbioctl, 10–76, 10–78

description, 15–157

function definition, 15–157

use as an alternative to wbflush on Alpha systems, 2–46

used to synchronize DMA buffers, 2–46

member

summary description of sel_queue structure field, 16–42

memory

relationship to device driver, 6–2

zeroing with bzero kernel interface, 9–13

memory address

defined, 2–32

description of address type that device drivers use, 2–32

memory barrier

discussion of, 2–48

discussion of mb interface on Alpha systems, 2–46

memory block

copying a memory block to I/O space with io_copyin kernel interface, 9–48

copying with io_copyio kernel interface, 9–52

copying with io_copyout kernel interface, 9–50

min_val member

summary description of cfg_subsys_attr_t structure field, 16–22

minor kernel interface

argument as related to call by cbclose, 10–44

argument as related to call by cbopen, 10–42

argument as related to call by cbread, 10–47

argument as related to call by cbstrategy, 10–55

argument as related to call by cbwrite, 10–51

description, 15–159

explanation of code fragment, 9–70

function definition, 15–159

minphys kernel interface

description, 15–160

function definition, 15–160

miscellaneous interface

category of kernel interface, 9–69

structure

allocation

using dynamic allocation technique, 2–36

using static allocation model 1 technique, 2–34

using static allocation model 2 technique, 2–35

local structure and variable definitions

description of code example for cb driver, 10–14 to 10–16

summary descriptions, 16–2t

used by autoconfiguration software, 7–13

used by loadable device drivers, 7–83

used in I/O operations, 8–1

used to register interrupts, 7–88

Subset Control Program

See SCP

subsystem

defined, 1–3

Subsystem_Description field

syntax description, 12–20

subyte kernel interface

description, 15–221

function definition, 15–221

supplying an SCP for /dev/cb device driver, 12–49

supplying an SCP for /dev/none device driver, 12–44

suser kernel interface

description, 15–224

function definition, 15–224

suword kernel interface

description, 15–226

function definition, 15–226

svatophys kernel interface

description, 15–227

svatophys kernel interface (cont.)

function definition, 15–227

swap_lw_bytes kernel interface

description, 15–229

function definition, 15–229

swap_word_bytes kernel interface

description, 15–229

function definition, 15–229

swap_words kernel interface

description, 15–229

function definition, 15–229

sysconfig

defined, 11–19

sysconfig.h file

defining CFG_OP_CONFIGURE constant, 10–32

defining CFG_OP_QUERY constant, 10–40

defining CFG_OP_UNCONFIGURE constant, 10–37

sysconfig.h header file

defines operation codes and data structures used in loadable driver configuration, 3–6

sysconfigdb

adds stanza.loadable to sysconfigtab database, 11–21

defined, 11–19

sysconfigtab database

comparison with stanza.loadable file fragment, 11–14f

defined, 7–2

example, 7–2

individual structures created from example, 7–4f

read by autoconfiguration software during autoconfiguration process, 7–2

W

wakeup kernel interface
description, 15–253
explanation of code fragment, 9–24
function definition, 15–253

wbflush kernel interface
use of mb interface as alternative on Alpha systems, 2–46

write device section
description, 3–17

write interface
relationship to d_write member of cdevsw structure, 8–11
setting up xxwrite in read and write device section, 3–18

write system call
causes driver's write interface to be called, 3–18

WRITE_BUS_D8 kernel interface
description, 15–255
function definition, 15–255

WRITE_BUS_D16 kernel interface
description, 15–255

WRITE_BUS_D32 kernel interface
description, 15–255

WRITE_BUS_D64 kernel interface
description, 15–255

WRITE_BUS_D16 kernel interface
function definition, 15–255

WRITE_BUS_D32 kernel interface
function definition, 15–255

WRITE_BUS_D64 kernel interface
function definition, 15–255

write_io_port interface
called by cbincled interface, 10–79
called by cbioctl interface, 10–75

write_io_port interface (cont.)
called by cbstart interface, 10–67
called by cbstrategy interface, 10–61
called by cbwrite interface, 10–52

write_io_port kernel interface
description, 15–258
explanation of code fragment, 9–46
function definition, 15–258

writing data to a device register
by calling write_io_port kernel interface, 9–45

writing SCP for /dev/cb device driver, 12–49

writing SCP for /dev/none device driver, 12–44

X

xclu member
formal description of driver structure field, 7–79
initialized for cb driver, 7–80f
summary description of driver structure field, 16–31

xx_configure driver interface
function definition, 17–10

xxcattach driver interface
function definition, 17–6

xxclose driver interface
function definition, 17–8

xxclose interface
example code fragment, 3–17

xxconfigure interface
example code fragment, 3–15

xxconfl1 bus configuration interface
function definition, 17–71

xxconfl2 bus configuration interface
function definition, 17–71

How to Order Additional Documentation

Technical Support

If you need help deciding which documentation best meets your needs, call 800-DIGITAL (800-344-4825) before placing your electronic, telephone, or direct mail order.

Electronic Orders

To place an order at the Electronic Store, dial 800-234-1998 using a 1200- or 2400-bps modem from anywhere in the USA, Canada, or Puerto Rico. If you need assistance using the Electronic Store, call 800-DIGITAL (800-344-4825).

Telephone and Direct Mail Orders

Your Location	Call	Contact
Continental USA, Alaska, or Hawaii	800-DIGITAL	Digital Equipment Corporation P.O. Box CS2008 Nashua, New Hampshire 03061
Puerto Rico	809-754-7575	Local Digital subsidiary
Canada	800-267-6215	Digital Equipment of Canada Attn: DECdirect Operations KAO2/2 P.O. Box 13000 100 Herzberg Road Kanata, Ontario, Canada K2K 2A6
International	————	Local Digital subsidiary or approved distributor
Internal[a]	————	SSB Order Processing – NQO/V19 *or* U. S. Software Supply Business Digital Equipment Corporation 10 Cotton Road Nashua, NH 03063-1260

[a] For internal orders, you must submit an Internal Software Order Form (EN-01740-07).

Reader's Comments

Digital welcomes your comments and suggestions on this manual. Your input will help us to write documentation that meets your needs. Please send your suggestions using one of the following methods:

- This postage-paid form
- Internet electronic mail: `readers_comment@zk3.dec.com`
- Fax: (603) 881-0120, Attn: UEG Publications, ZKO3-3/Y32

If you are not using this form, please be sure you include the name of the document, the page number, and the product name and version.

Please rate this manual:

	Excellent	Good	Fair	Poor
Accuracy (software works as manual says)	☐	☐	☐	☐
Completeness (enough information)	☐	☐	☐	☐
Clarity (easy to understand)	☐	☐	☐	☐
Organization (structure of subject matter)	☐	☐	☐	☐
Figures (useful)	☐	☐	☐	☐
Examples (useful)	☐	☐	☐	☐
Index (ability to find topic)	☐	☐	☐	☐
Usability (ability to access information quickly)	☐	☐	☐	☐

Please list errors you have found in this manual:

Page   Description

_____   _____

_____   _____

_____   _____

_____   _____

_____   _____

Additional comments or suggestions to improve this manual:

_____

_____

_____

_____

_____

What version of the software described by this manual are you using? _____

Name/Title _____ Dept. _____

Company _____ Date _____

Mailing Address _____

_____ Email _____ Phone _____

BUSINESS REPLY MAIL
FIRST–CLASS MAIL PERMIT NO. 33 MAYNARD MA

POSTAGE WILL BE PAID BY ADDRESSEE

DIGITAL EQUIPMENT CORPORATION
UEG PUBLICATIONS MANAGER
ZKO3–3/Y32
110 SPIT BROOK RD
NASHUA NH 03062–9987